The Study of Africa

Volume 2: Global and Transnational Engagements

Edited by
Paul Tiyambe Zeleza

CODESRIA

Council for the Development of Social Science Research in Africa

© Council for the Development of Social Science Research in Africa, 2007
Avenue Cheikh Anta Diop Angle Canal IV, BP 3304 Dakar, 18524 Senegal.
http:\\www.codesria.org

ISBN: 2-86978-198-9
ISBN 13: 978-2-86978-198-6

Typeset by Hadijatou Sy

Cover designed by Ibrahima Fofana based on the Adinkra symbol of knowledge, lifelong education and quest for knowledge.

Printed by

Distributed in Africa by CODESRIA

Distributed elsewhere by
African Books Collective, Oxford, UK
www.africanbookscollective.com

The Council for the Development of Social Science Research in Africa (CODESRIA) is an independent organisation whose principal objectives are facilitating research, promoting research-based publishing and creating multiple forums geared towards the exchange of views and information among African researchers. It challenges the fragmentation of research through the creation of thematic research networks that cut across linguistic and regional boundaries.

CODESRIA publishes a quarterly journal, *Africa Development*, the longest standing Africa-based social science journal; *Afrika Zamani*, a journal of history; the *African Sociological Review; African Journal of International Affairs* (AJIA); *Africa Review of Books; Identity, Culture and Politics: An Afro-Asian Dialogue* and the *Journal of Higher Education in Africa*. It copublishes the *Africa Media Review*. Research results and other activities of the institution are disseminated through 'Working Papers', 'Monograph Series', 'CODESRIA Book Series', and the *CODESRIA Bulletin*.

CODESRIA would like to express its gratitude to the Swedish International Development Cooperation Agency (SIDA/SAREC), the International Development Research Centre (IDRC), Ford Foundation, MacArthur Foundation, Carnegie Corporation, NORAD, the Danish Agency for International Development (DANIDA), the French Ministry of Cooperation, the United Nations Development Programme (UNDP), the Netherlands Ministry of Foreign Affairs, Rockefeller Foundation, FINIDA, CIDA, IIEP/ADEA, OECD, OXFAM America, UNICEF and the Government of Senegal for supporting its research, training and publication programmes.

Table of Contents

Acknowledgement

This book grew out of a seminar I ran while I served as Director at the Center for African Studies at the University of Illinois at Urbana-Champaign, 'Curricular Development Seminar in African Studies', in Fall 2002 for faculty and graduate students enrolled in the course on 'The Development of African Studies'. I would like to acknowledge the generous funding from the National Endowment for the Humanities (NEH) Grant ED-22151-01, which enabled me to bring more than twenty scholars from the US, Europe, Asia, and Africa. Many of the contributors to the seminar are included in this collection. I would also like to thank others who are not but came to the seminar: David Wiley, Ato Quayson, Charles Piot, Munene Macharia, Khabele Matlosa, Mahmood Mamdani, Linda Hunter, Keletso Atkins, Cheryl Johnson-Odim and Yassine Fall. I am indebted to Jamie McGowan, the Center's Assistant Director, and Sue Swisher, the Administrative Aide, for their hard work in the preparation of the grant proposal and the organization of the seminar, as well as Shana Wills, then an MA student in the Center who assisted with driving the guests to and from the airport. Several faculty opened their homes for the evening seminars and I would like to express my deepest thanks to all of them: Kathy Perkins, Kwaku Korang, Alma Gottlieb, Tom Bassett, Jan Nederveen-Pieterse, Sundiata Cha-Jua, Gale Summerfield, Adlai Murdoch, and Charles Stewart for their generosity. In this regard, I would also like to thank Cassandra Rachel Veney who kindly helped me host several of the seminars at our home. Due to publishing delays, some seminar participants or contributors to the collection published their presentations in other outlets but agreed to have their essays included in this volume. They include Li Anshan's 'African Studies in China in the 20th Century: A Historiographical Survey,' *African Studies Review* 48, 1 (2005): 59-87; Pearl T. Robinson's 'Area Studies in Search of Africa: The Case of the United States' in David L. Szanton, ed. *The Politics of Knowledge: Area Studies and the Disciplines* (2004); and Peter Probst's 'Betwixt and Between: African Studies in Germany,' *Afrika Spectrum* 3 (2005): 403-427.

Notes on Contributors

Aparajita Biswas is Professor in the Centre for African Studies, University of Mumbai, India. She has traveled extensively, attending African studies conferences in South Africa, Ethiopia, Mozambique, Australia, Russia, and Singapore. She was awarded a Visiting Fellowship by the International Development Centre, Queen Elizabeth House, University of Oxford, and was also associated with the UNESCO project on 'European Slave Routes in the Indian Ocean'. Her most recent book is *Post-Apartheid South Africa's Relations with the Neighboring Countries* (2005), and she has several recent articles on 'Energy Security Issues: Cooperation between India and African Countries' (2005), 'Non-Traditional Security Issues: Recent Trends in the Hydrocarbon Sector in the Indian Ocean Region' (2005), 'Small Arms Proliferation and Drug Trafficking in the Indian Ocean Region' (2005) and 'Japan's Relations with Africa' (2004).

Alan Cobley is Professor of South African and Comparative History at the University of the West Indies, Cave Hill Campus, Barbados. He has published widely on aspects of South African and Caribbean history. His books include: *Class and Consciousness: The Black Petty Bourgeoisie in South Africa, 1924 to 1950* (1990), *The African-Caribbean Connection: Historical and Cultural Perspectives* (1992), *Crossroads of Empire: The Europe-Caribbean Connection 1492-1992* (1994), *The Rules of the Game: Struggles in Black Recreation and Social Welfare Policy in South Africa* (1997), *The Caribbean Aids Epidemic* (2000), *Stronger, Surer, Bolder. Ruth Nita Barrow: Social Change and International Development* (2001).

Jean-Philippe Dedieu is currently a lecturer and PhD candidate in sociology at the École des Hautes Études en Sciences Sociales in France. In 2004, he was awarded a Fulbright Fellowship at the University of California at Berkeley. Apart from his contributions to the *Encyclopedia of Twentieth-Century African History* (2002), he has published various articles on African diasporas in France: 'US Exit, African Voices and Francophone Loyalty', *African Issues* (2002); 'Les élites africaines, enjeu de la diplomatie scientifique des États-Unis', *Politique étrangère* (2003); 'L'intégration des avocats africains dans les barreaux français', *Droit et société. Revue internationale de théorie du droit et de sociologie juridique* (2004); and 'L'impérialisme de la voix. Théâtre français en Afrique et comédiens africains en France', in *L'esclavage, la colonisation, et après* (2005).

Elizabeth Dimock is an Honorary Research Associate in the African Research Institute at La Trobe University in Melbourne. She has served variously as Treasurer, Secretary and Vice

President of the African Studies Association of Australasia and the Pacific. Her recent publications include, 'The Silence of African Women? A Christian Women's Protest in Buganda in 1931' in *The Post-Colonial Condition: Contemporary Politics in Africa* (1997) 'Women's Leadership Roles in the Early Protestant Church in Uganda: Continuity with the old order', in the *Australasian Review of African Studies* (2003), and *African Communities and Settlement Services in Victoria: Towards better Service Delivery Models* (2001). Her forthcoming publications include an anthology of primary sources on Africa, in a major six-volume series entitled *Women and Empire, 1750–1930: Primary Sources on Gender and Anglo-Imperialism* (Routledge, 2006).

Irina Filatova is a former head of the African Studies Department at Moscow State University (Russia) and head of the Department of History at the University of Durban-Westville (South Africa). She is now Professor Emeritus and Research Fellow at the University of KwaZulu-Natal, South Africa, and Professor of the State University in Moscow, Russia. She has widely published on African history and on the history of ties between Russia and South Africa. Among her books are *A History of Kenya* (1985) and *The Russians and the Anglo-Boer War, 1899–1902* (1999). She also co-edited a two-volume primary source collection *South Africa and the Communist International: A Documentary History* (2003).

Bogumil Jewsiewicki is a holder of the Canada research chair in comparative history of memory, Université Laval, Quebec, Canada, and member of the Centre d'études africaines, École des hautes études en sciences sociales, Paris, France. His extensive publications include *African Historiographies. What History for which Africa?* (1986), *A Congo Chronicle. Patrice Lumumba in Urban Art*, (1999), *Mami Wata. La peinture urbaine au Congo* (2003) and *Réparations, restitutions, réconciliations entre Afriques, Europe et Amériques*, special issue of *Cahiers d'études africaines* (2004).

Ronald Kassimir is Associate Dean of the New School for Social Research, and Associate Professor in its Department of Political Science. From 1996–2005 he was Program Director for Africa at the Social Science Research Council. He also directed the International Dissertation Field Research Fellowship Program and coordinated projects related to Youth and Globalization. He has published on civil society and politics in Uganda, and most recently is co-editor of *Intervention and Transnationalism in Africa: Global-Local Networks of Power* (2001), *Youth Activism: An International Encyclopedia* (2005), and *Youth, Globalization and the Law* (Stanford University Press, forthcoming).

Li Anshan is professor of the Institute of Afro-Asian Studies, School of International Studies, Peking University. He is also Vice-Director of the Centre for African Studies, Peking University and Vice Chair of Chinese Society of African Historical Studies. He received his PhD in history from the University of Toronto and has published in the *African Studies Review*, *The International Journal of African Historical Studies*, *Journal of Religious History*, and a variety of Chinese academic journals. He is the author of *Colonial Rule and Rural Protest: A Study of the Eastern Province in Colonial Ghana* (1998), *A History of Chinese Overseas in Africa*

(2000), *British Rule and Rural Protest in Southern Ghana* (2002), and *A Study on African Nationalism* (2004).

Mônica Lima is a doctoral student in History at Fluminense Federal University, teaches history at Cap/Federal University of Rio de Janeiro and at the Humanities Institute/Center of Afro-Asian Studies of the Candido Mendes University, Rio de Janeiro.

Tanya Lyons is the Academic Coordinator of the Globalization Program and a Lecturer in the School of Politics and International Studies at Flinders University, Adelaide, Australia. She is also an executive member of the African Studies Association of Australasia and the Pacific. Her publications include *Guns and Guerrilla Girls: Women in the Zimbabwean National Liberation Struggle* (2004); and 'Guerrilla Girls and Women in Zimbabwe's Liberation Struggle', in *Women in African Colonial History* (2002). She is also the co-author of several publications including *Africa on A Global Stage* (2006); 'Popular Youth Attitudes to Globalisation', *The Social Educator* (2004); and 'Developing Gender Mainstreaming and "Gender Respect"', *The Development Bulletin* (2004).

John McCracken recently retired from the University of Stirling in Scotland. He previously taught at the University of Rhodesia (now Zimbabwe, 1964), the University of Dar es Salaam (1965-69), and the University of Malawi (1980-83). His publications include *Politics and Christianity in Malawi, 1875-1940* (new edition 2000), 'British Central Africa' in the *Cambridge History of Africa* (Vol. 7, 1905-1940), and many articles in the *Journal of African History*, *Journal of Southern African Studies* and *African Affairs*. He has also helped to edit three collections of essays on Malawi including a special issue of the *Journal of Southern African Studies* (Vol. 28, 1, 2002). He is a past President of the African Studies Association of the United Kingdom (1990-92) and a member of the editorial board of the *Journal of Southern African Studies*.

James H. Mittelman is Professor, School of International Service, American University, Washington, DC, and Vice-President of the International Studies Association, 2006-2007. He is the author of *Globalization: Critical Reflections*, editor (1996), *Out from Underdevelopment Revisited: Changing Global Structures and the Remaking of the Third World* (1997), *The Globalization Syndrome: Transformation and Resistance* (2000); *Capturing Globalization*, coedited with Norani Othman (2001); and *Whither Globalization? The Vortex of Knowledge and Ideology* (2004).

Peter Probst is an associate professor in the departments of art history and anthropology at Tufts University, Massachusetts, USA. His current fields of interest are modernity, memory and the public sphere. He was trained in Germany and England and has taught at the Free University of Berlin, the Johann Wolfgang von Goethe University in Frankfurt/Main and the University of Bayreuth. Recent book publications include *African Modernities: Entangled Meanings and Current Debate* (2001), *Between Resistance and Expansion: Explorations of Local Vitality in Africa* (2004) and *Kalumbas Fest: Lokalität, Geschichte und Rituelle Praxis in Malawi* (2005).

Pearl T. Robinson is associate professor of African and African-American Politics at Tufts University. She is President (2006-2007) of the African Studies Association, USA, and a former Chair of the SSRC/ACLS Joint Committee on African Studies. She has served on the national boards of TransAfrica and Oxfam-America; as an advisor to the National Council of Negro Women's International Division and the African Academy of Science's Research Program on the Education of Women and Girls. She has been a Visiting Professor at Makerere University and at the University of Dar es Salaam, and a Research Affiliate of Abdou Moumouni University. Recent publications include 'Curriculum Co-Development with African Universities: Experiments in Collaboration across Two Digital Divides' (2004). Current projects include an intellectual biography of Ralph Bunche, and research on Islam and Female Empowerment among the Tijaniyya in Niger.

Ann Schlyter is an associate professor and director of the Centre for Global Gender Studies, School of Global Studies, Goteborg University, Sweden. She has a long experience of urban and gender studies in southern Africa and has focused her research on urban upgrading, housing, living conditions and everyday life for various groups, such as women-headed households, youth and elderly people. Her publications include the edited book, *Gender, Generation and Urban Living Conditions in Southern Africa* (2005), *Gender and Housing in Southern Africa: Emerging Issues* (2003),and *Multihabitation. Urban Housing and Everyday Life in Chitungwiza, Zimbabwe* (2003).

Jomo Kwame Sundaram is a prominent Malaysian economist currently serving as the United Nations Assistant Secretary General for Economic Development in the United Nations Department of Economic and Social Affairs (DESA). He was previously at the University of Malaya. He is the founder chair of International Development Economics Associates. He was also founder director of the independent Institute of Social Analysis (INSAN) until late 2004, President of the Malaysian Social Science Association (1996–2000). He has authored over 35 monographs, edited over 50 books and translated 11 volumes besides writing many academic papers and articles for the media. His better known recent books include *Privatizing Malaysia* (1995), *Southeast Asia's Misunderstood Miracle* (1997), *Tigers in Trouble* (1998), *Malaysia's Political Economy: Politics, Patronage and Profits* (1999), *Rents, Rent-Seeking and Economic Development* (2000), *Malaysian Eclipse* (2000) and *The New Development Economics* (2005).

Masao Yoshida is professor emeritus and former Director, Research Institute of International Studies, Chubu University. He previously taught at the Institute of Developing Economies where he served as director of the Area Studies Department, and at Rikkyo University, Nihon University, Osaka University, and Nagoya University. He was visiting professor at the universities of Dar es Salaam, Makerere (where he received his PhD in agricultural economics in 1972), California, and the Scandinavian Institute of African Studies, and consultant for Japanese missions to Egypt, Ethiopia, Kenya, Tanzania, and Southern Africa. He is the author of numerous articles and eight books, including *Agricultural Marketing Intervention in East Africa: A Study in the Colonial Origins of Marketing Policies, 1900–1965* (1984); *Economic Crises and Development Policies in African Countries in the 1980s* (1987); *Japanese Aid for the Agricultural Development in Africa* (1997), and *Contemporary History of East Africa* (2000).

Paul Tiyambe Zeleza is Professor and Head, Department of African American Studies at the University of Illinois at Chicago and Honorary Visiting Professor at the University of Cape Town. He has published scores of essays and has authored or edited more than a dozen books, including most recently *Rethinking Africa's Globalization* (2003), the *Routledge Encyclopedia of Twentieth Century African History, Leisure in Urban Africa* (2003), *Science and Technology in Africa* (2003) and *African Universities in the Twentieth Century* (2 volumes) (2004). He is the winner of the 1994 Noma Award for his book *A Modern Economic History of Africa* (1993) and the 1998 Special Commendation of the Noma Award for *Manufacturing African Studies and Crises* (1997). He has also published works of fiction.

Introduction

The Internationalisation of African Knowledges

Paul Tiyambe Zeleza

Almost invariably, the construction and conceptualisation of knowledge have social, spatial and temporal contexts and referents. Few would disagree that knowledge, whatever the prevailing disciplinary labels, is produced through specific paradigms that are developed by certain groups of people in particular places and periods. Knowledge production is, in this fundamental sense, a social practice marked by period and place, notwithstanding the vigorous, but often vain, attempts by some scholars to free their disciplines, specialties, theories and models from the supposedly suffocating confines of time and space. As even a cursory glance at the history of any discipline will show, and as was demonstrated in the previous volume, the disciplines and interdisciplines are rather porous and changing branches of knowledge; they are epistemic and social constructs whose intellectual, institutional, and ideological configurations are mediated and mapped by the unyielding demands of historical geography.

In the academies of Euro-America, I would like to submit, the argument between the interdiscipline of area studies, in which African studies is located, and the disciplines of the academic departments is essentially about the territoriality and temporality of knowledge and knowledge production: universality is claimed for the disciplines and contextuality for the area studies. And 'area' itself is parsed further: the disciplines are a preserve of the 'West' and 'area studies' of the 'Rest'. It is a hierarchical division of academic labour that is powerful and appealing to many, one that is institutionally sanctified in the Euro-American academy in the relatively low positioning of area studies faculty and programmes. It is reproduced in the perennial debates between the disciplines and the area studies, which are praised or pilloried for their propensity for descriptiveness and detail, local knowledge and exoticism, or complicity with imperialist impulses or multiculturalist political correctness. These characterisations, as will be demonstrated in the next section, are simplistic and seriously flawed.

As argued in the previous volume, African studies has both disciplinary and interdisciplinary dimensions, disciplinary in so far as it is the object of research, study, teaching and publications in specific disciplines and interdisciplinary in situations where these activities are institutionally organized in specific African studies units whether called—the administrative nomenclature varies—programmes, centres, institutes, or departments. These tendencies have a territorial dimension: within Africa itself there are few African studies programmes as such because Africa is lodged within the disciplines,[1] unlike what prevails in Euro-America where the area studies model was invented and African studies programmes provide a crucial institutional base. This parallels the relatively weak position in the American academy of American studies as an interdiscipline compared to the incorporation of American studies in the disciplines. In both cases, 'area studies' refers to, by and large, an 'outside' study, in the case of Africa study of the hegemonic imperial 'other', in the case of Euro-America the study of the colonial or postcolonial dependent 'other'.

There are other crucial differences in the organisation of 'area studies' in Africa and Euro-America: the latter's overdetermination of African knowledge systems remains palpable, while the African influence on Euro-American scholarship is quite negligible, notwithstanding the wistful claims made by the authors of *Africa and the Disciplines* (Bates, Mudimbe and O'Barr 1993). This situation points to the uneven and unequal ways in which the disciplines and interdisciplines are internationalised between the global North and much of the global South, including Africa. It suggests that the terms of global intellectual exchange, like the terms of trade for the so-called developed and developing economies, are decidedly unequal: African studies in the North is a peripheral part of the academy, whereas the Euro-American epistemological order remains central in the African academy. Since the colonial encounter, the construction of scholarly knowledge about Africa has been internationalised both in the sense of it being an activity involving scholars in various parts of the world and the inordinate influence of externally generated models on African scholarship.

More often than not the scholars who have tended to set the terms of debate and discourse in African studies, prescribing much of what is deemed authoritative knowledge, framing the methodological and theoretical terrain of the field, and shaping the infrastructures of scholarly knowledge production, are Euro-American rather than African. There is perhaps no other region in the world that has suffered more from what Paulin Hountondji (1997) calls 'theoretical extraversion' than Africa, where imported intellectual perspectives, preoccupations, and perversions play such a powerful role in scholarship, not to mention policy formulation and even popular discourse. This is a subject on which I have written extensively (Zeleza 1997, 2003, 2004, 2005). It would not be far-fetched to argue that the 'area studies' model, through which many African scholars educated in the global North were themselves trained, and through which academic relations between Euro-American universities and African universities are often organised, mediated or reproduced, played a critical role.

The chapters in this volume explore these issues: the ways in which Africa has been engaged in international studies and in international contexts, characterised by shifting analytical fads and different national tendencies. It is divided into three parts. The first part briefly explores the possibilities and perils of the area studies model as developed in the United States, a country with the largest academic system in the world and one of the largest African studies establishments outside of Africa itself, by examining some of the debates about area studies. In the second and third parts the introduction summarises and comments on the chapters in the volume. Part two looks at the study of Africa in international studies, that is, the state of African studies as seen through the paradigms of globalisation (Mittelman), transborder formations (Kassimir), and diaspora studies (Zeleza), as well as the implications of some of these paradigms for actual development processes in Africa (Sundaram), and the challenges of translation in transnational African studies scholarship (Dedieu). This is followed in the last part by analyses of African studies in different global regions: Europe—Britain (McCracken), France (Jewsiewicki), Germany (Probst), Sweden (Schlyter), and the former Soviet Union (Filatova); the Americas—the United States (Robinson), the Caribbean (Cobley), and Brazil (Lima); and finally the Asia-Pacific region—India (Biswas), Australia (Lyons and Dimock), China (Anshan) and Japan (Yoshida). Space simply does not allow for a more systematic analysis of African studies within Africa itself, a subject implied in some of the remarks that follow but which deserves an extended treatment in its own right.

The Possibilities and Perils of the Areas Studies Model

Histories of area studies, like academic histories in general, are revealing for what they say and leave out, what they seek to remember and to forget. They serve as weapons in the perennial institutional and intellectual struggles among disciplines and interdisciplines for material resources and reputational capital. These histories seek to mark boundaries, to stake positions, to confer authority, and in the case of area studies, to define the alleged contemporary crisis of the field and devise solutions appropriate to the protagonists. In areas studies histories written in the United States in the 1990s it is commonly assumed that the Second World War gave birth to 'area studies' in the American academy, and the cold war nurtured the interdiscipline, in response to the gruelling demands of global confrontation spawned by the two wars.[2] It followed that since the Cold War was now over, area studies had lost their *raison d'être*. Moreover, since much of the world was politically democratising and economically liberalising, knowledge of the world outside Euro-America could be inferred from the universal models of the disciplines, or the homogenising imperatives of globalisation.[3]

This narrative was quite appealing to right-wing ideologues who thought history was over; fiscally minded university administrators seeking programmes to cut; and social scientists desperate to acquire the analytical credentials of the natural sciences. However, it was a narrative that silenced other histories of area studies in the United States itself and in other world regions, as the contributions in this volume make abundantly clear. Writing about African studies, Pearl Robinson (1997: 169) eloquently contests the standard Cold War history of area studies:

> Debates about the future of African Studies seem to have little to do with the past as I know or have come to understand it. What I discern is a profusion of arguments linked to differing standpoints and designed to privilege new hierarchies of access to resources. Virtually all the prevailing reconstructions of African Studies begin with the Cold War and focus on the legacies of government- and foundation-funded Area Studies programs. Curiously, such accounts generally omit any reference to the long-standing tradition of African Studies at historically black colleges and universities, only rarely give a nod to African American professional and lay scholars of Africa, and seldom acknowledge the existence of epistemic communities based in Africa.

Robinson's contestation was echoed in a comprehensive compendium of area studies written at the height of the American 'area studies wars'.[4] Holzner and Harmon (1998) traced the roots of the area studies tradition to the nineteenth century. They explain:

> Prior to 1900, US 'research' about other parts of the world consisted of four traditions: the 'classical' tradition, which studied the ancient civilizations of Greece, Rome, and Egypt; the missionary movement, whose proponents traveled to other nations with the intent of encouraging conversion, but who were often anti-intellectual and explicitly limited the scope of inquiry into their host societies; a 'scientific racism' tradition that attempted to demonstrate the superiority of whites through comparison with and systematic examination of other races; and, finally, an anecdotal 'tradition' of relying on information about non-Western cultures from potentially unreliable travelers (Holzner and Harmon (1998:7).

During the late 1940s and 1950s when area studies became institutionalised, Gilbert Merkx (1995) contends that Cold War concerns were often used to achieve long-sought support for higher education in general and long-standing research on the non-Western world in particular.

There is no doubt that the Second World War and the Cold War had a profound impact on the development of area studies, and that the end of the cold war brought new contexts. But area studies, certainly African studies, antedated both wars. The area studies movement was bolstered by the need to overcome the isolationist and parochial tendencies of the American public and academy, increasingly seen as unbecoming and perilous for a superpower. The American public was woefully uninformed about the rest of the world, especially the newly independent countries of Africa and Asia, where the United States and the Soviet Union were locked in fierce combat to win hearts and minds. The need for information about these countries, including America's turbulent backyard, Latin America, as well as the Soviet bloc, was seen as essential in the struggle for global supremacy between the USA and USSR.

Reinforcing the national security imperative was the epistemological imperative to internationalise knowledge in the academy. While the link between social science and area knowledge goes back to the origins of some social science disciplines, such as sociology and anthropology, most of the disciplines remained resolutely ethno-centric, an intellectual deficiency syndrome that worsened as they aspired to 'scien-tific' status and concocted, from American experience, universal models and theo-ries that magically transcended the realities and diversities of global histories and geographies, cultures and societies, polities and economies. The theoretical conceit and parochialism of the disciplines reflected the imperial provincialism and ethno-centrism of the American public. Area studies were expected to overcome these deficiencies and to provide the public and academy with information about the non-Western world.

The interdiscipline was, therefore, infused with the twists and turns of American foreign policy, the projection of imperial power, in which knowledge of America and allied Europe more broadly was lodged within the disciplines, and that of the rest of the world was relegated to the area studies ghetto and inscribed with the pathologies of otherness. Consequently, the United States and Euro-America more generally were not considered an 'area,' which they obviously are, but at the very core of disciplinary knowledges, its experiences—rendered into stylised facts—and the epistemologies derived from them elevated into manifestations of the universal. So the pernicious fictions were born and bred that area studies were concerned with the parochial and the particular, while American studies, and their civilisational cous-ins, European studies, were disciplinary parables of the human condition. As Michael Chege (1997: 136-137) once admonished:

> It is also time for North America and Western Europe to be designated as "Area Studies" as well ... To that extent, calls for methodological rigor should not be dismissed offhand. The same applies to Western-based scholarship, to the extent that it is prepared to see itself objectively as one more "area" in which theory is validated or rejected. Such an approach would help short-circuit the sterile polemical debate on the relevance, or lack thereof, of Area Studies and still adopt a stridently critical demeanor concerning the reigning concepts of social science.

Often forgotten in the fictions of disciplinary superiority and the interdisciplinary lack of area studies was the simple fact that area studies faculty were both discipli-narians and interdisciplinarians: they were trained and held appointments in the disciplines. I discovered I was an area studies specialist only when I went to the United States to take up a job as director of the Center for African Studies at the University of Illinois (but my tenure home was in History). Before that in my previ-ous appointments in Canada, Kenya, Jamaica, and Malawi I had been known as a historian or a dilettante given the breadth of my intellectual interests. In short, area studies people in the American academy are far less parochial than the Americanists or Europeanists who wear monolithic disciplinary identities. An American can be a professor in most disciplines in the social sciences and humanities without knowing anything about non-western societies and countries; what is almost unheard of is an Africanist or an African professor who only knows the society she studies or comes from. Thus, it is not area studies people who need the rigour that comes from intellectual breadth and depth, but those in the ethnocentric disciplines.

The development of area studies was also tied to the fate of ethnic minorities in the United States. The 'scientific racism' that coloured much of the earlier work on non-Western societies was rooted in racist and discriminatory policies at home against the Native Americans, African Americans, and others. The exclusion of these populations from political and cultural citizenship, from the American mainstream, necessitated the separation of their ancestral cultures and continents from disciplinary narratives. In short, given the centrality of race in American society and politics, the eternal solitudes between blacks and whites rooted in slavery and segregation, it meant that the privileges and pathologies of the wider American social and intellectual order were reflected and reproduced with a ferocious investment of patronage, passions, and pain in African studies in a manner that was unusual even among the area studies programmes. More often than not, definitions and defamations of Africa were projections of attitudes to African Americans. The vocabulary used to depict the otherness and failed promises of Africa was often the same as that used for African Americans. This congruence of constructions and condemnations lay at the heart of the periodic contestations, often bitter, between Africans, African Americans, and European Americans in the study of Africa.

The shifting contexts, justifications, compositions, contents and predilections of area studies were neither peculiar to the area studies movement, nor to the United States. As shown in the previous volume, during the same period that area studies as an interdiscipline was developing, the disciplines were also undergoing important shifts, desperately seeking to redefine and differentiate themselves from each other and to gain ascendancy on the academic totem pole, to stake superior claims of the cognitive authority of science in a world so conscious of its modernity and dazzled by science and technology. Studies of knowledge production in other parts of the world would reveal, as is shown in this volume in the case of African studies in various world regions, similar tendencies, that the changing disciplinary and interdisciplinary architecture of knowledge occurs as much in the context of, and sometimes in response to, transformations in the epistemic and conceptual orders of knowledge as in the changing socioeconomic and political conditions of the wider society. In the case of the United States, the area studies movement has undergone five phases each characterised by its own dynamics, orientations, and dominant perspectives and shifting engagements between the interdiscipline and the disciplines and other interdisciplines, such as ethnic studies and women's studies, and interdisciplinary paradigms like cultural studies, postcolonial studies and diaspora studies.

The first phase was in the late nineteenth century and was characterised by competing racist Euro-American and vindicationist Afro-American traditions. The early twentieth century marked the second phase when African studies was dominated by African American scholar activists and the historically black colleges and universities whose work centred on the question of Africa's civilisational presence in the global concert of cultures. The Cold War era marked the third phase when the gravity of African studies shifted to European American scholars and the historically white universities. The foundations bankrolled the field together with the federal government's Title VI programmes of the US Department of Education and its analytical focus shifted to modernisation prescriptions. This phase was dominated at first by anthropology, the principal colonial science. History briefly took over from anthropology in the anti-colonialist wrath of decolonisation, and then political science and economics—yes the queen and aspiring king of the social sciences before their mathematical turn—assumed prominence in the great developmentalist drama of the early and euphoric postcolonial years. The turn of the 1990s ushered in the fourth phase—the post-Cold War era when area studies were deemed to be in crisis, a period that coincided with the ascendancy of the anti-foundationalist and representational discourses of postmodernism, postcolonial scholarship and cultural studies, which questioned the integrity of regional and cultural boundaries and identities and privileged hybrid, immigrant, and diasporic identities.

Four major critiques were advanced against area studies, each of which was vigorously and sometimes effectively rebutted by area studies practitioners. First, it was argued that area studies were a Cold War political project that had now outlived its usefulness. Second, area studies were 'merely "ideographic", primarily concerned with description, as opposed to the "nomothetic" or theory building and generalizing character of the core social science disciplines' (Szantzon 2004: 20-21). Third, some maintained that area studies scholars uncritically propagated the universalising or localising categories, perspectives, commitments, and theories of their imperialist interlocutors in the metropoles or their nativist informants in the postcolonies. Fourth, champions of globalisation contended that the apparently new world order of enhanced transnational economic, cultural, information, and demographic flows rendered the old structures of organising and producing knowledge in bounded regions increasingly obsolete. What was now required, in the place of old-fashioned area studies, it was argued, were international or global studies, or at the very least comparative regional studies.[5] The Social Science Research Council abolished its area studies committees and the foundations duly withdrew their area studies funding support and launched new initiatives on cross-regional and globalisation issues.[6] But the American triumphalism of the 1990s was brought to a sudden halt by the terrorist attacks of September 11, 2001. History was not over after all, and foreign cultures still existed that demanded understanding—translation—on their own terms. This ushered the fifth phase, marked by a return to the future of the national security imperative in area studies. The scientific pretensions of political science with its rational choice models, and the turgid postmodernist and postcolonial theorising of literary studies suddenly looked rather self-indulgent and unproductive.

Africa in International Studies

The chapters in the first part of the collection examine the engagements between African studies and various international studies constructs. This part opens with James Mittelman's fascinating interrogation of the implications for African studies of globalisation as a conceptual paradigm. From the 1990s there was an explosion in the literature on globalisation, seen both as a historical process of intensified transnational economic and cultural flows and interconnectedness and as an ideological project of global capitalism advancing the neoliberal agenda of liberalisation, deregulation and privatisation. Mittelman distinguishes between what he calls the para-keepers who contest the theoretical claims and policy aims of the globalisation paradigm and the para-makers who support them. As much else in scholarship, these divergences reflect not only different intellectual investments—ontological, methodological, and epistemological commitments—but also varied ideological, institutional, and even individual inclinations.

In the field of international studies the former include proponents of the realist, interdependence, and world systems perspectives and social democrats, for whom the processes associated with globalisation are not new, while the latter consist of an eclectic group of scholars who believe globalisation does constitute a new conceptual framework of examining the world and a new consciousness of experiencing the world. Whether or not globalisation represents a Kuhnian paradigm shift, there can be little doubt that it has reinforced the discontents and opened new analytical directions within international studies, a field traditionally focused on relations between nations and states as discrete entities and spaces. Mittelman highlights some of the major themes and traps of the globalisation paradigm, which is concerned with global problems, challenges and actors, transformations in global structures and the territorial configurations of power, and continuities and discontinuities with the past in the world order. But it suffers from conceptual promiscuity and lack of precision, tends to be overdetermined, reductive and insufficiently attentive to agency, and spawns new binaries as it simultaneously explodes the old dichotomies of international studies.

Nevertheless, the breadth of the globalisation paradigm's thematic and theoretical concerns—from economy to ecology, popular culture to transnational politics, cultural studies to political economy—is a potential source of critical strength, which gives it a transdisciplinary edge, the capacity to combat the fragmentation of knowledge. If the potential of globalisation studies is to be realised, Mittelman argues, there is need for more systematic conceptualisation of the varieties of globalisation and classification of globalisation schools, investigation into the implications of globalisation for disciplinary, interdisciplinary and transnational studies including development and area studies, and for curricular programming, as well as examination of its ethics in terms of what and whose values are being inscribed in globalisation as a process, a project, and a paradigm, and its structures of production as far as the locational and institutional inequalities in the construction of globalisation studies are concerned. African studies, Mittelman concludes, needs to interrogate and incorporate the globalisation paradigm more vigorously than it has so far; Africanist scholars have a responsibility to retell and remake the story of globalisation.

One of the fundamental issues raised by the globalisation problematic is the relationship, or rather the intersections between the local and the global, the external and the internal, the inside and the outside. Ron Kassimir argues in his chapter that globalisation is a very blunt instrument for conceptualising the global-local nexus, for disaggregating the various kinds of external-internal connections, and showing how they relate to one another. He reminds us of the central insight of dependency theory, that ever since the emergence of the world system the external is always already implicated in the local, although many dependency writers were wont to overemphasise external forces and underestimate local agency, and to depict the structural forces largely in materialist and economistic terms at the expense of their ideational, political, and cultural dimensions. He proposes the concept of transboundary formations as an analytical device to transcend the external-internal divide and capture the dynamics created by the intersection of forces emanating from various spatial, social, structural, and sectoral levels.

It is a framework that can yield useful hypothesis and provide insights in analysing concrete events and processes in which different institutions operate and intersect, where networks of people form and through which ideas and commodities are trafficked. Kassimir proceeds to illustrate this by looking at two sets of transboundary formations, first, the operations of the international aid regime, and second the illicit flows of so-called conflict diamonds. In the case of international aid, it is clear that as a mechanism of intervention, aid is already deeply implicated in the domestic development crises it seeks to alleviate, which are constituted and reproduced through the ongoing intersections between the providers, architects and advocates of aid and a range of other actors, including local government officials and business interests. As for the seemingly local political disorders that are often attributed to Africa's alleged affliction with primordial hatreds, the case of conflict diamonds bears testimony to the critical role played by the global demand and markets for commodities, cross-border smuggling of commodities and arms, and recruitment of mercenary forces in engendering and sustaining many a civil war and regional conflict.

The involvement of African studies and African scholars in setting the conceptual and methodological architecture of globalisation or international studies remains minimal. This is troubling enough for intellectual reasons: it is important for Africanists to inscribe their intellectual insights and interests in this ascending paradigm. But the matter goes beyond intellectual bragging rights. As a discursive project of neoliberalism globalisation has inspired policy interventions that have profoundly transformed Africa's development processes and prospects, whose costs for the continent have been truly horrendous. It is important for us to be reminded of this, that the struggle over ideas, over academic paradigms, involves competing visions, priorities, and policies on how best to organise society for specific social interests and projects. The chapter by Jomo Kwame Sundaram offers a sobering reminder of the heavy costs exacted on Africa's development by globalisation, specifically the doctrine of economic liberalisation espoused by the infamous 'Washington Consensus'. The neoliberal assault began at the turn of the 1980s with an escalating battery of serial and doctrinaire conditionalities—'getting prices right', 'getting good governance', and 'getting good institutions'—whose apparent absence was blamed for the increasingly evident failures of the structural adjustment programmes.

More than two and half decades after praying faithfully at the altar of neoliberalism, in much of Africa (and indeed the world as a whole) growth levels are slower than in the pre-adjustment days, poverty levels are higher, real wages have fallen, import substitution industrialisation has been replaced by de-industrialisation, exports and Africa's share of world trade have declined, capital inflows remain low and are dominated by speculative portfolio investment and capital flight continues unabated so that Africa has become a net exporter of capital. Structural maladjustment and its deflationary policies have weakened domestic capacities and put Africa on the low-productivity, low-growth path. The Washington Consensus is now largely discredited, certainly in Africa and in academic circles, as a strategy for development, let alone accelerated development as was originally promised in the notorious Berg report of 1981 and subsequent encyclicals from the international financial institutions. The epistemological delegitimation and the loss of certainty by the international financial institutions, as reflected in the adoption of an ever more eclectic assortment of new growth theories, offer a window of opportunity for new forms of economic research and policy-making in Africa based on a long term vision of sustainable development rooted in a comprehensive understanding of Africa's histories, political economies, institutions, challenges and needs.

Neoliberal globalisation has had more direct and contradictory consequences on African knowledge production systems. As is well known, structural adjustment programmes devastated African universities, which led to the massive migration of academics to other sectors at home or to institutions abroad (Zeleza and Olukoshi 2004). The growth of the African academic diaspora and of diaspora studies, especially in the countries of the global North, is the subject of Paul Tiyambe Zeleza's chapter. He argues that the African diaspora in general and its intelligentsia in particular has demonstrated the potential, which it has exercised during some key moments of modern African history, through the Pan-African movement for example, for a productive engagement with Africa. Africa's academic diaspora, itself a product of various cycles of capitalist globalisation including the current one, offers African academic systems a way of mitigating their peripherality, of negotiating new terms of engagement with the powerful research and publishing establishments that control international knowledge production, of minimising the negative and maximising the positive impacts of academic liberalisation, of modifying Africa's lopsided academic relations with external donors and scholarly gatekeepers, of mediating Africa's globalisation. The challenge for the contemporary African academic diaspora is to mediate continental Africa and diasporic Africa, the political and economic projects of Pan-Africanism and the cultural and discursive paradigms of diaspora and global studies.

Zeleza's chapter begins by trying to redefine African diaspora studies, suggesting the need for a global perspective that transcends the Atlantic framework, then it maps out the institutional, intellectual, and ideological dynamics of diasporic knowledge production, which is followed by an effort to historicise diasporic academic production and linkages with Africa during two crucial periods, the colonial and early post-independence eras. The final part of the chapter focuses on current trends and interrogates some of the typologies that have been advanced to characterise the orientations of the contemporary African academic diaspora based on their ideological inclinations, disciplinary affiliations, or research and publication preferences. A forceful case is made that the contemporary African academic diaspora is a critical mediator in the transmission of knowledges between Africa and the West, essential to the globalisation of African knowledges and Africanisation of global knowledges. As part of the new diaspora they are also a bridge between Africa and its historic diasporas, through whom Africa made enormous contributions to the very foundations of capitalist globalisation.

The epistemic communities in African studies are often divided by nationality, location and language. In this context the question of translation poses evident challenges; translation in the sense of cross-cultural access, reading and interpretation of scholarship on areas of mutual interest produced in different national intellectual traditions. Scholarship across national boundaries or epistemic communities, however constructed, especially in the human sciences, can be conceived as acts of translation, in which scholars grapple with foreign textual and lived experiences—languages, materials, and perspectives—and strive, if they are scrupulous, to understand them on their own terms and in terms that are also meaningful to their own cognitive universe and training. Translation is embedded in the very logic of area studies. Indeed, area studies can be seen, Alan Tansman (2004: 184) has argued persuasively, as a form of translation, 'an enterprise seeking to know, analyze, and interpret foreign cultures through multidisciplinary lens'. The question of the transnational translation of area studies textual products is the subject of Jean-Philippe Dedieu's captivating chapter that explores the problems of translation in France of work produced outside the Francophone world and in English by Francophone scholars resident in Anglophone countries. He shows that the reluctance to translate and engage foreign works, including Africanist texts, in France is rooted in a long and complex history.

Dedieu argues that French national identity consolidated itself, in part, through the selective domestication and consecration of foreign texts, as well as the imperial process of discursive colonisation, which created the 'translated men' of the colonies and the postcolonies who have increasingly found themselves excluded from France as a space of both territorial and linguistic sovereignty. More and more the Francophone scholars have migrated to the Anglophone world, especially to the United States because of restrictive French immigration policies and institutional racism. The relocated Francophone scholars are forced to produce works in English, which are not readily translated in France. The politics of translation reveals the methods of hospitality for the populations and the publications that are differentially allowed to cross the territorial and literary borders of France. This exclusion has not been confined to Francophone scholars, but also applies to American Africanist texts, and British authors in general. The disregard for American Africanist research, especially that connected with black studies, postcolonial studies and cultural studies, notwithstanding the inspiration some of these interdisciplinary perspectives have drawn from French theory, is based on a perceived epistemological divide between French republicanism and American multiculturalism, and French insularity and suspicion of US hegemony. The problems of the publishing industry in France simply reinforce the political logic of exclusion. The result is that major works produced in the United States, including those from Francophone scholars, tend to be ignored, dismissed, or take too long to be translated.

African Studies in Regional Contexts

The study of Africa has become increasingly global. There is now hardly a region where Africa is not taught in one way or another, where Africanist research is not conducted, where Africa does not feature in academic, popular, or political discourses. But there are enormous variations in the levels of regional and national expertise and commitment to African studies, partly predicated on different histories of economic, political, and cultural engagements with Africa, as well as the relative presence or absence of African diasporas. Also, the production and consumption of knowledges of Africa are filtered through the exceedingly complex, diverse and shifting prisms of local intellectual traditions, ideological tendencies, and institutional cultures. The result is that it is quite difficult to make valid generalisations about the state of or trends in African studies globally, except to say that nowhere does the field constitute a major area of scholarly attention. African studies and Africanists remain at the bottom of the academic ladder, even if in various countries they may stand on different rungs from the floor. This mirrors the position of Africa itself, whose international presence remains rather low save for moments of spectacular disasters, such as during the Rwanda genocide, or the periodic invocations of global panic as is the case with the HIV/AIDS pandemic.

The oldest African studies traditions tend to be found in countries with long colonial histories or large African diasporas or both. Knowledge of Africa, however distorted or self-serving it may have been, was an essential part of the colonial project. Similarly, knowledge of Africans, however deficient or stereotypical, was a constituent element of the emerging intellectual fabric of the settler societies based on African slave labour in the Americas. The chapters in this collection examine the development of African studies in some of these countries, including France and Britain, representing the old colonial superpowers, and Germany that lost its colonial empire after the First World War, and the United States, the Caribbean and Brazil, which contain large African diaspora populations. But as already noted, African studies has become a global enterprise, and some of the most dynamic centres can be found in European countries that have no colonial connections with Africa, such as Sweden and Russia, or Asian countries that have a shared history of European colonialism, such as India and Australia, and others that do not like China and Japan.

In his fascinating contribution, Bogumil Jewsiewicki offers a comparative trans-Atlantic, trans-linguistic mapping of the disciplinary evolution of African studies and its divergent trajectories in France and the United States. While the political and ideological inflatus for African studies is marked by the divergent historical relationship of each country to its African/Black Other, Jewsiewicki contends that a homology exists in terms of generational patterns and shifts in the development of African studies in both countries. These shifts, phases and generations in the United States saw the study of Africa informed successively by developments in Area Studies and Black Studies, while in the French situation, an early colonialist pedigree eventually gave way to a more centralised approach to African studies in various research units and clusters in the academy. Central to Jewsiewicki's explorations of the peculiarities of the development for African studies in the two countries is the existence of what he sees as a certain mnemonic function of Africa in each country. African studies developed and was disciplinarised in both contexts because of the existence of an Africa of memory for the two countries. This Africa harks back to slavery in the case of the United States and colonialism in the case of France.

If African Studies in the US was inspired and sustained by the political imperatives of superpower status and the presence of African Americans, in France it was initially stimulated by the aesthetic influences of African art on modernism whose global capital was Paris and later upheld by the ideology of anti-colonialism on the French left. Theory had greater import in French than in American African studies. It was only from the late 1960s that theory gained currency in the latter as anti-establishment students and faculty sought a new language of protest which they found initially in Latin American dependency theory and later in 'French theory'. In France, the prominence given to theory not only resonated with the tenor of French intellectual discourse, it also served as a means of differentiating French Africanists from colonial officials who launched the field of African studies. The investment in theory, largely Marxist, was facilitated by the absence of a recognised African political base in France, and theory functioned as an ideological expression of solidarity with Africa. While the events of September 11 in the United States promised to reinvigorate area studies, including African studies, in France the riots of November 2005 and attempts to sanitise or positivise the memory of colonisation have forced France to reckon with the place of Africa and Black people in its national imaginary which has implications for African studies in the country. One manifestation of this is the rediscovery, by the French academy, of cosmopolitan, migrant African intellectuals—the Manthia Diawaras, Mamadou Dioufs and Achille Mbembes.

The chapter by John McCracken outlines the broad changes that have taken place in African studies in recent decades in Britain. He recalls the perilous state of the field in the 1980s as the number of Africanist faculty dwindled and resources declined and Britain lost its pre-eminent position in African studies to other countries, especially the United States. Now looking back more than ten years after he delivered the 1992 presidential address at the biennial conference of the African Studies Association of the United Kingdom, McCracken happily finds that the pronouncements of the impending death of the field were greatly exaggerated. New programmes have been established and a spate of young faculty appointments made, student enrolments have risen, and high quality research is being produced. He singles out for illustration research in three areas: the Christian encounter with Africa, Africa and the environment, and African nationalism revisited. Particularly vibrant has been the expansion of African studies in the related fields of cultural and diaspora studies and in the new universities converted from polytechnics in the 1980s. Much of the energy propelling the growth of African studies, which also poses a challenge to the interdiscipline as conceived historically in Britain, is the expansion of the country's African and Afro-Caribbean communities. Among the challenges he identifies in addition to the perennial inadequacy of resources, is the need to develop more equitable and productive relations between the white and black British Africanists, as well between them and the African academics who have migrated to Britain since the 1990s and are part of new transnational African scholarly networks. He concludes on a cautious but hopeful note about the future.

In the annals of colonial history and European-African relations Germany is a little unique in that it was a colonial power but it lost its African empire after the First World War. It therefore occupies a peculiar position in European African studies lying between the colonial superpowers, Britain and France, and the smaller European powers like the Nordic countries that did not have African colonies. The history of African studies in Germany is as long as it is in Britain and France, but it lost its colonial scaffolding much earlier. Peter Probst's chapter presents a fascinating account of the ebbs and flows in the development of African studies in Germany. It has undergone several phases from its beginnings in the mid-nineteenth century when the field was founded by a small group of scholars and travellers. Although not yet institutionalised, African studies in Germany then was much more international and interdisciplinary than it became later. It was dominated by linguistics, a discipline that retained its supremacy until the early 1970s. During colonialism the growing band of German Africanists, many of whom were former missionaries, focussed largely on deciphering migration and diffusion among African cultural areas, themes that echoed scholarly preoccupations within Germany itself on German migrations and cultural formation. The field became institutionalised in the academy after the colonial period and became quite vibrant in the interwar years, during which anthropology and its functionalist approaches gained ground.

The first two decades after the Second World War was a period of restoration, reorganisation, continuation, and transformation, which saw the emergence of new disciplines especially literature and the arts, and politicisation of the field fuelled by the political pressures of decolonisation and anti-imperialist struggles in Africa and the rivalries between the two communist and capitalist Germany's. In 1969, the German Association of African Studies was formed at the instigation of young linguists seeking to transform their discipline by exposing it to other fields in African studies. Ironically, this ushered the demise of the dominance of linguistics, and the increasing 'social sciencing' of German African studies as history, law and political science gained prominence. Since unification in the 1990s, African studies in Germany has become both more differentiated and concentrated, thanks in part to funding formulas that favour the institutionalisation of thematic collaborative research centres. One result is that the disciplines are losing ground to interdisciplinary research. Another recent development whose impact on German African studies is likely to rise concerns the entanglement of national and supranational research agendas driven by the growing importance of the European Union project and the creation of EU-wide African studies networks, foreshadowed by the establishment of the Africa-Europe Group for Interdisciplinary Studies in 1991.

The Nordic countries had limited contacts with Africa before and during the colonial period, which were confined to church missions and sporadic trade adventures. Not surprisingly, Nordic researchers were on the periphery in European academic discourses on Africa dominated by scholars in the major European countries. The development of African studies in the Nordic countries largely coincided with African decolonisation and was marked by the formation of the Nordic Africa Institute in 1962 by the five Nordic ministries of foreign affairs. This is the subject of Ann Schlyter's chapter examining the development of African studies in Sweden. She argues that Swedish interest in Africa and African studies was motivated by the imperatives of small power global diplomacy, specifically political solidarity with the liberation movements in Southern Africa and economic support for development cooperation that was spawned by the ideological correspondence between the Swedish social welfare state project with the developmentalist state projects in the new states in Africa. Thus, Africanist research in Swedish universities and other institutions has had unusually strong financial support from the state, which is channelled through the Swedish Agency for Research Cooperation, originally an independent governmental body, but now a department within the Swedish development cooperation agency, Sida.

The close ties between research and development cooperation that has driven African studies in Sweden can be seen in the priority given to research on issues related to national resources, the environment and production of food, themes that received almost a third of Sida's funds in the second half of the 1990s. Also featuring high are health and medical research—they received a fifth of the funds. Thus, while African studies in Sweden is spread across a wide range of disciplines, the dominant fields tend to be those whose findings can be consumed by the development cooperation organisations, the main market of knowledge about Africa. The developmentalist thrust of Swedish research funding also means a premium is placed on capacity building in Africa and research cooperation with African scholars on the continent rather than encouraging African scholars to work and settle in Sweden. But Swedish Africanists have not been entirely confined to development-oriented research. Schlyter notes the growth of critical feminist and urban studies, and more recently work on human rights, conflict and democratisation, a clear indication that research in Sweden, despite its unique features, is responsive to political developments in Africa and theoretical tendencies elsewhere.

African studies has a long, fascinating history in the former Soviet Union. Before the Revolution of 1917 Russia's African scholarship consisted of translations and writings on Ethiopia and South Africa and was strongly anti-British and pro-African (Davidson and Filatova 2001). Soviet African studies started in earnest in the 1920s and underwent several phases that are delineated in comprehensive and insightful detail in the chapter by Irina Filatova. She argues that until the 1980s the field was dominated by the Soviet theory of anti-colonialism first formulated by Lenin and later revised by Stalin, which divided the world into oppressing and oppressed nations and sought to conceptualise the stages and revolutionary potential of the national liberation movement. Official theory framed all academic debates and political battles in Soviet African studies, a field that was controlled in the interwar years by the Comintern, where representatives from several African countries, beginning with South Africa, participated. The Comintern established the University of Eastern Toilers and other institutions that enrolled students from Africa. Much of the work of the early Soviet Africanists focussed on working class movements and activities, in which South Africa featured high, and debated in a highly ideological and scholastic manner whether or not an African bourgeoisie existed.

The writings of the Soviet Africanists in the 1920s and 1930s were inspired less by academic analyses of African realities than by theoretical and ideological concerns, so that African countries were often not differentiated from one another, a tendency that was reinforced by the fact that the Africanists did not travel to Africa unlike their western counterparts. But out of these very concerns and tendencies, Filatova shows, Soviet Africanists promoted comparative studies of Africa and pioneered the study of topics that did not interest western Africanists until the 1960s, such as the social structure of African societies, the social basis of African nationalism, the nature and possibilities of the postcolonial state, and other topics that were to characterise western Marxist writing on Africa. Soviet African studies entered a new phase in the 1940s and 1950s, thanks to decolonisation and the Cold War. The first generated debate about the nature of real and 'illusory' independence; the former was supposedly engendered by armed struggle and led by the proletariat and followed by reforms, especially nationalisation. The second inspired the need for allies among the newly independent states whose independence was increasingly portrayed as a progressive development and the working class was no longer accorded a leading role, but an active one, in the national liberation movements.

As the need for concrete information rose to inform Soviet policy towards the emerging African states, the work of Soviet Africanists became more empirical and theoretical generalisations gave way to more concrete analyses, a turn marked by the publication, in 1954, of *Peoples of Africa*, a huge study co-edited by the veteran Africanist Ivan Potekhin and Dimtrii Olderogge, in which ethnographic data occupied more space than political history. The work offered the first comprehensive history of African anti-colonialism published anywhere in the world. The trend established by 1960, Filatova informs us, lasted until the 1980s during which African studies boomed, with the establishment of African departments at several universities and institutes, and expansion to the study of languages, history, politics, economies, literature and cultures, areas in which Soviet academics made some original contributions. Since the mid-1980s African studies has felt the winds of liberalisation and the collapse of the Soviet Union, which was marked by the removal of ideological controls, freer travel to Africa, but there were also severe reductions in state funding. From the late 1990s, Davidson and Filatova (2006) observe, there has been a new momentum in Russian African studies and a revisiting of old and foray into new themes and topics of research.

As noted in the first part of this introduction, the United States boasts the largest concentration of African studies specialists outside of Africa itself. Consequently, the development of African studies in the US is unusually complex. The field has been marked by competing intellectual and ideological traditions, changing disciplinary and interdisciplinary configurations, shifting state mandates for area studies and civic engagements for African causes, and highly racialised contestations over resources, scholarly authority and the very boundaries of African studies among its main practitioners, European Americans, African Americans, and recent African immigrants. Pearl Robinson provides an exhaustive analysis of this rich, varied and tumultuous field. The construction of knowledge about Africa and the power to define and interpret it have been inextricably linked with American history, race relations, and the precarious status of African Americans. Robinson demonstrates that the Africanist enterprise has been characterised by the uneasy co-existence of at least three spatially-differentiated spheres of endeavour, what she calls the world of American research universities that typically focuses on sub-Saharan Africa, the world of diasporic Pan-African scholars, a polyglot realm that includes the historically black colleges and universities that engages the whole continent as well as the diaspora, and the world of African universities and research networks that generally defines Africa in continental terms.

African studies in the United States was pioneered by the scholar-activists belonging to the second tradition, who were ensconced at the HBCUs, especially Howard and Lincoln universities, from W.L. Hansberry to W.E.B. Du Bois to Ralph Bunche. It was not until the post-war era, during the Cold War, that the first tradition gained supremacy, supported by the federal government and foundation funding for area studies for US national security reasons and for the modernisation and internationalisation of the ethnocentric US disciplines. African studies centres and programmes were established at the historically white universities, beginning with Northwestern University in 1948, whose programme was headed by the anthropologist Merville Herskovits. In 1957 the African Studies Association was established. The division between the two traditions was loudly racial and epistemological, which was symbolised by the celebrated clash at the ASA Annual meeting in Montreal in 1969 over the racial composition and research content of white Africanist work. From the

1970s the third tradition began to assert itself as the traffic of African students to the US increased, and especially as the brain drain from Africa gathered momentum during Africa's 'lost decades' of the 1980s and 1990s when African universities were devastated by ill-conceived neoliberal divestments and deflations. This made the contestations within African studies even more complex and fierce, at the same time as significant disciplinary and theoretical transformations were occurring as exemplified by the rise of feminist studies and the 'posts'. A particularly critical development has been the return of diaspora studies, or rather the growing incorporation of diaspora in the research frameworks of white Africanist and immigrant African scholars, which Robinson believes bodes well for the future.

The development of African studies in the United States shares some parallels with the Caribbean. In fact, some of the scholar activists who pioneered African studies in the US were Caribbean immigrants. But as societies in which the African diasporas have historically constituted the majority of the population, the politics of African studies has been different, lacking the racial overtones of the American experience, and premised more on different degrees of identification with Africa. This is the subject of Alan Cobley's informative chapter, which traces the different tendencies in the development of African studies in the Caribbean. African studies were rooted in the inscription of Africa in Caribbean cultures and society from religion and diet to music and language, and from the creation of back to Africa imaginaries and movements to the construction of Afrocentric identities. Alongside this popular, organic African presence developed an intellectual tradition, the work of Caribbean intellectuals on African societies, cultures, and histories and their impact on Caribbean modernities and identities. Most of these intellectuals were activists as well, ranging from Marcus Garvey and George Padmore to C.L.R. James, Frantz Fanon and Arthur Lewis, who made significant contributions to the praxis of Pan-Africanism.

But the establishment of African studies as an academic discipline came relatively late during the era of decolonisation. The University of the West Indies was established in 1948 and nearly twenty years later the first academic programme in African history was established by Walter Rodney (1982), whose book, *How Europe Underdeveloped Africa* became the bible of European indictment for a whole generation of radicalised African and diaspora students, including mine. Gradually African studies courses were introduced in other disciplines and today Africa is taught in disciplines as diverse as history, literature, philosophy, education, French, economics and law. Moreover, the faculty include a growing number of African scholars who have migrated to the Caribbean in the last two decades. My first teaching job when I completed my doctorate in 1982 was at the Mona campus of the University of the West Indies in Jamaica. Cobley shows that the development of African studies has been uneven within the region. It is more advanced in the Anglophone than the Hispanic and Francophone Caribbean. In the Hispanic Caribbean research into the African heritage and connections was until recently actively discouraged because of myths of racial *creôlité*—the term used in the French Caribbean—or because it was seen as a threat to the construction of new, post-revolutionary societies as in Cuba.

The country with the largest African diaspora in the Americas is of course Brazil. It is also the country with the most refined national myth of 'racial democracy', an ideology that seeks to sanitise and silence Brazil's immense African demographic presence and cultural heritage. The chapter by Mônica Lima explores the teaching of African history and the history of Africans in Brazil. She notes that for a long time Brazilian historiography concealed and ignored the enormous contributions of African cultures and societies in the formation of Brazil. This was rooted in pervasive racism and attempts to whiten Brazilian society. When Africans and Afro-Brazilians appeared in the more progressive histories, they lost their specificity and disappeared into hapless objects of capitalist accumulation and pillage. They were reduced to helpless victims of foreign greed, a pitiable people subject to exploitation, domination, destruction, slavery, and oppression, rather than as historical subjects, active agents in the making and remaking of their own history and the history of Brazil as a whole. Protracted struggles against marginalisation—epistemic and economic, paradigmatic and political, conceptual and cultural, scholarly and social—finally led to the passage of a law in 2003 making the teaching of Afro-Brazilian history and culture as well as African history compulsory in the country's public and private schools. The rest of her chapter examines the challenges of turning this mandate into reality, the need to produce and disseminate complex, critical, and empowering histories of Africa and Brazil, in which the historicity and humanity of Africans and Afro-Brazilians are fully recognised, and that incorporate Afro-Brazilian connections to both Africa and the other Afro-American diasporas.

The global reach of African studies includes Asia and the Pacific, where several countries share varying degrees of historical and contemporary connections with Africa. One of these is India, which has had a long history of precolonial trading links and demographic and cultural flows with Eastern Africa and with Africa more generally through the circuits of British colonialism and anti-colonial struggles and the postcolonial solidarities of non-alignment and developmentalism. The chapter by Aparajita Biswas examines the development of African studies in India from the mid-1950s, whose growth owed much to the internationalist vision of India's leaders, especially Mohandas Gandhi and Jawaharlal Nehru, both of whom were Africanists in their own right. India's independence leaders believed fervently in Afro-Asian liberation and resurgence and stressed the need for a clear and critical understanding of the world and the imperative to develop a cadre of academic specialists on various world regions.

Thus from the outset African studies in India had strong state support. It was built on the success of the Indian Council of World Affairs and under the auspices of the Indian School of International Studies. A number of African studies centres were established at various universities with funding from the University Grants Commission, a statutory body for funding university education. Biswas briefly examines three of these centres (at the University of Delhi, Jawaharlal Nehru University, and Mumbai University), noting their considerable successes and continuing challenges. The constraints faced by African studies include bureaucratic and infrastructural impediments, insufficiency of funds, inadequate facilities for libraries and documentation, problems relating to teaching and student enrolment, the lack of coordination between the area studies centres and the Ministry of External Affairs, and the preponderance of political science and international relations at the expense of other disciplines.

Australia is another country in the Asia-Pacific region that shares close imperial ties with settler colonies in Africa, especially South Africa. In fact, as shown in the chapter by Tanya Lyons and Elizabeth Dimock, Australia's engagement with Africa began during the Anglo-Boer War when Australian troops fought on the British side. Events in South Africa have also had a direct academic impact: the years of the anti-apartheid struggles constituted the heyday of African studies in Australia and African migration to Australia has been dominated by waves of South African-born immigrants and others from the other former white settler colonies in the region— Zimbabwe and Namibia. It is also in South Africa that Australian universities have sought to establish a significant institutional presence in Africa. Unlike India and as we shall see below, China, African studies in Australia has never enjoyed state support. In fact, the rise of neoliberalism and Australia's embrace of Asia has drained official funding for Africa.

Lyons and Dimock discuss the development of African studies in Australia by looking at the role of the African Studies Association of Australasia and the Pacific formed in 1977, the results from a recent survey of the country's 38 public universities, two case studies of African studies centres at La Trobe University and the University of Western Australia, and relations between Africanists and NGOs and other interest groups. The picture is rather disquieting, notwithstanding the heroic efforts of the Africanists and the high quality of their work. The survey showed that only fourteen had any African studies in their teaching programmes, and Africa was more often treated in a comparative context than on its own. History has been the dominant discipline, but the study of African literatures has grown. The rise of the 'posts' in the 1990s invigorated cultural studies, media studies, and musicology. NGOs and African immigrants and students provide potentially valuable constituencies for the field. But the Africanist community remains small and rather beleaguered; it has lost members who have shifted to Asian studies or to the more favourable Africanist markets of the US and Britain.

The establishment of African studies in China from the late 1950s grew out of expanding ties between Africa and China in the aftermath of African decolonisation and the Chinese revolution and shared concerns against European imperialism and for rapid development. As in India, there was strong ideological and fiscal support from the state. Chinese intellectual interest in Africa started much earlier and has undergone important shifts since then as shown in Li Anshan's fine chapter. The history of African-Chinese contacts goes back to the frequent exchanges of products between China and Egypt in ancient times and through the first and second millennia up to the nineteenth century. But systematic studies of Africa began in modern times and were strongly influenced or mediated through Europe's growing colonial expansion in both Africa and China. During the first half of the twentieth century Chinese publications on Africa consisted of translations or editions of world geography covering some parts of Africa, travel writings that described places in Africa, and books about Egypt long respected as a great and old civilisation equivalent to China's own. It was only after the 1949 Chinese Revolution that African studies was institutionalised and started to flourish with the establishment of African studies centres in various universities and research institutions. Much of the work focussed on African nationalism. The translation of foreign publications expanded, but now preference was given to works by African nationalist leaders, serious works by western or Russian scholars, and reports to government and popular readers.

Anshan argues that the work produced during this period was more pragmatic than academic, largely generated in government units and history departments, and was done collectively. The Cultural Revolution (1966–1976) gravely undermined intellectual life in China as universities were closed for several years and student enrolment and instruction became excessively politicised. But work on Africa including translations, in which support for liberation movements in Southern Africa featured high, did continue. The end of the Cultural Revolution ushered in the most productive period for African studies. Nationalism continued to be a dominant topic of research, but in the 1980s there was greater interest on specific countries and topics from the Atlantic slave trade to the national bourgeoisie. In the 1990s the range of topics expanded to include socialism, democratisation, ethnicity, international relations, cultural studies, economic studies, Sino-African relations—and South Africa received a lot of attention. In addition to the exploding volume of scholarly works, numerous textbooks and reference materials including a general history of Africa and encyclopaedic works on African geography were produced. Clearly, African studies in China has grown from a politically oriented to an academically oriented interdiscipline and expanded the range of its thematic and topical focus and disciplinary coverage. But challenges remain, which include, according to Anshan, the need to improve contacts between Chinese and African scholars and communication between Chinese Africanists and the general public.

The development of African studies in Japan has been no less remarkable in recent years as shown in the chapter by Masao Yoshida, who notes that by 2001 membership of the Association of African Studies, which was established in 1964, had surpassed 700. This is attributed to the liberalisation of rules for establishing graduate courses in universities (previously regulated by the Ministry of Education) and the need for Africa-related expertise by the aid agencies. During a tour of several Japanese universities and research institutions in 2004 I was highly impressed by the quality and range of Japanese Africanist research. As elsewhere, African studies in Japan exhibits unique national features and preoccupations. One concerns the strong presence of natural scientists from zoology, primatology, botany, earth science, geology, and medical science. This rather unusual interdisciplinary engagement of social and natural scientists is complimented by the growing breadth of fields of study in the social sciences and humanities encompassing political science, law, economics, history, sociology, cultural anthropology, geography, agricultural science, literature, linguistics, arts and crafts, and music.

Towards the end of the paper Yoshida outlines the thematic focus in recent Japanese African studies scholarship in the key areas of social science research. In political studies the work of Japanese Africanists has concentrated on the issues of democratisation, civil society, conflict, and human security. In economic studies economic history and the economic crisis and free-market reforms of the 1980s and 1990s feature prominently. Particularly strong is research on agriculture and rural sociology focussing on the livelihoods or subsistence activities of farmers, herders and fishermen, relations between peasants and the national economy, the internal relations of rural communities, and the development of agricultural technologies. He argues that the preoccupation with community by Japanese Africanists comes out of the fascination and ambivalence among many Japanese about the existence of communal relations in their own society. The rural bias of Africanist research in Japan has meant that relatively fewer scholars study urban societies, but urban sociology and industrialisation studies that examine the dynamics of urban life, rural-urban linkages, the informal sector, small-scale and large-scale enterprises are growing.

Conclusion

Clearly, today African studies or the study of Africa is a vast international enterprise encompassing Africa itself, the former colonial powers of Western Europe, countries with large African diasporas in the Americas, as well as countries in Europe and Asia that have had no overt imperial relations with Africa. As a house of many mansions, a field with diverse, complex and infinitely fascinating disciplinary, interdisciplinary and global dimensions, the days when one country, one centre or one paradigm for that matter dominated African studies are long gone. For some this apparent fragmentation is a source of deep concern, for others it represents scholarly pluralisation that is a cause for celebration. For me it is a sign of the field's maturation. The key pitfalls and possibilities of African studies in the twenty-first century, I would argue, lie in the crises and changes in the systems of knowledge production in Africa itself and the emergence of new African diasporas—including the academic diasporas—riding on the ravages of neoliberal globalisation and the age-old solidarities of Pan-Africanism.

Fundamental to the future of African studies, or rather African and Africanist scholarship, is the revitalisation of African universities and scholarly communities on the continent that have been devastated by more than two decades of misguided structural maladjustment policies. In short, African studies—the production of knowledges on and about Africa—will, ultimately, only be as strong as African scholarship on the continent is strong.[7] For their part, the new academic diasporas are going to be crucial to the processes, however painful and difficult they may be, of establishing new, perhaps more equitable, transnational intellectual relations between Africa and the rest of the world. Much is indeed in flux in the architecture of knowledge production, dissemination, and consumption. The disciplines are in as much of a 'crisis'—undergoing profound changes—as the interdiscipline of area studies. For those of us committed to the study of Africa in whatever institutional arrangement of the contemporary academy (disciplinary departments or interdisciplinary programmes), and for whatever reason—epistemic, existential, or even economic—we must pay close attention to these changes and ensure that our beloved Africa is fully integrated in whatever intellectual configurations emerge in the new century.

Notes

1. Among the ones I am familiar with are: the Centre for African Studies at the University of Cape Town and the Institute for African Studies at the University of Ghana. At a recent conference I attended in Pretoria (26–28 February 2006) on African Studies, the absence of stand-alone African studies programmes across the continent was widely noted and the point was made that the issue was the 'Africanisation' of the existing disciplines and interdisciplines.
2. For recent studies on the development and challenges of area studies in the United States see the edited collections by Newil Waters (2000), Masao Miyoshi and H. D. Harootunian (2002), Ali Mirsepassi et al. (2003) and David Szanton (2004).
3. I offer a more detailed analysis and critique of the development of African studies in the United States in Zeleza (2003: 179-227).
4. This is the title of the book by Neil Walters (2000).
5. For a rather sardonic commentary on the explosion of globalisation studies from a publisher, see Peter Dougherty (2004), group publisher for the social sciences and senior economics editor at Princeton University Press.
6. In 1993, the Ford and the MacArthur Foundations launched a joint programme on globalisation, and the Mellon Foundation one on cross-regional issues. A few years later Ford launched its 'Crossing-Borders: Revitalizing Area Studies' programme. For a short and sharp critique of these initiatives and the fluid notion of globalisation driving them, see Hall and Tarrow (1998).
7. It is instructive that there are no African countries that I know of that actively sponsor African studies programmes around the world the way that the major countries in Euro-America do, and some Asian countries such as Japan, Korea and Taiwan do through the Japan Foundation, the Korea Foundation, and the Chiang Ching Kuo Foundation respectively which sponsor programmes in the United States, see Miyoshi (2002).

References

Bates, R.H., V.Y. Mudimbe, J. O'Barr, eds., *Africa and the Disciplines: The Contributions of Africa to the Social Sciences and Humanities*, Chicago and London: University of Chicago Press.

Chege, M., 1997, 'The Social Science Area Studies Controversy from the Continental African Perspective', *Africa Today* 44 (2): 133-142.

Davidson, A. and I. Filatova, 2001, 'African History: A View From Behind the Kremlin War', in L. Kropacek and P. Skalnik, eds., *Africa 2000: Forty Years of African Studies in Prague*, Prague, 51-70.

Dougherty, P. J., 2004, 'The Wealth of Nations: A Publisher Considers the Literature of Globalization', *The Chronicle of Higher Education. The Chronicle Review* 50 (45): B6.

Hall, P.A. and S. J. Tarrow, 1998, 'Globalization and Area Studies: When Is Too Broad Too Narrow?' *The Chronicle of Higher Education* 44 (20): B4-B5 23 January.

Holzner, B. and M. Harmon, 1998, 'Intellectual and Organizational Challenges for International Education in the United States: A Knowledge System Perspective', in John Hawkins et al., eds., *International Education in the New Global Era*, Los Angeles: International Studies and Overseas Programs, University of California, 31-63.

Hountondji, P., 1997, 'Introduction: Recentering Africa', in P. Hountodji, ed., *Endogenous Knowledge: Research Trails*, Dakar: CODESRIA, 1-39.

Merkx, Gilbert W., 1998, 'Graduate Training and Research', in John Hawkins, et al., eds., *International Education in the New Global Era*, Los Angeles: International Studies and Overseas Programs, University of California, 76-86.

Mirsepassi, A., A. Basu, and F. Weaver, eds., 2003, *Localizing Knowledge in a Globalizing World*, Syracuse, NY: Syracuse University Press.

Miyoshi, M. and H. D. Harootunian, 2002, *Learning Places: The Afterlives of Area Studies*, Durham, NC: Duke University Press.

Robinson, P. T., 1997, 'Local/Global Linkages and the Future of African Studies', *Africa Today* 44 (2): 169-178.

Rodney, W., 1982 [1972], *How Europe Underdeveloped Africa*, Washington, DC: Howard University Press.

Szanton, D., ed., 2004, 'Introduction: The Origin, Nature, and Challenge of Area Studies in the United States', in D. Szanton, ed., *The Politics of Knowledge: Area Studies and the Disciplines*, Berkeley: University of California Press, 1-33.

Tansman, A., 2004, 'Japanese Studies: The Intangible Act of Translation', in D. Szanton, ed., *The Politics of Knowledge: Area Studies and the Disciplines*, Berkeley: University of California Press, 184-216.

Walters, N. L., ed., 2000, *Beyond the Area Studies Wars: Towards a New International Studies*, Hanover and London: Middlebury College Press.

Zeleza, P. T., 1997, *Manufacturing African Studies and Crises*, Dakar: CODESRIA.

Zeleza, P. T., 2003, *Rethinking Africa's Globalization, Vol.1: The Intellectual Challenges*, Trenton, NJ: Africa World Press.

Zeleza, P. T. and A. Olukoshi, eds., 2004, *African Universities in the Twenty-First Century*, 2 volumes, Dakar: CODESRIA.

Zeleza, P. T., 2005a, 'Banishing the Silences: Towards the Globalization of African History', Paper presented at the Eleventh General Assembly of the Council for Development of Social Science Research in Africa, Maputo, Mozambique, 6–10 December 2005.

Zeleza, P. T., 2005b, 'Transnational Education and African Universities', *Journal of Higher Education in Africa* 3 (1): 1-28.

I

Globalisation Studies and African Studies

Chapter 1

Globalisation: An Ascendant Paradigm? Implications for African Studies

James H. Mittelman

This essay explores the questions: Does globalisation constitute an ascendant paradigm in International Studies, and what are its implications for African Studies?[1] Put in perspective, these questions go beyond the three 'great debates' in International Studies over ontology, methodology, and epistemology. Now, another debate, which focuses on globalisation as a paradigmatic challenge, is heating up, kindling theoretical controversies, and fusing the issues vetted in earlier rounds. The first debate was waged between 'realists' and 'idealists'; the second, 'traditionalists' and 'scientists'; the third, 'positivists' versus 'post-positivists,' or 'mainstreamers' versus 'dissidents' (in the terms of Lapid 1989; Wendt 1999:39; and Puchala 2000:136).

Now, it is time to move on. International Studies is on the cusp of a debate between those whom I will call *para-keepers*, observers who are steadfast about maintaining the prevailing paradigms and deny that globalisation offers a fresh way of thinking about the world, and *para-makers*, who bring into question what they regard as outmoded categories and claim to have shifted to an innovatory paradigm. This distinction is a heuristic for examining multiple theses. The ensuing heuristic argument does not posit a relation between two positions such that one is the absence of the other. Rather, between the keepers and the makers there are many gradations and dynamic interactions. These are tendencies, not absolutes.

In our field, ascendancy to a new *paradigm* would mark something other, or more, than the fourth, a successor, in a sequential progression of debates. True, building new knowledge may be a cumulative process; but it is not necessarily a linear one, and only occasionally involves paradigmatic rupture. To be sure, paradigms do not shift frequently, quickly, or easily. International Studies specialists are supposed to be the knowers, but, frankly speaking, often follow the doers in the sense that we trail events, even massive ones, as with our failure to anticipate the end of the Cold War, and still resist changing the paradigms in which many of us are invested.

If a paradigm in Kuhn's sense (1970) is understood to mean a common framework, a shared world view that helps to define problems, a set of tools and methods, and modes of resolving the research questions deemed askable, then globalisation studies makes for strange bedfellows. Perhaps constituting an up-and-coming subfield within International Studies, globalisation research brings together different types of theorists, with varied commitments and stakes.

No one would deny that globalisation is the subject of a rapidly proliferating theoretical literature. Notwithstanding its antecedents, primarily studies in classical social theory and world history and on the rise of capitalism, a scholarly literature on globalisation *per se* did not really exist before the 1990s. To a certain extent, globalisation is a synthetic concept—a reconstruction of precursor concepts through which analysts seek to comprehend reality. Clearly, this reconstruction is of recent vintage, and the literature and contestation over its importance go to the heart of our field: What is the fundamental problematic in International Studies? Primarily peace and war? Mainly what states do to each other? Rather, states and markets, a binary in much teaching and research on International Political Economy (even though Strange [1996, 1998] and others exploded it to include a wide variety of non-state actors)? Or, if globalisation really strikes a new chord, how does it change the problematic, and what are the implications for the ways in which disciplinary, cross-national, development, and area studies relate to our field?

For the purpose of addressing these issues, globalisation may be best understood as a syndrome of political and material processes, including historical transformations in time and space and the social relations attendant to them. It is also about ways of thinking about the world. Globalisation thus constitutes a set of ideas centred on heightened market integration, which, in its dominant form, neoliberalism, is embodied in a policy framework of deregulation, liberalisation, and privatisation.[2]

In this essay, then, the objective is to pull together the divergent positions, which heretofore are fragmented and may be found in many scattered sources, on the question of the ascendancy of these ideas and the formation of a new paradigm. I want to frame and sharpen the debate, and seek to strike a balance, though not necessarily midway, along a continuum, marked on either end by the resolute arguments put forward by the para-keepers and the more grandiose claims of the para-makers. In so doing, I will stake out postulates in globalisation studies, disclose inadequacies, and note the explanatory potential.

An Emerging Debate

In the evolving debate, it is worth repeating, there are different shadings on a spectrum, not a sharp dichotomy, between para-keepers and para-makers. Indeed, in time, the para-makers may become wedded to keeping their paradigm and experience attacks by other para-makers. To discern their positions in respect to globalisation, one can illustrate—not provide comprehensive coverage—by invoking explicit statements expressing the commitments of scholars and by examining logical extensions of their arguments, taking care, of course, not to do injustice to them.

The keepers are nay-sayers who doubt or deny that globalisation constitutes an ascendant paradigm. They include realists, interdependence theorists, social democrats, and some world-system theorists. Regarding globalisation as 'the fad of the 1990s' and as a model lacking evidence, Waltz (1999: 694, 696, and 700) declares that contrary to the claims of theorists whom he calls 'globalisers'—what I take to be a shorthand for globalisation researchers—'politics, as usual, prevails over economics'. Clinging to the neo-realist position that 'national interests' continue to drive the 'interstate system', advanced two decades before (Waltz 1979), he does not examine the foundational theoretical literature by 'globalisers' who worry about the same problems that concern him. Surprisingly, Waltz fails to identify major pioneering theoreticians (such as Giddens 1990; Harvey 1990; and Robertson 1992), opposing points of view, and different schools of globalisation studies. Waltz would probably find much to respect and much to correct in this work. Recalling Keohane and Nye's (1977) book, *Power and Interdependence*, Waltz's point (1999) is that the globalisers' contention about interdependence reaching a new level is not unlike the earlier claim that simple interdependence had become complex interdependence—i.e., countries are increasingly connected by varied social and political relationships and to a lesser degree by matters of security and force.

In fact, more recently, Keohane and Nye (2000: 104) maintained that contemporary globalisation is not entirely new: 'Our characterization of interdependence more than 20 years ago now applies to globalization at the turn of the millennium'. Thus, like complex interdependence, the concept of globalisation can be fruitfully extended to take into account networks that operate at 'multicontinental distances', the greater density of these networks, and the increased number of actors participating in them (Keohane and Nye 2000). In comparison to Waltz, Keohane and Nye reach beyond classic themes in politics to allow for more changes, and build transnational issues into their framework. However, like Waltz, Keohane and Nye (1998) posit that the system of state sovereignty is resilient and remains the dominant structure in the world. Implicit in their formulation is that the state-centred paradigm is the best-suited approach to globalisation; by inference, it can be adjusted so long as it is utilised in an additive manner—i.e., incorporates more dimensions into the analysis.

Not only do interdependence theorists (and neoliberal institutionalists, in Keohane's sense of the term, 1984) seek to assimilate globalisation to tried and tested approaches in International Studies, but also social democrats have similarly argued that there is nothing really new about globalisation. By extension, from this standpoint, a new theoretical departure is unwarranted. In an influential study, Hirst and Thompson (1999, echoing Gordon 1988) claim that the world economy is not really global, but centred on the triad of Europe, Japan, and North America, as empirically demonstrated by flows of trade, foreign direct investment, and finance. They argue that the current level of internationalised activities is not unprecedented; the world economy is not as open and integrated as it was in the period from 1870 to 1914; and today, the major powers continue to harmonise policy, as they did before. Leaving aside methodological questions about the adequacy of their empirical measures and the matter of alternative indicators (Mittelman 2000: 19-24), clearly Hirst and Thompson adhere to a Weberian mode of analysis consisting of a dichotomy between two ideal types, an inter-national economy based on exchange between separate national economies versus a full-fledged global economy. Taking issue with advocates of free markets whom, the authors believe, exaggerate globalising tendencies and want to diminish regulation, Hirst and Thompson, on the contrary, favour more extensive political control of markets—greater regulation.

World-system theorists also contend that there is nothing new about globalisation, a phenomenon that can be traced back many centuries to the origins of capitalism (Wallerstein 2000) or even longer. From this perspective, it is argued that the basic conflict is between a capitalist world-system and a socialist world-system. However, as will be discussed, the point of much globalisation research is to expand binaries such as the inter-national versus the global and capitalism versus socialism so as to allow for multiple *globalising* processes, including at the macroregional, subregional, and microregional levels as well as in localities. If anything, globalisation blurs many dualities—state and non-state, legal and illegal, public and private, and so on—that are customary in our field.

Coming down differently on the debate over globalisation *qua* paradigm are diverse theorists who resist pigeonholing into any particular tradition or traditions, yet all of whom support the proposition that globalisation constitutes a distinctive theoretical innovation. However difficult to categorise collectively they may be, this transatlantic group of authors signals the stirring of a paradigmatic challenge to International Studies. Emblematic of this position are the writings of four scholars with different commitments but whose position on new knowledge converges.

Representative of the innovatory stance is Cerny's (1996: 618) assertion that theorists are seeking an alternative to realism and that 'the chief contender for that honour has been the concept of globalisation'. Similarly, Clark's (1999: 174) *Globalization and International Relations Theory* makes the unequivocal argument that 'globalization offers a framework within which political change can be understood' and that 'if globalization does anything, it makes possible a theory of change'. Joining Cerny and Clark, Scholte (1999: 9) holds that '[c]ontemporary globalization gives ample cause for a paradigm shift', or, in another formulation, 'the case that globalism warrants a paradigm shift would seem to be incontrovertible' (p.22). Although Scholte does fill in some of the blanks, the question still is: What are the characteristics of this new paradigm?

While globalisation theorists have tentatively, but not systematically, responded to this question (an issue to which we will return), there is also a more guarded intervention in the debate over globalisation's status as a paradigm. Noting 'parametric transformations' in world order, Rosenau clearly sides with those who affirm that globalisation forms a new point of paradigmatic departure; however, he holds that his concept of globalisation is 'narrower in scope and more specific in content' than are many other concepts associated with changing global structures. According to Rosenau (1997: 80), globalisation refers to 'processes, to sequences that unfold either *in the mind* or in behavior' as people and organisations attempt to achieve their goals; emphasis added). In other words, globalisation is not only an objective trend, but also constitutes, or is constituted by, subjective processes. It is a mental, or intersubjective, framework that is both implicated in the exercise of power and in scholarship that informs, or is critical of, public policy. Certainly because of the need for greater theoretical, as well as empirical, precision, a qualified response to the question of the rise of a new paradigm is worthy of consideration. The route to this response will be a Kuhnian notion of what sparks paradigmatic transformations.

The Question of New Knowledge[3]

In his study of the history of the natural sciences, Kuhn (1970) famously argued that new paradigms appear through ruptures rather than through a linear accumulation of facts or hypotheses. Normal science, he claimed, is a means of confirming the type of knowledge already established and legitimised by the paradigm in which it arises. According to Kuhn, normal science often suppresses innovations because they are subversive of a discipline's fundamental commitments.

> No part of the aim of normal science is to call forth new sorts of phenomena; indeed those that will not fit the box are often not seen at all. Nor do scientists normally aim to invent new theories, and they are often intolerant of those invented by others. Instead, normal-scientific research is directed to the articulation of those phenomena and theories that the paradigm already supplies (Kuhn 1970: 24).

Or, to extrapolate, one might say that members of a shared knowledge community not only normalise certain types of questions, but also suppress the ability to raise them. Most important, Kuhn's insight is that only rarely do intellectuals refuse to accept the evasion of anomalies: observations at odds with expectations derived from prior theoretical understandings. A new paradigm emerges when the burden of anomalous phenomena grows too great and when there is incommensurability between competing paradigms to the extent that proponents of alternative frameworks cannot accept a common ground of assumptions.

Some observers dispute whether Kuhn's thesis, derived from the natural sciences, can be imported into the social sciences—and, I might add, into a field like International Studies, which is far more heterogeneous than disciplines such as physics. My concern here, however, is not the epistemological debate over the disparate means of discovery in respective branches of knowledge (see Lakatos 1970; Ball 1976; Barnes 1982). Rather, my contention, that globalisation is not only about 'real' phenomena, but also a way of interpreting the world, is more pragmatic.

To be sure, a Kuhnian perspective of the generation of knowledge is vulnerable insofar it is limited to social and psychological conditions within the scientific community, and does not give sufficient credence to socially constructed knowledge outside this community. The factors internal to the social sciences cannot be fully explained without reference to the external elements. There is nothing, however, to prevent joining Kuhn's insight about theoretical innovation with a broader analysis of social conditions. Moreover, unless one believes that International Studies is rapidly approaching a Kuhnian crisis, i.e., the overthrow of a reigning paradigm or paradigms—and I do not—then it is important to grasp the dynamic interface between established knowledge sets, including the structures (curricula, professional journals, funding agencies, etc.) that maintain and undermine them, and a potentially new paradigm. It would appear that even without a paradigm crisis, an ascendant paradigm could emerge.

For Kuhn, the transition to a new paradigm is all or nothing: 'Like the gestalt switch, it must occur all at once (though not necessarily in an instant) or not at all' (Kuhn 1970: 150; also pertinent are the nuances in is his subsequent work, 1977a; 1977b). In explaining transformations in this manner, Kuhn falls short insofar as he underestimates the tenacity of forerunner paradigms and their ability to modify themselves. By all indications in the social sciences, they fight back, usually with gusto. Nevertheless, by identifying the propellant of a new paradigm as the refusal to accept the evasion of anomalies in conjunction with the quest for an alternative, Kuhn has contributed powerfully to understanding theoretical innovation.

In this vein, it is well to recall Weber's (1949) '"Objectivity" in Social Science and Social Policy'. Like Kuhn, Weber indicated that the prevailing intellectual apparatus is in constant tension with new knowledge. According to Weber, this conflict is a propellant for creativity and discovery—concepts are and should be subject to change. However, there should also be a certain staying power in the intellectual apparatus that enables one to ferret out what is worth knowing. In other words, there is nothing worse than the fads and fashions that come in an out of vogue. In the end, Weber called for a mid-course between unyielding old concepts and unceasing shifts in paradigms.

Following Kuhn and Weber in the chase for paradigmatic advance, what are the anomalies in our field, and is globalisation a viable contender for fixing these imperfections?

Discomfort with International Studies

A discipline without complaints would be a non-sequitur. After all, scholars are trained in the art of debate; the skills of nuance are our stock-in-trade. That said, it is important to consider the specific anomalies within International Studies. Although some of these anomalies are perennial, it is no wonder that others have appeared, given monumental changes after the Cold War, and with the distinctive mix of global integration and disintegration at the dawn of a new millennium. While others could be cited, five anomalies seem most important, but can be considered only succinctly here.[4]

First, the term *International Studies* suggests a focus on relations between nations. But this is not so. The discipline has primarily concerned relations between states, the nation being only one of many principles of social organisation (Shaw 1994: 25; also Shaw 1999). Closely related, observers (for example, Rosenau 1997; Baker 2000: 366) have long argued that the conventional distinction between separate national and international spheres of activity is a misnomer. Nowadays, it is increasingly difficult to maintain the lines of demarcation between the domestic and the foreign realms, or between Comparative Politics and International Politics. Globalisation means that the distinction between them is hard to enforce. Increasingly evident are myriad forms of interpenetration between the global and the national—global economic actors even exist within the state, as with global crime groups in Russia or the International Monetary Fund/World Bank's structural adjustment programmes in developing countries.

Thus, a third discontent is opposition to the persistence of state centrism. From this angle, the case for an ontological shift springs from the anomaly between the objects of study seen through a realist or neo-realist lens and the globalists' vision of a polycentric, or multilevel, world order. New ontological priorities—an issue to which I will return—would consist of a series of linked processes. Toward this end, globalisation researchers are attempting to design a framework for interrelating economics, politics, culture, and society in a seamless web. Hence, in large measure a response to globalisation, some scholars have shifted attention to global governance: an effort to incorporate a broader ontology of structures and agents. The state is treated as one among several actors. It is not that state sovereignty is losing meaning, but the multilevel environment in which it operates, and hence the meaning of the concept, is changing.

Methodologically, the field of International Studies is based on the premise of territoriality, reflected in central concepts such as state-centred nationalism, state borders, and state sovereignty. Yet, with the development of new technologies, especially in communications and transportation, the advent of a 'network society' (Castells 1996), and the emergence of a 'nonterritorial region' (Ruggie 1993), there is a marked shift toward a more deterritorialised world. Hence, Scholte (1999: 17) has challenged 'methodological territorialism'—the ingrained practice of formulating questions, gathering data, and arriving at conclusions all through the prism of a territorial framework. Without swinging to the opposite extreme of adopting a 'globalist methodology' by totally rejecting the importance of the principle of territoriality, Scholte calls for a 'full-scale methodological reorientation', and concludes: '[T]hat globalisation warrants a paradigm shift would seem to be incontrovertible' (pp. 21-22).

Finally, there is the postmodernist complaint, which, arguably, has not really registered in our field.[5] As Said (1979) contends in regard to Orientalism, it is hard to erase certain representations of reality, for in Foucauldian terms, they take on the aura of authoritative expressions and are implicated in the exercise of power. Knowledge sets may thus operate as closed systems—what Caton (1999) terms 'endless cycles of self-referring statements'—thwarting counter-representations that might have the power to challenge normal knowledge. As scholars in International Studies, perhaps we should reflect on this allegation about collectively self-referential work, for we spend an enormous amount of time engaging in intramural debates over concepts, often without sufficient attention to the phenomena themselves. Still, it would be wrong to gloss over Said's insight that representations manifest as knowledge are tied to the establishment, maintenance, and exercise of power. In International Studies, probing Said's point about reflexivity involves shifting explanatory levels above and below the state—a characteristic of globalisation research.

Characteristics of Globalisation Studies

Globalisation theorists, of course, are not univocal. Inasmuch as their writings abound, there are different interpretations and considerable contestation. As Puchala aptly put it, '[C]onventional theories all have a table of outcomes that inventory what needs to be explained'. For example, the realist table of outcomes is chiefly wars, alliances, balances of power, and arms races. For liberals, the outcomes are regimes, integration, cooperation and hegemons (Puchala 2001). By contrast, the problematic that globalisation theorists seek to explain, while dynamic and open-ended, not invariant, may be gleaned from an emerging series of core, linked propositions. I will highlight six of them.

1.　Many contemporary problems cannot be explained as interactions among nation states, i.e., as International Studies, but must be construed as global problems. Although this claim is not unique to globalisation studies, at issue is a series of problems—for example, the rise of organised crime, global warming, and the spread of infectious diseases—partly within and partly across borders, partially addressed by states and partially beyond their regulatory framework.

2.　Globalisation constitutes a structural transformation in world order. As such, it is about not only the here and now, but also warrants a long perspective of time and revives the study of space. A preoccupation with what Braudel called 'the history of events'—the immediate moment—focuses attention on a frame that differs from the *longue durée*, an observation point that some researchers find advantageous for viewing the spatial reorganisation of the global economy.

3.　As a transformation, globalisation involves a series of continuities and discontinuities with the past. In other words, the globalisation tendency is by no means a total break—as noted, there is considerable disagreement about how much is new—but the contemporary period is punctuated by a large-scale acceleration in globalising processes such as the integration of financial markets, technological development, and intercultural contact.

4.　New ontological priorities are warranted because of the emergence of a dialectic of supra-state and sub-state forces, pressures from above and below. The advent of an ontology of globalisation is fluid, by no means fixed. It includes the global economy as an actor in its own right (as embodied, for example, in transnational corporations), states and interstate organisations, regionalist processes (at the macro, sub, and micro-levels), world cities, and civil society, sometimes manifest as social movements.

5. Given shifting parameters, the state, in turn, seeks to adjust to evolving global structures. States, however, are in varied positions vis-à-vis globalising forces, and reinvent themselves differently, the gamut of policies running from a full embrace, as with New Zealand's extreme neoliberal policies from 1984 to 1999, to resistance, illustrated by Malaysia's capital controls in 1998.

6. Underpinning such differences is a set of new, or deeper, tensions in world order, especially the disjuncture between the principle of territoriality, fundamental to the concept of state sovereignty, and the patent trend toward deterritorialisation, especially, but not only, apparent in regard to transborder economic flows. The horizontal connections forged in the world economy and the vertical dimensions of state politics are two dissimilar vectors of social organisation, with the latter seeking to accommodate the changing global matrix.

However schematically presented, the aforementioned, interrelated propositions put into question some of International Studies' ingrained ways of conceptualising the world. At present, although the attempts at reconceptualisation are in a preliminary stage of formulation, it is worth identifying the traps and confusions.

Discomfort with Paradigmatic Pretension

Barring caricatures of the concept *and* phenomena of globalisation—for example, it is totalising, inevitable, and homogenising, rather than, as many scholars maintain, partial, open-ended, and hybrid—surely there are grounds for discontent. For one thing, globalisation may be seen as a promiscuous concept, variously referring to a historical scenario, interconnections, the movement of capital, new technologies and information, an ideology of competitiveness, and a political response to the spread and deepening of the market. Hence, the complaint lodged earlier in this article: Observers (for instance, Kearney 2001) are crying out and striving for more analytical precision.

Moreover, globalisation is sometimes deemed overdetermined—too abstract, too structural, and insufficiently attentive to agency. From this perspective, it is thought that the logic is mechanically specified or mis-specified in that it is too reductive. For some, especially scholars carrying out contextualised, fine-grained research on particular issues and distinct areas, globalisation is regarded as too blunt a tool. After all, what does it leave out? What is not globalisation? In response, it may be argued that globalisation is mediated by other processes and actors, including the state. Furthermore, globalisation has a direct or indirect impact on various levels of social organisation, and becomes inserted into the local, thus complicating the distinction between the global and the local.

Another problem, then, is that the globalisation literature has spawned its own binary oppositions. On the one hand, as indicated, the phenomena of globalisation blur dichotomous distinctions to which International Studies has grown accustomed. For example, civil society now penetrates the state (as with members of environmental movements assuming important portfolios in government in the Philippines; and in several African countries, state substitution is abundantly evident—some so-called 'nongovernmental organisations' are sustained by state funding or, arguably, their agendas are driven by the state or interstate organisations). On the other hand, globalisation research itself presents new binary choices—'globalisation from above' and 'globalisation from below,' top-down and bottom-up globalisation, and so on— that certainly have heuristic value but must be exploded in order to capture the range of empirical phenomena.

How Far Have We Come?

It would be remiss not to join a discussion of the drawbacks to globalisation as an avenue of inquiry with its real gains, even if the nature of a new paradigm is tentative and being contested.

In the main, globalisation studies emphasises the historicity of all social phenomena. There is no escaping historiography: What are the driving forces behind globalisation, and when did it originate? With the beginnings of intercultural contact, the dawn of capitalism in western Europe in the long sixteenth century, or in a distinct conjuncture after the Second World War? Research has thus opened new questions for investigation and debate. And even if one returns to old issues, such as theories of the state, there are opposing views and vexing questions, especially in the face of public representations, such as Margaret Thatcher's attack on the 'nanny state'. Should the state be construed as in retreat (Strange 1996), as an agent of globalisation (Cox 1987), or, in an even more activist role, as the author of globalisation (Panitch 1996; from another perspective, Weiss 1998)? Taken together, the writings on these issues combat the fragmentation of knowledge. Not surprisingly, given the themes that globalisation embraces—technology, ecology, films, health, fast-food and other consumer goods, and so on—it is transdisciplinary, involving not exclusively the social sciences, but also the natural sciences, the humanistic sciences, and professional fields such as architecture, law, and medicine.

Arguably, within the social sciences, economic and political geographers (including Dicken 1998; Harvey 1999; Knox and Agnew 1998; Olds 2001; Taylor 1993; Taylor, Johnson, and Watts 1995; Thrift 1996) have carried out some of the most sophisticated research on globalisation. Even though the importance of spatial concerns is increasingly apparent, many International Studies specialists have not noticed the work of economic and political geographers.

For the purposes of teaching globalisation, one way to draw students into a subject that, after all, involves thinking about big, abstract structures, is to focus on spatial issues as they relate to the changes in one's own locale. Reading a collection of essays consisting of anthropological fieldwork at McDonald's restaurants in dif-

ferent Asian countries (Watson 1997), and then comparing the findings in the literature to their own fieldwork, including interviewing employees and customers at a
nearby McDonald's, my students are asked to analyse the cultural political economy
of globalisation: a production system, the composition of the labour force (largely
immigrants and members of minority groups in our locale), social technologies, and
the representations conveyed by symbols. The students pursue the question of meanings—the intersubjective dimensions of globalisation—in the writings of architects,
for example, on shopping malls and theme parks (Sorkin 1992), and by visits to local
sites.

Time permitting, consideration is also given to the legal and medical spheres.
Cyber-gangs and some novel types of crime do not neatly fit into the jurisdiction of
national or international law (see, for example, Sassen 1998). The field of public
health has called attention to the nexus of social *and* medical problems, especially
with the spread of AIDS. The tangible consequences of a changing global division
of labour and power include new flows and directions of migration, the separation
of families, a generation of orphans, and the introduction of the HIV virus into
rural areas by returning emigrants. As these topics suggest, globalisation studies identifies silences and establishes new intellectual space—certainly one criterion by which
to gauge an ascendant paradigm.

Pushing the Agenda

Notwithstanding important innovations, as a paradigm, globalisation is more of a
potential than a refined framework, world view, kit of tools and methods, and mode
of resolving questions. Where then to go from here? Although these are not the only
issues, the following challenges stand out as central to developing globalisation studies:

- Just as with capitalism, which has identifiable variants, there is no single, unified
  form of globalisation. Researchers have not yet really mapped the different
  forms of globalisation, which, in the literature is sometimes preceded by adjectival designations, such as 'neoliberal', 'disembedded', 'centralising', 'Islamic',
  'inner and outer', or 'democratic'. The adjectival labels are but hints at the need
  for systematic study of the varieties. Or should the object of study be
  globalisations?

- Closely related is the problem of how to depict the genres of globalisation
  research. What are the leading schools of thought? How to classify them so as
  to organise this massive literature and advance investigation? To catalogue
  globalisation studies according to national traditions of scholarship, by disciplinary perspective, or on single issues risks mistaking the parts for the whole.
  Avoiding this trap, Guillén (2001) decongests the burgeoning globalisation research by organising it into key debates: Is globalisation really happening, does
  it produce convergence, does it undermine the authority of nation-states, is
  globality different from modernity, and is a global culture in the making? In

another stocktaking, Held, McGrew, Goldblatt, and Perraton (1999) sort the field into hyper-globalisers who believe that the growth of world markets diminishes the role of states, sceptics who maintain that international interactions are not novel and that states have the power to regulate international economic flows, and transformationalists who claim that new patterns and an unprecedented configuration of global power relations have emerged. But there are other debates, major differences among policy research (Rodrik 1997), structural approaches (Falk 1999), and critical/poststructural accounts (Hardt and Negri 2000).

- What are the implications of globalisation for disciplinary and cross-national studies? How should these domains of knowledge respond to the globalisation challenge? It would seem that in light of the distinctive combinations of evolving global structures and local conditions in various regions, globalisation enhances, not reduces, the importance of the comparative method. However, there is the matter of exploring disciplinary and comparative themes within changing parameters and examining the interactions between these parameters and the localities.

- Similarly, what does globalisation mean for development and area studies? McMichael (2000: 149) holds that '[t]he globalization project succeeds the development project'. Surely development theory emerged in response to a particular historical moment: the inception of the Cold War, which, if anything, was an ordering principle in world affairs. After the sudden demise of this structure, development studies reached a conceptual cul de sac. Put more delicately, it may be worth revisiting development studies' basic tenets, especially apropos the dynamics of economic growth and the mechanisms of political power in the poorest countries, which have experienced a fundamental erosion of the extent of control that they had maintained—however little to begin with. This loss has been accompanied by changing priorities and reorganisations within funding agencies, a crucial consideration in terms of support for training the next generation of scholars, particularly apparent with regard to fieldwork for dissertations. Although some para-keeper area specialists have dug in their heels and have fought to protect normal knowledge in their domain, the task is to reinvent and thereby strengthen area studies.

- Insufficient scholarly attention has centred on the ethics of globalisation. The telling question is: What and whose values are inscribed in globalisation? In light of the unevenness of globalisation, with large zones of marginalisation (not only in a spatial sense, but also in terms of race, ethnicity, gender, and who is or is not networked), there is another searching question, Is globalisation ethically sustainable? What is the relationship between spirituality and globalisation, an issue posed by different religious movements? Which contemporary Weberian will step forward to write *The Neoliberal Ethic and the Spirit of Globalisation*?

- Emanating mostly from the West, globalisation studies is not really global. In terms of participating researchers and the focus of inquiry, there is a need for decentring. The literature on globalisation unavailable in the English language (for example, Ferrer 1997; Gómez 2000; Kaneko 1999; Norani and Mandal 2000; Podestà, Gómez Galán, Jácome, and Grandi 2000) is rarely taken into account in the English-speaking world. Still, only limited work has thus far emerged in the developing world, including studies undertaken by the Council for the Development of Social Science Research in Africa (1998), the National University of Singapore (Olds, Dicken, Kelly, Kong, and Yeung 1999), the Latin American Social Sciences Council (Seoane and Taddei 2001), and the Institute of Malaysian and International Studies at the National University of Malaysia (Mittelman and Norani 2001).

- Apart from the development of individual courses, there is a lack of systematic thought about the programmatic implications of globalisation for the academy. Does global restructuring warrant academic restructuring in the ways in which knowledge is organised for students? If a new paradigm is emerging, then what does this mean in terms of pedagogy and curriculum? Will universities—and their International Studies specialists—be in the forefront of, or trail behind, changes in world order? Will they really open to the innovation of globalisation studies?

To sum up, it is worth recalling that on more than one occasion Susan Strange held that International Studies is like an open range, home to many different types of research. Today, there is diversity, but surely one should not overlook the fences that hold back the strays. Mavericks who work in non-Western discourses, economic and political geographers, postmodernists and post-structuralists, not to mention humanists (whose contributions are emphasised by Alker 1996; Puchala 2000; and others), have faced real barriers.

It is in this context that globalisation studies has emerged as a means to explain the intricacy and variability of the ways in which the world is restructuring and, by extension, to assess reflexively the categories used by social scientists to analyse these phenomena. The para-keepers, to varying degrees, are reluctant to embrace globalisation as a knowledge set because some of its core propositions challenge predominant ontological, methodological, and epistemological commitments—what Kuhn referred to as 'normal science'. Again, not to dichotomise positions, but to look to the other end of the spectrum, para-makers advance a strong thesis about the extent to which a new paradigm is gaining ascendancy. The debate is fruitful in that it engages in theoretical stocktaking, locates important problem areas, and points to possible avenues of inquiry. It also helps to delimit space for investigation and to identify venues of intellectual activity. But, in the near term, there is no looming Kuhnian crisis in the sense of an impending overthrow that would quickly sweep away reigning paradigms. Given that systematic research on globalisation is only slightly more than a decade in the making, it is more likely that International Studies has entered an interregnum between the old and the new.

Although globalisation studies entails a putting together of bold efforts to theorise structural change, it would be wrong to either underestimate or exaggerate the achievements. Judging the arguments in the debate, on balance, a modest thesis is in order. The efforts to theorise globalisation have produced a patchwork, an intellectual move rather than a movement, and more of a potential than worked-out alternatives to accepted ways of thinking in International Studies. In sum, this fledgling may be regarded as a proto-paradigm.

Implications for African Studies

What does the emergence of this proto-paradigm mean for African Studies? Ironically, the power of globalisation is reorganising livelihoods and modes of existence throughout Africa, but African scholars based on the continent have not yet produced systematic research on the impact of contemporary globalising processes on their own societies. True, the Dakar-based Council for the Development of Social Science Research in Africa has commissioned studies, and African scholars working in the diaspora have contributed to globalisation research (Cheru 2002; Zeleza 2003); however, all in all, the output of research on globalisation by Africanists is not prodigious.

Whereas a number of African scholars have outstanding training in International Studies, in their home countries they are often pressed into carrying out applied research on the burning issues of the day. The demand for immediacy deflects attention from the long-term, macro-structural processes that constitute globalisation—the parametric transformations that drive the immediate issues. Some scholars, too, may be attracted by opportunities for employment or consultancies that are more lucrative than engaging in basic research offers. Moreover, the major funding agencies may not favour the 'big-picture' themes and may be disposed to more specific topics that they deem significant: in other words, a research agenda mostly driven outside the continent.

US efforts in developing countries to impose free-market democracy, militarily if need be, as with Washington's second Iraq war, underscore the importance of attempts to assert a plurality of cultural values and political forms in Africa. The power of globalisation is not only intensifying Western dominance of Africa's economic and cultural markets, but also further marginalising the continent. This does *not* mean that Africans are marginal agents in shaping or writing their own histories. Rather, the interrelated facets of Africa's marginalisation (*inter alia*, arms sales across borders, transnational crime, and worldwide finance, including debts structures) may be best understood as both metaphor and process. Metaphorically, a 'margin' is an outer edge if viewed from the centre. In this sense, 'margin' is a representation, an imaginary. In another usage, the margin is the point at which the returns from an activity barely cover its costs. This economic process is engendered by social relations of power.

Just as the subalterns in the West and Japan have produced acute social criticism and great insight into the workings of these societies, so too globalisation's margins offer vital observation points for identifying the main dynamics transforming world order. Africa can provide a sharpness of perception clouded at the centre. African studies has the potential to retell the story of globalisation. Still more important are the opportunities for remaking this story.

Notes

1. Parts of this chapter are taken from my article 'Globalization: An Ascendant Paradigm?', *International Studies Perspectives* 3(2002), pp. 1-14. I owe a debt of gratitude to Donald J. Puchala, three anonymous reviewers and the *International Studies Perspectives* editors, colleagues at the Research Program on Political and Economic Change/Institute of Behavioral Science at the University of Colorado in Boulder, and members of the Center for African Studies at the University of Illinois at Urbana-Champaign, for critical comments on drafts of this chapter. Thanks, too, to Patrick Jackson, who generously shared materials and insights—too numerous to pick up on entirely here.
2. The literature (for example, Beck 2000; Giddens 2000) suggests a number of other ways to come to grips with what constitutes globalisation.
3. This section draws from, and builds on, Mittelman (1997).
4. The question of the meaning of power and counter-power under globalisation is a topic too broad to examine here. I am exploring this theme elsewhere.
5. I have the strong impression, but cannot 'prove', that International Studies scholars, with notable exceptions (for example, Der Derian 1994; Peterson 1992; Sylvester 1994; Walker 1993), have been more insular in the face of incursions from postmodernism and post-structuralism than have those in the other social sciences.

References

Alker, H. R., 1996, *Rediscoveries and Reformulations: Humanistic Methods for International Studies*, Cambridge and New York: Cambridge University Press.

Baker, A., 2000, 'Globalization and the British "Residual State"', in R. Stubbs, G.R.D. Underhill and Don Mills, eds., *Political Economy and the Changing Global Order*, Second Edition, Ontario: Oxford University Press, 362-372.

Ball, T., 1976, 'From Paradigms to Research Programs: Toward a Post-Kuhnian Political Science', *American Journal of Political Science* 20 (February): 151-77.

Barnes, B., 1982, *T. S. Kuhn and Social Science*, New York: Columbia University Press.

Beck, U., 2000, *What Is Globalization?* Translated by Patrick Camiller, Cambridge, UK: Polity.

Castells, M., 1996, *The Rise of the Network Society*, Oxford: Blackwell.

Caton, S. C., 1999, *Lawrence of Arabia: A Film's Anthropology*, Berkeley: University of California Press.

Cerny, P. G., 1996, 'Globalization and Other Stories: The Search for a New Paradigm for International Relations', *International Journal* 51 (Autumn): 617-637.

Cheru, F., 2002, *African Renaissance: Roadmaps to the Challenge of Globalization*, London: Zed Books.

Clark, I., 1999, *Globalization and International Relations Theory*, Oxford and New York: Oxford University Press.

CODESRIA, 1998, 'Social Sciences and Globalisation in Africa', *CODESRIA Bulletin* 2 (December): 3-6.

Cox, R. W., 1987, *Production, Power and World Order: Social Forces in the Making of History*, New York: Columbia University Press.

Der Derian, J., ed., 1994, *International Theory: Critical Investigations*, New York: New York University Press.

Dicken, P., 1998, *Global Shift: Transforming the World Economy*, Third edition, New York and London: Guilford Press.

Falk, R., 1999, *Predatory Globalization: A Critique*, Cambridge, UK: Polity.

Ferrer, A., 1997, *Hechos y Ficciones de la Globalización [Facts and Fictions of Globalization]*, Buenos Aires: Fondo de Cultura Economica [Collection of Economic Writings].

Giddens, A., 1990, *The Consequences of Modernity*, Cambridge, UK: Polity Press.

Giddens, A., 2000, *Runaway World: How Globalization Is Reshaping Our Lives*, New York: Routledge.

Gómez, J. M., 2000, *Política e democracia em tempos de globalização*, Petrópolis, R.J., Brazil: Editora Vozes.

Gordon, D., 1988, 'The Global Economy: New Edifice or Crumbling Foundations?' *New Left Review* 168 (March-April): 24-64.

Guillén, M. F., 2001, 'Is Globalization Civilizing, Destructive or Feeble? A Critique of Five Key Debates in the Social-Science Literature', *Annual Review of Sociology* 27: 235-260.

Hardt, M., and A. Negri, 2000, *Empire*, Cambridge, Mass: Harvard University Press.

Harvey, D., 1990, *The Condition of Postmodernity*, Oxford: Basil Blackwell.

Harvey, D., 1999, *Limits to Capital*, London: Verso.

Held, D., A. G. McGrew, D. Goldblatt, and J. Perraton, 1999, *Global Transformations: Politics, Economics and Culture*, Cambridge, UK: Polity Press.

Hirst, P. and G. Thompson, 1999, *Globalization in Question: The International Economy and the Possibilities of Governance*, Second edition, Cambridge, UK: Polity Press.

Kaneko, M., 1999, *Han Gurouburizumu: Shijou Kaiku no Senryakuteki Shikou [Antiglobalism: Strategic Thinking on Market Reforms]*, Tokyo: Iwanami Shoten.

Kearney, A. T., 2001, 'Measuring Globalization', *Foreign Policy* 122 (January-February): 56-65.

Keohane, R. O., 1984, *After Hegemony: Cooperation and Discord in the World Political Economy*, Princeton: Princeton University Press.

Keohane, R.O., and J. S. Nye, Jr., 1977, *Power and Interdependence: World Politics in Transition*, Boston and Toronto: Little, Brown.

Keohane, R.O., and J. S. Nye, Jr., 1998, 'Power and Interdependence in the Information Age', New York: Council on Foreign Relations web site, *web.lexis-nexis.com/universe/printdoc/*

Keohane, R. O., and J. S. Nye, Jr., 2000, 'Globalization: What's New? What's Not? (And So What?' *Foreign Policy* 118 (Spring): 104-120.

Knox, P. and J. Agnew, 1998, *The Geography of the World Economy*, Third edition, London: Edward Arnold.

Kuhn, T. S., 1970, *The Structure of Scientific Revolutions*, Second edition, Chicago: University of Chicago Press.

Kuhn, T. S., 1977a, *The Essential Tension: Selected Studies in Scientific Tradition and Change*, Chicago: University of Chicago Press.

Kuhn, T. S., 1977b, 'Second Thoughts on Paradigms', in F. Suppe, ed., *The Structure of Scientific Theories*, Second edition, Urbana: University of Illinois Press, 459-482.

Lakatos, I., 1970, 'Falsification and the Methodology of Scientific Research Programmes', in I. Lakatos and A. Musgrave, eds., *Criticism and the Growth of Knowledge*, Cambridge, UK: Cambridge University Press, 91-196.

Lapid, Y., 1989, 'The Third Debate: On the Prospects of International Theory in a Post-positivist Era', *International Studies Quarterly* 33: 235-254.

McMichael, P., 2000, *Development and Social Change: A Global Perspective*, Second edition, Thousand Oaks: Pine Forge Press.

Mittelman, J. H., 1997, 'Rethinking Innovation in International Studies: Global Transformation at the Turn of the Millennium', in S. Gill and J. H. Mittelman, eds., *Innovation and Transformation in International Studies*, Cambridge, UK: Cambridge University Press, 248-263.

Mittelman, J. H., 2000, *The Globalization Syndrome: Transformation and Resistance*, Princeton: Princeton University Press.

Mittelman, J. H. and Norani Othman, eds., 2001, *Capturing Globalization*, London and New York: Routledge.

Norani, Othman, and S. Mandal, eds., 2000, *Malaysia Menangani Globalisasi: Peserata atau Mangasi? [Malaysia Responding to Globalization: Participants or Victims?]*, Bangi, Malaysia: Penerbit Universiti Kebangsaan Malaysia [National University of Malaysia Press].

Olds, K., 2001, *Globalization and Urban Change: Capital, Culture, and Pacific Rim Mega-Projects*, Oxford and New York: Oxford University Press.

Olds, K., P. Dicken, P. Kelly, L. Kong, and H. W. Yeung, eds., 1999, *Globalisation and the Asia-Pacific: Contested Territories*. London: Routledge.

Panitch, L., 1996, 'Rethinking the Role of the State', in J. H. Mittelman, ed., *Globalization: Critical Reflections*, Boulder: Lynne Rienner, 83-113.

Peterson, S., ed., 1992, *Gendered States: Feminist (Re)Visions of International Relations*, Boulder: Lynne Rienner.

Podestà, B., M. Gómez Galán, F. Jácome, and J. Grandi, eds., 2000, *Ciudadanía y mundialización regional: La sociedad civil ante la integración regional*, Madrid: CIDEAL.

Puchala, D. J., 2000, 'Marking a Weberian Moment: Our Discipline Looks Ahead', *International Studies Perspectives* 1 (Aug.): 133-144.

Puchala, D. J., 2001, Personal correspondence with the author, 30 January.

Robertson, R., 1992, *Globalization: Social Theory and Global Culture*, Newbury Park: Sage.

Rodrik, D., 1997, *Has Globalization Gone Too Far?* Washington, DC: Institute for International Economics.

Rosenau, J. N., 1997, *Along the Domestic-Foreign Frontier: Exploring Governance in a Turbulent World*, Cambridge, UK: Cambridge University Press.

Ruggie, J.G., 1993, 'Territoriality and Beyond: Problematizing Modernity in International Relations', *International Organization* 46 (Summer): 561-598.

Said, E.W., 1979, *Orientalism*, New York: Vintage.

Sassen, S., 1998, *Globalization and Its Discontents*, New York: New Press.

Scholte, J. A., 1999, 'Globalisation: Prospects for a Paradigm Shift', in M. Shaw, ed., *Politics and Globalisation: Knowledge, Ethics and Agency*, London and New York: Routledge, 9-22.

Scholte, J. A., 2000, *Globalization: A Critical Introduction*, London: Macmillan.

Seoane, J., and E. Taddei, eds., 2001, *Resistencias mundiales [De Seattle a Porto Alegre]*, Buenos Aires: Consejo Latinamericano de Ciencias Sociales.

Shaw, M., 1994, 'Introduction: The Theoretical Challenge of Global Society', in *Global Society and International Relations*, edited by M. Shaw, Oxford: Oxford University Press.

Shaw, M., ed., 1999, *Politics and Globalisation: Knowledge, Ethics and Agency*, London: Routledge.

Sorkin, M., ed., 1992, *Variations on a Theme Park: The New American City and the End of Public Space*, New York: Hill and Wang.

Strange, S., 1996, *The Retreat of the State: The Diffusion of Power in the World Economy*, Cambridge, UK: Cambridge University Press.

Strange, S., 1998, *Mad Money: When Markets Outgrow Governments*, Ann Arbor: University of Michigan Press.

Sylvester, C., 1994, *Feminist Theory and International Relations Theory in a Postmodern Era*, Cambridge, UK: Cambridge University Press.

Taylor, P. J., 1993, *Political Geography: World-Economy, Nation-State, and Locality*, New York: Wiley.

Taylor, P. J., R. J. Johnson, and M. J. Watts, 1995, *Geographies of Global Change: Remapping the World in the Late Twentieth Century*, Oxford: Blackwell.

Thrift, N., 1996, *Spatial Formations*, London: Sage.

Walker, R. B. J., 1993, *Inside/Outside: International Relations as Political Theory*, Cambridge, UK: Cambridge University Press.

Wallerstein, I., 2000, 'Globalization or the Age of Transition? A Long-Term View of the Trajectory of the World System', *International Sociology* 15 (June): 249-265.

Waltz, K.N., 1979, *Theory of International Politics*, Reading, MA: Addison-Wesley.

Waltz, K.N., 1999, 'Globalization and Governance', *PS: Political Science & Politics* 23 (December): 693-700.

Watson, J. L., ed., 1997, *Golden Arches East: McDonald's in East Asia*, Stanford: Stanford University Press.

Weber, M., 1949, '"Objectivity" in Social Science and Social Policy', in E. Shils and H. A. Finch, eds. and translated, *The Methodology of the Social Sciences* New York: Free Press, 49-112.

Weiss, L., 1998, *State Capacity: Governing the Economy in a Global Era*, Cambridge, UK: Polity Press.

Wendt, A., 1999, *Social Theory of International Politics*, Cambridge, UK: Cambridge University Press.

Zeleza, P. T., 2003, *Rethinking Africa's Globalization*, Vol. 1: *The Intellectual Challenges*, Trenton: Africa World Press.

Chapter 2

If You Are Part of the Solution, You Are Likely Part of the Problem: Transboundary Formations and Africa

Ronald Kassimir

Almost exactly a year after the towers fell in New York, war broke out in Côte d'Ivoire. In late September 2002, the *New York Times* carried a story on the removal of approximately 100 American children—sons and daughters of American Christian missionaries based in West Africa—who were studying at the International Christian Academy in the Ivoirien city of Bouaké, then engulfed in fighting between warring groups. The young Americans were escorted from Bouaké by French troops, who handed them over to American forces—these were the days before the build up to the Iraq war, and the French and American militaries were on more friendly terms. A colour photograph of several children inside a bus appeared on the front page of the *New York Times* (although the story itself ran on page 10) (Onishi 2002:10).

Many questions crossed my mind when I saw the photo and read the story, not least of which was just what are American Christian missionaries doing in places with large Muslim populations, and where most non-Muslims already have some kind of affiliation with one Christian denomination or another?[1] But three things stood out. First, what a strange imperial power the United States must be that when its citizens—children no less—are threatened, it removes them (with the help of the French!) rather than use its overwhelming force to secure order. Nineteenth century imperialists in Africa would not have passed up such an opportunity to impose their writ. (Nor did Ronald Reagan when American students were allegedly threatened in Grenada in the last decade of the Cold War, but that is another story.) Even after September 11, or perhaps because of it, the global hegemon was intent on picking its spots—which it did in Afghanistan and again in Iraq the following year.

A second observation was that the US was going in to protect *its* children, not Ivoirien children or other bystanders of the conflict. This was not unusual behaviour—powerful states tend to take direct care of their own and, perhaps, provide resources to non-governmental humanitarian agencies to take care of others. But it did drive home the idea that national citizenship, and the obligation of states (when they are able, of course) to take care of their citizens extra-territorially, was still an utterly commonsensical dimension of international relations. Far from being reduced by globalisation, nationality and statehood (of at least some states) are alive and well, perhaps even enabled in some ways by global connections.

Lastly, I wondered what would have been the reaction in New York on September 11, 2001, and the days after if an Ivoirien military force had arrived to remove Ivoirien citizens from a city devastated by terrorism. Of course the two situations are far from equivalent, but it was hard not to muse about how Americans would have reacted. And how that would have compared to how Ivoiriens in Bouaké must have reacted as they watched the bus filled with American mission kids pull away while they and their children remained in the middle of a war. This was not included in the *New York Times* report, but it is worth pondering.

While in the rest of this paper I consider ways of conceptualising the insinuation and entanglement of external forces in Africa, rather than the use of power to withdraw institutions of influence (like missions), I recount these musings in order to foreshadow one my of key points: that African 'crises' are not simply driven by internal dynamics but by the way those dynamics are already enmeshed in external relationships of one kind or another. When foreign governments or the international community decide to intervene, whether to remove American children or assist Ivoirien ones, it is analytically and practically naïve to view 'problems' or 'root causes' as simply local matters prior to the intervention. External forces are already implicated in local dynamics.

While in no sense could the conflict in Côte d'Ivoire be considered as produced by external forces,[2] there are demonstrably direct connections to other conflicts in the region partly fuelled by global markets in diamonds and timber (i.e., Sierra Leone and Liberia) not to mention small arms and mercenaries. In addition, the global economic context of severely fluctuating markets and exchange rates for Ivoirien primary products first fuelled migration from other parts of West Africa and has now depressed local economies in ways that generate conflicts over resources, land and labour in which those migrants are enmeshed. One might even argue that the discourse of 'ivoirité' that stigmatises Muslims and their political leaders as foreigners is itself a locally appropriated import of global discourses of indigeneity and its relationship to citizenship. Finally, Côte d'Ivoire's central role in France's Africa policy and the shifts in that role over the past decade, in particular in the period directly leading up to and following the outbreak of war, have clearly affected the political calculus of actors there in ways that may have created more space for the strategic use of violence. Again, none of these external elements have caused the war in Côte d'Ivoire. Rather, in their intersection with regional, national and local dynamics, they are constitutive—one cannot understand what has happened without considering their direct role and indirect shaping of putatively local imaginations, decisions, and practices.[3]

The impact of 'external' forces on the lives of Africans has been a predominant focus, even obsession, for scholars, policy-makers, and activists for at least a century, and perhaps going back as far as the slave trade and reactions to it by Africans and abolitionists in the West.[4] In particular, *how much* 'the external' influences or determines economic, social, cultural and political pasts, presents and futures in Africa drives a range of intellectual and political projects, and fuels debates about internalist versus external causes of crises, degrees and sources of Afro-pessimism, structure versus agency in the African context, and others.

One critique of this *how much* question centres on unpacking the distinction between external and internal, or outside and inside. A complementary strategy which I take up here, one that similarly problematises the external-internal distinction,[5] is to focus on *how* this influence takes place, rather than its extent in relation to other forces.

In getting to this point, I proceed as follows. First, I discuss why thinking about external-internal connections is poorly served by the meta-discussions and debates on globalisation. I then reflect on an analytical and political project pre-dating globalisation discourse and in some ways displaced by it: dependency theory. Dependency made (and, in new guises, still makes) the point about how the external is already implicated in the local in still useful ways, even if it overly privileged one external aspect and occasionally paid too little attention to diverse local structures and dynamics. Next, I discuss transboundary formations (TBFs) as a frame for imagining certain types of external-internal intersections. The notion of TBFs builds on insights from dependency theory (and its critics), international relations theory, and some of the flotsam and jetsam of discourses on globalisation. In doing so, it attempts to make certain kinds of intersections—those directly relevant to the production of authority and local orders—more tangible and amenable to empirical and comparative analysis.

Lastly, I return to the issue of how recognition of TBFs is relevant to the ways in which the international community intervenes in the region. One critical need in organising international assistance in Africa's economic and political crises (although not the only one) is to figure out how external dimensions (from development aid to global markets for 'blood diamonds') are part of the conjuncture of forces that produces crises in the first place.

Giving Globalisation a Rest

Whatever the other benefits of the recent scholarly dance with globalisation, it has called attention to the relationship between things 'inside' (a state, a community) and things 'outside' and, in some cases, to the ways in which this relationship is shaped by differences in wealth and power (Walker 1993). However, if one of the measures of the utility of an analytical construct is that two reasonably smart people (including those who typically disagree) will know they are arguing about the same thing then globalisation is a conceptual train wreck. So much time is required to define, clarify, qualify and position. Even figuring out how oneself and others are using the term—as an empirical phenomenon (is it happening or not? how much?), a unique feature of the contemporary moment (is it new? in what ways?) or a normative/political/ideological project (is it good or bad? for whom?)—is a burden. None of this denies the need to take a stand on these questions. However, for many analytical purposes, globalisation is a very blunt instrument.[6]

Why is it a good idea to extricate inside/outside, or internal/external relationships from the clutches of globalisation discourse? Not because some of the political and intellectual issues raised under the rubric of that discourse do not matter. Nor because the internal/external dichotomy is unproblematic—a point made in some versions of the discourse. But what is so difficult to do under the globalisation rubric is to figure out ways to disaggregate different kinds of global-local connections and how they relate to each other.[7] For this reason, aggregate kinds of questions such as how does globalisation affect Africa, or is it harmful or helpful to Africa can obscure much more complex phenomena.[8]

For example, Africa has very low rates of foreign direct investment (FDI) and accounts for a very small percentage of global trade (an ostensible indicator of de-linkage from global forces). Yet, Africa is 'integrated' into the global economy (both licit and illicit), at least in the sense that the continent is heavily affected by shifts in the latter. It receives fairly substantial amounts of overseas development assistance (ODA)—at least relative to FDI—and is deeply intertwined in global institutions from the UN to a wide range of NGOs devoted to development, relief and advocacy for a range of causes. Generalising about these kinds of connections (and many others) as 'globalisation' and debating whether more or less of 'it' is needed can lead analysts (and policy-makers) into making a false choice between 'internalist' and 'externalist' accounts of Africa's economic and political woes.

Thus, I want to assert that thinking about external-internal (read global-local if you like) connections and influences need not take place under the banner of globalisation as a master analytical construct or narrative.[9] I am not saying they should not do so; only that they need not. And that the result of this temporary separation can be some clarity that would be very useful for thinking about oft-troubled connections that African societies have with the world.

Giving Dependency Theory its Due

It is almost impossible to disentangle the fuzziness of the current usages and criticisms of globalisation from the struggles of the intellectual left under the weight of a neoliberal onslaught and the lacunae of its own theories as applied to the developing world. While there were clearly intellectually substantive internal divides and debates, the cluster of concepts such as dependency, underdevelopment, world systems, and neocolonialism provided a common language or discourse, one in which scholars, activists and even some policy-makers in Africa as well as without were quite conversant. Even among those who disagreed on political or intellectual grounds with this cluster of Marxist-inspired approaches, there was recognition that it was a worthy opponent. Mainstream scholars in international relations, for example, tested the claims of dependency theory, re-configured more formally as hypotheses, against the claims of neo-realism and other approaches. In other words, discussions about the non-local causes of African (and other) political economies were taken not only as polemics (although they were at times polemical, although more often labelled as such) but as serious positions within social scientific and policy discourse.[10] This legitimacy also filtered into international policy institutions, especially in the UN system but also among some (mostly northern European) donor governments.

This must all be somewhat hard to imagine for graduate students at US universities in the first decade of the twenty-first century! In reality, the core assumptions of and issues raised by dependency theory have not so much disappeared as they have been subsumed by different intellectual streams. The materialist claims and the focus on material interests were claimed by non-Marxist or highly heterodox Marxist political economists, while the emphasis on the properties of world system was taken up by globalisation theorists (although often without the materialist privileging of capitalism and its transformations).

Giovanni Arrighi (2002), one of the early pioneers of the dependency approach as it was applied to Africa, has recently provided a very candid and insightful reflection on what it got right and where it went wrong.[11] Only once in the article (at least as far as I could find) is the term 'globalisation' used, and it is modified by the phrase 'so-called' (Arrighi 2002: 34).[12] This echoes the scepticism toward globalisation discourse among some components of the 'old' left (Zeleza 2003: Chapter 1) Arrighi argues rather convincingly that, at least in terms of Africa, the key transformation in the global economy that drastically shaped on the continent's economic crisis took place in the 1970s, i.e. prior to the end of the Cold War—the moment often cited as the watershed that ushered in the current 'global era'.

More immediately relevant to concerns here is Arrighi's comparison of the New Political Economy (NPE, by which he means rational choice and institutionalist approaches) to the dependency approach. Surprisingly, he found some similarities, but also noted two key differences.

> Our variety of political economy ... paid far greater attention to the global context in which African developmental efforts unfolded; and it was far more neutral on the role of states in developmental processes' (Arrighi 2002: 11).

The contrast here centres firstly on how NPE, which strongly influenced the policies of the international financial institutions (IFIs), largely focussed on the internal causes of economic crisis and, secondly, that the principal culprit producing internal dysfunction was the state itself.

Neither of these two differences, it can be noted, depends upon the materialist foundations of classical Marxism. This is clear in the case of the latter, as the state was seen as the engine of economic growth in the earlier stages of development theory and has made a revival both in discussions of Asian capitalism and in the IFIs' belated discovery of governance and political institutions (Mkandawire and Soludo 1999). For the former, the incorporation of global processes into the explanation of Africa's problems did not need to be reduced to economic factors 'in the last instance', as evidenced by the frequent reference to the distorting impact of Cold War politics on Africa's development made often enough in both dependency work and more mainstream international relations.[13] Indeed, the best work in dependency theory did not shy away from politics. Terms and concepts such as neocolonialism, comprador elites and labour aristocracy were deployed to help understand the nature of regimes, their external linkages, and their social bases.

The point is that dependency theory was extraordinarily powerful and prescient in pointing to external factors that shaped not only economic outcomes, but political ones as well. At a time when understanding state- or local-level political outcomes in the more main streams of social science rarely looked at external influences on politics, dependency was in fact quite concerned with what could be called politics of globalisation (Zeleza 2003: Chapter 1), even if these concerns sat somewhat uncomfortably with its materialist assumptions. However, as a *de facto* theory of what we might now call global-local political linkages, it had several major problems and limitations.

First, the scope for agency on the part of the African ruling elites who were the principal gatekeepers between the external world and their societies was far greater than often implied in notions of compradors or puppets of global capitalism. Bayart's articulation of this critique of dependency is the key referent here, in part because its rootedness outside a neoliberal ideological base has made it influential in many parts of the intellectual left concerned with Africa. Bayart (2000: 219, 220), in fact, accepts 'the fact of dependency while eschewing the meanderings of dependency theory'. Similarly, while he accepts the systemic dimensions of the world economy as articulated by dependency theory, this 'does not mean that only "structure matters" as the dependency theorists would have us believe'. The notion of extraversion, in which elites use international economic and political relations to maintain and extend themselves in power, in some ways perfectly inverts the political logic of dependency theory (Bayart 1993).

Regrettably, this necessary critique of structuralist overkill often led to a reifying of 'local agency' in much of the recent post-structuralist work. Some globalisation discourses have contributed to this by equating 'global' with 'structure' and 'local' with 'agency'. What gets lost here is that there are *local structures* (political, economic, class-based, etc.) that intersect with external networks, resources and institutions. In this sense, the principal limitation of dependency theory is not its neglect of agency (however true that may be) but its assumption of the predominance of a world system. In other words, like material factors, the global systemic level itself was determinant 'in the last instance'. In an odd way, this paralleled the views of neo-realism in international relations theory, where the emphasis on levels of analysis privileged the state of anarchy at the global level as the key to explaining a range of political phenomena.[14]

Ultimately, though, the crucial shortcoming of dependency is that the range of external forces that impinge upon politics in Africa was circumscribed by a few key dispositions: the principal object of interest (i.e. the degree and nature of economic transformations) and the commitment to a kind of materialist analysis that focussed almost exclusively on private capital rather than public capital (i.e. foreign aid). In the event, a range of ideational and organisational connections that were and are having political (and also economic) consequences either were neglected or dismissed.[15] It is this neglect, and the aforementioned frustrations with globalisation discourse, that motivated the development of TBFs as a heuristic device. In a sense, TBFs builds on dependency's insights but attempts to encompass the range of external actors and the importance of non-economic forces.

Transboundary Formations

In an edited volume published at the end of 2001, my colleagues and I searched for a language and an approach for characterising intersections in which forces that cut across state, regional or continental boundaries were enmeshed with state and local institutions and organised groups. We were especially interested in the ways in which these intersections shaped the organization of power and authority in specific places, whether state capitals, rural communities, refugee camps, war zones, or enclaves managed by transnational corporations (Callaghy, Kassimir and Latham 2001). Our goals, alluded to in the previous section, were fairly straightforward. We wanted to find ways of showing how a dynamic was created by the intersection of forces emanating from various levels that was not reducible to understanding the world from only one of those levels. We wanted to provide conceptual breathing space for different kinds of forces: some of which look like the classic structures of global or local political economies, others of which look like the institutions, organisations, networks and movements that draw the attention of some sociologists, and still others which look like the flows of material objects, ideas, discourses, and cultural practices that engage much recent work in cultural studies and anthropology.

Inevitably, we developed some conceptual distinctions that we felt were useful and which captured the empirical examples analysed by contributors to the volume. Most important was the need to disaggregate both the kinds of forces that were intersecting and the different ways in which external forces became bound up with local processes of order and authority (also see Tarrow 2002). For the former, we particularly emphasised the distinction between whether actors or organisations were formally parts of states or not, and whether they were licit or juridical or not, and were careful not to equate the two. We argued that these distinctions were useful because

> ... all too often we have been faced with the assumption either that the juridical dimensions of states are the only places to look when analyzing structures of order

and authority, or that when states are apparently incapable of living up to the Weberian ideal type, 'real' authority lies in other institutions (Latham, Kassimir and Callaghy 2001: 15).

For the latter, we called attention to the multiple ways global forces insert themselves locally in politically relevant ways, what Latham called the 'differences in the nature of interactions that occur across boundaries' (Callaghy, Kassimir and Latham 2001: 71). In particular, he highlighted the differences between international arenas (international laws, conventions and public events that bear on what happens inside of states); transnational networks that allow something of value to be delivered across boundaries (for example, commodities, resources, small arms, diamonds, technical assistance, popular culture); and trans-territorial deployments as 'an installation in a local context of agents from outside that context' (for instance, refugee camps, peacekeeping, diplomatic or religious missions, transnational corporate factories or offices, etc.), and for which colonialism was the principal antecedent to current forms of intervention that take the form of direct deployments (p.75).[16] We posited that these kinds of distinctions could lead to the identification of different kinds of dynamics, local responses, and possibilities for learning from past actions, at least compared with a globalisation discourse that tends to flatten the radically different ways in which external institutions, ideas and practices have local consequences. TBFs are not offered as a new theory, but rather as a device for seeing patterns and potentially developing hypotheses about what kinds of intersections produce what kinds of effects, and how they happen. We felt that developing new tools was especially important given the extent and pluralising of old and new forms and mechanisms of intervention in the continent that has accelerated since the end of the Cold War: peacekeeping, post-conflict reconstruction, democratisation, building civil societies, anti-terrorism measures, economic and governance reform (including structural adjustment), development assistance, environmental preservation, disease control and delivery for medicines (such as anti-retroviral drugs for AIDS victims), religious missions, and international advocacy for a wide range of causes—whether debt relief, human, women's, children's, and indigenous rights, or opening of Western markets.

More broadly, our intent was not to deny to possibility of, or indeed the need to identify various forces as external or internal. Rather, it was to demonstrate that, much of the time, the mechanisms behind the reproduction or transformation of power relations 'on the ground' were not reducible to either external or internal causes, but to a complex intertwining of them.

Learning That the External Is Already Present

Compared to dependency, TBFs broaden the range of forces that intersect across boundaries, and do not privilege particular ones as determinative *a priori*. But they build on the central insight of dependency theory that the external is already part of the constitution of local realities. I have gone back to dependency here because globalisation discourse is so diverse that, while some treatments would readily affirm this aspect of global-local intersections, others would tend to see a relatively untouched periphery now penetrated by everything from the internet to hip hop to notions of human rights to foreign trade. Any notion that can simultaneously house such diametrically opposed views is simply not very useful for the purposes here.

The point here about external forces is similar to that made recently by Calhoun (2004: 376) in his critique of what he calls the emergency imaginary—'the deployment of the idea of emergency as a means of taking hold of these [mostly humanitarian] crises'. Specifically, he suggests that, among other effects, we note 'how it simultaneously locates in particular settings what are in fact crises produced at least partially by global forces, and dislocates the standpoint of observation from that of the wealthy global north to a view from nowhere'.[17]

Below I discuss two examples of TBFs in Africa—one centred on the formally licit (the international aid regime) and the other illicit (the flows of so-called conflict diamonds). The point is often made about how various kinds of interventions, especially humanitarian and development oriented ones, have unintended consequences.[18] Here I want to focus more on responses and adjustments to the consequences (unintended or not) of these TBFs on the part of at least some of the parties involved. The main responses noted take the form of advocacy networks that link global and local activists and act in the 'international arena', and yet they also may have distinct regulatory and governance dimensions to them.[19]

The current international regime of foreign aid, which constitutes a component of many TBFs, has tended to 'forget' the role of external forces in constituting the crisis that the regime, in principle, exists to rectify. A better understanding of the role of aid is critical in the African context given how central it is in both the overall composition of foreign capital flows in the region and in percentage of GDP per capita in most African countries, at least compared to other world regions.[20] Indeed, dependency theory, perhaps because of its roots in the analysis of Latin American development, did not focus much on the effects of external yet *public* flows of capital given in exchange for policy conditionalities—i.e. bilateral and multilateral foreign aid—on both developmental outcomes and the political balance of forces with African countries. Notwithstanding what has emerged as a very common image among development practitioners of 'aid dependency,' private capital (and especially FDI) was the core emphasis of dependency theory as development critique.

That the aid regime structures governance and authority relations in African countries is clear to all whether this involvement is applauded or criticised. However, the degree to which its institutions and their representatives are directly and even physically present in the exercise of authority—i.e. a transterritorial deployment—is less typically noted (but see Callaghy 2001). Van de Walle (2001:220-1) sharply describes this presence in the 1990s:

> Most African countries were overrun with donors and their activities at the sectoral level. It was not unusual for forty-odd bilateral and multilateral donors plus twice that many Western NGOs to be implementing over a thousand distinct aid activities, and essentially dominating if not taking over key government ministries. Entire

ministries were being marginalized from their own areas of responsibilities, with sectoral policy increasing designed in aid missions and donor capitals and implemented 'off-budget' by self-standing project units outside central government, which has lost its sense of accountability and responsibility.

He then goes on to examine the many perverse impacts on local institutional capacity in spite of strong rhetoric on behalf of capacity building, governance and local 'ownership'. Overall, donor interventions have 'allowed if not speeded up the withdrawal of governments from their development obligations ... Aid is increasingly substituting itself for the government' (p.228).

Chege (1998: 102) has made a similar point in raising the question of the accountability of international organisations when their power in places like Africa comes without organic links to the populations whose lives they shape, which ironically can include demands that African institutions become more responsive to their constituencies:

Very little attention has gone into examining the extent of transparency and accountability of international institutions operating in Africa, notwithstanding the profound responsibilities they have traditionally assumed in trying to fill the vacuum created by many decrepit and irresponsible national governments.

In raising this issue, my point is not that external factors like the aid regime are the principal causes of African economic woes. Rather, they are key components of the TBFs that, in intersecting with a range of other actors, constitute and reproduce the crisis. At the same time, they help to reinforce the internalist account of the crisis that can draw attention away from actions not directly involving African actors, policies and institutions that could also make a difference. Van de Walle notes that there is nothing new about this. As far back as the early 1980s, the shift to largely internalist explanations that became the principal rationale of structural adjustment programmes also ignored the aid regime of the 1960s and 1970s as a constitutive component of weak economic performance. '[T]he blame for the disappointing results was soon placed on the Africans themselves rather than on the aid system itself' (Van de Walle 2001: 212). [21]

Again, the issue is not blame in a causal sense so much as how problem-solving intervention in the continent either forgets its own past effects or ignores other external factors. Of course, one possible argument is that, given the current state and structure of global capitalism and especially its apparently dominant neoliberal bent, the aid regime can do nothing but reinforce these global tendencies. And it is impossible to dispute the policy constraints placed upon the region by the world economy and by changes in it over the last 30 years or so (Arrighi 2002; Mkandawire and Soludo 1999; and Mkandawire 1999). However, as recent debates over global trade and the World Trade Organization reveal, the system is itself riddled with contradictions. For example, one obstacle to Africa's further integration into the international trading system is the decidedly anti-liberal subsidies that Western governments provide to their agricultural producers. Advocacy groups, and even the IFIs themselves, have increasingly weighed in on the damage this does to reform efforts in regions like Africa that are being encouraged to export their way out of poverty. In a recent declaration, the heads of the IMF, World Bank and OECD stated: 'Donors cannot provide aid to create development opportunities with one hand and then use trade restrictions to take these opportunities away with the other'.[22]

Why the IFIs have only now come to aggressively involve themselves with this matter would itself be an interesting research question. There is clearly something about agricultural trade policies that brings out both passion and inconsistency across the political spectrum.[23] But the broader point is this: the interests and decisions of American and French farmers and the politicians who court their support shape Africa's economic situation. Thus understanding the latter needs to take account of the former.

A second example of the external dimensions of African TBFs that has been only belatedly recognised as intimately part of local political (dis)order is the global demand for commodities marketed by actors in civil wars and regional conflicts. While a set of intense and sometimes vituperative debates have been ongoing around the relative weight of 'greed and grievance' in explaining conflict in the 1990s, the role of external markets, cross-border smuggling of commodities and arms, and 'foreign' private security and mercenary forces have been established as constitutive components of the origins and especially the sustaining of conflicts.[24] Flows of diamonds and other minerals, arms, and warriors for hire have not only helped pay for the means of violence but enabled so-called warlords (in Liberia, Sierra Leone and Angola) and rebels and occupying armies (in the DRC) to establish and reproduce governance mechanisms of a particularly brutal type (Reno 2001).

A focus on these external dimensions of conflict have usefully complicated the reliance on 'primordial identities' or 'ancient ethnic hatreds' as the default explanation of conflicts so often applied to Africa in the international press and among some policy circles. The foci of much globalisation and international relations theorising on the post-Cold War environment is not misplaced here. Indeed, few observers would have looked away from the external dimensions of conflicts in the region during the Cold War when debates were about the merits of superpower intervention, not the fact of their influence on what were often labelled 'proxy wars'. If our understanding of those conflicts sometimes played down their rootedness in local struggles and interests, the coding of Africa as a place rife with impending ethnic violence in the1990s initially led to an occlusion of the external dimensions of transboundary conflict formations.

Most interestingly, and in some ways parallel to the IFIs' recent recognition of the deleterious effects of western agricultural subsidies, the issue of 'conflict', 'blood' or 'dirty' diamonds emerged in the late 1990s as important focus for global advocacy efforts.[25] This has ultimately evolved into an array of UN-sponsored certification mechanisms (i.e. certifying that diamonds sold in international markets were not smuggled from conflict zones) centred around what is known as the Kimberley

Process (established in 2000), and a range of other existing and potential enforcement mechanisms (Le Billon (2003). Two NGOs, Global Witness and Partnership Africa Canada, maintain vigilant monitoring of the main diamond firms and states' adherence to international agreements (for example, Belgium as well as African states), produce reports and promote awareness.[26]

Again, the idea is not that external forces are the sole or main cause for conflicts, their longevity, or their transformation into criminal enterprises. Rather, it is that the international community has recognised that, at least in this instance (and for other commodities such as drugs, timber and coltan), changes need to take place in Antwerp as well as Monrovia in order to constructively intervene in resolving conflicts.

Conclusion

A famous and oft-used adage from the 1960s is 'if you are not part of the solution, then you are part of the problem.'[27] Whether or not this is true, what I have tried to get at in this chapter is a twist on this chestnut—*if you are part of the solution, you are likely part of the problem.*

Clearly, who is the 'you' in this statement matters a lot, both analytically and empirically. Humanitarian NGOs, World Bank missions, religious organisations, transnational corporations and illegal arms merchants are likely to take very different perspectives to the intended and unintended consequences of their actions in Africa and elsewhere. One challenge, which this chapter does not take up, would be to map out these ranges of forces more systematically. We can make some rough distinctions—between actors who have no or only self-interested concern about the consequences of their actions, those who upon recognition of negative consequences reflect and attempt to change their behaviour, and global movements, often partnering with local organizations, that address problems caused by other global actors. By the logic of what has been argued here, the fact of local partnerships themselves is a signal that even these advocacy organisations are likely to have their own unintended effects.

It is systematic thinking about the range, diversity, intentions and consequences of these external forces and their local intersections that, I would argue, is one central task of re-thinking the study of Africa. For a variety of reasons, the rise of scholarly discourses of globalisation all too often produced either reactive or defensive responses on the part of social scientists working in or on the region. Many of us moved either to embrace some of these discourses (inheriting their incoherence or lack of specificity) or to assert the primacy of the local in the mistaken assumption that if one is arguing that external forces matter a lot, then local (and thus knowledge of the local) matter less. Others never gave up the ghost of dependency theory, but in the 1990s almost singularly focussed on the imposition of structural adjustment programmes to the exclusion of other features of the global economy, not to mention a range of post-Cold War political developments (and unfinished business that arose in the Cold War) that are not possible to ignore.

The polarisation of policy debate on Africa into 'internalist' and 'externalist' accounts in the 1990s is itself an important topic for a sociologist of knowledge to explore, as would be the related ways in which global gets equated with structure and local with agency in more rarefied academic discussions. But I would argue that the more pressing task is to look at concrete events and processes in which different institutions operate and intersect, where networks of people form and through which ideas and commodities are trafficked. Given how easily organisations from outside the region are able to operate in Africa—from arms merchants to missionaries to refugee camp managers to peacekeepers to corporate investors to social scientists (!)—the number and types of these intersections and networks are great. The degrees to which and the ways in which they (the intersections, not just the external part of the intersection) shape and re-shape individual lives, group dynamics and collective futures needs to be researched, not presumed. As noted in the previous section, there can even be practical, if certainly limited results from thinking about transboundary formations in this way. Powerful and well-intentioned external actors and institutions may even learn to deal better with the consequences of their actions, or with the actions of others not so well intentioned.

As I argued earlier, one can make a real contribution to an understanding of African development issues by studying the politics of American trade policy, and to understanding conflict in the region by examining the cultural and economic underpinnings of the world diamond market. This kind of work is not a substitute for understanding the local dimensions of economic crisis or a civil conflict. It is also not a substitute for understanding what becomes of an Ivoirien child in the midst of a war and in its aftermath, including how she might be affected by watching soldiers from another part of the world 'rescue' American children. The point is that we need to find ways of seeing these very different kinds of knowledges within a common frame if we are to treat complex questions of order and justice—global and local—with the care and urgency they merit.

Notes

1. This was not trivial given that the conflict in Côte d'Ivoire was playing out in ways that seemed to pit Christian/southern Ivoiriens against northern Muslims, many of whom were accused of not really being citizens but migrants from Burkina Faso.
2. Let alone caused by globalisation—which I argue below would be a meaningless assertion.
3. For recent analyses, see International Crisis Group (2003), and *La Côte d'Ivoire en guerre: dynamiques du dedans et du dehors*, special issue of *Politique Africaine* 89, 2003.
4. 'To Study Africa is to appreciate the long-term importance of the exercise of power across space, but also the limitations of such power' (Cooper 2001a: 190-191). See also Cooper (2001b).
5. To be clear, for me problematising the distinction is compatible with holding that some things are more external than others. The complicating of categories in this case does not eviscerate the need for them.

6. For a very helpful parsing of different streams of globalisation discourse as it relates to Africa, see Paul Tiyambe Zeleza (2003: Chapter 1).
7. For a similar point regarding the relationship between globalization and social movements, see Sidney Tarrow (2002).
8. As Cooper (2001: 195) succinctly puts it, 'The Question is whether the changing meaning over time of spatial linkages can be understood in a better way than globalization'.
9. I assert rather than argue, because the latter would require yet another definitional discussion of globalisation which, at least for purposes here, I want to avoid.
10. Partly for limits of space, I focus on theories of dependency and neo-colonialism and will note but not discuss two others: the field of international relations (IR) and the articulation of modes of production approach popular in Marxist anthropology in the 1970s and 1980s. While certainly influential, both mostly stayed within disciplinary debates (political science and anthropology, respectively).
11. An earlier and especially enlightening reassessment of the dependency debate is Colin Leys (1996).
12. The adjective 'global' is, however, used often and without qualification.
13. Of course, for the *dependistas* the Cold War was precisely about the world economy 'in the last instance'.
14. Work under the rubric of dependency did begin wrestling with these issues, although much more in studies of Latin America than Africa. Cardoso and Falleto (1969) emphasised the capacity of local structures to shape developmental and political outcomes, while Evans (1979) argued that the intersection of global and local structures could lead to economic transformations and shifts of some states in the global pecking order.
15. It should be noted that some dependency school theorists would ask today whether those who point out the plurality of external forces have a theory of which are the dominant influences, with the implication that the non-economic ones are either not as powerful as or are epiphenomenal of material forces.
16. The term 'trans-territorial' describes 'the movement of a social entity across the boundaries of a territory from some external place, where the entity retains in that territory its identity as external' (Latham 2001: 75).
17. Elsewhere in the paper Calhoun provides a lengthy discussion of the role of external forces in Sudan's lengthy civil war in ways that echo the imagery of TBFs and the argument presented here.
18. Peter Uvin (1998) remains a touchstone of this work, although many others have cropped up in recent years. See, for example, Sarah Kenyon Lischer (2003).
19. On advocacy networks, see Keck and Sikkink (1998). On the governance dimensions that often go beyond or around the frame of advocacy, see several chapters in Callaghy, Kassimir and Latham (2001).
20. For a detailed analysis, see Nicolas van de Walle (2001: Chapter 5). Also, see Arthur A. Goldsmith (2001).
21. It is worth noting that this point is premised on the notion that the pre-structural adjustment aid regime was very problematic—i.e. a different image than many critics of SAPs often hold. For a similar observation on the recent debate over NEPAD—the new development vision produced by African leaders, see Francis Owusu (2003: 1665), who

writes that NEPAD 'provides an opportunity for developed countries to participate in Africa's development efforts without admitting their role in creating the crisis'.

22. CalTrade Report, 2, 13, March 1–15, 2004, http://www.caltradereport.com/eWebPages/front-page-1063226666.html. See the website of KickAAS (Kick All Agricultural Subsidies) for extensive discussion and links on this issue. http://kickaas.typepad.com/

23. At least some anti-globalisation groups have their own contradictions in this regard, as they simultaneously critique trade liberalisation as a strategy and western agricultural policies that prevent African economies from effectively liberalising.

24. See Reno (1998), LeBillon (2003), Collier (2000), Berdal and Malone (2000), Mkandawire (2002), and Ellis (2003).

25. Particularly influential was the work culminating in a report out of the Canadian-based Sierra Leone Working Group. See Smillie, Gberie and Hazleton (2000).

26. A discussion of the conflict diamonds campaign as a transnational advocacy network appears in Mbabazi, MacLean and Shaw (2002).

27. The origin of this adage is Eldridge Cleaver, the American black nationalist. The actual quotation, taken from a speech he gave in 1968, is 'What we're saying today is that you're either part of the solution or you're part of the problem'.

References

Arrighi, G., 2002, 'The African Crisis: World Systemic and Regional Aspects', *New Left Review* 15: 5-36.

Bayart, J.-F., 1993, *The State in Africa: The Politics of the Belly*, London: Longman.

Bayart, J-F., 2000, 'Africa in the World: A History of Extraversion', *African Affairs* 99 (365): 217-267.

Berdal, M. and D. Malone, eds., 2000, *Greed and Grievance: Economic Agendas in Civil Wars*, Boulder, CO: Lynne Reinner.

Calhoun, C., 2004, 'A World of Emergencies: Fear, Intervention, and the Limits of Cosmopolitan Order', *Canadian Review of Sociology and Anthropology* 41 (4): 373-393.

Callaghy, T., R. Kassimir and R. Latham, eds., 2001, *Intervention and Transnationalism in Africa: Global-Local Networks of Power*, Cambridge: Cambridge University Press.

Callaghy, T. M., 2001, 'Networks and Governance in Africa: innovation in the debt regime', in T. Callaghy, R. Kassimir and R. Latham, eds., *Intervention and Transnationalism in Africa: Global-Local Networks of Power*, New York: Cambridge University Press.

Cardoso, F. H. and E. Falleto, 1969, *Dependency and Development in Latin America*, Berkeley: University of California Press.

Chege, M., 1998, 'Responsibility and Accountability by International Institutions: Sub-Saharan Africa in the 1990s', in F. Deng and T. Lyons, eds., *African Reckoning: The Quest for Good Governance*, Washington, DC: The Brookings Institution Press.

Collier, P., 2000, 'Doing Well Out of War: An Economic Perspective', in M. Berdal and D. M. Malone, eds., *Greed and Grievance: Economic Agendas in Civil Wars*, Boulder CO: Lynne Rienner Publishers.

Cooper, F., 2001a, 'What is the Concept of Globalization Good For? An African Historian's Perspective', *African Affairs* 100 (399): 189-213.

Cooper, F., 2001b, 'Networks, Moral Discourse and History', in T. Callaghy, R. Kassimir and R. Latham, eds., *Intervention and Transnationalism in Africa: Global-Local Networks of Power*, New York: Cambridge University Press.

Ellis, S., 2003, 'Violence and History: A Rejoinder to Mkandawire', *Journal of Modern African Studies* 41 (3): 457-75.

Evans, P., 1979, *Dependent Development: The Alliance of Multinational, State and Local Capital in Brazil*, Princeton: Princeton University Press.

Goldsmith, A.A., 2001, 'Foreign Aid and Statehood in Africa', *International Organization* 55 (1): 123-48.

International Crisis Group, 2003, *Côte D'Ivoire: The War is Not Yet Over*', ICG Africa Report No. 72, Freetown and Brussels.

Keck, M. E. and K. Sikkink, 1998, *Activists beyond Borders: Advocacy Networks in International Politics*, Ithaca: Cornell University Press.

Latham, R., 2001, 'Identifying the Contours of Transboundary Political Life' in T. Callaghy, R. Kassimir and R. Latham, eds., *Intervention and Transnationalism in Africa: Global-Local Networks of Power*, New York: Cambridge University Press.

Latham, R., R. Kassimir and T. Callaghy, 2001, 'Introduction: Transboundary Formations, Intervention, Order and Authority' in T. Callaghy, R. Kassimir and R. Latham, eds., *Intervention and Transnationalism in Africa: Global-Local Networks of Power*, New York: Cambridge University Press.

Le Billon, P., 2003, 'Getting it done: Instruments of Enforcement', in Paul Collier and Ian Bannon, eds., *Natural Resources and Violent Conflict: Options and Actions*, Washington, DC: World Bank.

Leys, C., 1996, *The Rise and Fall of Development Theory*, Oxford: James Currey.

Lischer, S.K., 2003, 'Collateral Damage: Humanitarian Assistance as a Cause of Conflict', *International Security* 28 (1): 79-109.

Mbabazi, P., S. J. MacLean and T. M. Shaw, 2002, 'Governance for Reconstruction in Africa: Challenges for Policy Communities and Coalitions,' *Global Networks* 21 (1): 31-47.

Mkandawire, T. and C. Soludo, 1999, *Our Continent, Our Future: African Perspectives on Structural Adjustment*, Dakar: CODESRIA.

Mkandawire, T., 1999, 'Crisis Management and the Making of "Choiceless Democracies"', in R. Joseph, ed., *State, Conflict, and Democracy in Africa*, Boulder, CO: Lynne Rienner Publishers.

Mkandawire, T., 2002, 'The Terrible Toll of Post-Colonial "Rebel Movements" in Africa: Towards an Explanation of the Violence Against the Peasantry', *Journal of Modern African Studies* 40 (2): 181-215.

Onishi, N., 2002, 'US Children Evacuated from Rebel-Held Ivory Coast City,' *New York Times*, September 26.

Owusu, F., 2003, 'Pragmatism and the Gradual Shift from Dependency to Neoliberalism: the World Bank, African Leaders and Development Policy in Africa', *World Development* 31 (10): 1655-72.

Reno, W., 1998, *Warlord Politics and African States*, Boulder, CO: Lyne Rienner Publishers.

Reno, W., 2001, 'How Sovereignty Matters: International Markets and the Political Economy of Local Politics in Weak States', in T. Callaghy, R. Kassimir and R. Latham, eds., *Intervention and Transnationalism in Africa: Global-local Networks of Power*, New York: Cambridge University Press.

Smillie, I., L. Gberie and R. Hazleton, 2000, *The Heart of the Matter: Sierra Leone, Diamonds & Human Security*, Ottawa: Partnership Africa Canada.

Tarrow, S., 2002, 'From Lumping to Splitting: Specifying Globalization and Resistance', in J. Smith and H. Johnston, eds., *Globalization and Resistance: Transnational Dimensions of Social Movements*, Lanham, MD: Rowman & Littlefield.

Uvin, P., 1998, *Aiding Violence: The Development Enterprise in Rwanda*, West Hartford, CT: Kumarian Press.

van de Walle, N., 2001, *African Economies and the Politics of Permanent Crisis, 1979-1999*, Cambridge: Cambridge University Press.

Walker, R.B.J., 1993, *Inside/Outside: International Relations as Political Theory*, Cambridge: Cambridge University Press.

Zeleza, P.T., 2003, *Rethinking Africa's Globalization, Volume I: The Intellectual Challenges*, Trenton, NJ: Africa World Press.

Chapter 3

Economic Liberalisation and Development in Africa

Jomo Kwame Sundaram

Over the past three decades, sub-Saharan African (SSA) income growth has barely kept pace with population growth. After a moderate increase in per capita income during the 1970s, SSA growth averaged 2.1 percent per annum in the 1980s and 2.4 percent in the 1990s, i.e. below the population growth rate. Despite a modest recovery after the mid-1990s, SSA per capita income at the turn of the century was ten percent below the level two decades earlier. Slow and erratic SSA growth has been accompanied by regressive income distribution trends (Geda 2005). The drop in average per capita income for the poorest 20 percent in SSA was twice that for the entire population between 1980 and 1995 (UNCTAD 2001:53).

For SSA, the new generation policies espoused by the 'Washington Consensus'—now involving 'getting prices right', 'getting institutions right' and 'good governance'—are still routinely offered as advice, if not imposed as conditionalities. Income levels in most of SSA are too low to generate the domestic resources needed for rapid growth. Meanwhile, under the Heavily Indebted Poor Countries (HIPC) initiative, only part of total debt is eligible for relief and, even then, only for some indebted countries. Furthermore, despite some recent acceleration in implementation, HIPC progress remains slow. As of June 2006, some ten years after the launch of the HIPC initiative, only 15 of the 32 African countries included in the HIPC list of 38, had reached completion.[1]

According to the World Bank, by 1998, a quarter of the population of the developing world, i.e. 1.2 billion people, were living below the poverty line of US$1 per day in 1993 purchasing power parity terms. Excluding China, where the number of poor has gone down with rapid economic growth, the number or poor people increased from 880 million in 1987 to 986 million in 1998. The number of poor in sub-Saharan Africa (SSA) rose from 217 million in 1987 to 291 million in 1998,

Table 1: Economic Trends in Sub-Saharan Africa

	1960 -65	1965 -70	1970 -75	1975 -80	1980 -85	1985 -90	1990 -95	1995 -2000	2000 -02
GDP per capita[a] An. Av. Gr. Rt.	2.76	2.37	1.79	-0.32	-1.9	-0.4	-1.43	0.68	0.75
Xs goods & services[b] An. Av. Gr. Rt.	6.91	4.25	0.81	4.46	0.18	2.86	3.28	4.73	1.79
Manufactured Xs (US$m) An. Av. Gr. Rt.								5.47	
X Price Unit Value Indices[c] (US$) An. Av. Gr. Rt.	1.4	0.27	21.12	22.45	-4.45	-2.22	1.86	-4.17	-1.78

	1960	1965	1970	1975	1980	1985	1990	1995	2000
Manufactured Xs (US$m)					4,683		29,699	38,757	

An. Av. Gr. Rt. (Average Annual Growth Rate)
[ab](const. 1995 US$); [c] These data are for the whole of Africa.

Table 2: Number of Poor in Africa

	% living on <$2/day 2001	Change in proportion and number of poor (<$1/day), 1981-2001	
		%	millions
World	53	-8	81
East Europe and Central Asia	20	15	70
Middle East and North Africa	23	2	19
Latin America and Caribbean	25	-3	3
East Asia and Pacific	47	-23	-252
Sub-Saharan Africa	77	2	134
South Asia	77	-9	106

Source: UN/DESA, 2005.

averaging around 46 percent of the SSA population over the period (World Bank, 2001b: 17, 23). The proportion of the population on less than US$1 a day in the least developed African countries has increased since the late sixties, rising from an average of 55.8 percent in 1965-69 to 64.9 percent in 1995-99 (UNCTAD 2002: Tables 19 & 20).

Over the last two decades, real wages have fallen and income inequality has risen as adjustment policies have hollowed out the nascent middle class in SSA. It is very difficult to reduce poverty through redistribution when average income levels are low, as in SSA. Hence, sustained poverty reduction can only proceed on the basis of rapid and sustained growth and job creation. However, the link between structural adjustment recommended by the Bretton Woods institutions (BWIs) and economic growth is generally weak, even when positive: of the 15 countries identified as core adjusters by the World Bank in 1993, only three were subsequently classified by the IMF as strong economic performers. And the exceptional cases of rapid growth among a few strong performers can be explained by special circumstances unrelated to structural adjustment policies.

Have Economic Reforms Helped Growth in Africa?

As is well known, the African development policy landscape has changed radically over the last three decades. Liberalisation and privatisation have replaced state controls and enterprises associated with import substitution. These failures can be traced to the displacement of strategic developmental thinking by policies of economic liberalisation. Ironically, while economic analysis during the pre-liberalisation developmental era seriously considered the impact of external factors on economic growth, the subsequent era, associated with globalisation, has tended to focus on 'domestic' determinants of economic performance. (More recently, this internal focus has gone beyond economic policies to include institutions, governance, rent-seeking, ethnic diversity, geography, etc.)

In 1981, the World Bank published the influential *Accelerated Development in Sub-Saharan Africa: An Agenda for Action*, often referred to as the Berg Report, after its principal author, Elliot Berg, from the University of Michigan's Economics Department. The document is seen as having set out the framework for subsequent economic reform led by the two Bretton Woods institutions over the last two decades in sub-Saharan Africa. The international sovereign debt crises from the early 1980s enabled the BWIs to impose the reform agenda as policy conditionalities for providing desperately needed credit in the face of the Volcker-induced world recession following the contractionary impact of raised US interest rates in the early 1980s.

While the International Monetary Fund (IMF) was generally responsible for short-term stabilisation programmes, the World Bank generally handled medium-term structural adjustment programmes (SAPs). These programmes were later dubbed as part of the Washington Consensus, also reflecting the economic policy preferences of the US leadership, particularly the Treasury Department. The Washington Consensus is generally associated with the global trend towards greater economic liberalisation since the 1980s, and has changed over time, largely in response to poorer economic performance throughout the world, especially in the developing countries, over the last two and a half decades. Despite Nobel laureate Joseph Stiglitz's acknowledgement that the Washington Consensus had failed and needed to be replaced by a reflationary and developmental post-Washington Consensus, there is little evidence of significant fundamental policy change despite growing dissent over those policies.

This is clearly reflected by remarks from the BWIs (for example, see *Finance & Development*, September 2002) with every hint of seeming economic success. The BWIs and their supporters have continued to deny that the poorer economic performance of the African region and the world in recent decades, can be directly attributed to the recommended or imposed policies pursued over the last two and a half decades. As the IMF put it, 'globalization is proceeding apace and SSA must decide whether to open up and compete, or lag behind' (Fischer et al. 1998:5). Or, as a World Bank economist has argued, 'If Africa is to reverse its unfavourable export trends, it must quickly adopt trade and structural adjustment policies that enhance its international competitiveness and allow African exporters to capitalize on opportunities in foreign markets' (Yeats 1997: 24). The key message of the BWIs to 'get prices right' through economic liberalisation is promoted as the conventional wisdom by media pundits. Commenting on the continuing stagnation of African per capita incomes, *The Economist* (2001: 12) argued that 'it would be odd to blame globalization for holding Africa back. Africa has been left out of the global economy, partly because its governments used to prefer it that way.'

Most African governments accepted the BWIs' policies, expecting the promised 'catalytic effect' on foreign capital inflows of the BWIs' stamps of approval. The actual response of private capital has, in the words of the World Bank, 'been disappointing' (quoted by Mkandawire 2005), although rates of return to FDI have generally been much higher in Africa than in any other region (Bhattacharya, et al. 1997; UNCTAD 1995, 2005). This, however, has not made Africa much more attractive to foreign investors, due to ill-specified and intangible 'risk factors'. Africa is systematically rated as more risky than warranted by economic indicators. Increased foreign investment into Africa has not increased Africa's share of global FDI flows. Although average annual inflows have increased five-fold, by 1998, the share of FDI going to sub-Saharan Africa (1.2 percent in 1999) was less than half its share in the mid-1980s (UNCTAD 2000).

However, from the mid-1990s, the BWIs began to claim success for their economic liberalisation and adjustment programmes. IMF officials suggested a 'turning point' (Fischer et al. 1998), claiming that the positive per capita growth rates of 1995-97 (averaging 4.1 percent) 'reflected better policies in many African countries rather than favourable exogenous developments' (Hernández-Catá 2000, quoted by Mkandawire 2005). Michel Camdessus, then IMF Managing Director, said at the 1996 annual meeting of the World Bank and the IMF, 'Africa, for which so many seem to have lost hope, appears to be stirring and on the move'. The World Bank President reported to his Board of Governors that there had been progress in the SSA, 'with new leadership and better economic policies' (Wolfensohn 1997). A senior IMF official, Alassane Ouattara (1997) claimed: 'A key underlying contribution has come from progress made in macroeconomic stabilization and the introduction of sweeping structural reforms', while a major World Bank (2000:21) report on Africa claimed there had been a turn around because of 'ongoing structural adjustment throughout the region which has opened markets and has a major impact on productivity, exports, and investment'.

The rise in FDI in the late 1990s was cited as evidence that the tide was turning (Pigato 2000),[2] although there is little evidence that the pattern of FDI is likely to bring about the sustained and broad-based economic growth and employment generation desperately needed in Africa (UNCTAD 2005). However, much of the investment in SSA went to South Africa and to mining, which is hardly influenced by macro-economic policy considerations. Some new investments have gone to expand or improve existing capacities, especially in natural monopolies (for example, beverages, cement and oil, gas and petroleum refining). Such expansion may have been stimulated by the short-lived spurt of growth that caused much euphoria, but later faded away. FDI has also been drawn by one-time opportunities associated with privatisation. For example, FDI to Ghana, once hailed by the BWIs as a 'success story', peaked with privatisation, with subsequent negative outflows. With the dismantling of protectionist barriers, import substituting activities have experienced de-industrialisation over recent decades. The end of the Multi-Fibre Arrangement (MFA) in 1995 and of its successor Agreement on Textiles and Clothing (ATC) in 2005 has brought an end to new investments in this sector, as many associated industries survive only due to the trade preferences enjoyed in the US and European markets, threatened by further trade liberalisation.

Also, highly speculative portfolio investment was attracted by temporary 'pull factors' such as high real domestic interest rates on Treasury Bills to finance budget deficits as well as temporary export price booms which attracted large export pre-financing loans (Kasekende et al. 1997). Mkandawire (2005) notes, with concern, the predominance of portfolio over direct investments, and acquisitions over 'green field' FDI, as possibly unintended consequences of the FDI policies adopted. Much recent FDI has involved acquisitions encouraged by privatisation, often on 'fire sale' terms. Such investments, which have declined since the late 1990s, accounted for about 14 percent of FDI flows into Africa. [3] Meanwhile, there has been relatively little for new greenfield investments actually creating other new economic capacities.

Incredibly, despite growing poverty, Africa has been a net exporter of capital. In 1990, 40 percent of privately held wealth was invested outside Africa (Collier and Gunning 1997; Collier et al. 1999; quoted by Mkandawire 2005). In the period 1970-96, capital flight from sub-Saharan Africa came to US$193 billion; with imputed interest, the total goes up to US$285 billion (Boyce and Ndikumana, 2000), compared to its combined debt of US$178 billion in 1996 (Mkandawire 2005). Ndikumana & Boyce (2002) argue that capital flight from Africa has been largely debt-fuelled though Collier et al. (2004) claims that serious financial capital flight from Africa has started to be reversed.

Even World Bank economists concede that the effects of financial liberalisation have been 'very small' (Devajaran, Easterly and Pack 1999). Incredibly, they argue that capital flight may indeed be good for Africa: 'The much-denigrated capital flight out of Africa may well have been a rational response to low returns at home ... Indeed, Africans are probably better off having made external investments than they would have been if they invested solely at home!' (Devajaran, Easterly and Pack, 1999:15-16), and conclude that there is 'over-investment' in Africa. Devajaran, Easterly and Pack (1999:23) argue that

> we should be more careful about calling for an investment boom to resume growth in Africa ... [and] about Africa's low savings rate ... [p]erhaps ... due to the fact that the returns to investment were so low. Also, the relatively high levels of capital flight

from Africa may have been a rational response to the lack of investment opportunities at home.

Table 3: Capital Inflows to Sub-Saharan Africa by Type of Flow and New Transfers, 1975-1998 (% of GNP)

Type of flow	Including Nigeria			Excluding Nigeria		
	1975-82	1983-89	1990-98	1975-82	1983-89	1990-98
Total net inflows	8.6	9.9	9.3	11.5	10	10.6
Official inflows	4.7	6.8	7.5	7.2	8	9.1
ODA grants [a]	1.7	3.3	5.4	2.6	4	6.4
Official credit	3.0	3.5	2.1	4.6	4.0	2.7
Bilateral	1.6	1.8	0.4	2.5	2.1	0.6
Multilateral	1.4	1.7	1.7	2.1	1.9	2.1
Private inflows	3.9	3.1	1.8	4.3	2	1.5
Interest payments	1.5	3.2	2.7	1.8	2.7	2.3
Profit remittances	1.4	1.1	1.1	1.1	1	1.2
Net transfer	5.7	5.6	5.5	8.6	6.3	7.1

Source: UNCTAD secretariat calculations, based on World Bank, *Global Development Finance, 2000* (CD-ROM). (a) This item corresponds to 'Grants' as defined by the World Bank in the source and excludes funds allocated through technical cooperation.

Mkandawire (2005) comments that this conclusion ignores the fact that the social benefits of citizens investing in their own country may exceed the private benefits accruing to individuals. These findings can also be contested on both methodological and econometric grounds. First, in the standard agreed approach in growth empirics, investment should be measured in international prices. However, the study used domestic prices, which generally overestimate investment rates because of the high cost of doing business in Africa. Second, they used cross-section regressions that do not account for country-specific effects. Such an omission can lead to inconsistent estimates.[4]

The little FDI drawn to Africa has largely been concentrated in the natural resource sectors. Such FDI has limited economic and developmental benefits because they usually do not:

* stimulate general, broad-based development;

* significantly expand employment opportunities;

* diversify exports away from primary commodities;

* facilitate meaningful transfer technology to recipient countries except for the limited purpose of more profitable resource extraction.

The logging of timber as well as agricultural expansion have been especially encouraged in recent years as the Washington Consensus effectively discourages (import-substituting) industrialisation for Africa. While generating temporary and dangerous (owing to the high incidence of logging 'accidents') work locally, such deforestation has also exacerbated water supply problems, droughts and desertification. More generally, corruption and ongoing resource conflicts in Africa have been fuelled by such foreign interest in the continent's natural resources.

African countries had been largely 'adjusted' by the late 1990s, with major changes in African economic policies and institutions. Africa has been 'liberalised' and opened to 'globalisation'. Most African countries experienced currency devaluations, trade liberalisation, privatisation as well as various market and investor friendly policies. Yet, improvements in the terms of trade and favourable weather conditions have explained improved economic performance much more than the BWI policies, underlining the continued vulnerability of African economies to external and transient factors.

The deflationary bias of the macroeconomic policies favoured by the Washington Consensus has put African economies on a low growth vicious cycle. Keynesians argue that the causal chain is from growth to investment to savings, and not the other way around. El Bedawi & Mwega (2000) and Mlambo and Oshikoya (2001) have found that the causality runs from growth to investment in Africa as well. Capital needs are essentially determined by expected output, i.e. investment demand is driven by expected growth. Meanwhile, 'endogenous growth theories' suggest that some 'determinants of growth' may themselves be dependent on growth.

Mkandawire (2002) argues that successful adjustment in Africa placed the continent on a 'low growth path'. He notes that oft-invoked 'determinants' of growth (for example, income growth) are themselves determined by growth (Macpherson and Goldsmith 2001), including the global growth slowdown of the last two decades (Easterly 2000). There is strong evidence that growth has been slower since the 1980s with liberalisation and globalisation in most of the developing world, including sub-Saharan Africa, compared to the previous two and a half decades (Weisbrot, Baker, Naiman and Neta 2000; Weisbrot, Naiman and Kim 2000; Weisbrot, Baker, Kraev, Chen 2001 and Weisbrot et al. 2005). Thus, slower growth has been attributed to the deflationary bias inherent in BWI stabilisation and adjustment programmes.

The investment patterns induced by economic liberalisation measures appear not to be associated with high economic growth. Historically, investment, growth and productivity have moved together, for instance, investment was associated with relatively high growth and significant total factor productivity gains in the pre-adjustment era (Rodrik 2001). The transformation due to economic liberalisation has instead brought economic stagnation, de-industrialisation and agricultural decline, rather than structural change induced by differential productivity gains and changing demand due to increasing incomes (Mkandawire 1988; Singh 1987; Stein 1992; Stewart 1994). Institutional Investor ratings for Africa deteriorated from 31.8 percent in 1979 to 21.7 percent in 1995 (Collier and Gunning 1997). The two countries that performed well were Botswana and Mauritius, both high growth economies not pursuing orthodox adjustment programmes.

Table 4: Africa: Savings and Investments, 1975-1999 (as % of GDP)

Indicator	1975-84	1985-89	1990-97	1998	1999
Gross Domestic Savings (GDS)					
Sub-Saharan Africa (SSA)	21.3	18.2	15.9	16	15.8
SSA minus S. Africa & Nigeria	15.3	13.4	11.1	12.7	12.6
Gross National Savings (GNS)					
Sub-Saharan Africa (SSA)	17.9	13.3	11	13.3	12.1
SSA minus S. Africa & Nigeria	12.1	8.4	4.9	10.4	8.5
Resource Transfer (GDS-GNS) Abroad					
Sub-Saharan Africa (SSA)	3.4	4.9	4.9	2.7	3.7
SSA minus S. Africa & Nigeria	3.2	5	6.2	2.3	4.1
Gross Domestic Investment (GDI)					
Sub-Saharan Africa (SSA)	22.9	17.7	17.3	18.8	18.4
SSA minus S. Africa & Nigeria	19.9	17.3	16.9	19.2	19.4
Resource Balance					
Sub-Saharan Africa (SSA)	-5	-4.4	-5.9	-3	-2.6
SSA minus S. Africa & Nigeria	7.8	4	5.9	-6.3	-6.3

Source: World Bank (2001a)

When other developing economies embarked on import substitution industrialisation, most of Africa was still under colonial rule. In fact, the import substitution phase in most of sub-Saharan Africa was relatively short, lasting barely a decade in many countries (Mkandawire 1988). Thus, trade liberalisation prematurely exposed African industries to global competition from mature industries, causing de-industrialisation. UNIDO notes that African countries had been increasingly gaining comparative advantage in labour-intensive manufacturing before such forced de-industrialisation. Given the BWI presumption that import substitution in Africa was bad, there was no attempt to see how the existing industries could form the basis for new export initiatives. Assuming that African import substituting industries had been protected for far too long, and would never become viable, let alone competitive, the policy was simply to abandon existing industrial capacity.

Hence, the share of manufacturing in GDP has fallen in two-thirds of the countries (Mkandawire 2005, Figure 4). The rates of growth of manufacturing value added have fallen continuously from the 1970s, and actually contracted by an annual average of one percent during 1990-97 (UNIDO p.245, quoted in Mkandawire 2005). UNIDO found that in ten industrial branches in 38 African countries, labour productivity declined by seven percent between 1900 and 1995. The decline in total factor productivity can be attributed to de-industrialisation.

Trade Liberalisation

African countries have not been exempt from trends in the international terms of trade which have moved against developing countries over the decades.

- The prices of primary commodities have declined against those of manufactures, as suggested by Prebisch and Singer more than half a century ago (see Ocampo and Parra 2006);

- The prices of tropical agricultural products compared to temperate agricultural goods have fallen, as observed by W.A. Lewis decades ago;

- Recent decades have also seen the decline of the prices of generic manufactures where access to industries has not been inhibited compared to manufacturing monopolies protected by strong intellectual property rights.

The likelihood of developing countries gaining from trade has been frustrated by protection and subsidies in most rich economies. For example, their tariff structures have been biased against developing countries. Hence, tariffs on imports between developed countries average only one percent. Meanwhile, tariffs on agricultural products from developing countries have been as high as 20 percent, while the tariffs on textiles from developing countries have been as high as 9 percent.

It is now generally acknowledged that economic growth is needed for trade expansion, rather than the other way round. Not surprisingly, the World Bank estimates a very modest contribution to economic growth of 0.6 percent by 2015 attributable

Table 5: Optimistic Projected Welfare Gains from Full Merchandise Trade Liberalisation

	TWG	GDCL	GDnCL	Agric., Food, & other primary	M
Global	254.3	139.6	114.7	167.51	86.8
Developed	146.2	96.6	49.6	121.84	24.4
Economies in transition	6.4	4.5	1.9	3.51	2.9
SS Africa	4.6	2.6	2.0	3.95	0.6
North Africa & Middle East	0.3	-1.0	1.2	-3.15	3.4
Latin America	35.7	17.9	17.8	23.03	12.7
Asian NICsChina	22.3	5.1	17.2	1.62	20.7
South Asia	15.4	9.0	6.4	5.72	9.7
Rest of the world	23.4	4.9	18.5	10.99	12.4

Source: Anderson et al. (2001)
Notes: Total Welfare Gains(TWG); Gains from Developed Countries' Liberalisation (GDCL); Gains from Developing Countries' Liberalisation (GDnCL) ; Agriculture, Food and Other Primary; Manufactures (M).

to full trade liberalisation based on what many would consider to be optimistic assumptions. Also, rapid resource reallocation to accelerate growth is unlikely without high rates of growth and investment in the first place. Even trade liberalisation advocate Jagdish Bhagwati urges the need for aid to compensate economies for the loss of tariff revenue and trade preferences associated with trade liberalisation as well as to build up production and export processing capacities to be available to take advantage of opportunities created by trade liberalisation.

The 'new trade theories' and evolutionary studies of technological development suggest that countries risk being 'locked' into permanent slow growth by pursuing static comparative advantage. It is now generally acknowledged that economic growth precedes export growth, while UNCTAD has long pointed to the importance of growth for trade expansion, more specifically, to an investment-export nexus that accounts for the failure of many countries to expand and diversify their exports. Rapid resource reallocation is generally not also feasible without high rates of growth and investment.

Before the recent liberalisation measures, monetary and other policies in East Asia ensured relative prices favourable to export industries (instead of non-tradables) with preferential interest rates supporting investment and economic restructuring. Export promotion strategies have generally involved an investment-export nexus, including measures to promote public investment, subsidised inputs (from state-owned enterprises and with preferential special exchange rates), direct subsidies (including tax incentives), selective credit allocation and other industrial policy instruments (Akyüz 1996). Government instruments for stimulating investment and industrial development have been severely eroded by economic liberalisation measures.

Mkandawire (2005) notes that, from the outset, the advent of the WTO trade regime was expected to entail losses for Africa, especially with the loss of preferential treatment (from erstwhile colonial rulers and the European Union under the Lome Convention). Trade liberalisation under WTO auspices has significantly reduced policy options utilised by developmental states, especially for industrial or investment policy (Adelman and Yeldan 2000; Panchamukhi 1996; Rodrik 2000a), though some (for example, Amsden 1999) would still argue that the WTO regime still leaves room for industrial policy initiatives.

Gains from Agricultural Trade Liberalisation?

A major premise of the Berg Report was that Africa's comparative advantage lies in agriculture. If only the state would stop 'squeezing' agriculture through marketing boards and price distortions (also see Bates), agricultural producers would respond, enabling export-led growth. Recent changes in Africa's exports indicate no general increase in output in activities in which African countries ostensibly have a 'revealed' comparative advantage. Indeed, after two decades of reforms, the most striking trend has been a lower African share of global non-oil exports to less than half what it was in the early 1980s (Ng and Yeats, quoted by Mkandawire 2005).

Contrary to current popular wisdom, it is not clear how much Africa would gain from agricultural trade liberalisation. After all, many food importing African countries would be worse off without subsidised food imports while very few economies are likely to be in a position to significantly increase their exports. African agricultural production and export capacities have been undermined by the last three decades of economic contraction and neglect. Severe cuts in public spending under structural adjustment caused significant deterioration of infrastructure (roads, railway systems, etc.) and undermined potential supply response (UNECA 2003), even though numerous micro studies have confirmed the importance of good infrastructure for trade facilitation (Badiane and Shively 1998; Abdulai 2000). As Table 6 shows, existing estimates of the overall welfare effects from multilateral agricultural trade liberalisation do not point to significant gains, but on the contrary, suggest the likelihood of some losses.

Table 6: Selected Estimates of Welfare Effects from Multilateral Agricultural Trade Liberalisation

	50% tariff cut	50% domestic support cut	Elimination of export subsidies
Laird, et al. (2003)			
World	27.5	..	-4.0
Developed Countries	11.1	..	1.9
Developing countries	8.2	..	-2.9
NICs + China	4.4	..	-0.2
South Asia	0.3	..	0.0
SS Africa	0.2	..	-0.4
North Africa and ME	3.0	..	-2.2
Others	0.3	..	-0.2
Dimaranan, et al. (2004)			
Developing countries	..	-0.36	..
Asia	..	-0.11	..
Latin America	..	0.14	..
North Africa & Middle East	..	-0.27	..
SS Africa	..	-0.13	..

Sources: Laird et al. (2003) and Dimaranan et al. (2004)

In the 1980s and 1990s, Africa's export collapse has involved 'a staggering annual income loss of US$68 billion—or 21 percent of regional GDP' (World Bank 2000, quoted by Mkandawire 2005). However, 'Africa's failures have been developmental, not export failure per se' (Helleiner 2002a: 4). Rodrik (1997) argued that Africa's 'marginalisation' is not due to trade relative to GDP, although this is low by cross-national standards. Given its geography and its per capita income level, Africa trades as much as is to be expected. Indeed, 'Africa overtrades compared with other developing regions in the sense that its trade is higher than would be expected from the various determinants of bilateral trade' (Coe and Hoffmaister 1999; Foroutan and Pritchet 1993).

Table 7: Africa: Destination of Exports (% of total)

	1990-2002 Av.	1999-2001 Av.
Africa	4	5
European Union	64	52
United States	17	19
Asia	10	16
Other	6	9

Source: UN Comtrade

Meanwhile, by the end of the 1990s, the few gains from trade generally acknowledged were of a one-off character, often reflecting switches from domestic to foreign markets without much increase in overall output (Helleiner 2002a, 2002b; Mwega 2002; Ndulu et al. 2002). In some cases, manufactured exports increased even as the manufacturing sector contracted. 'No major expansion occurred in the diversity of products exported by most of the Sub-Saharan African countries ... Indeed, the product composition of some of the African countries' exports may have become more concentrated. Africa's recent trade performance was strongly influenced by exports of traditional products which appear to have experienced remarkably buoyant global demand in the mid-1990s' (Ng and Yeats: 21, quoted by Mkandawire 2002).

Despite the unrealism of using the World Bank's CGE model, Taylor and von Arnim (2006) show that Africa will not gain, on balance, from trade liberalization. Their exercise suggests that:

- If trade elasticities are less than stipulated by the Bank, sub-Saharan Africa experiences welfare losses even assuming the absence of macroeconomic shocks.

- If the current account can respond to trade liberalization and imports exceed exports, Africa will experience a worsening trade balance.

- If the government's fiscal deficit is incorporated into the analysis, fiscal balances in Africa will often worsen as they improve in the rest of the world.

- If employment and income can vary, they may increase in sub-Saharan Africa, but together with trade deficits and foreign debt, which will in turn make the gains sustainable.

Tropical Fate?

The World Bank (1993:77) noted that temperate countries grew on average by 1.3 percentage points more than tropical countries during the 1965-90 period, after controlling for other factors. The study explains this significant shortfall in terms of the greater prevalence of disease, poorer soils, more frequent typhoons and other natural calamities in the tropics.

Surprisingly, the study seems to be oblivious to W.A. Lewis's (1969; 1978) pioneering work on the economic performance of the tropics. As Lewis (1978) has shown, tropical exports grew faster than temperate zone exports during the last period of global liberalisation from the end of the last century. For the period 1883-1913, for example, French Indochina, Thailand, British Ceylon, West Africa, French West Africa and Madagascar all had average annual export growth rates of five percent or more, while Brazil had 4.5 percent. The comparable rates for temperate settlements, the USA and Northwest Europe were 4.3, 3.8 and 3.5 percent respectively.

While the tropics generally had more modest export bases than the temperate zone to begin with, this also suggests that the tropics were better able to respond to export demand despite the disadvantages they faced. Lewis emphasised that not all tropical countries were able to seize opportunities from increased export demand. He suggests that the exports in greater demand were largely water-intensive; hence, only those areas with enough water to substantially increase their exports were able to take advantage of the new opportunities. The more arid tropical grassland areas, for example in Africa, thus could not benefit from the increased demand for tropical products.

While some Southeast Asian newly industrialising countries and some other tropical countries have also grown rapidly since the sixties, most countries in the tropics have fared badly in recent decades. It is not enough simply to attribute the tropical growth shortfall to 'pests, diseases, typhoons and other natural calamities', though such factors may not have been unimportant.

Lewis observed that the terms of trade for tropical exports deteriorated badly against temperate exports. In the half century between 1916 and 1966, for example, the index for natural rubber fell from 100 to 16. This suggests that productivity gains in the tropics were largely lost to worsening terms of trade, and the situation was worse where few productivity gains were made.

Many observers (for instance, Intal 1997) have suggested that sub-Saharan Africa has lagged behind in terms of agricultural development since the sixties due to inadequacies in agricultural R&D and infrastructure, crop and agronomic considerations and macroeconomic conditions. He argues that higher temperate agricultural productivity has partly been due to long, sustained and larger investments in agricultural R&D, which temperate LDCs (for example, Chile, Korea and Taiwan) have been better able to take advantage of. The tropical Green Revolution in rice farming since the sixties has mainly benefited irrigated farms in Southeast and South Asia, while drier agriculture in Africa has generally been left behind.

However, the Southeast Asian success with tree crop agriculture offers some hope. This experience suggests that significant investments in tree crop agricultural R&D (for example in rubber, oil palm and cocoa) as well as rural infrastructure have made possible productivity gains in tree crop agriculture as well. The geographic and climatic specificities of agriculture imply that for imported agricultural varieties and technologies to be successfully adopted, there is a great need for effective adaptive investments in R&D and extension. Unfortunately, many governments have neglected or under-funded agriculture.

Resource Curse?

The Sachs's ADB (1997) study also suggests that natural resource wealth is bad for growth. Curiously, the study defines natural resource abundance in terms of the ratio of net primary product exports to GDP in 1971, without distinguishing extractive non-renewable natural resources (especially minerals) from agricultural products. The so-called Dutch Disease mainly involves the former, which tend to be very capital-intensive and only involve a small proportion of the population in extraction of the resource. Consequently, the added income accrues to a few while appreciation of the country's currency affects the entire population.

Agricultural exports generally involve much more of the population, and increased income usually accrues to all involved, diffusing the adverse consequences of currency appreciation. The Southeast Asian high performing economies have been major agricultural exporters, helping offset problems associated with the mineral exports of Malaysia and Indonesia, in sharp contrast to, say, Nigeria. Generally better macroeconomic management has also helped, especially to offset the tendency to indulge in expenditure on non-tradables.

Wage Competitiveness?

Intal (1997) has argued that the marginal labour productivity—and hence, the opportunity cost—of farm labour for manufacturing is higher in land-abundant African economies compared to land-scarce Asian economies even though average labour productivity is usually higher in the latter. Hence, it is unlikely that the former will be able to compete with the latter in labour-intensive manufactures. The Malaysian experience suggests that labour-scarce, land-abundant economies can only be competitive in skill-intensive, rather than unskilled labour-intensive manufactures, requiring considerable investments in human resource development.

The situation in much of Africa suggests that not unlike Indian labour, African labour may also not be competitive in wage/productivity terms in both agriculture and industry. With full employment not assured following trade liberalisation, there is the real possibility of both de-industrialisation as well as de-agriculturalisation in much of Africa with greater trade openness.

Changed Role of the State

The economic reforms of recent decades have fundamentally transformed the nature and role of African governments. While many of these reforms were imposed, some were adopted by domestic elites who saw their interests best advanced by such reforms. As a consequence, African governments' fiscal means have been considerably reduced, constraining their potential developmental as well as redistributive capacities even for governments which might be so inclined.

Meanwhile, taxation systems have generally become far less progressive, if not more regressive. On the other hand, government spending has also become less progressive, if not also more regressive. A relatively smaller share of government expenditure goes to the social sector, and even here, reforms have made social spending less progressive. Although even World Bank research has found targeting to be costly and largely ineffective (Mkandawire 2005), 'donors' continue to urge targeting, thus undermining social solidarity and the political sustainability of such social benefits. Not surprisingly then, high-income countries spend 2.5 times as much of national income on health, education and welfare compared to low-income countries (UN/DESA 2005), further exacerbating the consequences of inequalities in the latter. This is reflected in Africa's low enrolment rates at both primary and secondary school levels (see Table 8).

Table 8: Enrolment rate by region and school level, 2001

Indicator	Highest	Lowest
Net Primary Enrolment Ratio	95.6% L. America + Caribbean	62.8% Sub-Saharan Africa
Net Secondary Enrolment Ratio	89.2% N. America + W. Europe	21.3% Sub-Saharan Africa

Source: UN/DESA (2005).

Measures of unemployment in Africa are not deemed to be very meaningful, not only because of the limited statistical capacities of most governments, but also because unemployment is rarely an option for survival in low-income economies, offering few, if any, social benefits to the unemployed. Thus, the vast majority are often under-employed due to limited resources for productive self-employment. Millions have migrated to urban areas, seeking and adopting different economic survival strategies in the face of very limited employment opportunities in the formal urban economy, whether in the debilitated public sector or in the private sector, following the de-industrialisation in the continent over recent decades. Not surprisingly then, informal employment remains highest in sub-Saharan Africa among the regions of the world.

Table 9: Share of informal workers in the non-agricultural workforce by region

Region	% Share
Latin America & Caribbean	51
Asia	65
North Africa	48
Sub-Saharan Africa (excl. S. Africa)	78

Source: UN/DESA (2005).

Inequality, Poverty, Violence and Conflict

There are a few general explanations for violence and conflict, but much violence and conflict may be related to poverty and inequality, although the links between inequalities, poverty and extreme aspects of social disintegration beg better understanding and explanation. Some recent analyses point to relations between inequality, poverty, violence and conflict (for example, see the figure below), involving complex links among reduced growth and development, poverty, lack of opportunities, inequalities (including so-called 'horizontal' inequalities between cultural groups, regions, etc.), authoritarian governance and armed conflict, often for resource control (Mkandawire 2005; Collier et al 2003: 11-50).

Figure 1: The probability of relapse into civil war within five years rises with poverty

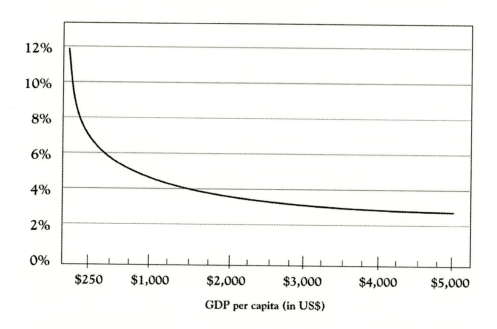

Source: UN/DESA, RWSS, 2005.

New Challenges

Developments since the 1980s have fundamentally changed the environment and conditions for developmental states attempting to pursue selective industrial or investment policy. Most importantly, economic liberalisation—at both national and international levels—has seriously constrained the scope for government policy interventions, especially selective industrial promotion efforts. This is especially apparent in international economic relations, but is also true of the domestic policy environment, where WB and IMF policy conditionalities as well as WTO and other obligations have radically transformed the scope for national economic policy initiatives.

There has been a widespread, sweeping and rapid opening up of trade, investment, finance and other flows. Very often, such liberalisation has been externally imposed by the Bretton Woods institutions as part of conditions laid down to secure access to emergency credit during the debt crises of the 1980s, and more recently, in the wake of more currency and financial crises. Various policy packages for (price) stabilisation in the short term or for structural adjustment in the medium term have involved such conditionalities. The new political, intellectual and policy environment which emerged during the 1980s—under Reagan and Thatcher—led to the so-called 'Washington Consensus', which has promoted such policy reform despite repeated failures to improve economic growth and development, let alone social equity and welfare.

This has been especially true of much of Latin America and Africa, which experienced a 'lost decade' of economic growth in the 1980s following (sovereign) debt crises and ensuing 'stabilisation' and 'structural adjustment' reforms, usually imposed by the international financial institutions. The 1990s were only slightly better, with a few spurts of high growth here and there which have been touted as proof of the success of the Washington Consensus, when precisely the opposite has been true. While the Washington Consensus has been challenged, if not discredited in academic circles, it continues to constitute the ideological basis for economic analysis and policy-making in developing countries, especially in Africa, Latin America and other smaller economies.

Invariably, the circumstances of such policy changes as well as the limited policy capabilities of the governments concerned have meant that little preparation—in terms of a pro-active strategy or transitional policies to anticipate and cope with the implications of sudden exposure to new international competition—has been undertaken. Few of the investment policy instruments of the past are viable or feasible options today, including many used successfully in post-war East Asia. Most of the main industrial policy tools were used by the advanced industrial economies, including those that now deny such selective industrial promotion to others. Indeed, most advanced economies still have a plethora of policies and institutions involved in research and development (R&D), skills training, investment promotion and infrastructure provision, for instance for the new information and communication technologies (ICT).

Such policies and institutions are probably necessary, but certainly not sufficient for stimulating and sustaining economic growth and structural change for developing countries to try to 'catch-up'. Additional initiatives are urgently needed to prevent such economies—already at a historical disadvantage in various respects—from falling further behind the industrially more developed economies of the North, as well as the other newly industrialised economies that have emerged in recent decades.

Moving Forward

The preceding discussion strongly suggests that much of the ostensible conventional wisdom regarding African development and poverty is not only wrong, but often harmful. For example, IMF research has recently acknowledged that international financial liberalisation has not improved growth, but has instead exacerbated volatility. For Africa, net capital outflows, facilitated by such liberalisation, have exceeded ODA inflows—not only a net, but even on a gross basis.

Worse still, there is strong evidence that some of the economic policy advice given to and conditionalities imposed on governments in the region have reflected vested interests and prejudices. In recent years, much emphasis has been given to promoting FDI even though experiences elsewhere show that FDI generally tends to follow, rather than lead, domestic investments. Not surprisingly, there continues to be limited FDI, mainly in the minerals sector, with limited employment and other benefits. Nonetheless, the economic policy reforms have enhanced the profitability and protection of FDI while reducing the trickle-down benefits to the domestic economies of such enclave investments.

Available evidence suggests that the gains from trade liberalisation will be modest for the world economy, and the gains for Africa are hardly assured as trade liberalisation is not necessarily welfare-enhancing for all. There is also considerable evidence that the main winners from agricultural trade liberalisation will be the existing big agricultural exporters of the Cairns group from North America, Australasia, Southeast Asia and the Southern Cone of Latin America. Nonetheless, many well-meaning NGOs have joined in the chorus calling for agricultural trade liberalisation as a gain for Africa. Thankfully, other NGOs have helped developing countries to try to ensure that the Doha Round is truly developmental, by ensuring the policy space for trade and other policy instruments for development.

In view of the pervasive influence of such erroneous and harmful policy advice and conditionalities, it has become crucial to increase 'policy space' for governments to be able to pursue policies for development. Countries need to be able to choose or design their own development strategies as well as to develop and implement more appropriate development policies. Besides enhancing policy space, it is also crucial to be able to increase resources for development. The removal of the huge debt overhangs of the poorest countries through debt relief is an important step in this direction. Prolonged and massive increases in ODA are also needed to kick-start investments and growth, and, in the longer term, to reduce the continent's resource gap and dependence on aid (UNCTAD 2006). Three decades of economic stagnation, contraction and increased poverty have also taken a huge toll on the continent's economic, social and political fabric, and pro-active efforts are urgently required in order to build new capacities and capabilities for development.

As economic growth and development do not necessarily reduce poverty and inequalities, special efforts will need to be made to ensure such outcomes. The United Nations' Millennium Development Goals (MDGs) provide some specific welfare targets and indicators for this purpose. Enhanced social expenditure should be universal as far as possible to ensure broad public support and thus sustainability, but selective targeting including affirmative action measures may be needed to overcome long-term discrimination, marginalisation and neglect. After all, progress towards achieving the MDG indicators may still bypass the poor as the rising tide of economic development does not lift all boats equally.

The MDGs are important for and mutually reinforce the UN's broader Development Agenda, derived from the UN's global summits and conferences, especially since the 1990s, such as the Earth Summit in Rio de Janeiro in 1992, the Population and Development Conference in Cairo in 1994, the Beijing conference on women in 1995, the Monterrey Conference on Financing for Development and the Johannesburg conference on Sustainable Development of 2002, among others. This agenda has been reiterated and given greater coherence by the Millennium Declaration of 2000 and the Outcome Document of the Summit in September 2005.

Acknowledgement

I wish to thank Eloho Otobo for proofreading and helping me improve the paper and Noelle Rodriguez, Suzette Limchoc and Carl Gray for their suggestions as well.

Notes

1. This part has been heavily drawn from Mkandawire (2002).
2. As Mkandawire (2002) observes, this paper seeks to 'help boost SSA's image as an investment location' (Pigato 2000: 2), explaining the positive conclusions painstakingly promoted despite data suggesting otherwise.
3. In 1998 alone, privatisation in SSA attracted US$684 million of FDI (UNCTAD). Such one-off sales explain the jump in FDI in the 1990s, but by 1999, privatisation-related FDI had slowed down.
4. I owe these observations to my colleagues, Carl Gray and Oumar Diallo, who have also provided other valuable comments and suggestions.

References

Abdulai, A., 2000, 'Spatial price transmission and asymmetry in the Ghanaian maize market', *Journal of Development Economics*, 63: 327-349.

Adelman, I. and E. Yeldan, 2000, 'Is this the End of Economic Development?', *Structural Change and Economic Dynamics*, 11: 95-109.

Akyüz, Y., 1996, 'The Investment-Profit Nexus in East Asian Industrialization', *World Development*, 24 (3): 461-470.

Amsden, A., 1989, *Asia's Next Giant*, Oxford University Press, New York.

Amsden, A., 1999, 'Industrialization under New WTO Law', UNCTAD X High Level Round Table on Development: Directions for the Twenty-First Century, Bangkok.

Ariff, M. and H. Hill, 1985, *Export-oriented Industrialization: The ASEAN Experience*, Allen and Unwin, Sydney.

Badiane, O., and G. Shively, 1998, 'Spatial integration, transport costs, and the response of local prices to policy changes in Ghana', *Journal of Development Economics*, 56: 411-431.

Bhagwati, J., 1988, 'Export-promoting trade strategy: issues and evidence', *World Bank Research Observer* 3 (1), January: 27-57.

Bhattacharya, O., P. Montiel and S. Sharma, 1997, 'Can Sub-Saharan Africa Attract Private Capital Flows?', *Finance and Development*, June: 3-6.

Bird, G., 2001, 'IMF Programmes: Do They Work? Can They Be Made to Work Better?', *World Development*, 29 (11): 1849-1865.

Boyce, J.K. and L. Ndikumana, 2000, 'Is Africa a Net Creditor? New Estimates of Capital Flight from Severely Indebted Sub-Saharan African Countries, 1970-1996', Political Economy Research Institute, University of Massachusetts, Amherst.

Bradford Jr., C. I., 1990, 'Policy Interventions and Markets: Development Strategy: Typologies and Policy Options', in G. Gereffi and D. Wyman, eds., *Manufacturing Miracles: Paths of Industrialization In Latin America and East Asia*, Princeton NJ; Princeton University Press.

Chang, Ha-Joon, 1994, *The Political Economy of Industrial Policy*, Basingstoke: Macmillan.

Coe, D. and A. Hoffmaister, 1999, 'North-South Trade: Is Africa Unusual?', *Journal of African Economies*, 8 (2): 228-256.

Collier, P. and J.W. Gunning, 1997, *Explaining African Economic Performance*, Oxford, Centre for the Study of African Economies, Oxford University.

Collier, P. and J.W. Gunning, 1999, 'Why Has Africa Grown Slowly?', *Journal of Economic Perspectives*, 13 (3): 3-22.

Collier, P., A. Hoeffler and C. Patillo, 1999, 'Flight Capital as Portfolio Choice', Washington DC: IMF.

Collier, P., V.L Elliot, H. Hegre, A. Hoeffler, M. Reynal-Querol and N. Sambanis, 2003, *Breaking the Conflict Trap: Civil War and Development Policy*, New York: Oxford University Press.

Collier, P., A. Hoeffler, and C. Pattillo, 2004, 'Africa's Exodus: Capital Flight and the Brain Drain as Portfolio Decisions', *Journal of African Economies*, 13: 15-54.

Collins, S.M., and B.P.Bosworth, 1996, 'Economic growth in East Asia: Accumulation versus assimilation', Brookings Papers on Economic Activity, 2: 135-203.

Devajaran, S., W. Easterly, and H. Pack, 1999, *Is Investment in Africa Too Low or Too High? Macro and Micro Evidence*, Washington, DC: World Bank.

Easterly, W. and Levine, R., 1995, *Africa's Growth Tragedy*, Washington, DC: World Bank.

Easterly, W., 2000, 'The Lost Decades: Developing Countries Stagnation in Spite of Policy Reform, 1980-1998', *Journal of Economic Growth* 6: 135-157.

Economic Commission for Africa (ECA), 2004, *Economic Report on Africa, 2004: Unlocking Africa's Trade Potential*, Addis Ababa: ECA.

Elbadawi, I. and F.M. Mwega, 2000, 'Can Africa's Saving Collapse Be Reversed?', *World Bank Economic Review*, 14 (3): 415-443.

Fischer, S., E. Hernàndez-Catà, E. and M.S. Khan, 1998, 'Africa: Is this the Turning Point?', Processed, World Bank, Washington DC.

Foroutan, F. and L. Pritchet, 1993', Intra-Sub-Saharan African Trade, Is It Too Little?', *Journal of African Economies* 2 (1), May: 74-105.

Gerschenkron, A., 1962, *Economic Backwardness in Historical Perspective*, Cambridge, MA: Harvard University Press.

Helleiner, G. K., 2002a, 'Introduction', in Helleiner, G. K., ed.., *Non-traditional export promotion in Africa: Experience and issues*, London: Palgrave.

Helleiner, G. K., ed., 2002b, *Non-traditional Export Promotion in Africa: Experience and issues*, New York, Palgrave.

Hernández-Catá, E., 2000, 'Raising Growth and Investment in Sub-Saharan Africa: What Can Be Done?', Washington DC: International Monetary Fund.

Intal, Ponciano S. Jr. 1997, 'Comments on Chapter 2 of the Emerging Asia Study: AEconomic Growth and Transformation@, 'Emerging Asia' seminar, Manila, Asian Development Bank, 1-2 September.

Jalilian, H., and J. Weiss, 2000, 'De-industrialization in sub-Saharan: Myth or Crisis?', in H. Jalilian, M. Tribe and J. Weiss, eds., *Industrial Development and Policy in Africa*, Cheltenham, UK: Edward Elgar.

Kasekende, L., D. Kitabire, and M. Martin, 1997, 'Capital Inflows and Macroeconomic Policy in Sub-Saharan Africa', in Helleiner, G. K., ed.., *Capital Account Regimes*, London: Macmillan.

Killick, T., 1992, 'Explaining Africa's Post Independence Development Experiences', Biennial Conference on African Economic Issues, Lome.

Kim, Jong-Il, and L. Lau, 1994, 'The Sources of Economic Growth of the East Asian Newly Industrialized Countries', *Journal of the Japanese and International Economies* 8 (3): 235-271.

Krugman, P., 1994, 'The Myth of Asia's Miracle', *Foreign Affairs* 73 (6): 62-78.

Lewis, W. A., 1969, *Aspects of Tropical Trade, 1883-1915*; Wicksell Lectures, Stockholm: Almqvist & Wicksell.

Lewis, W. A., 1978, *Growth and Fluctuations, 1870-1913*, London: Allen & Unwin.

Lindauer, D.L. and A. D. Valenchik, 1994, 'Can African Labor Compete?', in David L. Lindauer, and Michael Roemer, eds., *Asia and Africa Legacies and Opportunities in Development*, San Francisco: ICS Press.

Little, I.M.D., 1981, 'The Experience and Causes of Rapid Labour-intensive Development in Korea, Taiwan Province, Hong Kong and Singapore, and the Possibilities of Emulation', in E. Lee, ed., *Export-led Industrialization and Development*, Asian Employment Program, International Labour Organization, Geneva, International Labour Organization.

Little, I.M.D., 1994, 'Trade and Industrialization Revisited', *Pakistan Development Review*, 33 (4): 359-389.

Loayza, N., K. Schmidt-Hebbel, and L. Servén, 2000, 'Saving in Developing Countries: An Overview', *The World Economy Review*, 14 (3): 393-414.

Madavo, C. and J.-L. Sarbib, 1997, 'Africa on the Move: Attracting Private Capital to a Changing Continent', *The SAIS Review*, 7 (2): 111-126.

McPherson, M. F., and A. A. Goldsmith, 2001, 'Is Africa on the Move?', Cambridge, MA: Belfer Center for Science & International Affairs, John F. Kennedy School of Government, Harvard University.

McPherson, M. F., and T. Rakovski, 2001, 'Understanding the Growth Process in Sub-Saharan Africa: Some Empirical Estimates, African Economic Policy', Cambridge MA: Belfer Center for Science & International Affairs, John F. Kennedy School of Government, Harvard University.

Milanovic, B., 2002, 'The Two Faces of Globalization: Against Globalization As We Know It', Washington DC: World Bank.

Milanovic, Branko, 2005, *Worlds Apart*, Princeton NJ: Princeton University Press.

Mkandawire, T. and C. Soludo, 1999, *Our Continent, Our Future: African Perspectives on Structural Adjustment*, Trenton NJ: African World Press.

Mkandawire, T., 1988, 'The Road to Crisis, Adjustment and de-Industrialization: The African Case', *Africa Development*, XIII (1).

Mkandawire, T., 2002, 'The Terrible Toll of Post-colonial "Rebel Movements" in Africa: Towards an Explanation of the Violence against the Peasantry', *Journal of Modern African Studies* 40 (2): 181-215.

Mkandawire, T., 2005, 'Maladjusted African Economies and Globalization.' *Africa Development* XXX (1& 2): 1–33.

Mlambo, K., and T. W. Oshikoya, 2001, 'Macroeconomic Factors and Investment in Africa', *Journal of African Economies*, 10 (2): 12-47.

Mosley, P., T. Subasat, and J. Weeks, 1995, 'Assessing Adjustment in Africa', *World Development*, 23 (9): 1459-1473.

Mwega, F. M., 2002, 'Promotion of non-traditional exports in Kenya', in G. K. Helleiner, ed., *Nontraditional export promotion in Africa: Experience and Issues*. New York, Palgrave.

Myrdal, G., 1968, *Asian Drama*, 3 volumes, New York: Pantheon.

Naya, S., et al., 1989, 'ASEAN-US Initiative', Singapore: Inst of Southeast Asian Studies.

Ndikumana, L., and J. K. Boyce, 2002, 'Public Debt and Private Assets: Explaining Capital Flight from Sub-Saharan African Countries', Working Paper No. 32, Political Economy Research Institute, University of Massachusetts, Amherst.

Ndulu, B. J., J. Semboja, and A. Mbelle, 2002, 'Promotion of non-traditional exports in Kenya', In G. K. Helleiner, ed., *Non-traditional export promotion in Africa: Experience and issues*, New York: Palgrave.

Ng, F., and A. Yeats, 2000, 'On the recent Trade Performance of Sub-Saharan African Countries: Cause for Hope or More of the Same?', Africa Region Working Paper Series No. 7, Washington, DC: World Bank.

Ocampo, J.A. and M.A. Parra, 2006, 'The Commodity Terms of Trade and their Strategic Implications for Development', in Jomo K.S. ed., *Globalization Under Hegemony: The Changing World Economy*, New Delhi: Oxford University Press.

Ouattara, A., 1997, 'The Challenges of Globalization for Africa', Southern African Economic Summit Sponsored by the World Economic Forum, Harare.

Panchamukhi, V., 1996, *WTO and Industrial Policies*, Geneva: UNCTAD.

Perkins, D., 1994, 'There are at least three models of East Asian development', *World Development* 22 (4): 655-661.

Pigato, M., 2000, 'Foreign Direct Investment in Africa: Old Tales and New Evidence', Washington DC: World Bank.

Przeworski, A., and J. Vreeland, 2000, 'The Effects of IMF Programs on Economic Growth', *Journal of Development Economics*, 62: 385-421.

Rodrik, D., A. Subramanian, and F. Trebbi (2002) 'Institutions Rule: The Primacy of institutions over integration and geography in economic development.' IMF Working Paper No. 02/189, African Dept., November, International Monetary Fund, Washington, DC,

Rodrik, D., 1994, 'Getting interventions right: How South Korea and Taiwan grew rich', Cambridge, MA: NBER Working Paper No. 4964, December, National Bureau of Economic Research

Rodrik, D., 1995, 'Trade strategy, investment and exports: Another look at East Asia', Working Paper No. 5339, November, Cambridge, MA: National Bureau of Economic Research.

Rodrik, D., 1997, 'Trade Policy and Economic Performance in Sub-Saharan Africa', Stockholm, Swedish Foreign Ministry.

Rodrik, D., 1998, 'Saving Transitions', Cambridge, MA: Kennedy School of Government, Harvard University.

Rodrik, D., 2000a, 'Can Integration into the World Economy Substitute for a Developing Strategy?', Paris: World Bank ABCDE-Europe Conference.

Rodrik, D., 2000b, 'Saving Transitions', *The World Bank Economic Review*, 14 (3): 481-507.

Rodrik, D., 2001, 'The Global Governance of Trade as If Development Really Mattered', Cambridge, MA.

Sachs, J., and A. Warner, 1995, 'Natural Resource Abundance and Economic Growth', HIID Discussion Paper No. 517A, Cambridge, MA: Harvard Institute for International Devt.

Sender, J., 1999, 'Africa's Economic Performance: Limitations of the Current Consensus', *Journal of Economic Perspectives*, 13 (3): 89-114.

Singh, A., 1982, 'Industrialization in Africa: A structuralist view', in Fransman, M., ed., *Industry and Accumulation in Africa*, London: Heinemann.

Singh, A., 1986, 'The IMF-World Bank policy programme in Africa: A commentary', in P. Lawrence, ed., *The World Recession and the Food Crisis in Africa*, London: James Currey/ Review of African Political Economy.

Singh, A., 1987, 'Exogenous shocks and de-industrialization in Africa: Prospects and strategies for re-industrialization', in RISNODEC. African Economic Crisis, New Delhi, RIS.

Singh, A., 1999, 'Should Africa promote stock market capitalism?', *Journal of International Development*, 11 (3): 343-367.

Stein, H., 1992, 'De-industrialization, Adjustment and World Bank and IMF in Africa', *World Development*, 20 (1).

Stewart, F., 1994, 'Are Short-term Policies Consistent with Long-Term Development Needs in Africa?', in G. A. Cornia, and G. K. Helleiner, eds., *From Adjustment to Development in Africa: Conflict, Controversy, Convergence, Consensus?*, London: Macmillan.

Stiglitz, J. E., 1998, 'More Instruments and Broader Goals: Moving toward the Post-Washington Consensus', UNU/WIDER Lecture, Helsinki: World Institute for Development Economics Research, United Nations University.

Taylor, L. and R. von Arnim , 2006, 'Computable general equilibrium models of trade liberalization: The Doha debate', Draft paper for Oxfam UK, 8 January, Center for Economic Policy Analysis, New School University, New York.

The Economist, 2001, 'Globalisation and its Critics: A Survey of Globalisation', *The Economist*, September 29: 5-6.

Toye, John, 1987, *The Dilemma of Development*, Oxford: Blackwell.

UN/DESA, 2005, *The Inequality Predicament: Report on the World Social Situation, 2005*, New York; United Nations Department of Economic and Social Affairs.

UNCTAD, 1987, *Handbook of Trade Control Measures of Developing Countries. Supplement: A Statistical Analysis of Trade Control Measures of Developing Countries*, Geneva: United Nations Conference on Trade and Development.

UNCTAD, 1995, *Foreign Direct Investment in Africa—1995*, Geneva: United Nations.

UNCTAD, 1998, *Trade and Development Report, 1998*, Geneva: United Nations.

UNCTAD, 2000, *World Investment Report, 2000: Cross-border Mergers and Acquisitions and Development*, Geneva: UNCTAD.

UNCTAD, 2002, *Economic Development in Africa: From Adjustment to Poverty Reduction: What is New?*, UNCTAD/GDS/AFRICA/2, Geneva: United Nations Conference on Trade and Development.

UNCTAD, 2005, *Economic Development in Africa: Rethinking the Role of Foreign Direct Investment.*, Geneva: UNCTAD.

UNCTAD, 2006, *Doubling Aid: Making the 'Big Push' Work.*, Geneva: UNCTAD.

UNECA, 2003, The ECA and Africa: Accelerating a Continent's Development, Addis Ababa: United Nations Economic Commission for Africa.

UNIDO, 1999, 'Domestic Capacity-Building for Enhancing Productivity and Competitiveness in Africa', in A. Sall, ed., *The Future Competitiveness of African Economies*, Paris: Karthala.

Wade, Robert, 1990, *Governing the Market*. Princeton: Princeton University Press.

Weisbrot, Mark, Dean Baker, E. Kraev and J. Chen, 2001, 'The Scoreboard on Globalization 1980-2000: Twenty Years of Diminished Progress', Washington DC: Center for Economic and Policy Research.

Weisbrot, Mark, Dean Baker, R. Naiman and G. Neta, 2000a, 'Growth May Be Good for the Poor—But Are IMF and World Bank Policies Good for Growth?', Washington, DC: Center for Economic and Policy Research.

Weisbrot, Mark, R. Naiman and J. Kim, 2000b, 'The Emperor Has No Growth: Declining Economic Growth rates in the Era of Globalization', Washington, DC: Center for Economic and Policy Research,
http://www.cepr.net/images/IMF/The_Emperor_Has_No_Growth.htm

Wolfensohn, J., 1999, 'A Proposal for a Comprehensive Development Framework', Washington, DC: World Bank.

Wolfensohn, J. D., 1997, 'The Challenge of Inclusion', Address to the Board of Governors, Hong Kong, Washington, DC: World Bank.

World Bank, 1981, *Accelerated Development in Sub-Saharan Africa: An Agenda for Action*, Washington, DC: World Bank.

World Bank, 1981b, *World Development Report 1981*, New York: Oxford University Press.

World Bank, 1983, *World Development Report 1983*, New York: Oxford University Press.

World Bank, 1993, *The East Asian Miracle: Economic Growth and Public Policy*, New York: Oxford University Press.

World Bank, 1994, *Adjustment in Africa: Reforms, Results and the Road Ahead*, Washington, DC: World Bank.

World Bank, 1997, *World Development Report 1997: The State in a Changing World*, New York: Oxford University Press.

World Bank, 2000, *Can Africa Claim the 21st Century?*, Washington, DC: World Bank.

World Bank, 2001a, *Global Development Finance 2001*, Washington, DC: World Bank.

World Bank, 2001b, *Global Economic Prospects*, Washington, DC: World Bank.

Yeats, A. J. et al., 1997, 'Did Domestic Policies Marginalize Africa in International Trade?', *Directions in Development*, Washington, DC: World Bank.

Young, A., 1994, 'Lessons from the East Asian NICs: A contrarian view', *European Economic Review* 38 (3-4): 964-973.

Young, A., 1995, 'The tyranny of numbers: Confronting the statistical realities of the East Asian growth experience', *Quarterly Journal of Economics* 110 (3): 641-680.

Chapter 4

African Diasporas and Academics:
The Struggles for a Global Epistemic Presence

Paul Tiyambe Zeleza

The African academic diaspora, however defined, has never been larger than it is now, and it continues to grow rapidly. According to some estimates since 1990 an average 20,000 highly educated Africans, among them academics, have been migrating to the global North every year. That much is clear, but far less so are the causes, courses, and consequences of this expansion, specifically the implications for knowledge production in and on Africa. Depending on one's developmentalist anxieties, globalist or cosmopolitan affectations, Pan-Africanist aspirations, or analytical predispositions toward international skilled labour migration (the 'brain drain' of popular and policy discourse), the academic diaspora can be seen as either a liability depriving Africa of desperately needed professionals trained at enormous cost, or an asset providing the continent crucial connections to the global North that can facilitate transfers of capital (technological, financial, cultural and political), and help mediate, in terms of knowledge production, the globalisation of African scholarship and the Africanisation of global scholarship.

This essay seeks to discuss the role that the African academic diaspora in the United States plays and can play in African knowledge production. Needless to say, as a social formation this diaspora is quite complex in its composition and it exhibits contradictory tendencies in its practices, so that it is difficult to make generalizations about its politics or engagements. Nevertheless, I am inclined to argue that in general the diaspora, both the historic and contemporary diaspora, and its intelligentsia in particular, has the potential, which it has exercised during some key moments of modern African history, through the Pan-African movement for example, for a productive and progressive engagement with Africa. The challenge is to decipher the tendencies and instances among the academic diaspora in contemporary times— a conjuncture characterised by the vast and complex processes and projects of capitalist globalisation, technological change, and new economies of knowledge production and the production of knowledge economies—that can be mobilised for African intellectual development at multiple spatial and social scales, from the local to the global and from generation to gender.

The essay is divided into four parts. It begins by trying to define the diaspora, for it seems to me it is important to distinguish between dispersal and diaspora and the historic and contemporary diasporas and the connections between them. This is followed by an attempt to contextualise the academic diaspora, to map the institutional, intellectual, ideological, and individual dynamics of diasporic knowledge production. The third part makes an effort to historicise diasporic academic production and linkages with Africa during two crucial periods, the colonial and early post-independence eras. The final part focuses on current trends and interrogates some of the typologies that have been advanced to characterise the orientations of the contemporary African academic diaspora.

In conclusion, the essay suggests the ways in which intellectual communities and networks based both in the diaspora and on the continent, such as the Council for the Development of Social Science Research in Africa (CODESRIA), can most productively engage each other. It cannot be overemphasised that the rising international migration of Africa's professional elites and intellectuals may indeed be a curse if dismissed and ignored, but it can be turned into a blessing if embraced and utilised. It is generated by, and inserts Africa into, contemporary processes of transnationalisation and globalisation, which follow and reinforce the old trails of Pan-Africanism. The challenge for Africa is how to rebuild the historic Pan-African project, spawned by the global dispersal and exploitation of African peoples over the centuries, by creatively using the current migratory flows of African peoples, cultures, capacities, and visions and the contemporary revolution in telecommunications and travel technologies. It is an old challenge in a new age that requires responses and solutions that are both old and new (Zeleza 2003: 170).

Redefining African Diaspora Studies

There are several conceptual difficulties in defining the African diaspora, indeed in defining the term diaspora itself (Zeleza forthcoming). Diaspora, I would suggest, simultaneously refers to a process, a condition, a space, and a discourse; the continuous processes by which a diaspora is made, unmade and remade, the changing conditions in which it lives and expresses itself, the places where it is moulded and imagined, and the contentious ways in which it is studied and discussed. It entails a culture and a consciousness, sometimes diffuse and sometime concentrated of a 'here' separate from a 'there', a 'here' that is often characterised by a regime of marginalisation and a 'there' that is invoked as a rhetoric of self-affirmation, of belonging to 'here' differently. The emotional and experiential investment in 'here' and 'there' and the points in between, indeed in the very configurations and imaginings of 'here' and 'there' and their complex intersections obviously change in response to the shifting material, mental, and moral orders of social existence. Diaspora is simultaneously a state of being and a process of becoming, a kind of voyage that encompasses the possibility of never arriving or returning, a navigation of multiple belongings, of networks of affiliation. It is a mode of naming, remembering, living and feeling group identity moulded out of experiences, positionings, struggles, and imaginings of the past and the present, and at times the unfolding, unpredictable future, which are shared or seen to be shared across the boundaries of time and space that frame 'indigenous' identities in the contested and constructed locations of 'there' and 'here' and the passages and points in between.

If the term diaspora is to retain analytical specificity it has to be conceived in some bounded way, but not too narrowly if it is to remain useful for comparative study. In a broad sense, a diasporic identity implies a form of group consciousness constituted historically through expressive culture, politics, thought and tradition, in which experiential and representational resources are mobilised, in varied measures, from the imaginaries of both the old and the new worlds. Diasporas are complex social and cultural communities created out of real and imagined genealogies and geographies (cultural, racial, ethnic, national, continental, transnational) of belonging, displacement, and recreation, constructed and conceived at multiple temporal and spatial scales, at different moments and distances from the putative homeland. A diaspora is constructed as much in the fluid and messy contexts of social existence, differentiation and struggle, as in the discourses of the intellectuals and political elites. Its development involves the mobilisation and appropriation of what Jacqueline Brown (1998) calls 'diasporic resources'—cultural productions, people, and places and their associated iconography, images, ideas, and ideologies.

Given the multiplicity of historical conditions in which diasporic identities can be moulded, there cannot but exist different African diasporas whose complex relationships and exchanges, including the trafficking of the notion of diaspora itself or Africanity, are entwined in the very construction of the various diasporas. It is in the metropolitan centres, in the interstices of the 'overlapping diasporas', to use Earl Lewis's (1995) term, that different diasporas connect, communicate and sometimes compete most intimately, thereby refashioning themselves and creating and commodifying new transnational diasporic cultures mediated by national, ethnic, religious, class, and gender identities.

There are several dispersals associated with African peoples over time. Colin Palmer (2000) has identified at least six, three in prehistoric and ancient times (beginning with the great exodus that began about 100,000 years ago from the continent to other continents), and three in modern times, including those associated with the Indian Ocean slave trade to Asia, the Atlantic slave trade to the Americas, and the contemporary movement of Africans and peoples of African descent to various parts of the globe. Our tendency to privilege the modern diasporic streams, especially the last two, is a tribute to the epistemic and economic hegemony of the Euro-American world system which spawned them and created what Tiffany

Patterson and Robin Kelley (2000) call 'global race and gender hierarchies' within which African diasporas are situated and often discussed.

It is quite instructive that the term African diaspora only emerged in the 1950s and 1960s in the United States, although African diasporas existed long before then in different parts of the world, and African peoples were mobilised using other terms, such as Pan-Africanism. One author complains that the discursive politics of the term diaspora has 'imposed a US and English language-centered model of black identity on the complex experiences of populations of African descent' (Edwards 2000: 47). But even African diasporic histories focussed on the wider Atlantic world are partial in so far as African migrations and diaspora communities also emerged in the Mediterranean and Indian Ocean worlds of Southern Europe and Asia (Blakely 1986; Alpers 2000; Hunwick and Powell 2002; de S. Jaysuriya and Pankhurst 2003). Michael West (2000: 62-3) has even suggested that if black internationalism, in the ontological sense, did not originate in Africa, we also need to think of a 'Black Pacific', an entity if 'properly constructed, would include not just communities of African descent along the Pacific coast of North, Central, and South America, but also, presumably, black communities with no known ties to Africa—in historic times, that is—elsewhere in the South Pacific, such as Fiji, Papua New Guinea, and Australia, communities that only began to join the black internationalism earnest in the 1960s'.

The conflation of hegemony and discourse can be seen in the pre-eminent position occupied by African Americans in diaspora studies, despite the fact that the largest community of diaspora Africans in the Atlantic world, indeed globally, is in Brazil, not in the United States. Such is the popular fascination and scholarly preoccupation with the African American diaspora that they remain in the foreground even in texts that set out to destool them, such as Paul Gilroy's (1993) *The Black Atlantic*, itself a monument to Anglophone self-referential conceit and myopia. If Africa is largely a silent primordial presence in Gilroy's *Black Atlantic*, the historic Atlantic African diaspora is pilloried by Kwame Appiah's *In My Father's House* in his ill-tempered charge against the supposedly racialist Pan-Africanisms of Alexander Crummell and W. E. Du Bois.[1] In fact, it can be argued that except in the obligatory histories of Pan-Africanism and nationalism, the historic African diaspora tends to be ignored in much African scholarly discourse. Instead, far greater concern is expressed for the travails of the contemporary African diaspora in the North, but even here the discourse is firmly rooted in the economistic preoccupations of development studies, rather than the culturalist politics of diaspora studies (Zack-Williams 1995).

It is critical for African scholars on the continent to become more engaged in diaspora studies, to help in mapping out the histories and geographies of African global migrations, dispersals, and diasporas which are so crucial to deepening our understanding of both African history and world history for intellectual and ideological reasons, developmental and cultural considerations. African migrations to the

North, especially Western Europe and North America are increasing (Zeleza 2000, 2002). Many of these migrants are constituting themselves into new diasporas, whose identities involve complex negotiations with the host African diaspora communities and their countries of origin. If the diasporas of enslavement—the historic diasporas—had no choice but to see themselves in Pan-Africanist terms whenever they identified with Africa, the diasporas of colonialism and neocolonialism—the contemporary diasporas—are more disposed to see themselves in pan-national, or even pan-ethnic, terms. It cannot be taken, for granted, therefore, that the contemporary diasporas are more Pan-Africanist than the historic diasporas, which is one more reason for the different diasporas to engage each other and for institutions on the continent to engage both.

In a country such as the United States, there are in fact at least four waves of African diasporas: first, the historic communities of African Americans, themselves formed out of complex internal and external migrations over several hundred years; second, migrant communities from other diasporic locations, such as the Caribbean that have maintained or invoke, when necessary or convenient, national identities as Jamaicans, Puerto Ricans, Cubans, and so on; third, the recent immigrants from the indigenous communities of Africa; and finally, African migrants who are themselves diasporas from Asia or Europe, such as the East African Asians or South African whites. Each of these diasporas, broadly speaking, has its own connections and commitments to Africa, its own memories and imaginations of Africa, and its own conceptions of the diasporic condition and identity. The third group is, in turn, sometimes divided by the racialised codifications of whiteness and blackness, sanctified in the colonial cartographies of North Africa and sub-Saharan Africa, and by US immigration law under which North Africans are classified as white.

This merely points to the complexities of the African diasporas and challenges of studying them and underscores Kim Butler's (2000) point that 'conceptualizations of diaspora must be able to accommodate the reality of multiple identities and phases of diasporization over time'. She offers a simple but useful schema for diasporan study divided into five dimensions: '(1) reasons for, and conditions of, the dispersal; (2) relationship with homeland; (3) relationship with hostlands; (4) interrelationships within diasporan groups; (5) comparative study of different diasporas'. For Darlene Clark Hine (2001) black diaspora studies need to have three features: a transatlantic framework, an interdisciplinary methodology, and a comparative perspective. I would agree with the last two and revise the first that African diaspora studies need to have a global framework.

Contextualising the Academic Diasporas

Knowledge production by the African academic diaspora, as for other academics, is conditioned by various structural and epistemic imperatives over which they do not always have much control. The contexts and constraints that shape academic production are subject to changes emanating as much from the academy itself as from the wider society. As is well known by now, in recent years the academy almost everywhere has been undergoing massive transformations tied to shifting internal and external mandates and missions.[2] Since it is not possible in a chapter such as this to discuss these changes in much detail, I will try to outline an analytical framework that might help us capture their essential features and dynamics. Knowledge production systems involve the intricate interplay of institutional, intellectual, ideological, and individual factors.

Academic institutions can be classified according to their physical location (rural, urban, or metropolitan), fiscal base (private, public, or for-profit), academic structure (doctorate-granting, master's, baccalaureate, associates, or specialised),[3] and cultural composition (historically white, historically black, or women's). The intellectual enterprise itself can be distinguished in terms of its disciplinary organisation (humanities, social sciences, sciences, or professions), theoretical orientation (positivist, post-structuralist, feminist, etc.), and methodological considerations (empirical, experimental, ethnographic, textual, etc.). Ideology in the academy, often reflecting the ebbs and flows of wider social thought and movements, shapes intellectual discourses and practices from research and teaching to faculty hiring and publishing.

The dominant ideologies have included, among many others, racism and liberalism in the American academy, and nationalism and developmentalism in the African academy, while Marxism has found succour in both at certain times. Besides these ideological tropes, for Africanists in the American academy, including African diaspora academics, the knowledge they produce might also be framed by their attitudes to the grand ideas and images of the 'West', 'Africa', the 'Third World', 'the North', 'the South', 'globalisation', and 'transnationalism', or the diasporic demands and dreams of Pan-Africanism or Afrocentricism. As for the last factor, there can be little doubt that individual traits, values, and idiosyncrasies, especially the social inscriptions of gender, class, race, nationality, ethnicity, age and even religion and sexuality influence academics' ideological and theoretical proclivities, their institutional and disciplinary preferences, and their research and publication practices.

Clearly, the variables to consider in charting the contours of knowledge production by academics in general and African diaspora academics in particular are too complex for glib generalisations, whether those inspired by the solidarities of Pan-Africanism or the solitudes of Afro-pessimism. To my knowledge, no comprehensive data has been collected identifying the location of the African diaspora academics, from all the four diasporic waves I identified earlier, in the matrix of institutional, intellectual, ideological and individual factors outlined here. Much of what is known even about contemporary African academic migrants is anecdotal, for little systematic research has been conducted on their demographic and social composition, occupational and institutional affiliations, let alone their ideological orientations and personal inclinations. The data problems are compounded by the fact that the universities are losing their monopoly over scholarly production to other institutions and agencies, thanks to the changes associated with capitalist globalisation, namely, the liberalisation and privatisation of the universities themselves and the commercialisation and commodification of knowledge in the wider economy and society, so that academics are no longer confined to the universities and tracking them is no easy task. For example, I know of many African diaspora academics working for NGOs, foundations, and think tanks in the United States.

Notwithstanding these limitations, several broad observations can be made about African diaspora academics. I will limit myself to the United States the country with which I am most familiar and where abundant data exist on the higher education system. It is quite evident that their numbers in the American academy are relatively small and their influence is rather limited.[4] If this is true of the historic diaspora as a whole, it is even more so for the contemporary academic diaspora. According to the 2005-6 *Almanac of the Chronicle of Higher Education*, the total number of full-time Black faculty members (US citizens and resident aliens) at US universities and colleges was 33,137 out of 631,596 in Fall 2003, or a mere 5.2 percent, far below their share of the national population, estimated at 12.8 percent.[5] Interestingly, Asians, with only 4.1 percent of the total US population, outnumbered Black faculty by nearly 8,000. No less telling is the fact that Black faculty made up only 3.2 percent of full professors. The 5,343 Black professors comprised 16.1 percent of the total Black faculty, while 21.7 percent were at the rank of associate professor, 28.6 percent were assistant professors, 20.4 percent were instructors, and 13.2 percent were lecturers and other.[6]

The exact share of the contemporary African academic diaspora among black (and other) faculty is not known, but it is most likely small, although it is growing. The proportion of African migrant academics at the historically black colleges and universities (HBCUs) is probably within the range of the 13 percent that make up 'other minorities and foreigners' at these institutions (58 percent of HBCU faculty are African American and 29 percent white) (Johnson and Harvey 2002). Needless to say, the HBCUs tend to be a lot poorer and have heavier teaching loads than the white research universities. While courses on Africa are taught regularly at many historically white universities (HWUs), compared to the latter the HBCUs are less internationalised in terms of their curricula, study abroad, and faculty exchange programmes. Furthermore, they seem to place a higher premium on the professions and sciences than the humanities and social sciences. It has also been said that they are generally conservative politically, ideologically, and socially, a lingering tribute to their vocational and religious foundations, precarious funding, and mission to vindicate and improve the 'race', to build a black professional elite.[7]

Black faculty continue to find themselves relatively marginalised in the historically white universities, despite all the rhetoric about affirmative action spawned by the aborted promises of civil rights. Robin Wilson tells us that about half of the black faculty 'work at historically black institutions. The proportion of black faculty members at predominantly white universities—2.3 percent—is virtually the same as it was 20 years ago' (Wilson 2002: A10). It is not unusual on the large campuses with more than 30,000 students and thousands of faculty to find less than a 100 black faculty, or entire departments without a single black faculty member, especially in the Eurocentric bastions of the humanities (philosophy and classics), the dismal queen of the social sciences (economics), the assorted mandarins of the natural sciences (physics, chemistry, mathematics and biology), and the new high-tech inter-disciplinary frontiers from information technology and biotechnology to nanotechnology and environmental technology.

While much is heard, and sometimes done, about internationalisation and Afri-can studies courses and programmes have expanded remarkably in the last three decades, Africa and recent African migrants find themselves engulfed in America's eternal racial war, buffeted between the competing demands of white hegemony (manifested in the much-bemoaned control of African studies programmes by Eu-ropean Americans) and black struggle (articulated in the often beleaguered efforts to build viable and respected African American studies programmes).[8] I have writ-ten at length elsewhere of the frequently bitter contestations—which are simultane-ously political, pecuniary and paradigmatic—between migrant Africans, African Americans, and European Americans in the study and construction of Africa (Zeleza 2003: Chapter 5).

If the relations between the contemporary African academic diaspora and Euro-pean Americans are marked by questions of race and intellectual authority, between migrant Africans and African Americans they centre on nationality and institutional access. It is not uncommon for the historically white universities to hire the recent African immigrants over African Americans in order to serve affirmative action and save themselves from combative race relations. As immigrants and indigenes, the two African diasporas are driven by different memories and materialities of colonised and underdeveloped Africa and racialised and developed America, of being abroad and at home, by different motivations and moralities of personal and public engagement, national and transnational sentiments and solidarities. Not sur-prisingly, relations between these diasporas are characterised by the conflicting emo-tions and realities of accommodation, ambiguity, and animosity.[9]

Historicising Diasporic Academic Production and Linkages

The diaspora has been a critical site of knowledge production on Africa for a long time, and this history might hold salutary lessons as we seek to strengthen the en-gagements among the different waves of the diaspora and between them and Af-rica. As both a place and a project, a cultural and cognitive community, the diaspora has provided an unusually fertile space for imagining and writing Africa. Pan-Africanism, the progenitor of the numerous territorial nationalisms in Africa and the Caribbean, emerged out of the diasporic condition experienced by the diasporas of enslavement and exposure to the diasporic experience for the diasporas of colo-nialism. During the late nineteenth and early twentieth centuries, as colonialism reconfigured the global civilisational presence of Africans and reconnected Africa to its diasporas, the latter became crucial to the (re)constructions of Africa as an idea, Africa as an object of study, Africans as academics, and Pan-Africanism as a project.

The idea of Africa—descriptions, meanings, images and discourses about Africa—as inscribed by both Africans and non-Africans has mutated in various historical and geographical contexts from ancient times to the present (Zeleza 2005). By the end of the nineteenth century, in the emerging 'colonial library', as V. Y. Mudimbe (1998) calls it, the African paradigm of negative difference was firmly entrenched, as immortalised in G. W. F. Hegel's imperious dismissal of Africa as the incarnation of the 'Unhistorical, Undeveloped Spirit'. Assaulted for centuries by European racial and epistemic violence, it is not surprising that Africans in the diaspora, rather than those on the continent, were the first to launch protracted and passionate struggles for epistemological and political liberation, in which the vindication of Africa, as a human and historical space, was central. To be sure, there were those who reproduced the narratives of derision, who yearned for unconditional assimilation and Africa's erasure from their memories and bodies. And even among those who longed for Africa's redemption many had internalised the civilisational binaries of the Western epistemological order and they believed Africa would only be liberated from its current backwardness by the 'modernised' diaspora returning to the 'backward' motherland.

Notwithstanding such ambiguities, or even contradictions, so well-noted by several commentators (Davidson 1992; Korang 2004; and Mudimbe 1988), the vindicationist tradition, represented most powerfully in the writings of W. E. B. Du Bois (1970, 1976, 1994), William Leo Hansberry (1974, 1977), and Edward Blyden (1857, 1967, 1971), to mention just a few, sought to emancipate African societies and cultures from the cognitive and colonial apparatuses of European imperialism, a struggle that still continues. It is quite remarkable, indeed, how little the defamations and defences of Africa have changed since the late nineteenth century, a tribute to the enduring power of Eurocentrism, thanks to Western hegemony in the world capitalist system, and a sobering reminder that the struggles to liberate Africans at home and abroad must continue.

The texts of the vindicationist writers constituted one foundational stream for contemporary African studies. This is the Pan-African tradition whose analytical scope and scheme varied from the Africanist tradition that emerged after the Second World War. 'Rejecting the dichotomies on which Africanist scholarship would later be constructed', Michael West and William Martin (1997: 311) state, African diaspora scholars 'connected ancient Africa to modern Africa, Africa north of the Sahara to Africa south of the Sahara, and, especially, the African continent to the African diaspora. They tended to concentrate on broad political, religious, and cultural themes that transcended national and continental boundaries in the black world'.

They were preoccupied with the fundamental questions of Africa's purity and parity, as Kwaku Korang (2002) has so perceptively observed; purity in terms of Africa's autonomy and authenticity and parity in terms of Africa's progress and modernity, of creating what Blyden called an 'African personality', an African ontology and epistemology that was both distinctly African and worldly in the context of an overriding European epistemic and existential presence that constantly sought to create and consume an African difference or alterity inscribed with inferiority. These large civilisational and cultural questions were generally shed from the African studies of the post-war Africanist tradition, in which the modernisation paradigm—packaged in a variety of ideological and theoretical but decidedly positivist trajectories—assumed ascendancy, which resonated with the developmentalist preoccupations of postcolonial Africa.

In pre-civil rights America where segregation was legal and colonial Africa where universities were few (mostly concentrated in South Africa and North Africa), the HBCUs provided the most auspicious home for the study of Africa by both African Americans and Africans from the continent. It was at these colleges and universities that the serious and systematic study of Africa was pioneered, courses on African peoples established, and monographs and journals published long before the historically white universities, in pursuit of national security, disciplinary excitement or belated multiculturalism, discovered African studies or diaspora studies. As is clear from Joseph Harris's (1993) masterly collection, *Global Dimensions of the African Diaspora*, there are few significant intellectual or political figures in early twentieth century African American or Anglophone African history who did not study, teach, or were inspired by or had some dealings with an HBCU. The cases of Kwame Nkrumah and Nnamdi Azikiwe at Lincoln University in Pennsylvania, or medical doctors such as Hastings Kamuzu Banda at Meharry medical school in Nashville, Tennessee are emblematic of the thousands of Africans who received their university education in the United States during the first half of the twentieth century when segregation kept the doors to the white universities shut (Veney 2003, 2004).

Thus, diaspora academic institutions were in the forefront of producing knowledge and personnel, counter-hegemonic discourses and developmental capacities for the diaspora itself and Africa. The transformative role of the diaspora in terms of knowledge production is nowhere as evident as it is in the settler and re-captive settlements of Liberia and Sierra Leone during the late nineteenth and early twentieth centuries. Much has been written about the initiatives, choices, and adaptations the Americo-Liberian and Sierra Leonean Krio intelligentsia, both secular and religious, made as teachers and evangelists to reconcile their dual, and in some cases triple, heritage as a community with claims to Africa, the West, and sometimes Islam, to nativity, modernity and difference. They were led by the indomitable iconoclast Edward Blyden whose voluminous writings laid the foundations of twentieth century Pan-Africanist thought. As Toyin Falola (2001) has demonstrated in his suggestive history of *Nationalism and African Intellectuals*, Blyden was eagerly emulated and debated by his contemporaries and later by the Negritude writers and post-independence nationalists.

The thought and praxis of these intellectuals (there were as yet not many academics on the continent because there were few universities) demonstrated the umbilical relationship between Pan-Africanism and nationalism, the intricate web of ideas, images, individuals, values, visions, expressive culture, and institutional practices circulating in the elite cosmopolitan, not to say globalised, circles of Africa and the diaspora. Pan-Africanism would later develop different spatial and social referents, but in the late nineteenth and early twentieth centuries it was pre-eminently a trans-Atlantic phenomenon. The lead taken by the African diaspora in the Caribbean and the United States in organising Pan-Africanism can be attributed to the fact that racial ideologies there were more severe than in Latin America. Also, Britain was a colonial superpower and later the United States became a global superpower (Zeleza 2003).

Transatlantic Pan-Africanism was articulated most concretely in the first half of the twentieth century through political movements and the traffic in expressive culture. The movements included W. E. B. Du Bois's elitist Pan-African Congresses, Marcus Garvey's populist conventions and bungled 'Back to Africa' scheme, and a whole range of organisations formed by African students and African American activists, such as Paul Robeson's Council on African Affairs, especially in the aftermath of the 1935 Italian invasion of Ethiopia—the beacon of successful African resistance and freedom from colonialism—which enraged and galvanised the Pan-African world. The trans-Atlantic circulation of expressive cultural practices, from music to dress to language, were powerful signifiers of black cosmopolitanism, and in highly racialised colonies such as South Africa, African American cultural forms were adopted as performative tools that disconnected modernity from whiteness by subverting, mocking, and reversing the 'racial time' of white modernity 'that locked Africans into static "uncivilized native" categories' (Kemp and Vinson 2000: 14).

Clearly, Pan-Africanism involved far more than trans-Atlantic political discourse and engagement, it also represented the globalising cultural flows between Africa and its diaspora, in which cultural imports and exports were traded in complex circuits of exchange throughout the trans-Atlantic world. The circulation of many forms of popular music from rumba and jazz, to reggae and rap is fascinating story that has been told by many, so is that of the connections between the literary movements of Africa and the diaspora, most significantly the Harlem Renaissance and the Negritude movement in the 1920s and 1930s, as well as the religious linkages from the role of diaspora missionaries and models in the spread of Christianity and the growth of Christian independency (also called independent churches) to Africa's contribution to the development of diaspora religions, such as Candomble, Santeria, Voodoo, and Rastafarianism. In short, an African cosmopolitanism emerged in the trans-Atlantic world. Cosmopolitanism here refers to a cultural phenomenon that is both local and transnational, social islands of practices, material technologies, conceptual frameworks, and lifestyles that circulated internationally but were localised in their production and consumption.[10]

As the storms of decolonisation gathered momentum in Africa and the Caribbean and desegregation in the United States, trans-Atlantic Pan-Africanism entered a new phase, in which it was increasingly supplanted by new Pan-Africanisms and territorial nationalisms. To be sure, reverberations between these nationalisms and Pan-Africanisms continued. For example, the nationalist achievements in Africa and the Caribbean inspired civil rights struggles in the US, while civil rights activists in the US provided crucial support to liberation movements fighting against recalcitrant settler regimes in Southern Africa by applying pressure on the American state and capital (Nesbitt 2004). But there was no denying that other Pan-Africanisms were rising, both in practice and in discursive terms.

The most significant discursive intervention was Gilroy's notion of the Black Atlantic, a form of Pan-Africanism that is largely confined to celebrating the creativity and construction of new cultures among the African diasporic communities in the Anglophone world of the United States and Britain, excluding continental Africa. The other Pan-Africanisms were as much conceptual as they were organisational, namely, continental, sub-Saharan, Pan-Arab, and global. The first has focused primarily on the unification of continental Africa. The second and third have restricted themselves to the peoples of the continent north and south of the Sahara, and in the case of Pan-Arabism, extended itself to western Asia or the so-called Middle East. Gamal Abdel Nasser proudly saw Egypt at the centre of three concentric circles linking the African, Arab, and Islamic worlds. The last, which seeks to reclaim African peoples dispersed to all corners of the globe, is the weakest in organisational terms, although it is assuming intellectual salience as diaspora scholars seek to map out the dispersal of Africans in the Indian Ocean and Mediterranean worlds and configure their African diasporic identities.

The political transformations associated with the nationalist and civil rights struggles transformed the institutional bases of Pan-African academic knowledge production and linkages. The terrain changed significantly for the independence generation of African students both at home and abroad. In their countries they were no longer confined to the awfully few regional universities belatedly set up by the colonial states as new national universities were established, while in the United States they were no longer limited to the HBCUs as the white universities were officially desegregated. What they gained in access, they lost in scope. In other words, unlike the pre-independence generations, the postcolonial generations of African students and even faculty often lacked exposure to Pan-Africanizing experiences of the old regional universities and the HBCUs, even if they might express Pan-African sentiments about Africa's common future and the need for greater unity and sympathise with civil rights struggles in the diaspora.

Despite its proverbial failures to realise the fruits of *uhuru* or independence, territorial nationalism succeeded in turning the cartographic contraptions bequeathed by colonialism into objects of desire and discord for the increasingly despondent citizens and professional elites—including academics—of the postcolonial state. If decolonisation engendered nationalist identities (notwithstanding the fissiparous tendencies of ethnicity) for continental Africans, the enfranchisement that came with desegregation in the United States strengthened national identity among African Americans (even though racism persisted). Thus, encounters between postcolonial Africans and post-civil rights African Americans were increasingly mediated by territorial nationalisms that were far more muted during the era of Nkrumah and Du Bois.

Tendencies of the Contemporary Academic Diaspora

The contemporary African academic diaspora has to engage and negotiate with multiple constituencies as academics, as immigrants in another country, and as emigrants from specific African countries.[11] As predominantly academics of colour, to use the American nomenclature for racial minorities, they must learn to climb the slippery poles of the highly racialised American academy, and come to grips with the complex institutional, intellectual and ideological imperatives of the largest and most diversified and differentiated higher education system in the world.

As immigrants, they confront, on the one hand, the legal issues of their resident status, now further complicated by the imposition of a stringent homeland security regime following the terrorist attacks in New York and Washington on September 11, 2001.[12] On the other hand, there are the infinitely thorny challenges of social adjustment, which require them to navigate the contours of race, ethnic and gender relations in the United States, to negotiate relations with the dominant white society and with African Americans as well as with other immigrants (including those from their own countries, other African countries and elsewhere in the African diaspora, especially the Caribbean), and to ascertain their participation in the country's social and political affairs.

As emigrants, they face unending demands from home, both real and imagined, ranging from the intimate obligations to family and friends, often to provide financial and moral support, to the more abstract compulsion to defend and promote Africa in a country where things African are routinely denigrated and demonised. In fact, the devaluation of Africa frequently seems to parallel the depreciation of their own qualifications and status, a condition that induces acute agonies and tortured adaptations, as they are forced to pay an additional cultural tax for being African usually on top of the racial tax that African Americans have always paid for being black, while for the women among them there is an extra gender tax.

The number of African immigrants in the United States has been increasing steadily since 1970 for reasons we cannot go into here, except to point out that this is related to changes in migration pressures in Africa itself and immigration conditions and law in the United States. According to the latest US 2000 Census there were 861,000 African born residents in the United States; their numbers had reached 1.5 million by 2005. While this number may appear large and has more than quadrupled since 1990, it only represents a mere 3 percent of the foreign born population (estimated at 33 million, which accounted for about 11 percent of the total US population, the highest since 1930). An indication that many African residents are recent migrants is demonstrated by the fact that the median length of their residence is 10.2 years while the proportion of naturalised citizens is 37 percent, both of which are lower than for most of the other major regions.[13]

Where African migrants trump everybody else, including native-born Americans is in education. In 2000, 94.9 percent of African-born residents age 25 and older had completed high school or more education, compared to 86.6 percent for native-born Americans, and 67 percent for all foreign-born residents. Among the African-born residents, 49.3 percent had a bachelor's degree or more as compared to 25.6 percent for the native-born population and 25.8 percent for the foreign-born population as a whole.[14] Clearly, African residents in the United States constitute the most educated population in the country, while residents from America's historic backyard in Mexico, Central America, and the Caribbean have the lowest educational levels. The relatively high levels of education among the African-born residents compared to African Americans might be one source of tensions between the two groups as it translates into class divisions and prejudices. This phenomenon represents an historic inversion in that it is the recent African arrivals, not the long-settled diaspora populations that seem, disproportionately, to possess the cultural capital of western modernity and benefit from the latter's civil rights struggles which expanded minorities' access to education and material opportunities.

Not surprisingly, African-born residents are mostly to be found in the professions, despite the proverbial stories of Africans with PhDs driving taxis in New York, Washington, or other major American cities. In 2000, more than a third, 36.5 percent to be exact, were in a managerial and professional specialty, 22.1 percent in technical, sales and administrative support, 19.6 percent in service occupations, 4.2 percent in precision production, craft and repair, and the remaining 17.1 percent were labourers, fabricators and operators. In contrast, the occupational distribution for residents from—using the US Census classifications—Latin America, the Caribbean, Central America, Mexico and South America—are weighted to the less professional and managerial occupations and include sizeable groups in farming, forestry and fishing. Yet, in terms of household income and poverty rates, African residents tend to do less well than their educational levels would seem to suggest.[15]

The irony cannot escape anyone: Africa, the least educated and most underdeveloped continent in the world has the most educated population in the world's most developed country. This gaping mismatch, a testimony to the asymmetrical linkages between Africa and the North that fuel the 'brain drain', is undoubtedly a tragedy, but it can potentially be turned to Africa's favour if effective strategies are developed to transform the 'brain drain' into 'brain gain' or to turn it into what some have called 'brain mobility'. The latter involves building expatriate knowledge networks and establishing connections between the migrant professionals and their countries or regions of origin, which can facilitate the exchange of information and knowledge and the transfer of skills (Granovetter and Sweedberg 1997).

The African academic diaspora, as cultural producers, have an important and specific role to play in brokering relations between Africa and the North, in 'Africanizing' the Atlantic. They must resist the seductions of the Northern academies to become native ventriloquists, complicit 'others' who validate narratives that seek to marginalise Africa. Nor should they let themselves be manipulated as a fifth column in the North's eternal racial wars by disavowing the protracted struggles of historic African diaspora communities for the full citizenship of racial equality, economic empowerment, and political power. There is need to devise effective strategies, which I have outlined at length elsewhere, that might be used to turn the contemporary African academic diaspora from liabilities into assets for African intellectual development in terms of the triple mission of the academic enterprise—research, teaching, and service (Zeleza 2003: 161-70).

Prescriptions, of which Africa always gets in abundance, of course often sink in the quick-sands of reality, in this case the realities of both the African and American academies and knowledge production systems. One issue is to look at the actual linkages that have been established between the two, and the other the profile of the contemporary African academic diaspora in the United States, who are by no means homogeneous and whose tendencies can facilitate or hinder productive and progressive linkages with their colleagues on the continent. Earlier I alluded to linkages between the HBCUs and Africa. These linkages of course continue, although since the 1950s and 1960s they have increasingly been eclipsed by the entry of the historically white universities, bankrolled by the foundations and the state itself (for example, through the federally funded Title VI area studies programmes) into African studies and academic exchanges with African institutions.

Briefly, the patterns of academic exchange between the United States and Africa have been unequal, patterns that the contemporary processes and projects of globalisation are helping to reinforce and recast. Historically, academic exchanges between the United States and Africa have involved student and faculty exchange programmes, short-term training programmes, and technical assistance for specific projects. Since the 1990s new patterns of academic exchange and mobility between American and African universities began to emerge. Three can be identified: first, the growth of what is called 'transnational' education (often involving the establishment of overseas university branches of American universities); second, the globalisation of American scholarly societies (expanding their global reach by aggressively recruiting foreign members, including from Africa); and third, the expansion of online education (using the Internet to export curricula and instructional expertise, especially in the lucrative fields of science, engineering, and business) (Zeleza 2003; Samoff and Carrol 2002).

It is not easy to identify the tendencies among the contemporary African academic diaspora. There is of course no shortage of impressionistic accounts of their politics and scholarship. For example, Falola (2001: 282) has observed that 'like all communities they have their tensions, petty rivalries, and resentments toward members who are perceived to be especially successful', and he discusses how they deal with the questions of identity politics and scholarly audience, singling out the experiences of Manthia Diawara, Es'kia Mphahlele and Nawal el Saadawi. However, his tantalising distinction between 'migrants as revolutionaries', as people with 'alternative allegiances' and as 'agents of culture', is not further developed.

The Kenyan scholar, Francis Njubi Nesbitt (2003), offers a more compelling typology of the African academic diaspora. He has argued that the Duboisian 'double consciousness' of African migrant intellectuals in the North, which is spawned by the contradiction between their high academic achievements and an inferiorised identity in America's unyielding racial hierarchy and between their alienation from Africa (where they are often condemned for abandoning their countries) and the need to come to terms with their Africanity and to promote Africa, produces three 'types' of migrant intellectuals: the comprador intelligentsia, the postcolonial critic, and the progressive exile.

Members of the comprador intelligentsia cynically use their Africanity to authenticate the neocolonial and neoliberal agendas of the international financial institutions; they are infamous for defending the global order and condemning African countries for corruption, 'tribalism', and ineptitude. For their part, the postcolonial critics see themselves in a mediating role, as expert interpreters of the African experience to the West and transmitters of the ever-changing panorama of Euro-American perspectives—from liberalism, modernisation, Marxism, dependency, and the 'posts' (postmodern, post-structural, and postcolonial)—to Africa and to 'explain' the African experience. The progressive exiles seek to use their space of exile to develop a dignified Pan-African identity by unabashedly promoting African knowledges and participating in the liberation struggles of both the diaspora and their countries of origin. Njubi suggests Ngugi wa Thiong'o as the paragon of the progressive exile and Kwame Anthony Appiah for the postcolonial critic, and one could point to George Ayittey (1992, 1998) as the quintessential comprador intellectual.

When Njubi presented this paper at a major conference of African social scientists in Kampala, Uganda, some participants pointed out that the categories could be expanded or were not mutually exclusive, a point the author himself in fact emphasised. 'Intellectuals who consider themselves progressives in one context', he wrote, 'find themselves allied with global capital and neocolonial forces in another. Take the case of the independence generation ... It is this generation that gave us hopeful theories like African personality, Consciencism, and African Socialism. Yet, once they returned home from exile and seized the reigns of power, an alarmingly large number of them abandoned their progressive politics for the worst forms of neocolonial clientilism and despotism' (Njubi 2002: 74).

Undoubtedly, one could come up with other typologies based on different criteria. Njubi's classification primarily refers to the contemporary African academic diaspora's *ideological positioning* toward African liberation. They could also be classified in terms of their *disciplinary orientation*—as humanists, social scientists, scientists, and professionals—each of which has a bearing on the kinds of research they conduct and the possible collaborations they can establish with colleagues and institutions on the continent because each of these organisational branches in the academy has its own intellectual requirements and institutional and reputational resources. For example, research in the humanities is more poorly financed than in the sciences, and scholars in the literary disciplines can conduct their textually-based research without ever going to Africa, which would be frowned upon for historians or anthropologists who need to conduct empirical and ethnographic research. Also, in many social science and humanities disciplines it is common to work individually, while in many of the sciences collaboration is often necessary given the cost of the research apparatus and the kind of academic culture that has evolved in the sciences.

The permutations and implications of the disciplinary schema as a basis for organising knowledge production and classifying academics and assessing the nature of their potential or actual engagements with Africa obviously deserve consideration. Yet, one cannot resist the search for a more comprehensive typology that incorporates as many of the dynamics that frame academic knowledge production as possible. Earlier we identified four of these—the institutional, intellectual, ideological, and individual factors. With this in mind I would propose, very tentatively it must be stressed, three broad classifications of African diaspora academics: the Pan-Africanists, the Americanists, and the globalists, based on the organisation and content of their research, publishing, and teaching practices. Members of the first group conduct their research and derive their research agendas, and do their publishing and sometimes their teaching (conventional and electronic) in both Africa and the United States, while the second are largely focused on the United States in their research, publishing, and teaching practices, and the third are connected to multiple sites besides the United States and Africa. Needless to say these 'choices' are driven as much by ideological and individual predispositions as by institutional and intellectual predilections and material incentives.

It cannot be overemphasised that this is a rather rudimentary typology, that many people straddle these categories at different times in their careers. Indeed, many African academics circulate between Africa and the United States as students, faculty, or visitors. It simply underscores the fact that for African diaspora academics located in the United States, it is not just their *personal politics* toward Africa and its struggles that are important as far as knowledge production is concerned. Equally important, perhaps even more so, are their *academic practices*, which do not always coincide with their personal inclinations or ideologies. A more comprehensive typology would in fact also help us to differentiate among those in the historic African diaspora who are engaged in African studies, and identify the tendencies in the two diasporas that continental research networks and organisations might fruitfully engage for mutual benefit. Beyond these 'natural constituencies' of Africa in the United States, there are of course the European American Africanists, and many others who have more than a nodding acquaintance or interest in knowledge produced in and on Africa. The African knowledge production enterprise in the global North is indeed a house of many mansions.

Conclusion: What Role for Continental Institutions?

There can be little doubt that the contemporary African academic diaspora in the United States and elsewhere in the global North is becoming a force to reckon with in knowledge production on Africa. It is also becoming more conscious of itself as a diaspora, of the many ties that bind it together and to the historic diasporas and to Africa, but also of the many tensions that tear it apart internally and from the other diasporas and the continent. This is a diaspora often brought to the United States through chain migration (after studying or working in other countries, including foreign countries in Africa), so that it has rich reservoirs of transnational experiences and empathies.

Indeed, the revolution in telecommunications and travel, which has compressed the spatial and temporal distances between home and abroad, offers this diaspora, unlike the historic diasporas from the earlier dispersals, unprecedented opportunities to be transnational, to be people of multiple worlds, perpetually translocated, physically and culturally, between several countries or several continents. They are able to retain ties to Africa in ways that were not possible to earlier generations of the diaspora. Lest we forget many of the people who have worked for continental research institutions and networks, such as the Council for the Development of Social Science Research in Africa (CODESRIA), including the current and past two executive secretaries, not to mention the universities, have had their sojourns in the diaspora. Thus, many African institutions of higher education and research networks are not only Pan-African in theory or in fact, but beneficiaries and beacons of intellectual energies from and for the diaspora.

African universities and research institutions remain peripheral in the international knowledge system by any measure—faculty size, student enrolments, research output—and they are unusually dependent on external sources for resources, models, and paradigms. As globalisation and its gospel of neoliberalism and market fundamentalism penetrate the ivory towers or the brick walls of academe this system is becoming more competitive and entrepreneurial than ever, which threatens to erode further Africa's global intellectual standing, autonomy, and production. The academic diaspora, itself a product of various cycles of capitalist globalisation including the current one, offers African academic systems a way of mitigating their peripherality, of negotiating new terms of engagement with the powerful research and publishing establishments that control international knowledge production, of minimising the negative and maximising the positive impacts of academic liberalisation, of modifying Africa's lopsided academic relations with external donor and scholarly gatekeepers, of mediating Africa's globalisation.

The challenge for these institutions is to recognise and strengthen their diasporic connections and commitments. As Philip Altbach (2003: 146) notes, 'developing a consciousness of the importance of the diaspora is an important first step ...' The understandable tendency to feel that those who have abandoned the homeland are somehow suspect needs to be eliminated, and efforts must be made to involve diaspora scholars and scientists in the development of science and universities. There is, after all, a significant degree of patriotism and commitment to the country of origin among most expatriate scholars and scientists. Institutionally, this entails giving the diaspora, both the contemporary and historic, a voice in the governance and deliberations of the regional continental and perhaps even some of the national institutions, a subject that was raised forcefully by several participants at CODESRIA's 10th General Assembly with reference to CODESRIA itself. The mechanics of doing this are of course problematic, but the principle should not be. Intellectually, the challenge is also to incorporate diaspora academics in continental and regional research networks, institutes, and publishing programmes. There might be reluctance if resources are seen in zero-sum terms, but this need not be so if it is understood, and insisted upon, that the diaspora has access to and should harness and channel its resources to these research activities.

A compelling case can be made for joint research and publishing projects between African academics based on the continent, the contemporary African academic migrants or diaspora, and the academics from the historic African diaspora. There are enormous benefits to be repeated on both sides: the exchange of internally positioned knowledge with externally positioned knowledge can reveal the 'blind spots' of each position and foster greater reflexivity and intellectual enlightenment. Such exchanges need to be underpinned by a commitment to Pan-Africanism, both what St. Clair Drake (1993) calls Pan-Africanism with a small 'p' and Pan-Africanism with a big 'P'.[16] The former consists of symbolic affirmations of African identity by ordinary people in Africa itself and the diaspora, while the latter entails organised resistance and solidarity, resistance against global imperialisms and racisms and fostering solidarity among African peoples, sometimes invoked in the name of race (racial Pan-Africanism) or in the name of the continent (continental Pan-Africanism), invocations that are not always compatible. The challenge for the contemporary African academic migrants or diaspora is to mediate continental Africa and diasporic Africa, the political and economic projects of Pan-Africanism and the cultural and discursive paradigms of diaspora studies, the imperatives of physical and psychological return to Africa through positive and productive identification with Africa.

For their part, African universities and research networks have a responsibility to promote critical and informed public debate and discussion about African issues globally and relations between Africa and its diasporas. In building more effective linkages with the African diaspora, deliberate efforts ought to be made to include academics from all the branches of knowledge—the humanities, social sciences, natural sciences, professional fields, and the various interdisciplinary areas, not only because it makes eminent intellectual sense in this era of furious disciplinary reconfigurations, but also to tap into the intellectual energies of the African academic diaspora working in all these areas who are seeking active collaborations with African colleagues. I am often quite amazed at the exciting research being conducted on the burning issues confronting Africa today by diaspora academics outside the traditional humanities—and social science-dominated circles of North American African studies.

Many of these academics already collaborate with colleagues and institutions on the continent. Indeed, many of us in the diaspora maintain strong personal linkages with colleagues in Africa and we will continue to do so. The challenge and opportunity for African institutions and for us is to channel and enrich these engagements through more structured arrangements, by creating organised, inclusive and energising intellectual relations that can help rebuild the historic Pan-African project in these new turbulent times of ferocious capitalist globalisation. Over the past four decades African institutions of higher education and research networks have undergone many trials, tribulations and triumphs in building viable African learning and research communities. It is time they set their sights to help (re)shape the world of Africa's own academic diaspora, which is crucial to the struggles over scholarly knowledge production on and in Africa, and for Africa's global reach. That might be their singular contribution to Pan-Africanism and Africa's globalisation in the new century.

Notes

1. For insightful critiques of Paul Gilroy's *The Black Atlantic* see Ntongela Masilela (1996), Michael J. C. Echeruo (1999), and Laura Chrisman (2000). And for Kwame Anthony Appiah's (1992) *In My Father's House*, see Nkiru Nzegwu (1996), Femi Taiwo (1995), and Tsenay Serequeberhan (1996).
2. For a surveys of the changes in the academy in Africa and globally see Paul Tiyambe Zeleza and Adebayo Olukoshi (2004) and Paul Tiyambe Zeleza (forthcoming).
3. This is the classification used by the Carnegie Foundation for the Advancement of Teaching, which is the leading typology of American colleges and universities. See http://www.carnegiefoundation.org/classification/. Needless to say, different classifications of higher educational systems operate in different countries.
4. For studies of blacks in the American academy see Joy James and Ruth Farmer (1993), Lee Jones (2000), and Valora Washington and William Harvey (1989).
5. *The Chronicle of Higher Education*, Almanac, August 26 (2005:26). These classifications are problematic in so far as they conflate racial (Black), geographical (Asian) and linguistic (Hispanic) categories. For example, there are many Hispanics who are 'Black'. For the purposes of this paper there are additional problems in that while many African immigrants would fit into the category 'Black', immigrants from North Africa and African immigrants of European and Asian descent would be excluded; similarly African diaspora immigrants from Asia and Europe might be excluded.
6. Of 33,137 the Black faculty 16,270 were men and 16,867 were women; and women made up 35.9 of the professors, 46.4 of the associate professors, 54.8 percent of the assistant professors, 49.6 percent of the instructors, and 46.9 percent of the lecturers and other.
7. For histories of the HBCUs see Charles V. Willie and Ronald R. Edmonds (1984), James D. Anderson (1988), Julian B. Roebuck and Komanduri S. Murty (1993), and Serbrenia J. Sims (1994).
8. For some interesting studies on the struggles of African American, Afro-American, Africana, or Black studies—the nomenclature is itself indicative of the field's contestations and continued search for a viable identity—see some of the following: Abdul Alkalimat (1990), Mario Azevedo (2003), Manning Marable (2000), Elliot P. Skinner (2000), Margaret Barrett and Philip Carey, (2003), and Makasa Kasonde (2001).
9. Recent examples of conflict between African migrants and African Americans include the widely publicised altercations at Virginia State University, an HBCU, in which the

institution's black president was accused of demoting African American heads of department in favour of foreign-born faculty, including Africans, under a reorganisation. See Robin Wilson (2001). In a different twist an African-Lebanese man from West Africa sued Loyola College in Maryland in federal court after he was turned down for a position allegedly on the grounds that black faculty members were pressuring for the hiring of an 'African-American that was visibly black'. See Roger Clegg (2002). For a detailed examination of these relations, see Zeleza (2006).

10. On the influence of African American cultural practices in South Africa see Zine Magubane (2003) and on cosmopolitanism in Zimbabwe as expressed through music see Tom Turino (2003).

11. See the following recent studies on African immigrants in the United States: John A. Arthur (2000), Brent K. Ashabranner and Jennifer Ashabranner (1999), Jacqueline Copeland-Carson (2004), JoAnn D'Alisera (2004), and April Gordon (1998).

12. For a discussion of the implications of this, see Ali A. Mazrui (2002), Cassandra R. Veney (2004), Zeleza (2003) and *The Chronicle of Higher Education*, 'Special Report, Closing the Gates', April 11 (2003): A12-A25.

13. The median length of residence years for US residents born in the following regions are as follows: Europe 25 years, Asia 14.3 years, Latin America 13.5 years, Caribbean 17.6 years, Central America 12.9 years, Mexico 12.8 years, South America 13 years, Northern America (mostly refers to Canada) 24.8 years, and other 13.2 years. Comparable figures of naturalised citizens among the foreign-born resident population from the other regions are as follows: Europe 52 percent, Asia 47.1 percent, Latin America 28.3 percent, Caribbean 46.5 percent, Central America 21.1 percent, Mexico 20.3 percent, South America 38.6 percent, Northern America 43.1 percent, and other 24.3 percent. See US Census Bureau, *Profile of the Foreign Born Population in the United States* (Washington, DC: US Census Bureau, 2001), 19-21.

14. Comparable figures for the other regions in terms of proportion of those with high school or more education are: Europe 81.3 percent, Asia 83.8 percent, Latin America 49.6 percent, Caribbean 68.1 percent, Central America 37.1 percent, Mexico 33.8 percent, South America 79.7 percent, Northern America 85.5 percent, and other 50.8 percent. As for the proportions of those with a bachelor's degree or more the figures are: Europe 32.9 percent, Asia 44.9 percent, Latin America 11.2 percent, Caribbean 19.3 percent, Central America 5.5 percent, Mexico 4.2 percent, South America 25.9 percent, Northern America 36.2 percent, and other 10.5 percent. See US Census Bureau (2001: 36-7).

15. In 2000 they earned an average $36,371 as compared to $41,733 for residents from Europe, $51,363 for Asian-born residents, $36,048 for the foreign-born altogether, and $41,383 for native-born Americans. In terms of poverty rates, it was 13.2 percent for African-born residents, 9.3 percent for European-born, 12.8 for Asian-born, 21.9 percent for Latin American-born, 20.6 percent for Caribbean-born, 24.2 percent for Central America-born, 25.8 percent for Mexico-born, 11.5 percent for South America-born, 7.4 percent for Northern America-born, and 17.8 percent for other (US Census Bureau 2001: 36-7).

16. He offers a fascinating rationale and programme for collaborative research that will enhance both diaspora studies and Pan-Africanism.

References

Alkalimat, A., 1999, *Paradigms in Black Studies: Intellectual History, Political Meaning and Political Ideology*, Chicago: Twenty-first Century Books and Publications.

Alpers, E., 2000, 'Recollecting Africa: Diasporic Memory in the Indian Ocean World', *African Studies Review* 43 (1): 83-99.

Altbach, P. G., 2003, 'African Higher Education and the World', in D. Teferra and P. G. Altbach eds., *African Higher Education: An International Reference Handbook*, Bloomington and Indianapolis: University of Indiana Press.

Anderson, J. D., 1988, *The Education of Blacks in the South, 1860-1935*, Chapel Hill: University of North Carolina Press.

Appiah, K. A., 1992, *In My Father's House: Africa in the Philosophy of Culture*, New York: Oxford University Press.

Arthur, J. A., 2000, *Invisible Sojourners: African Immigrant Diaspora in the United States*, Westport, CT: Praeger, 2000.

Ashabranner, B. K. and J. Ashabranner, 1999, *The New African Americans*, North Haven, CT: Linnet Books.

Ayittey, G. B. N., 1998, *Africa Betrayed*, New York: St. Martin's Press, 1992, and *Africa in Chaos*, New York: St. Martin's Press.

Azevedo, M., ed., 2003, *African Studies: A Survey of Africa and the African Diaspora*, Third edition, Durham, NC: Carolina Academic Press.

Barrett, M. and P. Carey, 2003, *Diaspora: Introduction to Africana Studies*, Dubuque, Iowa: Kendall/Hunt

Blakely, A., 1986, *Russia and the Negro: Blacks In Russian History and Thought*, Washington, DC: Howard University Press.

Blyden, E. W., 1857, *A Vindication of the African Race: Being a Brief Examination of the Arguments in Favor of African Inferiority*, Monrovia: G. Killian.

Blyden, E. W., 1967, *Christianity, Islam and the Negro Race*, Edinburgh: Edinburgh University Press.

Blyden, E. W., 1971, *Black Spokesman: Selected Published Writings of Edward Wilmot Blyden*, Hollis R. Lynch, ed., London: Frank Cass.

Brown, J. N., 1998, 'Black Liverpool, Black America, and the Gendering of Diasporic Space', *Cultural Anthropology* 13 (3): 291-325.

Butler, K. D., 2000, 'From Black History to Diasporan History: Brazilian Abolition in Afro-Atlantic Context', *African Studies Review* 43 (1): 127.

Chrisman, L., 2000. 'Rethinking Black Atlanticism'. *Black Scholar* 30 (3/4): 12-17.

Clegg, R., 2002, 'When Faculty Hiring Is Blatantly Illegal', *The Chronicle of Higher Education* November 1: B20.

Copeland-Carson, J., 2004, *Creating Africa in America: Translocal Identity in an Emerging World City*, Philadelphia: University of Pennsylvania Press.

D'Alisera, J., 2004, *An Imagined Geography. Sierra Leonean Muslims in America*, Philadelphia: University of Pennsylvania Press.

Davidson, B., 1992, *The Black Man's Burden: Africa and the Curse of the Nation-State*, New York: Times Books.

de S. Jaysuriya, S. and R. Pankhurst, eds., 2003, *The African Diaspora in the Indian Ocean*, Trenton, NJ: Africa World Press.

Drake, St. Clare, 1993, 'Diaspora Studies and Pan-Africanism', in J. Harris, ed., *Global Dimensions of the African Diaspora*, Second edition, Washington, DC: Howard University Press, 451-514.

Du Bois, W. E. B., 1970, *Black Reconstruction in America*, New York: Athenaeum.

Du Bois, W. E. B., 1976, *The world and Africa*, Millwood, NY: Kraus-Thomson Organization.

Du Bois, W. E. B., 1994, *The Souls of Black Folk*, New York: Dover.

Echeruo, M. J. C., 1999, 'An African Diaspora: The Ontological Project', in I. Okpewho, C. B. Davies and A. A. Mazrui, eds., *African Diaspora. African Origins and New World Identities*, Bloomington and Indianapolis: Indiana University Press, 3-18.

Edwards, B.H.., 2000, '"Unfinished Migrations": Commentary and Response', *African Studies Review* 43 (1): 47-50.

Falola, T., 2001, *Nationalism and African Intellectuals*, Rochester: University of Rochester Press.

Garibaldi, A., ed., 1984, *Black Colleges and Universities: Challenges for the Future*, New York: Praeger.

Gilroy, P., 1993, *The Black Atlantic. Modernity and Double Consciousness*, Cambridge, MA: Cambridge University Press.

Gordon, A., 1998, 'The New Diaspora—African immigration to the United States', *Journal of Third World Studies* 15 (1): 79-103.

Granovetter, M. and R. Sweedberg, 1992, *The Sociology of Economic Life*, San Francisco: Westview Press.

Hamilton, K., 2003, 'Challenging the Future of Black Studies', *Black Issues in Higher Education* 20 (2): 38-9.

Hansberry, W. L., 1974, *Pillars in Ethiopian History*, J. E. Harris, ed., Washington: Howard University Press.

Hansberry, W. L., 1977, *Africa and Africans as Seen by Classical Writer*, Washington: Howard University Press.

Harris, J., ed., 1993, *Global Dimensions of the African Diaspora*, Second edition, Washington, DC: Howard University Press.

Hine, D. C., 2001, 'Frontiers in Black Diaspora Studies and Comparative Black History: Enhanced Knowledge of Our Complex Past', *The Negro Education Review* 52 (3): 101-108.

Hunwick, J. and T. Powell, 2002, *The African Diaspora in the Mediterranean Lands of Islam*, Princeton: Markus Wiener Publishers.

James, J. and R. Farmer, eds., 1993, *Spirit, Space & Survival: African American Women in (White) Academe*, New York: Routledge.

Johnson, B. and W. Harvey, 2002, 'The Socialization of Black College Faculty: Implications for Policy and Practice', *The Review of Higher Education* 25 (3): 297-314.

Jones, L., ed., 2000, *Brothers of the Academy: Up and Coming Black Scholars Earning Our Way in Higher Education*, Sterling, Virginia: Stylus Publishers.

Kasonde, M., 2001, 'African American Studies: An African Scholars View', *Contemporary Review* 278 (1624): 272-5.

Kemp, A. D. and R. T. Vinson, 2000, 'Professor James Thaele, American Negroes, and Modernity in 1920s Segregationist South Africa', *African Studies Review* 43 (1): 141.

Korang, K. L., 2003, 'Intellectuals: Colonial', in P. T. Zeleza and D. Eyoh, eds., *Encyclopedia of Twentieth Century African History*, London and New York: Routledge, 268-274.

Korang, K. L., 2004, *Writing Ghana, Imagining Africa: Nation* and *African Modernity*, Rochester, NY: Rochester University Press

Lewis, E., 1995, 'To Turn as on a Pivot: Writing African Americans into a History of Overlapping Diasporas', *American Historical Review* 100 (3): 765-787.

Magubane, Z., 2003, 'The Influence of African American Cultural Practices on South Africa, 1890-1990', in P.T. Zeleza and C. R. Veney, eds., *Leisure in Urban Africa*, Trenton, NJ: Africa World Press, 297-319.

Marable, M., 2000, *Dispatches from the Ebony Tower: Intellectuals Confront the African American Experience*, New York: Columbia University Press.

Masilela, N., 1996, "'The Black Atlantic" and African Modernity in South Africa', *Research in African Literatures*, 27 (4): 88-96.

Mazrui, A.A., 2002, 'Brain Drain Between Counterterrorism and Globalization', *African Issues* XXX (1): 86-89.

Mudimbe, V. Y., 1988, *The Invention of Africa: Gnosis, Philosophy, and the Order of Knowledge*, Bloomington and Indianapolis: Indiana University Press.

Mudimbe, V. Y., 1994, *The Idea of Africa*, Bloomington and Indianapolis: Indiana University Press.

Murdoch, J., 1997, 'Towards a Geography of Heterogeneous Associations', *Progress in Human Geography* 21 (3): 321-337.

Nesbitt, F.N., 2004, *Race for Sanctions: African Americans against Sanctions, 1946-1944*, Bloomington and Indianapolis: Indiana University Press.

Njubi, Nesbitt F., 2003, 'African Intellectuals in the Belly of the Beast: Migration, Identity, and the Politics of Exile', *African Issues* XXX (1): 70-75.

Nzegwu, N., 1996, 'Questions of Identity and Inheritance: A Critical Review of Kwame Anthony Appiah's *In My Father's House*', *Hypatia* 11: 175-201.

Owolabi, K. A., 1995, 'Cultural Nationalism and Western Hegemony: A Review Essay of Appiah's Universalism', *Africa Development* 20: 113-123.

Palmer, C., 2000, 'The African Diaspora', *Black Scholar* 30 (3 /4): 56-59.

Patterson, T. and R. D. G. Kelley, 2000, 'Unfinished Migration: Reflections on the African Diaspora and the Making of the Modern World', *African Studies Review* 43 (1): 11-45.

Roebuck, J. B. and K. S. Murty, 1993, *Historically Black Colleges and Universities: Their Place in American Higher Education*, Westport, CT: Praeger.

Serequeberhan, T., 1996, 'Reflections on *In My Father's House*', *Research in African Literatures* 27: 110-118.

Sims, S. J., 1994, *Diversifying Historically Black Colleges and Universities: A new higher education paradigm*, Westport, CT: Greenwood Press.

Skinner, E. P., 2000, 'Transcending Traditions: African, African-American and African diaspora studies in the 21st century—the past must be the prologue', *Black Scholar* 3 (4) 4-11.

Taiwo, F., 1995, 'Appropriating Africa: An Essay on New Africanist Schools', *Issue: A Journal of Opinion* 23: 39-45.

The Chronicle of Higher Education, 2003, 'Special Report, Closing the Gates', April 11: A12-A25.

Turino, T., 2000, *Nationalists, Cosmopolitans, and Popular Music in Zimbabwe*, Chicago: University of Chicago Press.

Turino, T., 2003, 'The Middle Class, Cosmopolitanism, and Popular Music in Harare, Zimbabwe', in P. T. Zeleza and C. R. Veney, eds., *Leisure in Urban Africa*, Trenton, NJ: Africa World Press, 321-341.

US Census Bureau, 200,) *Profile of the Foreign Born Population in the United States*, Washington, DC: US Census Bureau.

Veney, C. R., 2003, 'The Ties That Bind: The Historic African Diaspora and Africa', *African Issues* XXX (1): 3-8.

Veney, C. R., 2004, 'Building on the Past: African and American Linkages', in P. T. Zeleza and A. Olukoshi, eds., *African Universities in the Twenty-First Century. Vol. 1: Liberalization and Internationalization*, Dakar and Pretoria: CODESRIA Book Series, 263-279.

Washington, V. and W. Harvey, 1989, *Affirmative Rhetoric, Negative Action: African-American and Hispanic Faculty at Predominantly White Institutions*, Washington, DC: George Washington University.

West, M., 2000, '"Unfinished Migrations": Commentary and Response', *African Studies Review* 43: 1: 61-64.

West, M. O. and W. G. Martin, 1997, 'A Future with a Past: Resurrecting the Study of Africa in the Post-Africanist Era', *Africa Today* 44 (3): 297-308.

Willie, C. V. and R. R. Edmonds, eds., 1978, *Black Colleges in America: Challenge, Development, Survival*, New York: Teachers College Press.

Wilson, R., 2002, 'Stacking the Deck for Minority Candidates? Virginia Tech has diversified its faculty, but many professors there doubt the efforts are fair—or even legal', *The Chronicle of Higher Education* July 12: A10.

Wilson, R., 2001, 'A Battle Over Race, Nationality, and Control at a Black University. At Virginia State U., black Americans and black Africans each see bias from the other side', *The Chronicle f Higher Education* July 27: A8.

Zack-Williams, A., 1995, 'Development and Diaspora: Separate Concerns?' *Review of African Political Economy* 65: 349-358.

Zeleza, P. T., 2000, 'African Labor and Intellectual Migrations to the North: Building New Transatlantic Bridges', Paper presented at the African Studies Interdisciplinary Seminar, Center for African Studies, University of Illinois at Urbana-Champaign, February.

Zeleza, P. T., 2002, 'Contemporary African Migrations in a Global Context: Towards Building the Black Atlantic', Paper Presented at the 10[h] CODESRIA General Assembly, Kampala, December.

Zeleza, P. T., 2003, 'Academic Freedom in the Neo-Liberal Order: Governments, Globalization, Governance, and Gender', *Journal of Higher Education in Africa* 1 (1): 149-194.

Zeleza, P. T., 2003, *Rethinking Africa's Globalization. Vol.1: The Intellectual Challenges*, Trenton, NJ: Africa World Press.

Zeleza, P. T., 2005, 'Africa: The Changing Meanings of "African" Culture and Identity', in E. Abiri and H. Thörn, eds., *Horizons: Perspectives on a Global Africa*, Göteborg, Sweden: National Museum of World Cultures and Göteborg University, 31-72.

Zeleza, P. T., forthcoming, 'Knowledge, Globalization and Hegemony: Production of Knowledge in the 21st Century', in S. Sörlin and H. Vessuri, eds., *Knowledge Society and Knowledge Economy: Knowledge, Power and Politics*, New York: Palgrave-Macmillan.

Zeleza, P. T., forthcoming, *Africa and Its Diasporas: Dispersals and Linkages.*

Zeleza, P. T., 'Pan-Africanism', in P. T. Zeleza and D. Eyoh, eds., *Encyclopedia of Twentieth Century African History*, London and New York: Routledge, 415-418.

Zeleza, P. T. and A. Olukoshi, eds., 2004, *African Universities in the Twenty-First Century*, Volume 1: *Liberalization and Internationalization*; Volume 2: *Knowledge and Society*, Dakar: CODESRIA.

Zeleza, Paul Tiyambe, 2006, 'Diaspora Dialogues: Engagements Between Africa and its Diasporas', Keynote address presented at the Conference on the New African Diaspora: Assessing the Pains and Gains of Exile', organized by the Department of Africana Studies, Binghamton University, April 7-9.

Chapter 5

The Problem of Translation in African Studies: The Case of French

Jean-Philippe Dedieu (translated by Maymoena Hallett)

MAN must use MEN language to carry dis message ...SILENCE BABEL TONGUES: recall and recollect BLACK SPEECH.—Bongo Jerry quoted by Edward Kamau Brathwaite, *History of the Voice*, 1984.

From the moment when, because of restrictive French migratory policies and the collapse of the African educational system, many Francophone African researchers have progressively become researchers living in the United States (Dedieu 2002), a question emerges: will their works, increasingly written in English, come back to France? In other words, will their works be translated into French? Will the corpus under which they now fall be offered to Francophone readers? The obvious paradox should not deceive us as regards the significance of this question. It brings to a close the last identifiable possibilities of a space and the resources of voice for African immigrants in France. It assigns translation a challenge which would be wholly its own: the hospitality of a language that welcomes these historically marginalised speakers in a last gesture, or the intention that it disguises: the ostracism of a language which rejects them in an ultimate exclusion. 'The place from where one emits speech, from where one emits the text, from where one emits the voice, from where one emits the scream, that place is immense', specifies Edouard Glissant (1996:29), then adding in a closure, 'but this place one can close it....' Posing the question of translation pertains to a topology of national culture which structures itself as much with the asylum granted to populations in its space of territorial sovereignty as with the welcome reserved for texts in its space of linguistic sovereignty.

The hospitality is in effect not only reduced to the legal norms which set the conditions of stay imposed on nationals of a foreign country, to the professional practices which dismiss to the margins the eternally profane of immigrant origin, to the managerial procedures that stimulate the selective import of specialists by the professional depopulation of southern countries or to the bureaucratic conducts which reject the petitions written by political refugees (see Noirel 1991: 274-290; Bloomaert 2001). In a larger sense, hospitality is an act of translation which composes a comprehension device by the act of listening to a speech and the reception of its speaker in the construction of a common space. It is thus possible to advance an argument according to which, by structural homology, the politics of translation reveal the methods of hospitality which are not only deciphered to those populations allowed to cross the territorial borders of France, but also in view of the texts admitted in translation across her 'literary border'.[1] The analysis of selections made from among innumerable foreign textual indexes permits in fact the revealing of the will of reformation, or the reproduction of the political consensus which institutions try to establish on the migratory question and, by extension, on the minority question.

'Linguistic hospitality' then follows the definition Paul Ricoeur (1999) gives and can hope to remain this 'work of translation, conquered by means of intimate resistances motivated by the fear, even hate, of the foreigner, seen as a threat directed at our own linguistic identity' (15-16). In this ideal sense, translators are as much smugglers as intercessors of foreign literary, legal, economic or political traditions. For example Jean Bazin, Alban Bensa, Pierre Bourdieu or Denise Paulme, sociologists, philosophers or anthropologists have thus, as translators or editorial collection leaders, also directly collaborated on this strategic asylum through the mobilisation of their linguistic, cultural and social capital. They have allowed for no longer having to 'converse from different linguistic hedges' (Mudimbe 1994: 3) according to the formula of Valentin Mudimbe but for a dilation of the places of knowledge and recognition. However, as generous as this definition of linguistic hospitality is, it should not conceal the marginal position of the translator's function in the processes of translation which cross editorial policies, the logic of economy and institutional practices. The incorporation of foreign texts in a national language pertains to the constituting of state-controlled symbolism and to political consensus. The naturalisation of literary taste, economic preference or civic sensitivities is linked to these practices which are concealed from public attention and scientific observation. The translation is in effect an institutional ritual all the more magical since the name and the translation copyright are subordinate to those of the authors (Venuti 1995: 353) and an extreme opacity conceals the editorial strategies of translation (Dirkx 1999: 74).

To the *mystery* of social movements stemming from immigration which succeed in making themselves recognised by public opinion corresponds as much to the *enigma* of translation which according to the usual formula, *finds its public*. To mobilise an opinion or to find a public: these two configurations of communication have in common the offering of resources of discursive practices and collective identification and therefore, the capacity to generate innovations or to consolidate orthodoxies. 'As translation constructs a domestic representation for a foreign text and culture,' notes Lawrence Venuti (1998: 68),

> it simultaneously constructs a domestic subject, a position of intelligibility that is also an ideological position, informed by the codes and canons, interests and agendas of certain domestic social groups ... A calculated choice of foreign texts and translation strategy can change or consolidate literary canons, conceptual paradigms, research methodologies...

For these reasons, the advent or the postponement of a translation is also the outcome of the economic as well as political assessment of its legitimacy in a national context.

The national identity which consolidates itself by the selective domestication and consecration of foreign texts is well exemplified in French history. If the construction of its political sovereignty was built in the age of classicism by the rejection of Spanish and Italian barbarisms and the appropriation of Greek and Roman classics, the ideological constitution of the nation-state leaned during the nineteenth century towards the annexation of texts intended to offer it a conceptual frame. The introduction to the French of the works of Vico by J. Michelet or those of Herder by E. Quinet are revealing of translation practices which articulated the formation of national culture and the reflection on national identity in a paradoxical dynamic of extra-national import. The constitution of cultural capital and its direct corollary, linguistic capital, allowed France in return to distribute the imperialism of her universals. In this way, the imperial process of discursive colonisation can be interpreted as the creation of an auxiliary linguistic space. This aim at linguistic homogenisation by the recusal of African languages and the imposition of the French language permitted the creation of a subsidiary rhetorical space which for the purpose of a simplified exercise of structural subordination, purely and simply did away with the symbolic and material costs of translation.[2]. The perversity of this historical process has rendered speakers of the former colonial empires 'translated men', according to the expression of Salman Rushdie, continually searching for legitimacy and literary consecration (Casanova 1999:192-193).

The economic argument regularly presented by the consecration authorities defending their selective procedures of translation reveals the liberalisation of the economic sectors of publishing which has undermined the durability of the French publishing sector, has accentuated the usual shifts of translations and has led to a true process of de-translation (Julien et al. 1999). The apparent rationality of this argument, however, tends to overlook the fact that the financial logic intensifies the political logic at work in the processes of translation (Bourdieu 1999). The belated French publication of Eric Hobsbawm's book *Age of Extremes: The Short Twentieth Century 1914-1991*, which appeared in Great Britain in 1994, is an example particularly remarkable since the historian's previous works were mostly available in French. Whereas this book was translated or in the process of being translated into the majority of European Union languages, France was one of the rare countries whose editorial structures ruled this out (see Hobsbawm 1999: 28-29). The special edition of the magazine *Le Débat* devoted to this postponement is revealing of the correlation between financial and ideological logics. In his apologia, Pierre Nora who *represented* French publishing under the title of collection director at Gallimard itemised the accounting and commercial reasons which had led to the recusal of this editorial project before underlining the preoccupation which he had had of being in conformity with the civic sensitivity *of the moment*: the context of reception. 'France having been the country longest and the most deeply stalinized', he wrote, 'decompression, at the same time, accentuated the hostility towards everything which, closely or from afar, reminds one of this former age of philosovietism or procommunism, including the most open marxism' (Nora 1997: 94). The work, which was finally translated owing to a partnership between the Belgian publishers *Complexe* and *Le Monde Diplomatique* permitted a renewal of the experience without national relocation in the case in point. Furthermore, in 2000, the newspaper associated itself with Fayard in order to naturalise into French Edward Said's *Culture and Imperialism*, a founding reference in Anglo-American postcolonial research.

In light of the stakes assigned to translation in the constitution of the national habitus, it is important to detail the sociological determinants which have driven French researchers to disregard the advances made in American research, to which are now linked the works of African researchers who have settled in the United States. Since the independence of former colonies in Africa, the dialogue which had been established between French and American Africanist research has been considerably reduced. The emergence since the 1960s of massive immigration from African countries formerly under colonial administration, from which was constructed Africanist research, and the consolidation at the turn of the 1980s of an institutional racism in France drove Africanist researchers to determine themselves according to modes that reflect generational, epistemological and also linguistic divides.

From One Generation to the Next

The generational divide finds its source in an increased professionalisation of research in France, in particular of Africanist research. If this field of study emerged at the turn of the last century under the impulse of colonial administrators, subsequent generations were closely implicated in a 'militant and teleological perspective' (Bernault 2001: 128) in the struggle for independence. This found support in the 'colonial situation' as analysed in a founding text by Georges Balandier and resulted in active involvement in the process of decolonisation. Until the 1970s, this engagement remained a constant in French Africanist research, fostered in the main by Marxist researchers (Terray 1992). It was however rapidly confronted by post-independence disenchantments, by the African authoritarian regimes, by the undermining of academic liberties and by the constant support of France for these autocracies in spite of the stillborn hope of the accession to power of François Mitterrand (Bayart 1984). This disillusionment was as much a reason to question the militancy with which the postcolony had been stranded as it was to leave a deeply altered land. Following the example of more belated withdrawals from the African continent by researchers such as Gérard Althabe, Marc Augé or Marc Abélès who promoted French anthropology (Abélès 1999), Georges Balandier (2002) analysed his own defection as the desire not to be compromised in the inextricable relations which tied France to her former colonies. He insisted on the fact that his withdrawal was less linked to the 'regret of an extinct Africa, or nearly extinct since the 1960s, than the feeling that a form of treason was fermenting in passions nourished in post-war years' (Balandier 2002:4).

However, if the African political situation placed French researchers who specialised in this geographical area in an uncomfortable position, the French political situation furthermore placed them in a delicate situation. Indeed, the turn of the 1980s saw a dramatic rise of xenophobia in France which coincided with the reinforcement of laws imposing greater migratory control on African migrants. This configuration constituted a major scientific and professional challenge to Africanists in that this social circumstance was now imposed on citizens of countries where they had made their debut and gained experience and legitimacy; in that it was exercised within the national space of the institutional practice of their profession; and finally in that it applied to students come to train in France, and often within their own research institutions. In spite of this trinity, which would have legitimised a more active commitment, Africanist institutions revealed a remarkable slowness in involving themselves in the migratory question. The bitter note written by Emmanuel Terray (1986) at the end of a symposium organised in the mid-1980s by the French Association of Anthropologists on the theme 'Towards a pluricultural France' is revealing of this French reticence:

> Considering the object and the stake of the symposium—the problems posed by emigration and cultural intermixing, the rise of racism—why do these prevail? Why have the internal quarrels of the profession taken over? Why especially this indifference on the part of the great majority? One must go back to the reasoning expressed here three years ago by the initiators of the enterprise. I will only speak on my behalf; I had estimated at the time that the progress of intolerance and xenophobia in France should question and unsettle anthropologists particularly for several reasons. First of all, the victims of this growing xenophobia are above all nationals of countries where many amongst us have worked: a certain feeling of responsibility towards them seemed natural to me. Moreover, anthropology can be defined as an effort to understand the Foreigner: from the relationship our society entertains with him, we should have, so it seems to me, asked to intervene in our capacity as 'experts on difference and otherness'. In either case, and notwithstanding ideological and political divides, this was the profession that should have been appealed to ... at the origin of the ethnological vocation, there was often a passionate attention turned to 'third-world' and decolonisation problems; it was at the time of the Algerian war, and a considerable number of future anthropologists were more or less intensely committed militants. For all these reasons, there actually was then, at least among the

youngest generation, a community of anthropologists who felt or believed itself invested with a kind of clerical function, as soon as the problems of the other, the foreigner, difference, xenophobia and racism were raised. Our illusion was to think that which was true twenty-five years ago is still true today (Terray 1986:11-13).

Since this disillusioned hint, anthropologists, mostly those of Africanist training, have investigated the field of migratory research. Rémy Bazenguissa-Ganga, Christophe Daum, Alain Morice, Christian Poiret, Catherine Quiminal, Jean Schmitz and Mahamet Timera have worked, among others, on the transnational communities of Congolese, Malian and Senegalese, notably Soninke, migrants particularly. Didier Fassin, Jean-Pierre Dozon and Laurent Vidal gave to their works dedicated to the anthropology of health in Africa a comparative perspective by being interested in the problems of health of African migrants on French soil. At the end of the 1990s they expressed some clearly radical positions in the collective works which brought them together (Fassin et al. 1997:278; Balibar et al. 1999:123).

An Epistemological Divide

This brief generational outline of Africanist research cannot, however, fully account for the various stances taken in the field of research. Some theoretical orientations have also indirectly impacted on the positions taken by researchers on the migratory question. Works on ethnic groups coordinated by Jean-Loup Amselle and Elikia M'Bokolo (1985:225) and then by Jean-Pierre Chrétien and Gérard Prunier (1989:435) were important moments in French research for better understanding by means of an act of deconstruction the manipulation of this concept within the French colonial context. The impact this research had on the construction of Africanist epistemology was not without repercussion for their field of application within the French migratory context. Mistrust of reified adherences, reticence towards the use of ethnic and racial categories in French public or scientific discourse as much as distancing from American multiculturalism can also be understood as the basis for this theoretical configuration whose validity has been cruelly confirmed at the time of the Rwandan genocide and, more recently, during the Ivory Coast conflict (Chrétien 1997: 400; Vidal 1991: 180). Relying on his previous work, Jean-Loup Amselle (1996: 179) demonstrated through a reading of Foucault the aporia of the French system of representation which pretends not to recognise the rights of minority groups while founding the constitution of its history on 'race wars'. Even if his research is read as an attempt to understand the failure of a republican model in crisis, it nevertheless puts *French assimilation* and *American multiculturalism* back to back.

It is through the diffraction of these theoretical orientations that one can read the uneasy reception of American works, most notably the negative reactions to the translation of *Black Athena* by Martin Bernal whose aim is to demonstrate the concealment of the African roots of Ancient Egypt, and the collective editorial initiative which in France backfired on the American release. Published in the United States in 1987, the first volume of *Black Athena* was translated by the Presses

Universitaires de France in 1996 in a general collection edited by two philosophers, Etienne Balibar and Dominique Lecourt. Without provoking in France a welcome as passionate as it did in the United States, a response initiated by Jean-Pierre Chrétien, François-Xavier Fauvelle-Aymard and Claude-Hélène Perrot (2000: 402) was nevertheless forthcoming. Gathering more than twenty mainly French and American authors, with a complete absence of contributions from African researchers in a work supposedly countering ethnocentrism, *L'Afrocentrisme* is unfortunately representative of French research that does not succeed in setting up a true dialogue with Southern research, only a contradictory one, and participates in fact in the reproduction of the relative resentment of African researchers towards their French colleagues.

This strong French mobilisation around Afrocentrism tends by analogy to discredit the African studies done in the United States both in terms of recruitment and in terms of work. It integrates with a reductive French reading of the American academic field interpreted as the basis of a reified communitarianism. If the corpus of *black studies, cultural studies* or *postcolonial studies* has in fact remained perfectly suspicious, the most stinging attacks led by American conservative intellectuals (Allan Bloom [1987], Dinesh D'Souza [1992], or Arthur Schlesinger [1993]) against multiculturalism were translated into French soon after their original publication. The enthusiastic welcome reserved for these publications in public debate and relayed by excellent media coverage (Granjon 1994) reflects, via the translatory practice, the reproduction of French 'spectral universalism' (Schor 2001: 48).

In this context of mistrust, Africanists have hardly participated in the extensive dialogue between Anglo-American and French academic research (Coquery-Vidrovitch 1997). Work undertaken in the United States has been received with a scepticism which penalises accordingly comparative research which could have been conducted about the modes of integration of immigrants in France and in the United States (Collomp 1999; Green 1999). Postcolonial studies conducted in the United States are largely unappreciated in France. They remain less translated even though an 'impression of a neutralization of the critical discourse in France' (Piriou and Sibeud 1997: 12) is felt by some French researchers, as is the selective construction of a 'truth compatible with patriotic paradigms' (Liauzu 2002: 53). The gap remains immense in spite of sudden and fragmentary attempts at rehabilitation (see Ghasarian 1998).

This contradictory transatlantic reception is not new. It highlights the relative French tension towards the influence American critical works exert on its history. The analysis brought forward in *Cahier d'Etudes Africaines* (1980) of William B. Cohen's *The French Encounter with Africans: White Response to Blacks, 1530-1880*, published in 1980—some years before the work by Henri Brunschwig, *Noirs et Blancs dans l'Afrique Noire Française*—is laudatory of its contribution to the scientific racism at work in France yet it blames Cohen (186-187) for importing American categories:

> although it is difficult, it specifies, to criticize a study which is valid and scientific as a whole, one could however quibble with Professor Cohen who, in writing within the

American context, perhaps has the tendency to give too much importance to the concept of racism, detecting it where one would rather note the influence of economic and social factors.

When the book was published in French in 1981 (Cohen 1981), a review, this time damning, in the pages of the daily *Le Monde* sanctions in a nationalistic tone the scientific quality itself of the work:

> [T]he author of *Français et Africains* is only interested in the hexagonal racism between 1550 and 1880. But his obvious desire to attack French culture as a whole leads to an overflow of the significance of this period, making xenophobia in general, and the horror of Blacks, in particular, the structural elements, irremovable from our national tradition, a sort of anthropological malediction (Todd 1982: 16).

If the works dedicated to Africa continue to be counted and commented on in scientific journals, the more specifically postcolonial corpus is hardly in the same position. Alice Conklin's (1997) *A Mission to Civilize: the Republican Idea of Empire in France and West Africa, 1895-1930* was the object of a critical treatment at the very least elusive: 'this book does not escape the clichés of a certain American school, less historic than sociological, whose shortcomings do not fail to irritate those who do not have the sensitivity of a seraglio' (*Cahiers d'Etudes Africaines* 1980: 151). The absence of translations into French of works which have marked Anglo-American research in the last twenty years, such as those of, inter alia, Frederick Cooper, Ann L. Stoler, Anthony Appiah, Paul Gilroy and Stuart Hall, is particularly notable. At the heart of this research, Francophone African and Caribbean researchers, such as Irène Assiba d'Almeida, Manthia Diawara, Valentin Mudimbe or Michel-Rolph Trouillot, who having immigrated to the United States, occupy a peculiar position, having 'change[d] their language' (Mudimbe 1994: 165) and practising 'the pain and the perverse pleasure of writing in a second language' (Trouillot 1995: xv).

A Linguistic Recess

Efficient articulation between scientific and migratory policies has in fact contributed to the erosion, to the benefit of the United States, of the place of France in the geographical area traditionally under its influence. This diplomacy, based on scientific exchanges, pertains not only to the relative autonomy of American research, which has hence become both international and national, but also to the forced indexing and dependence of French research on the latter.[3] Despite the fact that French researchers are particularly aware of the powerful ties between research and politics—since these are at the very origin of French ethnology—the reception reserved for African researchers in American research establishments is more than often considered the basis for minority domestic politics which has the tendency to diminish the credibility of this research and thereby reduces the incitement to translation. In an unfortunate formulation, Jean-Loup Amselle (2001) in his latest work, supposes that 'Africanism as a discipline is more and more threatened by the African-Americans and the Africans who claim their place within the Western academic system on the basis of their phenotypical appearance' (108-109).

This critique, which is regularly expressed to counter the demands of African researchers for a better representation in establishments of French research, tends to make one forget that whereas the North American continent brings together international research and national research by offering a particularly calculated hospitality to Southern researchers, France withdrew into its own domestic territory, henceforth amply provincialised. Social sciences are particularly victim to a strong research pauperisation which contributes to rigidifying the national character of their scientific market. While the recent official report by Maurice Godelier on *L'Etat des Sciences de l'Homme et de la Société en France* ('The State of Human Sciences and Society in France') (2002) noted the weak hexagonal comparative or interdisciplinary approach, it also specified that the considerable absence of translations into French of foreign works effected a crippled scientific deliberation and the withdrawal of researchers into their own domestic market. Conversely, the difficulties that French researchers encounter in exporting their works are also sizeable. Preoccupied with Anglo-American supremacy to the detriment of other languages, and constrained to a nearly compulsory bilingualism, the Conseil National du Développement des Sciences Humaines et Sociales (1999) nevertheless recognised the necessity of adapting itself, with public help, to translation and the recruitment of scientific translators. The new linguistic balance of power places speakers and more specifically French researchers in a position which appears to close history by projecting them into auto-translation.

This unpublished linguistic asymmetry is paralleled by an asymmetry in terms of discourse. If the canon of African studies has completed the canon of African-American studies in order to give the latter the academic legitimacy it was lacking politically, a critical space has as a result amply opened itself in the United States. This rhetorical space paradoxically bases itself not only on the contribution of French theories, acclimatised in crossing the Atlantic while remaining marginal in France (Duell 2000), but also on the recruitment of researchers transatlantically naturalised while they remained inadmissible in France. The geopolitical power of translation found at work in these strategies which come, via physical and textual translation, to participate in the narrative construction of a minority discourse in the United States. Conversely, the French institution's capacity for resistance in hearing this discourse is found even in the absence of translation into French of the postcolonial canon, whether written in English by Anglophone authors or by Francophone writers become Anglophone. The condition of the exiled intellectual is two-fold, since the linguistic and geographical exile is enclosed in one last exile, one last grief: the impossibility of returning in translation into their own language or the language of their first scientific works.

The rare translations of the corpus of *black studies*, *post-colonial studies* or *cultural studies* are paradoxically typical of researchers or collections occupying a relatively off-centre position in the eyes of the French Africanist institution. *True France* (1995) by Herman Lebovics (1995) was published in a collection edited by one of the main French immigration historians, Gérard Noiriel. In 1996, the work by James Clifford *The Predicament of Culture*, published in 1988 in the United States, was published by the Paris École Nationale Supérieure des Beaux Arts, under the patronage of a philosopher, Yves Michaud (Clifford 1996). Paul Gilroy's *Black Atlantic* was published by a tiny publishing house specialising in music history ten years after its original publication (Gilroy 2003).

Cultural ferrymen can also be found equally among researchers or publishers accumulating social and linguistic capital distributed between the United States and France, and on the African continent. In 2001, *In Search of Africa* by Manthia Diawara was finally translated into French by the publishing house Présence Africaine, a tireless broker of the African diaspora. In 2002, Thomas C. Spear, professor at CUNY and translator of Edouard Glissant (1999), published with Karthala a selection of texts (Spear 2002) which brought together contributions from researchers and French-speaking authors, particularly those settled in the United-States. Through a series of negotiations and adjustments, the title of the collection was successively *De la pollution culturelle française* ('The pollution of French culture'), then *Traces de la culture française* ('Traces of French culture'), before settling for *La culture française vue d'ici et d'ailleurs* ('French culture as seen from here and elsewhere'). It is not the least of paradoxes of this work to have been prefaced by these words by Edouard Glissant:

> The French language is emboldened by these commentaries, this gossip, these confessions, torments and vague consents which demarcate its uses in the world. It has thickened nowhere and is contaminable everywhere, there lies its privilege. It serves everyone and everyone is free to revoke it or to incline it towards other desires (Spear 2002: 3).

It is indeed these 'other desires' which are mobilised in the partnership established between the French publisher Karthala and the SEPHIS, a program of cooperation on history and development funded by the Netherlands Ministry of Development Cooperation for 'encouraging the formation of a South-South network directed towards comparative historical research on long-term processes of change'. This alliance has allowed for the introduction in France, with a delay of more than twenty years, of the founding works of the group of the *Subaltern Studies* initiated by, among others, Ranajit Guha and Gayatri Spivak, translator into English of some works by Jacques Derrida (see Derrida 1976). It is two African researchers educated in France but now connected to American institutions, Mamadou Diouf and Ousmane Kane, who, by commencing, in the case of the former, publishing work, and, in the case of the latter, translation work, have offered French-speaking readers this important work (Diouf 1999). According to the long preface written by Mamadou Diouf, the choice of this translation presents itself as the will to undertake on behalf of African historiography a critical approach similar to that presented for Indian historiography. By extension, this enterprise permits itself to be endowed with the theoretical resources necessary for the dissipation of the colonial inheritance weighing on the construction of African history, in Africa or in France. For lack of being perfectly naturalised, its reading is already a beginning of hospitality. It has often been noticed that the Franco-American dialogue has been marred by misreadings. Prior to misreading, however, the chance of a proper reading should be offered.

Notes

1. In a sociological study devoted to translation, Pascale Casanova (1999: 179-180) emphasises that: 'The consecration, in the form of recognition by the autonomous critique, is a sort of crossing over of the literary border. To cross this invisible line means to be submitted to a sort of transformation ... The consecration of a text is the metamorphosis, almost magical, of plain material into "gold", into absolute literary value...'
2. Henri Brunschwig (1982: 105-123) has well demonstrated to what extent the training of indigenous interpreters is vital in the enterprise of colonisation. Within the contemporary European context, the linguistic heterogeneity of the European Union poses numerous difficulties for the construction of a true political identity. The importance of budgets allocated to the translation of deliberations and official documents thus definitely consecrates, by economic necessity and political lobbying, the supremacy of English.
3. In the social sciences in 1997, 17.2 percent of quotations in scholarly American publications came from foreign works, against 74.6 percent for the French for a worldwide average of 39 percent (Gingras 2002: 38).

References

Abélès, M., 1999, 'How the Anthropology of France has Changed the Anthropology in France: Assessing New Directions in the Field', *Cultural Anthropology* 14 (3): 404-408.

Amselle, J.-L., 1996, *Vers un multiculturalisme français: l'empire de la coutume*, Paris: Aubier.

Amselle, J.-L., 2001, *Branchements. Anthropologie de l'universalité des cultures*, Paris: Flammarion.

Amselle, J.-L. and E. M'Bokolo, 1985, *Au cœur de l'ethnie: Ethnie, tribalisme et Etat en Afrique*, Paris: Syros.

Balandier, G., 2002, 'De l'Afrique à la surmodernité un parcours d'anthropologue. Entretien', *Le Débat* January-February: 118: 4.

Balibar, É., M. Chemillier-Gendreau, J. Costa-Leroux, and E. Terray, 1999, *Sans-papiers: l'archaïsme fatal*, Paris, La Découverte.

Bayart, J.-F., 1984, *La politique africaine de François Mitterrand*, Paris: Karthala.

Bernault, F., 2001, 'L'Afrique et la modernité des sciences socials', *Vingtième siècle* 70.

Bloom, A., 1987, *L'âme désarmée*, translated by Paul Alexandre, Paris, Julliard.

Bloomaert, J., 2001, 'Investigating Narrative Inequality: African Asylum Seekers' Stories in Belgium', *Discourse and Society* 12 (4): 413-450.

Bourdieu, P., 1999, 'Une révolution conservatrice dans l'édition', *Actes de la Recherche en Sciences Sociales* 126-127: 3-28.

Brunschwig, H., 1982, *Noirs et Blancs dans l'Afrique noire française ou comment le colonisé devient colonisateu: 1870-1914*, Paris: Flammarion.

Cahiers d'Etudes Africaines, 1980.

Casanova, P., 1999, *La République mondiale des Lettres*, Paris: Le Seuil.

Chrétien, J.-P., 1997, *Le défi de l'ethnisme: Rwanda et Burundi, 1990-1996*, Paris: Karthala.

Chrétien, J.-P. and G. Prunier, eds., 1986, *Les Ethnies ont une histoire*, Paris: Karthala.

Claudine V., 1991, *Sociologie des passions: Rwanda, Côte d'Ivoire*, Paris, Karthala.

Clifford, J., 1996, *Malaise dans la culture : l'ethnographie, la littérature et l'art au XXe siècle*, translated by Marie-Anne Sichère, Paris: École nationale supérieure des Beaux-Arts.

Cohen, W. B., 1981, *Français et Africains: les Noirs dans le regard des Blancs: 1530-1880*, translated by Camille Garnier, Paris: Gallimard.

Collomp, C., 1999, 'Immigrants, Labor Markets, and the State, a Comparative Approach: France and the United States, 1880-1930', *The Journal of American History* 86 (1): 41-66.

Conklin, A. L., 1997, *A Mission to Civilize: The Republican Idea of Empire in France and West Africa, 1895-1930*, Stanford: Stanford University Press.

Conseil National du Développement des Sciences Humaines et Sociales, 1999, *Rapport annuel d'activité*, Paris, Ministère de l'Education nationale, de la Recherche et de la Technologie

Coquery-Vidrovitch, C., 1997, 'Réflexions comparées sur l'historiographie africaniste de langue française et anglaise', *Politique africaine* juin: 91-100.

D'Souza, D., 1992, *L'éducation contre les libertés: politiques de la race et du sexe sur les campus américains*, translated by Philippe Delamare, Paris: Gallimard.

Dedieu, J.-P., 2002, 'US Exit, African Voices and Francophone Loyalty', *African Issues* XXX (1): 66-9.

Derrida, Jacques, 1976, *Of Grammatology*, translated by G. C. Spivak, Baltimore: Johns Hopkins University Press.

Diouf, M., ed., 1999, *L'historiographie indienne en débat: colonialisme, nationalisme et sociétés postcoloniales*, translated by O. Kane, Paris: Karthala; Amsterdam: SEPHIS.

Dirkx, P., 1999, 'Les obstacles à la recherche sur les stratégies editorials', *Actes de la Recherche en Sciences Sociales* 126/127.

Duell, J., 2000, 'Assessing the literary; intellectual boundaries in French and American literary studies', in M. Lamont and L. Thévenot, eds.,, *Rethinking Comparative Cultural Sociology: Repertoires of Evaluation in France and the United States*, New York: Cambridge University Press, 94-124.

Fassin, D., A. Morice, and C. Quiminal, eds., 1997, *Les lois de l'inhospitalité: Les politiques de l'immigration à l'épreuve des sans-papiers*, Paris, La Découverte.

Fauvelle-Aymar, F.-X., J.-P. Chrétien and C.-Hélène Perrot, eds., 2000, *Afrocentrismes: l'histoire des Africains entre Egypte et Amérique*, Paris: Karthala.

François J., T. Marchaisse, M. Gendreau-Massaloux and M. Prigent, 1999, 'Lettre ouverte sur la politique de la traduction', *Esprit* 253: 108-118.

Ghasarian, C., 1998, 'A propos des épistémologies postmodernes', *Ethnologie française* XXVIII (4): 563-577.

Gilroy, P., 2003, *L' Atlantique noir: Modernité et double conscience*, translated by Jean-Philippe Henquel, Paris: Kargo.

Gingras, Y., 2002, 'Les formes spécifiques de l'internationalité du champ scientifique', *Actes de la Recherche en Sciences Sociales* 141-142: 31-45.

Glissant, E., 1996, *Introduction à une Poétique du divers*, Paris: Gallimard.

Glissant, E., 1999, *Faulkner, Mississipi*, translated by B. Lewis and T. C. Spear, New York: Farra, Straus and Giroux.

Godelier, M., 2002, *L'Etat des Sciences de l'Homme et de la Société en France et leur rôle dans la construction de l'espace européen de la recherché*, Paris: La Documentation Française.

Granjon, M.-C., 1994, 'Le regard en biais. Attitudes françaises et multiculturalisme américain (1990-1993)', *Vingtième siècle. Revue d'histoire* 43 (July-September): 18-29.

Green, N. L., 1999, '*Le Melting-Pot*: Made in America, Produced in France', *The Journal of American History* 86 (3): 1188-1208.

Hobsbawm, E., 1999, 'L'Age des extrêmes' échappe à ses censeurs', *Le monde diplomatique* September: 28-29.

Lebovics, H., 1995, *La vraie France: les enjeux de l'identité culturelle, 1900-1945*, translated by G. de Laforcade, Paris: Belin.

Liauzu, C., 2002, 'Interrogations sur l'histoire française de la colonization', *Genèse* 46 (March): 53.

Mudimbe, V., 1994, *Les corps glorieux des mots et des êtres: esquisse d'un jardin africain à la bénédictine*, Paris: Présence africaine.

Mudimbé, V., 1994, *Les corps glorieux des mots et des êtres*, Paris: Présence Africaine.

Noirel, G., 1991, *La tyrannie du national*, Paris: Calmann-Lévy.

Nora, P., 1997, 'Traduire: nécessité et difficultés', *Le Debat* 93 (January-February): 93-95.

Piriou, A. and E. Sibeud, eds., 1997, *L'Africanisme en questions*, Paris: Centre d'Etudes Africaines et Ecole des Hautes Etudes en Sciences Sociales.

Ricoeur, P., 1999, 'La paradigme de la traduction', *Esprit* 253: 15-16.

Schlesinger, A. M., 1993, *La désunion de l'Amérique: réflexions sur une société multiculturelle*, translated by Françoise Burgess, Paris: Liana Levi.

Schor, N., 2001, 'The crisis of French Universalism', *Yale French Studies* 1000: 43-64.

Spear, Thomas C., ed., 2002, *La culture française vue d'ici et d'ailleurs: treize auteurs témoignent*, Paris: Karthala.

Terray, E., 1986, 'A propos des anthropologies', *Journal des anthropologues* 25: 11-13.

Terray, E., 1992, 'French Marxist Anthropology', in V. Mudimbe, ed., *The Surreptitious Speech. "Présence Africaine" and the Politics of Otherness 1947-1987*, Chicago, The University of Chicago Press, 249-256.

Todd, Emmanuel, 1982, *Le Monde*, 19 February: 16.

Trouillot, M.-R., 1995, *Silencing the Past: Power and the Production of History*, Boston: Beacon Press.

Venuti, L., 1995, *The Translator's Invisibility: A History of Translation*, London: Routledge.

Venuti, L., 1998, *The Scandals of Translation: Towards an Ethics of Difference*, London: Routledge.

II

African Studies in Regional Contexts

Chapter 6

African Studies:
France and the United States

Bogumil Jewsiewicki
(translated from the French by Pius Adesanmi)

The constitution of specialised knowledges on African societies into a domain of university research occurred first in Great Britain. The doctrine of indirect rule, which functioned through locals, facilitated access of the colonised to higher education in Europe as well as the United States and also allowed, subsequently, for the founding of universities in the colonies. The imperative of training 'native' manpower for churches, the civil service, teaching, and the intensification of this trend through the intervention of American churches accentuated its utilitarian character. African Anthropology as well as African History was thus engaged early by university scholars, alongside non-academic actors: administrators, missionaries, etc. They did not shy away from practical objectives; from the 1950s, studies of the past were invoked to support the recognition of the natives' capacity for self-governance and independence.

The International African Institute (IAI) was founded in London in 1926 in the spirit of collaboration among colonial powers. Its initial aim was to deploy knowledge in the service of education, based on linguistic and ethnographic research. At the end of the Second World War, for which the Germans were blamed and isolated, the IAI became first a site of collaboration between old colonials who were soon replaced by Western academics, and later by the first African scholars to work on Africa. French actors close to colonial circuits played an important role in this context.

The Institute published *Africa*, the main international journal on Africa, especially in anthropology. In 1960, the *Journal of African History*, launched by Cambridge University Press to prepare the publication of *Cambridge History of* Africa—which was to take another twenty years to appear—opened up overseas studies (especially oriental studies) to research on Africa. When the School of Oriental and African Studies was founded at the University of London (in 1939 through the transformation of the School of Oriental Studies whose new Africa department was initially funded by the Rockefeller Foundation), several British anthropologists and sociologists were already engaged in research on contemporary Africa, due in part to the significant presence of white Anglophone communities in Africa (especially in South Africa and Rhodesia). These communities considered themselves 'African' and their interests were thus linked to a modernisation imbricated with urbanisation and industrialisation. Between the Rhodes-Livingstone Institute in Northern Rhodesia (Zambia) and the University of Manchester emerged a dynamic anthropology of contemporary Africa which influenced Georges Balandier (1952), whose methodological inaugural essay was published in *Africa* in 1952.

Africa, Object of Study

With some delay, France as well as the United States joined the ferment of university research on Africa, each approaching the subject in its own way and for its own peculiar reasons. However, half a century later, one can now acknowledge the influence of American policy on the institutional directions which disciplinary contributions in African studies took around a cultural axis. The experience of the Second World War and the environment of the Cold War led the American establishment to a preoccupation with the weakness of knowledge generation in American universities with regard to the diverse societies and cultures of the world. This concern gave birth to Area Studies programmes, initiated in 1946 by the Carnegie Corporation and embraced by the major private foundations. To establish Area Studies programmes and promote research on areas which, altogether, covered the world with the exception of the United States, several universities, including the biggest ones, received private and government funding, sourced among others by the defence sector and the intelligence services (in 1944, the Council on African Affairs held a conference, 'For a New Africa', in New York). This explains why the first generation of Africanists, almost exclusively white, was later bitterly criticised by African Americans for having served 'imperialist' interests.

In the contexts of reconstruction aid to Western Europe and the Atlantic Charter, the big American foundations also invested in university training structures and in research on the old continent of Europe. Fernand Braudel benefited from this for the 6th section of the Ecole pratique des hautes études (later to become the École des hautes études en sciences sociales, EHESS). This later led to the creation of interdisciplinary centres, each of which focussed on a geographical area. One notable component was the Centre d'etudes africaines, the major training site of French academic Africanists, with the exception of political scientists.

If we leave aside former colonial administrators (Hubert Deschamps, Yves Person, and Robert Cornevin, who never held a university position), the first generation of French Africanists—Georges Balandier, Gilles Sautter, Paul Mercier, Raymond Mauny, and Henri Brunschwig—comprised few individuals who were rapidly promoted to the status of trainers and masters. The second generation chose sub-Saharan Africa mostly through an anti-colonial engagement often motivated by the rejection of the Algerian war, after an initial, often accidental contact with sub-Saharan Africa while working as expatriate interns during military service, for example. Many of them established their African careers in the context of ORSTOM that had just emerged from a colonial utilitarianism against which it often revolted (its predecessor, the Office de recherche scientifique coloniale, was created in 1943; in 1947, it offered Balandier its support for his first field work). Claude Messailloux recalls that the choice of Africa in his own case was an accident due to his knowledge of English and the availability of funds for fieldwork.

Paradoxically, this generation which conferred a global reach on African studies never received any specific training in this domain. Even at the doctoral level, the degree is made up of disciples. Today, on the verge of retirement, they have controlled the field for a good quarter of a century, contrary to their few masters whose institutional influence was short lived. Despite the fact that the Centre d'études africaines of the EHESS and the centres at University of Paris-1 and Paris-7 were created by geographers, historians, and a sociologist, anthropology was the discipline of choice of French African studies in the 1970s and 1980s. It was fashioned as economics more because of its roots in Althusserian Marxism than any real focus on economics as a subject of study. It was also an anthropology practised—especially with regard to its luminaries—by philosophers who trained at the École normale, rue d'Ulm, where Louis Althusser was then teaching.

Even if historians were not trained at the doctoral level at the EHESS, the arrival of Catherine Coquery-Vidrovitch on the scene, the entry of Elikia M'Bokolo, Jean-Louis Triaud's links with the Maison des sciences de l'Homme or those of Jean-Pierre and Françoise Raison with the Centre d'Etudes Africaines placed the Centre at the heart of French Africanism in the 1970s and 1980s. The Centre publishes *Cahiers d'études africaines*, the major French Africanist journal with a global reputation. But, in France, African history developed essentially outside of EHESS, especially in the 1980s when the attraction of economic anthropology began to wane.

Contrary to what obtains in the Anglo-Saxon world, the history of the precolonial period has never been successfully established in France as a distinct methodological, or even simply empirical field. Despite the originality of the contribution of anthropologists such as Marc Auge, Jean Bazin, Michel Izard, Emmanuel Terray; despite the reputation of the historians working at the Centre de recherches africaines of Paris-1—Chretien, Person, Perrot—no school emerged. Devise attempted an experiment of articulation of African archaeology and history which did not survive his departure. The orientation of this centre was then close to the 'usable past' current of Terence Ranger and Jan Vansina's 'oral tradition as history', famous everywhere but almost unknown in France, except at Paris-1. At Paris-7, under the aegis of Catherine Coquery-Vidrovitch, African history took a comparative turn, inspired by theses of underdevelopment and third worldism, before moving towards the longitudinal study of development. In the last few years, Aix-en-Provence, which previously limited itself to the history of the neocolonial tradition, has acquired a reputation in the history of the Muslim societies of West Africa.

French political scientists working on Africa have for long been caught in the institutional and political web occasioned by the transfer of colonial institutions to governmental cooperation with Africa. In the 1980s, a revolt of young researchers led by Jean-François Bayart radically altered the landscape and resulted in the founding of a new journal, *Politique Africaine*. A very dynamic group emerged around the ideas of a historian, Michel de Certeau. This group, whose members worked mostly at the *Centre d'etudes et de relations internationales* of the *Fondation nationale des sciences politiques*, were very critical of the French African policy of that period. After a period in Bordeaux, the editorial board of *Politique africaine* is now at the Centre in Paris-1. At the CERI, research on Africa is henceforth organised around the new journal, *Critique internationale*, which privileges comparative perspectives. For French Africanist political scientists, and also geographers like Michel Coquery and Jean-Pierre Raison, comparative and historical perspectives are very important. Considering the fact that among the anthropologists, some, like Bazin, have always been very close to historians while some, like Terray, returned to historical perspectives while yet others like Jean-Pierre Dozon and Didier Fassin employ historical and comparative perspectives, it is arguable that such perspectives are specific traits of French Africanism.

Africa in the Memories of the United States and France

Decolonisation, the Cold War, the acquisition of sovereignty by 'modern' African states, and transnational social movements energised by a utopian vision of global social justice: it is in this climate that African studies emerged as a research and an academic domain. In the United States, images and symbols of Africa thus circulate within two distinct networks which evoke two separate collective memories which the civil rights movement problematised rather than brought into contact. For many blacks, especially intellectuals, mother Africa is the cradle, Egypt, and the origin of civilisation where whites raped Africans before condemning them to slavery and oppressing them through colonisation. For whites, Africa is the land of barbarity which corrupts and is incapable of producing anything other than slaves and buffoons. Whoever glosses over this memory and its effect on the treatment to which blacks were subjected would be incapable of grasping the extraordinary hostility which greeted Joseph Conrad's (2005) *Heart of Darkness* in the context of literary (postcolonial) studies.

The civil rights struggle and the fight for desegregation could have produced new representations and symbols, different from the two preceding ones. But the Africanism of Melville Herskovits, anthropologist and student of Franz Boas, who was struggling for a common ground for African and Black studies—later, African American studies—did not succeed in the venture. Rather, political and institutional dynamics separately reactivated certain segments of each memory and this resulted in the separation of African studies and African American studies, or the inclusion of the former in the latter. At the end of the 1960s, the African Studies Association almost split into two associations, one black and the other white, leading to the departure of the Canadians who formed a separate association. Since then, in the United States and elsewhere, care is taken to maintain the equality of black and white, men and women, and the Association is an important pressure group.

American interest in Africa is political and is recognised as such by all. With the exception of Native Americans who until very recently were relegated to reservations and oblivion, all Americans admit having come from somewhere else. Reference to the extra-American origin of ancestors, no matter how distant it is in the past, is part of Americanity. Scholarly and academic disputations about the content of history curriculum and literary canons have accentuated the importance of Africa for African Americans and this allows for a better balance of the multiculturalist mosaic.

In the United States, Africa and its decolonisation constitute an example of the affirmation of America as a moral force of contemporary history. It is not only about support for decolonisation and for freedom as the natural right of Africans. The decolonisation of black Africa is supposed to be a therapy for curing America permanently of one of its foundational maladies: racial discrimination. The powerful social movement in favour of civil rights made decolonisation, and later the anti-apartheid struggle, a factor in the moral redress of American society. Herskovits, the man recognised as the father of African studies in the American academy, underscored already in the 1950s the necessary links between knowledge of African societies and the recognition of the cultural, social and economic contribution of American citizens of African origin.

The situation is different in France where interest in Africa was without doubt activated initially by aesthetic considerations, which considered primitive art as the inspiration and inflatus of the modernism that had its global capital in Paris. This is illustrated by the Paris of the 1930s, the Paris of Michel Leiris and the African expeditions, and also the Paris of Josephine Baker (considered African because she was black). The Paris of this period reinforced Gauguin's quest for a reinvigoration of 'civilisation' in the truth of the primitive. French interest in Africa also resulted from a rejection of all exploitation in favour of equality and fraternity, in favour of an anti-fascist and anti-capitalist attitude that saw market liberalism as a source of inequality as opposed to American-type freedom. This is what connects the grand inter-war inquiries of Andre Gide and Albert Londres and the anti-colonialist tradition which resulted from the third worldism of the 1970s. Emmanuel Terray is the incontestable leading example of the commitment of French Africanists to the struggle against exploitation and inequality, wherever they exist, including the diversion of urgent attention from Africa to Eastern Europe and, also, action on the fate of undocumented immigrants in France.

At the risk of sounding banal, it can be argued that the Africa of the United States politically correct and legitimate from the Christian point of view, is a mother who nurtures her children who rely on her. The Africa of France on the other hand is young, black and resplendent. Her bare breasts suggest closeness to nature and her strength derives from the desire she generates. This aesthetic and sexual force is universal as evidenced in the negritude model. Thus, the election of Leopold Sedar Senghor to the French Academy underscores the inclusive universality of the French language rather than the contribution of Africa. To this sentiment of an aesthetic debt to primitivism without which modern art would not have been born was added, after the Second World War, the conscience of the culpability of the political system produced by the French Revolution. This system betrayed its founding ideals through the colonial adventure.

From Marxism to Multiculturalism

It is symptomatic that French Africanists faced historical reality only after the years of uncertainty about the intellectual authority upon which their work was based: it is the analysis of the colonial situation by Georges Balandier (1955)[1] which formed the foundational text of African studies in France, at least in the principal form it took in the 1970s. The aura of Althusser and the enthusiasm for an autopsy of the world using the scalpel of Structuralism-Marxism eclipsed for a long time this specificity of French Africanism which consisted in an understanding of the colonial situation as the key moment in understanding sub-Saharan Africa, as Jean Copans (1991) opines.

It is necessary to draw attention to the contrast between two traditions constructed by signs attributed to marked historical situations, and between two founding fathers of African studies: the United States and France. Melville Herskovits and Georges Balandier represent respectively the realisation of the liberal ideal of emancipation and equal opportunities, and redemption from the original sin against the ideal of the universality of Man. Besides, in the establishment of fields of knowledge, American pragmatism, which was the first to embark on institutional restructuring in the academy, contrasts with the pursuit in France of a universal devolving from the transformation of theory and the progression of ideology and aesthetics.

The American university world is a market. When African studies appeared as a new product in this market at the beginning of the 1960s, it was necessary to establish rules of engagement and evaluation, etc. Funding from the Area Studies development programme was based on competition; star scholars were therefore needed to attract students and gain a proper footing in the competition for funds. Promising scholars, especially British and Belgians, were hired, centres and programmes were founded and numerous students were attracted by doctoral scholarships. For reasons that bear no repeating here but which are related to the mechanisms of this funding market, African Americans were mostly absent from the picture. The exigencies of the politics of Area Studies and the ambient pragmatism shaped hiring and evaluation criteria in a system in which the value of a faculty was directly reflected in his/her annual salary. There was therefore little or no place for theory, except for classification aimed at managing reality.

Yet, the new generation, that of doctoral students in the 1960s, attacked American as well as global interests in a way that necessitated ideology, at least on the political level. Thus, this generation manifested a huge thirst for theory and this turned its attention towards Latin American theories of dependency. This explains why French African studies were prized by American Africanists. This marks the commencement of the longstanding attraction for French Theory. It is beyond the brief of the present chapter to discuss its ramifications but a brief overview of the conditions of emergence of Africanism in France with a view to understanding its origin is necessary. Despite the fact that these conditions were similar to those surrounding the birth of African studies in the United States, they led to the emergence of a very different academic field in France.

Newness and marginality also made it incumbent on scholars who took to African studies in France to demonstrate the pertinence of the field and gain recognition for it. Devoid of an internal political base as exists in the United States, young actors confronted two possibilities: a theoretical investment which considers Africa as a polemical site with a universal scope; or contribution to the creation of solidarity, the principal criterion of evaluation in France. At least since the Dreyfus affair, taken as the advent of intellectuals, solidarity has become the chief position for thought in the political and civil arenas, evidence of a scholar's prestige. Disciplinary knowledge counts for little whereas grand theory, so close to ideology when used externally, is potentially rich in effects.

Alongside this structural factor, circumstances exclusive to African studies strongly contributed to its embrace of theory. In the 1960s, Western Europe experienced a pervasive sense of guilt for not having prevented the explosion of fascism and for having been complicit in colonialism and its dirty wars for such a long time. Yet, knowledge of Africa at the time came mainly from ex-colonials. Their knowledge being pragmatic and utilitarian, it became necessary to distance oneself from it. The concept of the colonial situation and the move, related to an anthropological history of the Manchester School applied to the rural-urban transition, offered rich possibilities in an intellectual context in which Marxism was the principal source of theoretical inspiration. African examples gave meaning to the profound difference between past and present and paved the way for the suggestion of modalities of action. As the theorisation of transition—from feudalism to capitalism, from capitalism to socialism—was the order of the day, African studies approached from the perspective of the colonial situation regained extra vigour in the public arena. African studies harboured ideological interventions and engagements in political actions in France as in Africa. Following their declared positions, many young Africanists of ORSTOM returned to France with a warning never to return to the countries they had just left. Many of them, such as Francoise Raison-Jourde, had to make do with working henceforth on documents while others, such as Gerard Althabe, swapped the African field for France. Others, such as Emmanuel Terray, opted for neighbouring countries.

From the second half of the 1960s, the American student milieu and some young scholars, pitched against the political establishment, the American social order, and American foreign policy on the underdeveloped parts of the world in particular, lacked a theoretical and ideological base. French theory, based on a Marxism that was more structuralist than Marxian, and certainly not Leninist, arrived just in time, especially as the young French academics of the time were not competitors in the American market. The theoretical power attendant on the combination of the initial African field work, the reformist Marxist historicism (with the Polish historian of the transition, Marian Malowist), and the prestige of French research (namely Fernand Braudel), is evidenced in the success of Immanuel Wallerstein who was expelled from the American university system during the protests on university campuses only to make a triumphant return.

African studies in the United States, confirming its specific identity and its weight, both at the international and national levels—the African Studies Association has more than three thousand members—explored the theoretical gains of French research to structure a disciplinary field in the face of multiculturalism and postmodern relativism. In France, the double engagement which characterised the Africanist work of Balandier, a description attentive to the most contemporary stakes, and the universalistic perspective, resulted in two approaches which became increasingly separate and distant from each other. The attention given to immediate reality inspired political engagement and investment in education in the most general sense of the term. Enhanced by an interpretive view of the world and by the position of the intellectual as society's guide, theory facilitated the move towards reflection of a philosophical nature. This move was accompanied by a change of terrain, especially among anthropologists: Africa was eclipsed by a contemporary or 'historical' West.

The first attitude is felt mostly among historians and, to a lesser extent, among geographers. Among the historians, Catherine Coquery-Vidrovitch occupies an important position. Co-author, with Henri Moniot, of the first university level French textbook of African history which appeared in 1974 in the prestigious collection 'Nouvelle Clio', she is mostly devoted to syntheses, both general and thematic (Coquery-Vidrovitch 1997, 2005). Elikia M'Bokolo (1985, 2004) and the late Jean Devisse,[2] also published joint and individual monographs. With their preference for monographical research, these three historians, as well as Françoise Raison-Jourde (a graduate of the Ecole normale whose dissertation was directed by a non-Africanist historian), invested enormously in the training of academics from Francophone Africa; together they groomed several dozen African students at the doctoral level. Even if Catherine Coquery-Vidrovitch came from the EHESS and Elikia M'bokolo belonged there (he was Director of the Centre for African Studies), historians came from other traditions external to the EHESS. But ambitions and engagements of the *Annales* school continued to determine their professional choices. Catherine

Coquery-Vidrovitch is the most visible in American African Studies, even winning the Distinguished Africanist Award of the African Studies Association in 2000.

In the United States, multiculturalism has a more important influence on African studies than American postmodernism. The latter mostly characterises literary studies and anthropology. Francois Furet rightly sees in this more political rather than heuristic representation a new version of the nineteenth century American liberal utopia of a non-national society. This society would be united partly by the market and a neutral complex of political and juridical norms guaranteed mostly by the judiciary. At all levels, courts are rather perceived as an emanation of the concerned societies, the ethico-political voice of each community guaranteed by a jury. Thus, the judiciary would guarantee 'real' equality as opposed to 'formal' equality which devolves from the legislature and the executive.

Since the 1990s, we have witnessed the transformation of the American dream into a planetary ideology under the guise of globalisation. The national as framework of emancipation is receding while the non-political community (*indigenes*, homosexuals, etc.), which supposedly survived the assault of the nation-state, becomes more and more legitimate. In analyses of Africa, the state is singled out as a factor of underdevelopment, responsible for the failures of independence. There is a consensus today that there is a 'false start in Africa', to borrow the title of Rene Dumont's (1966) famous book. More than the structures of inequality which undergirded the formation of our world, the nation-state, decolonisation's Greek gift, is held responsible for the false start. Basil Davidson (1992), loyal companion of all independence movements and national liberation struggles in Africa, the most famous promoter of the deep historicity of the state in Africa, published a sort of admission of error in 1992—an admission applicable to his generation. *Black Man's Burden* (a play on the famous slogan of the colonial *mission civilisatrice* of the British) holds the nation-state—already responsible for the European tragedies of the twentieth century—responsible for the failure of contemporary Africa.

Mention must be made in passing that the definitive condemnation of the nation-state as a political structure is not a common practice among French Africanists, even those working on the Horn of Africa where there are no longer nation-states; or in the Great Lakes where states have replaced the civil nation with regional or ethnic nations. There is however a distinction to be made between political scientists and historians on the one hand (insofar as Achille Mbembe was a member of French Africanism in the 1990s) and anthropologists who claim to be students of Balandier on the other. The former place emphasis on the indiscipline (Mbembe) which empties the political order of all substance; they also focus on the gangrene of the formal state occasioned by local mechanisms of sociability and survival. Having become famous, Jean-François Bayart's (1993) book, *The State in Africa: The Politics of the Belly*, was quickly translated into English. On the contrary, the authors of the edited volume, in which contributions from Balandier's former students were assembled after a colloquium organised in Balandier's honor by the Centre for African Studies, subscribed to the idea of the state as a factor of historicity. This, in my opinion, is an extension into the diachronic comparatism of postcolonial situations which Mamadou Diouf practises and the post-Soviet comparatism of French geographers and political scientists.

However, the call to historicise ethnicity, a structure of sociability which has been perceived by Africanists as the public enemy of the state since the 1960s, came from the Centre for African Studies and was heard later by the historians at Paris-1. Alongside Terray's dissertation, whose publication took years, *In the Heart of Ethnicity*, a very influential volume edited by Amselle and M'Bokolo (1999) confirmed the shift to dynamic social analysis in the long term. Jean-Loup Amselle (1998) is the only one among the Africanist anthropologists of the EHESS to participate actively and durably in the introduction of the multiculturalist paradigm of reading. *Mestizo Logics*, his often cited book in the United States, found continuity in two other books which confirmed the position of the author in the new field of French language academic multiculturalism.

Politically correct multiculturalism's call, aimed mostly at a domestic American audience, to destroy the sources of power of the dead white males, was progressively extended to English language postcolonial studies. Furet calls it 'a liberal utopia arising from the ruins of the communist utopia, human rights revenge on Marxism', which replaced third worldism, underdevelopment, and other paradigms of the 1970s and 1980s. More of a political tone in France, Michel Foucault's (2005) exhortation on the importance of the site of enunciation (attributed to his homosexuality in the United States) discredited those who spoke about communities to which they did not belong. Following this logic, since a huge majority of those who made French African studies famous in the academy belong to the category of white European males, they would have nothing more to say about the victims. The objectification of the subjectivity of historical experience, which indelibly marks a society in its social body as well as its memory, replaced the universalising power of theory as evidenced by Jean-Paul Sartre (2004). Yet, without post-structuralism and without the contribution of Marxist anthropology (in its economic character), which lent themselves to diverse usage, this revenge on European universalism could not have been feasible.

Generational shifts occurred in France a decade later than in the United States. It is a question of age: the generation of Jan Vansina, Philip Curtin, and Ivor Wilks stands between Georges Balandier and Marc Augé. Their replacement ensured the future of African studies. Presently, the place of those who consider themselves Africans differentiates African studies in France and the United States. In the last thirty years in the United States, the ranks of Africanists—African Americans or recent African immigrants—have swelled. In France, given the very limited number of available positions, candidates of African origin who have been hired in the last three years are relatively numerous. At Paris-7, two of the three advertised positions were given to African candidates; another candidate of African origin was hired at Lille. These appointments probably constitute half of the advertised positions during this period. The influence of these mostly young appointments on the orientation of African studies will increase with time. The growing proportion of French citizens of African origin could increase the internal political importance of the field.

Another point: the terrorist attacks of 9/11 have modified the attitude of the US administration to university scholars. The *New York Times* of November 20, 2001 remarked that contrary to the initial attitude of the Bush administration, which selected the President's scientific advisor very late and slightly reduced his position in the hierarchy, numerous contacts have just been made with several American academies of science in order to re-establish links. It is highly likely that a movement comparable to the promotion of Area Studies will emerge in the social sciences, so long as the tendency to replace the conception of the United States as manager by a different conception of it as partner in the construction of the world is maintained. African studies may come out of this strengthened, especially as influential Africanists like Jane Guyer (2001) director of the Program for African Studies at Northwestern University founded by Herskovits until 2001—have never renounced the idea of Area Studies. In France, a renaissance of African studies will depend on the ability of one of the existing centres to ensure its leadership. After Jean-Francois Bayart's tenure as Director of CERI, there are few candidates for this role while myriad misgivings of the past make the task difficult for the old, experienced actors.

African Studies in the Face of Memory and a Forgotten Africa Caught Between Atlantic and Mediterranean Political Imaginaries

The recent (2005) riots in the suburbs of big cities in France were followed by debates on the topicality of the colonial past and its place in the historical consciousness of the French nation.[3] Some characteristics of the links between French memory and Africa—following V. Y. Mudimbe's (1988) sense of the latter in *The Invention of Africa*[4]—thus came to light. I will limit my remarks to the presence, until very recently absence, of Africa and Africans in the historical consciousness of the Republic. The slave trade and colonisation, two major historical facts of the modern world, will be examined in their connection with the political imaginary of France and the place which black Africa occupies in it.[5] Asia, the Caribbean, the Indian Ocean, and the Pacific all have specificities with regard to their place in the historical consciousness of the French as citizens of the Republic and in relation to the slave trade and colonisation. I will not discuss this here. Despite the claims of academic research to autonomy, the dominant political imaginary influences the state of research and profoundly impacts on the relation between the dissemination of research findings and political memory.

I deem it necessary to broach the relationship of the French to Africa through the Republic. Even if in the economic, social, and perhaps, political spheres, the place of the Republic has waned, it remains central in the French national imaginary and in historical consciousness. I will thus speak of France in the restricted sense of the French Republic, and of the French in sense of citizens of the Republic.[6] The Republic and the Revolution of 1789 are two sites of memory par excellence (Nora

1997, 1999).[7] As from the Revolution as site of memory, the Republic gave birth to modern France and prides itself for having disseminated to the world its democratic ideals and the notion of human rights. The French national imaginary of the Republic and the Revolution, as sites of the construction and dissemination of the universality of Man, is crucial to any understanding of the relationship to Africa and black people. Historical facts such as Napoleon's denial of revolutionary values while restoring slavery in Saint-Domingue and the colonising Republic are not integrated into French memory.[8]

Thus, the acceptance of Africans as citizens of the Republic in France—present somewhat like neighbours—conflicts with the political memory of the Republic. It thus becomes difficult to understand that the memory of slavery is part of the identity—it is even its veritable site of memory today—of Caribbeans. The French could find it astonishing that memory of colonisation constitutes the site of memory of black Africans, especially those who did not experience it. But to call on citizens of the Republic not to remember the Revolution or the Republic, since they are both of the past, would irritate the French. But paradoxically, people pretend not to understand why Caribbeans and black Africans are hurt by appeals to get over their 'outdated' memories of slavery and colonisation.[9] Particularly in recent times, while political identities are resolutely (re)constructed on the memory of collective trauma, the negation of the centrality of the memory (which is not history) of slavery and colonisation to the political identity of Francophone blacks is surprising.

This forgetting of the mnemonic heritage of the close Other in France (the situation is different with African Americans whose memory of slavery and segregation is recognised) can be explained through two mutually reinforcing phenomena. On the one hand, French political identity is conflated so much with the Republic that the citizen must love it passionately, and collective memory (as opposed to history) cannot be allowed to acknowledge major betrayals of the principles of the Revolution.[10] On the other hand, the universal mission of France, supposedly conferred on it by the Revolution, prevents any remembering (inscribed in collective consciousness and not only in history books) of discontinuities in the adhesion to its principles. This is how forgetting,[11] albeit negation, of the memory of the Other has long allowed to see only harmony at the site in which the political schizophrenia of the exceptionality of national memory, vector of a the universal mission, resides.[12]

We know since Fernand Braudel (1996) who, like other successful authors, stated with authority what is generally known, that the world of French historical imaginary is first and foremost Mediterranean. As was the case in the Roman Empire, black Africa and its inhabitants constitute its margins. On the contrary, North Africans, despite being Muslims and thus historical enemies, belong to the Mediterranean and not Africa. In political memory, they are accorded historical reality while Africans only come into the picture as value-laden representations. The first relation, sealed in memory by the hot iron of violence, is nevertheless corporeal while the second is experienced as an imaginary. Thus, when blacks present themselves politically as foreigners, France welcomes them with open arms. Once they make no claims to belong to the Republic, they enjoyed the same quality of acceptance as other refugees and without racial prejudice. The 'Paris noir' of the interwar years, which Bennetta Jules Rosette (2001) has worked on, comes to mind. Several African Americans and Caribbeans, including colonial 'subjects' of France, found a land of liberty and equality in the Paris of that period. The situation changed radically with the end of French colonial empire. Immigrants from former colonies wanted to become citizens of the Republic, neighbours of other citizens, whereas the Republic could only offer them the frustration of feeling like its 'natives' once there.

The difference between the Anglo-Saxon imaginary of the Atlantic world and the French imaginary of the Mediterranean world accounts for the big difference with regard to the place reserved for the memories of the Atlantic slave trade and colonisation. They are inscribed in the constitution of the first universe, their violence trails it. On the contrary, the contemporary imaginary of the Mediterranean evokes classical slavery and thus de-links the Atlantic slave trade from race and then constructs modern imperialism as an extension of Roman imperialism. Collective amnesia thus becomes manifest alongside the surprise of discovering that the heirs of the enslaved and the colonised (descendants are the ones who chose their ancestors in the postmodern world) are offended.[13] The riots in the suburbs and the insult in the infamous paragraph of the bill of 23 February 2005, which requires teaching the benefits of colonisation, imposed a debate on the memory of slavery (there are still attempts at dissolving it in the general memory of slavery as a phenomenon) and colonisation in the public sphere. The Centre national de la recherche scientifique created in a few weeks a research unit on slavery and the slave trade,[14] a venture it has been unable to undertake for so many years. Yet, we still have not come close to an acceptance of the fact that it is legitimate for French citizens to construct their political identity not on the Revolution and the Republic but on acts of betrayal of their principles which slavery and colonisation represent.

In debates among scholars who are neither racists nor avid nationalists, historical knowledge is still deployed to justify, sometimes even to support, constructed forgetting, whether it is the Algerian war[15], colonisation, or the Atlantic slave trade. In the country where *Realms of Memory* (Nora 1997) was a best-seller, it is unnerving to hear intellectuals combat memory with historical arguments or attempt to invalidate the process of remembering the political amnesia of a historical fact through the assertion of knowledge of its history.

In this context, African studies—including the militant left—could only seek its legitimacy in the universalisation of an Africa taken as a particular case. Either one embarked on aestheticisation following Leiris and Rouche, or one grasped the primitivism of Africa in order to discover the truth of Man's universality. French Marxist anthropology constructed around the concept of mode of production devoted itself completely to the second option. Claude Meillassoux's (1991) brilliant works on slavery are a good example of the trend. French historians of colonised Africa have always preached in the desert because the knowledge they try to disseminate to the public either fell into the black hole of amnesia or was caught in the maelstrom of denunciation, thus bouncing off the shell of collective forgetting.[16]

Lastly we must recall that the academic works in English that are best placed to open a debate on the memory[17] of slavery and colonisation—principally, Mudimbe and Martin Bernal—have not been translated. Yet, Mudimbe's *The Invention of Africa* has more to say on the place of Africa in the French imaginary than in the Anglo-Saxon[18] imaginary.

In the last few months, the French university world has begun the process of (re)discovering 'its' black intellectuals. Those who trained professionally in France before leaving and who are still considered part of that world. The Manthia Diawaras, Mamadou Dioufs, Achille Mbembes—just to cite those three—return to France this time as 'foreigners', renowned academics in US or South African universities. From the 'Black Paris of artists' in the 1930s, we are now at the 'intellectual Paris of African origin', both made up of 'false' foreigners but who no longer inconvenience Republican memory.

Glossary of Acronyms and Translator's Notes

CERI—Centre for International Relations, affiliated to the *Fondation nationale des Sciences politiques.*

Fondation Nationale des Sciences Politiques—National Foundation for the Study of Political Science.

Centres d'etudes africaines—Centre for African Studies, affilated to the EHESS.

EHESS—School of Advanced Social Sciences.

Ecole Normale, rue d'Ulm—Based at Ulm Street in Paris, one of the most prestigious French institutions that has produced the leading names (philosophers, anthopologists, etc.) in French Thought.

ORSTOM.—The French Institute of Scientific Research for Development in Cooperation. ORSTOM was a French-owned public service organisation under the joint authority of the Ministry of Research and the Ministries of Cooperation and Development. With a budget of nearly one billion francs, ORSTOM had a staff of 2,500. It recently became the IRD (Institute of Research for Development).

Paris-1, Paris-7, etc—In the heavily centralised French system, after May 1968 the former Sorbonne was divided to more than ten universities located in Paris area and named numerically.

Notes

1. On Balandier's contribution to African Studies see *Afrique plurielle, Afrique actuelle. Hommage à Georges Balandier*, Paris: Kartahala 2000, on Balandier as sociologist, *Georges Balandier : lecture et relecture, Cahiers internationaux de sociologie*, vol. CX, Paris: Presses universitaires de France 2001.
2. French representative on the editing board of the UNESCO *History of Africa*.
3. For some aspects of this debate, see the volume edited by Claude Liauzu and Gilles Manceron (2006). The social and political discomfort makes translating into an effort for

the critical self examination of the state of French research on both African studies as well as slavery and slave trade studies in France. The Centre national de la recherche scientifique supported two conferences held in Paris, in June 2006 on the state of slavery and slave trade studies in France (blacks of North African diaspora in France or worldwide not included) and in late November 2006 on the state of African studies in France. In both cases invitations seemed to be addressed to French scholars and no comparative perspective seemed to be invited.

4. French publishing houses do not consider this book to be of interest for the French public. Yet, Mudimbe's analysis, rooted in the purest French intellectual tradition, is more than ever topical in France. Reactions to this book in French are marginal to the university world as is the case with Kasereka Kavwahirehi's (2006) *V. Y. Mudimbe et la ré-invention de l'Afrique.*

5. This dimension largely undermined the baseless controversy occasioned by an edited Caribbean volume, which accused Olivier Petre-Grenouilleau (2004) of the negation of crimes against humanity in his book. The constant confusion of history and memory of slavery transformed it into a dialogue of the deaf.

6. In France, debate about politics is necessarily a debate about Revolution and Republic. Jean-Fabien Spitz (2005) is the most recent intervention, after the works of Marcel Gauchet (1989, 1995, and 2005); of Pierre Rosanvallon (2000, 2004).

7. Pierre Nora's entire work, a reconstruction of French national historical consciousness around memory, is organised around the Republic.

8. The indignation of Emmanuel Le Roy Ladurie (among other major French historians) against the abstention of the French government from the Napoleonic celebrations (*Le Figaro* of 1 January 2005, p.14) is only equalled by the anger in some Caribbean milieus against a figure they considered a slaver. This marks a veritable crisis of the suburbs.

9. Or that they should accept as sufficient reparation the recent transfer of the remains of Alexandre Dumas to the Pantheon: his mixed blood and descent from a line of slaves on the mother side were 'forgotten' for a long time. On the question of reparations, see the recent issue of *Cahiers d'etudes africaines* (nos. 173-174, 2004) which I edited: 'Reparations, restitutions, reconciliations'.

10. To gauge the importance of the Revolution as a national ideological monument, it is necessary to grasp the intensity of the tremor occasioned by the publication of Francois Furet's (1981) *Interpreting the French Revolution. The Passing of an Illusion: the Idea of Communism in the Twentieth Century* (Furet 2000) was, in a way, a sequel.

11. Ernest Renan underscored how indispensable forgetting is to the success of the permanent referendum that is the nation. The famous book, *Que'est-ce qu'une nation?* was reissued in 1993 in paperback (Paris Pocket)

12. Informed interrogations of the issue have no way of coming to public attention: the book by Patrick Weil and Stephane Dufoix (2005, is a good example. Another research work, conducted for several years by a group led by Pascal Blanchard, Nicola Bancel and Sandrine Lemaire (2005) (mostly on racial prejudice) had no better luck with this same public until the recent crisis suddenly gave it a new lease of life. Also see Nicolas Bancel, Pascal Blanchard and Francoise Verges (2003).

13. This is completely different from the Anglo-Saxon imaginary of the Atlantic which has now been appropriated by blacks under the rubric of the Black Atlantic, the Atlantic slave

trade serving as its foundational event. Paul Gilroy (2000) can be cited as the most successful of an impressive list of works from William L. Andrews and Henry Louis Gates (1999), Paul Lovejoy and David V. Trotman (2003), Paul Lovejoy (2000), Kristin Mann and Edna Bay (2005), James Walvin (2000), Adam Potkay and Sandra Burr (1995), J. Lorand Matory (2005), Joan Braxton and Marie Dietrich (2005), John Cullen Gruesser (2005), Toyin Falola and Mat D Childs (2004), Gesa MacKenthun (2004), etc. The black Atlantic has also been appropriated today in the Brazilian imaginary, Alberto da Costa e Silva (2003). I am grateful to Ana Lucia for this reference.

14. RTP Slavery (the Americas, Africa, Europe), Forms, political, economic systems, and social productions.

15. Among French historians of the African continent, Benjamin Stora is the only one who effectively takes into consideration the dimension of memory and to distinguish it from the historian's work. For several years, he has done pioneering work aimed at removing the histories of the Algerian war and colonial Algeria from the shadow of the academy. His last book (Stora 2005) is worth mentioning. I believe that the Algerian War and colonial Algeria feature in French political memory but this fact says nothing for Africa and blacks who are absent from the imaginary of the Mediterranean. With regard to publications on sub-Saharan Africa, mention must be made of Jean-Pierre Dozon (2003).

16. Also see the journalism of François-Xavier Verschave (1999). There also very meritorious efforts of young scholars like Sophie Dulucq and Colette Zytnicki (2003). Unfortunately, such efforts have changed nothing in the relationship of history and memory. In the last instance, it is encouraging to note that the book was published by the Société Francaise d'histoire d'Outre-mer (the French Association for the study of overseas history).

17. I underscore this point because it is works in English which opened up public debate and brought the memory of Vichy to the front burner.

18. Journals such as *Politique Africaine* and *Cahiers d'etudes africaines* have changed a lot but they belong more to the Atlantic universe of African studies today than to the French or Mediterranean academic worlds.

References

Amselle, J-L & E. M'Bokolo, eds., 1999, *Au coeur de l'ethnie*, Paris: Découverte, new edition 2005.

Amselle, J.-L., 1998, *Mestizo Logics: Anthropology of Identity in Africa and Elsewhere*, translated by Claudia Royal, Stanford CA: Stanford University Press

Andrews, W. L. and H. L. Gates, eds., 1999, *Pioneers of the Black Atlantic: Five Slaves narratives from the Enlightenment 1772-1815*, New York: Civitas Books.

Balandier, G., 1952, 'Approche Sociologique des "Brazzavilles Noires": Étude préliminaire', *Africa* 22 (1): 23-34.

Balandier, G., 1955, *Sociologie actuelle de l'Afrique noire*, Paris: Presses universitaires de France.

Bancel, N., Pascal Blanchard and Francoise Verges, 2003, *La Republique coloniale. Essai sur une utopie*, Paris: Albin Michel.

Bayart, J-F., 1993, *The State in Africa: the Politics of the Belly*, London and New York: Longman.

Blanchard, P., N. Bancel and S. Lemaire, 2005, *La fracture coloniale. La societe francaise au prisme de l'heritage coloniale*, Paris: La Découverte.

Braudel, F., 1996, *The Mediterranean and the Mediterranean World in the Age of Philip II*, Berkeley, California: California University Press.

Braxton, J. and M. Dietrich, 2005, *Monuments of the Black Atlantic: Slavery and Memory*, Munich: Lit Verlag.

Cahiers internationaux de sociologie, 2001, *Georges Balandier: lecture et relecture,*, vol. CX, Paris: Presses universitaires de France.

Chanson-Jabeur, C. & O. Goerg, eds., 2006, *'Mama Africa': Hommage à Catherine Coquery-Vidrovitch*, Paris: L'Harmattan.

Conrad, J., 2005, The *Heart of Darkness*, New York: Norton.

Copans, J., 1991, *La longue marche de la modernité africaine*, Paris: Karthala.

Copans, J., M. Godelier, S. Tornay, C. Backes-Clement, 1971, *Anthropologie science des sociétés primitives ?* Paris: Le Point de la Question.

Coquery-Vidrovitch, C. & H. Moniot, 1974, *L'Afrique noire depuis 1800 à nos jours*, Paris: Presses universitaires de France, new revised and expanded edition 2005.

Coquery-Vidrovitch, C., 1997, *African Women. A Modern History*, New York: Westview Press/ Harper Collins.

Coquery-Vidrovitch, C., 2005, *The History of African Cities South of the Sahara: from the Origins to Colonization*, translated by Mary Baker, Princeton, NJ: Markus Wiener Publishers.

da Costa e Silva, A., 2003, *Um Rio Chamado Atlantico—A Africa no Brasil e o Brasil na Africa*, Rio de Janeiro: Ed. Nova Fronteira.

Davidson, B., 1992, *The Black Man's Burden: Africa and the Curse of the Nation-state*, New York: Times Books.

Dozon, J-P., 2003, *Frères et sujets. La France et l'Afrique en perspective*, Paris: Flammarion.

Dulucq, S. and C. Zytnicki, eds., 2003, *Decoloniser l'Histoire? De l'histoire coloniale aux histoires nationales en Amérique latine et en Afrique*, Paris: Société Française d'Histoire d'Outre-Mer.

Dumont, R., 1966, *L'Afrique noire est mal partie*, Paris: Seuil.

Falola, T. and M. D. Childs, eds., 2004, *The Yoruba Diaspora in the Atlantic World*, Bloomington: Indiana University Press.

Ferro, M., 1996, *Histoire des colonisations*, Paris: Seuil.

Ferro, M., ed., 2004, *Le livre noire du colonialisme*, Paris: Hachette.

Foucault, M., 2005, *The Order of Things. An Archaeology of the Human Sciences*, London and New York: Routledge.

Francois-Xavier Verschave, especially, 1991, *La Francafrique: le plus long scandale de la Republique*, Paris.

Furet, F., 1981, *Interpreting the French Revolution*, New York: Cambridge University Press.

Furet, F., 2000, *The Passing of an Illusion: the Idea of Communism in the Twentieth Century*, Chicago: Chicago University Press.

Gauchet M., 1989, *La revolution des droits de l'Homme*, Paris: Gallimard.

Gauchet M., 1995, *La révolution des pouvoirs*, Paris: Gallimard.

Gauchet M., 2005, *La condition politique*, Paris: Gallimard.

Gilroy, P., 2000, *The Black Atlantic: Modernity and Double Consciousness*, Cambridge: Harvard University Press.

Goerg, O., 1991, 'L'historiographie de l'Afrique de l'Ouest: tendances actuelles', *Genèses* 6: 144-160.

Gruesser, J.C., 2005, *Confluences: Postcoloniality, African American Literary Studies, and the Black Atlantic*, Athens: University of Georgia Press.

Guyer, J. I., 2001, 'Revitalising area studies: The transformation of interdisciplinarity', *PAS* (Program of African Studies. Nothwestern University), 12 (1): 2-3.

Guyer, J. I. and D. L. Mack, 1998, 'Living Tradition in Africa and the Americas: The Legacy of Melville J. and Frances S. Herskovits. A Sourcebook to the [PAS Jubilee] Exhibition', PAS Working Papers, Number 4, Evanston, IL: Program of African Studies, Northwestern University .

Guyer, J. I., 1998, 'PAS: Perspectives on the beginning', *PAS* 9 (1): 1-2.

Jewsiewicki, B., 2001, 'Pour un pluralisme épistémologique en sciences sociales; à partir de quelques expériences de recherche sur l'Afrique centrale', *Annales. Histoire. Sciences sociales*, 56 (3): 625-642.

Jules Rosette, B., 2001, *Black Paris. The African Writer's Landscape*, University of Urbana and Chicago: University of Illinois Press.

Jules-Rosette, B., 2007, *Josephine Baker in Art and Life: The Icon and the Image*, Chicago: University of Illinois Press.

Kavwahirehi, K., 2006, *V. Y.Mudimbe et la Re-invention de l'Afrique*, Paris: Rodopi.

Lamont, M. and L. Thévenot, eds., 2000, *Rethinking Comparative Cultural Sociology. Repertoires of Evaluation in France and the United States*, Cambridge: Cambridge University Press.

Liauzu, C. and G. Manceron, 2006, *La colonization, la loi et l'histoire*, Paris: Syllepse.

Lorand Matory, J., 2005, *Black Atlantic Religion : Tradition, Transnationalism and Matriarchy in the African Candomblé*, Princeton: Princeton University Press.

Lovejoy, P., ed., 2000, *Identity in the Shadow of Slavery*, New York: Continuum International Publishing.

Lovejoy, P. and D. V. Trotman, eds., 2003, *Trans-Atlantic Dimensions of Ethnicity in the African Diaspora*, New York: Continuum International Publishing.

M'Bokolo, E., 1985, *Afrique au XXe siècle*, Paris: Seuil.

M'Bokolo, E. et al., 2004, *Afrique noire: histoire et civilisation du XIXe siècle à nos jours*, Paris: Hatier.

MacKenthun, G., 2004, *Fictions of Black Atlantic in American Foundational Literature*, London: Routledge.

Mann, K. and E. Bay, eds., 2005, *Rethinking the Black Diaspora: The Making of a Black Atlantic World in the Bight of Benin and Brazil*, London: Frank Cass.

Meillassoux, C., 1991, *The Anthropology of Slavery*, London: Athlone.

Mudimbe, V. Y., 1988, *The Invention of Africa: Gnosis, Philosophy, and the Order of Knowledge*, Bloomington: Indiana University Press.

Nora, P., 1999, *Rethinking France: Les lieux de memoire*, Chicago: Chicago University Press.

Nora, P., ed., 1997, *Realms of Memory*, New York: Columbia University Press.

Petre-Grenouilleau, O., 2004, *Les traites negrieres: Essai d'histoire globale*, Paris: Gallimard.

Potkay, A. and S. Burr, eds., 1995, *Black Atlantic Writers of the Eighteenth Century: Living the New Exodus in England and the Americas*, London: Palgrave Macmillan.

Raison, F., 1991, *Bible et pouvoir à Madagascar au XIXe siècle*, Paris: Kartthala.

Rosanvallon, P., 2000, *La démocratie inachevée, histoire de la souveraineté du peuple en France*, Paris: Gallimard.

Rosanvallon, P., 2004, *Le modèle politique francais.la société civile contre le jacobinisme de 1798 a nos jours*, Paris: Gallimard.

Sartre, J-P., 2004, *Critique of Dialectical Reason. Theory of Practical Ensembles*, London: Verso.

Spitz, J-F., 2005, *Le moment républicain en France*, Paris: Gallimard.

Stora, B., 2005, *La gangrene et l'oubli: La memoire de la guerre d'Algerie*, Paris: La Découverte.

Verschave, F-X., 1999, *La Francafrique: le plus long scandale de la Republique*, Paris: Stock.

Walvin, J., 2000, *Making the Black Atlantic: Britain and the African Diaspora*, London: Cassel.

Weil, P. and S. Dufoix, eds., 2005, *L'esclavage, la colonisation, et après... France, Etats-Unis, Grande Bretagne.* Paris: Presses universitaires de France.

Chapter 7

New Directions in African Studies in the United Kingdom

John McCracken

In September 1992, I had the privilege of delivering the Presidential address at the biennial conference of the African Studies Association of the United Kingdom (ASAUK) on the theme 'African history in British universities: past, present and future' (McCracken 1993). At that time, many academics were concerned at the extent of the damage inflicted on African Studies in Britain by large-scale cut-backs from the late 1970s; it therefore seemed appropriate to review the condition of the subject. Signs of contraction were not hard to find. Between 1977 and 1982, the proportion of the Social Science Research Council budget spent on African Studies had fallen from 2.3 to 0.8 percent. Faced in the early 1980s by severe cuts in government funding, universities had slashed travel grants, reduced library book funds and forced some of the most able scholars in the country into early retire-ment. Postgraduate numbers had declined, in part as a consequence of the steep rise in overseas fees and the subsequent reduction in the number of African postgradu-ates studying in Britain. Between 1985 and 1989 the overall number of Africanists teaching in British universities had fallen by 16 percent. It was hardly surprising that in 1986, at the height of the cuts, Michael Twaddle had speculated as to whether there would still be any African Studies left to teach in British universities by the year 2000 (Twaddle 1986). Tony Hopkins, writing a year later, had been even more pessimistic. Despite the achievements made by the pioneers, 'the subject is dying because its practitioners are fading away' (Hopkins 1987).

In 1992 my own conclusions were, albeit cautiously, more up-beat. African Stud-ies had weathered the storms of the 1980s much more successfully than might have been expected, I argued. Despite the fears of contraction regularly expressed, it remained the case that African history (my own discipline and the one with which I was most directly concerned) had maintained a significant presence in Britain's higher educational system, taught in nearly half of the universities in place by the mid-1980s and continuing to attract undergraduates in significant numbers. Temporary falls in postgraduate numbers at Birmingham's Centre of West African Studies (perhaps the most prestigious of the new African Studies centres founded in the wake of the 1961 Hayter Report) were more than balanced by a growth in postgraduate numbers at Oxford, particularly in the field of southern African history. Furthermore, while Britain could no longer claim the central position in the study of Africa that it had held in the 1950s and 1960s, important research continued to be published in abundance. As I was at pains to demonstrate, the proportion of articles by British-based historians published in the *Journal of African History* and the *Journal of Southern African Studies* had declined significantly in the 1980s, partly as a consequence of the growth of American and South African research centres. But to a greater extent than ever, the work of British Africanists was impacting more widely on the writing of history through the production of major monographs and seminal articles by scholars such as Ranger (1985), Marks (1994), Iliffe (1987), Berman and Lonsdale (1992), and Vaughan (1991). Weaknesses continued to exist, including the virtual collapse of precolonial African history, once, under the leadership of Roland Oliver at SOAS, the shining strength of British Africanist scholarship, but now consigned almost everywhere to a minor role, though sustained by a small group of able scholars, including McCaskie (1995) and Law (1991). However, there were compensating strengths in the quality and popularity of modern South African history, though I expressed concern that too heavy a concentration on South Africa could result in a reduction of our knowledge of the rest of the continent. Moreover, there was a danger that the political transformation of South Africa would result in a waning of popular interest in Britain and the collapse of once influential paradigms. To a significant extent, African Studies in British universities since the 1960s had been invigorated and strengthened by the large-scale recruitment of South African refugees from apartheid. Would this continue in the future? If not, did African Studies in British universities have the capacity to reproduce itself? How successful were we being in recruiting the brightest and the best? African Studies in Britain, I suggested, stood 'at a cross roads, capable of advancing if it grasps the opportunities now available but also in danger of shrinking into insignificance if it fails to adapt' (McCracken 1993).

More than ten years later, with the year 2000 now well behind us, it has become clear that earlier apocalyptic predictions can safely be laid to rest. Writing at the turn of the millennium, John Lonsdale emphasised the deep problems that continue to exist. Reporting on a survey he had made in response to a query from the Foreign Office Research Department which had become worried by the lack of knowledge of Africa among the British newspaper-reading public, he pointed to the continuing concern over high overseas students fees, the decline, at least in older universities, of Africanist staffing and the loss of language-teaching capacity, particularly at SOAS where such major languages as Bemba, Fulani, Mende and even Shona were no longer taught (Lonsdale 2000a).[1] In the United States, as I discovered on my visit to the University of Illinois at Urbana-Champaign to deliver this paper, it is still possible for a state university to purchase copies of well over 30 contemporary African newspapers for its Africana library, as well as a host of locally produced publications, official and non-official. In Britain, by contrast, so Lonsdale comments:

> Librarians can no longer go on book-buying trips to Africa as some once did; there is a growing dialogue of the deaf, therefore, between British and African scholars with segregated bibliographies. The crucial ephemera and daily newspapers of to-day are being lost to us (and with them the history of today by future historians) (Lonsdale 2000).

A particular concern expressed by a number of Lonsdale's correspondents is the relatively low professional status accorded in successive Research Assessment Exercises (the major mechanism through which research funding is distributed to universities) to interdisciplinary area studies. Universities, in consequence, tend to transfer resources to core disciplines where Africanists are often marginalised.

Yet as Colin Bundy (2002:61-73), the then Director of SOAS, noted in 2002, concern at pressure on resources must be tempered by recognition of the continued resilience of African social science in Britain. The closure in the early 1990s of York University's lively Centre of Southern African Studies (the site of the most memorable conference I have ever attended[2]) was a grievous blow. But at Edinburgh, under the leadership of Kenneth King, the once-troubled Centre of African Studies has taken on new life as an institution focused particularly on developmental issues. African history appears to have been weakened at SOAS, recently, by the retirement or departure of several of its leading stars. However, at Durham, in a curious reverse of the norm, several new appointments in African history have been made at the very time that steps have been taken to close the university's prestigious Centre of South Asian Studies. Wherever one turns, fears that the subject would be unable to reproduce itself have proved groundless. Instead, there is good reason to argue that, all the way from Oxford to Stirling and taking in Bristol and Keele, excellent young academics have been appointed of a quality at least equalling and often surpassing that of those they have replaced. Of equal importance has been the growth of Africa-related posts, often in the field of cultural and disaporic studies, in the new universities, most of them former polytechnics created in the 1980s. Thus, while in certain areas, language teaching in particular, academic provision has undoubtedly declined, in others, notably in cultural studies and in studies relating broadly to development, there has been an overall increase in the number of teachers and students.

In his article, Bundy (2002: 64) is at pains to distinguish pressures that result from a shortage of material resources from 'epistemological pressures', the 'various ways in which the intellectual foundations of the study of Africa have been called into question'. Of immediate concern is 'the apparent fallibility of theoretical approaches or modes of explanation in dealing with African realities'. Jolted by the successive collapse of theories of modernisation, of underdevelopment, of modes of production and of structural adjustment, social scientists in a variety of disciplines have either abandoned the field altogether or else retreated into ever more abstract and technical study—a trend particularly prevalent among economists. In the humanities, the influence of postmodernism and postcolonialism has been equally problematic. Work in this tradition has been genuinely valuable in the light it has thrown on the nature of evidence and on the need to explore alternative meanings. However, it has also tended to divert attention away from the study of material factors—crucial for a real understanding of Africa—to a more dubious and, in some senses, more superficial engagement with discourse.

Yet if British Africanists are in general a chastened lot, less confident than they once were in their ability to provide definitive answers to Africa's problems, they have also demonstrated in the last decade an impressive ability to come up with new analyses on a variety of different topics. Some indication of the range of that work was demonstrated in five lively survey articles (by no means confined to British Africanist scholarship alone) published in the centenary issue of *African Affairs* in April 2000 and covering such issues as the African diaspora, Africa and the world, medicine, Christianity and the environment (*African Affairs* 2000). No comprehensive description of this research can be attempted here but, from a purely personal perspective, three areas stand out as being particularly worthy of attention: the Christian encounter with Africa, Africa and the environment, and African nationalism revisited. Like other research that could be cited with equal validity, this work demonstrates the importance of the interchange of ideas within the global Africanist community. Seen from outside, it may be that British Africanist scholarship has distinctive qualities distinguishing it from work elsewhere. Seen from within, one of its most important features is its permeability as demonstrated in the regular contacts made by Africanists in Britain with fellow-scholars in Africa, the United States and increasingly in northern Europe.

The Christian engagement with Africa has long been a fruitful area of study for British Africanists but it was revitalised from the mid-1990s onwards by the appearance of a number of distinguished publications. Adrian Hastings's (1995) wide ranging survey, *The Church in Africa 1450–1950*, must be included among this group as a work that links the best scholarship of earlier decades with the most fruitful insights of the present. Written by a scholar who in a long and variegated career combined committed social activism with the most rigorous academic standards, *The Church in Africa* demonstrate at a continental level the need to give equal weight to the social and religious environment out of which the European missionaries came and the political and spiritual world inhabited by African Christians.

Hastings's insistence on the need to focus on the African roots of Christianity is also apparent in two more recent works based respectively in north-eastern Zimbabwe and in western Nigeria. David Maxwell's (1999) *Christians and Chiefs in Zimbabwe: A Social History of the Hwesa People* is representative of the best scholarship produced by a new generation of young historians of Zimbabwe: locally focused, making extensive use of oral as well of written sources and sensitive to theory. But it must cede pride of place to John Peel's (2000) path-breaking study, *Religious Encounter and the Making of the Yoruba*, quite simply the richest and most coherent account now available on why a particular group of Africans turned to Christianity and what kind of Christians they became. The exceptionally fertile sources available to Peel—including 86 detailed journals written before 1889, nearly half of them by African missionaries—ensure that few scholars working in other areas will be able to replicate the rich detail provided in this book on the nature of the Christian encounter and the dialogue with indigenous Yoruba ideas. Equally, however, few scholars will fail to be influenced by Peel's demonstration that religious change in Africa has to be understood not just though attention to missionary endeavour or colonisation but, crucially, through attention to 'the endogenous development of African societies' (Peel 2000: 2).

For some scholars, interest in religious change blends seamlessly with interest in Africa's changing environment. Terence Ranger, for example, one of the pioneers in arguing that due weight has to be given to religion in understanding the history of African people, is also one of the pioneers in asserting the importance of cultural factors in the making of African landscapes. *Voices from the Rocks* (1999), his attempt to historicise the Matopos Hills, is notable for the way in which it extends its analysis beyond changing European representations of the Matopos to an understanding of the hills as a site of intense symbolic struggle involving both whites and blacks.

Ranger's concerns are paralleled by an 'avalanche of studies' (Beinart 2000: 279) dealing with human relationships with the African environment. Some of these follow Ranger in his fascination with the linkages between culture and representation, landscape and identity. Others, many of them encouraged by William Beinart at Oxford, explore the history of scientific and intellectual engagements with the environment. It is an indication of the growing interest in the area that the conference on 'African Environments: Past and Present' held at Oxford in 1999 attracted over 90 papers, many of which have been published in one or other of two collections (Beall et al. 2000; Beinart and McGregor 2003). Several of these question conventional interpretations of environmental degradation as being related to population growth and inappropriate farming techniques. But they also tend to move beyond blanket condemnations of colonial science to a more nuanced position in which at least some colonial scientific initiatives are regarded as being worthy of serious attention (for a detailed study see Beinart 2003; see also Mackenzie 1998).

In his paper, 'The State of African Studies 2000', John Lonsdale (2000a:3) notes that 'UK Africanist political science seems weak by comparison with the USA and France'. The judgement is a harsh one, ignoring some distinguished work. Nevertheless it remains the case that greater insights have been produced on culture, consciousness and identity in recent years than on the old staples of politics and political economy. Participants at an 'Away Day' held by the editorial board of the *Journal of Southern African Studies* in 2003 were virtually unanimous in concluding that while the retreat from neoliberalism and postmodernism opened up possibilities for a return to serious study of political economies, at present few papers in this tradition are being sent to the journal. More rewarding perhaps are the new approaches to nationalism being taken by a variety of scholars. Once presented as the grandest of grand narratives, the study of nationalism virtually disappeared from academic agendas for three decades before re-emerging in recent times in a number of revisionist guises. Richard Rathbone (2000) in *Nkrumah and the Chiefs* has led the way in demonstrating the continuing importance of chieftaincy at a time when, in the view of many commentators, it had been sidelined by the advance of mass nationalism. Other historians, including Terence Ranger (1995) in his study of the Samkange family, have returned to the social and intellectual roots of nationalism, to explore its ambivalent relationship with both democracy and authoritarianism (see also McCracken 1998).

Of particular interest are local studies, extending research into previously neglected areas, revealing alternative scenarios to those presented in dominant narratives, throwing light on once marginalised groups and demonstrating previously overlooked divisions. Ranger has often been criticised as a provider of 'nationalist historiography' in the sense that he has attempted to link early episodes of resistance in Zimbabwe to the emergence of a popular and unified nationalist movement. In his most recent monograph, however, *Violence and Memory* (2000), written jointly with Jocelyn Alexander and JoAnn McGregor, the tone is very different. As in Ranger's earlier work, this study of the forests of the Shangani Reserve emphasises the importance of the shared experiences of its inhabitants, many of them evicted into the area from other parts of Matabeleland. But it also provides an unsparingly bleak depiction of the character of rural nationalism, much of it drawn from the extensive field research of Alexander and McGregor, as expressed both in the war of independence and in the violent struggles of the 1980s.

Studies of this type frequently inter-relate with the myriad investigations of African popular culture, undermining the dichotomy between 'traditional' and 'modern', which have been published in the last two decades. They include among their number Karin Barber's account of Yoruba popular theatre (Barber 2001) and Stephanie Newell's discussion of literary culture in Ghana (Newell 2002).

What are the main challenges and opportunities facing African Studies in Britain at the beginning of the twenty-first century? First to be considered must be the growing interest in imperial and diasporic studies as evinced not only in a wealth of new scholarly publications and academic courses but also in the making of television series, the launching of seminar programmes and the opening of museums. Back in the early 1960s, when African history first made its mark in British universities outside SOAS, it did so often at the expense of imperial history and in the conviction that Africa, like Asia, could be understood only if studied from within, rather than as part of a survey of 'Europe and the Wider World'. In similar vein, Oliver and Fage (1962) in their path breaking *Short History of Africa* turned their backs on earlier accounts by Du Bois and others that had emphasised the centrality of the African diaspora to African history by providing a narrative largely focused on activities in the continent itself.[3] What was relevant was defined more by geography than by culture or race.

Against this background, Bundy (2002: 72) is right to emphasise as a development worthy of special mention 'the rising interest in and sophistication of enquiry into diasporas, trans-national communities, the identities and interactions of people of African descent'—though it is important to note that in Britain this has been accompanied by a revival of interest in empire based only partly on old-fashioned nostalgia. For many years, Manchester University Press's well-known Studies of Empire series, under the general editorship of John Mackenzie, has demonstrated a scholarly concern for expanding our knowledge of the imperial experience. Recently, however, other developments have emerged alongside Mackenzie's initiative including the opening of the long projected Museum of Empire at Bristol and the holding of a succession of conferences and seminars on maritime history, often involving African historians, at the National Maritime Museum at Greenwich. Niall Ferguson's (2003) recent television series on Empire, made with more than half an eye on the American market, demonstrates an attempt to channel this interest into a more popular arena. It was followed in 2004 by a further series on Scotland's empire, exploring themes that once would have been considered only of academic concern.[4]

For Africanists in Britain these developments pose both the threat of a retreat to the popular margin and also the challenge of extending knowledge of Africa to hitherto untouched constituencies. One scenario would involve the descent of African studies into the academic aridity of the late 1950s (hinted at in some postcolonial analyses) where studies of attitudes towards Africa take pride of place over those concerned with the actions and beliefs of Africans themselves. The other would involve the fruitful association of Africa with wider oceanic studies, exemplified by the international collaborative project, 'The Development of an African Diaspora: The Slave Trade of the Nigerian Hinterland', linked in turn to the UNESCO 'Slave Route' Project (publications relating to this include Law and Stickrodt 1999). Whether the opportunities will be fully grasped will depend at least in part, as Lonsdale has noted, on the ability of African Studies to make itself fully relevant to Britain's African and Afro-Caribbean communities (Lonsdale 2000b: 16). It will also require British Africanists to continue to engage in discussions in the wider public forum. At this of all times, there can be no excuse for allowing fashionable neo-conservative interpretations of empire to go uncontested. Equally, so Bundy (2002: 73) insists, there is every reason to continue to analyse African realities with 'rigorous, even ruthless honesty'.

The second challenge facing British Africanists concerns their relationship with Africa's beleaguered academic community. The complex connections between colonialism, decolonisation and the rise of African Studies in Britain have not yet been fully dissected.[5] But it would be difficult to deny that, in a variety of sometimes contradictory ways, the growth of Africanist scholarship in the UK, at least up to the 1970s, was powerfully affected by Britain's position as a colonial and ex-colonial power. On the available evidence, in the first decade after African independence, links between government agencies and African Studies centres in the United States were very much closer than they ever were in Britain. Nevertheless, British academics benefited from institutional connections which allowed a good few to obtain employment in Africa's newly founded universities, just as institutions like SOAS and the Centre of West African Studies at Birmingham were invigorated by the flow of able young African postgraduates to their doors.

Thirty years on, the situation is bleaker though by no means devoid of hope. High overseas fees serve as a disincentive to African students; British postgraduates seem to spend less time on research in Africa than previously; fewer British Africanists have worked in African universities. Quite often, employees of aid-NGOs such as Oxfam have greater first-hand experience of Africa than have academics. Michael Crowder's (1987: 109) much quoted warning from 1987 of 'the creation of two separate and compartmentalised worlds of Africanists, African and non-African' looks ominously perceptive.

Pessimism, however, must be tempered by recognition of positive developments. If the brain drain from Africa has weakened scholarship there, it has also resulted in the emergence of a group of African scholars, resident mainly in America but with representatives now in Britain, who go out of their way to maintain fruitful links with universities and research centres in their countries of origin (Zeleza 2002). In its reconstituted form, the British Institute in Eastern Africa now plays an active role in bringing together African, European and American social scientists in workshops and conferences held in Eastern Africa (for a recent example see Burton 2002). The *Journal of Southern African Studies* has set an example for other British-based Africanist journals in contributing to the costs and organisation of a variety of conferences in Africa. The publisher, James Currey, arguably Britain's most worthwhile contribution to Africanist scholarship, has established joint publishing ventures with a number of African-based firms, thus ensuring that at least some recent monographs produced abroad will be available in Africa at affordable costs. Similarly, many books published in Africa can now be purchased in London through the enterprise of the Africa Book Centre. Academics are increasingly involved in collaborative enterprises, among them Terence Ranger, whose involvement with Ngwabi Bhebe, as joint editors of a two volume study of Zimbabwe's Liberation War (Bhebe and Ranger 1995a; 1995b), may be cited as an example of this type of partnership at its best. Zimbabwe, however, also presents a disconcerting example of the political pressures to which a relationship of this kind can be subject. A conference organised in Harare in 1996 on the challenging theme of 'Nationalism, Democracy and Human Rights' resulted in 2001 in the publication of a volume of essays looking at precolonial and colonial legacies of democracy in Zimbabwe (Bhebe and Ranger 2001). Two further years were to elapse, however, before the appearance of the companion volume (Ranger 2003), focused on nationalism and democracy in more recent times. Even then, only 100 copies were initially produced. At a time when a generation of thoughtful, energetic Zimbabwean historians are being marginalised or forced to take jobs elsewhere, there can be no place for revisionist studies of nationalism, only for 'patriotic history' as defined by President Mugabe.[6]

Meanwhile, leading academic members of the energetic British-Zimbabwe Society find themselves increasingly employed providing background information for lawyers handling the cases of Zimbabweans seeking refuge in Britain.

In most accounts of African Studies in Britain the golden age is almost always in the past and the crisis is almost always in the present. My conclusion is different. British African Studies today is in a fragile condition, under-resourced, under-appreciated, both in the world of academe and of government, and lacking, at times, in confidence. Yet, as I have attempted to demonstrate, it is also currently producing an impressive range of thoughtful and sophisticated monographs, many written by a new generation of Africanist scholars. There is every reason to believe that it will continue to develop, intellectually vibrant in a culturally more variegated form than ever.

Notes

1. For an expanded version of this memo see Lonsdale (2000b: 13-20).
2. This conference, organised by Landeg White and Jack Mapanje in September 1993, brought together most of the major actors in the Cabinet Crisis in Malawi of 1964 with a variety of writers and historians.
3. This point was made by Robin Law at a conference on Du Bois and Fanon, Stirling University, 2002.
4. The central stimulus behind this series was the publication of Michael Fry, *The Scottish Empire* (Tuckwell Press, East Lothian, 2001).
5. Much has been written on anthropology, though less on other disciplines. An excellent recent discussion is provided in Schumaker (2001). See also Kuper (1983). For a wider perspective see Rimmer and Kirk-Greene (2002).
6. The story is told in Ranger (2004).

References

Alexander, J., J. McGregor, T. Ranger, 2000, *Violence and Memory. One Hundred Years in the 'Dark Forests' of Matabeleland*, Oxford: James Currey.

Barber, Karin, 2001, *The Generation of Plays,* Bloomington: Indiana University Press.

Beall, J., W. Beinart, J. McGregor, D. Potts and D. Simon, eds., 2000, 'African Environments: Past and Present', *Journal of Southern African Studies* 26, 4: 595-871.

Beinart, W., 2000, 'African History and the African Environment', *African Affairs* 99 (395): 269-302.

Beinart, W., 2003, *The Rise of Conservation in South Africa. Settlers, Livestock and the Environment 1770-1950*, Oxford: Oxford University Press.

Beinart, W. and J. McGregor, eds., 2003, *Social History & African Environments*, Oxford: James Currey.

Berman, B. and J. Lonsdale, 1992, *Unhappy Valley: Conflict in Kenya and Africa*, 2 Volumes, London: James Currey.

Bhebe, N. and T. Ranger, eds., 1995a, *Soldiers in Zimbabwe's Liberation War*, London: James Currey, Harare: University of Zimbabwe Publications.

Bhebe, Ngwabi and Terence Ranger, eds., 1995b, *Society in Zimbabwe's Liberation War*, London: James Currey, Harare: University of Zimbabwe Publications.

Bundy, C., 2002, 'Continuing a Conversation: Prospects for African Studies in the 21st Century', *African Affairs* 101, 402: 61-73.

Burton, A., ed., 2002, *The Urban Experience in Eastern Africa c.1750-2000*, special issue of *Azania*, XXXVI-XXXVII, Nairobi: British Institute in Eastern Africa.

Crowder, M., 1987, '"Us" and "Them": The International African Institute and the Current Crisis of Identity in African Studies', *Africa* 57, 1: 109-122.

Ferguson, N., 2003, *Empire: How Britain made the Modern World*, Harmondsworth: Penguin Books.

Fry, M., 2001, *The Scottish Empire*, East Lothian: Tuckwell Press.

Hastings, A., 1995, *The Church in Africa 1450-1950*, Oxford: Clarendon Press.

Hopkins, A.G., 1987, 'From Hayter to Parker: African Economic History at Birmingham University, 1964-86', *African Affairs* 86, 342: 93-101.

Iliffe, J., 1987, *The African Poor. A History*, Cambridge: Cambridge University Press.

Kuper, A., 1983, *Anthropology and Anthropologists: The Modern British School*, London: Rouledge & Kegan Paul.

Law, R., 1991, *The Slave Coast of West Africa 1550-1750. The Impact of the Atlantic slave trade on an African society*, Clarendon Press: Oxford.

Law, R. and S. Stickrodt, eds., 1999, *Ports of the Slave Trade (Bights of Benin and Biafra)*, Stirling: Centre of Commonwealth Studies, University of Stirling.

Lonsdale, J., 2000a, 'The State of African Studies, 2000', memo for Richard Lavers (FCO), ASAUK Newsletter, 5, 19: 1-5.

Lonsdale, J., 2000b, 'African Studies in the United Kingdom', African Studies Association of Australasia and the Pacific, *Review and Newsletter* 22, 2: 13-20.

Mackenzie, F., 1998, *Land, Ecology and Resistance in Kenya, 1880-1952*, Edinburgh: Edinburgh University Press.

Marks, S., 1994, *Divided Sisterhood: Race, Class and Gender in the South African Nursing Profession*, Basingstoke: Macmillan.

Maxwell, D., 1999, *Christians and Chiefs in Zimbabwe. A Social History of the Hwesa People c. 1870s-1990s*, Edinburgh: Edinburgh University Press for the International African Institute.

McCaskie, Tom, 1995, *State and Society in Precolonial Asante*, Cambridge: Cambridge University Press.

McCracken, J., 1993, 'African History in British Universities: Past, Present and Future', *African Affairs* 92 (367): 239-53.

McCracken, J., 1998, 'Democracy and Nationalism in Historical Perspective: The Case of Malawi', *African Affairs* 97: 231-49.

Newell, Stephanie, *Literary Culture in Colonial Ghana: How to Play the Game of Life*, 2002, Bloomington: Indiana University Press

Oliver, R. and J. D. Fage, 1962, *A Short History of Africa*, Harmondsworth: Penguin Books.

Peel, J. D. Y., 2000, *Religious Encounter and the Making of the Yoruba*, Bloomington: Indiana University Press.

Ranger, T., 1985, *Peasant Consciousness and Guerrilla War in Zimbabwe: A comparative study*, London: James Currey.

Ranger, Terence, 1995, *Are We Not Also Men? The Samkange Family and African Politics in Zimbabwe 1920–64*, Oxford: James Currey.

Ranger, Terence, 1999, *Voices from the Rocks. Nature, Culture and History in the Matopos Hills of Zimbabwe*, Oxford: James Currey.

Ranger, Terence, ed., 2003, *The Historical Dimensions of Democracy and Human Rights in Zimbabwe*, Volume II, Harare: University of Zimbabwe Publications.

Ranger, Terence, 2004, 'National Historiography, Patriotic History and the History of the Nation: The Struggle over the Past in Zimbabwe', *Journal of Southern African Studies*, Edinburgh, 30, 2: 215-34.

Rathbone, R., 2000, *Nkrumah and the Chiefs. The Politics of Chieftaincy in Ghana 1951–60*, Oxford: James Currey.

Rimmer, D. and A. Kirk-Greene, eds., 2002, *The British Intellectual Engagement with Africa in the Twentieth Century*, Basingstoke: Macmillan and the Royal African Society.

Schumaker, L., 2001, *Africanizing Anthropology. Fieldwork, Networks and the Making of Cultural Knowledge in Central Africa*, Durham and London: Duke University Press.

Twaddle, M., 1986, 'The State of African Studies', *African Affairs* 85, 340: 444-5.

Vaughan, M., 1991, *Curing their Ills: Colonial Power and African Illness*, Cambridge: Polity Press.

Zeleza, P. T., 2002, 'The Politics of Historical and Social Science Research in Africa', *Journal of Southern African Studies* 28, 1: 1-21.

Chapter 8

Betwixt and Between: African Studies in Germany[1]

Peter Probst

Compared to the excited debate of the early 1990s it has by now become a truism that globalisation did not just begin with the explosion of electronic media and the neoliberal expansion of capitalism after the fall of the Berlin wall. After the initial excitement a certain sobering effect has set in which has led many led to ask whether globalisation is really the right concept to deal with the complex issues involved at all (Cooper 2001). Nevertheless, it cannot be ignored that if not the world in general, at least the domain of science has indeed become more and more a global project. Being part of that project, African studies is no exception. On the other hand, the very persistence of area studies demonstrates the resilience of the local, local traditions of African studies included. Just as the nation state has not become obsolete, certain national features have survived and continue to play a role.

Given this situation, writing about African studies in Germany can be seen as a lesson in academic ethnicity. It is certainly no coincidence that an encompassing history of African studies in Germany is yet missing.[2] Keenly suspicious of any attempt to create a hierarchical structure, what holds the various segments of African studies in Germany together is a notion of their togetherness based upon an historical narrative explaining disciplinary kinship relations. Like in other (ethnic) groups, both the notion and the narrative are primarily invoked vis-à-vis others in this way providing internal solidarity and mutual help in case of attacks from the outside. When probing deeper into the official story, however, it rapidly becomes apparent that the different segments all have their own rival and conflicting versions of what happened in the past and what is going on in the present.[3]

Thus, writing about African studies in Germany is to some degree writing about a convenient fiction based upon the dubious appeal to the territorial confines of the nation state. Rather than presuming the existence of a clear-cut, distinctive unit,

what we find when we talk about African studies in Germany is an array of different, even contradictory approaches followed by members of an 'imagined community' (Anderson 1991). As such, the causes and dynamics giving rise to this community apply to a regional approach in African studies just as much as they do to the
study of ethnicity in general. On the other hand, it needs to be accepted that the task
of deconstructing the nation state also has its limits. Whatever we may think of the
categories a group of people employ to endow themselves with a distinct history and
identity, the fact is that these histories and identities do exist and continue to work.
Accepting this premise, the very dynamics of these identities should allow us to
identify certain features which distinguish the emergence and *changing* characteristics
of African studies in Germany from developments in other countries. In other
words, what need to be taken adequately into account are the processual elements
involved in this complex. After all African studies in Germany today is not only
profoundly different than it was during its 'classical period' in the first decades of
the last century. Compared to other players in the European league of African
studies it has also a special status.

What distinguishes the present scene of African Studies in Germany from many
other national scenes in Europe is probably best described by referring to its peculiar position of being 'betwixt and between'.[4] That is to say, while Germany shares its
long established history of African studies with that of France and Britain, the
position it has is between these two major spheres of influence; belonging neither to
the Anglophone nor to the Francophone traditions, but rather moving and manoeu-
vring constantly between the two while at the same time maintaining a big yet somewhat concealed territory of its own. This again sets it apart from other smaller
European countries like Sweden, Denmark or the Netherlands. In contrast to the
situation in these countries, the mere size of the German-speaking population (Germany, Austria, parts of Switzerland) has allowed it to give rise to a viable, self
sustained academic space not necessarily dependent on publication strategies in foreign languages.[5] Given the increasing dominance of English as the scientific lingua
franca, the effect is that for the international public unable to read German, the
wide range of Africa-related research in Germany published in German has become to some extent rather hidden.

The visible parts, however, which do exist refer to the highly competitive milieu
from which they evolve. Major recently published monographs of German Africanists
in the US and Britain include, for instance, Wolgang Bender's (1991) and Veit
Erlmann's (1991, 1996) studies on modern African music and South African performance; Heike Behrend's (1999) ethnography of war in Northern Uganda; Roman Loimeier's (1997) analysis of Islamic reform and political change in northern
Nigeria; Guenter Schlee's ethno-historical study of ethnicity in Kenya (Schlee 1989);
Fritz Kramer's (1993) work on the relationship between spirit possession and African art or the studies of Bernd Heine and his colleagues in the field of cognitive
linguistics (Heine, Claudi and Huennemeyer 1991, Heine 1997), to name just a few.
In addition there are numerous important edited volumes on topics like the making

of African landscapes (Luig and von Oppen 1998); African languages (Heine and Nurse 2000); new local historiographies from Africa (Harneit-Sievers 2002) and spirit possession and power (Behrend and Luig 1999); the dynamics of violence (Elwert, Feuchtwand Neubert 1999); everyday life in colonial Africa (Jones 2002); ethnicity in Ghana (Lentz and Nugent 2000); or visual media and the debate on African modernities (Behrend 2001, Deutsch, Probst, Schmidt 2002). Other examples which could be cited are from German Africanists studying conflict (Elwert 2001); ethnicity and language (Schlee 2001); spirits and spirit possession (Luig 2001); work (Spittler 2001) and nomadism (Scholz 2001) in the new edition of the *International Encyclopedia of Social Sciences*. Last but not least, there are several important works published in French ranging from issues like village politics and the state in Benin (Bierschenk and de Sardan 1998); the coping with crisis and hunger among the Tuareg in Niger (Spittler 1993); to literary issues like the legacy of Patrice Lumumba in Francophone African Literature (Riesz & Halen 1997).

All of these studies stem from a dynamic scene very different from the one that existed during the 'classical period' of German African studies when the work of scholars like Carl Meinhof, Diedrich Westermann, Richard Thurnwald and Leo Frobenius served as well-selling export ideas to other countries.[6] Surely, not only the interests and research agendas have changed, but also the very conditions which allowed such 'flows' to work. In the first decades of the twentieth century, Africa-related research had not yet reached the high degree of differentiation as we experience it today. Being relatively few in number and with German, French and English still existing on more or less equal terms it was easier to follow the developments both in other countries as well as in other disciplines. Given these factors, it can be claimed that African studies in general was probably not only more international but also more interdisciplinary than it is nowadays. Or, to put it in other words, right from the start, African Studies was characterised by a keen awareness of mixtures and movements, contacts and connections, not only between Africa and the rest of the world but also between Africanists themselves. Going all the way back to the mid-nineteenth century, what stood out in the German version of this tradition was the quite remarkable prominence given to linguistics and language. The reasons for this were rooted in German history wherein a language-based notion of folk or nation had to make good the perceived lack of a political nation state. As a result, the approach favoured in Germany of seeing language rather as an expression of cultural values and ideas than a mirror of abstract logical operations became very attractive for groups which perceived their situation in similar ways.[7]

Although the importance of linguistics has remained—most of the places in Germany where Africa-related research is taking place today have linguists in their midst, for example, Bayreuth, Berlin, Cologne, Frankfurt, Hamburg, Leipzig, Mainz, and Munich—today the discipline has lost its formerly leading role. Ironically, the relative decline was in a way self-induced for, as I am going to show further below, the very framework in which this loss of importance took place had been created by linguists themselves. The story behind this is the establishment of the German African Studies Association in 1969. Initially conceived and dominated mainly by linguists as a forum for new ideas and new inter-disciplinary work, the focus soon shifted in favour of members coming from the social sciences. In view of the fact that this process of 'social sciencing' African studies in Germany is up to now unbroken, it would be tempting to take the year 1969 as a suitable starting point for providing an insight into that somewhat mysterious box called 'African Studies in Germany'. In terms of the phases African studies has undergone, the result does not differ much from the development in the US recently outlined by Jane Guyer (1996). The three eras Guyer has distinguished for the US context apply to the German scene just as well, and probably to many others.[8] Yet, as I mentioned above, the history of Africa-related research in Germany transcends the beginning of its formal institutionalisation by far. In fact, depending on the various dates one sets to mark its beginning one gets different pictures with different histories and different players. The multiple traditions which resulted belong together. Deeply entangled as they are their various forms, the interactions and intensities outline the scope of what, with all due reservation, might be called 'African Studies in Germany'.

Given this complex situation, the following essay is organised into four parts. In the first part I will briefly outline the 'primal scene'. As with many other African creation stories, the story of African studies in Germany too has its legendary sites and ancestors, places where it all began and figures who made it all happen. The second part focuses on the time between the wars, the so-called 'classical period' of German research on Africa, while the third part analyses the development from the end of the Second World War to the reunification of the two Germanys. In the fourth and final part I will give an overview of the current developments and conclude with a note of the future role of German African studies within the European context.

Formation and Migration

African studies in Germany began during the second half of the nineteenth century. The names commonly mentioned in this context are many.[9] While some refer to early travellers like Heinrich Barth (1821-1865), others stress the importance of scholars like Friedrich Ratzel (1844-1904). Both came from geography, a discipline which together with linguistics provided the scientific basis on which the steadily incoming reports and artefacts from Africa were interpreted.

An important factor in this interpretation was the importance given to the role of diffusion and migration. Thus Ratzel (1982) saw the history of mankind as a history of mixtures and movements, contacts and connections. The central problem herein was not so much migration as such but rather the relationship between diffusion and migration, how culture could diffuse *without* migration.[10] The solution to this question was a combination of the economic insight into the circulation of goods and the idealistic argument that objects or goods are forms inhabited by ideas, a notion later taken up also by Frobenius. Using the Africana collection of the Ethnological Museum in Leipzig as an empirical basis, Ratzel not only intended to prove his 'migration' theory by the analysis of African bows, but also tried to come up with a culture historical differentiation and grouping of African people (Ratzel 1889). Even before Ratzel's migration theory, the Austrian Friedrich Mueller, a professor of Sanskrit and comparative philology at the University of Vienna, had outlined a linguistic migration model for the African continent in which the invasion of the so-called Hamites from the north played a central role (Müller 1876-1888). Thought to originate from Asia, the Hamites were seen to be superior to the authochtonous African societes, pushing them not only further south but also leading to a great variety of mixed languages.

In terms of their social appeal, both studies had their roots in the specific conditions of the early nineteenth century when the practice of emigration had been declared a hopeful solution for the increasing social, economic and political problems resulting from the industrialisation process which Germany, at that time still a predominantly rural society, was going through. Campaigns were organised persuading the lower middle class and the landless peasantry to migrate to foreign countries where they were supposed to form farming enclaves. Thus between 1835 and 1855 roughly two million people left Germany and migrated mainly to North America and South America, a minor portion to Australia and Russia. It was in this very context, the experience of migration as part of a lived social reality became a crucial formative factor in the emergence of African studies in Germany.[11]

The academic outcome was the study of the so-called 'culture areas' (*Kulturkreise*), an approach most often associated Leo Frobenius (1873-1938). Conceived as an integral spatially bounded unit characterised by specific cultural traits, Frobenius first developed his ideas by studying the distribution of various African artefacts and religious institutions (Frobenius 1898a&b). On the basis of these results he distinguished between three culture areas or provinces (Upper Guinea, Congo region and Lower Guinea and Southwest Africa). Lacking any university degree, his work initially was given a highly critical reception. Soon after, however, it was taken up and developed further by two young assistants at the Ethnological museum in Berlin, Bernhard Ankermann and Wilhelm Graebner. Both tried to connect the idea of the culture area (*Kulturkreis*) with that of cultural strata (*Kulturschichten*). In a famous meeting at the Berlin society of Ethnology, Anthropology and Prehistory, they explained their approach (Ankermann 1905, Graebner 1905). The research strategy thus consisted of three steps: sorting out the various components constituting different cultural geographical provinces or culture areas, trying to identify the origins of the elements forming culture areas, and analysing the latter according to their historical relationship with one another. Seen in this perspective, Africa was thought to be a result of cultural mixing due to a long period of successive immigrations originating mainly from the East—from Arabia and India all the way to Indonesia. Although the results that this approach produced were acknowledged as mere speculation, the firm belief was that the doubts could be removed if only the methods could be improved. The self-understanding was a positivistic one orientated to the work of philology and history which served as a kind of role model for the newly emerging ethnological museums. By likening the ethnographic objects they collected to the written texts and documents on whose interpretation the historical and philological sciences were based, ethnological museums understood themselves as scientific laboratories providing insight into the (pre)history of non-literate cultures. Criticism with regard to the dangers of this approach came from Frobenius. In attendance at the meeting where Ankerman and Graebner presented their work, he insisted that it was not enough to look merely at the outer forms of certain culture elements. What counted for Frobenius was the coherent idea, the total world view that a bow, an arrow, a club, or a shield embodied. Recalling the old insight that objects were forms inhabited by ideas, he argued that the focus was not the object as such but the relationships between the objects in which the essential pattern or *Gestalt* of a culture would reveal itself. In his view, to perceive and recognise this hidden quality was ultimately a gift of intuition and imagination not a matter of method.

The difference in the two positions just outlined reflected a long-established tension in the cultural and intellectual milieu of late nineteenth century German society which had its effects also in the newly emerging field of African studies. The relationship between Frobenius, on the one hand, and Ankerman and Graebner, on the other, needs to be understood in the light of the argument that German romanticism, of which Frobenius can be seen a representative, was actually an undercurrent of the Enlightenment, not its opposite. Given this argument, it is not surprising to detect such a basic tension not only in the field of anthropology but also in the field of philology. Thus in the early formative period of the study of African languages in Germany the romantic impulse focussing on the organic vitality of the *Volksgeist* expressed in songs, fairy tales, poetry and other performative, notably oral, genres met with the ambitions of a comparative philology analysing the grammatical rules and structures of spoken African languages whose results were interpreted along the taxonomic models developed in the natural sciences.[12] Where one position referred to Humboldt and Herder, the other referred to Schleicher and Schlegel. Existing side and by side, both fields were actually seen to complement each other, with the evolutionist and diffusionist paradigms providing the necessary framework for the historical development and origins of African languages and cultures. Thus in his *Nubian Grammar* the Berlin Egyptologist Richard Lepsius took over Mueller's model and standardised it into a triadic classification which distinguished between the southern Bantu languages based on classes, the northern Hamitic languages based on gender, and a third mixed zone resulting from of the interactions between Hamitic and Bantu languages (Lepsius 1880). Both models, that of Mueller and Lepsius, were actually an inversion of the Biblical stories about Babel and Noah which had inspired the classificatory scheme of early nineteenth century comparative philology.[13] This strong Biblical imagery in the early academic treatment with African languages was visible also in the sources available. Initially, the material for linguistic research—dictionaries, linguistic descriptions, word lists, collections of epics, songs, folktales, etc.—stemmed almost exclusively from missionaries. Not surprisingly then, it was mainly missionaries and churchmen who at the end of the nineteenth century made the study of African languages an academic subject.

In 1887, seven years after Lepsius's *Nubian Grammar* and two years after the Berlin conference at which Germany had entered the colonial league, the Institute for Oriental Languages was established at the Friedrich-Wilhelm-University (now Humboldt University) in Berlin. The Institute's primary aim was to provide practical knowledge for the German traders, planters and government officials serving in the new colonies. The teaching therefore focussed mainly on Swahili as the lingua franca in German East Africa. However, interest was also given to the study of Swahili literature and the linguistic analysis of African languages in general. One outcome was the establishment of the linguistic journals such as *Zeitschrift für Afrikanische Sprachen* and *Zeitschrift für Afrikanische und Ozeanische Sprachen*. Among those who published their work in these journals was Carl Meinhof (1857-1944), one of the most eminent scholars in African linguistics in the first half of the twentieth century. Working originally as a vicar interested in African languages, Meinhof became an academic when his first major study, *An Outline of the Phonetics of Bantu Languages*, earned him a position at the Institute of Oriental Languages in Berlin, first as a lecturer and in 1905 as a professor. Meinhof's comparative phonology broke new ground and opened up the door for research on Bantu languages (Meinhof 1909, 1915). In 1907 he left Berlin and moved to Hamburg where he became director of the department of colonial languages at the newly opened Colonial Institute. Institutionally, this new body in Hamburg stood in direct competition with the Institute of Oriental Languages in Berlin. On a scholarly level, however, co-operation prevailed. Thus shortly after his arrival in Hamburg Meinhof began a collaboration with Diedrich Westermann, another former missionary, who in 1910 had been appointed professor in the Department for Oriental Languages in Berlin. What followed was the academic institutionalisation of African studies in Germany. In 1916 the Ethnological museum in Berlin had divided their hitherto joint African and Oceanic collection and established an independent Africa department with Bernhard Ankermann as its first director. In 1919, after the foundation of the University of Hamburg, Meinhof obtained the first chair of African languages. Another six years later, in 1925, Diedrich Westermann was appointed to the first chair of African languages and cultures at Berlin University.

Imagination and Instrumentalisation

At the end of the nineteenth and the beginning of the twentieth century the colonial experience was characterised by a high degree of global interconnectedness and an interwovenness with the 'fabric of world economy' (Thurnwald 1910). The railway network had increased exponentially, German companies had their offices in all parts of the world, and the economic dependence on foreign exports was much higher than today (Sombart 1927). In this highly dynamic milieu of contacts and connections, diffusionism was seen to be a kind of cultural geology which attempted to order the surface chaos resulting out of the overall cultural mixture by sorting out its various elements according to the historical sequence by which the different cultural 'flows' had crossed one another.

The distinct political features of this approach, which actually made it very much a German answer to globalisation, are perhaps best illustrated by Leo Frobenius.[14] As indicated above, Frobenius conceived the study of 'culture areas' in Africa primarily as a morphological task. Heavily influenced by the philosophy of vitalism and its focus on 'life' as a root metaphor of early twentieth century Europe, he understood cultures as living organisms which followed the eternal circle of birth, maturation, old age and death. Being organisms, cultures were also seen to be endowed with a certain energetic patterns or forces, Frobenius's famous *paideuma*, which enabled them to act upon or 'seize' individuals (Frobenius 1921). To identify the specific elements constituting this force was seen to be a matter of ethnographic analysis and diffusionist comparison, yet to get a feeling of its 'seizure' (*Ergriffenheit*) was ultimately not a matter of method and science but an aesthetic operation based upon 'introspection' (*Tiefenschau*). Much as this approach was indebted to the ideas of German romanticism, it invoked the old resentments against the 'state machines' (Johann Gottfried Herder), France and England.[15] Thus the fatal hostility that Frobenius claimed to have discovered in Africa between 'Hamitic' and 'Ethiopic' cultures was seen to mirror an encompassing binary principle governing world history in general. In this way the 'Hamitic' force in Africa, which Frobenius associated with pastoralists and magic, warriors and state builders and which spatially corresponded with Meinhof's distribution of Hamitic languages, underlay also the materialistically and rationalistically orientated cultures of England and France. In contrast, the 'Ethiopic' force associated with farming and religion, planting, and mysticism, spatially corresponding with Bantu and Westermann's Sudanic languages, was seen to be the spiritual force or 'soul' impregnating Germany and Russia. As it is well-known, the political appeal of the programme proved to be a success not only in Germany, where the exiled Kaiser Wilhelm II figured as Frobenius's most prominent supporter, but also in Africa itself. Thus Frobenius's culture morphology found its way into Senghor's and Césaire's concept of *négritude* in the same way as Levy-Bruhl's ideas of 'primitive mentality' was integrated into Placide Tempels's 'Bantu philosophy'. Both sides argued for the ontological difference of the African mind, using the reference to vitality as a sort of conceptual tool whose own intellectual history allowed it to find and formulate a position of difference very much along the same lines as the concept had been developed in Europe.[16]

Between Frankfurt, the seat of Frobenius's Institute of Cultural Morphology, and Vienna, where Fathers Wilhelm Schmidt and Wilhelm Koppers had built up a hardly less influential school of culture history (Schmidt and Koppers 1924), there were many other German scholars following similar projects. Yet African studies during the inter-war period in Germany entailed much more than a focus on culture history alone. It comprised also scholars who were inclined to functionalism. A case in point for this dual nature of African studies in Germany was the relationship between Diedrich Westermann and Richard Thurnwald (1869-1954). As mentioned above, Westermann had first worked as a missionary in Togo before entering the academic world. Thurnwald, roughly the same age as Westermann, had begun his career with anthropological fieldwork in Papua New Guinea. Both met in 1925 at Berlin University where Thurnwald, already 56 years of age, had been appointed to a professorship. Thurnwald's lectures on general anthropology, sociology and social psychology caught the interest of Westermann, who saw in Thurnwald's knowledge and experience a valuable asset for coming to terms with the tasks of developing a contemporary approach in social research on Africa. Thus, when in 1927 Westermann was appointed co-director of the International Institute of African Languages and Cultures in London and—a year later—editor of the Institute's journal *Africa*, he saw to it that Thurnwald became a member of the executive council of the Institute.[17]

Thurnwald's functionalist approach and his interests in social change fitted well into the Institute's colonial agenda. Right from the start the focus was on the *changing African*. The general aim was to come to terms with colonial modernity. The ambience of decay, disintegration, and dissolution depicted as being characteristic of much of early twentieth century Africa resembled strongly the perception of fragmentation, fluidity, and fusion analysed by German writers like Simmel, Benjamin, and Kracauer as dominant features of early twentieth century Europe (Frisby 1986). Indeed, processes of urbanisation and industrialisation applied to both continents and their implications and consequences were thus the main issue of research on both sides. There was, however, a crucial difference. While the above mentioned authors writing on modernity in Europe accepted the experience of fragmentation and shock [*chock*] (Walter Benjamin), resulting from overwhelming experiences of ever new sensations, authors on colonial modernity in Africa fought against it and looked for means to reinstall social cohesion and equilibrium.[18]

Thurnwald's own contribution to this task consisted of a sociological field study that he and his wife carried out between 1930 and 1931 in what is now Tanzania. Funded by the International Africa Institute, the focus was on the emergence of a *New Civilisation* resulting from contacts and relationships between *Black and White in East Africa* (Thurnwald 1935).[19] The approach underlying the study was a fusion of different perspectives stemming mainly from French social psychology, German culture history, and British functionalist anthropology, making it difficult to give the study a definite label. When the book finally appeared in 1935, it failed to have a major impact. However, as another indirect outcome of the Tanzania study, Thurnwald's use of the concept of 'acculturation' became a success (Thurnwald 1932). For Thurnwald the Tanzanian study was not a starting point. Rather it added empirical evidence to the idea of human society and social change he had developed over the course of years (Thurnwald 1931-1935). Citing historical and anthropological examples, Thurnwald argued that societies tend to have alternating rhythms of negative and positive attitudes towards foreign cultures. Within these waves, acculturation entails decision processes about which aspects of a foreign culture to reject and eliminate or to adopt and transform to fit core cultural norms and practices. On the basis of these decisions Thurnwald saw acculturation as a process proceeding in four stages ranging from withdrawal, imitation, *Völkertod* (ethnic death) to recovery understood as a blend of the old and new, making a culture viable and compatible with the contemporary world.

While in this way Thurnwald's contribution to African studies remained restricted to an important stimulating factor for US American research on Africa, notably that of Melville Herskovits (Herskovits 1937),[20] Westermann's work was much more directly involved in practical matters. As co-director of the Institute and editor of its journal Westermann steered a strictly interdisciplinary course, combining linguistic, anthropological and ethnological studies. Inclined more to the British doctrine of indirect rule than to the French approach of cultural assimilation, he saw his own linguistic competence as part of a general language policy which aimed to influence the realm of moral education and political development. In 1933 he published, together with Ida Ward, the handbook *Practical Phonetics for Students of African Languages* (Westermann and Ward 1934). A year later followed *The African today* (with a foreword by Frederick Lugard) which actually started the African Institute's African Studies Series (Westermann 1934). The plea for a more person-focussed perspective was expressed also in *The African Explains Witchcraft*, a collection of articles which Westermann had initiated for the 1935 volume of *Africa*, as well as in his *Africans tell their lives* (Westermann 1938), a number of biographical sketches in which he tried to oppose the dominant colonial perspective by giving the anonymous colonial subject a concrete face and individual history. Though it might be possible here to detect a line going from the Christian missionary idea of *Naechstenschaft*, most explicitly formulated by Bruno Gutmann—another German missionary, linguist, anthropologist working among the Chagga in Tanzania (Gutmann 1932, 1966)—to the radical anthropological self-critique in terms of Johannes Fabian's influential concept of 'co-evalness' (Fabian 1983), the attitude in all these works was nevertheless strongly paternalistic.

Certainly, the finding does not differ all too much from the way how the established colonial power relations between master and servant were invoked in other parts of Europe at that time. What needs to be explained, however, is the strength of this colonial practice and imagery in a country which, after all, had already lost its colonies as a result of the First World War. The answer to that goes back to the mid-1920s when, in response to the Versailles treaty, the 'colonial idea' had experienced a distinct revival. New colonial societies were established aiming to prepare Germany's victorious return to the colonial league. Step by step the 'colonial idea' encroached also the academic domain. Thus the hitherto mainly philological orientation in African studies changed more and more to a culture-orientated focus. In 1933, for example, after the fascists' seizure of power, the Institute of Oriental Studies at Berlin became an *Auslandshochschule*, a kind of Foreign Service Academy. Its main aim was now to teach 'nation sciences' (*Nationenwissenschaften*) aiming to provide practical insights into the specific cultural and psychic conditions of the lost colonies which were soon to become part of the 'Third Reich'. Given this context, African studies in Germany actively involved itself in the revanchist agenda of the Nazi regime by trying to document its own colonial usefulness.[21] Despite prominent examples, it would be misleading, however, to see all members of African studies as playing an active role in Hitler's Germany. The appropriate picture was rather, as Dostal (1994) has called it, 'silence in darkness'.

Politicisation and Transformation

As in many other social study fields in post-war Germany, the first two decades of African studies were a time of restoration and reorganisation, continuation and transformation. The climate was characterised by the results of the political and territorial split between East and West Germany. Given this division, the two academic landscapes differed profoundly. Interactions practically did not exist. The so-called 'Cold War' forbade any exchange. Yet, in the beginning from the late 1940s until the late 1960s it was just this very difference which made the division of African studies in Germany two sides of the same coin. Not only was the long-established holistic and historical orientation maintained, the ideological programmes dominating in the two spheres complemented each other. Thus, while in the East the turn to Marxism-Leninism provided a paradigm which tied research and teaching on African colonial history to a chiliastic vision of the future, in the West the turn to positivism within African culture history created an ambiance that encouraged dropping the burden of the past.

With the reopening of the universities in the late 1940s the old pre-war personnel in African Studies had remained more or less the same.[22] As a result the old interests and paradigms dominating the disciplines before the war remained more or less unchanged as well. When in 1952 for example Diedrich Westermann's *History of Africa* appeared, this history was still one conceived mainly as culture history (Westermann 1952).[23] Seen from this perspective, recent events and single actors, as famous as they might have been during their time, became negligible. What mattered were general historical traits and big encompassing cultural units or provinces transcending the deeds of individuals. It is therefore not astonishing that new ideas did not arise within the traditional centre of African studies, i.e. linguistics and anthropology, but on the fringe of the established disciplines.

One such discipline was literature, with Janheinz Jahn (1918-1973) as one of its most popular and most effective representatives. Jahn was trained in theatre studies, art history and Arabic. His interest in Africa was more or less incidental (Schild 1974, Lindfors and Schild 1976). In 1951 he heard a lecture at the Institute Française in Frankfurt where Senghor spoke on the 'new negro poetry' (*la nouvelle poésie nègre*). Listening to Senghor's talk marked the beginning of his untiring collection and translation of African literature. In 1954 Jahn edited *Black Orpheus*, a collection of modern African poetry (Jahn 1954). Three years later followed the anthology *Rumba Mcumba* (Jahn 1957), another year later appeared his most famous and influential book *Muntu: An Outline of Neo-African Culture* (Jahn 1958). *Muntu* was not meant to be scientifically correct, it was a political statement. Drawing heavily on the ideas of Leo Frobenius and Placide Tempels, Jahn argued for the existence of a highly dynamic pan-African aesthetic practice driven by the rhythm of 'tribal' drums and nourished by ancient ideas about the mystery of life. Rather than having become diminished, the manifold mixtures experienced particularly during colonial times were seen to have strengthened this practice, leading to new ways of aesthetic expression. From this point of view, Jahn mapped an aesthetic topography of African culture which comprised dance, poetry, literature, religion, and music ranging from the African home land across the *Black Atlantic*, to use a current notion, all the way to the US, Cuba, and Brazil.

Due to Jahn's highly idiosyncratic way of blending Fanon and Frobenius, Kenyatta and Kagame into one powerful notion of Africaness, the reception of *Muntu* was highly controversial. Critics pointed to the manifold weaknesses and contradictions inherent in his essentialist argument. Yet as valid as these criticisms were, what *Muntu* stood for was a radical change in the Western perception of Africa. Whereas in the past Africa had been seen as continent which, in the words of Frobenius, 'had always received but had never given', *Muntu* provided a counter-model, one that allowed people to see African cultures in a positive light, and not in terms of the manifold imperialist versions of inborn passivity and submissiveness or in terms of the colonial ideas ranging from the Darwinist image of the colonised as prey to the functionalist notion of a sick patient infected by a contagious modernity. What *Muntu* presented instead was an image of Africa as a strong and healthy Other facing the West on eye-level. As it is well-known, post-independence Africa turned out to be quite different from the picture Jahn had depicted. Civil wars, dictatorial regimes, and political oppression on the African continent and the experience of the student movement back home pushed Jahn's work into the background making way for studies in the field of political science, sociology, and history (Ansprenger 1961; Bley 1968; Geiss 1968; Grohs 1967; Tetzlaff 1970).

Up to then, the two main disciplines with which African studies in Germany had begun, linguistics and anthropology, had not formed a joint association.[24] With the growing politicisation of German society, however, this eventually changed. In 1969 the German Association of African Studies (VAD) was founded in Marburg. The initiative for this came from a group of young linguists who stood in critical distance to the field of African studies in Germany at that time. As a move to overcome its traditional concentration on linguistics the 'young Turks', as some of old professors labelled the dissidents, widened the term *Afrikanistik* thus opening the field for representatives of other disciplines dealing with Africa. The new association was to send out a signal. It became a venture to new shores, a rebellion against the essentialising politics of the past. The constitution of the association stated that *Afrikanistik* should be conceived as a contemporary, interdisciplinary, critical, and self-reflexive project actively engaged in collaboration with African colleagues (VAD 1970).

The Marburg conference marked the beginning of an increasing trend in the 'social sciencing' of African studies in Germany.[25] Together with the process of decolonisation in Africa this tendency led to increasingly different understandings with respect to the 'function' of *Afrikanistik*. While in the East answers to such questioning were clearly defined by the state ideology, in the West they became a source of conflict. During the 1972 conference of the German association of Africanists, the hitherto latent tensions within the association broke out openly. Adherents of Marxist positions rejected the label *Afrikanistik* for being nothing more than '... the useless attempt to turn a geographical signification into a problem' (Hinz 1976: 217). Similar to the developments in other Western countries, what was demanded instead was a political idea of African studies informed by an acute awareness of Africa's attempts to resist the neo-imperialist and capitalist ambitions of the West. As a result, African studies was seen to have the responsibility to help and assist African countries in this very resistance. Faced with such a demand, those linguists who had once initiated the VAD increasingly felt that the original aim of the association had failed.[26] The intention to discuss genuine linguistic questions in an open, constructive dialogue with other disciplines was perceived as having lost the interest of the audience. Moreover, the self-understanding of Africanists was much more indebted to a rigorous inductive approach, a fact which made it more and more difficult to find common ground with members of other disciplines who, as the linguists thought, followed all too often preconceived theoretical concepts (cf. Möhlig 1976). In 1978 the founders of the VAD therefore formed their own conference platform, the so-called *Afrikanistentag* in Cologne.[27] In contrast to the VAD conferences, the bi-annual meetings of the linguists, much more than the anthropologists, henceforth maintained the historical focus as part of their discipline's legacy.[28]

In the 1970s, with new people, new subjects and new research issues coming up, the academic landscape became more colourful. In Bayreuth for example a focus on *new literatures* at the departments of English and Romance languages was established by János Riesz, Richard Taylor and Eckard Breitinger, whose work set the standard for subsequent ventures at other universites.[29] Equally in Bayreuth, Ulli Beier established Iwalewa house, a hybrid institution modelled after Beier's famous *mbari* clubs in Yorubaland, Nigeria, focussing on contemporary African art, literature, and music. In Mainz, where the chairs of anthropology and sociology, W.E. Mueller and Gerhard Grohs, managed to secure the library of Janheinz Jahn, a stimulating milieu for research on decolonisation, the study evolved of new elites, modern African literature, popular music and art. In Heidelberg, a number of young lawyers formed the African Law Association with the aim of spreading knowledge about the laws of the various jurisdictions on the African continent and to encourage studies of African law. With an anthropological focus, the study of African law became also a major feature at the anthropology departments in Munich and Muenster (Schott 1978, 1980). Taking over the chair of African linguistics from Oswin Köhler at the University of Cologne, Bernd Heine introduced the new field of socio-linguistics. At the Free University of Berlin, Franz Ansprenger focussed his chair at the Institute of Political Science on the study of African states. Last but not least, in Hamburg, Hannover and Bremen, Helmut Bley, Leonhard Harding and Immanuel Geiss founded new history courses under the rubric of overseas history, concentrating mainly on African colonial and economic history in the former German colonies (Geiss 1976).

With a focus on feudalism, state formation, and Marx's Asiatic mode of production, colonial and precolonial African history was a main topic in East Germany as well.[30] Contrary to the improvement of political relations between East and West Germany, however, academic exchanges between the two factions of African Studies remained rare and, if they happened, then only on an individual, personal level. The same held true for other fields of African studies. They often came to a standstill due to political restraints and a lack of funds for travelling and the acquisition of new literature. In some fields, however, it was just the very isolation from the West which allowed research in the East to break new ground. A case in point is the development in the field of literature and theatre studies. Due to the official socialist solidarity with the 'African brother states', not only a lively activity in the sector of translation set in, but the study of new dramatic and literary forms of expression also became a legitimate research subject. While Jahn had invoked Frobenius, a fact which very much blocked the recognition of his work in the departments of English and Romance languages and placed him among Africanists, East German scholars like Burkhard Forstreuther (1975) and Joachim Fiebach (1979, 1986) followed Bertholt Brecht.[31] The result was a new approach to writing about contemporary African theatre and literature which in many ways preceded the so-called postcolonial turn long before concepts like carnevalisation or hybridity became popular figures of thought in cultural studies and literary theory.

When in 1989 the German Democratic Republic collapsed, scholars like Fiebach thus found it relatively easy to enter the West German domain of African studies. In general, however, East German scholars were confronted with an academic landscape whose institutions allowed the integration of 'strangers' only in few cases. Profoundly different principles governed the social production of scientific knowledge and discoveries in the two Germanies (Krauth 1998). While in the East the aims of scientific research had been clearly defined by the state, in the West state institutions like the German Research Foundation, public and private funding bodies like the Volkswagen and Thyssen foundations, and research organisations like the Max Planck and Leibnitz societies guaranteed the existence of a more or less autonomous, self-regulating scientific system. The subsequent transformation of African studies in East Germany proceeded along the lines of its integration into this West German system. Although from a systemic point of view it was a necessary modernisation process, seen from the perspectives of the individuals concerned, the abstract nature of such an argument was often perceived as one legitimising injustice, awkward compromises, and academic imperialism and colonisation.

Today, after the profound remodelling and restructuring of the East German academic landscape, the former tensions have made way for a very vivacious and productive scene Many of the institutions survived and not a few of them used the chance to build up a new competitive profile. At the Centre for Modern Oriental Studies Berlin, for example, an institution which originally evolved from a section of the Academy of Sciences of the GDR and which is now funded by both the State of Berlin and the German Research Foundation, Africa-related research has moved towards the fertile terrain of culture and history, focussing now on social space and collective memory in a translocal and transnational perspective. At the nearby Humboldt University, Westermann's old site, three newly created chairs in language, literature, and history now form the Department of African studies, giving it a distinct profile indebted to cultural studies and postcolonial theory. Teaching and research here are closely linked to the institute of anthropology at the Free University of Berlin, where the main themes are the study of religion, transnational relations, gender ethnicity, and violence. Together, the two institutions have successfully revived the Berlin tradition of African studies. In Leipzig, another former GDR centre of African studies, research has shifted to a close alliance between linguistics, history, economics and politics. Complementary to the development in Leipzig, Africa-related research conducted at the newly established Max Planck Institute of Social Anthropology in Halle, only a few kilometres away from Leipzig, concentrates on issues of legal pluralism, ethnicity, and the state.

This is just a glimpse of the present situation in the former eastern part of Germany, including the West Berlin scene. To describe all the manifold Africa-related research activities taking place in the various other universities in Germany in detail would transcend the limited space of this chapter by far. What I set out to do in the remaining pages is therefore to restrict myself to a number of—in my view—important features which characterise the present state of affairs.

Differentiation and Concentration

It is surely the case that the history I have given of African studies in Germany from the 1960s onwards differs in many respects from Jane Guyer's (1996) history of African studies in the US. However, the basic pattern in terms of an initial focus on basic research on newly emergent Africa, followed by a development agenda, shows clear parallels with the German case. Indeed, it seems likely that the same finding can be detected in other countries as well. Thus assuming that Guyer's 'three eras' do have a wider currency, her last era, the experience of marginalisation and the dominant image of collapse, should be found in the German context as well. No doubt, the seemingly endless list of features powerfully inscribed into the Western perception of Africa, ranging from the AIDS pandemic all the way to the Zimbabwe conflict, have truly conjured an image of collapse in Germany too. Given this situation, it would be interesting to see if a specific German response and correlation to that perception does exist, and if it exists, how it is shaped.

Before I set out to answer this question I will briefly outline the regional specialisations on which the possible responses are based. In general, the German landscape of African studies shows a clear focus on West and East Africa. A list of the African countries in which senior members at the main centres of African Studies have conducted field research in the past five years illustrates this pattern.

Bayreuth	Benin, Burkina Faso, Côte d'Ivoire, Egypt, Ghana, Mali, Malawi, Morocco, Niger, Nigeria, Tanzania, Malawi, Mozambique, Sudan
Berlin, Free University	Benin, Ethiopia, Ghana, Mali, Sudan, Zambia
Berlin, Humboldt	Burkina Faso, Sudan, Tanzania, Zimbabwe
Cologne	Kenya, Namibia, Tanzania, Uganda
Frankfurt	Ghana, Burkina Faso
Hamburg	Cameroon, Ethiopia, Tanzania, Uganda
Leipzig	Nigeria, Sudan
Halle	Kenya, Somalia, Sudan, Tanzania
Mainz	Benin, Ghana, Mali, Ethiopia, Congo, South Africa, Chad
Munich	Nigeria, Sudan

The research themes in the context of this regional specialisation vary greatly, but certain key features can be detected. At the risk of over-simplification, it can be argued that issues like violence, conflicts, corruption, ethnicity, disaster, and the African state dominate present social science research on Africa in Germany. While in this way the situation presumably does not differ much from the one in other countries, what is specific in the German context are probably two main features. One is the emphasis given to the detailed historical analysis of the conflicts in question for which for the strongly linguistically informed ethno-historical work of Guenther Schlee (1999, 2002) on the modern politics of ethnic inclusion and exclusion among pastoralists in Somalia, southern Ethiopia and northern Kenya, and Carola Lentz's (1997, 1998, 2000) studies of settlement histories, land rights and ethnicity in northern Ghana can be seen as prominent examples. The other, more general feature concerns the way power and violence are conceptualised. A crucial source in this context is the writings of the German sociologist Heinrich Popitz (1969, 1992). Inspired by both Marx and Weber, Popitz belonged to a tradition of German cultural sociology which oscillated between philosophy, psychology and anthropology with scholars like Norbert Elias, Helmuth Plessner and Dieter Claessens being its most prominent representatives. Popitz's own theoretical reflections circulated mostly around *phenomena of power* (Popitz 1992). Following a processual perspective, he focussed on the formation of power, the establishment of norms, the stages through which the state acquired the monopoly of violence, and the control and limitation of violence. His insights have turned out to be highly influential in recent German research on the postcolonial state in Africa. Important examples in this context are Georg Elwert's (1997) studies on venality, morality, and markets of violence and Thomas Bierschenk's (2000a&b) analysis of political decentralisation in Benin. Those who made Popitz's work popular in the German Africanist milieu, however, were two former students of his, Trutz von Trotha and Gerd Spittler.

Both used his writings as an analytical instrument in their analysis of the French (Spittler 1981) and German (von Trotha 1994) colonial state in Niger and Togo respectively. Having produced students of their own, the influence of Popitz on German Africanist research within the realm of sociology and anthropology sees destined to last.[32]

Quite a different picture is conveyed by the role of political science and economics in German African Studies. Compared to the situation in the 1970s and 1980s, the disciplines are losing ground. At present, chairs of political science focussing specifically on Africa are found only at Leipzig and Hamburg. With respect to the situation of economics the situation is even worse. The reasons for this situation are without doubt manifold. Partly, however, they lie in the rather weak cooperation with anthropology, sociology and history, an approach taken, for example, in the study of African law at Bayreuth University. Certainly, a processual approach, based on intensive fieldwork, often conveys a different picture of the situation on the ground than the one produced by a classical institutional analysis which stands the danger of affirming and reproducing the powerful imagery of collapse and decay presently dominating perceptions of Africa in the West.

Given the often expressed need to correct that image, when it comes to appointments and the establishment of chairs, the respective policy seems to follow other interests. In fact, it is deplorable that up to now chairs in the fields of African arts and music do not exist. Certainly, there is Iwalewa House at Bayreuth university with its internationally acclaimed collection of modern African art, and the archive of modern African music at the University of Mainz which, as mentioned above, houses also the Janheinz Jahn library. Neither institution, however, is endowed with chairs.[33] Rather, the teaching of African art and music is part of the general curriculum, connected with anthropology and African literature. Again, the reasons for this outcome are manifold. Much has to do with role of museums which, at least in the beginning, have dominated the scene in this regard. Also mainstream African studies has followed more the study of crises and conflicts as outlined above. Yet in view of the fact that Popitz at the end of his days turned his interests more and more to the study of imagination and the realm of the fantastic this turn should have its effect on German African studies as well. With the rise of new research agendas concentrating now on media and visual culture the scene has changed drastically, demanding a proper place on the institutional level as well.

Current research following along such lines of interest (Behrend and Wendl 1999; Behrend 2001; Förster 2001; Förster and Okome forthcoming; Röschenthaler 2004; Probst 2001, 2004; forthcoming; Wendl 2001, 2004) is closely connected to the work of Fritz Kramer (1993). Formerly in the anthropology department in Berlin, then a professor at the Academy of Fine Arts in Hamburg, Kramer has influenced teaching and scholarship in African Studies in Germany in a way equal to that of Popitz, but this influence articulated itself in a different domain. In the early 1980s, together with Bernhard Streck, he initiated an extensive Sudan research programme which has yielded numerous monographs on the ways Dinka, Nuba or

Koma experienced and acted upon the situation of change, violence and crisis.[34] Working rather at the margins of anthropology with strong affinities to philosophy and art history, his main impact, however, is based on thinking across, or rather between, the disciplines. In this way he illuminated new horizons and stimulated a number of highly interesting studies of which Richard Rottenburg's (2002) recent sophisticated 'parable' about the mutual fictions and cultural translation processes in the world of development aid is one of the best examples.

Based on his own anthropological research in Tanzania and Germany, Rottenburg followed the modern demands of a multi-sited ethnography, investigating the 'traffic in culture' (Marcus and Myers 1995). As problematic as such a strategy might be in the case of anthropology, other disciplines have followed it with more ease. Thus, in religious studies, for instance, researchers at Bayreuth University have adopted it to study the spread of Pentecostal churches from Nigeria to Germany. A global network perspective is used in the fields of geography and Islamic studies, equally at Bayreuth, to study past and present processes in the establishment of Islamic law and education in Tanzania and the current transnational trade relations of Tanzanian entrepreneurs dealing with jewels and gems. Employing the notion of 'seascape', historians at the Centre for Modern Oriental Studies in Berlin are investigating cultural interactions across the Indian Ocean between Swahili and Gujarat in India. An important role in this context have been also the archaeological research activities in Cologne and Frankfurt/Main on rock paintings in Southern Africa and settlement history in West Africa.

Numerous other examples illustrating current German Africanist research in the 'traffic in cultures' could be given. The point they refer to affects the very heart of African studies. If African studies are part of areas studies, what is meant with 'area' exactly? Does it have its borders at the shores of the Atlantic or the Indian Ocean? Is someone who is doing research on members of the 'African diaspora' in Cuba, the US or Brazil not part of the (imagined) community of African studies any longer? Debates on this matter can be found in the German context as well. Yet it seems to me that the German situation still differs from the US one (Berger 1997; Alpers and Roberts 2002). The crisis which affected areas studies in the US during the 1990s did not hit the German scene that hard. While there are several reasons for this, one major factor was and still is the German funding situation in terms of the existence of special collaborative research centres funded by the German Research Foundation fostering inter-disciplinary work within a framework of a specific research agenda on a long-term basis.[35]

The existence of these centres seems to have had not only a stabilising effect on African studies— making it a bit more relaxed about the threat of becoming obsolete—but has also led to certain centralisation processes within the German landscape of African studies. Given that the programmes operate for a length up to twelve years, they can generate or consolidate jobs and distinct local research profiles. Since this requires not only a sustained effort on the part of individual members to maintain the quality of research but also the support of the university and the authorities of the federal states, centres are embedded in a changing political environment which makes the success of research dependent also on extra-academic factors. The following list shows the old and new centres which have been established over the past years.[36]

- Bayreuth: 'Identity in Africa' (1984-1997), 'Local Action in Africa in the Context of Global Influences' (2000-present);

- Cologne: 'Arid Climate, Adaptation and Cultural Innovation in Africa' (1995-present);

- Frankfurt/Main: 'Culture Development and Language History in the West African Savannah' (1988-2003);

- Hamburg: 'Processes of Social Transformation and their Mastering in Africa' (1999-2002);

- Mainz: 'Processes of Change in Historical Fields of Tension in Northeast Africa and West Asia' (1997-present).

New centres are bound to arise. Currently, a strong focus exists on studying and fostering South-South relations. Already, a respective research unit has been established in the context of the collaborative research centre at Bayreuth University. Other activities along this line concern the assistance in establishing an intra-African science network and the improvement of academic collaboration between German and African institutions. A new programme in this respect has been launched only recently by the VW Foundation. Among those who designed the VW programme was Mamadou Diawara, professor of anthropology at Frankfurt University and founder of Point Sud, an autonomous research institution located at Bamako, Mali, focussing on local knowledge and developing new modes of interaction amongst countries of the South. Besides Mamadou Diawara, another prominent figure is Said Khamis. Teaching African literature at Bayreuth University, Said Khamis invests his energies in the strengthening of academic collaboration in the field of Swahili studies. Similar initiatives could be listed. What they amount to is the determined effort on the side of German African studies not only to study but also to counter the 'African crisis'.

Outlook

At the beginning of this contribution I employed Victor Turner's famous formula of 'betwixt and between' to characterise the position of African studies in Germany within the European context. Having reached the end, I want to conclude with a reflection on the possible future of this position. Two possible scenarios seem to prevail.

Given the growing importance of the European Union as a common political and economic project, the corresponding notion of a common European identity may come to serve as a kind of filter through which differences between research activities taking place inside and outside of Europe are perceived and negotiated. In fact, the existence of AEGIS (Africa-Europe Group for Interdisciplinary Studies), a London-based network of Africanist institutions of the European Union which was established in 1991, can be seen as a direct outcome of this development. Currently, the network consists of fourteen institutes coming from twelve European countries (Belgium, Denmark, France, Germany, Great Britain, France, Italy, Portugal, Spain, Sweden and Switzerland). Certainly, the number is still small. But it can be argued that the present situation simply represents an early phase in the formation of a more encompassing European Association of Africanists modelled on the African Studies Association in the US.[37]

On the other hand, there is the example of APAD. Based in Marseille, France, and founded roughly around the same time as AEGIS,[38] APAD stands for *Association Euro-Africaine pour l'Anthropologie Changement Social et du Développement*. Even though membership in APAD is open, the majority of members come from the Francophone sphere. British researchers are in the minority. Of course, being mostly concerned with developmental issues, the objectives of APAD are different from that of AEGIS. Nevertheless, the difficulties of APAD in bringing Anglophone and Francophone scholars together indicate some of the problems AEGIS might face as well.

Given this situation, it might well be that the position of African studies in Germany of being 'betwixt and between' will last for some time. It depends on the perspective one takes whether one sees this as positive or negative. In view of Victor Turner's ideas about liminality, there is every reason to be relaxed and focus on the creative power the position entails as a zone full of possibilities.

Notes

1. The present text benefited from comments and critique I received from a number of friends and colleagues. Femi Abodunrin, Thomas Bierschenk, Michael Bollig, Jan Georg Deutsch, Adeleke Durotoye, Andreas Eckert, Johannes Fabian, Carola Lentz, Ute Luig, Gudrun Miehe, Onookome Okome, János Riesz, Klaus Schubert, and Achim von Oppen all read and commented on a first version of this paper. I would like to thank all of them, stressing, of course, that the responsibility for all shortcomings and errors is solely mine.
2. This is not to say that such histories do not exist. So far, however, they have come only from outside. For a recent example, see Diallo (2001).
3. See the lively debate on the state of affairs of African studies in Germany in the recent issues of *Africa Spectrum* (Engel 2003, Bierschenk 2003, Reh 2003).
4. I am grateful to Carola Lentz and Thomas Bierschenk for drawing my attention to the importance of this feature.
5. For an overview of the range of Africa-related books and journals published in German see the website of two German publishing houses focussing on Africa-related research: Ruediger Koeppe Verlag (http://www.koeppe.de/) and LIT Verlag (http://www.lit-verlag.de/kataloge/afrika_2002.pdf). In addition see also the website of the Institute of African Affairs in Hamburg (http://www.duei.de/iak/show.php). The Institute functions as the base of the German Association of African Studies and is publishing

the association's journal *Africa Spectrum*. The association has its own website: http://www.vad-ev.de/. For more information see the appendix.

6. The influence of Frobenius on Senghor's notion of *négritude* is just one prominent example (Riesz 2002). Another is the German influence on American (cultural) anthropology through scholars like Franz Boas, Robert Lowie, Edward Sapir, and Alfred Kroeber (see Stocking 1996).

7. As it is well known, members of the Harlem renaissance in the US, for example, looked particularly to the early German pioneers of African studies as a source of inspiration and courage for their own project of creating a Black nation (Irek 1994a, b).

8. According to Guyer, the first era was marked by basic research on newly emergent Africa and the independence struggles, the second era was characterised by a development agenda, while the third and still lasting era is one in which the image of marginality and total collapse dominates the public perception of Africa.

9. See Essner (1985) and Marx (1988).

10. I would like to thank Johannes Fabian for the clarification of this point.

11. In his autobiography, Ratzel (1966) himself hinted at the relationship between his migration theory and the fact he grew up in a poor rural area region in the south-west of Germany where most of the early German migrants during that time came from.

12. A telling example of this position is Meinhof's short article on *Sprache und Volkstum* in the first volume of *Africa* (Meinhoff 1927). For an overview of the historical relationship between *Afrikanistik* and general linguistics, see Miehe (1996).

13. Ham, Chem and Japhet, the three sons of Noah, gave their names to the distinction between Hamitic, Semitic and Japhetic languages. While the latter were seen to be those populating the East, the former was seen to be the ancestor of peoples populating the South, i.e. Africa. The reason was the curse Noah laid on Canaan, the son of Ham, which destined him to eternal slavery. Mueller's and Lepsius's redefinition of the Hamites as coming originally from Asia thus not only 'whitened' Egypt; it deprived Africans also of their Biblical ancestor, thereby distancing Africa further from the West. Only later, with the work of Leo Frobenius, the Hamitic theory experienced yet another inversion, this time directed against the West, particularly France and England (see Rottland 1996).

14. A good contextualisation of Frobenius's work is given by Kramer (1985, 1986) and Streck (1995, 1999). For Frobenius's biography see Heinrichs (1998).

15. A similar argument has been made by Conte (1988) with respect to the differences between French and German approaches in the study of African history.

16. On this point see also Probst and Spittler (2004: 9ff).

17. Among the thirteen founding members of the Institute's editorial board four were from Germany and Austria: Karl Meinhof, Fathers Paul Schebesta and Wilhelm Schmidt, and Ludwig Schachtzabel, the successor of Bernhard Ankermann as director of the Africa department at the Ethnological Museum at Berlin.

18. See Probst, Deutsch and Schmidt (2002).

19. In terms of its conceptual approach Thurnwald's idea of change basically followed Malinowski's programme of culture contact which he had outlined in the Institute's *Five Year Plan of Research* (African International Institute 1932). Methodologically, however, the study was based not on participant observation but on questionnaires and surveys.

20. During a visit to the US in 1932 Thurnwald gave lectures at Yale and Northwestern University where he also met with Melville Herskovits with whom he discussed the concept of acculturation (Melk-Koch 1989: 268f).

21. A telling example of this ambition was Hermann Baumann. As an anthropologist belonging to the second generation of the German culture history school, Baumann's aim was to reshape the old *Kulturkreis* concept not only by focussing on the distribution of material artefacts but also by taking into account the role of landscape and language. Already in 1934, at that time still working at the Ethnological museum in Berlin, he had published an article in *Africa* in which he had outlined his ideas (Baumann 1934). In 1939, one year after the so-called *Anschluß* of Austria to Germany, Baumann moved from Berlin to Vienna to take over the chair of anthropology there. The former incumbent, Kopper, a close ally of Father Wilhem Schmidt, had been expelled in the course of the political purification programmes. With Baumann came a strong proponent of the Nazi ideology. Shortly after his arrival in Vienna he published the handbook *Voelkerkunde von Afrika* (Baumann, Westermann and Thurnwald 1940). The scope of the book clearly conformed to the new demands. Organised into three parts, Bauman wrote on culture history, Westermann on language and education, and Thurnwald on colonial intervention and social change. All the three texts were impregnated by the revanchist and expansionist plan to re-appropriate and reconquer the lost colonies. Thus Westermann, who had lost his position as co-director of the International African Institute with the outbreak of the war in 1939, affirmed the colonial master-servant relation and Thurnwald revived the old resentment against France when he criticised the French colonial policy of assimilation. Of all three authors, however, Baumann exemplified the new milieu most explicitly (Baumann 1940). His text is an oppressive blending of the idea of culture province, the linguistic model of a Hamitic invasion, and the new paradigm of race biology with its programmes of race breeding and genetic manipulation. For other studies see Fischer (1990), Hauschild (1996), Linimayr (1994), Mosen (1991), and Streck (2000).

22. In Frankfurt, Adolf Ellegard Jensen, a student of Froebenius who had succeeded him after his death in 1936 as director of the Frobenius Institute, became incumbent of the new chair of anthropology in 1947. In 1947, Westermann was reinstalled as the director of the Institute of Oriental Languages in Berlin. In Hamburg, August Klingenheben, who had succeeded Meinhof in 1936, continued to hold the chair until 1954. In the same year Hermann Baumann, who had held the chair of anthropology in Vienna until 1945, resurfaced in Munich as chair of anthropology at the newly established institute of anthropology.

23. Actually, Westermann had started to work on the book already in the early 1940s. In the turmoil of the war, however, the completed manuscript as well as the printing plates were lost, so that Westermann rewrote the book anew after the war.

24. Of course, there were lobbies, for example, in West Germany the Institute of African Affairs in Hamburg and the German African Society in Bonn. However, their purpose was more of an applied and practical nature in terms of serving as political and economic consultants for the German government. In fact, it was not the least the strongly con-

servative character of the German African Society against which the new association was directed.

25. The trend is clearly reflected in the early VAD conferences. While the first conference focussed on problems of interdisciplinary collaboration, the second conference was devoted to the notion of Africanity (*Afrikanität*) and theoretical problems of socialism in Africa (Grohs 1971). In the centre of the discussion stood the difference between Senghor's and Jahn's political vision of *negritúde* and Nyerere's practice of African socialism in the shape of *ujamaa*. Participants analysed the translation and appropriation of Western political concepts into Swahili and deconstructed Senghor's and Jahn's hidden agenda. Those who dominated the discussions were sociologists, political scientists, and anthropologists. In contrast to the first meeting linguists were now in minority. In the following years the trend in 'social sciencing' African studies continued. During the third VAD meeting in 1971, the conference theme was on ethnic minorities and nation building in Africa (Hinz 1974), the fourth conference on problems of social sciences in Africa (Benzing 1975), while the fifth annual conference discussed methods of Africanist research and teaching in Germany (Benzing & Bolz 1976).

26. Especially Bernd Heine, Wilhelm Moehlig, and Hermann Jungraithmayr.

27. For a short account of the history of this platform, see (Möhlig 1995).

28. By the late 1970s the grand narratives of culture history had been duly buried. The last major work indebted to this tradition was Hermann Baumann's posthumously published *Die Völker Afrikas und Ihre Traditionellen Kulturen* (Baumann 1975). See, however, the revival and modification of this research in Sweden (Jacobson-Widding 1984, Zwernemann 1983.)

29. For a biographical account of these developments see Riesz (2003) and Breitinger (2003).

30. For the history of this research tradition see Büttner (1992).

31. The courses Janheinz Jahn gave at the university of Frankfurt took place in the Frobenius Institute, thus in the department of anthropology, not that of English.

32. At the anthropology departments in Munich and Bayreuth, Kurt Beck and Georg Klute are carrying this tradition further.

33. At Iwalewa House, after Ulli Beier retired in 1997, Till Förster had taken over the directorship. Having moved to the University of Basle, Switzerland, Tobias Wendl is now the new director. In Mainz, the centre for modern African music is embodied in the tireless activities of Wolfgang Bender.

34. An overview of the programme is given in (Kramer & Streck 1991).

35. The German Research Foundation started these programmes back in 1964. In the beginning they comprised mostly research initiatives in the natural sciences. From the late 1980s, however, African studies came onto the scene as well.

36. For more information, see the web-sites of these centres in the appendix.

37. A certain indication for the validity of such an argument was the first AEGIS European conference scheduled for 29 June to 3 July 2005 in London.

38. I would like to thank Thomas Bierschenk for relating his experiences with APAD.

Appendix: List of universities and disciplines with a strong Africa focus

Universities	African Languages	Anthropology	Archaeology	Geography	History	Islamic Studies	Law	Literature	Economics	Political Science	Religious Studies	Sociology
Bayreuth	x	x		x	x	x	x	x	x		x	x
FU Berlin		x		x								
HU Berlin	x		x		x	x		x				x
Cologne	x	x	x	x	x			x				
Frankfurt/M.	x	x	x	x	x			x				
Halle		x					x					
Hamburg	x	x	x	x	x					x		
Hannover					x							
Leipzig	x	x			x			x	x	x		
Mainz	x	x				x		x				
Munich	x	x						x				x

References

International African Institute, 1932, 'A five year plan of research', *Africa* 5: 1-13.

Alpers, E. and A. Roberts, 2002, 'What is African Studies? some reflections', *African Issues* 30 (2): 11-18.

Anderson, B., 1991, *Imagined Communities: Reflections on the Origin and Spread of Nationalism*, London: Verso.

Ankermann, B., 1905, 'Kulturkreise und Kulturgeschichten in Afrika', *Zeitschrift für Ethnologie* 37: 53-90.

Ansprenger, F., 1961, *Politik im schwarzen Afrika: Die modernen politischen Bewegungen in Afrika französischer Prägung*, Köln.

Baumann, H., 1934, 'Die afrikanischen Kulturkreise', *Africa* 7: 129-142.

Baumann, H., 1940, 'Völker und Kulturen Afrikas', in H. Baumann, R. Thurnwald and D. Westermann, eds., *Völkerkunde von Afrika mit besonderer Beruecksichtigung der kolonialen Aufgabe*, Essen: Verlagsanstalt, 3-374.

Baumann, H., ed., *Die Völker Afrikas und ihre traditionellen Kulturen*, Wiesbaden: Steiner.

Baumann, H., R. Thurnwald, and D. Westermann, eds., 1940, *Völkerkunde von Afrika mit besonderer Beruecksichtigung der kolonialen Aufgabe*, Essen: Verlagsanstalt.

Behrend, H., 1999 [1993], *Alice Lakwena and the Holy Spirits: War in Northern Uganda*, Oxford: James Currey.

Behrend, H., ed., 2001, 'Photographies and Modernities in Africa', *Visual Anthropology* 14 (3).

Behrend, H. and U. Luig, eds., 1999, *Spirit Possession, Power and Modernity*, Oxford: James Currey.

Behrend, H. and T. Wendl, eds., 1999, *Snap me One: Studiophotographen in Africa*, Muenchen: Prestel.

Bender, W., 1991, *Sweet Mother. Modern African Music*, Chicago: University of Chicago Press.

Benzing, B., ed., 1975, *Beiträge zu den Problemen und Tendenzen der sozialwissenschaften in Afrika*, Hamburg: Buske.

Benzing, B. and R. Bolz, eds., 1976, *Methoden der afrikanistischen Forschung und Lehre in der BRD*, Hamburg: Buske.

Berger, I., 1997, 'Contested boundaries: African Studies approaching the millennium', *African Studies Review* 40 (2): 1-14.

Bierschenk, T, and J.-P. O. de Sardan, eds., 1998, *Les pouvoirs aux villages: Le Bénin rural entre démocratisation et decentralization*, Paris: Karthala

Bierschenk, T., 2000a, 'Introduction: Les courtiers entre développement et État', in T. Bierschenk, J.-P. Olivier de Sardan, and J.-P. Chauveau, eds., *Courtiers en développement: Les villages africaines en quête des projets*. Paris: Karthala, 5-42

Bierschenk, T., 2000b, 'Herrschaft, Verhandlung und Gewalt im modernen Afrika: Zur politischen Soziologie einer afrikanischen Mittelstadt (Parakou, Benin)', *Afrika-Spektrum* 34: 321-348.

Bierschenk, T., 2003, 'Brauchen wir mehr Afrika-Politologen und weniger Aethiopisten?', *Africa-Spectrum* 38 (2): 243-248.

Bley, H., 1968, *Kolonialherrschaft und Sozialstruktur in Deutsch-Südwestafrika, 1894-1914*, Hamburg: Rowohlt.

Breitinger, E., 2003, 'Afrikanische Literatur und deutsche Universität: Eine Polemik', in F. Veit-Wild, *Nicht nur Märchen und Mythen: Afrika Literatur als Herausforderung*, Trier: Otto & Kornelius, 164-174.

Büttner, T., 1992, 'The development of African historical studies in East Germany: an outline and selected bibliography', *History in Africa* 19: 133-146.

Conte, E., 1988, 'Verfehlte Begegnungen: Deutschand, Frankreich—Unterschiedliche Ethnologie, Unterschiedliche Geschichtsauffassung Afrikas', in N. E. Conte, ed., *Macht und Tradition in Westafrika: Französische Anthropologie und Afrikanische Geschichte*, Frankfurt: Campus, 9-48.

Cooper, F., 2001, 'What is the concept of globalization good for?', *African Affairs* 100: 189-213.

Diallo, Y., 2001, 'L'africanisme en Allemagne hier et aujourd'hui', *Cahiers d'Etudes Africaines* 161 (XLI-1): 13-43.

Deutsch, J. G., P. Probst and H. Schmidt, eds., 2002, *African Modernites: Cherished Meanings and Entangled Debate*, Oxford: James Currey.

Dostal, W., 1994, 'Silence in the darkness: German ethnology during the nationalist socialist period', *Social Anthropology* 2: 251-262.

Elwert, G., 1997, 'Gewaltmärkte: Beobachtungen zur Zweckrationalitaet der Gewalt', in T. von Trotha, ed., *Soziologie der Gewalt*, Opladen: Westdeutscher Verlag, 86-101 (special issue of *Koelner Zeitschrift fuer Soziologie und Sozialpsychologie*, No. 37).

Elwert, G., S. Fechtwang and D. Neubert, eds., 1999, *Dynamics of Violence: Processes of Escalation and De-Escalation in Violent Group Conflicts*, Sociologus Berlin: Duncker & Humblot.

Elwert, G., 2001, 'Conflict, anthropological perspective', in N. Smelser and P. Baltes, eds., *International Encyclopedia of the Social and Behavioral Sciences*, Amsterdam: Elsevier: 2542-2547.

Engel, U., 2003, 'Gedanken zur Afrikanistik: Zustand und Zukunft einer Regionalwissenschaft', *Africa-Spectrum* 38 (1): 111-123.

Erlmann, V., 1996, *Nightsong: Performance, Power and Practice in South Africa*, Chicago: University of Chicago Press.

Erlmann, V., 1991, *African Stars: Studies in South African Performance*, Chicago: University of Chicago Press.

Essner, C., 1985, *Deutsche Afrikareisende im 19 Jahrhundert*, Stuttgart: Steiner.

Fabian, J., 1983, *Time and the Other: How Anthropology Makes its Object*, Columbia: Columbia University Press.

Fiebach, J., 1979, *Kunstprozesse in Afrika: Literatur im Umbruch*, Berlin: Akademieverlag.

Fiebach J., 1986, *Die Toten als die Macht der Lebenden: Zur Theorie und Geschichte von Theater in Afrika*, Berlin: Henschel Verlag.

Fischer, H., 1990, *Völkerkunde im Nationalsozialismus: Aspekte der Anpassung, Affinität und Behauptung einer wissenschaftlichen Disziplin*, Berlin: Diedrich Reimer Verlag.

Förster, T., 2001, 'Wiedersehen mit den Toten: Eine Ethnographie der Medien in Westafrika', in H. Behrend, ed., *Geist, Bild Narr: Zu einer Ethnologie kultureller Konversionen. Festschrift fuer Fritz Kramer*, Berlin: Philo, 155-171.

Förster, T. & O. Okome, eds., forthcoming, *Modes of Seeing: The Popular Video in Africa*.

Forstreuter, B., ed., 1975, *Gedichte*, Berlin: Volk und Welt.

Frisby, D., 1986, *Fragments of Modernity*, Oxford: Polity Press.

Frobenius, L., 1898a, *Die Geheimbünde Afrikas: Eine Ethnologische Studie*, Hamburg: Verlagsanstalt u. Druckerei A.-G.

Frobenius, L., 1898b, *Der Ursprung der Afrikanischen Kulturen*, Berlin.

Frobenius, L., 1921, *Paideuma: Umrisse einer Kultur-und Seelenlehre*, München: C. H. Beck.

Frobenius, L., 1933, *Kulturgeschichte Afrikas: Prolegomena zu einer historischen Gestaltlehre*, Zürich: Atlantis.

Geiss, I., 1968, *Panafrikanismus: Zur Geschichte der Dekolonisation*, Frankfurt: EVA.

Geiss, I., 1976, 'The study of African history in Germany', in C. Fyfe, ed., *African Studies since 1945: A Tribute to Basil Davidson*, London: Routledge, 209-219.

Grohs, G., 1967, *Stufen afrikanischer Emanzipation: Studien zum Selbstverständnis*,

Grohs, G., ed., 1971, *Theoretische Probleme des Sozialismus in Afrika*, Hamburg: Buske.

Graebner, F., 1905, 'Kulturkreise und Kulturgeschichten in Afrika', *Zeitschrift für Ethnology* 37: 28-52.

Gutmann, B., 1932, *Die Stammeslehren der Dschagga*, 3 Vols., Muenchen: Beck.

Gutmann, B., 1966, *Afrikaner—Europaer in naechstenschaftlicher Entsprechung*, Stuttgart: Evangelisches Verlagswerk.

Guyer, J., 1996, *African Studies in the United States*, Atlanta: ASA Press.

Harneit-Sievers, A., ed., 2002, *New Local Historiographies from Africa and South Asia*, Leiden: Brill.

Hauschildt, T., ed., 1996, *Lebenslust und Fremdenfurcht: Ethnologie im Dritten Reich*, Frankfurt: Suhrkamp.

Heine, B., U. Claudi, and F. Huennemeyer, 1991, *Grammaticalization: A conceptual framework*, Chicago: University of Chicago Press.

Heine, B., 1997, *Cognitive Foundations of Grammar*, New York, Oxford: Oxford University Press.

Heine, B. and D. Nurse, eds., 2000, *African Languages: An Introduction*, Cambridge: Cambridge University Press.

Heinrichs, J., 1998, *Die fremde Welt, das bin ich: Leo Frobenius, Ethnologe, Forschungsreisender, Abenteurer*, Wuppertal: Hammer.

Herskovits, M., 1937, 'The significance of the study of acculturation for anthropology', *American Anthropologist* 39: 259-264.

Heyden, U. van der, 1999, *Die Afrikawissenschaften in der DDR. Eine akademische Disziplin zwischen Exotik und Exempel: Eine wissenschaftsgeschichtliche Untersuchung*, Münster/Hamburg/London: LIT Verlag

Hinz, M., ed., 1974, *Ethnische Minoritäten im Prozess Nationaler Integration in Afrika*, Hamburg: Buske.

Hinz, M., 1976, 'Thesen zur Posiumsdiskussion Afrikanische Afrikanistik', in B. Benzing, ed., *Methoden der afrikanistischen Forschung und lehre in der BRD*, Hamburg: Buske., 217-218.

Irek, M., 1994a, 'From Berlin to Harlem: Felix von Luschan, Alain Locke and the New Negro', iIn W. Sollors and M. Diedrich, eds., *The Black Columbias. Defining Moments in African American Literature and Culture*, Cambridge, MA: Harvard University Press, 174-184.

Irek, M., 1994b, *The European Roots of the Harlem Renaissance*, Münster: Lit Verlag.

Jacobson-Widding, A., 1984, 'African folk-Models and the application: modified research design and progress report of the Research Programme on African Cultures sponsored by the Swedish Council for Research in the Humanities and Social Sciences', *Uppsala Working Papers in African Studies*, No. 1.

Jahn, J., 1954, *Schwarzer Orpheus: Moderne Dichtung afrikanischer Völker beider Hemisphären*, München: Carl Hanser.

Jahn, J., 1957, *Rumba Macumba: Afrocubanische Lyrik*, München Hanser.

Jahn, J., 1961 [1958], *Muntu: an Outline of Neo-African Culture*, Marjorie Grene (Übers.), London: Faber & Faber.

Jones, A., ed., 2002, 'Everyday life in colonial Africa', *Journal of African Cultural Studies* 15 (1): 93-103.

Kramer, F., 1985, 'Empathy—reflections on the history of ethnology in pre-fascist Germany: Herder, Creuzer, Bastian, Bachofen, and Frobenius', *Dialectical Anthropology* 9: 337-347.

Kramer, F., 1986, 'Die Aktualität des Exotischen: Der Fall der "Kulturmorphologie" von Frobenius und Jensen', in R. Faber and R. Schlesier, eds., *Die Restauration der Götter: Antike Religion und Neo-Paganismus*. Würzburg: Königshausen and Neumann, 258-270.

Kramer, F., 1993 [1987], *The Red Fes: Art and Spirit Possession in Africa*, London: Verso.

Kramer, F. and B. Streck, 1991, *Sudanesische Marginalien*, Muenchen: Trickster.

Krauth, W. H., 1998, 'Die Asien- und Afrikawissenschaften in der DDR', in W.H. Krauth and R. Wolz, eds., *Wissenschaft und Wiedervereinigung: Asien-und Afrikawissenschaften im Umbruch*, Berlin: Akademie Verlag, 443-466.

Lentz, C., 1998, *Die Konstruktion von Ethnizität: Eine politische Geschichte Nord-West Ghanas, ca. 1870-1990*, Köln: Köppe.

Lentz, C., 1997, 'Creating ethnic identities in north-western Ghana', in C. Govers and H. Vermeulen, eds., *The Politics of Ethnic Consciousness*. London: Macmillan, 31–89.

Lentz, C., 2000, 'Of hunters, goats and earth-shrines: settlement histories and the politics of oral tradition in northern Ghana', *History in Africa* 27: 193–214.

Lentz, C. and P. Nugent, eds., 2000, *Ethnicity in Ghana: The Limits of Invention*, London: Macmillan.

Lepsius, R., 1880, *Nubische Grammatik. Mit einer Einleitung über die Völker und Sprachen Afrikas*, Berlin.

Lindfors, B. and U. Schild, eds., 1976, *Neo-African Literature and Culture. Essays in Memory of Janheinz Jahn*, Mainzer Afrika-Studien, 1, Wiesbaden: B. Heymann, 1976.

Linimayr, P., 1994, *Wiener Völkerkunde im Nationalsozialismus*, Frankfurt: Peter Lang.

Loimeier, R., 1997, *Islamic Reform and Political Change in Northern Nigeria*, Evanston, IL: Northwestern University Press.

Luig, U., 2001, 'Anthropology of spirits', in N. Smelser and P. Baltes, eds., *International Encyclopedia of the Social and Behavioral Sciences*, Amsterdam: Elsevier, 2542-2547.

Luig, U. and A. von Oppen, eds., 1997, *The Making of African Landscapes*, Paideuma, Mitteilungen zur Kulturkunde Vol. 43, Wiesbaden: Steiner.

Marcus, G. and F. Myers, eds., 1995, *The Traffic in Cultures*, Berkeley: University of California Press.

Marx, C., 1988, *Völker ohne Schrift und Geschichte: Zur historischen Erfassung des vorkolonialen Schwarzafrika in der deutschen Forschung des 19.und fruehen 20. Jh*, Stuttgart: Steiner.

Meinhof, C., 1909, *Grundriß einer Lautlehre der Bantusprachen nebst einer Anleitung zur Aufnahme von Bantusprachen*, Leipzig, Berlin.

Meinhof, C., 1915 [1910], *An Introduction to the Study of African Languages*, New York: E.P. Dutton.

Meinhof, C., 1927, 'Sprache und Volkstum', *Africa*, Vol. 1, 1-8.

Melk-Koch, M., 1989, *Auf der Suche nach der menschlichen Gemeinschaft. Richard Thurnwald*, Berlin: SMPK.

Miehe, G., 1996, 'Vom Verhältnis zwischen Afrikanistik und Allgemeiner Sprachwissenschaft', *Paideuma* 46: 267-284.

Moehlig, W. J. G., 1976, 'Zur Methode der afrikanistischen Afrikanistik', in B. Benzing, ed., *Methoden der afrikanistischen Forschung und Lehre in der BRD*, Hamburg: Buske, 163-184.

Moehlig, W. J. G., 1995, 'Der Afrikanistentag ein Forum aktueller Forschung', in A. Fleisch and D. Otten, eds., *Sprachkulturelle und Historische Forschung in Afrika*, Köln: Koeppe, 9-12.

Mosen, M., 1991, *Der koloniale Traum. Angewandte Ethnologie im Nationalsozialismus*, Bonn: Holos Verlag.

Müller, F., 1876-1888, *Grundriss der Sprachwissenschaft*, 4 vols., Wien.

Popitz, H., 1969, *Prozesse der Machtbildung*, Tuebingen: Mohr.

Popitz, H., 1992, *Phänomene der Macht: Autorität, Herrschaft, Gewalt, Technik*, Tübingen: Mohr.

Probst, P., 2001, 'Bild und Weltbild', in H. Behrend, ed., *Geist, Bild Narr. Zu einer Ethnologie kultureller Konversionen: Festschrift für Fritz Kramer*, Berlin: Philo, 207-223.

Probst, P., G. Deutsch. and H. Schmidt, 2002, 'Cherished visions and entangled meanings', in G. Deutsch, P. Probst and H. Schmidt, eds., *African Modernities*, Oxford: James Currey, 1-17.

Probst, P. and G. Spittler, 2004, 'From an anthropology of astonishment to a critique of anthropology's common sense: an exploration into the notion of local vitality in Africa', in P. Probst and G. Spittler, eds., *Between Resistance and Expansion*, Muenster/Hamburg/London: Lit Verlag, 1-32.

Probst, P., 2004, 'Schrecken und Staunen: Nyau Masken der Chewa im Kontext der Konjunktur des Okkulten und der Medialisierung der Gewalt in Afrika', in T. Wendl, ed., *Africa Screams: Das Böse in Kino, Kunst und Kult*, Wuppertal. Hammer.

Probst, P., ed., forthcoming, *The Audience of Images. Visual Publics in Africa and Beyond*.

Ratzel, F., 1882, *Anthropo-Geographie oder Grundzuege der Anwendung der Erdkunde auf die Geschichte*, Stuttgart.

Ratzel, F., 1889, 'Die Afrikanischen Boegen—Ihre Verbreitung und Verwandtschaften', *Abhandlungen der Koeniglichen Saechsischen Gesellschaft der Wissenschaften, philologisch-historische Classe*, Band XIII, Nr. 111, 291-343.

Ratzel, F., 1966, *Jugenderinnerungen*, München.

Reh, M., 2004, 'Plädoyer für eine Stärkung der Afrikaforschung, die afrikanische Sprachen als gesellschaftliches Gestaltungs-Interpretations- und Ausdrucksmedium ernst nimmt', *Africa-Spectrum* 23: 249-251.

Riesz, J., 2002, 'Senghor and the Germans', *Research in African Literatures* 33 (4): 25-37.

Riesz, J., 2003, 'Afroromanistik', in F. Veit-Wild, ed., *Nicht nur Mythen und Märchen: Afrika-Literaturwissenschaft als Herausforderung*, Trier: Otto and Kornelius, 153-168.

Riesz, J. and P. Halen, eds., 1997, *Patrice Lumumba entre Dieu et Diable: Un héros africain dans ses images*, Paris: Karthala.

Röschenthaler, U., 2004, 'Die Ambivalenz des Außergewöhnlichen', in T. Wendl, ed., *Africa Screams: Das Böse in Kino, Kunst und Kult*, Wuppertal: Hammer.

Rottenburg, R., 2002, *Weit hergeholte Fakten: Eine Parabel der Entwicklungshilfe*, Stuttgart: Lucius and Lucus.

Rottland, F., 1996, 'Hamiten, Neger, Negritude: Zur Geschichte der afrikanistischen Klassifikation', *Paideuma* 42: 53-62.

Schild, U., 1974, 'Janheinz Jahn, 1918-1973', *Research in African Literatures* 5: 194-195.

Schlee, G., 1989, *Identitities on the Move: Clanship and Pastoralism in Northern Kenya*, Manchester: Manchester University Press.

Schlee, G., 1999, 'Nomades et Etat au Nord Kenya', in A. Bourgeot, ed., *Horizont nomades en Afrique Sahélinenne*, Paris: Karthala, 219-239.

Schlee, G., 2001, 'Ethnicity and Language', in *International Encyclopedia of Social and Behavioral Sciences*, Amsterdam: Elsevier, 8285-8288.

Schlee, G., 2002, 'Régularités dans le chaos: Traits récurrents dans l'organisation politoco-religieuse et militaire des Somalis', *L'Homme* 161: 17-49.

Schmidt, P. W. and W. Koppers, 1924, *Völker und Kulturen*, Regensburg: Habbel.

Scholz, F., 2001, 'Nomads/Nomadism in History', in *International Encyclopedia of Social and Behavioral Sciences*, Amsterdam: Elsevier, 10650–10655.

Schott, R., 1978, 'Das Recht gegen das Gesetz: Traditionelle und moderne Rechtssprechung bei den Bulsa in Nordghana', in F. Kaulbach and W. Krawietz, eds., *Recht und Gesellschaft*, Berlin: Dunker and Humblot.

Schott, R., 1980, 'Triviales und Transzendentes: Einie Aspekte afrikanischer Rechtstraditionen unter besonderer Beruecksichtigung der Bulsa in Nordghana', in W. Fikentscher, H. Franke and O. Koehler, eds., *Entstehung und Wandel rechtlicher Traditionen*, Freiburg.

Sombart, W., 1927, *Das Wirtschaftsleben im Zeitalter des Hochkapitalismus*, Berlin: Dunker und Humblot.

Spittler, G., 1978, *Herrschaft über Bauern: Die Ausbreitung staatlicher Herrschaft und einer islamisch-urbanen Kultur in Gobir (Niger)*, Frankfurt am Main.

Spittler, G., 1981, *Verwaltung in einem afrikanischen Bauernstaat: Das koloniale Französisch Westafrika 1991-1939*, Freiburg.

Spittler, G., 1993 [1989], *Les Touaregs face aux sécheresses et aux famines: Les Kel Ewey de l'Aïr, (Niger) (1900-1985)*, Paris: Karthala.

Spittler, G., 2001, 'Work: anthropological aspects', in N. J. Smelser and P. B. Baltes, eds, *International Encyclopedia of the Social and Behavioral Sciences 24*, Amsterdam: Elsevier 16565-16568.

Stocking, G., ed., 1996, *Volksgeist as Method and Ethic: Essays on Boasian Ethnography and the German Anthropological Tradition*, Madison: University of Wisconsin Press.

Streck, B., 1995, 'Entfremdete Gestalt: Die Konstruktion von Kultur in den zwei Frank-furter Denkschulen', in T. Hauschild, ed., *Lebenslust und Fremdenfurcht: Ethnologie im Dritten Reich*, Frankfurt: Suhrkamp, 103-120.

Streck, B., 1999, 'Leo Frobenius oder die Begeisterung in der deutschen Völkerkunde', *Paideuma* 45: 31-43.

Streck, B., ed., 2000, *Ethnologie und Nationalsozialismus*, Gehren.

Strecker, I., 1988, *The Social Practice of Symbolization: An Anthropological Analysis*, London: Athlone Press.

Tetzlaff, G., 1970, *Koloniale Entwicklung und Ausbeutung: Wirtschafts und Sozialgeschichte Deutsch-Ostafrikas 1885-1914*, Berlin.

Thurnwald, R., 1910, 'Rezension von C.E. Woodrufs "Expansion of Race", *Archiv für Rassen- und Gesellschaftsbiologie*', Vol. VII: 658.

Thurnwald, R., 1931-1935, *Die Menschliche Gesellschaft in Ihren Ethno-Soziologischen Grundlagen*, 5 Vols., Berlin and Leipzig.

Thurnwald, R., 1932, 'The Psychology of Acculturation', *American Anthropologist* 34: 557-569.

Thurnwald, R., 1935, *Black and White in East Africa*, London: IAI.

Von Trotha, T., 1994, *Koloniale Herrschaft: Szur soziologischen Theorie der Staatsentstehung am Beispiel des Schutzgebietes Togo*, Tübingen: Mohr.

VAD, ed., 1970, *Interdisziplinäre Afrikanistik*, Hamburg: Buske.

Veit-Wild, F., ed., 2003, *Nicht nur Mythen und Märchen: Afrika-Literaturwissenschaft als Herausforderung*, Trier: Otto und Kornelius.

Wendl, T., 2001, 'African art and performance on video and film', in H. Cole, ed., *The Grove Encyclopedia of African Art*, London: MacMillan.

Wendl, T., 2004, *Africa Screams. Das Böse in Kino, Kunst und Kult*, Wuppertal: Hammer.

Westermann, D., 1934, *The African To-day*, London.

Westermann, D., 1938, *Afrikaner erzählen ihr Leben*, Essen: Essener Verlagsanstalt.

Westermann, D., 1940, 'Sprache und Erziehung', in H. Baumann et al., eds., *Völkerkunde von Afrika*, Essen: Essener Verlagsanstalt, 375-454.

Westermann, D., 1952, *Geschichte Afrikas: Staatenbildung südlich der Sahara*. Köln: Greven.

Westermann, D. and I. Ward, 1934, *Practical Phonetics for Students of African Languages*, London.

Zwernemann, J., 1983, *Culture History and African Anthropology: A Century of Research in Germany and Austria*, Stockholm: Almquist and Wiksell.

Chapter 9

Research on Africa: A Swedish Perspective

Ann Schlyter

This paper provides a short overview of Swedish research on Africa, with a special focus on gender perspectives. It further comments on the development cooperation policy of Sweden and the European Commission and on research on urban issues. The focus is motivated by my own experiences of urban and gender research in southern Africa. The paper points out the connection between research on Africa, development cooperation and the broader political context.

Studies in Colonial Africa

The early history of studies on Africa in Europe or by Europeans is closely interlinked with the history of trade. For example, in the eighteenth century in Naples, an institute was founded in order to support trade with Ethiopia by training trade partners and by collecting information on the markets. With the slave trade, colonisation and the extraction of resources, the encounters between Europe and Africa became less and less equal. Travellers, explorers, and a growing number of scholars of various blends formed the images of Africa in Europe.

From a distance and as a first generalisation one might say that natural scientists and ethnographers played an important role in colonisation, as they provided information for the utilisation of resources in Africa—besides slaves. The colonial masters needed information about local social conditions and power relations, specifically so with the model of 'indirect rule' applied by the British.

Certainly, knowledge production is always situated in power relations. But looking closer, the situation becomes quite complex. One reason is the relative independence of university studies. In the academic world there was a quest for great narratives, even for 'laws' to which all human beings adhered. Cross-cultural comparison was a basis for generalisations and early anthropology was based on a belief in biological and social evolution. Africans were seen as backward, and studies in Africa were seen as a way to understand the human pre-historic past.

Occasionally anthropologists took the side of the colonised in opposition to the colonial administration. They tried to protect local populations against damaging of various kinds. However, their perspective was often to preserve and protect what they saw as the genuine, traditional 'tribal' life against the threat of modern influences. The urban anthropologists of the Rhodes-Livingstone–Manchester school developed a line of argument very different from those who wanted to write monographs of a 'tribe'. They used aggregated information and extended case histories in a way that became standard also in development studies and they introduced the network concept in analysing social change.

Studies on Behalf of Neo-colonialism, Solidarity, or for Academic Interest

In the 1960s, at the time of African independence, there were only a few universities on the continent. National universities were built more or less as annexes to European ones. It was a slow process to broaden education, as it had to start with recruitment to secondary schools. Ideas of pursuing 'local knowledge', and the provision of schools with a curriculum that taught skills for African everyday life came up, but few were tested in practice. The idea was dismissed as an underhand way of providing a second-class education for Africans.

Gradually, Africans have taken over the control of their universities, and the debate on how this control actually is reflected in knowledge production continues today. Many examples show how a lack of resources makes it impossible to formulate a research agenda grounded in the needs and experiences of the society.

In the decolonisation process the colonial powers developed their global policy with the aim of maintaining dominance through trade and culture. The Nordic countries, with no colonial history, tried to position themselves and become players on the arena. Trade between Africa and the Nordic countries was small, and has remained so. Development aid was provided in the name of international solidarity, in contrast with charity, a horizontal relation between partners who are essentially equals. As Prime Minister of a small non-allied country, Olof Palme raised his voice for all small and non-aligned countries.

Development aid had, and still has, wide popular support in Sweden as a gesture of international solidarity. In the liberation movements in Southern Africa and against apartheid, national development aid using public funds was actually channelled to the liberation movements (Sellström 2002).

The development cooperation agencies became the dominant funding organisations of research on Africa. The distribution of research funds to various disciplines conducting research on Africa became closely related to the needs of the development agencies and the shifting paradigms of development aid.

Research was always dependent on those providing funds; nevertheless a degree of academic independence could simultaneously be maintained. In the 1960s researchers revived the efforts to construct grand narratives, especially the French, who worked with generalised models of the pre-capitalist, non-capitalist, or African mode of production. The British were more focussed on local modes of production or local economies and with a more empirical and practical touch. Marriage and kinship had always been a theme of anthropological studies, and in the 1970s these studies were combined with the mode of production discourse, producing work on domestic modes of production and on reproduction. This interest led to more studies on women's status and the domestic division of labour. Researchers in the Nordic countries participated in these academic discourses, but largely on the periphery.

From the Cold War to Structural Adjustment

In the Cold War era, military force as well as the development of social welfare was used in the struggle to obtain allies in Africa. The US and Europe intervened directly or indirectly to remove unwanted leaders, while after their instalment dictators such as Mobutu were supported for decades. The French intervened in Africa many times with military force. But these actions were disguised by the silence of the Cold War. Only the support for apartheid was widely exposed to the public in Europe, thanks to the strong anti-apartheid movement.

In this climate it is not surprising that development discourses were de-politicised, and development cooperation was a bureaucratic exercise outside of the democratic process. African states became dependent on aid. Ministries negotiated aid projects, totalling in value to more than the national budgets of the countries concerned, but outside parliamentary control. Lacking the stabilising effect of social movements backing up the policies, the developmental states became vulnerable to all the theories, paradigms and whims of the development agencies and their consultant researchers. Seen from such a perspective, researchers enjoyed great influence, while the African countries were not left alone long enough to really work anything through.

However, to see welfare policy and development aid solely as an element in the Cold War is certainly not fair. The demands on states from below for providing schools and health facilities were enormous. The policies of the nationalist parties' post-independence policies have been thoroughly criticised. Mkandawire (1998) and Aina (2002) also find reason to note the complexity in the challenges African governments faced, and also see their progress. The Swedish social democratic welfare state project had many ideological currents in common with the developmentalist state projects in the new states in Africa. Both had a strong social engineering component.

Effective reforms of social engineering have to be based on well-grounded information. Social research was developed to provide the necessary data. The Anglo-Saxon tradition of positivist research in the form of huge quantitative studies was widely adopted in Africa. Of course, quantitative information was needed in planning, but given the fact that the capacity to meet demand usually was quite insufficient, the exact numbers may have been less important. Under-theorised develop-ment projects reduced many huge surveys to tables with comments. There was a huge gap between the grand theories and applied studies.

In the 1980s, with the switch from political to economic domination, much of the discursive power became vested in the World Bank and the IMF. With the strong neo-liberal convictions of their experts, studies of local conditions became almost superfluous. European development aid organisations followed suit with some delay, although with a reluctance to leave social services such as health and educa-tion to the market.

Swedish Support to African Studies

As a contemporary of many African countries, the Nordic Africa Institute recently celebrated its fortieth anniversary by inviting a number of outstanding African re-searchers. Swedish contacts with Africa had until the middle of the last century been limited to church missions and sporadic trade adventures. The Nordic Africa Insti-tute has developed into an environment of intensive encounter with colleagues in the networks of African researchers built within the various programmes. Some of the programme researchers are Africans who have obtained their posts in competi-tion on the global market (Adebayo Olukoshi, Erika Sal, and Amin Kamete). This is not how it started. It was an initiative primarily aiming at informing a Nordic public about Africa, and at supporting Nordic students in conducting studies on Africa. Gradually, the Institute developed as a research milieu with a mandate to support Nordic and African scholars outside the Institute as well, for example, with library services and travel grants. In line with this, all research posts at the institute are temporary, so that researchers return to home institutions in the Nordic countries or in Africa.

The five Nordic ministries of foreign affairs own the Institute. On the council, which defines the themes of the research programmes, there are representatives for both the ministries and the Nordic research society. Beyond this administrative ap-paratus, researchers have the academic freedom to define their work within wide themes, such as poverty, rural-urban connections, large cities, conflicts, or sexuality. Also within the universities the funding procedures are such that it is possible to channel funds towards specific themes or problem areas. Theoretically, research on Africa can be funded by any research funding body, but in practice most projects are funded by the Swedish Agency for Development Cooperation.

The Swedish Agency for Research Cooperation (SAREC) was originally an inde-pendent governmental body. Now it is a department within the Swedish develop-ment cooperation agency, Sida. Sida/SAREC's first mandate is to support capacity building for knowledge production within the developing countries. Ninety percent of the funds for research are directed to universities and research institutions in developing countries.

The strong emphasis on development cooperation for the support of African research environments is, if not unique in Europe, at least most pronounced in Sweden. While other countries have scholarships for African studies, it was decided about thirty years ago that Sweden should support capacity building in Africa instead. There were several good reasons, one related to language, another to the brain drain. At that time Swedish universities did not offer courses in English, and it was seen as a waste to force Africans to learn Swedish. The reluctance of many students to return to their country of origin was also noted.

Today, there are many Masters' programmes that bring African students to Sweden for short periods. Some doctoral students come to Swedish universities for various 'sandwich' courses, working jointly with their home universities in Africa. This policy is also specific to Sweden. Norway, for example, offers many scholarships. With increasing global cooperation and a circular migration among researchers of all nationalities, the policy of keeping African students and researchers out of Sweden may need to be reconsidered. The Swedish intellectual environment is deprived of a valuable input, but a change in the Swedish policy is not expected during the coming years, as a parliamentary commission on Swedish policy for global development has proposed no change.

Africa today has many excellent and outstanding researchers. Still, their situation is not easy and support to African universities is more necessary than ever. Research expenditures in Africa are only 0.2 percent of registered GNP; and only 0.8 percent of the world's scientific publications are published in Africa (UNESCO 1999). Most donors want to support special research programmes but shy away from core funding of universities. Regional councils and organisations such as CODESRIA and SAPES have offered a way for African researchers to receive funds from donors and develop independent research as African governments turned their backs on higher education (Wohlgemuth 2002).

A Stock-taking of African Studies

In the late 1990s on behalf of the government I conducted a stock-taking exercise of African studies in Sweden. The investigation revealed that research on Africa was spread over the country, and over a multitude of institutions at both the main universities and the small regional ones. There was also a wide distribution across different disciplines, notably anthropology, cultural geography, agriculture, economy, sociology of law, urban and housing studies, 'theme institutions' for water and energy, medicine and many others (Högskoleverket 1998). Most of the studies were undertaken for doctoral theses. However, Swedish students' interest in Africa should not be overrated. Only 0.3 percent of the students who utilised the possibility to study abroad with the Swedish economic support system went to Africa. The Swedish connection to East and Southern Africa in development cooperation is clearly reflected in research interests. Tanzania was the most frequently researched country, followed by Kenya, South Africa, Zambia and Zimbabwe. A tendency for an increased interest in West Africa could be noted.

Research in Sweden is funded by research councils. Also, university teachers have, if they want to do research, to apply for funds on a competitive basis. The main funding organisation of African studies in Sweden is Sida/SAREC, which in this capacity functions as a research council. Ten percent, or about $12m, of Sida/SAREC's funds for research are channelled to Swedish researchers. The rationale for using aid money for this purpose is to keep a basis of knowledge about Africa and other developing countries in Sweden. The research is supposed to be 'development relevant', but is not necessarily useful in development cooperation in the short run. There is still a degree of academic freedom, although the research themes largely followed the changes in paradigms in development cooperation. Curiously enough, academic research on development cooperation as such is rather rare.

During the second half of the 1990s, almost a third of Sida's research funds to Swedish-based researchers were awarded to research on issues related to natural resources, the environment and the production of food. Also health and medical research enjoyed a high priority: almost a fifth of the funds. Within departments of economics research focussed on trade, small-scale business and regional economic cooperation. The anthropologists followed the international trends of interest in identities, ethnicity and religion. Only small sums were directed towards urbanisation and migration. This is in line with the Swedish anti-urban tradition in development cooperation. More surprising was the tiny amount allocated to research on education, although education has always had a high priority in Swedish aid. Media research was also small, although there was a considerable high interest among young researchers. This was manifested in the number of applications for studies on media submitted for travelling grants at the Nordic Africa Institute.

There is a regular flow of PhD theses on Africa presented, which shows a great interest among students. However, after their doctorate examination, there are very few who manage to obtain funds to continue in the field. There are few university institutions for African studies. The only departments in Sweden are at Göteborg University; one is for African languages, the other is a Centre for African Studies with the aim to stimulate research on Africa and cooperation with African researchers at the university. The centre conducted an inventory of African studies at its own university and found that during the 1990s almost forty dissertations were defended (Närman 2001). The main department for these studies was the Department of Economics, Peace and Development, Human and Economic Geography, and of Social Anthropology.

Gender Studies

Although democracy and gender equality had become goals of Swedish development cooperation, the theme of democracy occupied only about a tenth of the researchers in the 1990s, and research on gender issues was almost negligible. The official line was that gender should be mainstreamed into all research, but the inventory did not reveal that this was the case (Högskoleverket 1998). If gender was mainstreamed into the research projects at all, it was carefully hidden from project titles and key words.

Internationally, 'Gender and development' has become an established concept for an area of study generated within or in close connection to international development cooperation. It can be described as starting with a concern for women in development projects. The discourses have developed in dialogue with development practice around themes such as economic efficiency, poverty alleviation, population policies, land policies, reproductive health, and good governance, to mention only a few. Research in this field has helped to develop concepts such as participation and empowerment, and has also critically evaluated how they are used in practice. Contemporary research on women's rights and the girl children's rights, domestic violence, and trafficking in women are themes in line with the priority areas of the Beijing Platform for Action.

Following a parliamentary decision in 1996 that gender equality was an aim in Swedish development cooperation, Sida discussed experiences and produced policy documents (Sida 1998, a, b, c & d). Sida had been in the forefront in working with women's and gender issues since mainstreaming was adopted in line with the strategy recommended in the Beijing Platform for Action. The mainstreaming represented a shift in thinking about women, from women as a target group of development assistance to gender equality as a development objective (Schalkwyk et al. 1996).

Many consultancy reports and policy documents on gender have been produced on behalf of bilateral and other development cooperation organisations. Nevertheless, reporting on the implementation of these policies has remained poor. Hannan (2000: 220) concludes that 'in recent years there has been a preference within bilateral agencies for development of simplified tools and quantifiable targets in the gender equality efforts, rather than a focus on the more political aspects of promotion of gender equality'.

The need for both academic and applied research on the theme is obvious, but there has been no strong academic home for such studies. Research in departments for gender studies in Sweden has been very responsive to international theoretical influences but at the same time narrowly focussed on Swedish conditions. The feminist researchers in Sweden have been in dialogue with European and North American colleagues but have few other contacts. When the Swedish scientific council arranged a meeting on tendencies in gender research in 2002, studies were presented on immigrants to Sweden which used postcolonial theoretical frameworks and highlighted the way that gender and race intersected, but there was no research on the agenda related to development or to Africa.

Gender studies on Africa have been located in departments of other disciplines, notably anthropology and of development studies. There are also exceptional studies in departments of other disciplines often carried out by researchers of African origin. Sida has so far not seen it as its task to support the Swedish academic environment for global gender studies, which could combine consultancy with an academic theoretical development, but has rather engaged British and Canadian consultants.

Doctoral students dominate academic research on gender. The great interest among young researchers was obvious when in 2000 a seminar was arranged in Uppsala with the theme 'Power, Resources, and Culture in a Gender Perspective— Towards a Dialogue between Gender Research and Development Practice'. The database of the Nordic Africa Institute in early 2003 yielded about forty hits on Swedish research on gender. About half of these references were studies on reproductive health, including medical research on AIDS. Many of the others were doctoral students working on, for example, urban livelihoods and welfare.

Swedish researchers strive to work with African researchers, but it is not always easy to find the right form for fruitful cooperation. I have been privileged to work with a Sida/SAREC supported research cooperation programme that has been running since 1991: 'Gender Research on Urbanisation, Planning, Housing and Everyday Life'. Eventually it was Africanised and is now based in Lesotho. During three phases almost fifty researchers in southern Africa have been involved in the programme activities, and the results have been published in three volumes. The Nordic Africa Institute furnishes institutional support for research cooperation between the Institute and African researchers. A successful programme with wide networking focuses on gender, sexuality and society (Arnfred 2000). A programme on gender and age in African cities was initiated at the Institute in 2003.

To an increasing degree, African researchers are locally recruited to do commissioned research for international aid organisations and carry out gender research in Africa. In most countries there are many highly competent gender researchers. Their research results are turned into recommendations and directly fed into development work. With a strong inclination among African researchers to conduct useful work, this is generally perceived as positive. However, there is obviously also a risk that research questions are formulated as a consequence of the needs of development organisations, while the local scientific community has few resources to set the agenda and formulate research questions outside of, or critical of, the context of development projects.

Having emphasised the close relation with development cooperation, I must also mention that there are critical studies which do not accord well with research utilising the concepts of gender and development. Instead of making an effort to put emancipatory and liberatory content in the concepts, some researchers reject them totally. Swedish researchers follow the discourses in Africa and among the African diaspora, such as for example, Nzegwu, who contests the concept of gender on basis of it being introduced by Western feminist researchers hostile to men. She dismisses the definitions of gender that refer to dynamic social, cultural and power relations, claiming that at a deeper level everything that initiated the theoretical articulation of gender remains intact and 'regardless of feminist claims that gender is a social category it is fundamentally biological' (Nzegwu 2001:113). With this I think she threw the baby out with the bathwater, as gender can be a useful tool in analysing social constructions that can be changed for the benefit of women. However, it is acknowledged that several distinguished researchers in, or with roots in, postcolonial countries have made important contributions to the discourse about feminism, pointing to the fact that what may be a radically liberating piece of writing or action in one area can act as a colonising agent in another.

European-African Research Cooperation

The history of European studies on Africa differs somewhat between countries. The colonial powers had their special ties and interests. The Dutch gave up their colonial interest in Africa in the nineteenth century, and the development of African studies the Netherlands was similar to the one in the Nordic countries (Abbink 2001). One of Europe's larger centres for African studies is situated in Leiden. Many European universities have experienced stagnant or even shrinking budgets. Institutions are affected by the need for quick marketable knowledge—and this market regarding Africa is mainly to be found among development cooperation organisations.

Most research on Africa in Europe is formulated within or in dialogue with the development cooperation agenda, although probably less so in the humanities and in anthropology. As far as I know, there is in Europe no similar organisation or department as Sida/SAREC, aiming specifically at research capacity building in Africa. The development cooperation agencies buy studies of African universities, and hire consultants. Sometimes they are given a free hand and time to develop their own research questions within a theme, but most often the questions are formulated by the agency.

Centres of African studies in Europe have joined in an organisation called Aegis, Africa-Europe Group for Interdisciplinary Studies. This body was formed to strengthen the voice of Africanists in Europe. Apart from the objective of strengthening the academic discourse, there was the hope of being able to tap funds from the European Commission for research efforts. However, in the latter respect the organisation has not been particularly successful. Funds have been raised for a few seminars and 'watch' missions but not for real research, and Aegis has remained a network for scholarly exchange. The European Union's development cooperation has been concentrated on infrastructure and on humanitarian aid. This effort has been rather inefficient and the outcome of promises of reforms has not yet been assessed. The European Science Foundation ran, until last year, an interdisciplinary programme in the humanities and social sciences called Asian studies, but there was nothing similar for African studies.

Urban Studies

It might be unfair to focus a discussion on Europe-Africa research cooperation to the urban sector, because the rural bias in European, and not only Swedish, development cooperation is reflected in a weak tradition of European-African urban research work. Urban studies are often close to planning and implementation, and therefore the European input tends to be closely allied with development cooperation.

European researchers have networked to enhance the weak research area. In 1982, a meeting was arranged by three European institutions: the Groupe de Recherches et d'Echanges Technologique (GRET), Paris, the International Institute of Environment and Development, London, and the Institute for Housing Studies, Bouwcentrum, Rotterdam. In re-reading the report from this seminar one is struck by the changing ideological climate (GRET et al. 1982). The role of European researchers was critically scrutinised, and it was agreed that they should support the production of locally based knowledge by promoting contact and dialogue with and between Third World researchers. After twenty years of domination of a totally different discourse within urban studies, a similar critical perspective is again emerging, this time within the N-AERUS network. N-AERUS is a multi-disciplinary network of researchers and experts working on urban issues in developing countries. It was created in March 1996 with the objective to mobilise and develop European institutional and individual research and training capacities on urban issues in the South. N-AERUS will work in association with researchers and institutions in developing countries.

The City Summit held in Istanbul in 1996 produced a Plan of Action within the framework of the Habitat Agenda. The Agenda provides a good starting point, but it has hardly been as effective a tool as was hoped. Cities and towns are growing in size and number. Unauthorised structures and activities constitute an increasing part of the urban set up. Urban people struggle to arrange their everyday life amidst problems of basic services. Urban poverty is increasing. The work of the UN Centre for Human Settlement, Habitat, in cooperation with local governments, has far from begun to match the enormity of urban problems.

Habitat in its continued work has taken on the challenge of focussing on the social dimensions of urbanisation, and especially on urban poverty and homelessness. Equity and social justice were proposed as basic principles, and it is recommended that effects on women's conditions should be used as primary indicators of the success of interventions. There are quantifiable findings that women are critical role-players in the fields of concern for Habitat.

The researchers in the network N-AERUS gathered in Venice in 1999 to discuss and analyse current concepts used by the most influential international development co-operation organisations. Concepts and paradigms used in their policy programmes and declarations are the tools which are used for change. A sign of the weakness of research is that the researchers responded to concepts coined by the agencies, not the other way round. The European Commission was in the process of formulating its first Urban Development Policy for Co-operation. Proposed goals were urban economic growth, social equity and poverty reduction, and sustainable environmental development. Transparent and accountable urban governance based on participatory democracy and effective urban management was to be supported as well as partnerships between public, private and community sectors. This was compared to the World Bank view of cities as marketplaces for the countries' economies

The actors in the global urban area display many similarities in their use of concepts and in the way they look at the world. Partnership is a term that is present in all their programmes. But there are also differences—at least in emphasis. The European programme emphasises social equity more than the World Bank, but perhaps less so than Habitat. Only Habitat recognises the crucial role of women explicitly. The European Commission's policy emphasised the environment more than the World Bank, which saw competitiveness and bankability as criteria for sustainability.

The European researchers had formulated demands on independent urban research, but still at the 1999 N-AERUS meeting the focus was on development co-operation. However, only a very small sector of urban development in this urbanising world is touched by development aid projects. There is still very little research on urban development outside of such projects. I would guess that at least 90 percent of the research reports on urban issues that are produced in Africa are generated within development co-operation. This is a problem, not primarily because researchers tied to urban projects may be biased, but because the questions generated by development aid may not be the same questions as those generated from the internal urban dynamics, from local authorities, from residents and from urban actors.

Sanders (1992) pointed out the Eurocentric bias in the study of African urbanisation. He was of the view that studies on urbanisation in Africa have been more interdisciplinary than other urban studies. Nevertheless, they have not succeeded in shedding much light on the nature of the urbanisation process. The bias is embedded in dichotomies like formal/informal, and concepts like development. Even if Portes, Castells and Benton (1989) wrote more than a decade ago that conceptual advances in understanding the urban informal economy in Africa would be impossible unless we were willing to abandon the comfort of familiar definitions and theories, these concepts still dominate research. The very concept of development is under attack. Aina (2002) defends the concept of development against both what he sees as left- and right-wing arguments. He notes that development was not the aim during the structural adjustment period, neither within the neo-liberal ideology nor in practice. Rather, adjustment and the creation of market mechanisms were the goals. He would like to see a return to the emancipatory and liberatory aspects of development.

New Directions

This short and selective review of research on Africa in Sweden and in Europe has shown the close ties between research and development cooperation. To identify emerging directions in research it may be wise to look not only at the research environments but also at the changes in political context.

At the end of the Cold War many of the old African dictators fell from power, no longer able to play off one superpower against another. To build a new, more democratic state order turned out to be a conflict-ridden process. Internal conflicts surfaced, often dressed in ethnic or religious colours. All over the continent voices were raised in the struggle for human rights, and for the acknowledgement that human rights are also for women. What then are the responses at the European and Swedish political level to these developments in Africa?

While in the 1960s and 1970s more than two-thirds of the European Commission's development aid was directed to Africa, by the end of the 1990s it was only one-third. The total annual level had reached almost US$ 8 billion (Nauckhoff 2000). This movement away from Africa is hardly in line with the development goals of poverty reduction, and in discussions on a new development cooperation policy the Commission declared that the focus on poverty would be improved by increased support to the poorest countries, and also by a focus on the poor population in middle income countries, taking a poverty perspective in all cooperation efforts. Priority areas of cooperation that have been proposed include: trade, regional integration, macroeconomic policy, transport, food security and institutional capacity. But the announced process of revitalisation is expected to continue to be slow, as the past has shown how ineffective the Commission's work has been.

The Swedish parliament has established a committee to propose a new policy for global development (Globkom 2002). The committee's recommendations are in line with those of the European Commission. Poverty reduction had been the goal of Swedish development cooperation since the start, and now it is to be re-emphasised. A policy for a positive development all over the world has to be coherent, working towards the same aim in, for example, trade and agricultural policies as in development cooperation. This is far from the case as regards the policies of the European Union. The concept of global public goods has been adopted as a label for a new area of development work: it includes the environment and issues such as health and the 'global financial architecture'. Although the committee acknowledges the development of a global knowledge society, its view on knowledge production is unclear. In certain sections knowledge is seen as goods that just can be transferred in partnership with business. There is, generally, in development cooperation circles a deeper and more complex understanding of knowledge.

Having interviewed a number of Swedish academics within different disciplines about how they see the tendencies within their fields, I must conclude that research in Sweden continues to be very responsive to political developments. That is not to say that there is one-way communication. Certainly there is some dialogue, and policy-makers want to base their decisions on well-grounded information and research findings. But research is a slow process and, for example, in the late 1990s, I was surprised to find that few researchers worked with issues of democratisation and the relationship to economic transformation and external pressures. Working in Africa I had often confronted with the contradiction between in the demands for democracy and the dictates of banks and international organisations. Why elect leaders if they could not listen to the voters' preferences but were forced to implement a structural adjustment policy? Now, the research community has caught up, and there are massive research efforts being put into this field of research. Democratisation processes are related to other areas of research such as human rights, conflict resolution, and the utilisation of natural resources. Research on democratisation is being widened to include multi-disciplinary studies of political parties, trade unions, civil society and social movements.

A dramatic increase in research on conflict and risk can partly be attributed to the events of September 11, 2001. To some degree, this trend makes a focus on poverty and Africa more diffuse, but research on African conflicts and their roots in poverty, religion, ethnicity or natural resources has also increased.

Similarly, the concept of global public goods is now more widely considered to be central. Programmes on environmental issues and HIV/AIDS which are situated in Africa might be counted in this category. Research on poverty has for a long time been widely researched within the framework, for example, of urban livelihoods and food security systems. Research findings have had an impact on reformulation of policies at, for example, the World Bank. While there is still a severe lack of understanding of how informal and shortage economies works, there is also concern among researchers about the consequences of a narrow focus on the poor in research on Africa.

The Sida/SAREC, has for some years invited proposals on special areas of concern in order to stimulate research in specific areas. Human rights have been one such area; forestry, urban development, education and ITC have been amongst the others. Gender research in Sweden has been rather weak; only recently in 2003 did Sida/SAREC announce its intention to support a network of gender researchers in order to strengthen the field.

Urban sector research has been strengthened, although there is no strong research support for this in Sweden. European urban researchers within N-AERUS have organised a seminar under the heading, 'Beyond the neo-liberal consensus on urban development: other voices from Europe and the South'. The need to go further than to criticise structural adjustment programmes is widely felt and the search for alternatives to the neo-liberal agenda has begun. It is also symptomatic that the voices are both from Europe and the South. In all fields of research there is a tendency for Swedish researchers to establish a real and working cooperation with local researchers. Knowledge production in Africa is still often initiated by the needs of the development cooperation agencies. It is time that Africans set their own agenda of research.

Post-script

Since this chapter was presented the situation of African studies in Sweden has improved in many respects. The Nordic Africa Institute continues to be the main institution and its library provides service all over the Nordic countries. The Centre for African Studies at Göteborg University gives courses in African studies and runs a master course in Africa and development cooperation. The centre has consolidated its position within the newly formed School of Global Studies which is also the home of a Centre of Global Gender Studies. A network for Gender and Development research has more than eighty members whereof about twenty are Africanists. More than half of these researchers on gender in Africa are doctors, a fact that bears witness to an increase in the possibility to get funding for post-doctorate research. The GRUPHEL project has now in 2007 reached its end; five books and numerous research reports have been published by the Institute for Southern African Studies, National University of Lesotho. For the administration of future Sida/SAREC support to gender studies a model relying on African institutions to take over the assessment process for selection of projects worthy of funding has been discussed for years. With the increasing excellence of African research departments cooperation with European researchers improves and enhances the quality of research. Aegis has started to arrange biannual European Conferences on African Studies (ECAS). The theme of the conference in 2007 will be "African Alternatives: Initiative and Creativity beyond Current Constraints".

References

Abbink, J., 2001, 'African studies in the Netherlands', *African Research and Documentation*, No. 87.

Aina, T. A., 2002, 'Scales of Suffering, Orders of Emancipation: Dilemmas of Democratic Development in Africa', Paper presented to the Nordic Africa Institute Fortieth Anniversary Conference, 'Knowledge, Freedom and Development, Uppsala 1-3 September.

Arnfred, S., 2000, Presentation of the Research Programme 'Gender, Sexuality and Society in Africa', Uppsala, the Nordic Africa Institute, www.nai.uu.se.

Castells, M., 1997, *The Information age, Economic Society and Culture. Volume II: The Power of Identity*, Oxford, Blackwell Publishers.

Globkom, 2002, *En rättvisare värld utan fattigdom. Betänkande av den parlamentariska kommittén om Sveriges politik för global utveckling*, Stockholm, Statens offentliga utredningar.

Gret et al., 1982, *Report of a Meeting of West European Institutions Involved in Research in Third World Housing and Settlements Issues*, Paris: Groupe de recherche et d'échange technologique; London: International Institute for Environment and Development; Rotterdam: Institute for Housing Studies.

Hannan, C., 2000, *Promoting Equality Between Women and men in Bilateral Development Cooperation: Concepts, Goals, Rationales and Institutional Arrangements. Part One: Theory, Practice and Priorities for Change*, Lund: Lund University, Department of Economic Geography.

Högskoleverket, 1998, *Utbildning och forskning för strategisk internationalisering: Redovisning av ett regeringsuppdrag*, Stockholm: Högskoleverket.

Mkandawire, T., 1998, 'Thinking About Developmental States in Africa', Paper presented at the conference on 'Institutions and Development in Africa', Tokyo.

Nauckhoff, E., 2000, *EUs utvecklingssamarbete*, Stockholm: Styrelsen för internationellt utvecklingssamarbete, Sida.

Nzegwu, N., 2001, 'The Politics of Gender in African Studies in the North', in C. R. Veney and P. T. Zeleza, eds., *Women in African Studies: Scholarly Publishing*, Trenton and Asmara: Africa World Press, 111-146.

Närman, A., 2001, 'Introduction', in A. Närman and J. Ewald, eds., *Göteborg University in Africa*, Göteborg: Göteborg University, Centre for African Studies.

Portes, A., M. Castells, and L. A. Benton, eds., 1989, *The Informal Economy: Studies in Advanced and Less Developed Countries*, Baltimore: Johns Hopkins University Press.

Sanders, R., 1992, 'Eurocentric Bias in the Study of African Urbanisation: A Provocation to Debate', *Antipode* 23 (3): 203-213.

Schalkwyk, J., H. Thomas and B. Woroniuk, 1996, *Mainstreaming: A Strategy for Achieving Equality Between Women and Men. A Think Piece*, Stockholm: Swedish International Development Cooperation Agency.

Sellström, T., 2002, *Sweden and National Liberation in Southern Africa, Vol. II: Solidarity and Assistance 1970-1994*, Uppsala: The Nordic Africa Institute.

Sida, 1998a, *A Brief Presentation of Swedish Work and Policies on Gender Equality*, Stockholm: Swedish International Development Cooperation Agency.

Sida, 1998b, *Kvinnor och män. Sidas program för jämställdhet*, Stockholm: Swedish International Development Cooperation Agency.

Sida, 1998c, *Striking the Balance*, Stockholm: Swedish International Development Cooperation Agency.

Sida, 1998d, *Gender Equality in Bilateral Development Cooperation*, Stockholm, Swedish International Development Cooperation Agency.

UNESCO, 1999, *Statistical Year Book*, Paris: United Nations.

Wohlgemuth, L., 2002, 'Universities in Sub-Sahara', *Journal für Entwicklungspolitik, African Empowerment: Knowledge and Development*, 1 (18): 69-80.

Chapter 10

Anti-Colonialism in Soviet African Studies (1920s–1960)

Irina Filatova

Soviet Africanists produced hundreds of books, the majority of which never reached the reader outside the Soviet Union and are now thoroughly forgotten. There were multiple reasons for this situation. Soviet Africanists had little first-hand knowledge of African realities; some of their works were purely ideological and some were politically expedient. All Soviet publications were subject to strict state censorship and in addition (or as a result) authors tended to self-censor themselves. Soviet realities in general were not conducive to debate outside the framework of official doctrine, or to the development of new ideas. The language barrier was, of course, an additional problem, for translations were rare and the choice of books for trans-lation was usually ideologically or politically motivated. However, some topics that Soviet Africanists worked on—or rather the ideas they put forward—were to have a long life, gained a following abroad and became a part of the ideology of many national and social movements in Africa. Anti-colonialism was one such topic. Thus, for example, 'strategic tasks', the timing of each of the two stages of revolution—national-democratic and socialist, the 'mobilisation of motive forces', the 'education of the masses', the relationship between the 'cadres' and the 'masses', the leading role of a particular class or party at a particular stage of the revolution—were all notions derived from the Soviet theory of anti-colonialism, and they are still pas-sionately discussed in South Africa today. Why did these ideas prove so attractive to those who fought and won anti-colonial struggles—and what did Soviet African studies contribute to them?

The Soviet Theory of Anti-Colonialism and Soviet African Studies in the 1920s and 1930s

The Soviet theory of anti-colonialism—rather the part of it pertaining to national liberation movements—was first formulated by Lenin in his *Preliminary Draft Thesis on the National and the Colonial Questions* for the Second Congress of the Communist International in 1920. It was later developed in his article, '"Left-Wing" Communism—an Infantile Disorder', in his speech to the Second All-Union Congress of Communist Organisations and Peoples of the East, and in his speeches and reports to the Third and Fourth Congresses of the Comintern. Later, Stalin significantly modified some of Lenin's ideas, and the Sixth and Seventh Congresses of the Comintern made further modifications. In the 1950s, when many Asian and the first African countries became independent, the changing international situation resulted in the transformation of the theory, and in the early 1960s it acquired the form in which it lasted until the mid-1980s. The transformation of the official theory is important for this topic, for during the Soviet era all academic debates and political battles around problems of anti-colonialism could take place only on the basis of this official theory.

The main points of Lenin's theory as expressed in the *Report of the Commission on the National and the Colonial Questions* (written on the basis of Lenin's *Draft Thesis*) to the Second Comintern Congress were as follows:

(i)   The world consists of oppressing and oppressed nations (not only classes); the former are a small minority; the latter, a huge majority;

(ii) After the First World War 'relations between nations ... are defined by the struggle of a small group of imperialist nations against the Soviet movement and Soviet states with Soviet Russia at the head';

(iii) 'Any national movement can only be bourgeois-democratic by nature, for the main mass of population of backward countries consists of peasantry...' This point provoked a heated debate in the Commission on the National and the Colonial Questions to which the *Theses* were presented for discussion. The members of the Commission thought that the term 'bourgeois-democratic' did not reflect the difference between reformist and revolutionary movements. 'Very often (probably in most cases)', the Commission stated, 'while the bourgeoisie of exploited nations supports national movements, it simultaneously fights against all revolutionary movements and revolutionary classes in agreement with, i.e. together with the imperialist bourgeoisie'. Thus, the term 'national-revolutionary movements' was substituted for 'bourgeois-democratic movements'. This meant that in principle communists could support 'bourgeois liberation movements in colonial countries', but only when 'these movements were truly revolutionary, when their representatives will not prevent us from educating and organizing the peasantry and the broad exploited masses in the spirit of revolution'.

(iv) In pre-capitalist conditions, in the absence of a proletariat, the experience of peasant councils on the outskirts of Russia should be applied. Peasants would understand such a 'form of applying communist tactics', but 'the proletariat of the advanced countries can and should help the backward toiling masses'. First of all this applies to the proletariat of Soviet republics.

(v) The capitalist stage of development is not unavoidable for 'the backward people who get their freedom now', for 'the victorious proletariat' will wage systematic propaganda among them, and Soviet governments[1] 'will render them assistance with all means at their disposal'.

(vi) Communist parties should work not only in their own countries but in the colonies as well. 'The greatest betrayal' of the member parties of the Second International lay exactly in the lack of action in this direction (Lenin 215-220).

All points seem clear here, except, perhaps, the second one: what did Russia's position on the international arena have to do with the colonial question? In fact, this was the crux of Lenin's approach: although Russia did not fit into the category of oppressed nations, it was a victim of the same few but powerful oppressing nations. Thus the main idea of the theses: socialist Russia and anti-colonial movements were natural allies—despite the fact that anti-colonial movements were bourgeois by nature—and as such should act together in a united front against imperialism, because (a) bourgeois movements in colonies could be national-revolutionary if they allowed communists 'to educate' the masses and lead them; and (b) under the leadership of communists in the colonies themselves, in the metropoles and, first and foremost, in Soviet Russia itself the most 'backward' colonial peoples, i.e. those that had not reached the capitalist stage of development, might avoid going through it.

By the mid-1920s Lenin's theses had undergone substantial transformation. While Lenin stressed the possibility and even the desirability of an alliance with the colonial bourgeoisie, as long as it did not hamper communist propaganda, the Fifth Congress of the Comintern in 1924 rejected the idea that the national bourgeoisie in colonies could have any anti-colonial potential. Moreover, even socialists who agreed to support colonial reform rather than outright revolution in the colonies, were now called 'national reformists'. Soon those who wholeheartedly supported anti-colonial revolutions, but not under the banners of the Comintern, were denounced as the worst enemies of all—'Trotskyists'.

These changes were, of course, initiated at the very top. The Party's national policy was now defined by Stalin who had begun his ascent to the Party leadership from an article on this very topic. Stalin did distinguish between the bourgeoisie of imperialist countries and the 'national bourgeoisie' of colonial and dependent countries, as did Lenin. The latter, Stalin (1952: 11) wrote, 'could support the revolutionary movement in their countries against imperialism at a certain stage and for a certain time'. However, by the mid-1920s the Soviet leadership rejected the possibility of an alliance with bourgeois parties and movements, even temporary ones, and even in the colonies. Already in his first article on the national question, *Marxism and the National Question* published in 1913, Stalin (1949: 49) declared that '... generally the proletariat does not support the so-called "national-liberation" movements because until now all such movements have acted in the interests of the bourgeoisie and corrupted and confused the class consciousness of the proletariat'.

This article was included in the 1946 edition of Stalin's works, which meant that he did not change his position on this issue until the last years of his life.

In the 1930s Stalin developed his idea of the hegemony of the proletariat in the national-liberation struggle. In his article, *The International Nature of the October Revolution*, Stalin (1952: 245) wrote: 'The era of liberation revolutions in colonies and dependent countries has come, the era of the awakening of the proletariat of these countries, the era of its hegemony in revolution'. Lenin's approach was thus in effect abandoned, although it was never mentioned either by Stalin or by multiple Soviet interpreters of the works of the classics.

Origins and Development of African Studies

Soviet African studies emerged in the late 1920s and early 1930s,[2] during the upsurge of Stalin's campaign against 'national reformism'. The views of the first Soviet Africanists were greatly influenced by a curious combination of Lenin's theory ('united front') and Stalin's fight to stamp out 'national-reformism' and to step up the idea of proletarian leadership in national-liberation revolutions.

Several events stimulated Soviet interest in Africa. From 1921 the Communist Party of South Africa actively participated in the work of the Comintern. During the 1920s representatives of different African countries, first of all, South Africa, worked in various organisations of the Comintern, studied in its schools and participated in its meetings and congresses. In 1928 the Sixth Congress of the Comintern adopted the creation of an 'independent Native republic' in the Union of South Africa as the main goal and the main slogan for the CPSA,[3] thus attracting the attention of researchers to the problems of this country and of the whole continent. From the late 1920s one of the Comintern's schools, the Communist University of Eastern Toilers (KUTV), began to enrol groups of students from Africa; some South Africans studied at the Lenin School, another Comintern educational institution. In 1929 a research wing of KUTV, the Academic Research Association for the Study of National and Colonial Problems (NIANKP), opened a study circle on African socioeconomic problems.

There were only a handful of Africanists in the Soviet Union at the time, and even fewer of them specialised in problems of anti-colonialism. Only five people studied these or related subjects: a Hungarian, Endre Sik (in the Soviet Union he was known as Andrej Alexandrovich Shiik), Georgi Yevgenievich Gerngros, Nikolai Mikhailovich Nasonov, Ivan Izosimovich Potekhin and Alexander Zakharovich Zusmanovich. They were all connected to the Comintern and based their work not only on Party documents and Lenin's and Stalin's works, but also on Comintern publications, lectures and discussions about the East and, to a lesser extent, about the 'Negro problem' in the United States. Speeches and publications on the 'national-colonial question' by such Comintern theoreticians as Ludwig Magyar, Georgi Ivanovich Safarov and Otto Kuusinen, provided the 'academic' context in which a new academic discipline grew and developed. These people were the ones who set the tone, and their publications are testimony to the political atmosphere in which first Soviet Africanists worked.

The style of Ludwig Magyar, deputy head of the Eastern Secretariat of the Comintern's Executive Committee, was academic, but even for him colonies were a field of political battles, rather than of academic analysis. His articles usually began with conclusions. This is, for example, the beginning of his article on national reformism: 'In the developed capitalist countries social democracy is the main social basis of the bourgeoisie, while in the colonies our main enemy, the main social basis of imperialism—I stress, *social*—is national reformism'. The article presented a cogent argument in favour of the thesis (which was, as we now know, wrong) that the national bourgeoisie 'does wage the struggle, but cannot wage a consistent revolutionary struggle', and as a result would never achieve national liberation (Magyar 1933: 24, 28).

Georgi Safarov (1934: 18-19), another deputy head of the Eastern Secretariat, wrote like a real pogromist: '... it is necessary to arouse the hatred and the fury of the masses against any imperialist violence and against concrete agents of imperialist violence. The struggle should be directed against definite, concrete governing institutions, organs and methods of the imperialist state ... It is necessary to be able to concentrate the forces of destruction, hatred and indignation of the masses upon every representative of violent power'. Safarov went even further in his denunciation of the national bourgeoisie than Magyar, when he wrote that it was becoming 'fascist'. He called for 'revolutionary dictatorships' with communist parties at their head to be established in colonies on the basis of the 'mobilization of the destructive forces of the revolutionary proletariat' (Safarov 1934: 28-29).

The atmosphere of a theoretical and later of a real physical pogrom was not conducive to the deep study of any problems, but particularly not of the problems of contemporary history. In evaluating the works and behaviour of the founders of Soviet African studies it is impossible to ignore this factor. The question is whether they wrote despite this atmosphere or because of it; and whether they contributed something really new and valuable to their discipline that went beyond the Comintern's scholastics, in this case in the study of anti-colonialism.

At the first meeting of the African study circle at NIANKP, Endre Sik, who at that time worked for the Comintern,[4] presented a programme for the study of Africa—the first ever in Russia (Sik 1930a). The study of anti-colonialism occupied a large place in the programme, although Sik's main topic, as defined by the name of the study circle, was socioeconomic problems. Even the very need to study these problems was explained by the fact that the core of Lenin's approach to the 'national-colonial question' was the principle of the right of nations to self-determination, and that the application of this principle to the countries that had not yet formed nations, i.e. had not created their own national bourgeoisie, had not been properly studied (Sik 1930a: 88).

'Until now the Comintern and its sections [i.e. foreign communist parties - I.F.] have paid very little attention indeed to the question about the most backward colonial countries like Black Africa', wrote Sik. 'We have been too interested in the burning issues of China, India and other colonial countries ... But our Marxist-Leninist revolutionary philosophy does not recognise and does not allow any hierarchies in respect of colonised countries ... In the near future we have to do everything to fill this gap. We must do this immediately and unconditionally, because in the colonial peoples of Black Africa, who are more exploited and oppressed than any other, we have potential allies in our struggle against the imperialist system, for these most backward and undeveloped peoples, who, as a rule, do not have a more or less developed proletariat, are the most defenceless victims of world imperialism' (Sik 1930a: 88-89).

The programme contained sections on the 'History of the Opposition of Native Tribes to the Capitalist Occupation' and on 'Liberation Movements and Organisations of the Oppressed Peoples of Black Africa' (Sik 1930a: 99). Sik (1930a: 96-97) also mentioned 'non-capitalist development' in Africa which, according to him, would be possible because African peoples did not have 'native capitalism'. Thus, in Sik's interpretation the study of social structures of African societies, and first of all, of the existence or non-existence of a local bourgeoisie, was firmly connected with the understanding of the nature and role of African peoples in the struggle against imperialism, which in his view was tantamount to their role in world history. In effect Sik repeated here Lenin's points with the exception of the bourgeois nature of national movements. In his view there was no bourgeoisie in Africa, and little possibility that it would ever emerge. According to Lenin, if there is no bourgeoisie, there is no nation; and if there is no nation, there is no national movement. Within the framework of class-based Marxist-Leninist theory any social or political movement had to have a class definition; it could not be simply a revolutionary liberation movement. In the case of Africa such movements could not called either 'bourgeois' or, even less so, 'proletarian', so Sik simply avoided any definitions.

Sik's (1930b) article 'Black Africa on the Revolutionary Road', published in 1930, became the first Soviet study devoted directly to anti-colonial movements in Africa. However, there is not much anti-colonialism in it. Sik described the colonial exploitation of African peoples and their hard economic situation. Anti-colonialism in his view was a natural and logical outcome of exploitation—logical to such an extent that there was no need to prove the connection. So, he described only one strike and quoted only one, though quite radical, declaration by an African leader: the young Jomo Kenyatta.

It is quite possible that Sik did not know about African religious movements, Afro-Christianity, etc., but he made no mention of African political parties either (with the exception of the East African Union in connection with the strike)—and he must have read or heard about them: Josiah Gumede, the leader of the African

National Congress, visited Moscow in 1927. There could be only one reason, i.e. that such parties were considered to be neither revolutionary, nor anti-imperialist, and thus did not merit a mention from the point view of the anti-imperialist struggle.

If, in Sik's view, some developments in African societies could compromise their image, he explained them away by colonial exploitation or by imperialist provocations. Thus, he wrote that the clashes between Shona and Ndebele were the result of provocation on the part of British imperialism, the purpose of which was 'to stifle their rebellious mood' (Sik 1930b: 244).

During the 1930s Sik (1966) worked on his doctoral thesis, *The History of Black Africa*. [5] If this monumental work had been published when it was written, it would have opened a new era in the development of African studies throughout the world. Sik described the history of the continent in its entirety: all its regions, all its history as it was then known, from the beginning to the 1930s. Moreover, he attempted to present African peoples as the subjects, not the objects of history. For today's reader this attempt may look crude and naïve, and in many instances Sik simply failed, for his simplistic Comintern Marxism was certainly Euro-centric, but in the 1930s nobody else even tried.

Naturally, anti-colonialism occupied an important place in this work. Sik collected an enormous (for the time) amount of material about opposition to colonisation, strikes, anti-colonial religious movements and about the political organisations of dozens of African countries. The manuscript also contained Sik's ideas on the nature and periodisation of liberation movements. Unfortunately, this work was published only in 1966 (in Hungary, but in French and English), when not only Sik's ideological approach but also much of his material was completely outdated, and his mistakes only too obvious. It is unlikely that Sik had the time and energy to change much of his original text for publication: at that time he occupied one of the highest positions in the Hungarian government. Yet because of this delay it is difficult to judge Sik's views and approaches of the 1930s on the basis of this publication.

The first Soviet publications on Africa were authored by Georgi Yevgenievich Gerngross, who published under the pen-name 'Yug' (in Russian 'South'). In the late 1920s and early 1930s he published four books: *Imperialism on the Black Continent* (Yug 1929); *The Union of South Africa: Essays* (Yug 1931a); *British Colonies in East Africa* (Yug 1931b); and *Imperialism and Colonies* (Yug 1932).

Despite this impressive list of publications and the work he did at NIANKP (he was not a full-time employee), Gerngross remained unknown. Well-educated and a non-Party member, he was an outsider among the Soviet Africanists of the time. His father had been a Tsarist general (a fact that his colleagues might not have been aware of), and his fate was sealed: he was arrested and in 1937 shot.

None of Gerngros's books was devoted directly to anti-colonialism, but he touched upon this topic, mostly in his book about South Africa, which contained several chapters on this topic. He wrote about the activities of the Industrial and Commercial Union (the first big African Trade Workers Union) and described the ANC and other African political organisations. He thought, however, that the future belonged 'neither to the peaceful slogans of liberal national native organisations and nor to uncoordinated actions of individual trade unions, but to the power of the proletariat that would be able to unite these hapless masses in a mighty gust'. 'All these national congresses', he continued, 'leagues of Negro communities, European-Native associations, conferences of non-European clergymen, and other similar organisations that call on the black population to fight by legal means through petitions, parliamentary questions, etc.... all such organisations in fact assist the white bourgeoisie'. The Communist Party, Gerngross wrote (1931a: 158-9), was the only one which called for 'a new method of struggle'—the anti-imperialist revolution, at the basis of which was 'the agrarian question'.

The importance of the 'agrarian question' (in effect, the land question) was not Gerngross's own idea. Comintern theoreticians of anti-colonialism often wrote about the coming 'agrarian revolutions' in Asia, where, according to them, this form of struggle was the most obvious, for peasants constituted the majority of the population there.[6]

Gerngross paid special attention to the slogan of the independent Native republic. He published the full text of the Resolution of the Sixth Congress of the Comintern on South Africa and quoted the speech at the Congress of the South African communist S.P. Bunting, one of the leaders of CPSA, who turned against the slogan. He also gave his own thoughts about the slogan and the reaction to it among South Africa's black and white population (Yug 1931a: 160-61).

Gerngross's manner slightly differed from that of his colleagues: his books were academically better, contained more concrete material, less theorising, and none of the labelling that was typical of the time. But his political line fully coincided with the Comintern's official line, particularly where anti-colonialism was concerned. It is difficult to know how sincere he was when he wrote about the appeasing role of non-proletarian organisations in anti-colonial movements, of the need for hegemony of the proletariat and the communist parties in the anti-imperialist revolutions even in colonial countries, and of the independent Native republic as the only correct goal of struggle. Whatever his motives, towing the line did not save his life.

The best known Soviet Africanists of the 1930s who wrote on anti-colonialism were Potekhin[7] and Zusmanovich. In 1932-36 they published numerous articles on Africa (mostly on South Africa), and in 1933, a co-authored monograph (Zusmanovich, Potekhin, and Jackson 1933), *The Labour Movement and Forced Labour in Negro Africa*[8] (their third co-author was Albert Nzula, the first black secretary of the CPSA, who at that time was studying at the Lenin School in Moscow and later died there of pneumonia; his alias and pen-name was Tom Jackson).

The structure of this book inaugurated a pattern followed by other Soviet Africanists for years to come: failures of the economy; colonial exploitation and hardships experienced by the African population; anti-colonial movements from 'more primitive' forms, such as peasant movements and uprisings, to trade union movements and finally communist movements, where they existed.

The problems of anti-colonialism occupied approximately half of the book. The text was academically uneven. Some parts presented completely new material, while others gave a biased, even distorted, picture of reality. Thus, in the chapter 'Peasant Movements and Uprisings in Colonies' the authors gave a detailed description of Kimbangist clashes with the police, but not of the movement itself, neither its goals, nor its religious nature. Only the economic grievances of the followers were listed, and Simon Kimbangu himself was not even mentioned. Moreover, the assertion by the Belgian authorities that the movement was 'extremely conservative and religious by nature' was called 'hypocritical'.

The authors did not say that militancy—uprisings, bloody clashes with the police and the army—was the only 'correct', or even the preferable form of anti-colonialism, but other forms simply do not merit a mention. There were, however, two exceptions: early signs of the struggle for land in Kenya and the role of the CPSA in the peasants' movement in South Africa. The latter was completely removed from reality. 'The Communist Party', asserted the authors, 'leads the struggle of peasant committees. It also organises labourers on plantations and on the farms; simultaneously it attracts industrial workers to render assistance to peasants in their struggle' (Zusmanovich, Potekhin, and Jackson (1933: 101). We do not know the distribution of labour among the authors, but Nzula could not have read this chapter, let alone written it: he would have known better.

On the other hand, two chapters, 'The Trade Union Movement in Negro Africa' and 'The Economic Struggle of the Working Class in Negro Africa' contain concrete and detailed information on trade union organisations (by industry) in South Africa and in several West African colonies, as well as detailed accounts of strikes. One is left with the impression that this information could only be provided by a participant, or drawn from systematic reading of local newspapers (which was quite possible: KUTV received not only national but several provincial newspapers from South Africa).

Anti-colonial theory, as the authors saw it, was presented in the chapter 'The Struggle for Independence and National Reformism'. For the first time in Soviet literature they clearly outlined the concept of a two-stage revolution as applied to the African continent. They wrote: 'the struggle for land and the war for national liberation constitute the contents of the first stage of the revolution in Negro Africa'. This stage, according to them, would be bourgeois-democratic, and so would the independent Native republics created as its result. However, already during this stage 'the proletariat ... will have to introduce significant social initiatives—the nationalisation of mining enterprises, railways, banks, etc'. The second stage, according to the authors, would begin in the Union of South Africa 'through gradual transformation of this agrarian-nationalist, bourgeois-democratic revolution into a socialist revolution; the process of strengthening of socialist elements against the Native bourgeoisie will constitute its economic content ... and the process of the transition of revolutionary-democratic dictatorship of proletariat and peasantry into the dictatorship of the proletariat, its political content'. As for the rest of the African continent, there, the authors wrote, 'anti-imperialist revolution and the support of the countries under proletarian dictatorship will create the possibility of non-capitalist development of peasant economies' (Zusmanovich, Potekhin, and Jackson 1933: 165-6).

The authors also offered an analysis of the 'driving forces of the revolution' and of the social structure of African societies, equally detailed and equally remote from reality. They disagreed with Sik about the existence of a local bourgeoisie: while, they said, it was correct that there was no industrial bourgeoisie in Africa, there were 'local exploiters', who were represented by 'a commercial and money-lending bourgeoisie and "tribal" chiefs'. According to them, the proletariat was the only group of the population which could really rise against imperialism. The commercial bourgeoisie was a faithful ally of imperialism, while tribal chiefs could have differences with it. The intelligentsia was in principle against imperialism, but was not consistent enough, because it mostly consisted of the children of tribal chiefs. The ANC was called a national-reformist organisation, whose social basis was provided by chiefs and the intelligentsia. But the policy of the Congress was discussed in detail, with quotations from its resolutions and from the articles of its members published in the local media, including *Umteteli Wabantu* (Zusmanovich, Potekhin, and Jackson 1933: 166, 170-74).

Two other examples of 'national-reformist' organisations were Ghana's Aborigines' Rights Protection Society and Kenya's Gikuyu Central Association. Unbelievably, the authors thought that the main task of 'communists and revolutionary-minded workers' was 'to expose the treacherous activities of these organisations systematically and daily'. But their programmes were analysed on the basis of first-hand sources with quotations from documents and such details as, for example, 'the possibility of the emergence of revolutionary opposition inside the Gikuyu Central Association'. What this possibility was remained unclear, perhaps the purported return to Kenya of Jomo Kenyatta, who was to finish his course at KUTV in 1933. Whatever it was, such details were certainly impressive for the time (Zusmanovich, Potekhin, and Jackson 1933: 174-79).

Zusmanovich and Potekhin continued their crusade against national reformism in their articles published in the mid-1930s. The main topic of these works was the class analysis of the supposed social base of the anti-colonial revolution. Who would constitute a united anti-colonial front? In some cases Zusmanovich (1935a: 149) wrote that it would be 'a united front of the working class, the peasant masses and the urban poor against the imperialist-feudal bloc, against the treacherous Native bourgeoisie', in others, that this would be a united front of 'Native and white workers' (Zusmanovich 1935b: 41). In his view there could be no alliance with the bourgeoisie, with the exception of the 'petty bourgeoisie' which according to Marxist terminology of the day meant peasants. In compliance with the Comintern theory Zusmanovich wrote that 'the only class capable of uniting the national revolutionary front of struggle is the Native proletariat supported by the most oppressed masses of the European[9] proletariat'. 'The national liberation revolutionary movement in

South Africa', he assumed, 'could lead to the formation of the independent Native republic only under the leadership of the working class' (Zusmanovich 1935b: 42-43).

Zusmanovich thought that there was a national—'Native'—bourgeoisie in South Africa, consisting of 'traders, sub-lessees, etc.' According to him it could not lead a national-liberation revolution not just because, like any bourgeoisie, it was an unreliable ally, but also because it was not an industrial bourgeoisie, for only a local industrial bourgeoisie could have interests different from those of the imperialists. Zusmanovich was a firm opponent of Sik's idea that there was no bourgeoisie in Africa at all. 'We must understand absolutely clearly', he declared, 'that to deny the existence of a Native bourgeoisie logically leads to denying the need of the struggle for the hegemony of the proletariat in the anti-imperialist revolution' (Zusmanovich 1935b: 38-9).

An independent Native republic was, for Zusmanovich, the cornerstone of his scenario of anti-colonial revolution. This republic would emerge as a result of an 'agrarian revolution' and of the 'liberation from the imperialist yoke'—thus it would be bourgeois-democratic by nature. The creation of such a republic would not lead to the lowering of living standards of the white proletariat. On the contrary, it would raise living standards of black workers to those of white workers; and the rights of white workers would be protected as the rights of a national minority. However, Zusmanovich wrote, because this bourgeois-democratic republic would not be governed by the proletariat, the proletariat 'would not stop at the independent Native republic, and would go further, transforming it into a Soviet socialist republic'. This would be not a national-democratic revolution under the hegemony of the proletariat, but a socialist revolution under its dictatorship (Zusmanovich 1935b: 43-44, 46-48).

Potekhin was interested in two questions in connection with the anti-colonial revolution: 'the Native bourgeoisie', like Zusmanovich, and South African political organisations. Both were analysed in his article, 'National Reformism in the Union of South Africa'. Potekhin's view of the African bourgeoisie in South Africa was less dogmatic than Zusmanovich's, although in principle they agreed. For Potekhin, South Africa had no 'national' industrial bourgeoisie, because there was no national industry (which meant that Potekhin considered all industry in South Africa to be foreign). Before the arrival of the British, he wrote, the only accumulation of capital was 'the accumulation of feudal property by tribal chiefs'. Later on the emergence of a 'national bourgeoisie' was hampered by the fact that South Africa was 'not only a colony, but also a dominion'. He did not explain what he meant by this, but it is clear from the context that his idea was close to what Joe Slovo later called 'colonialism of a special type'—a colony and a colonial power in one country. Even so, Potekhin wrote, the process of accumulation of 'Native' capital had started, and he showed its sources, its nature, and its political role. His conclusion was that the 'native bourgeoisie' was a 'class in the making', but that its role 'in the socio-political life of the Native society was much bigger than its economic significance' (Izotla 1934a: 84-88).

When it came to political organisations, both Zusmanovich and Potekhin used labels rather than academic analysis and their assessments notably hardened since the time of their co-authored book. Without hesitation Zusmanovich (1935a: 152) now called the African National Congress 'a feudal-comprador time-server to impe- rialism', and placed his main hopes on the radical opposition to its leadership (Zusmanovich 1935b: 36). Potekhin, too, denied the ANC the status of a 'national- reformist' organisation which both authors attributed to it before. 'There are repre- sentatives of the Native bourgeoisie and intelligentsia in it', wrote Potekhin, but 'tribal chiefs who constitute the social basis of imperialism [in South Africa – I. F.], play the leading role in it'. If the Congress fought for the extension of 'tribal lands', for Potekhin it was the struggle for 'greater opportunities of feudal exploitation of the peasantry by the chiefs'; if it campaigned to lower government taxes, according to Potekhin, it was only in order to increase the taxes collected for the chiefs' cof- fers. With great regret Potekhin noted that the ANC 'still had a significant influence on the toiling Native masses' (Izotla 1934a: 83-92).

According to Potekhin the real national reformist organisation was the ICU, the Industrial and Commercial Workers' Union. He analysed its policy, its internal frictions and splits, and the political tendencies within each of its fragments. As in case of the ANC, he did not see anything positive in its activities that were aimed at improving the situation of its members. The only correct way forward for him was to strike (Izotla 1934a: 102).

On the other hand, both authors weighed in to support the CPSA leadership. Neither mentions the fact of a deadly internal struggle within the Party caused by the Comintern's interventions, but both denounce communists who were expelled from it for objecting to the Comintern's methods of 'Bolshevisation' and to the slogan of an independent Native republic. Potekhin called them 'Bunting's counterrevolutionary leadership' (Izotla 1934a: 91), and Zusmanovich, 'counter- revolutionary opportunists from Bunting's camp' (1935a: 158).

Both Zusmanovhich and Potekhin saw the African situation in a similar way, through the prism of the Comintern's policy, as did Sik and Gerngross. There were small differences of interpretation and sometimes bitter arguments over small de- tails, but all the Comintern's Africanists followed its line. The difference was that for Sik and Gerngross Africa was an object of academic study within the framework of a particular ideological doctrine, while for Zusmanovich and Potekhin it was a field of political battle, yet another region which had to be won for the revolution. Zusmanovich's works were more theoretical, Potekhin's more concrete. In their article both, but particularly Potekhin, gave direct instructions to their CPSA col- leagues on how to wage propaganda, on what they should or should not do (Izotla 1934b).

Zusmanovich soon paid for his theorising dearly: in the middle of 1935 the Comintern's line made such a sharp turn that Zusmanovich did not manage to follow it in time. The Seventh Congress of the Comintern rejected the policy of the Sixth Congress, having returned, in effect, to Lenin's formulations. This meant that the 'united front' was no longer 'proletarian', but rather 'popular'; that national reformists were now allies; that in the South African case the independent Native republic was now a taboo; that most of the 'Buntingists' were no longer enemies; and that some even had to be allowed to rejoin the party. In fact the changes were not all that sudden—they started months before the Congress, while the preparations were going on. It seems, however, that Zusmanovich believed so deeply in the independent Native republic and in the 'proletarian' interpretation of the united front that he simply failed to grasp the depth of the changes before it was too late. In an article published in 1935 he still wrote: 'Some comrades have wrongly interpreted the united front as a reconciliation with national-reformists, because they saw the tactics of a united front as a rejection of irreconcilable struggle against national reformist compromising' (Zusmanovich 1935b).

At the Congress itself Zusmanovich's KUTV student, Josie Mpama, represented the CPSA. Her speech was prepared for her by Zusmanovich and by another student, also a South African communist, Lazar Bach—a fact she tearfully disclosed to the Comintern's commission of enquiry, where she was invited to explain why she had distorted the line. Zusmanovich had put into her speech several pages of apologia for the proletarian united front, not a popular one, and at the end had added the cherished goal of the creation of an independent Native republic. Zusmanovich was removed from his position of a Head of the African Section of KUTV. Bach soon paid for his mistakes with his life. The main accusation against him was not connected with South Africa, but this distortion of the line added weight to his sentence. Zusmanovich's position was offered to Potekhin, but soon both were expelled from KUTV altogether for organising a lecture by a visiting South African journalist, who (it was reported) was a Trotskyist. In fact, he wasn't, but for both Potekhin and Zusmanovich their expulsion was a blessing in disguise. Had they remained in position longer, they would, most probably, have perished in the camps together with hundreds of their former colleagues and students (Davidson et al 2003: 18).

With that the African section at KUTV was closed and Comintern's African studies effectively ceased. Zusmanovich and Potekhin were to return to their subject only in the new era, after the War.

Soviet African Studies in the 1930s

It is difficult to assess Soviet African studies in the 1930s, particularly in relation to the discipline of African studies in Western countries of the day. Unlike their Western colleagues Soviet Africanists did not travel to Africa. The Comintern did send secret emissaries to South Africa but they did not publish the results of what they observed, they only wrote reports for the Comintern's Executive Committee, or, in some cases, directly to Stalin; but those remained, of course, completely secret even within the closed Comintern system. Soviet Africanists had no experience of African realities, and their publications were extremely scholastic. Their views, or at least the views expressed in their publications, were completely subordinate to the ideological dogma and political directives of the Comintern, and because of this even their theoretical constructs were much less interesting than they might have been, had they resulted from independent research and debate, even within the context of the same ideology.

It would be wrong to say that there was no debate at all. During the 1920s and even in the early 1930s there was a lot of debate, but it was strictly limited to interpretations of the official line, and at any moment could get the participants into trouble. To give just one example: a heated theoretical battle was fought by Nasonov and Sik in the pages of the *Revolutsionnyi Vostok* journal. In 1929 Sik, who at that time was studying the problem of race relations, published a critical review of Nasonov's article about the 'Negro problem' in the USA. Nasonov replied with a crushing criticism of Sik's views in general and of his approach to the race problem in particular. Both sides accused each other of a lack of understanding of Marxism and an inability to apply its principles to the race problem.

Sik knew the empirical material better but Nasonov was a stronger demagogue. After much bickering Nasonov gained a complete victory over his opponent by publishing a crude but devastating review—in effect a political report—of Sik's book *The Race Problem and Marxism* (Nasonov 1929, 1930; Sik 1929, 1930c). For several years after this Sik was a whipping boy for whoever cared to denounce him, until finally the *Revolutsionnyi Vostok* published his repentant letter, in which he admitted that all the accusations against him were correct, gave a detailed account of where and how he was wrong, and explained that his theory was 'objectively directed against the programme and policy of the Comintern', although how this showed in his text was not clear. Sik finished his letter with a call: 'I and those comrades who in this or that way, or in this or that aspect supported my views must consider it to be their Bolshevik duty to admit our political mistakes without any reservations, categorically to dissociate ourselves from them, to overcome them and to be in the forefront of the struggle against distortions of Marxist-Leninist theory and of the Comintern line in these questions' (Sik 1933: 217-18).

After this nobody was willing to discuss the race problem in the US for a long time to come. And this was a great pity: the questions raised during the discussion were interesting: what was the social nature of the American black population: was it a class or a race; what was a race generally; what were the goals of the struggle of American blacks: independence or integration; how did the Comintern's slogan of an independent black republic for the 'black belt' states of the USA fit in this struggle, and so on.

Perhaps, the main problem with Soviet studies of anti-colonialism in the inter-war years was that Africanists did not see the analysis of African realities as their main goal. What they wrote was, in effect, practical recommendations for the

Comintern and for the communists and other 'progressive forces' on the continent. Their works had, quite openly, an applied character. As true Cominternians they believed that they knew the correct and final answer to any question, if not personally, then through the collective wisdom of the Party and the undisputed correctness of its ideology. The task was simply to show why and how this particular answer was correct in order to persuade others.

Thus in effect ideology was the main obstacle to the development of Soviet African studies, but paradoxically it was precisely this ideology which led Soviet Africanists to raise and discuss problems which their Western colleagues began to discuss only years later, thanks in part to the Soviet influence. This is true first of all about anti-colonialism. In the 1930s Soviet Africanists presented the African trade union movement, strikes, clashes in the rural areas, etc., as a part of a wider anti-colonial movement which they saw as central to Africa's contemporary history. Their Western colleagues did not discuss these topics—certainly not in this light—until much later. Even in the 1960s, when the first Western works on anti-colonialism had already emerged, an anti-colonial writer like Terence Ranger (1968: 438-39) could note that Soviet historians had begun to study this topic earlier, though, of course, he could not know about publications of the 1930s, and based his judgment only on what had been written in the 1950s and early 1960s.

The Comintern's wisdom was the same for all countries, irrespective of the concrete situation in each of them. Different countries were just 'examples', concrete manifestations of the general laws of historical development. Stalin wrote: 'specific features only supplement general features' and insisted that communist parties should base their work on these general laws and not on specific situations. This explains why Soviet Africanists of the 1930s did not pay much attention to the differences between the African countries about which they wrote. They tended to stress only what these countries had in common, which often led to distortions of reality. The only details that interested them were those connected with uprisings, clashes with the police, strikes, and sometimes repression against communists, trade union leaders, etc. Paradoxically, this academically invalid approach resulted in the comparative analysis of events in different countries—a method then used in the West only by social anthropologists.

Soviet Africanists were also the first to analyse the social basis of African political organisations. Of course, this analysis could hardly be valid because they had only three categories, defined by the Comintern, to describe the whole spectre of political, religious and social movements in the colonies: feudal-bourgeois; national reformist; and national revolutionary—besides the communist, of course. Moreover, they used social terms directly transferred from European capitalist societies, which could not reflect the social realities of African colonial societies (proletariat; rural proletariat; peasantry; industrial bourgeoisie; commercial bourgeoisie, etc.).

The international connections of the Comintern, its almost unlimited financial possibilities and indeed, the whole nature of its work created unique possibilities for research. In their publications Soviet Africanists refer to primary sources (documents and materials of political parties, government documents, documents of various colonial commissions, etc.) and to local newspapers of varying ideological backgrounds (the *Rand Daily Mail*, *Umteteli Wabantu*, *Umsebenzi*, etc.), as well as the press of the metropoles and the latest specialist literature. In this respect they were sometimes more closely in touch with events than their Western counterparts. Thus Potekhin published his review of a book by the South African trade unionist, William Ballinger, virtually immediately after it appeared in the bookshops (Izotla 1935b).

Moreover, the Comintern's Africanists worked in close and permanent contact with representatives of African countries studying at KUTV or at the Lenin School or working in Comintern's various organisations. There were not only communists among them, but also trade unionists and representatives of other political parties. Zusmanovich, Potekhin, Sik and Nasonov taught them, worked together with them in the African circle of NIANKP, and co-authored publications with them. The book by Zusmanovich, Potekhin and Nzula was only one of several examples of such cooperation.

On the one hand such cooperation meant that Soviet Africanists had a permanent access to fresh information not only from written sources but also from participants in events. This meant that some of their publications (notably Gerngross's and Potekhin's), particularly those devoted to political organisations and trade unionism, contained solid, detailed and sometimes even unique data.

On the other hand they became, at least in part, participants in events themselves, because, without a doubt, their ideology influenced their African students and colleagues, future leaders of anti-colonial and communist movements on the continent. Many years later J. B. Marks, chairman of the CPSA, said of Potekhin: 'I consider Ivan Izosimovich Potekhin my teacher ... We were students, and Potekhin was our professor. He gave us lectures on Russian history and on British colonial policy in Southern Africa, and also seminars on current political problems. As I remember Potekhin now, he was then an energetic young academic, a born lecturer and a hard worker, who, while teaching us, never missed an opportunity himself to study'.

Moses Kotane, general secretary of the CPSA, had this to say about Potekhin: 'I knew him from 1933 ... Our professors were Zusmanovich, Sik and others, and then came Potekhin. I have known him well both as a person and as a talented young academic ... We had long and very interesting conversations, and every time he showed a deep understanding of the most complicated problems of South Africa. His contribution to research proved very great, because he was one of the first to approach these problems from a Marxist position—at a time when bourgeois academics dominated Africanist research'.[10]

Another channel of their influence was their publications in foreign languages, particularly in the *Negro Worker*, the journal of the International Trade Union Committee of Negro Workers, which was distributed in Africa. Translations of some of their articles were also published in *Umsebenzi* (Potekchin 1932; Izotla 1935b; A.Z. 1935a; A.Z. 1935b).

This influence was not undisputedly for the good. The debate on the existence or non-existence of an African bourgeoisie, on the nature of the independent Native republic (for example, on the question of why the proletariat, which is supposed to lead the first stage of the revolution, should give power to somebody else after its victory) and on other theoretical issues, started in Moscow, was transferred to South Africa and, combined with the Comintern's 'bolshevisation' of the CPSA, nearly destroyed the party. Kotane and Marks themselves belonged at that time to different camps within the CPSA and sent messages to Moscow, each calling its wrath down on their respective opponents (Davidson, et al. 2003).

Yet, the fact remains that, leaving ideology aside, in the 1930s Soviet Africanists worked in a way in which their Western colleagues began to work only in the late 1950s and early 1960s, when they moved to African universities, began to publish in African media and to create schools of their students and followers. In the early 1930s Moscow had such a school, which made its own—unrecognised—input into African studies, and perhaps even (through its ideological influence) into political events on the continent. True, the Soviet Africanists of the 1930s used a turgid, ideological language which renders their works almost unreadable today but through communist publications and through the African leaders who worked with them, their approaches and assessments, among other factors, pushed the next generation of Africanists to study new topics, such as the social structure of African societies and anti-colonialism, the social basis of African nationalism and the nature and possibilities of the state in postcolonial Africa. These were to become dominant concerns for all Africanists in the 1960s.

'Winds of Change' in Soviet African Studies: The Late 1940s and 1950s

Inevitably, the changed post-war world altered the approach of official Soviet ideologists to problems of anti-colonialism. In the first years after the war no official documents on this topic appeared because the institutions that might have generated them were gone. The Comintern had been dissolved in 1943 (although in practice it had already ceased to function in 1937), and no congresses of the CPSU were held until 1952. However, academic publications, particularly those coming from the very top of the Soviet Academy of Sciences, hinted at changes in the official approach to this topic.

One could sum up the contents of such publications in two words, 'crisis' and 'collapse'. Several Soviet monographs and collections of article on colonialism were published in the late 1940s-early 1950s, and all had one of these words in the title. At first it was 'crisis', and by the late 1950s it was usually 'collapse'—a fair enough reflection of the accelerating process of decolonisation.

According to Soviet theoreticians, the new feature of anti-colonialism was the fact that 'broader and broader masses of people ... are drawn into the national liberation struggle ... even at the most remote corners of the colonial world' (Zhukov 1949: 4). According to academician Yevgenii Mikhailovich Zhukov, head of the Institute of General History and of the Department of History at the Academy of

Sciences, Madagascar was such a remote corner, for the only example of this process in his book was the 1947 uprising in that country. Listing the new features of anti-colonialism after the war, Zhukov did not quote any official documents (because there were none), but rather articles by the late Andrei Zhdanov, one of the top Soviet ideologists of the 1940s and by the British communist Palme Dutt. Both stressed the upsurge of the armed struggle, and Dutt also listed the creation of independent republics in Vietnam and Indonesia, 'the introduction' of African peoples to the struggle and the strengthening of the role of the working class, trade unions and communist parties in the leadership of liberation movements (Zhukov 1949: 5,6). The independence of Vietnam and Indonesia apart, there was not much new here. And a long quotation from 'Comrade Stalin's teaching on the stages of the Chinese revolution' allowed Zhukov to leave untouched the interpretation of the two stages of a national liberation revolution (Zhukov 1949: 14).

However, in other respects Zhukov's work was quite innovative. For the first time the Soviet theory of anti-colonialism had to face the phenomenon of independence as one colony after another changed its status. This phenomenon had to be interpreted and incorporated into the existing theoretical constructs. It was necessary to define the nature of Soviet relations with the new states. It would seem that the Soviet Union would hail the liberation of colonial countries—after all, this had been the main goal of the Comintern and Soviet policy. But in reality everything turned out to be more complicated. The problem was that few new countries acquired their independence according to the scenario created for them by the Comintern, a scenario still in force after the war. According to this, they could reach independence only under the hegemony of the proletariat, led by local or friendly communist parties, whereas in fact they often achieved it under the leadership of those whom the Comintern denounced as 'feudal compradors', not even national reformists! It was impossible to admit that something was wrong with the theory, so something had to be wrong with the newly liberated countries. Thus Soviet theoreticians greeted their birth without fanfare. If a colony obtained its independence not under the leadership of the working class then, according to Zhukov, this independence was 'formal' or 'illusory'. 'Colonial status, i.e. first of all the economic enslavement of a country by imperialism', he wrote, 'is fully compatible with its formal equality and even with "independence"' (Zhukov 1949: 21). Burma and India were given as examples of this 'illusory' independence.

The idea of illusory independence was further developed by one of the main Soviet specialists in the theory of anti-colonialism, V. A. Maslennikov. In 1953 he wrote: '... One of such manoeuvres [by the ruling classes of the colonial countries— I. F.] is granting of a fictitious independence to colonies. Granting this so called "independence", imperialists recruit to power the most venal groups of landowners and bourgeoisie, and through them suppress the national liberation movement and increase colonial exploitation' (Maslennikov 1953: 3). In another work Maslennikov gave his list of such 'fictitiously' independent countries: Philippines, Burma, Ceylon, India and Pakistan. He even wrote about the 'national liberation movement' in India as something separate from the Congress Party, three years after India had proclaimed its independence under Congress rule (Maslennikov 1952:44, 45). Palme Dutt also omitted independence from his list of new factors in the post-war anti-colonial movement. Moreover, he did not even mention the independence of India and Burma. Indonesia and Vietnam were mentioned but only because they had achieved their independence in a prolonged and bloody armed struggle. However, not all was well even with these countries. For example, in Indonesia 'bourgeois nationalist agents of imperialism deny the common laws of social development and demand the creation of "specific ways and laws" for every country, stemming from its specific features', wrote Zhukov. He explained with disarming sincerity what was wrong with this: 'The exaggeration of specific feature in the development of each country is aimed directly at attempting to separate colonial and dependent countries from the democratic and anti-imperialist forces led by the Soviet Union' (Zhukov 1949: 18).

It was precisely the closeness of former colonies to the Soviet Union, not their independence *per se*, that defined the Soviet attitude to them in the early post-war years. Indeed, at war's end the Soviet government even attempted to take over some former Italian colonies, in order 'to show, what a socialist colony could be', until these attempts finally failed in 1947 (Davidson and Mazov 1999).

As in the 1930s, the armed struggle remained the preferred form of anti-colonialism, because in theory it was bound to bring the liberated countries into the socialist camp. After the war this was asserted even more openly. This is how I. M. Lemin (1951: 9), author of a monograph, *The Aggravation of the Crisis of the British Empire after the Second World War*, described this process: 'The peoples of colonial and dependent countries rise up to fight imperialism, arms in hand, they win their independence, create a popular democratic power and join the mighty camp of socialism, democracy and peace'.

The leading role of the proletariat in the national liberation movement was still considered the main condition for its success. Lemin (1951: 9) even wrote about this as if it was a reality, not a wishful theoretical construct: 'The working class, whose numbers, discipline, political influence and authority have increased to a huge degree, now leads the national front of struggle'. Indeed, all post-war Soviet theoreticians of anti-colonialism asserted that the role of proletariat in anti-colonial movements had grown, and Lemin thought that this was one of the three new features of national liberation movements at the time, the other two being the broadening of the front of struggle and the creation of national liberation armies (Lemin 1951: 46).

The 'national bourgeoisie' still occupied a significant place in the post-war works on anti-colonialism, and it was still thought that social divisions within it were bound to define its attitude to national liberation. Lemin (1951: 10), for example, wrote that: 'While the struggle unfolds, the national bourgeoisie gets split. The big bourgeoisie, closely connected with foreign banks and monopolies, which is ready to compromise, betrays national interests and forms a bloc with imperialism. The other part of the bourgeoisie, the petty and middle, which suffers from the domination of foreign colonialists, participates in the united national anti-imperialist front'.

Despite the resolutions of the Seventh Comintern Congress and the experience of the united front during the war, immediately after the war the attacks on Social Democrats were renewed. 'Right wing socialists—the most vicious enemies of the people', wrote Maslennikov, 'are active accomplices of imperialist monopolies ... suppressors of the oppressed peoples' (Maslennikov 1952: 44).

Some aspects of this theory remained in use until Gorbachev's perestroika changed the priorities of Soviet foreign policy. Others, however, had to be changed or withdrawn much sooner. Zhukov's thesis that former colonies could not be really independent if they were not closely connected with the Soviet Union was soon replaced with a list of particular reforms. A country could be considered really independent if it began a land reform, nationalised the banks and fought for peace together with the Soviet Union and its allies. The most important of these reforms was nationalisation. In the 1950s and early 1960s this reform alone could earn a former colony the approval of Soviet theoreticians (Maslennikov 1952: 32, 34). And, despite all the differences between the really independent and 'fictitiously' independent countries, they were all finally recognised, together with the working class of developed countries, as 'a part of a united front against the common enemy'. 'In the course of successful liberation struggles colonies stop being the most important reserve and source of power of imperialism and turn into the most important reserve and component of the great camp of peace, democracy and socialism, led by the Soviet Union', wrote Lemin (1951: 10).

Armed struggle was another aspect which soon had to change its nature, although it did not lose its allure to many Soviet writers on anti-colonialism until the collapse of the Soviet Union. In 1949 a meeting of the Information Bureau of Communist Parties (Cominform)—a modest successor of the Comintern—took place in Hungary. It introduced a new notion of peace as a factor uniting foreign supporters of the USSR ('peace front'; 'struggle for peace'; 'supporters of peace', etc.). 'For the first time in the history of humanity', a Cominform document ran, 'there emerged an organised peace front, led by the Soviet Union—the stronghold and standard-bearer of world peace. The courageous call of communist parties, declaring that peoples will never fight against the first socialist country in the world, against the Soviet Union, is spreading wider and wider among the popular masses of capitalist countries'.[11]

Of course, this concerned first of all the peace movement in the capitalist world, which became, according to the authors, another factor of the crisis of capitalism, on condition that it was directed by the USSR. But as a result the thesis of armed struggle as the preferred method of anti-colonial movement had to be used with caution, particularly after October 1952, when the CPSU 19th congress for the first time declared the possibility of peaceful co-existence with capitalist countries. The thesis could not be cancelled but offensive struggle was now transformed into defensive struggle. Thus, having said that the creation of national liberation armies was a new feature of anti-colonialism after the war, Maslennikov (1952:46) immediately explained that 'the creation of these armies came as a response to the attempts by imperialists to suppress national liberation movements'.

Another new feature of Soviet political doctrine after the war was anti-Americanism. As far as anti-colonialism was concerned, the USA was, on the one hand, accused of 'expansionism with the purpose of capturing British and French colonies', and on the other, of 'leading the reactionary imperialist front against national liberation movement' (Maslennikov 1953: 38).

In the late 1940s and early 1950s Potekhin (who had returned to African studies) also wrote several theoretical articles. After the war he became deputy director of the Institute of Ethnography of the USSR Academy of Sciences. He was not a professional interpreter of the official line, which may be why his theoretical writing was even less sophisticated than the others. He stressed the role of the proletariat in the anti-colonial movement (quoting Stalin), described 'open armed struggle' as the sign of the crisis of the colonial system (quoting Zhdanov) and accused 'the big bourgeoisie of the most developed colonies' of 'direct betrayal of the national interests of their countries' (proving it by another quote from Stalin). Of course, he thought that the independence of several Asian colonies 'did not resolve the main tasks ... of the national liberation movement'. As an example of the 'correct' national liberation movement in which 'under the working class leadership the struggle for national independence merges with the struggle for all-round economic and political renovation of the country', Potekhin quoted the 1948 programme of the Indian Communist Party which, among other things, demanded the nationalisation of banks and big industries' (Potekhin (n.d. 5-7). Having merged the two stages of the national liberation revolution into one, Potekhin in effect repeated what Stalin originally said about national liberation movements: there was no reason for the proletariat (i.e. communist parties) to support them, unless they could be turned into socialist movements.

In his article, 'V. I. Lenin on the National Liberation movement in Colonial and Dependent Countries', Potekhin (1950b) again wrote not so much about Lenin's approaches to the topic, but rather those of Stalin and of Soviet post-war ideologists. He quoted some (but not all) of Lenin's points on anti-colonialism from his *Theses on the National-Colonial Question* and his work *Imperialism as the Highest Stage of Capitalism* and simply continued with Stalin's ideas from *The Foundations of Leninism*, as if all these works were one organically connected whole. One of the omitted points was the bourgeois-democratic nature of the national liberation movement. The point emphasised the most, however, was the possibility that the newly-liberated countries might by-pass the capitalist stage of development and choose a 'non-capitalist way of development'. There was no doubting that 'non-capitalist' for Potekhin meant 'socialist' in the Soviet sense: at the end of the article he even offered a term for 'the new state form of the dictatorship of proletariat' in former colonies—'people's democracies', as in the new socialist countries of Eastern Europe. However, most attention in his work was paid to denouncing American aid to 'underde-veloped countries', much more than even to denouncing the metropoles themselves.

Perhaps the most important of Potekhin's theoretical works on anti-colonialism at the time was his paper for Stalin's seventieth anniversary presented at the special meeting of the Academic Council of the Institute of Ethnography. Much of its contents and style was a reflection of the time: one could see how the stifling atmos-phere of the late 1930s was back. Potekhin wrote that the 'strictly scientific' Soviet theory of anti-colonialism was created by the 'leading light of science', Stalin, while Lenin only 'outlined its main features'. According to him, its main point was that 'the solution of the colonial question, the liberation of the oppressed peoples from colonial slavery, was impossible without proletarian revolution and the overthrow of imperialism'. He even reproached those intellectuals from colonial countries who refused to support this idea and proved their mistakes by quoting Stalin. However, immediately after this he pointed out that the national bourgeoisie could at some stage support colonial revolutionary movements, and even mentioned a 'special strategic stage of the colonial revolution—the stage of the national anti-imperialist front' (Potekhin 1950a: 24-7).

It is easy to accuse Potekhin of a lack of consistency and even of academic dishonesty. Unlike the pre-war scholastic but logical theory, Soviet post-war theoreti-cal constructs were generally full of contradictions, juggling and distortions of the original texts, even the texts of the 'classics of Marxism'. Before the war the striving to get to the bottom of every theoretical problem continued until 1937, despite the unfolding terror. In the 1940s and 1950s this momentum was completely lost, and Soviet theoreticians seemed to care more about choosing correct quotations for their publications and omitting incorrect ones. Sadly, in the Humanities a prominent academic who had reached a certain position could not escape being a theoretician: 'theoretical' articles were a requirement of the status.

However, theoretical logic and consistency were not only hampered by the politi-cal climate. Soviet leaders now needed concrete information about the newly liber-ated countries, for they had to establish relations and do business with them, and concrete facts did not fit into such schemes easily. Potekhin's article on Stalin's theory may be the best proof of this, because the second part of it is based on concrete material. It was still full of generalisations: Potekhin spoke about 'African society', and not 'societies'; about indirect rule in British colonies in general, although with concrete examples; the same about 'African chiefs'. Moreover, just as in the 1930s, all groups in African societies had to be presented to Soviet readers in the categories understandable to them. Chiefs, for example, had to be 'feudal or semi-feudal', 'peasants' were 'petty bourgeois', workers were the 'proletariat'—and the only specific feature of this proletariat was that 'it was young and had not accumu-lated experience of political struggle'.

Sometimes Potekhin still wrote about events not as they were, but as they ought to be. One example was his assertion that after the war the influence of the 'feudal-aristocratic elite' in Africa was collapsing. The proof given was the events of the late

1940s in Buganda. However, Potekhin was honest, or tried to be: neither in this article, nor in his later works did he write anything that directly contradicted the facts. Thus, having quoted Stalin on the hegemony of the proletariat in the national-liberation movement, he still wrote: 'at present the leading role in the national-libera-tion movement of the majority of colonies of Tropical and South Africa belongs to the national bourgeoisie and national intelligentsia' (Potekhin 1950a: 26-28, 30-31, 34). In an article published in 1956, when the situation in Buganda changed, he recognised, though reluctantly, that his understanding of the situation of chiefs in African societies had been wrong (Potekhin 1956).

Perhaps one of the most difficult of Potekhin's tasks at that time was to ascribe political characteristics to African leaders: he could not fail to understand that not only Soviet leaders and diplomats but he too would soon have to face these leaders in person. Potekhin wrote about many of them, for example, of Nnamdi Azikiwe and Kwame Nkrumah with qualified sympathy. They were revolutionaries, and in Potekhin's system of values this was the highest status that a human being could aspire to. However, their revolution was only national, not a social one, and not all of them were ready for radical measures, particularly armed struggle. Azikiwe, for example, had declared his adherence to non-violence, and Potekhin denounced him as a 'petty bourgeois national reformist'. Other African leaders were also rebuked for their 'desire to keep the movement within the framework of colonial legality'. For Potekhin, the smashing of European shops during a demonstration in Ghana was the highest point of the anti-colonial movement in that country (Potekhin 1950a: 32-34). Whatever his generalisations, even these theoretical works leave no doubt that Potekhin learnt a lot more about African societies than he knew about them in his Comintern years.

In the early 1950s the contemporary problems of the African continent were studied not only in the Institute of Ethnography under Potekhin, but also in the Institute of Economics of the USSR Academy of Sciences. In 1952 and 1953 the Institute published two big works connected with anti-colonialism in Africa. Both were disappointing.

The book by Irina Pavlovna Yastrebova became, and for many years remained, the most detailed Soviet study of the Union of South Africa. Although it was called *The Union of South Africa after the Second World War*, in effect Yastrebova described the economic and political history of the country from the early twentieth century on-ward (Yastrebova 1952: 203). The book was extremely rich in detail: it seems that the author left out nothing, no meaningful fact or event. But it is not easy to read: it is full of propaganda-style clichés and stock phrases, and all its details do not lead to a valid analysis, and as a result the scale and the real meaning of events are dis-torted. Thus, Yastrebova called the National Party 'fascist', but the word 'apartheid' did not enter the text. The policy of Smuts's government was subjected to even harsher criticism than that of the NP: the author did not distinguish between the two at all. Another example: following the priorities of Soviet foreign policy of the time Yastrebova paid much attention to South Africa's peace movement. Such a movement, led by communists, did indeed exist in South Africa but in the early 1950s it was extremely marginal both to the country's politics and even to those communists who were still free.

Yastrebova wrote about it as if she was unaware of the reality, although the banning of the CPSA was, of course, well covered in the book: 'Peaceful demo-cratic forces in South Africa understand that the struggle for peace is the duty of all progressively-minded citizens, who must join the struggle by protesting decisively against all acts of preparation for the new war by the imperialist camp, particularly by the American imperialism'.

Yasterbova's approach to anti-colonialism and her view of the social basis of national liberation movements and of particular parties did not differ from that of Potekhin. But Potekhin's text was livelier and more interesting than Yastrebova's. One reason could be that Potekhin used many more first-hand sources: Yestrebova refered only to the British communist paper, *The Daily Worker*, and *The Guardian* which was run by South African communists. There were no references to South African sources and only two or three references to non-communist periodicals and publications. This was not the fault of the author: it was extremely difficult to get such publications in the Soviet Union at the time, and quoting 'reactionary' 'bour-geois' sources was extremely dangerous. Either because of his position or for some other reason Potekhin could afford to write differently.

The collection of articles, *The Imperialist Struggle for Africa and the Liberation Move-ment of Peoples* dealt directly with anti-colonialism. Both Lemin and Yasrebova con-tributed chapters to it, both simply repeating the main points of their previous publications, tailoring them even more strictly to suit Soviet orthodoxy (Vasiliieva et al., 1953).

The biggest achievement of Soviet African studies in the early 1950s was a huge volume *The Peoples of Africa*, published by Potekhin and Dmitrii Alexeievich Olderogge (1954), head of the Leningrad school of Africanists, who mostly studied African languages and ethnography. This enormous (730 large format pages) book was written by a handful of authors with most articles authored by the two editors themselves. In volume, if not in contents, it could only be compared with Hailey's *An African Survey*.[12] Ethnographic data occupied more space in it than political his-tory, but each regional part ended with chapters on anti-colonialism, written mostly by Potekhin. These chapters presented detailed information about political parties, labour and religious movements, strikes and uprisings and dealt with the whole spectrum of anti-colonial movement from the colonial occupations to the mid-1950s. In effect this was the first history of African anti-colonialism, not only in the Soviet Union, but anywhere in the world.

There was no theorising in these chapters. Theory was dealt with in the introduc-tion and then left more or less alone, which, of course, makes the concrete material presented in it much more valuable and interesting. One reason for this was that by then Potekhin had accumulated a vast knowledge of his subject, which allowed him to select and present his material expertly. The other was doubtless the simple fact that Stalin died in March 1953, and the volume went to the printers only in September 1954, by which time the ideological climate had already softened considerably.

Potekhin's other great achievement of the time was his second doctoral thesis devoted to the process of ethnic consolidation in South Africa.[13] Whether one agreed with the author's conclusions or not, this work was a major contribution to the debate on the South African nation, in which Potekhin himself actively participated.[14] In this work Potekhin presented anti-colonialism as a major factor in the process of the consolidation of the national consciousness of South Africa's Bantu-speaking communities.

This work, like *The Peoples of Africa*, is fully based on concrete material. Thus, despite his desire, in the spirit of Soviet Marxism, to raise every problem of the continent to the level of high theory, it was actually Potekhin who inaugurated a new 'empirical' approach in the Soviet treatment of anti-colonialism.

The late 1950s saw a transformation of Soviet interpretations of anti-colonialism. It was in these years that a new Soviet strategy in Asia and Africa was forged, the main principles of which remained practically unchanged until the early 1990s. The major change lay in the realisation of the huge value to the USSR of the political independence of the newly liberated countries and the recognition of the importance of maintaining an alliance with them in the situation of the Cold War. By the late 1950s it had become obvious that the Soviet Union and these countries, irrespective of their ideologies and policy, had some common geo-political interests. The success (from this point of view) of the Bandung Confernce and of the Cairo Solidarity Conference of Asian and African countries,[15] and the support that Soviet initiatives often received from these countries in the United Nations, confirmed the collective value of this new strategic alliance for the Soviet Union and created a new political environment within which the USSR could act with great effect.

The change was hardly less dramatic than that brought by the Seventh Comintern Congress. The 1957 meeting of representatives of Communist and working class parties—another attempt to revive Comintern's practice of working out a common strategy for the world communist movement—paid little attention either to anti-colonialism or to the newly-liberated countries. The next such meeting, however, though convened only three years later, declared that the importance of the collapse of the 'system of colonial slavery under the pressure of the national liberation movement' was 'second only to the formation of the world socialist system'. The meeting stated that 'Communists always recognised the progressive, revolutionary significance of wars for national liberation', but simultaneously they stressed that in the new global situation different forms of struggle were possible, both military and political, 'depending on condition in each country'. Moreover, the working class was no longer accorded a leading role in the national liberation movements, only an active one.

Of course, bringing former colonies into the socialist camp remained the ultimate goal. The ideal scenario for them was the creation of a state of 'national democracy' led by 'the united national democratic front of all patriotic forces of the nation'. According to this plan the role of the proletariat in such a state would gradually grow, the national bourgeoisie would align itself with 'internal reaction and imperialism', the assistance of socialist countries and communist parties of the world would play 'the decisive role' in strengthening national independence, and the 'popular masses' would gradually realise that 'non-capitalist development' was 'the best way to improve their condition'. The difference was that even where this could not be achieved, anti-colonialism was now recognised as a progressive development.[16]

Potekhin's writing on anti-colonialism in the late 1950s and early 1960s reflected the pace of change. His articles on this subject published in 1958 and 1959 were still full of clichés from the previous era. All Africa's problems for Potekhin still stemmed from colonialism and the United States; everything about anti-colonialism and almost everything about the new African states was good, and whatever the metropoles offered was a plot to extend their control of Africa (Potekhin 1958). As before, he still denounced African politicians who thought that it was possible to reach independence through the ballot box: he was still convinced that the overthrow of a colonial regime was impossible 'within the framework of colonial legality' (Potekhin 1959). However, in 1960 Potekhin's approach underwent a dramatic change. In his long article, 'The Characteristic Features of the Collapse of the Colonial System in Africa', he wrote, for the first time in his long academic career, that the national liberation movement was 'universal' and 'popular' by nature and that in new conditions it was possible 'to gain independence by peaceful, constitutional means'. Of course, he immediately added that 'to deny the oppressed peoples their right to initiate and use violence' would mean to give colonialists the right to do whatever they pleased, and the fact that they themselves denounced violence meant precisely that using it was the right thing to do.

Not even the documents of the 1960 Summit of the world's Communist parties could make Potekhin lose his belief in the potential of the African proletariat, which he termed a 'powerful force' in the anti-colonial movement. Yet simultaneously he had to admit that it 'has not yet become the political leader of the broad popular masses'. Amazingly, the most revolutionary class in African societies was now ... the intelligentsia. Not only was it leading parties and non-governmental organisations, but its 'best representatives' were also spreading Marxism on the continent. It looks as if Potekhin himself did not believe what he had written, for he immediately corrected himself: as before, 'the intelligentsia was mostly connected with feudal and bourgeois circles'; a context in which its progressive role looks even odder.

Of course, Potekhin mentioned that anti-colonial revolutions could not be considered complete until all survivals of the colonial legacy in all spheres of life were removed, a process, in which the world socialist system was 'always ready to render all-sided and selfless assistance'. The problem, and this was a complete novelty, was that not only the imperialists were to blame for Africa's woes. Among those who opposed reform Potekhin mentioned not just African feudalists and capitalists, but also the 'sabotage' by several new governments. African allies were not criticised in the Soviet Union until the mid-1980s, but Potekhin did it in 1960 when their record was tainted with just one bloodless coup. In some countries, he wrote, 'even those norms of bourgeois democracy that had been won by the hard struggle of the toiling masses during the colonial period, have now been eliminated' Potekhin (1960: 16-21; 27-28).

It is next to impossible to judge individual views of Soviet historians and political scientists who published works on such politically sensitive issues as anti-colonialism during the Soviet era. One can never know for certain what the authors truly believed, what they found it necessary to say and what was added by the editors. Such questions became particularly relevant not only in connection with another article on the collapse of the colonial system in Africa, this time written by Apollon Borisovich Davidson. Even in the article for a highly censored political magazine, *Mezhdunarodnaia Zhizn*, Davidson (1960) managed to keep his individual style: interesting quotations, a broad selection of concrete material and brilliant erudition. Yet the meaning of the article and the author's approach to the topic were similar to those of Potekhin, even of pre-1960 Potekhin (Davidson 1960).

Fortunately this was not the only publication of Davidson's at the time. His book, *The Ndebele and Shona in the Struggle against British Colonisation,* was published two years earlier, but it was this book that opened a new page in Soviet writing on anti-colonialism. There were no theoretical generalisations in it, and just one (appropriate) quotation from Lenin in the introduction. Instead there was a thorough analysis of concrete events, based on the extensive use of primary sources (including British Blue Books, memoirs, and materials drawn from British and Russian media) and practically the whole of the available literature. There was nothing in this book that could make the Soviet censors unhappy, yet it was a different history of anti-colonialism: concrete events and people in all their complexity, no empty generalisations; the starting point of this book was research, not theory (Davidson 1958).

Even now, almost forty years later, this book reads well, just as a good history should. It is difficult to believe that it was written only six years after Yastrebova's book: they belong to different eras. Potekhin knew it: the same year as Davidson's book was published he wrote to Lionel Forman: 'Yasrebova's book is old, you'll find nothing worth attention in it...' (Forman and Odendaal: 191).

Several other works which touched on the subject of anti-colonialism were published in the late 1950s by the new generation of Soviet Africanists. The most significant was a long piece by Roza Nurgaliievna Ismagilova (1956), 'The Peoples of Kenya under Colonial Rule', in which a whole chapter was devoted to the history of anti-colonialism in that country, from the first political parties to the Mau Mau uprising. This work was based on a broad range of sources, well- researched and well-written. Ismagilova did not quote the details of Mau Mau rituals, but concentrated instead on British reprisals because, according to her, she did not trust the reports of bourgeois media on this subject. This was, however, the only lack of balance in her otherwise academically solid work.

Conclusion

Until the late 1950s the Soviet theory hampered the study of anti-colonialism as it was, and not as theoreticians wanted it to be. Despite this in the 1930s it was this ideology that introduced new academic approaches to Africa, and brought about the study (albeit mostly theoretical) of new topics. But by the 1950s the innovative potential of this ideology was exhausted. Concrete knowledge of African anti-colonialism accumulated much faster in the West than in the USSR, and although the Soviet Africanists of the 1950s knew more about Africa than their predecessors in the 1930s, the limitations of ideology and censorship prevented them from developing a deeper understanding of African societies at a time when it was particularly important. Moreover, in the 1950s the theoretical dogma, adjusted to accommodate the changing realities, lost its internal logic, although not its scholastic nature. For many decades it caused some Africanists to distort conclusions based on research, to apply crude schemes to an obstinately resistant reality, or just led them to be satisfied with a simple repetition of its main points, slightly seasoned with additional facts. But in the 1950s another way emerged: the complete separation between theory and research. Five pages of theory ('bowing to the icons' as the joke ran) and then one was free to write what one wanted, within well known limits, of course.

The crude labelling style of the 1930s underwent a major revamp. In the 1950s and early 1960s even official documents were written in a flowery style, with many epithets and metaphors, some of them set in stone (thus, communist sympathy for the fighters for independence was always 'ardent'; their support always 'active'; the plans of imperialists were always 'crazy'; the Chinese people were always 'great' (until 1959, of course). There was also a lot of 'love', mostly the love of colonial peoples for the Soviet Union. There was something in that era that required romantic images.

African realities were romanticised too. K. Ivanov (1960: 27)—this was the pen name of Vladimir Semionovich Semionov, later a deputy foreign minister—wrote for example: 'Next to the peasant towers the distinctive figure of the African worker, sometimes half-peasant, some-times half-intellectual ... Those who do not see this figure, extremely poor, but cheerful, optimistic, full of faith in the future and often drawing his confidence from the example of the great Soviet Union and other socialist countries—see almost nothing in Africa'. It was exactly the desire to see more in African anti-colonialism than this mythical figure, which led the new generation of Soviet Africanists of the late 1950s to drop theoretical generalisation and refer to primary sources instead.

Today, after six decades of African independence and the collapse of the Soviet Union, the problems of anti-colonialism of the 1930s-1950s look different. Direct comparisons would be inaccurate and inappropriate, but looking back at the studies of anti-colonialism of those days could help our understanding of what happened to the USSR and beyond its borders. But one should sound a cautionary note too. Then Soviet Africanists thought that they knew everything about anti-colonialism.

Now, when we assess their works, it seems to us that we know all the answers—but we may be just as wrong.

While it is easy to be scornful of the Soviet Africanists of the 1930s to the 1950s, the fact is that they left a significant trace in world African studies. They found a real gap in Western writing on Africa at their time and, indirectly, spawned a whole further generation of Marxist writing on Africa, this time by Western scholars. One wonders how much of Russian Africanist writing of today will have such a long life.

Notes

1. Before the creation of the Union of Soviet Socialist Republics in 1924, several independent states with Soviets at their head emerged on the territory of the former Russian Empire, as well as in Hungary, Bavaria, etc.
2. Russian periodicals (mostly Comintern-affiliated) published several articles by South African communists even before then. See Davidson (1972: 588).
3. Member parties of the Comintern were not independent organisations, they were considered to be national branches of this international organisation. This justified the practice of the Centre making all policy decisions for member parties.
4. For the detailed analysis of E. Sik's works see Davidson (1981).
5. The second edition of these two volumes supplemented by another two was published in 1971-1974.
6. See, for example, P. Mif (1935: 7).
7. For a detailed analysis of Potekhin's works see A. B. Davidson (1974).
8. English translation (abridged and not very accurate): A. T. Nzula, I. I. Potekhin, A. Z. Zusmanovich. *Forced Labour in Colonial Africa*. London 1979.
9. In this case 'European' meant local white.
10. These reminiscences of Marks and Kotane were recorded by Dr. Leo Rytov in Moscow in 1972 and published in *The African Communist*, the journal of the SACP, in 1973, no. 54, in connection with Potekhin's 70th anniversary.
11. *Soveshchaniie Informatsionnogo biuro kommunisticheskikh partii v Vengrii vo vtoroj polovine noiabria 1949 g. (Meeting of the Information Bureau of Communist Parties held in Hungary in the second half of November, 1949)*. Moscow, 1949, p. 13.
12. M. Hailey. *An African Survey*. London, 1st ed. 1938; 2nd ed. 1957.
13. A part of it was published in a series of occasional publications by the Institute of Ethnography (Potekhin 1955).
14. See, for example, S. Forman and A. Odendaal (1992).
15. The USSR participated as an Asian country.
16. *Dokumenty soveshchaniia predstavitelei kommunistichskikh i rabochikh partii (Documents of the Meeting of Representatives of Communist and Workers' Parties)*. Moscow, 1960.

References

A. Z. (A. Zusmanovich), 1935a, 'Does a Class of Native Bourgeoisie Exist in South Africa?', *The Negro Worker* 5 (5).

A. Z. (A. Zusmanovich), 1935b, 'Once Again about the Native Bourgeoisie in South Africa', *Umsebenzi* 13 July.

Davidson, A. B., 1958, *Matabele i Mashona v borbe protiv angliiskoi kolonizatsii, 1888-1897 (The Ndebele and the Shona in the Struggle against British Colonisation, 1888-1897)*, Moscow.

Davidson, A. B., 1960, 'Krusheniie kolonialnoi sistemy v Afrike' (The Collapse of the Colonial System in Africa), *Mezhdunaronaia zhizn* 11.

Davidson, A. B., 1972, *Yuzhnaia Afrika: stanovleniie sil protesta.1870-1924 (South Africa: birth of protest. 1870-1924)*, Moscow: Nauka Publishers.

Davidson, A. B., 1974, 'I. I. Potekhin i sovetskaia afrikanistika' (I. I. Potekhin and Soviet African Studies), *Sovetskaia etnografiia* 4.

Davidson, A. B., 1981, 'Endre Sik', *Narody Azii i Afriki* 2.

Davidson, A. B., S. V. Mazov, eds., 1999, *Rossiia i Afrika: dokumenty i materialy, XVIII v.-1960 (Russia and Africa.: Documents and Materials, 18th century-1960)*, vol. 2, Moscow.

Davidson, A., I. Filatova, V. Gorodnov, S. Johns, eds., 2003, *South Africa and the Communist International: a documentary history. 1919-1939*, vol. 1, London: Frank Cass.

Forman S., A. Odendaal, eds., 1992, *Lionel Froman. A Trumpet from the Housetops. Selected writings*, Athens, Ohio: Ohio University Press.

Hailey, M., 1938, *An African Survey*, London, second edition 1957.

Ismagilova, R. N., 1956, 'Narody Kenii v usloviiakh kolonialnogo rezhima' (The Peoples of Kenya under Colonial Rule), *Afriaknkii etnograficheskii sbornik*, Moscow.

Ivanov, K., 1960, 'K sotsialno-ekonomicheskoi kharakteristike sovremennogo kolonializma' (On the Socio-economic Characteristics of Modern Colonialism), *Mezhdunarodnaia zhizn*, 10.

Izotla, J. (I. Potekhin), 1934a, 'Natsional-reformizm v YuAS' (National Reformism in the Union of South Africa), *Revoliutsionny Vostok* 4 (26).

Izotla, J. (I. I. Potekhin), 1934b, 'Umsebenzi' – tsentralnyi organ Kommunisticheskoi partii Yuzhnoi Afriki, 1933-1934' ('Umsebenzi' – the Central Organ of the Communist Party of South Africa), *Revolutsionnyi Vostok* 5 (27).

Izotla, J. (I. I. Potekhin), 1935a, 'Agentura britanskogo imperializma v riadakh natsionalnogo dvizheniia v Yuzhnoi Afrike' (Agents of British Imperialism in the Ranks of the National Movement in South Africa), *Revolutsionnyi Vostok* 1 (29).

Izotla, J., (I. Potekhin), 1935b, 'On the Question of the Native Co-operative Societies in South Africa', *The Negro Worker* 5 (1).

Lemin, I. M., 1951, *Obostreniie krizisa Britanskoi imperii posle vtoroi mirovoi voiny (The Aggravation of the Crisis of the British Empire after the Second World War)*. Moscow.

Lenin, V. I., 1950, Doklad komissii po natsionalnomu i kolonialnomu voprosam, 26 iiulia (Report of the Commission on the National and the Colonial Questions, 26 July), in V. I. Lenin, *Sobraniie sochinenii (Collected Works)*, fourth edition, vol. 31, Moscow.

Magyar, L., 1933, 'O natsional-reformizme' (On National Reformism), *Revolutsionnyj Vostok*, 6 (21).

Maslennikov, V. A., 1952, *Uglubleniie krizisa kolonialnoi sistemy imperializma (The Deepening of the Crisis of the Colonial System of Imperialism)*, Moscow.

Maslennikov, V.A., 1953, 'Natsionalno-osvoboditelnoie dvizheniie v kolonialnykh i polukolonialnykh stranakh' (The National Liberation Movement in Colonial and Semi-colonial Countries), in: V. A. Maslennikov, ed. *Uglubleniie krizisa kolonialnoi sistemy imperializma posle vtoroi mirovoi voiny (The Deepening of the Crisis of the Colonial System of Imperialism after the Second World War)*, Moscow.

Mif, P., 1935, 'Problemy gegemonii proletariata v kolonialnoi revolutsii' (Problems of the Hegemony of the Proletariat in the Colonial Revolution), in: *Sbornik 3-4, Kolonialnyie problemy. (Collected Essays 3-4. Colonial Problems)*, Moscow: Institute of World Economy and World Politics.

Nasonov, N., 1929, 'Negritianskaia problema v Severo-Amerikanskikh Soiedinennykh Shtatakh' (Negro Problem in the North American United States), *Revolutsionnyi Vostok* 6.

Nasonov, N., 1930, 'Rasovaia problema i marksizm v ponimanii tov. Shiika' (Race Problem and Marxism as Understood by Com. Sik), *Revolutsionnyi Vostok* 9/10.

Potekchin, I., (I. Potekhin), 1932, 'The Unemployed Movement in South Africa', *The Negro Worker* 11-12.

Potekhin, I. I., n.d., *Obosreniie krizisa kolonialnoi sistemy imperializma i zadachi sovetskoi etnografii: avtoreferat doklada (Aggravation of the Crisis of the Colonial System of Imperialism and the Tasks of Soviet Ethnography. Thesis of the paper)*, n.p.

Potekhin I. I., 1950a, 'Stalinskaia teoriia kolonialnoi revolutsii i natsionalno–osvoboditelnoie dvizheniie v Tropicheskoi i Yuzhnoi Afrike' (Stalin's Theory of the Colonial Revolution and the National Liberation Movement in Tropical and South Africa), *Sovetskaia etnografiia* 1.

Potekhin, I. I., 1950b, 'V. I. Lenin o natsionalno-osvoboditelnom dvizhenii v kolonilnykh i zavisimykh stranakh' (V. I. Lenin on the National Liberation Movement in Colonial and Dependent Countries), *Sovetskaia etnographiia* 2.

Potekhin I. I., 1955, *Fromirovaniie natsionalnoi obshchnosti yuzhnoafrikanskikh bantu (The Formation of the National Community of the South African Bantu)*. Moscow.

Potekhin, I. I., 1956, 'Politicheskoie polozheniie v stranakh Afriki' (The Political Situation in African Countries), *Sovetskoie vostokovedeniie* 1.

Potekhin, I. I., 1958, 'Raspad kolonialnoi sistemy v Afrike' (The Collapse of the Colonial System in Africa), *Kommunist* 17.

Potekhin, I. I., 1959, 'Afrika obryvaiet tsepi kolonializma' (Africa Breaks the Chains of Colonialism), *Mezhdunarodnaia zhizn* 2.

Potekhin, I. I., 1960, 'Kharakternyie cherty raspada kolonialnoi sistemy imperializma v Afrike' (Characteristic Features of the Collapse of the Colonial System in Africa). *Problemy vostokovedeniia* 1.

Potekhin I. I., D.A. Olderogge, eds., 1954, *Narody Afriki (The Peoples of Africa)*. Moscow.

Ranger, T. O., 1968, 'Connections Between 'Primary Resistance' Movements and Modern Mass Nationalism in East and Central Africa', *Journal of African History*, IX (3): 438-439.

Safarov, G., 1934, 'Imperialisticheskoie gosudarstvo i natsionalno-kolonialnaia revolutsiia' (Imperialist State and the National-Colonial Revolution), *Revolutsionnyj Vostok* 3 (25).

Sik, A., 1929, 'K voprosu o negritianskoi probleme v SASSH' (On the Question of Negro Problem in the NAUS), *Revolutsionnyi Vostok* 7.

Sik A., 1930a, 'K postanovke marksistskogo izucheniia sotsialno-ekonomicheskikh problem Chernoi Afriki' (On the Foundations of Marxist Study of Socio-Economic Problems of Black Africa), *Revolutsionnyi Vostok* 8.

Sik, E., 1930b, Chernaia Afrika na revolutsionnom puti (Black Afirca on the Revolutionary Road), *Revolutsionnyi Vostok* 8.

Sik, A., 1930c, 'Zamechaniia na kritiku tov. Nasonova' (Notes on Com. Nasonov's criticism). *Revolutsionnyi Vostok* 9/10.

Sik, A., 1933, 'Pismo v redaktsiiu 'Rev. Vostoka' (Letter to the Editorial Board of the Rev. Vostok), *Revolutsionnyi Vostok* 1 (17).

Sik, E., 1966, *The History of Black Africa,* vols. 1-2. Budapest: Akadémiai Kiadó, 1966, second edition 1971-1974.

Stalin, I. V., 1949, *Sochineniia (Works),* vol. 1, Moscow.

Stalin, I. V., 1952, *Sochineniia (Works),* vol. 10, Moscow.

Vasiliieva, V. Ya., I. M. Lemin, V. A. Maslennikov, eds., 1953, *Imperialisticheskaia borba za Afriku i osvoboditelnoie dvizheniie narodov (The Imperialist Struggle for Africa and Peoples' Liberation Movement),* Moscow.

Yastrebova, I. P., 1952, Yuzhno-Afrikanskii Soiuz posle vtoroj mirovoi voiny (The Union of South Africa after the Second World War), Moscow.

Yug (G. Ye. Gerngros), 1929, *Imperialism na chernom kontinente (Imperialism on the Black Continent),* Moscow.

Yug (G. Ye. Gerngros), 1931a, *Yuzhno-Afrikanskii Soiuz: Ocherki (The Union of South Africa: Essays),* Moscow-Leningrad.

Yug (G. Ye. Gerngros), 1931b, *Britanskiie kolonii v Vostochnoj Afrike (British Colonies in East Africa),* Moscow-Leningrad.

Yug (G. Ye. Gerngros), 1932, *Imperialism i kolonii (Imperialism and Colonies),* Moscow.

Zhukov, Ye. M., 1949, 'Obostreniie krizisa kolonialnoi sistemy posle vtoroi mirovoi voiny' (Aggravation of the Crisis of the Colonial System after the Second World War), in: Ye. M. Zhukov, ed. *Krizis kolonialnoi sistemy (The Crisis of the Colonial System).* Leningrad.

Zusmanovich, A., 1935a, 'O nekotorykh voprosakh kommunisticheskogo dvizheniia v Yuzhnoi Afrike' (On Some Problems of the Communist Movement in South Africa), *Revolutsionnyj Vostok* 2 (30).

Zusmanovich, A., 1935b, 'Antiimperialisticheskoie dvizheniie i borba za iedinyi front v Yuzhnoi Afrike' (The Anti Imperialist Movement and the Struggle for a United Front in South Africa), in: *Materialy po natsionalno-kolonialnym problemam* (Materials on the National-Colonial Problems), Moscow: NIANKP 6 (30).

Zusmanovich, A, I. Potekhin, T. Jackson, 1933, Prinuditelny trud i profdvizheniie v negritianskoi Afrike (Forced Labour and Trade Union Movement in Negro Africa). Moscow.

Chapter 11

Area Studies in Search of Africa:
The Case of the United States

Pearl T. Robinson

Whatever the field of inquiry, the best scholarship aims to change the way we think about its subject. Thus a comparative assessment of African Studies in the American academy must, in the final analysis, ask what kinds of new thinking have resulted from this enterprise. The Cold War rationale for area studies, with its geopolitical criteria for establishing priorities, gave us a world of regional hierarchies calibrated by relative power, levels of culture, and ideological cleavages. From the perspective of the area studies establishment, Africa's place at the bottom of those hierarchies was never in question. Yet the assumptions behind that marginality—and the contestations they engender—have combined to produce the rich, varied and tumultuous terrain that configures the current landscape of African Studies.

This is a complicated geography, fragmented into non-contiguous spatial arrangements. But it hasn't always been that way. Hence, to fully understand the intellectual history of African area studies, one must acknowledge the existence of, and tease out, the relationships among, at least three spatially-differentiated spheres of endeavour: (i) the *World* of US Research Universities, particularly the top research tier, which is the domain of the major Title VI African Studies Centers;[1] (ii) the *World* of Diasporic Pan-Africanist Scholars—a highly polyglot realm that includes the Historically Black Colleges and Universities (HBCUs), which were the first US institutions of higher learning to introduce African Studies into the curriculum; and (iii) the *World* of African Universities and Research Networks. Each of these *Worlds* has its own complex sociology of intellectual pace-setters, respected elders, epistemological debates, citation conventions, overlapping memberships, and identity politics configured around a mix of symbolic and substantive associations with the production and validation of knowledge about Africa. Research agendas differ. Moreover, funding sources have generally treated these spaces as separate and distinct.

It should come as no surprise to find that scholars working in these varied realms define the boundaries of 'Africa' (i.e., the region of study) differently. Africanists trained at mainline universities in the US typically focus on Africa south of the Sahara. Diasporic Pan-Africanist scholars engage with continental Africa and the African Diaspora, often taking as given a link between the two. Scholarly communities connected to African universities or research networks generally define Africa in continental terms. A notable exception was apartheid South Africa, which remained isolated from the major currents and communities of African scholars until the advent of majority rule in the early 1990s.

To be sure, these boundaries are constantly challenged and in flux. And sometimes the politics of boundaries spark hotly contentious debates. One such flare-up occurred at the University of Cape Town (UCT) in 1998, when the Social Sciences and Humanities Faculty decided to launch a new core course on 'Africa' for the first year students. It fell to Mahmood Mamdani, a Ugandan national, to draw up the initial course outline. Mamdani had recently moved to South Africa to assume an appointment as the A. C. Jordan Professor of African Studies at UCT. Stunned when the Faculty rejected his course proposal and adopted instead an alternative syllabus prepared by a three-person committee of long-time UCT academics, he went public with his critique. The committee favoured approaches and literature honed in the *World* of Western Research Universities. Mamdani accused his South African colleagues of failing to come to grips with the question of how Africa should be taught in a post-apartheid University. His retort was a discourse of spatial analysis:

> [T]he syllabus reproduces the notion that Africa lies between the Sahara and Limpopo (Mamdani 1998a: 14) ... and that this Africa has no intelligentsia worth reading (Mamdani 1998b: 46) ... The idea that Africa is spatially synonymous with equatorial Africa, and socially with Bantu Africa, is an idea produced and spread in the context of colonialism and apartheid (1998a: 14).

Underlying this denunciation of UCT's curriculum reform project was a more fundamental critique of a set of hierarchical assumptions about race, historical agency, and human development.[2] Though Mamdani lost the skirmish, he gained a public airing for his larger point, and in so doing expanded the intellectual space for thinking more broadly about research agendas, pedagogy, and the legacy of apartheid in the South African academy. At the same time, thanks to the Internet, this debate travelled and was picked up by the African studies community in the USA.

The contention that South African academics downplay the significance of scholarship by African intellectuals from equatorial Africa rests largely on an indictment of institutional racism.[3] However, explanations for the marginalisation of Africanist scholars within the US academy are at once more subtle and more complex. Consider, for example, this personal revelation published by Harvard political economist Robert Bates in the Comparative Politics section newsletter of the American Political Science Association:

When I started out in political science in the late 1960s, comparative politics was marginal to the broader discipline. The sense of marginality was heightened by my location at Caltech, where the social sciences were marginal to the Institute; political science marginal within the social sciences; and the study of American politics king (Bates 1996: 1-2).

Africa's place at the bottom of that hierarchy goes without saying.

Bates's self-portrait of his early marginalisation in academia is telling testimony of the difficulties faced by a theoretically-oriented Africanist determined to make his mark in the mainstream of political science. Over the years, he responded to this predicament by engaging the most 'scientific' of the social science disciplines on their own terms: honing field-based techniques for a comparative political economy of rational choice, exploring interdisciplinarity by crafting analytical narratives, marshalling game-theoretic reasoning to solve behavioural puzzles, and eventually picking up the quantitative tools of formal modelling. Along the way, he served on the board of the US African Studies Association, co-edited a book on the contributions of African studies to the disciplines, proclaimed the death of area studies,[4] promoted Africa as 'the development challenge of our time', and eventually landed a chair as Eaton Professor of the Science of Government at Harvard University, where he is an active member of Harvard's Committee on African Studies and a Faculty Fellow at the Center for International Development. His book *Africa and the Disciplines* (Bates, Mudimbe, and O'Barr 1993), seeks to justify the place of African studies in the American university on the basis of contributions to theory and basic knowledge, thus moving away from the Cold War rationale and sidestepping alternative justifications grounded in multiculturalism (see O'Keefe 1999: 62). Increasingly acerbic in his critique of the traditional area studies model, Bates has attempted to re-invent African studies in the image of a discipline-based American academy, and in so doing, to reposition himself, by virtue of theoretical and methodological contributions in the social sciences, from the margins to the centre.

In fact, time and again we find that a creative response to a particular mindset about the place of Africa in a hierarchy of values becomes the driving force behind a move into new intellectual territory. Another powerful example of this triggering encounter is offered in the testimony of Nigerian-born social anthropologist Ife Amadiume:

My initial reaction of anger and disbelief came when I was an undergraduate reading social anthropology in Britain in the second half of the 1970s. As the data were gathered selectively, and interpreted and applied according to the point of view and the politics of that period, which had to justify conquest and the subjection of indigenous people and their culture to foreign rule, the material produced was inevitably racist ... If non-Western cultures were described as primitive, barbaric, savage, etc., one can image how women in these cultures were presented. To early anthropologists, evolutionists that they were, 'primitive' women stood at the lowest end of the scale, described as no better than beasts and slaves, while the Victorian lady stood at the apex (Amadiume 1987:2).

Although this reference to 'early anthropologists' occurs in a context that evokes the work of late nineteenth century evolutionists, Amadiume argued that old assumptions die hard. A revulsion to such representations planted the seeds for her own seminal work on sex and gender in an African society.

Amadiume took as a point of departure the construction of global feminism advanced by female academics and Western feminists of the 1960s and 1970s. What troubled her was the way some of the theorists and activists were appropriating and interpreting bits of data from Africa and elsewhere in the Third World in their writings about motherhood, marriage and the family. Particularly irksome was the universalising assumption of women's social and cultural inferiority that, in her view, enabled white feminists to 'fanaticise' a measure of superiority over African women (Amadiume 1987:1-10). As a corrective, Amadiume articulated the need for more empirically based social histories of the many thousands of societies worldwide that have never been studied by anthropologists.[5] Her own doctoral dissertation research on the Nnobi Igbo and subsequent book, *Male Daughters, Female Husbands*, were paradigm-making in this regard. Framed in terms of the new wave of women's studies that emphasised the social construction of gender, Amadiume's work took this form of analysis to a new level. Both the subject and method of her research brought to light data that reveal how the flexibility of Igbo gender construction affected women's access to economic resources and positions of power through the institutions of male daughters and female husbands. Indeed, only after British colonialism and the influences of Christianity introduced the more rigid gender ideology of the West did women in Nnobi society come to experience their maternal and domestic roles as constraining and unrewarding.

At the time, Amadiume's interpretation of her own research findings was at odds with the position of feminist theorists who held that maternal and domestic roles account for the subordination of women worldwide.[6] Dismissive of this theory for its lack of a broadly based socio-cultural analysis she insisted that the Nnobi data prove the contrary (Amadiume 1987:191). Denouncing the 'racist' and 'disrespectful trivialization' of feminist analysis grounded in categories and conceptual systems of a Western epistemological order, Amadiume rejected the logic that sought to reposition Africa within this hierarchy. Instead, she set out to generate a different type of knowledge about African women and societies. By so doing, she emerged as an important contributor to what Valentin Mudimbe (1988: xi) calls 'African discourses on otherness and ideologies of alterity'. Debates over whether female status is a cause or an effect of cultural values will no doubt continue. Meanwhile, Ife Amadiume has pioneered the production of a body of work that reaches beyond African studies and compels us all to rethink *feminism* as a cultural construct.

Mamdani, Bates, and Amadiume: their personal narratives illustrate how the field of African studies is both constrained and propelled by discourses of knowledge and power on and about Africa. As scholars, each responded to Africa's marginality by confronting assumptions of hierarchy that make it acceptable to perceive this marginality as though it were common sense (see Hoare and Smith 1971). In *The Invention of Africa*, Mudimbe (1988) uses an approach guided by Foucauldian archaeology to uncover what lies beneath the development of African studies as a discipline. His analysis reveals the prevalence of hierarchy as an organising principle and confirms the difficulty of transforming the types of knowledge produced about Africa (Mudimbe 1988: x-xi). Yet Diasporic Pan-Africanist scholars, for reasons of their own history, location and social position, have often willingly embraced 'rejected forms of wisdom' concerning Africa. And it was through their *World* that African Studies first entered the US academy.

The remainder of this chapter examines the development of African studies in the USA, from its introduction in the historically Black colleges and universities (HBCUs) toward the end of the nineteenth century through its move into the academic mainstream. The study of Africa found an early home in the disciplines of archaeology and anthropology. Later, helped by the interdisciplinary wedge of foundation- and government-supported area studies programmes, teaching and research on Africa made inroads across the broader curriculum. As we shall see, the rationale for African studies has shifted over time, while efforts to combat notions of hierarchy and the reality of marginalisation have profoundly influenced its intellectual agenda.

African Studies: The Early Years

In 1873 William Tracy, a prominent member of the New York Colonization Society, wrote to William Dodge suggesting that either Lincoln Institute in Pennsylvania or Howard University in Washington, D.C. should establish a department of African Studies and recruit Edward Blyden from Liberia to teach Arabic language and African culture. Tracy and his friend Dodge, a white philanthropist and benefactor of black colleges, were dismayed that the African American students at these institutions showed so little interest in Africa. They reckoned that courses on African civilisations and cultures would promote race pride and thus motivate some of these students to become missionaries in Africa, or to take up the work of African recolonisation (Bond 1976: 494-5).

The idea of recruiting Blyden was consistent with the mission of a select group of black colleges founded in the antebellum South to educate freed slaves. In contrast to the numerous schools and normal academies set up to provide basic literacy and teacher training, institutions such as Fisk, Howard, Lincoln, Wilberforce, Morehouse, Spelman, and Atlanta University offered their best students a classical education that, to paraphrase W. E. B. Du Bois, sought 'to furnish the black world with adequate standards of human culture and lofty ideals of life' (Du Bois 1902: 292; see also Richardson 1980). Blyden, a West Indian black educated in England, was a professor in the College of Liberia and a Minister of the Ashum Presbyterian Church in Monrovia. Widely respected for his knowledge of Hebrew, Greek, Latin, French, German, Italian and Arabic, he was the author of several well-known works on Africa (Blyden 1862; 1869a; 1869b; 1888; 1903). Though a frequent visitor to the United States and the recipient of several honorary degrees from US institutions, he settled and remained permanently in Liberia and Sierra Leone. It was not until Leo Hansberry joined Howard University's History Department in 1922 that one saw the beginnings of a coherent approach toward a programme in African Studies at an HBCU.

Hansberry arrived with an intellectual agenda. Troubled by the influence of social Darwinism, he sought to dispel derogatory myths and stereotypes about African culture and peoples by affirming the significance of African civilisation (Harris 1974: 4-18). Convinced that Howard had a special role to play in changing popular misconceptions, he urged the development of a programme in African studies on the grounds that it offered the University 'the most promising and immediate opportunity to distinguish itself as a leader in the general cause of public enlightenment' (Hansberry cited in Harris 1974: 9-10). Despite some resistance, a series of courses on 'Negro Civilizations of Ancient Africa' became part of an African Civilization Section in Howard's History Department.[7] Hansberry's lectures typically addressed aspects of state-building, nation-building, or statecraft and their applications.

When Ralph Bunche joined Howard's Political Science Department in 1928,[8] he brought an interest in Africa viewed through the then contemporary lenses of imperialism, colonialism, and proto-nationalist movements. His dissertation, defended in 1934, compared colonial rule in a League of Nations mandated area, French Togoland, with that in a French colony, Dahomey.[9] It was one of the earliest scholarly works on colonial administration.

Ralph Bunche was the first African American to receive a PhD in political science from Harvard University. Determined to establish his credentials as a modern social scientist, he used his dissertation as a platform to refute the myth of racial hierarchy as an explanation for imperialism. His research design combined comparative political analysis, economic determinism, and hypothesis-testing to investigate whether the type of colonial administration made a difference in the life of the native. Fieldwork supported by a Rosenwald Fellowship enabled him to gather data on the internal dynamics of French colonial administration in the two settings. Finding little difference between the two, he then marshalled evidence to argue that French economic interests shaped colonialism in both Dahomey and Togo. For this ground-breaking study, Bunche won Harvard's Toppan Prize for the year's best dissertation in political science.

During the period between the two World Wars, Hansberry and Bunche, each in his own way, contributed to making Howard University a critical site for the study of Africa in the US. Hansberry's courses were popular with students. He organised symposia and lectured widely to audiences outside the University. Bunche was an active scholar, taught courses on imperialism and on colonialism in Africa, and attracted international scholars to Howard for a conference he organised in 1936 on 'The Crisis of Modern Imperialism in Africa and the Far East' (Henry 1999). In

1934, when Hansberry and others formed the Ethiopian Research Council to mobilise American support for Ethiopia's efforts to resist the Italian invasion, Bunche served as the organisation's advisor on international law (Harris 1974: 24). Although the two men never collaborated to establish an interdisciplinary centre for African Studies—indeed, they moved in different circles at Howard[10]—their pioneering efforts had ripple effects and connected with a scattering of developments at other institutions.

Lincoln University in Pennsylvania is a case in point. From its founding as the Ashum Institute in 1856, Lincoln had always educated significant numbers of African students.[11] Its educational programme reflected the expectation that many graduates would 'glorify God' through their work in Africa, as missionaries or otherwise. Nonetheless, the enrolment of Benjamin Nnamdi Azikiwe from Nigeria in 1929 and of Francis Kwame Nkrumah from the Gold Coast in 1935 infused new meaning into Lincoln's Africa mission. Azikiwe transferred to Lincoln from Howard, where he had studied African History with Hansberry and Political Science with Bunche.[12] He later played a role in recruiting Nkrumah to Lincoln. First as student leaders and then as instructors, both these future heads of state sought to equip themselves, and the general student body, with knowledge that would hasten the liberation of Africa.[13] They found inspiration in their studies of political philosophy, anthropology, race relations and imperialism. And they drew elements from Africa's rich cultural endowments to fashion the fundamentals of a new African nationalism. While a student, Azikiwe lobbied successfully for the introduction of a course on Negro history at Lincoln. Serving briefly as an instructor after graduating, he taught the course himself, using an approach that connected the past with the present by juxtaposing the history and cultures of Africa with the struggles of New World blacks.[14]

By the early 1930s, material on both early Africa and colonial Africa began to make its way into the liberal arts curriculum at leading black colleges. For instance, a two-semester Negro history offering at Spelman College for women surveyed Ancient Africa, the slave trade and US slavery, the Civil War, Reconstruction, the partitioning of Africa, Haiti and Cuba, and 'the Negro in America today'.[15] W. E. B. Du Bois introduced a course on Ancient Africa at Atlanta University in 1936. Then the publication in 1939 of his book *Black Folk: Then and Now*, written expressly for use in schools, combined in one comprehensive volume a history of the African past with contemporary debates on the slave trade, emancipation, the political control of Africa, and the future of world democracy (Du Bois 1939).[16] Du Bois's stated objective was to correct the belief that 'the Negro has no history' (Du Bois 1939)[17] When the book appeared, it was widely reviewed and its reception generally sympathetic—with at least one commentator noting its 'success in demolishing concepts of racial inferiority' (cited in Aptheker 1975: 14). The intersection of race and history so prevalent in Du Bois's *Black Folk* was a harbinger of contentious debates that would later clutter the intellectual landscape of African Area Studies. For in the US, the power to define and interpret knowledge about Africa has been inextricably linked with American history, race relations and the precarious status of the African American.

For decades, the treatment of African history at the HBCUs typically sought to promote race pride and combat race prejudice by recovering the glories of Africa's past. Then in 1930 the anthropologist Melville Herskovits turned this approach on its head by proposing to treat the New World as an historical laboratory to study the presence of Africanisms and their functions (Herskovits 1930). Rejecting the conventional wisdom that American blacks had lost all vestiges of their African cultural heritage, he mapped out a multi-faceted research agenda for studying the conditions under which African culture 'has maintained itself under stress and strain' (150). Years later he explained the importance of establishing the existence of African survivals in the New World as follows:

> To give the Negro an appreciation of his past is to endow him with the confidence in his own position in this country and in the world ... which he can best attain when he has available a foundation of scientific fact concerning the ancestral cultures of Africa and the survivals of Africanisms in the New World ... [W]hen such a body of fact, solidly grounded, is established [and] this information diffused over the population as a whole, [it] will influence opinion in general concerning Negro abilities and potentialities, and thus contribute to a lessening of interracial tensions (Herskovits 1958: 32).

By declaring the systematic study of Africans in the New World 'a matter of utmost scientific importance', Herskovits (1930: 150) held out the promise of contributing answers to 'some of the basic questions that confront the study of man'. This boldly ambitious research agenda helped secure a place for Africanist anthropologists squarely in the academic mainstream and ultimately gained recognition for its author as the pre-eminent American scholar of Africa. At the same time, it set forth criteria for establishing a scholarly hierarchy around issues of credibility and scientific authority. Understanding how these issues played out at Howard University can shed light on the complex power/knowledge dynamics that accompanied the development of African area studies in the US.

In 1925 the young Herskovits went to Howard as a lecturer in anthropology. A recent Columbia University PhD and student of Franz Boas, he was at the time a National Research Council Fellow in Biological Sciences working on the problem of variability under black-white racial mixing. At Howard, he found Leo Hansberry preparing to launch courses on ancient African civilisations, and the philosopher and cultural critic Alain Locke advancing his concept of 'The New Negro'. Locke, a Harvard-trained PhD and the first black Rhodes Scholar, considered the Harlem Renaissance of the 1920s the flowering of a New Negro Movement based on a growing race consciousness, self-confidence and sophistication among urban blacks. He attributed these traits to the development of an independent black cultural tradition that blended 'a deep-seated aesthetic endowment' from the ancestral African past with the folk traditions of American blacks, then 'blossomed in strange new forms' (Locke 1925: 254).

Herskovits initially dismissed this claim of cultural uniqueness, preferring instead to emphasise 'the Negro's Americanism'. In an essay on black urban culture included in Locke's edited volume *The New Negro: An Interpretation*, he reported having found in Harlem 'not a trace of Africa' (Herskovits 1925: 359). However after moving to Northwestern University in 1927, Herskovits reversed himself on the matter of African survivals, reporting that various research findings from his fieldwork in Dutch Guyana, Haiti, and Trinidad 'repeatedly forced revision of prevailing hypotheses'.[18] He would henceforth become a lifelong student of African cultural retentions in the New World.

What distinguished the work of Herskovits and his associates from that of other earlier proponents of African cultural survivals was a solid grounding in a research programme designed to gather evidence, generate theories, and test hypotheses (Herskovits 1930: 145-156). Alain Locke also encouraged scientific approaches to the study of black people. Although a humanist, he saw in science an antidote for the stereotype of the Old Negro—a figure whom, in Locke's view, the American mind seemed always to consider 'from the distorted perspective of a social problem' (Locke 1925: 3-4). However as the discourse of positivism swept the US academy, broad generalisations, reliance on secondary sources, and interpretive analyses were no match for purportedly *objective* observations based on primary source data gathered in the field. And in this context, an eminent philosopher such as Locke was marked by his *subjective* motivation as a 'race' man. Hence his scholarship could be dismissed, rightly or wrongly, as polemical, exaggerated, or merely interpretative commentary.

Hansberry's situation was more fragile. He never earned a doctorate,[19] lacked the requisite political support at Howard, was unable to get to Africa for fieldwork until 1953,[20] and had to self-finance most of his instructional projects. In 1932, the same year he received an MA from Harvard, Hansberry sought advice on whether, as a black American, he might have difficulty joining a British archeological expedition to Egypt. A letter from Dows Dunham of Boston's Museum of Fine Arts confirmed his apprehension:[21]

> To be perfectly frank with you, if I were in charge of such an expedition, I should hesitate long before taking an American Negro on my staff ... I should fear that the mere fact of your being a member of the staff would seriously affect the prestige of the other members and the respect which the native employees would have for them ... (quoted in Harris 1974:13).

Dunham's response conveyed the increasingly prevalent view in American Africanist circles that racially mediated hierarchies affected access to data and determined success in the field. Ironically, Hansberry was caught in a conundrum that used subjective criteria such a motivational bias and racialised authority structures to determine who was suitable for training and who could be trusted to carry out objective fieldwork in Africa.

By the 1940s, historically black colleges were no longer the pacesetters of Africa-related curriculum development in American higher education. Specialists on Africa remained few, but they began to surface at major research universities. Anthropology and archaeology more than any other disciplines took centre-stage as the legitimisers of knowledge about Africa. And Herskovits, recognised for his expertise on both Continental and New World blacks, became a gatekeeper for research and training opportunities in African American as well as African studies. Not until the publication in 1939 of E. Franklin Frazier's *The Negro Family in the United States* did Herskovits face a significant challenge to the scholarly merits of his work on African survivals. That challenge was launched from Howard University.

Franklin Frazier arrived at Howard in 1934 as Professor and Chair of the Sociology Department. Trained at the University of Chicago where he received his PhD in 1931, he put great store in the discipline and skills of sociological research. His abiding concern with the progress, organisation, and functions of the black American family was wedded to an insistence that behaviours could be understood only in terms of the social conditions that shaped them. And in this regard he was among the most strident critics of the notion of African survivals. Frazier effectively rekindled the debate over African cultural survivals in the New World, this time taking Herskovits to task for a lack of scientific rigour.

Rejecting as fatally flawed the attempts to build theory on inferences drawn from 'scraps of memories' and 'fragments of stories concerning Africa', Frazier argued instead that the conditions of life in the United States destroyed the significance of the slaves' African heritage (Frazier 1939). This position was by no means without controversy, for it stood to undermine all who would use Africa to counter the myth that American blacks have neither a past nor a history. But Frazier found explanations of behaviour that rely on race and African culture problematic. According to Charles Henry (1999: 60), an astute analyst of African American political culture, 'Frazier denie[d] the possibility of African survivals in order to refute the biological claims that Black deviance from [the] middle-class family norm [was] due to the less-evolved status of the Black race'. This prospect led him to refute the evidence of Africanisms among US blacks, and to develop an alternative theory to explain why and how the conditions of plantation slavery in the American South caused subsequent generations to lose all meaningful connection to their African cultural heritage. In response, Herskovits spent the next 30 years sharpening his conceptual apparatus, honing more sophisticated theoretical arguments, and developing the first consistent applications of the ethnohistorical method, as he sought to validate the thesis of African cultural survivals.

What is striking, and peculiarly American, about this early period of African studies in the US was the synergism generated by the movement of ideas and individuals between the historically Black colleges and the mainstream research universities. Major scholars in both *Worlds* took notice of each other's work, engaged each other in debates, and generally functioned as part of a connected, albeit compartmentalised, epistemic community. Trans-disciplinary exchanges were the rule. Moreover, the legacy of slavery and the meanings of history served to bridge African and African American Studies, and at times facilitated cross-fertilisation that was paradigm-making.

What cannot be denied—and this too is peculiarly American—is the enormous resource gulf and racial divide that precipitated the development of distinct *Worlds* of African studies within the US academy. Through the early 1930s, an African American scholar could only expect to get funding from three sources: the Rosenwald Foundation, the General Education Fund, and Phelps-Stokes (Huggins 1990:72). In the Preface to *Black Folk*, Du Bois apologised for producing a book that 'is not a work of exact scholarship' but, rather, 'as good as I am able to command with the time and money at my disposal' (Du Bois 1975: vii). Bunche, who did his dissertation fieldwork with a Rosenwald Fellowship, was more fortunate. He received a grant from the Social Science Research Council (SSRC) in 1936 to study the effects of colonial rule and Western culture on Africans. What's more, the SSRC took the unusual step of making a two-year award, stipulating that he acquire the anthropological training deemed necessary to successfully undertake research on acculturation.[22] And Bunche remained the only African American funded by a private foundation to make a research trip to Africa until the 1950s. As for Hansberry, it was 1953 when he received a Fulbright Fellowship that finally got him to Egypt, Ethiopia and Sudan for field research.

Given the circumstances, it is indeed remarkable that serious academics were able to engage in productive, creative, and even contentious dialogue across this chasm. Whether at an HBCUs or a major research university, scholars in the field of African studies worked against the backdrop of a broader set of assumptions about human development, cultural hierarchies and social marginality. Some did more than their share to contribute to the proliferation of marginalising discourses through the production of knowledge about Africa. But the best of the lot were concerned to change the way people think about Africa.

Institutionalising Basic Research

In 1995 the Ford Foundation engaged Jane Guyer to prepare a report on African studies in the United States. Guyer, who had recently moved to Northwestern as director of the Program of African Studies and professor of anthropology, was keen to establish that scholarly interest in Africa significantly pre-dates the Cold War phase of area studies. To this end, she picked up the story in the 1930s, when Africa gained currency as a laboratory for investigators interested in human behaviour and cultural factors. Using a periodisation structured around a distinction between theoretically-driven basic research and more practically-oriented policy research, she chronicled the entrance of African studies into the mainstream academy.

Guyer's account explains how two sets of forces converged to prepare the ground for constituting Africa as an academic field. These included scientific concerns derived from classic history, basic studies in linguistics, social theory and evolutionary theory together with late colonialism's interest in modernisation. For some two decades, scholars working in anthropology, archaeology, palaeontology and linguistics were able to have considerable influence on research agendas in their respective disciplines (Guyer 1996). Initially few in number, they began building an interdisciplinary canon of African studies. During this period Africa found itself at the vortex of disciplinary conventions based on distinctions between the study of Western and non-Western societies, 'tribal' peoples and high civilisations, and cultures deemed agents of history versus those construed as ahistorical or frozen in the past.[23] To be sure, many of the perspectives advanced by those pioneering Africanists have now succumbed to the scrutiny of contemporary intellectual challenges (Mudimbe 1988; see also Said 1979). Nevertheless, Guyer does well to remind us of a moment when mutually intelligible discourses emerged around a shared interest in the diversity of human societies and their dynamics of change (Guyer 1996: 5).

Over time, the institutional landscape of African studies evolved from clusters of individual professors with a scholarly interest in Africa to the proliferation of formally organised programmes devoted to the study of Africa.[24] For instance, Hansberry's courses on Negro Civilizations of Ancient Africa were housed within Howard's History Department and emphasised the connections between Ancient Africa and equatorial Africa (Harris 1974: 3–30). When Herskovits moved to Northwestern in 1927, he introduced the first African Program offered as part of a liberal arts curriculum in an American university. In this setting the boundary was Africa south of the Sahara and the scope primarily anthropological. Yet from the beginning, Northwestern devoted considerable resources to developing a comprehensive library of Africana, a repository that today is unparalleled as a resource for scholars working in wide-ranging disciplines.

The Second World War marks a watershed in the expansion of African studies into the American academic mainstream. The shifting currents became noticeable as early as 1941, when the University of Pennsylvania set up a Committee on African Studies (CAS) with a mandate to focus on modern Africa. Conyers Read, a professor of history, had left Penn to go to work for the new Office of the Coordinator of Information (COI) in the Library of Congress.[25] The COI was soon transformed into the Office of Special Services (OSS), and Read headed the British Empire Section of its Research and Analysis Branch. Efforts to recruit staff made him keenly aware of the paucity of scholars knowledgeable about emerging developments across the African continent. The CAS sought ways to address this situation.

The group at Penn was an interdisciplinary Committee drawn from the departments of political science, economics, linguistics, geography, earth sciences and botany. This mix of disciplines signalled a different scholarly orientation toward Africa, one that no longer privileged the history of ancient civilisations or the anthropology of small-scale societies. Its members fashioned a graduate curriculum that combined courses on contemporary African issues with instruction in African languages— Swahili for East Africa and Fanti for West Africa. Kwame Nkrumah, then a graduate student at Penn, helped mobilise support for the establishment of an Institute of African Cultures and Languages (Bond 1976: 507). As one of a new generation of ardent African nationalists, he seized the opportunity to associate with an initiative that would bring Africa out of the shadows and into the academic mainstream. But more than anything else, geopolitical concerns, stoked by the war effort, gave rise to Penn's foray into African area studies.

Meanwhile, Read recruited Howard University's Ralph Bunche to fill the position of Africa specialist in the Office of the COI. Bunche's multidisciplinary, graduate level training in political science and anthropology; dissertation and post-doctoral fieldwork in Africa; and a vast interracial network of personal contacts in Africa, Europe and the US made him, ironically, the only American scholar of Africa deemed fully prepared to meet the academic requirements of this sensitive national security assignment.[26] When the OSS was up and running, Bunche joined a team that included two historians, two economists, a China expert, a Russia expert, a South America specialist, and an expert on Germany.[27] Their mission: 'to provide the President and key military officials with the information necessary to fight the war' (Henry 1999:124).

Within months Bunche morphed from an outspoken critic of New Deal policies into a dispassionate foreign policy insider. His new intelligence duties were extensive: He gathered information about African colonial policies and problems; race relations in British Africa; events in French, Portuguese and Spanish Africa; and the situation in Liberia. He prepared documents and country guides, including maps, for American troops who would be deployed in South Africa, North Africa and West Africa. He offered advice on how to handle the impact of US racial attitudes on the war effort. And he counselled the need for Americans to understand African points of view, particularly African nationalism and African attitudes toward the war (Henry 1999:126). Ultimately, the substantive and operational concerns of the researchers who staffed the OSS influenced the profile of what was to become the wartime foreign area specialist. And in many respects, Bunche set the standard. After a year on the job he won high praise from Read as 'the ablest man in his field in America and was the only staffer in the British Empire Section to receive an A-1 performance rating' (Conyers Read to William Langer, October 29, 1942, cited in Henry 1999:127).

When the SSRC's Committee on World Regions issued a report in 1943 calling for a new strategic approach to area studies training, its recommendations reflected thinking that had been honed in the heat of battle. Anticipating US responsibilities in the post-war world, the Committee pressed the case for training 'thousands of Americans' who would combine professional and technical competence with 'knowledge of the languages, economies, politics, history, geography, peoples, customs, and religions of foreign countries', Japan, China, and Latin America were identified as priority regions. More to the point, the need for social scientists grounded in the different regions of the world was equated to the requirements for 'military and naval officers familiar with ... actual and potential combat zones' (SSRC n.d.: 143, cited in Wallerstein 1997:195). Following this rationale, it seemed only logical that the onset of the Cold War in 1945 should affect an abrupt shift in area priorities to the Soviet Union and China.[28]

But another debate was stirring within the SSRC. Initially keen to embrace geopolitical considerations in its advocacy of area studies, the Council began to refine its position. A new advisory committee on World Area Research, chaired by Robert Hall, expressed concern with a war-time model of area studies that stressed 'content without scientific principles'. There was a sense that the SSRC should not be in the business of promoting educational programmes that veer from the objectives of a liberal arts education, or neglect training for basic research. As a corrective, the Hall committee called for a national programme of area studies that would eventually work toward complete world coverage and be undertaken by 'first-class centers of study' (Hall 1947: 17-18, cited in Wallerstein 1997: 199-200). Given the impossibility of doing everything at once, the Committee proposed a phase-in using global power relations and notions of cultural hierarchy as ordering principles. The following recommendations from its 1947 report anticipate how fine lines of distinctions might be drawn:

> The relative power of an area is one important consideration. Does the area in question generate an excess of power ... or does it simply submit to the power exerted from other areas? Another consideration lies in the level of culture existing in an area. Presumably we have more to gain from the study of China or India than we have from, say, the Congo Basin or New Guinea (Hall 1947: 17-18).

Social Darwinism buttressed by the principles of *realpolitik* accentuated the marginalisation of Africa. Nevertheless, the proposition held that serious scholars of the Congo along with many other regions of the globe could be found to advance the development of a universal social science (Wagley 1948, cited in Wallerstein 1997: 205). The assumption that sub-Saharan Africa held little attraction for American academics in fields other than anthropology simply meant that the critical social science disciplines would have actively to recruit students to work on contemporary African issues. For the necessary resources, private philanthropy stepped into the breach.

Grant programmes of the Carnegie Corporation and the Rockefeller Foundation have actively fostered international studies in US higher education since the 1930s. Though Africa was never a major target of these early initiatives, Herskovits and his Africanist colleagues at Northwestern received funding from Carnegie in 1948 to start a Program on African Studies (PAS) and to build up graduate offerings in economics, geography, history and political science. That same year the SSRC launched its first programme of area research training fellowships, again with funding from Carnegie. But it was the Foreign Area Fellowship Program (FAFP), launched by the Ford Foundation in 1952, that marked the beginning of a coherent strategy to support individuals as well as institutions committed to specialising in the contemporary cultures of major foreign areas.[29] The basic architecture comprised four pillars: fellowships for research and training, area studies centres, professional associations for the area studies communities, and area studies committees appointed jointly by the SSRC and the American Council of Learned Societies (ACLS) (Silbey 1995-6: 98-99).

Africa as an area field became established and spread into major research universities as part of this comprehensive strategy. In line with the Hall Report's recommendation that these new programmes should be undertaken by 'first class centers of study,' Harvard University was approached, but declined to host a major African Area Studies centre. So in 1953 Ford funded the start-up of a totally new graduate level African Studies Program at Boston University and also awarded modest support to Howard University to establish an MA degree programme in African Studies.[30] Howard, an HBCU, was not considered a major research university, but its track record and longstanding involvement with the study of Africa could not be denied. Nevertheless, the prevailing view of influential scholars such as Herskovits, as well as decision-makers at key funding agencies, held that African Americans could not be relied upon to produce scientifically objective research on Africa. Two years later Northwestern's PAS received an institutional strengthening grant. Then in 1957 a group of 36 American Africanists representing a variety of disciplines met in New York City to discuss the formation of a professional association. They founded the African Studies Association (ASA) as a national membership organisation. Melville Herskovits was elected its first president. At this point, three of the four pillars were in place.

While these developments in African studies and other area studies fields were consequential, advocates of international studies considered the job to be done immense and the overall funding level grossly inadequate (Benett 1951). The SSRC began casting about for a way to secure federal funding without government control. Ironically, the Soviet Union obliged. The launch of Sputnik on 4 October 1957 created a national security crisis with implications for American higher education. Congress responded by passing the 1958 National Defense Education Act (NDEA). Under Title VI of the NDEA, area studies centres around the country receive grants for core support to programmes, student fellowships, library resources, and language faculty (many of the instructors of African languages have been non tenure-track). The grants are subject to competitive renewal every three years and have resulted in the designation, at various times, of more than twenty US universities as National Resource Centers for Africa.

Appointment in 1960 of a Joint Committee on African Studies (JCAS) by the SSRC and the ACLS marked the coming of age of the African area field. Other joint committees had already been set up for the Slavic area (1948), Asia (1949), the Near and Middle East (1951), China (1959), and Latin America (1959).[31] Initially these groups of scholars administered grant-in-aid programmes for their respective regions. Later they assumed responsibility for research planning as well. Within a short period of time the JCAS was functioning to broaden and alter the orientation of what began as a Cold War area studies agenda.

At the same time another, more troubling development was underway. As African area studies moved more solidly into the academic mainstream, the historically black colleges and universities were increasingly marginalised—if not excluded—from the enterprise. Each piece of the architecture (FAFP, Title VI Centers, the ASA, and the JCAS) carried resource endowments that were largely denied to these earliest advocates of African studies. Training and research fellowships for dissertations as well as faculty post-docs almost always went to candidates from major research universities. When the first Title VI Centers for Africa were designated, Howard University was passed over. Moreover, the founders of the ASA set up a two-tiered membership structure in which voting membership was limited to a Roster of Fellows who had to apply for admission on the basis of past academic achievement and experience in the Africa field. Taken on their own, these various measures were consistent with the goal of establishing the area fields at 'first class centers of study.' However, they also served to de-link the new Africa field from its historical roots in the United States, and to constitute African area studies as a *World* unto itself.

Establishing Research Agendas

Once the architecture was in place, the best scholarship succeeded in changing the way we think about Africa. The initial mission seemed simple: to fill in the map with knowledge. Yet unlike specialists of many other world regions, Africanists must frequently confront the marginality of their region in the realm of ideas. This intellectual challenge has generated a remarkably steady stream of works that raise epistemological questions about the nature and grounds of knowledge. It has pushed researchers to invest in methodological approaches and to devise logical constructs, analytical categories, theoretical arguments and discursive modes that enable them more accurately to explain and interpret African realities. These strategies have affected research agendas in myriad and profound ways, offering up theoretical insights and practical understandings with implications that carry far beyond African studies.

Projects sponsored by the area research training fellowships during the 1950s concentrated on fundamentals and were designed in large part to enable American researchers to familiarise themselves with contemporary issues in late colonial Africa. Some of the topics investigated were similar to those tackled by Ralph Bunche when he was an active scholar: colonial administration, acculturation, emerging leaders, and developments in South Africa. Others were more immediately current: political development, urbanisation, and political institutional transfer. A concerted effort was made to shift the gaze of the anthropologists away from the traditions of 'tribal' societies and onto the new dynamics of socio-cultural change. More political scientists were attracted into the field.

Modernisation theory was the dominant paradigm in the 1950s and early 1960s, and African societies were prime candidates for its application. But the task for empirical research was to explain the mechanism of change, and on this score the data from Africa were decidedly mixed. The excitement associated with the appearance of David Apter's (1955) *The Gold Coast in Transition* was due at least in part to the sense that Apter told a story of *Africa rising*:

> This book, a case study of political institutional transfer ... deals ... with the Gold Coast, an area marked by singular success in the transformation from a tribal dependency to a parliamentary democracy, a success which has aroused major interest throughout the world (Apter 1955: iii).

Apter believed that this transition of the Gold Coast colony into independent Ghana under the charismatic leadership of Kwame Nkrumah would cause the world to look at Africa differently. In many respects he was right—although not in the ways anticipated. Even so, it was not long before the proliferation of fieldwork on modernisation would produce its own critics.

Sylvester Whitaker, Jr. began his studies of political change in Northern Nigeria with a 1957-58 area research training fellowship. The eventual publication of *The Politics of Tradition: Continuity and Change in Northern Nigeria, 1946-1966* (1970) helped to explode a host of purported certainties about the modernisation process. With an ironic twist, his argument acknowledged the hierarchal premise of political modernisation then proceeded to attack the unilinear assumptions of a model that sees conflict between modernity and tradition as inevitable:

> ... [T]he principal objection to the prevailing notion of modernization is that it unsoundly rests on a strictly a priori assumption that for all societies there is only one direction of significant change, culminating in the essentials of modern Western society. This conceptual attachment to a unilinear model of change ... places the societies that one is most familiar with or admiring of at the top of a descending scale of human virtue (Whitaker 1970: 3).

Whitaker's book contributed much to our understanding of the role of tradition in contemporary politics in general and to Nigerian politics in particular. It also marked the ascendance of a revisionist critique of modernisation theory, which in turn gave way to a wave of new theoretical and methodological departures coming from both the humanities and the social sciences.

This rupture in the basic programme of African area studies dates from 1968 and will be discussed in greater detail below. It came in the wake of a rush of unsettling developments, including the 1965 overthrow of Ghana's Kwame Nkrumah; a 1966 *coup* in Nigeria that escalated into the Biafran secession and a three-year civil war; prolonged drought and famine in the Sahel (1968-72); and a troubling secular decline in food production.

In the midst of this spreading turmoil, behavioural responses of elites and ordinary Africans alike were multifaceted and often strategic. Individually and collectively, they developed survival mechanisms, tailored and husbanded resources, selectively innovated and repudiated, manipulated the urban environment, reinterpreted old understandings, developed new solidarities, and equivocated (Whitaker 1983: ix). Postcolonial Africa posed numerous puzzles that could not be adequately addressed within the modernisation framework. Henceforth, no single paradigm would be able to dominate the field or control the research agenda in its hegemonic embrace.[32] With a push from the Joint Committee on African Studies (JCAS), pluralisation of the research agenda became the new mantra. In the process, a gap opened and began to widen between African area studies and the national security agenda of Cold War area studies.

Cold War African Studies

The conventional view that African area studies developed largely free from the influence of Cold War concerns is only partially accurate. It is based on the assumption that no vital US interests were at play in the region (Guyer 1996: 5; see also Wallerstein 1997). However in matters of policy, where you stand depends on where you sit. By 1962 the State Department's *Guidelines for Policy and Operations* in Africa had concluded that Africa was 'probably the greatest open field of maneuver in the world-wide competition between the [Sino-Soviet] Bloc and the non-Communist world' (Department of State 1962: 1) Moreover, the treatment of America's African-descended population was considered a serious liability in the context of East-West competition, particularly in the light of the Soviet Bloc's anti-colonialist and anti-imperialist reputation (Department of State 1962: 5).

A close reading of the security issues delineated in the 1962 Africa *Guidelines* suggests the outlines of a research agenda for Cold War African studies. Its major strategic objective was 'denial to the Sino-Soviet Bloc of military bases and, to the maximum extent practicable, of military influence in any African country' (Department of State 1962: 21). North Africa and the Horn of Africa were singled out for their strategic location and importance in securing NATO's southern flank. Nigeria was identified as a moderate 'bellwether' country with potential for exerting positive influence on the African continent. Tanganyika, Ivory Coast, Sudan and Senegal seemed capable of being included in this category. Among the subjects highlighted as essential to the long-term success of US Africa policy were information about leadership dynamics; trade union movements; trends in education, social and economic development; factors affecting the shape of political institutions; and African perceptions of race relations.

In short, Cold War exigencies created a demand for knowledgeable and sophisticated American analysts capable of projecting the US position on world issues in terms consistent with local African attitudes and preoccupations (Department of State 1962: 35). Hence, national security served as a rationale for the generous funding that paved the way for African area studies into the academic mainstream. That the Cold War never became a dominant motif is due in large part to bottom-up agendas articulated in the various *Worlds* of African Studies—and to the dialectics of change (Wallerstein 1997).

Proliferating Research Agendas

A review of the African area research supported by the SSRC beginning in the 1950s reveals the imprint of a Cold War agenda. Discernible in the early years, it receded with the proliferation of new thematic, theoretical, and methodological frameworks. By 1953 a shift from the hegemony of anthropology to a flux in the disciplinary mix from year to year was evident. Overall, during the 1950s, at least 10 FAFP research awards for Africa went to anthropologists. However available data show that between 1953 and 1960, only four of these fellowships went to anthropologists, while five went to political scientists, one to a geographer, and one to a historian. [33] But it was the establishment of the Joint Committee on African Studies (JCAS) in 1960 that placed a multidisciplinary group of Africanist scholars in a position to allocate resources in ways that would broaden and reconfigure the general orientation of the field. The Committee's writ was Africa south of the Sahara. Its geopolitical boundaries made no allowance for Africa's diaspora. Through its dual role as a research planning vehicle and a selection committee for dissertation and post-doctoral grants, the JCAS began to override the Cold War agenda with scholarly and practical concerns that ranged widely across the social sciences and humanities.

The 1960s

The Committee launched its research planning activities by convening small interdisciplinary conferences and workshops. These initial meetings were largely strategic mapping exercises, pulling together the current state of knowledge and research activity in a given area. The themes were an eclectic mix: urbanisation in Africa, the role of the traditional artist in contemporary African societies, competing demands for labour in traditional African societies, African architecture, African intellectual reactions to Western culture, and sub-national politics. Results were published in edited books, special issues of journals, and as review articles with the expressed intention of directing attention of researchers to these areas.

Consistent with the SSRC's general orientation to establish area studies at 'first class centers of study,' members of the Africa Committee were drawn from top research universities. For the first decade and a half, at least 50 percent of those appointed were based at institutions designated NDEA Title VI African Studies Centers. Unwittingly, the combination of this locational bias, the convention of separating Egypt from sub-Saharan Africa, and the de-linking of the African area field from its diaspora distanced critical constituencies of African American scholars and students from the African Studies mainstream. It was not until 1969, after Black Power advocates disrupted the annual meeting of the African Studies Association (ASA) in Montréal, that the JCAS re-examined its position on the issue of boundaries and considered broadening the scope of its work to include Africa in the New World. But after exploratory talks, little changed. The committee members opted to continue limiting their focus to continental Africa below the Sahara. But they also successfully lobbied the SSRC to create a new Committee on African American Societies and Cultures. Though this proved to be a short-term venture, from 1968 to 1972 a separate SSRC committee with its own budget, staff, and research planning activities represented the *World* of Diaspora Pan-Africanist scholars.

The 1970s

The events at the ASA meeting in Montréal left their mark on programmatic agendas in African Studies for the next decade and beyond. Diaspora blacks accused white scholars of controlling access to knowledge about their African homeland. Progressives faulted the ASA for its policy of political neutrality. Together, critics accused the African studies establishment of cozying up to colonial governments, remaining silent about the injustices of apartheid, and condoning a whole host of abuses that weighed heavily against the welfare of Africans. Donor agencies were taken to task for financing such developments. Reactions were many and varied. Two new organisations were born: the African Heritage Studies Association (AHSA) and the Association of Concerned Africa Scholars (ACAS).[34] The ASA opened up its membership, made room in its annual meetings for panels organised by the ACAS, and created a new journal to accommodate scholarly debates on politically charged issues.[35]

In this climate, The Ford Foundation was compelled to take another look at both the impact and the outcomes of its training support for Africanists through the FAFP and found an unanticipated trend. The number of African American recipients of these SSRC administered fellowships, although never high, had suffered a secular decline. Because the opportunity to do fieldwork is critical to a successful scholarly career in African studies, this development gave weight to the contention that the *World* of African Area Studies supported the access of white scholars—to the detriment of blacks. To address this situation, Ford established the Middle East and Africa Field Research Program (MEAFP) for African Americans. Although the MEAFP was phased out after eight years, it has proved the single most effective vehicle devised to date to encourage talented African Americans to pursue careers as scholars of Africa.[36]

The reaction of the Joint Committee to the criticisms hurled at Montréal was deliberate and multifaceted, but side-stepped the issue of African American exclusion. Rethinking its purpose, the JCAS opted to diversify its membership *internationally*, initiate a new *domestic* programme of regional research seminars, and change the eligibility requirements for dissertation fellowships to allow support for non-US citizens. In this politically charged atmosphere, critical policy areas became the hook for efforts by US-based Africanists to engage scholars in Africa. This new focus was at least in part donor-driven, as significant levels of funding became available for projects designed to address issues affecting African development. The JCAS launched new research planning activities, identifying the crisis in African agriculture, problems of health and disease, and the breakdown in local-level governance and service delivery as subjects that could benefit from the interdisciplinary approaches of areas studies specialists. Special SSRC grant programmes of post-docs, dissertation fellowships and conferences sought to interest more scholars in the North in studying these problems.[37]

By the early 1970s it was no longer tenable for strategic actors in African area studies to ignore the region's looming crisis in higher education. Politicisation of the universities, the erosion of academic freedom, the drying up of financial resources, and the early phase of the brain drain were all taking a toll (Ekeh 1975; Diouf and Mamdani 1994). With a push from the Ford Foundation, the JCAS turned its attention to the research needs of African scholars and what might be done to help meet those needs. For the first time, the Committee reached out and established formal ties with the *World* of African universities and research institutions, welcoming B. J. Dudley from the University of Ibadan (Nigeria) and Sekene Mody Cissoko from the University of Dakar (Senegal) in 1973. These new JCAS members facilitated the launch of SSRC training institutes in Africa that provided instruction in the use of quantitative methods and computer applications in the social sciences. The first of these institutes was held at the University of Ibadan during the summer of 1976, and it set the model of including graduate students from US universities doing fieldwork in the region.

A proliferation of research, policy and training agendas further relaxed the grip of the Cold War on African area studies. By the late 1970s the development crisis loomed so large that *it* had become the focal point of uneasy tension between theoretically-driven and pragmatically-oriented researchers (Guyer 1996: 6-7). As funding for development institutes and applied departments expanded, resources available for basic research became increasingly scarce. Some critics of this trend linked government funding for policy relevant research with Cold War clientage and support for dictators. But for the pragmatists, US-AID supported initiatives such as the Sahel Development Program created new opportunities for people with degrees in African Studies at a time when the area studies bubble of academic jobs had burst.

Meanwhile the publication in 1974 of two prize-winning books by prominent scholars of Africa underscored the start of a new round of challenges to the disciplines and their conventions for studying social change. One, Immanual Wallerstein's *The Modern World System: Capitalist Agriculture and the Origins of the European World Economy in the Sixteenth Century*, was awarded the American Sociological Association's Sorokin prize in 1975. The other, Elliott Skinner's *African Urban Life: The Transformation of Ouagadougou*, was co-winner that same year of the African Studies Association's Herskovits prize. Both are mature works by senior scholars who first went to Africa in the 1950s and later rose to prominence in their respective disciplines.

Skinner, an anthropologist, broke new ground with his study of urbanisation in Ouagadougou by connecting the daily lives and outlooks of ordinary Africans with the larger, global socioeconomic trends shaping the modern world. Writing in the preface to *African Urban Life*, he took his discipline to task for undervaluing the multidimensionality of the African subject. The message was clear and to the point:

> This book appears at a time when the ethics of individual anthropologists are being severely questioned, and when the relevance of our discipline to the modern world is seriously challenged ... Third World peoples ... can now insist that anthropologists view them in all their humanity and deal with all their problems rather than highlight only some aspects of their societies and cultures. Moreover, these people reject the notion that it took the West to make them conscious of themselves. To the contrary, they are now reasserting their humanity after being considered objects by the West (Skinner 1974: vii).

Wallerstein, a sociologist, zeroed in on two problematic aspects of disciplinary distinctions: the unit of analysis and the parcelisation of knowledge. The book's overarching thesis grew out of his own intellectual trajectory as a regional specialist. As Wallerstein explains, having first gone to Africa to study the process of decolonisation, he became deeply interested in the fate of these new states *after* independence. Analytic questions turned his attention to the broader category of 'states in the period after formal independence but before they had achieved something that might be termed national integration' (Wallerstein 1974). The logic of this line of inquiry then led him to examine early modern Europe and the process of modernisation. He eventually resolved that Africa's story was embedded in the larger story of social change and the world as a social system. Hence the *Epilogue* to *The Modern World System* calls for an end to artificial divisions of knowledge:

> When one studies a social system, the classical lines of division within social science are meaningless ... They make certain limited sense if the focus of one's study is organizations. They make none at all if the focus is the social system. I am not calling for a multidisciplinary approach to the study of social systems, but for a unidisciplinary approach (Wallerstein 1974: 11).

Wallerstein and Skinner, each in his own way, drew attention to the need for more critical reflection about the relationship between area studies and the disciplines. Ironically, these clarion calls came at about the same time that institutional support for area studies had levelled off, and disciplinary forces were becoming more aggressive in the competition for faculty positions and tenure.

By 1977 the JCAS had dropped the expectation that its grant recipients would necessarily do fieldwork and began welcoming proposals for comparative theoretical research in non-field settings. This move reflected the changing demands for career advancement faced by the younger cohort of Africanist scholars at major research universities. Indeed, regional specialists faced a double bind: an increasingly tight job market, plus the control of most academic positions by disciplinary departments rather than area studies centres. And in the departments, theory was king. Beyond the pressure to publish, involvement in theoretically oriented work was weighted more heavily in the criteria for tenure and promotion. As Guyer acknowledged in her assessment of African area studies, this turn of events had positive as well as negative consequences:

> [T]he return to the library did allow us to concentrate on the big picture, the long term and the essential conceptual and analytical issues ... The unforeseen result ... was the decreasing regular involvement of the theoretical wing in day-to-day Africa, and a certain myopia about the current state of Africa on the part of some in the academy (Guyer 1996: 7).

In short, theorising the study of Africa took on a life of its own.

The 1980s

The 1980s saw the launch of a particularly successful attempt to create a new canon, one characterised by theoretical paradigms that crossed disciplinary boundaries, attention to constellations of issues germane to the Africa region, and a rethinking of conceptual tools and methods. Between 1981 and 1994, this thrust was shaped and advanced in a series of 21 research overview papers commissioned by the JCAS and published in the *African Studies Review*. These 'state of the art' reviews initially stressed strategically chosen themes (for example, the household and gender analysis, Africa's agrarian crisis, health and healing, political economy and the state). However their most enduring legacy has been the impact of the ten or so papers commissioned with the specific intent of raising the profile of the humanities in African studies. For more than a decade, review articles on philosophy and social thought, literature and oral traditions, the visual and popular arts, history and social processes, religious movements, and performance studies served as prime sites for debates and paradigmatic shifts in African area studies.[38]

This was, as well, a period when American universities reaped enormous benefits from Africa's brain drain. Perhaps the single most influential scholar to emerge from an extraordinarily gifted talent pool was Valentin Mudimbe—philosopher *cum* cultural critic. Mudimbe left Lovanium University in Zaire for Haverford College in Pennsylvania before moving to Duke University as R. F. DeVarney Professor of Romance Studies, professor of comparative literature, and professor of cultural anthropology. Recruited to the JCAS in 1981, he was asked to write an overview paper surveying African philosophy. The resulting essay, 'African gnosis: philosophy and the order of knowledge' (Mudimbe 1986), is breathtaking in its range. An expanded version of this overview paper was published as *The Invention of Africa: Gnosis, Philosophy and the Order of Knowledge*, a book that immediately catapulted its author into the ranks of America's most distinguished paradigm-setting Africanists. A co-winner of the 1989 Herskovits prize, Mudimbe's *Invention* combines a sophisticated perspective on traditional African thought with a Foucauldian analysis of power, knowledge and discourse, to construct an argument about epistemological shifts in the study of Africa as a scientific discipline 'from the perspective of wider (Darwinian) hypotheses about the classification of beings and societies'.

Thus a number of developments converged during the 1980s to elevate the prominence of theory in the works of Africanists operating in the academic mainstream. Moreover, as the growing ranks of postmodernist and postcolonial researchers moved into area studies across the board, a shared discourse of theoretical understandings facilitated trans-regional dialogues and meta analyses, although sometimes at the expense of close attention to facts on the ground. On the upside, this infusion of new conceptual frameworks heightened the visibility of a few of the more theoretically inclined African scholars (for instance, Mudimbe, Achille Mbembe, Paulin Hountondji, and Kwame Anthony Appiah) (see Appiah 1992; Mbembe 1992; Hountoundji 1983),[40] and facilitated their incorporation into the American academy as world class intellectuals.[41] On the downside, the tilt toward higher-level abstractions accentuated longstanding cleavages between theoretically focussed and empirically oriented scholars.

Some critics have derided this trend as the privileging of knowledge distanced from the daily lives and struggles of African people (see Mamdani 1990; Owomoyela 1994). That debate is ongoing. Even so, for nearly two decades the intellectual centre of gravity for African area studies was defined by the cross-disciplinary, humanities-centred canon forged in the 1980s. Almost immediately, the influence of the research overview papers could be seen in the works of Herskovits Prize laureates writing about religion: James Fernandez, *Bwiti: An Ethnography of the Religious Imagination in Africa* (1982); philosophy and social thought: Paulin Hountondji, *African Philosophy: Myth and Reality* (1983), T. O. Beidelman, *Moral Imagination in Kaguru Modes of Thought* (1986), Mudimbe, *The Invention of Africa* (1988), Kwame Anthony Appiah, *In My Father's House: Africa in the Philosophy of Culture* (1992); visual and popular arts: Johanes Fabian, *Power and Performance: Ethnographic Explorations through Proverbial Wisdom and Theatre in Shaba, Zaire* (1990), and Susan Mullin Vogel, *Baule African Art, Western Eyes* (1997); and history and social processes: John Iliffe, *The African Poor: A History* (1987), Jonathan Glassman, *Feasts and Riot: Revelry, Rebellions and Popular Consciousness on the Swahili Coast, 1856-1888* (1995), Keletso Atkins, *The Moon Is Dead! Give Us Our Money! The Cultural Origins of an African Work Ethic, Natal, South Africa, 1843-1900* (1993), and Nancy Rose Hunt, *A Colonial Lexicon: Of Birth Ritual, Medicalization, and Mobility in the Congo* (1999).

The 1990s

The end of the Cold War and the concomitant failure of regional specialists to predict the demise of the Soviet Union ultimately called into question the geopolitical rationale that had carried the area studies enterprise for some 40 years. One of the unanticipated consequences of this crisis of legitimacy was the opening up of intellectual space along myriad new fronts. This was certainly the case for African area studies.

Africanists interested in conflict and its resolution began migrating to the field of security studies, bringing with them rich lodes of theoretical and empirical analyses on topics ranging from ethnic conflict to state collapse. Crawford Young's 1976 book, *The Politics of Cultural Pluralism*, together with I. William Zartman's 1995 volume *Collapsed States*, became essential reading for anyone seeking to understand post-Cold War developments in East and Central Europe (Young 1976; Zartman 1995). Shifting currents in the academy also created space for strong theorists to make more visible the contributions of Africa research to major developments in the core disciplines. Take, for example, economist Paul Collier's chapter in the 1993 Bates, Mudimbe and Jean O'Barr volume, *Africa and the Disciplines*. Sounding like a salesman making a pitch to bottom-line university administrators, Collier describes advances that place African research at the forefront of several major developments in his field:

> Africa is a gold mine to economics because its economic history has been so extreme: booms, busts, famines, migrations. Because there are so many African countries, often following radically different economic policies, Africa offers a diversity ideally suited to the comparative approach, which is the economist's best substitute for the controlled experiment. Until recently this potential has not been realized ... However, the situation is rapidly changing (Collier 1993:58).

The contrast between Collier's emphasis on disciplinary contributions and the rationales for area studies articulated during the Cold War signals the beginning of a new era.

Along with disciplinary knowledge, gender analysis gained a steadier foothold in African area studies during the 1990s. To be sure, Africanists in the *World* of research universities have always heralded at least a few scholars who placed women at the centre of their work. At least four of the 45 winners of the Herskovits Prize between 1960 and 2000 adopted women or gender as an explicit focus: Margaret Strobel's *Muslim Women in Mombasa, 1980-1995* (1979); Claire Robertson's *Sharing the Same Bowl* (1984); Luise White's *The Comforts of Home: Prostitution in Colonial Nairobi* (1990); and *Cutting Down Trees: Gender, Nutrition and Agricultural Change in the Northern Province of Zambia, 1890-1990* by Henrietta L. Moore and Megan Vaughn (1994). In recent years, epistemological contributions honed in the field of women's studies have posed increasingly strident challenges to the gender-neutral paradigms that have guided the study of Africa.

Feminist research methods and objectives are concerned with giving voice to the women studied. The researcher generally prefers an ethnographic approach, seeks to be more egalitarian and collaborative, and strives to both hear and amplify what is being said. The devices of feminist scholarship have come to include life histories, testimonies, multiple authorships, and oral histories. Anthropologist Gwendolyn Mikell, writing in the Introduction to her 1997 edited volume *African Feminism: The Politics of Survival*, explains that the new feminist scholarship is committed to revealing how African women 'think of themselves' as they grapple with 'affirm(ing) their own identities while transforming societal notions of gender and familial roles' (Mikell 1997:1).

A more recent development to emerge from this reflective methodology accords high value to the practice of reciprocity, played out in terms of accountability to people interviewed and greater respect for research subjects. Political scientist Aili Tripp has gone so far as to urge feminist scholars to re-think the hierarchies of power that structure their relations with the women they study by incorporating these women into the process of *theorising*. Relating a personal epiphany while doing fieldwork on women's politics in Uganda, Tripp recalls:

> ... I found, as one who is deeply interested in women's agency, that I needed to pay attention to how women analyzed their own circumstances ... I had to find ways of engaging in mutual learning and dialogue and take people seriously at a conceptual level, not simply as a source of data (Tripp 2000: xxiii).

Although Tripp has consistently engaged the work of African feminist scholars and seeks their feedback on an ongoing basis, she found that 'theorizing at the grass-roots' provided a unique opportunity to create new knowledge together with the women she was studying. The book that resulted from this research, *Women and Politics in Uganda*, won the American Political Science Association's 2001 Victoria Schuck Award for the best book published on women and politics. Gender analysis and disciplinary knowledge come together in this penetrating study about how women's political activity can be embedded in multipurpose organisations.

Many more voices from the slow but steady stream of African émigré scholars who arrived during the 1990s are now also being heard above the din. Mamdani moved to Columbia University in the city of New York. Amadiume took up a position at Dartmouth College in Hanover, New Hampshire. The Malawian historian, essayist, and novelist Paul Tiyambe Zeleza has emerged as a particularly active presence. He left a position in Canada to become Professor of History and Director of the Title VI African Studies Center at the University of Illinois, Champaign-Urbana. Zeleza's *A Modern Economic History of Africa, Volume I* (1993) won the 1994 Noma Award for Publishing in Africa. The jury citation praised the book for 'its bold and convincing challenge to hitherto accepted orthodoxies, terminologies, and interpretations, about the nature and development of African societies and economies'. A few years later he published *Manufacturing African Studies and Crises*, a provocative and at times irreverent collection of essays that examined African studies and those who study it.

Through empirical research and critical essays, *Manufacturing African Studies* makes visible the separateness of the *Worlds* of African studies and the power hierarchies that structure their different realities. Analysing the contents of five leading English-language African studies journals between 1982 and 1992,[42] Zeleza concludes that Africanist publishing is largely a preserve of white male scholars, while research by African scholars rarely appears in Western academic media (Zeleza 1997: 61). He attributes these imbalances to structures of power that are articulated with spatial, gender, racial and ethnic hierarchies. Moreover, he insists that the only solution to the intellectual marginalisation of Africa in the production of knowledge about Africa lies in Africans developing and sustaining their own publishing channels.[43]

Bringing the Diaspora Back In

Security studies, gender studies, and a greater emphasis on disciplinary knowledge: these are three of the hallmarks of post-Cold War African area studies. When the SSRC phased out the JCAS in 1996, an Africa Regional Advisory Panel (RAP) was established in its place. The RAP facilitates dialogue and the development of shared research themes among US-based Africanists and networks of African scholars located on the continent. This new direction reflects the SSRC's efforts to become more truly international in its client base. Still, the burning question at the start of this new millennium is whether the study of Africa as a scientific discipline will continue to be fragmented into different, separate *Worlds*.

In balance, it is clear that the Joint Committee on African Studies succeeded in its mission of giving intellectual coherence to Africa as a field of study. By promoting interdisciplinary graduate training, encouraging the study of African languages and literature, overseeing fellowship programmes for graduate and post-doctoral fieldwork, and giving its imprimatur to context-sensitive research, the Committee did a great deal to channel Africa into the US academic mainstream.

Yet the JCAS was also constrained by the networks of its members. The Committee did well to recruit scholars from Europe, Africa and a more diverse cross-section of North American universities and research institutes. These additions facilitated connections with a larger universe of regional specialists and intellectual currents. Regrettably, my own tenure as the only African American to chair the JCAS (1991-93) occurred during the Committee's final years, and hence was essentially a holding operation. But more importantly, the outreach efforts never extended to Historically Black Colleges and Universities in the US. And as greater numbers of black faculty and students were recruited by majority white universities, it became easier for the institutional pillars of the African area studies establishment to justify their exclusion of the HBCUs from African Studies networks.[44] A list of the institutional affiliations of JCAS members from 1960 through its phase-out in 1996 is telling: not a single scholar based at an HBCU ever served on the Committee.[45]

One can always identify the occasional individual whose networks straddle two or more of the *Worlds* of African studies. Therefore the issue of absence/exclusion is posed here in institutional terms in order to shed light on the assumptions and exclusionary consequences of practices involved in bounding the academic mainstream. Because of the strategic role played by the SSRC in the development of area studies as far back as the 1940s, the universities represented on its various Joint Committees map the ecology of each region's academic high ground. The absence of HBCUs from the Council's African Area Studies landscape became part of a process that transformed what were once permeable lines of differentiation into walls of separation. Opportunities for the kinds of formative interactions that the young Herskovits had with senior scholars at Howard in the 1920s and 1930s were indeed rare by the 1980s. Missed opportunities in the wake of this disconnect remain a matter for speculation. Yet ironically, the consequences of separate development may have been more liberating than deleterious for the field of African Diaspora Studies.

When Historian Joseph E. Harris convened the First African Diaspora Studies Institute (FADSI) at Howard University in 1979, the JCAS was preparing to launch its research overview papers. Postmodernism and a new postcolonial paradigm were beginning to drive much of the theoretically oriented work in the humanities. And rational choice theory had found an opening through the social sciences in Africa. However Harris's project was more empirically grounded. Participants in the FADSI were invited to consider the meanings, relevance and location of boundaries as diasporas impinge on the economies, politics, and social relations of both homeland and the host country or area (Harris 1996: 7). Papers presented at that inaugural session were published in *Global Dimensions of the African Diaspora Studies Institute* (1982) edited by Harris. This seminal volume, with case studies from Europe, Asia, Africa and the Americas, laid the groundwork for a re-evaluation of the dispersion of Africans across the globe. Its co-authors treat these diasporas as dynamic and push us to think about Africa and its population movements in relational terms. The Second African Studies Diaspora Institute (SADSI) met in Kenya in 1981 with a mostly African audience. What SADSI did was to reach out and link that way of thinking about Africa's population movements—i.e., in dynamic, relational terms—to continental African scholars.[46]

Situating FADSI's genesis squarely in the *World* of Diasporic Pan-Africanist scholars, Harris explained the intellectual roots of African diaspora studies as follows:

> African-American social scientists and humanists have had at the core of their research on Africa and blacks generally ... the motivation to change the way of thinking about both. That motivation linked the black or African world to the struggle for human rights. Thus most university educated African-American scholars have employed research concepts and methodologies to discover and present 'the facts' ... [in order] to educate and thus bring about change through another way of understanding. This commitment expressed itself in pan-African approaches to the study of Africa and led to the evolution of the diaspora concept. ... Hansberry, Rayford Logan, Bunche and others conveyed this in their teaching and research at Howard University (Harris 2002).

Two years after the publication of *Global Dimensions*, sociologist Ruth Simms Hamilton and historian Leslie Rout, Jr. co-founded the African Diaspora Research Program (ADRP) at Michigan State University. This project enlarged the purview of Africa diaspora studies with a model that incorporates in-depth comparative historical analysis into a conceptualisation of the African diaspora as a global social formation. Four intersecting components frame the ADRP's approach to the analysis of global identity formation: (i) geosocial mobility and displacement, (ii) Africa-diaspora-homeland connections, (iii) relations of dominance and subordination, and (iv) cultural production and endurance (Simms Hamilton 1997; forthcoming). This formulation marked a major departure from the longstanding legacy of Herskovits's research programme on African retentions in the New World, and his emphasis on links to West Africa (Herskovits 1958). The former orientation had relied heavily on work in cultural anthropology, history, and the visual and performing arts. By fostering research on modes of dispersion other than slavery, and by emphasising the global sociological dynamics of the African diaspora, the ADRP spurred interest in contemporary economic, social and political realities. What is more, institutionalised African Diaspora Studies took root at Michigan State alongside one of the original Title VI African Studies Centers, creating opportunities for synergism (African Diaspora Research Project 1993).

Harris and Simms Hamilton are major figures in the *World* of Diasporic Pan-Africanist scholars. Both attended HBCUs: Harris, a product of Howard, studied with Hansberry; Simms went to Taladega College, where there was no focus on Africa.[47] Both found their way to Northwestern as doctoral students in the early 1960s: Harris went there to specialise in African History; Simms Hamilton's initial interest was mainstream sociology. Exposure to the *World* of African area studies at Northwestern led her to enrol in African studies courses, including language study, and eventually to conduct dissertation fieldwork on urban sociology in Ghana. Harris broke new ground with the publication of *The African Presence in Asia* (1971), an examination of the East African slave trade to Asia. He then broadened his research agenda to include two-way migration patterns, particularly emphasising the trajectories of voluntary population movement by African origin peoples around the globe. Simms Hamilton's foray into African studies from a disciplinary base anticipated developments that would be promoted as 'new' in the 1990s. Her role as Director of the ADRP has involved overseeing a programme that trains scholars in African Diaspora Studies, promotes scholarship on the African diaspora, and facilitates curriculum enrichment. The ADRP publishes *Connexões*, a newsletter that is distributed to more than 50 countries in Europe, Africa, Asia and the Middle East.

The launch of the Howard Institute, of Michigan State's ADRP, as well as the publication of Yale art historian Robert Farris Thompson's *Flash of the Spirit* (1983) were part of the same critical moment. These projects, grounded in the study of Africa, sowed the seeds for a renaissance in African Diaspora studies. With frames of analysis that elicit thick description in tandem with comparative and interpretive work, each in its own way operates on the assumption that linkages tying the diaspora to Africa must be articulated and are not inevitable (Patterson and Kelley 2000: 20). Farris Thompson's pioneering text, which documents the richness of detail and moral wisdom of Yoruba, Bakongo, Fon, Mende and Ejagham art and philosophy, and examines their fusion with other elements overseas, pointed the way for diaspora studies to look more closely at ethnicity and cultural identities *within* Africa (Patterson and Kelley 2000: 16).

Today, the networks of scholars growing out of these stirrings in African Diaspora Studies generally differ in several important ways from those fostered by the traditional African area studies model: The HBCUs are recognised as major sites of activity, scholars of Africa north as well as south of the Sahara are part of the mix, and pride of place is given to specialists in local/global linkages, regardless of whether they are trained as Africanists. Take, for example, Ronald Walters, a leading specialist in African American politics who served as head of Howard University's Political Science Department for more than a decade before moving to the University of Maryland in the 1990s. Walters followed Farris Thompson as Chair of the SSRC's short-lived Committee on African American Societies and Cultures, the post-Montréal Committee that was phased out in 1972. His *PanAfricanism in the African Diaspora* (1993) is framed around a central question: *What forces drive people of African descent to continue identifying with the source of their origin?* In this work, the *linkages* between Africa and its diasporas—real and imaginary—are the unit of analysis. Surveying the politics of cultural mobilisation in the US, the Caribbean, and Britain, Walters weaves together many local stories of African legacies and their re-invention in the cause of political empowerment and community development. This is clearly not a book that would fit the rubric of African area studies. Nor was it meant to be.

However, a millennial year article by Harvard historian Emmanuel Akyeampong written to mark the hundredth anniversary of the Royal African Society, declares that it is time to 'rethink the boundaries of African Studies as well as the definition of who is an African' (Akyeampong 2000: 213). Arguing that the late twentieth century has given rise to 'a unique African who straddles continents, worlds and cultures', he characterises today's world of globalised capital and culture as terrain where Africa and its diaspora 'exist in a closer physical union than in any previous period' (188).

Following this logic, the metamorphosis of identity has emerged as a prominent theme in diaspora studies in general, and African diaspora studies in particular (Patterson and Kelley 2000: 19-24). Indeed, some of the most inspired scholarship in the field examines processes of identity transformation over time. Michael Gomez's *Changing Our Country Marks: The Transformation of African Identities in the Colonial and Antebellum South* (1998) is an extraordinary achievement in this regard. Gomez, an anthropologist with strong interdisciplinary training, especially in history, has mined the wealth of data now available thanks largely to some 70 years of African area studies scholarship to produce a work that emphasises the crucial role played by the African background of slaves in the determination of African American identity. Consider his sources: secondary literature on North American slavery and the transatlantic slave trade, anthropological theory on the acculturative process, historical and anthropological studies on West and Central Africa, and a corpus of primary materials consisting of runaway slave advertisements from southern newspapers.[48] The result is an historical account of the ethnogenesis of African American identity in Charleston, South Carolina that is impressive in its breadth eclectic in its methodological sophistication.

Revisiting the Herskovits/Frazier debate and the methodologies that informed their divergent positions, Gomez builds on, and discards, aspects of both. Acknowledged is the enduring contribution made by Herskovits's use of the comparative analytical approach to New World slave societies as he sought to validate the thesis of African cultural survivals. But Gomez rejects Herskovits's conclusion that in the few cases where Africanisms persisted in the US, they were 'almost never directly referable to a specific tribe or definite areas' (cited in Gomez 1998, Chapter 1). Gomez then embraces Frazier's view that the debate should turn on an analysis of the organisation and functions of the black family in America and the social conditions that shaped them. But he dismisses Frazier's conclusion that the conditions of life in the US destroyed the significance of the slaves' African heritage.

In the end, facets of conceptual and methodological approaches pioneered by both Herskovits and Frazier made it possible to recover the cultural, political, and social background of regions in Africa directly affected by the slave trade, and to show how a distinct African American cultural identity emerged through a process of forging family life under the difficult conditions of slavery. Gomez's treatment of ethnicity, based on scholarship that was not available to Herskovits or Frazier, provides traction for explaining the resilience of African cultures in the New World. His development of a methodology for examining continuity through the lens of ethnicity is a major contribution to research on cultural survivals, a topic that has found new audiences through the resurgence of diaspora studies.

It is well to remember that Melville Herskovits devoted a life-long research programme to African cultural survivals in the New World—in short, to African diaspora studies. However the area studies model that emerged in the aftermath of the Second World War moved the diaspora from the centre to the margins of the new African studies canon. Ironically, even the African Studies Association took the position that books about Africa's diasporas would not be eligible for its prestigious Herskovits Prize. This paradox was finally put to rest during the deliberations of the ASA Committee charged with making the 2002 award.

Bringing the diaspora(s) back in is opening up the study of Africa in exciting new ways. It is giving rise to a host of new sites of intellectual activity in which scholars are variously theorising African diasporas; collaborating around major research agendas; doing all manner of innovative, interdisciplinary, comparative research; reading each others' work; engaging each other in debates; and either envisaging, launching or strengthening research institutes. Beyond Europe, the New World, and Asia, contemporary studies of African diasporas stretch into Indian Ocean societies, the Islamic world, and virtual spaces (Alpers 1997; Patterson and Kelley 2000: 13-14). For example, the Afro-diasporic historian Robin D. J. Kelley has teamed up with historian Tiffany Ruby Patterson in a highly ambitious project that treats the African diaspora as a unit of analysis in a larger process of migrations in world history.[49] Their goal: to move beyond narratives of displacement and launch a research agenda for the new millennium, conceptualised in terms of black globality and its connections to other forms of internationalism.[50] In a paper presented at the 1999 annual meeting of the ASA, Kelley and Patterson mapped out a conceptual framework that emphasises:

(i)   The historical construction of the African diaspora;

(ii)   The development of a disaporic identity and its social, cultural, and political manifestations;

(iii)   The contributions of black migrant and colonial intellectuals to rethinking the modern West; and

(iv)   The continual re-invention of Africa and the diaspora through cultural work, migrations, transformations in communications, as well as the globalisation of capital (Patterson and Kelley 2000: 13).

(v)   To this list I would add a fifth, introspective, connection to globality: the construction (by Africans) of imaginary 'spaces' associated with areas outside of Africa that become part of extraverted strategies for personal mobility and betterment.

This last category evokes the notion of virtual diasporas—i.e., spaces where one can obtain access to personalised channels within global markets, or be 'wired' into Western culture without permanently leaving the homeland. It directs attention to a particular kind of response to economic globalisation and cultural marginalisation, one that is anchored in the realm of the imagination yet extends into the socio-cultural and economic empowerment strategies of daily life. These virtual diasporas are rendered palpably real in work such as economic historian Yvette Djachechi Monga's (2000) article 'Dollars and lipstick: the United States through the eyes of African women'. Here, she details the ways in which the varying strata of Cameroonian women in her research are able to 'redefine or symbolically reinvent their lives' (201) by appropriating certain signs of American culture. Strategies run the gamut from investing in the future by arranging to give birth in the United States to children who will become American citizens, to buying made-in-America beauty products through reliable trading networks that can authenticate the source. According to Djachechi Monga, the United States becomes a 'vessel' into which these women 'pour their dreams' (193).

At the dawn of a new millennium we find that widening networks of diaspora scholars are straddling the various *Worlds* of African Studies, making connections across continents or across racial divides (for a discussion of African American Africanists, see Robinson and Skinner 1983). Michael Gomez is one of many examples: An African American Africanist who studied with Joseph Harris at Howard, he held positions at historically black Spelman College and the University of Georgia at Athens before to moving to New York University, where he joined a stellar group of African diaspora scholars that includes the Africanist historian Fredrick Cooper[51] and Afro-diasporic historian Robin D. J. Kelley. At an institutional level, there are stirrings that would breathe new life into the 1981 SADSI initiative, which resulted in the introduction of courses on the African Diaspora at the Universities of Zambia, Zimbabwe and Malawi. In an essay entitled 'Imagining Pan-Africansim in the 21st Century', Zeleza proposes the establishment of African Diaspora Studies centres at African universities. Such centres would further alter the conventional boundaries of African area studies as scholars in Africa undertake research and teaching about Africans and people of African descent who straddle continents, worlds and cultures. These centres might also serve as bridges for linking African scholars and black scholars in the diaspora in a common intellectual project. He promotes such collaboration as a way to begin redressing the hegemony of white male scholars in the production of Africanist knowledge (Zeleza 1997: 518).

As new directions in diaspora research further problematise our conventional notions about geographic boundaries and point to the effects of globalisation processes on all facets of life, the institutional landscape of African studies in the US is changing as well. Hence we are witnessing the launch of twentieth-first century research centres related to Africa yet different from the Title VI centres in their various missions and geographical reach. For instance, the University of Maryland's Driskell Center for the Study of the African Diaspora, established in 2001, is committed to scholarly endeavours that promote 'a full understanding of African and African American life'. To this end it will encourage research that is inter- and multidisciplinary and that bridges the humanities, performing and visual arts, and social sciences. The start up of UCLA's Globalization Research Center-Africa (GRCA) in 2002 signals yet another departure from the conventional area studies model. GRCA will foster research on the impact of global forces on African societies, on the influence of African societies on globalisation processes, and on cross-national and cross-cultural comparisons of global processes as they relate to Africa. The founding directors of both these centres—Eileen Julien at Maryland and Edmond Keller at UCLA—are African area studies specialists whose long records of scholarship and intellectual activism straddle three *Worlds* of African Studies.[52] While director of the University of Illinois' African Studies Center, Zeleza involved the Center in the project of institutional transformation at universities in Africa, and advocated the development of Pan-Africanist networks that 'consciously cross the various boundaries of scholarly production and communication' to engage burning issues related to Africa wherever they are raised (Zeleza 1997: 518).

Thus we have come full circle. Research agendas that highlight the contributions of black migrants and colonial intellectuals to the making of the modern West, or that explore the ways in which African societies influence globalisation processes, are framing alternatives to the assumption of Africa's marginality. Diaspora studies and research on globalisation are bringing to light new understandings of present-day Africa. And some of the work being done in these fields is contributing to epistemological shifts in the study of Africa as a scientific discipline. In spite of these trends, however, who validates knowledge about Africa remains a point of contention (Zeleza 1997: 61).

Whether African diaspora(s) studies or studies of globalisation will emerge as sites for connecting the various *Worlds* of African studies remains an open question. Whatever the case, the best scholarship on Africa will continue to emerge from context-sensitive research rooted in the specificities of the region's diverse and varied cultural, political, socioeconomic, and gender realities. The era of Cold War area studies has ended. But the contributions of research in Africa to the disciplines and to more practically-driven policy issues are ongoing. Meanwhile, explaining and framing alternatives to Africa's present-day marginality remains a fundamental mission of African studies.

Notes

1. Title VI of the National Defense and Education Act established area studies centres with funding from the US Department of Education.
2. Mamdani argued that the course developed by his UCT colleagues implied that Africa had no social history before the presence of the white man on the continent, revealed an ignorance of key debates in the equatorial African academy, and used a textbook informed by debates in the North American academy. These points were addressed and refuted by UCT Professors Martin Hall and Johann Graaff, who defended their course design. See Hall (1998) and Graaff (1998).
3. Institutional racism, as distinct from individual racism, lays the blame on processes, legacies, and patterns that flow from established conventions and may operate at a subconscious level.
4. Specifically, Bates (1996: 1) wrote that '... within the academy, the consensus has formed that area studies has failed to generate scientific knowledge'.
5. Citing Maurice Godelier in 1987, Amadiume reports that there could be as many as 10,000 societies, of which anthropologists had studied between 700 and 800.
6. Regarding feminist scholars who support the theory that maternal and domestic roles account for the universal subordination of women, Amadiume references Rosaldo (1974), Sanday (1974), Chodorow (1974), and Ortner (1974), all in Rosaldo and Lamphere (1974).
7. Three offerings formed the core: Negro Peoples in the Culture and Civilizations of Prehistoric and Proto-Historic Times, Ancient Civilizations of Ethiopia, and The Civilization of West Africa in Medieval and Early Modern Times.
8. Ralph Bunche taught at Howard University from 1928 to 1941. He joined the faculty. in 1928 upon receiving his MA from Harvard and established Howard's Political Science Department. He completed his Ph.D. in 1934.
9. In Rivlin (1990), the following chapters are especially instructive on Bunche's career as an Africanist scholar: Nathan Irvin Huggins, 'Ralph Bunche the Africanist'; Lawrence S. Finkelstein, 'Bunche and the colonial world: From trusteeship to decolonization'; Charles P. Henry, 'Civil rights and national security: the case of Ralph Bunche'; and Martin Kilson, 'Ralph Bunche's analytical perspective on African development'.
10. In the 1930s, Bunche was part of a remarkable group of black scholars at Howard known as the Young Turks: Alain Locke, E. Franklin Frazier, Sterling Brown, Abram Harris, Charles Houston and William Hastie. These were men of exceptional intellect and academic credentials who, except for racism, would have had appointments at major

research universities. Prolific scholars and leftists, they were the epitome of Du Bois's 'talented tenth'.

11. Lincoln's founding mission included the training of Africans and African Americans who would become part of the governing elite in the new Republic of Liberia and work with the Presbytery of West Africa. The first African student enrolled in Lincoln in 1857; he came from Liberia. In its first hundred years, Lincoln graduated 159 African students. They came from Liberia (39), South Africa (22), Nigeria (58), Sierra Leone (18), the Gold Coast (14), Kenya (3), and one each from Ethiopia, French Cameroon, Gabon, South West Africa, and Uganda.

12. Explaining why he moved from Howard to Lincoln, Azikiwe recounts that in contrast to Howard, Lincoln had a reputation for training people who would 'minister to the needs of Africa' by involving themselves with operations on the ground (Bond 1976: 499-50).

13. Kwame Nkrumah became Prime Minister and then President of Ghana, which gained its independence in 1957. In 1960, when Nigeria attained independence, Nnamdi Azikiwe became its first President.

14. The Negro in History: 'This course ... considers, first, the anthropological and ethnological background of the Negro; second, the part played by the Negroid races in Egypt, Nubia, Ethiopia, India, and Arabia; third, the role of the Negro in medieval times in Songhai, Ghana, Melle, etc.; and fourth, the contemporary Negro in Africa, the West Indies, Latin America, and the United States. Instructor, Mr. Azikiwe' (*Lincoln University Herald* 1933-34: 46).

15. This course was cross-listed and open to the men of neighbouring Morehouse College, *Annual Catalogue 1933-34*, pp. 81-82.

16. Prior to the publication of *Black Folk*, the basic text was Carter G. Woodson's *The African Background Outlines or Handbook for the Study of the Negro* (1936).

17. Du Bois wrote the manuscript of *Black Folk* while a Professor of Sociology at Atlanta University, an HBC specialising in graduate studies.

18. In Herskovits (1958: 6-7; 300-301) he details how he came to reverse his position on the significance of African retentions.

19. Hansberry received a BA degree from Harvard in 1921 and a Harvard MA in 1932.

20. In 1953 he became a Fulbright Research Scholar and spent a year doing fieldwork in Egypt, Sudan and Ethiopia.

21. Dunham had been a trusted advisor to Hansberry since his undergraduate days at Harvard. He sought advice about whether being black might disqualify him from joining an expedition to Egypt being planned by the English Egyptologist F. L. Griffeth. See Harris (1974: 12-14).

22. Following a programme worked out with the SSRC, Bunche travelled to Northwestern to study with Herskovits, to the London School of Economics to study with Bronislaw Malinowski, and to the University of Cape Town to study with Isaac Shapera. See Henry (1999: 75).

23. In the traditional division of labour, anthropology focused on 'primitive peoples,' while Oriental studies were the domain of non-Western 'high civilisations'. Traditional ethnography sought to reconstitute or preserve knowledge of pristine cultures, and

critics of Orientalism point to a presumption that non-Western civilisations are incapable of autonomous modernisation. See Immanuel Wallerstein (1997: 198-199).

24. Much of the discussion of the institutional expansion of African Studies programmes in the US is based on Hill (1967: 65-88).

25. The OCI later became the Office of Strategic Services (OSS), which was the precursor to the CIA.

26. For an in-depth view of Bunche's extensive South Africa contacts, see Robert Edgar, *Ralph Bunche: An African-American in South Africa* (1992). Bunche published four scholarly articles (1934; 1936; 1939; 1941) on colonial Africa and nationalist responses.

27. Economists Charles Hitch and Emile Dupres, Russian expert Gerald Robinson, China expert Burton Faho, historians Conyers Read and Hajo Halborn, South American agent Maurice Halperin, and German expert Herbert Marcuse.

28. Among the early advocates of the Cold War shift in regional priorities was Harvard University's Committee on Educational Policy. See *Report of the Subcommittee on Language and International Affairs* (1945) cited in Wallerstein (1997: 201-202).

29. The FAFP was created to support American graduate students and to facilitate doctoral and post-doctoral field research opportunities.

30. William O. Brown, a sociologist and specialist on African affairs at the US State Department, became the first Director of the new Boston University program. E. Franklin Frazier was named Director of the Program at Howard. From 1953 to the early 1970s, BU received nearly $1.2 million from the Ford Foundation for its African Studies Program. By contrast, Howard University received a total of $70,000 from 1954 to 1962.

31. Joint committees for Japan (1967), Korea (1967) and Eastern Europe (1971) were established after the Joint Committee on African Studies.

32. Although the rational choice modellers predict victory, the paradigm has generated a host of critics. See Bates' challenge in the *APSA-CP Newsletter*, as well as Elster (2000) and Bates (2000).

33. Data on all SSRC International Doctoral Research Fellowships (not just those for study in Africa) from 1965 to 2000 (N = 540) show substantial fluctuations in the disciplinary mix, with economics and political science receiving smaller percentages of the awards today than they did in the 1960s; anthropology and economics in 1965 received roughly equal shares, while two decades later anthropology's proportion had increased substantially, while that of economics had declined. It appears that the shares awarded to anthropology and to history were inversely related, which may be a result of shifts in review committee composition. See figure 1 on p. 9 of SSRC's Items & Issues, (2001). Thanks to David Szanton for drawing my attention to these comparative statistics.

34. The African Heritage Studies Association is an autonomous association catering to people of African descent. The Association of Concerned Africa Scholars functions as an activist caucus within the ASA.

35. *Issue: A Journal of Opinion* began publication in 1971.

36. I was one of a critical mass of African American scholars who benefited from an MEAFP awards. Several from my cohort have provided extraordinary service to the field of African Studies as well as to their respective disciplines. Three have served as Directors of African Studies Centers (Edmond Keller at UCLA, Sheila Walker at the University of Texas -Austin; and Gwendolyn Mikell at Georgetown). Two are past presidents of the

ASA (Keller and Mikell). Mikell is also the Senior Fellow for Africa at the Council on Foreign Relations and was the founding president of the Association of African Anthropologists. Keller is the founding director of UCLA's Globalization Research Center-Africa. Ernest J. Wilson III is Director of the Center for International Communications and Conflict Management at the University of Maryland College Park and a past director of the University of Michigan's Center for Research on Economic Development.

37. SSRC annual reports for the 1970s.

38. An energetic advocate of the Humanities thrust was JCAS member Ivan Karp, curator of African ethnology at the Smithsonian, who, together with Charles Bird, convinced Indiana University Press to launch a new series on African Systems of Thought.

39. See introductory quote at the start of this article.

40. See, for example, Appiah (1992), Ch. 5, pp. 137-157; and Mbembe (1992). Paulin Hountoundji's *African Philosophy: Myth and Reality* (1983) and Appiah's *In My Father's House* (1992) won the ASA's Herskovits Prize in 1984 and 1993, respectively.

41. In this regard, the contrast with the 1970s, when the Joint Committee's relationship to African scholars was framed in terms of a rescue operation, is most striking.

42. The journals are *The Journal of Modern African Studies, African Studies Review, Research in African Literatures, Canadian Journal of African Studies,* and *Journal of African History.*

43. Zeleza has managed to negotiate these power hierarchies in his own professional life by tacking back-and-forth between Africa, the Caribbean, Canada and the US, and by refusing to publish his scholarly work in Western outlets.

44. I thank Joseph Harris for insisting on the importance of this development (Personal e-mail communication).

45. The records show several instances of individuals at HBCUs being brought in to serve on various screening panels or fellowship selection committees.

46. One result was the establishment of courses on the African diaspora at the Universities of Zambia, Zimbabwe and Malawi. Joseph Harris, personal communication with author, 10 July 2002.

47. Joseph Harris attended Howard University, where he was a student of Leo Hansberry. Ruth Hamilton is a graduate of Talladega College in Talladega, Alabama.

48. Announcements of runaway slaves frequently assigned ethnic identities. Gomez (1998) was able to roughly match overall patterns of slave importation with references to specific individuals and communities.

49. Anthropologist Jonetta Cole, an African American Africanist, was president of Spelman College when Gomez and Patterson were recruited to the faculty.

50. Their frameworks for understanding black internationalism in the modern world are (i) the trans-Atlantic system, (ii) Diaspora, (iii) international socialism, (iv) women's peace and freedom, (v) anti-colonialism, (vi) Third World solidarity, and (vii) Islam.

51. Fredrick Cooper (1981) authored the first JCAS African Research Overview paper on the theme 'Africa and the world economy'.

52. Eileen Julien, a specialist in Comparative Literature, has served as president of the African Language and Literature Association, and as Director of the Dakar-based West African Research Consortium. Political Scientist Edmond Keller is a past president of the African Studies Association and served for a decade as Director of UCLA's Title VI African Studies Center. Both are African Americans.

References

African Diaspora Research Project, 1993, *A Report on Progress, 1986-1993*.

Akyeampong, E., 2000, 'Africans in the diaspora: the diaspora and Africa', *African Affairs* 99 (395): 183-215.

Alpers, E., 1997, 'The African diaspora in the northwest Indian Ocean: reconsideration of an old problem, new directions for research', *Comparative Studies in South Asia, Africa and the Middle East* 17 (2): 61-80.

Amadiume, I., 1987, *Male Daughters, Female Husbands: Gender and Sex in an African Society*, London and New Jersey: Zed Books.

Appiah, K. A., 1992, 'The postcolonial and the postmodern', from *In My Father's House: Africa in the Philosophy of Culture*, New York and Oxford: Oxford University Press, 137-157.

Apter, D. E., 1963, 'Preface', in *Ghana in Transition*, New York: Atheneum.

Bates, R. H., 1996, 'Letter from the President: area studies and the discipline', *APSA-CP Newsletter* 7 (1): 1-2.

Bates, R. H., 2000, 'The analytic narrative project', *APSR*, September.

Bates, R. H., V. Y. Mudimbe, and J. O'Barr, eds., 1993, *Africa and the Disciplines: The Contributions of Research in Africa to the Social Sciences and Humanities*, Chicago: University of Chicago Press.

Benett, W. C., 1951, *Area Studies in American Universities*, New York: Social Science Research Council.

Blyden, E., 1862, *Liberia's Offering*, New York: J. A. Gary.

Blyden, E., 1869a, *Liberia: Past, Present and Future*, Washington City: McGill & Witherow Printers.

Blyden, E., 1869b, *The Negro in Ancient History*, Washington City: McGill & Witherow Printers.

Blyden, E., 1888, *Christianity, Islam and the Negro Race*, London: W. B. Whittingham & Co.

Blyden, E., 1903, *Africa and Africans*, London: CM Philips.

Bond, H. M., 1976, *Education for Freedom: A History of Lincoln University, Pennsylvania*, Lincoln University, PA: Lincoln University.

Bunche, R., 1934, 'French educational policy in Togo and Dahomey', *Journal of Negro Education* 3 (1).

Bunche, R., 1936, 'French and British imperialism in West Africa', *Journal of Negro History* 21 (1).

Bunche, R., 1939, 'The land equation in Kenya Colony', *Journal of Negro History* 24 (1).

Bunche, R., 1941, 'The Irua ceremony among the Kikuyu of Kiamba District, Kenya', *Journal of Negro History* 26 (1).

Chodorow, N., 1974, 'Family structure and feminine personality', in M. Z. Rosaldo and L. Lamphere, eds., *Women, Culture and Society*, Palo Alto: Stanford University Press.

Collier, P., 1993, 'Africa and the study of economics', in R. H. Bates, V. Y. Mudimbe, and J. O'Barr, eds., *Africa and the Disciplines: The Contributions of Research in Africa to the Social Sciences and Humanities*, Chicago: University of Chicago Press, 58-82.

Cooper, F., 1981, 'Africa and the world economy', *African Studies Review* 24 (2/3): 1-86.

Diouf, M. and M. Mamdani, eds., 1994, *Academic Freedom in Africa*, Dakar, CODESRIA Book Series.

Du Bois, W. E. B., 1902, 'Of the training of black men', *The Atlantic Monthly* 90 (DXXXIX, September), pp. 289-297.

Du Bois, W. E. B., 1939, *Black Folk Then and Now: An Essay in the History and Sociology of the Negro Race*, New York: Henry Holt and Company.

Du Bois, W. E. B., 1975, *Black Folk: Then and Now*, Millwood, NY: Kraus-Thomson Organization Ltd.

Edgar, R., ed., 1992, *Ralph Bunche: An African-American in South Africa*, Athens: Ohio University Press.

Ekeh, P., 1975, 'Colonialism and the two publics in Africa: a theoretical statement', *Comparative Studies in Society and History* 17: 91-112.

Elster, J., 2000, 'Rational choice history: a case of excessive ambition', *APSR*, September.

Frazier, E. F., 1939, *The Negro Family in the United States*, Chicago: University of Chicago Press.

Gomez, M., 1998, *Exchanging our Country Marks: The Transformation of African Identities in the Colonial and Antebellum South*, Chapel Hill: University of North Carolina Press.

Graaff, J., 1998, 'Pandering to pedagogy or consumed by content: brief thoughts on Mahmood Mamdani's "teaching Africa at the post-apartheid University of Cape Town"', in M. Mamdani, M. Hall, N. Hartman, and J. Graaff, eds., *Teaching Africa: The Curriculum Debate at UCT*, Cape Town: University of Cape Town, Centre for African Studies, 51-56.

Guyer, J. I., 1996, *African Studies in the United States: A Perspective*, Atlanta: African Studies Association Press.

Hall, M., 1998, 'Teaching Africa at the post-apartheid University of Cape Town: a response', in M. Mamdani, M. Hall, N. Hartman, and J. Graaff, eds., *Teaching Africa: The Curriculum Debate at UCT*, Cape Town: University of Cape Town, Centre for African Studies.

Hall, R. B., 1947, *Area Studies: With Special Reference to Their Implications for Research in the Social Sciences*, New York: Social Science Research Council.

Harris, J., ed., 1974, *Pillars in Ethiopian History: The William Leo Hansberry African History Notebook, Volume I*, Washington DC: Howard University.

Harris, J. E., 1971, *The African Presence in Asia: Consequences of the East African slave trade*, Evanston, IL: Northwestern University Press.

Harris, J. E., ed., 1982, *Global Dimensions of the African Diaspora*, Washington, DC: Howard University Press.

Harris, J. E., 1996, 'The dynamics of the global African diaspora', in A. Jalloh and S.E. Maizlish, eds., *The African Diaspora*. Arlington, TX: Texas A & M University Press.

Harvard University Faculty of Arts and Sciences, 1945, *Report of the Subcommittee on Language and International Affairs*, November 12.

Henry, C. P., 1999, *Ralph Bunche: Model Negro or American Other?* New York and London: New York University Press.

Lincoln University Herald, 1933-34.

Herskovits, M. J., 1925, 'Americanism', in A. Locke, ed., *The New Negro: An Interpretation*, New York: Albert and Charles Boni.

Herskovits, M. J., 1927, 'Acculturation and the American Negro', *Southwestern Political and Social Science Quarterly*, 8, 211-225.

Herskovits, M. J., 1930, 'The Negro in the New World: the statement of a problem', *American Anthropologist* (New Series) 32 (1): 45-155.

Herskovits, M. J., 1958, *The Myth of the Negro Past*, Boston: Beacon Press.

Herskovits, M. J., 1936, 'The Significance of West Africa for Negro Research', *Journal of Negro History* 21(1): 15-30.

Hill, A. C., 1967, 'African studies programs in the United States', in V. McKay, ed., *Africa in the United States*, New York: Macfadden-Bartell Corp.

Hoare, Q. and G. N. Smith, eds., 1971, *Selections from the Prison Notebooks of Antonio Gramsci*, New York: International Publishers.

Hountoundji, P., 1983, *African Philosophy: Myth and Reality*, Bloomington: Indiana University Press.

Huggins, N. I., 1990, 'Bunche the Africanist', in B. Rivlin, ed., *Ralph Bunche: The Man and His Times*, New York and London: Homes & Meier.

Locke, A., 1925, 'The legacy of the ancestral arts', in A. Locke, ed., *The New Negro: An Interpretation*, New York: Albert and Charles Boni.

Mamdani, M., 1990, 'A glimpse at African studies, made in USA', *CODESRIA Bulletin* (2): 7-10.

Mamdani, M., 1998a, 'Statement to the faculty of social science and humanities, 13 March 1998', in M. Mamdani, M. Hall, N. Hartman, and J. Graaff, eds., *Teaching Africa: The Curriculum Debate at UCT*, Cape Town: University of Cape Town, Centre for African Studies.

Mamdani, M., 1998b, 'Is African studies to be turned into a new home for Bantu Education at UCT? Seminar on the Africa core of the foundation course for the Faculty of Social Sciences and Humanities', in M. Mamdani, M. Hall, N. Hartman, and J. Graaff, eds., *Teaching Africa: The Curriculum Debate at UCT*, Cape Town: University of Cape Town, Centre for African Studies.

Mbembe, A., 1992, 'Provisional notes on the postcolony', *Africa* 62 (1): 3-7.

Mikell, G., 1997, ed., *African Feminism: The Politics of Survival in Sub-Saharan Africa*, Philadelphia: University of Pennsylvania Press.

Monga, Y. D., 2000, 'Dollars and lipstick: the United States through the eyes of African women', *Africa* 70, no.2, 192-208.

Moore, H.L. and M. Vaughn, 1994, *Cutting Down Trees: Gender, Nutrition, and Agricultural Change in the Northern Province of Zambia, 1890-1990*, Portsmouth, NH: Heinemann, London: James Currey, Lusaka: University of Zambia.

Morehouse College, *Annual Catalogue 1933-34*.

Mudimbe, V. Y., 1986, 'African gnosis: philosophy and the order of knowledge', *African Studies Review* 23 (2/3): 149-233.

Mudimbe, V. Y., 1988, *The Invention of Africa: Gnosis, Philosophy, and the Order of Knowledge*, Bloomington and Indianapolis: Indiana University Press.

O'Keefe, M., 1999, 'Emerging Africa: coming to terms with an overlooked continent', *Harvard Magazine* 101 (4) March–April.

Ortner, S. B., 1974, 'Is female to male as nature is to culture?' in M.Z. Rosaldo and L. Lamphere, eds., *Women, Culture and Society*, Palo Alto: Stanford University Press.

Owomoyela, O., 1994, 'With friends like these: a critique of pervasive anti-Africanisms in current African studies epistemology and methodology', *African Studies Review* 37 (3): 77-101.

Patterson, T. R. and R. D. G. Kelley, 2000, 'Unfinished migrations: reflections on the African diaspora and the making of the modern world', *African Studies Review* 43 (1): 11-45.

Richardson, J. M., 1980, *A History of Fisk University, 1865-1964*, Tuscaloosa, AL: University of Alabama Press.

Rivlin, B., ed., 1990, *Ralph Bunche: The Man and His Times*, New York and London: Homes & Meier.

Robertson, C. C., 1984, *Sharing the same bowl? A socioeconomic history of women and class in Accra, Ghana*, Bloomington: Indiana University Press.

Rosaldo, M. Z., 1974, 'Women, culture and society: a theoretical overview', in M.Z. Rosaldo and L. Lamphere, eds., *Women, Culture and Society*, Palo Alto: Stanford University Press.

Rosaldo, M. Z. and L. Lamphere (eds.) *Women, Culture and Society*, Palo Alto: Stanford University Press.

Said, E., 1979, *Orientalism*, New York: Vintage Books.

Sanday, P. R., 1974, 'Female status in the public domain', in M. Z. Rosaldo and L. Lamphere, eds., *Women, Culture and Society*, Palo Alto: Stanford University Press.

Silbey, E., 1995-6, *Social Science Research Council: The First Fifty Years*, Social Science Research Council: Annual Report, 23-70.

Simms Hamilton, R., 1997, 'Toward a conceptualization of modern diasporas: exploring contours of African diaspora social identity formation', in H. E. Schockman, E.-Y. Yu, and K. Songs, eds., *Contemporary Diasporas: A Focus on Asian Pacifics*, University of Southern California Center for Multiethnic and Transnational Studies Occasional Paper Series, Monograph Paper No. 3, Vol. II.

Simms Hamilton, R., ed., forthcoming, *Routes of Passage: Rethinking the African Diaspora*, East Lansing, MI: Michigan State University Press.

Skinner, E. P., 1974, *African Urban Life: The Transformation of Ouagadougou*, Princeton: Princeton University Press.

SSRC Committee on World Regions, 2001, *World Regions in the Social Sciences: Report of a Committee of the Social Science Research Council*. New York: Social Science Research Council

Strobel, M., 1979, *Muslim Women in Mombasa, 1890-1975*, New Haven: Yale University Press.

Tripp, A. M., 2000, *Women and Politics in Uganda*, Oxford: James Currey, Kampala: Fountain Publishers, and Madison: University of Wisconsin Press.

United States Department of State, 1962, *Guidelines for Policy and Operations, Africa*, March, Secret, declassified 5/7/76.

Thompson, R. F., 1983, *Flash of the Spirit: African and Afro-American Art and Philosophy*, New York: Vintage Books.

Wagley, C., 1948, *Area Research and Training: A Conference Report on the Study of World Areas*, No. 6, New York: SSRC, June.

Wallerstein, I., 1974, *The Modern World System: Capitalist Agriculture and the Origins of the European World Economy in the Sixteenth Century*, New York: Academic Press.

Wallerstein, I., 1997, 'The unintended consequences of Cold War area studies', in N. Chomsky et al., *Cold War and the University: Toward an Intellectual History of the Postwar Years*, New York: New Press.

Walters, R., 1993, *PanAfricanism in the African Diaspora: An Analysis of Modern AfroCentric Movements*, Detroit: Wayne State University Press.

Whitaker, Jr., C. S., 1970, *The Politics of Tradition: Continuity and Change in Northern Nigeria 1946-1966*, Princeton: Princeton University Press.

Whitaker, Jr., C. S., 1983, 'Foreword', in P. T. Robinson and E. P. Skinner, eds., *Transformation and Resiliency in Africa*, Washington, DC: Howard University Press.

White, L., 1990, *The Comforts of Home: Prostitution in Colonial Nairobi*, Chicago: University of Chicago Press.

Woodson, C. G., 1936, *The African Background Outlines or Handbook for the Study of the Negro*, Washington, DC: The Association for the Study of Negro Life and History.

Young, M. C., 1976, *The Politics of Cultural Pluralism*, Madison: University of Wisconsin Press.

Zartman, I. W., ed., 1995, *Collapsed States: The Disintegration and Restoration of Legitimate Authority*, Boulder and London: Lynne Rienner Publishers.

Zeleza, P. T., 1993, *A Modern Economic History of Africa, Volume 1: The Nineteenth Century*, Dakar: CODESRIA.

Zeleza, P. T., 1997, *Manufacturing African Studies and Crises*, Dakar: CODESRIA.

Chapter 12

'Returning to the Caribbean by way of Africa': African Studies in the Caribbean in Historical Perspective[1]

Alan Cobley

In the introduction to their edited collection on the state of African studies in the United States at the end of the 1990s, entitled, *Out of One, Many Africas*, William Martin and Michael West (1999) identify three intellectual traditions or paradigms which have shaped the discourse on the study and meaning of Africa. They label these (i) the 'Africanist' paradigm, associated with the emergence of 'African studies' as an academic subject since the 1950s and represented in universities today by a cohort of mainly white Western males of a certain age; (ii) the 'continental' para-digm, associated with a body of scholarship investigating the African condition gen-erated by postcolonial African academics from universities in Africa; and (iii) the 'transcontinental' paradigm, the oldest of the three since it emerged as a 'defense of the African past' in the black Atlantic world during the nineteenth century, which is 'spearheaded' by Africans of the diaspora. According to their reading of the current situation in the United States, the 'Africanist' paradigm has fallen on hard times due to the declining strategic interest in Africa at national, governmental and interna-tional levels since 1990. This has been accompanied by a dramatic shrinkage in available research funding for Africanist scholars and cutbacks in African studies programmes throughout the country. Similarly, the 'continental' tradition, which had sought to combat the 'hubris and racial arrogance of Africanist scholars' in the 1960s and 1970s, has struggled since that time in the face of crippling economic constraints on the African continent associated with structural adjustment, including low pay and inadequate or neglected infrastructure for research. Alone among the three paradigms, the 'transcontinental' tradition, having progressed from its earliest 'vindicationist' phase up to the middle of the twentieth century, and having survived the condescension and neglect of the ascendent Africanist academy in the 1970s and 1980s, re-emerged with renewed vigour in the 1990s, on the back of an 'African cultural renaissance' among people of African descent. Ultimately, Martin and West (1999: 30-31) suggest it is the popular interest and energy surrounding this last development that is likely to sustain, renew and redirect African studies as a project in the United States for the immediate future; for good measure they also suggest that this future must include a re-connection between African studies as practised and understood in Africa and its diaspora.

By contrast with this struggle for the soul of African studies to the North, in the Caribbean islands and many of the surrounding territories, where people of African descent have formed a decided majority since the eighteenth century, African studies could never have developed except as a part of a visceral movement to reconnect with the African motherland. Similarly, at an ideological level, African Studies in the Caribbean was born in the conceptual space identified by Paul Gilroy (1995) as 'the Black Atlantic'. This 'transcontinental' tradition, as Martin and West call it, was the progenitor of a local 'Africanist' tradition, because it valorised African studies and forced an entry for it into the academy within the region. Uniquely, however, this was a radicalised version of the 'Africanist' tradition in which the practitioners were predominantly scholar-activists who recognized the implications of their work for the communities they served and who sought to promote political action in those communities based on their conclusions. This article will seek to trace these developments.

The African Connection

The history of the transatlantic trade which brought millions of Africans to the Americas as slaves is deeply grained in the identity of Caribbean people. It represents the second great holocaust to have shaped Caribbean culture and historical memory after the genocidal war waged against the indigenous Amerindian population by the early waves of European settlers. Estimates by historians of the number of Africans ripped from their homes to feed the voracious appetite of the transatlantic slave trade over more than three and a half centuries range from ten million to over a hundred million souls. The calculations are complicated by the huge numbers of people who are believed to have died en-route to a life of slavery in the Americas: many were killed resisting enslavement or perished in the forced marches to the coast; still others succumbed to ill-treatment, hunger and disease in the 'slave factories' on the African coast while waiting to be transported, or died as a result of the horrors of the 'Middle Passage' in the crammed holds of slave ships. The ill-usage, hunger and unremitting toil which characterised plantation slavery throughout the Americas ensured that mortality rates among African slaves were always extremely high, so that there was a constant demand for fresh supplies (Klein 1999: 166-167). Based on figures compiled by Philip Curtin and David Eltis, Herbert Klein suggests that at least ten million African slaves were landed in the Americas in the period up to the 1860s. Of these at least four million were landed in ports in the Caribbean.[2]

Table 1: Estimates of African Slave Arrivals in the Caribbean by Region 1500–1870

British West Indies	French West Indies	Dutch West Indies	Danish West Indies	Spanish America*
1,635,700	1,699,700	437,700	47,400	1,662,400

* Includes Spanish West Indies, Central and South America.
Source: Klein 1999, Appendix, Table A-2.

A broad, non-specific, popular 'Afro-centric' consciousness was one of the most enduring, if unanticipated, and—from a European point of view—unwelcome, legacies of the transatlantic slave trade in the Caribbean. Despite the best efforts of generations of slave masters, overseers, missionaries, white settlers and colonial officials, myriad traces of African influence remain in societies and cultures across the region, although often they are present in distinctive, creolised forms. This is not merely a reflection of the fact that people of African descent today constitute the majority in many of the islands and territories of the region.[3] It is also a testimony to the enduring struggle of enslaved Africans across centuries to preserve their heritage and foster an identity in ways which rejected the hegemonic power of those western values, practices, and belief systems that were embedded in the European-controlled societies of the colonial Caribbean.[4]

Among these African influences are examples of religious belief and practice, ranging from the *Vodún* and *Shango* cults in Haiti, and *Santería* in Cuba, which appear to have survived in almost pure form since being imported to the region from West Africa four hundred years ago, to syncretic Christian sects such as the Spiritual Baptists in Trinidad and *Pukamina* in Jamaica, or, for that matter, the forms of worship in black Pentecostal churches almost everywhere. Hand in hand with aspects of African religion goes the survival of African patterns of thought, represented in the modern Caribbean in attitudes to life, and death, nature, the environment and the spirit world, or more concretely, parcelled up and passed on in proverbs. Traces of African epistemology and cultural practices are also present in many Caribbean societies through the continuing appeal to folk medicine or '*obeah*' when Western medicine fails, or is so expensive as to be out of reach of the common folk. Similarly, a whole basket of Caribbean musical genres, from *kaiso*, *zouk*, and salsa to reggae and dance hall, reflect both continuities and productive re-engagements with African roots. Perhaps most pervasive of all is the influence of African languages on the rhythms of Caribbean speech at the structural level of syntax and grammar, as well as more obviously in the retention of African words in the Caribbean lexicon or the transliteration of African metaphors and phrases.[5]

Against this background, it is not surprising to find that aspirations to return to the African continent were often voiced during the course of slave revolts, or that a few (albeit mostly unsuccessful) physical attempts were made to achieve this. Where this return was not achieved in life, some hope to achieve it in death: archaeologists excavating slave cemeteries, such as that found at Newton Plantation, Barbados, suggest that burials were aligned so that the head of the deceased faced eastwards, pointing back across the Atlantic whence they had come. Occasionally this popular 'Afro-centric' consciousness bubbled to the surface even after the ending of slavery in the Caribbean; when King JaJa of Opobo (in modern Nigeria) was exiled to the eastern Caribbean at the end of the nineteenth century, his presence sparked a popular sensation and public demonstrations among people of African descent in Grenada, St. Vincent and Barbados. The legend of his sojourn in the Caribbean endures in a popular folk song (Cox 1998).

With the growing popular interest in issues of identity in the West over the last 25 years, it is not surprising that many people of African descent in the modern Americas are anxious to know more about their African heritage. This impulse was part of the reason for the African cultural renaissance in the United States noted by Martin and West. A similar impulse has focussed popular interest in Africa among Caribbean people of African descent. Unfortunately, historians are rarely able to supply precise information on the origins of individual families or particular populations of African descent because it was in the nature of the slave trade that each human cargo shipped to the Americas could be drawn from a wide mixture of sources. In any case, such records as do exist on the sources of slave cargoes are both inaccurate and incomplete. When these practical problems are combined with the effects of the systematic efforts of the slave owners to strip African slaves of their culture, as well as to dehumanise them in other ways, the problem of defining origins becomes peculiarly intractable. It is against this background that the emergence of a generalised concept of shared African identity among the populations of African descent in the Caribbean must be understood.

In the Caribbean, then, the 'transcontinental' tradition identified by Martin and West is, in the first instance, not an intellectual movement but a popular, organic tradition in which significant African-derived populations have engaged continuously and creatively with their African heritage.

'The Black Atlantic' and the Intellectual Origins of African Studies in the Caribbean

From the eighteenth century onwards a handful of the millions of Africans who had been caught up in the Transatlantic slave trade and transported to the Americas began to set down their experiences of enslavement, and of the African societies they had left behind. The writings of this new, westernised black intellectual elite mirrored and articulated the continuing popular sense of connection with Africa among African peoples of the diaspora, whilst, at the same time, contributing to the growing political and philosophical debate on, and the campaign against, the institution of slavery in the western world. Works by individuals such as James Albert Ukawsaw Gronniosaw, Ignatius Sancho, Ottobah Cugoano and Olaudah Equiano were among the first to attempt to present the western world with a view of the African continent and its peoples that was not motivated by racial prejudice, avarice, or Christian evangelical fervour, and that did not pander to assumptions of Western cultural superiority.

Olaudah Equiano, who spent his youth and early manhood years working as a slave within the plantation system encompassing the Caribbean islands and the Southern United States, devoted the first chapter of his autobiography to a description of his home in West Africa, from which he had been taken as a child. In explaining his reasons for doing so, he articulated the yearnings of generations of enslaved Africans in enforced exile in the West:

> I hope the reader will not think I have trespassed on his patience in introducing myself with some account of the manner and customs of my country. They had been implanted in me with great care, and made an impression on my mind, which time could not erase, and which all the adversity and variety of fortune I have since experienced served only to rivet and record; for, whether the love of one's country be real or imaginary, or a lesson of reason, or an instinct of nature, I still look back with pleasure on the first scenes of my life, though that pleasure has been for the most part mingled with sorrow (Edwards 1989: 15).

Thus the origins of the modern discipline of African studies can be said to lie in the black Atlantic world, in Africa remembered by its enslaved children, and in the subsequent engagement of black intellectuals with modernity in the West as they struggled to give meaning to concepts of the Enlightenment such as justice, freedom, and equality in the second half of the eighteenth century. From that time on, generation upon generation of Caribbean intellectuals of African descent have played a key role in developing not only a scholarly understanding of African cultures, societies, and history but also a politicised consciousness of the African continent and its peoples, both within the Caribbean basin and in the wider framework of the Western world. As a result, there was never a point in the Caribbean where the twin aims of scholarship on Africa and advocacy for Africa decisively diverged.

In the hundred years from the mid-nineteenth century up to the mid-twentieth century numerous African-Caribbean intellectuals contributed to this emerging tradition. They included, to name some of the more prominent examples, Edward Wilmot Blyden (Danish West Indies), Henry Sylvester Williams (Trinidad), Marcus Garvey (Jamaica), C. L. R. James (Trinidad), George Padmore (Trinidad), Frantz Fanon (Martinique), and Aimé Césaire (Martinique). The themes of black identity, culture, and identification with the African 'motherland', as well as the strategic question of promoting political mobilisation in defence of Africa, were central to the work of all these figures, although their approaches often varied widely (Fanon, for example, became deeply committed to the violent anti-colonial struggle in Algeria and dismissed what he saw as the deradicalising 'nativism' of the 'Negritude' movement espoused by his compatriot Césaire).[6] Pan-Africanism as an organised political movement also owes much to this African-Caribbean intellectual tradition. It was the Trinidadian lawyer Henry Sylvester Williams who founded and acted as Secretary of the first ever Pan-African Congress held in London in 1900, while the Jamaican Marcus Garvey founded the Universal Negro Improvement Association and African Communities League in 1914 as a vehicle for his message of 'Africa for the Africans' and black self-improvement. Garvey's copious writings in the columns of his newspaper *The Negro World* were particularly important in valorising and popularising discussion of African history, culture, and politics among people of African descent, and among rising westernised African elites in colonial Africa itself.[7]

The lives of Williams and Garvey, like that of James, Fanon and others, exemplify another important contribution made by African-Caribbean intellectuals to debates on Africa during the first half of the twentieth century. They carried new and challenging perspectives on colonial Africa and the African diasporic condition to the metropoles as part of the increasingly important wave of African-Caribbean migration to North America and Western Europe.[8] In London and Paris in particular, black West Indian and West African nationalist elites formed a vibrant intellectual community during the 1930s and 1940s. They studied each other's societies, compared perspectives and traded analyses on the nature of colonial rule, a process which sowed the seeds for an effective ideological challenge to colonialism on both sides of the Atlantic. The vehicles for this discourse were many and varied, including meetings, debates, newspaper articles, small-circulation journals, and even letters, yet together they constituted a devastating critique of contemporary colonial societies in Africa and the Caribbean. There was no parallel for it in the formal academic sphere, where African societies were still viewed largely as a collection of anthropological curiosities, and in which the Caribbean featured hardly at all.

Flowing from this fertile season of intellectual interaction in the metropoles, and anticipating the call made by Martin and West for a reunification of African continental and transcontinental traditions by half a century, a generation of African-Caribbean intellectuals including Frantz Fanon, C.L.R. James, Ras Makonnen and Arthur Lewis would put themselves and their professional skills at the disposal of various African nations that were engaged in the painful transition to independence during the 1950s and 1960s. In the process they sought to broker a new understanding of, and a new relationship between, Africa and the West. This ranged from Fanon's (1967) shocking and profound discussion of the psychology of the colonial condition, and particularly the role of racism in producing what he described as 'the depersonalised self', to Lewis's (1939; 1950; Lewis et al. 1951) seminal contributions on the economic aftermath of empire and the problems of development planning.

W. Arthur Lewis is an outstanding example of a West Indian scholar-activist of African descent during these years who combined his scholarship with advocacy for, and engagement with, Africa. A winner of the Nobel Prize for his contributions to economics, who was also knighted, his many publications on aspects of development planning included the classic pamphlet *The Industrialisation of the British West Indies* (1950), which introduced the concept of 'industrialisation by invitation', and a short pioneering historical study of labour organisation in the West Indies entitled *Labour in the West Indies: The Birth of a Workers' Movement* (1939).[9] A close friend and ally of many in the independence generation of African leaders, in March 1950 he resigned from the Colonial Economic Development Council in London in protest at the British Government's treatment of Seretse Khama, who had been deposed as chief of the Bangwato (a people in the British Protectorate of Bechuanaland) in the wake of a commission of enquiry into Khama's marriage to a white woman. Lewis explained his position in a letter to the Manchester *Guardian*: 'I consider the Socialist Government's action... to be dishonest in suppressing the report; cowardly in surrendering to South African policies which are certain to cause the disintegration of the Empire; and insulting to the 400 million coloured subjects of the Empire' (quoted in Hyam and Henshaw 2003: 183). The following year, he articulated his concerns about the future of Africa in a book he co-authored with Michael Scott, Martin Wight and Colin Legum, *Attitude to Africa* (1951), which was described as 'a survey of the main problems of British Africa, suggesting the lines of policy that any British government should follow in the years ahead.'. Over a decade later, he wrote about his time spent in Ghana as Chief Economic Advisor to Kwame Nkrumah in *Politics in West Africa* (1965).

African Studies as an Academic Discipline in the Caribbean

Despite these powerful organic intellectual traditions—or perhaps because of them—the inauguration of African studies as a formal academic discipline in the West Indies had to await the era of decolonisation. Prior to this time, such provision as was made for higher education in the Caribbean had been for the purpose of propagating empire. The first foundations for higher learning in the Hispanic and Anglophone Caribbean had been concerned with training clergy to minister to the growing communities of European settlers and Christianised slaves; it was only in the twentieth century, in the period between the two World Wars, that the establishment of institutions for the training of local elites to fill positions as teachers, civil servants, and other white collar professionals in the colonies was considered for the first time (Cobley 2000).

However, one academic work stands out in the period prior to the Second World War as an attempt to bring an 'African studies' perspective to the study of the colonial Caribbean. *Warning From the West Indies: A Tract for the Empire* (1938) by the South African social scientist W. M. MacMillan was, in effect, a comparative study of conditions in the colonial Caribbean and colonial Africa. MacMillan's message was that the failure to address critical development needs had caused widespread economic stagnation and social decay in the Caribbean, and that an imminent political crisis could only be averted if urgent remedial action was undertaken. The perilous conditions in the British West Indies were a warning of what might follow in British Africa if similar problems there were not addressed. His thesis caused something of a sensation in the British Colonial Office when an outbreak of riots in the West Indies shortly after the book was published appeared to bear out his thesis. Discussion of this work formed part of the background to the passage of the Colonial Development and Welfare Act in 1940.

Immediately after the Second World War, resources from the Colonial Development and Welfare Fund were used to assist in the establishment of the University College of the West Indies (UCWI) in Jamaica, which was opened in 1948. It was one of several University Colleges established in the colonies around the same time following the recommendations contained in the Report of the Asquith Commission in 1944. The others were all in Africa.[10] Initially the curriculum for the UCWI was devised in England, and it awarded degrees accredited by the University of London. There was little room for discussion of Africa in the early days, and little interest in doing so on the part of a mainly British academic staff. However, within months of gaining its own charter as a degree-awarding institution in 1962, finally breaking the colonial link with Britain, steps were being taken at the renamed University of the West Indies (UWI) to develop local expertise in African History. It was no surprise that this development occurred under the leadership of Sir Arthur Lewis, who had been recalled from Nkrumah's Ghana to serve as the new University's first Vice Chancellor. Just a year later, in 1963, a brilliant young Guyanese graduate of the University of the West Indies named Walter Rodney was sent from the Mona campus in Jamaica to study for a doctorate in African history at the School for Oriental and African Studies (SOAS) in London. While at SOAS he completed a doctorate entitled 'A History of the Upper Guinea Coast 1545-1800', supervised by Richard Gray.[11] After gaining his doctorate in 1966 Rodney's first teaching job was a temporary post at the University College of Dar es Salaam. In his letter of application to Professor Terence Ranger, then Head of Department at Dar es Salaam, Rodney explained his plans: 'My main commitment is to the University of the West Indies, to which I will return in October 1967 to help start a programme in West African Studies. My interest therefore is in a temporary post...' (quoted in Lewis 1998: 43-44).[12] As he told members of the Institute of the Black World several years later: 'I understood it to be my role to return to the University of the West Indies to teach African history and to relate to our people on the African question. Specifically, I was returning to the Caribbean by way of Africa. This is how I always saw it' (quoted in Hill 1990: 33).

In his letter to Ranger, Rodney also included a description of the history programme which he had passed through in Jamaica. This gives an interesting picture of the place occupied by Africa in the curriculum at that time:

> The History courses ... were based on the general pattern of the University of London. There were nine final papers, to be written after three years. Two of these were in English History between 1487 and 1945, and there was a similar arrangement for European History. The West Indies and the Americas accounted for two further courses of the usual kind. 'Reconstruction' after the Civil War in the USA was the special topic which introduced the use of source materials, and this comprised two

papers. Finally, there was a translation paper, involving two languages. The course in New World history occasioned a very marginal interest in West Africa, so that I have done most of my reading in that subject since my arrival at the School of Oriental and African Studies in October 1963 ... (quoted in Lewis 1998)[13]

Having completed a year teaching at Dar es Salaam, Rodney duly returned to Jamaica to take up a post at UWI in October 1967. At the same time as he began to develop an academic programme in African history, he also began speaking regularly at public events hosted by members of the Rastafarian community (then in a ferment after the visit of Haile Selassie to Jamaica in April 1966) and a variety of other black consciousness groups. He also gave a series of lectures on Black Power to members of the Student's Union on the Mona Campus.[14] Given the long intellectual tradition of the 'Black Atlantic' of which he was part, it was almost inevitable that Rodney's training as an Africanist should launch him directly into the debates about black identity then raging in Jamaica.

However, the politically conservative Jamaican Government became alarmed by the spectre of a radical 'Black Power' movement on its doorstep; in October 1968 it took the opportunity of Rodney's attendance at a Black Writers' Conference in Montreal to bar his re-entry. The move led to riots in Jamaica. After this rebuff, Rodney returned to Dar es Salaam, where he stayed until 1974. During this period he published his most famous work, *How Europe Underdeveloped Africa* (1972). His decision to return to the Caribbean in 1974 was prompted by an offer of a job as Professor of African History at the University of Guyana. When he arrived in Guyana, however, he found that his appointment had been blocked by the authoritarian Forbes Burnham regime. Nevertheless, Rodney felt compelled to stay on in Guyana to work as a member of the radical opposition to Burnham. He was assassinated by a car bomb in Georgetown, Guyana in 1980.[15] Some years after his death, a proposal was made in 1988 to establish a Research Institute in African, Asian, Caribbean and Related Studies at the University of Guyana, but this never left the drawing board due to lack of funding. Nevertheless, courses in African history and literature have been offered as part of the curriculum there on a regular basis since the early 1970s.[16]

Meanwhile, African Studies had developed apace in the West Indies. In 1965 Rodney was followed from UWI to SOAS by two other young Guyanese graduates, Alvin Thompson and Winston McGowan. Both returned to the Caribbean to take up teaching posts at the University of Guyana (in 1969 and 1970 respectively). While McGowan remained in Guyana, Thompson moved to the Cave Hill Campus of the UWI in Barbados in 1972. He was largely responsible for the development of an undergraduate programme in African history there.[17] By 1990 the History Department at Cave Hill included three members with expertise in African History out of a total membership of eight, including Richard Goodridge, a Barbadian who was sent by the department to complete his doctorate in West African History at the University of Ibadan in Nigeria. In 2000 the History Department at Cave Hill offered a taught Masters in history with a specialisation in African History for the first time.

The controversy which had surrounded Rodney and the development of African studies in Jamaica was echoed in Trinidad when efforts were made to introduce an African studies programme at the UWI's St. Augustine Campus. The pioneer at St Augustine was the Grenadian-born historian Fitzroy Baptiste, who arrived in Trinidad in October 1968, at the height of student demonstrations to protest Rodney's exclusion from Jamaica, to become the first staff member of the Institute of African and Asian Studies. The Institute had been formally established by UWI in 1963 as the brainchild of Dr Eric Williams, the Prime Minister of Trinidad and Tobago. Williams hoped that it would foster a spirit of mutual respect among the people of his newly independent country, the population of which was almost evenly split between people of African and Asian descent.[18] However, in 1970 a 'Black Power Uprising' in Trinidad coincided with a mutiny by members of the Trinidad and Tobago Regiment. In the ensuing State of Emergency, several UWI academics were detained or subjected to harassment, including Baptiste. In the aftermath of these events, according to Baptiste, Williams and his party, The People's National Movement (PNM), 'had a concern lest the search for identity by the African and Asian components in newly independent Trinidad and Tobago might end up in what [Williams] termed "Mother Africa" and "Mother India" and, thereby, detract from the goal of nation-building'.[19] Against this background, Williams established an Education Commission to review the schools curriculum in Trinidad and Tobago, and especially to advise on the future role of 'Afro-Asian Studies'. The Valdez Commission recommended the inclusion of 'Afro-Asian Studies' in the curriculum for both Junior and Senior Secondary Schools; however, it specified that the overall aim should be 'to use Afro-Asian Studies and cultural forms to foster an appreciation for our national unity and not to produce divisions'.[20] In these circumstances, the teaching of African and Asian Studies at St. Augustine was left in a politically ambiguous position and was starved of resources by both the university and the government for much of the next two decades. Eventually, the Institute was dissolved in the early 1990s, with the history courses being subsumed into the History Department and other aspects of the programme being taken over by other departments. After this disaggregation, the 'Asian' component fared somewhat better than the 'African' component because the local Indian community and the Government of India provided funds for both a Visiting Professor of Indian Studies and a lectureship in Hindi at St. Augustine. No similar resources were forthcoming for African studies. Nevertheless, a range of courses in African and Asian studies are still offered regularly at St. Augustine, and an undergraduate Major combining the two areas remains on the books.

One means by which African Studies has been sustained at UWI has been through the recruitment of a steady trickle of African scholars to teach African specialities within the framework of other disciplinary majors. This trend began in the 1970s and has been continued up to the present. At the time of writing African scholars are teaching on all three of UWI's campuses in disciplines as diverse as history, literature, philosophy, French, education, economics and law.

Interest in and study of aspects of African history and society grew in parallel with a burgeoning academic interest in African survivals in Caribbean culture during these years. Studies which arose out of this interest included work on African linguistic survivals and religious practices in the Caribbean, as well as African influences on the creative and performing arts, such as Calypso music, poetry and dance. Among the central figures in these developments were Edward Kamau Brathwaite, Mervyn Alleyne, Maureen Warner Lewis, and Rex Nettleford.[21] A key early vehicle for such work was the African Studies Association of the West Indies, formed in Jamaica in 1967 (Walter Rodney served briefly as its treasurer). The Association had a somewhat chequered existence, but it published eight issues of its own *Bulletin* between December 1967 and December 1976. The *Bulletin* was reborn as the *Caribbean Journal of African Studies* in 1978, but only one issue appears to have been published.[22] A lasting legacy of these efforts was the introduction of a variety of courses in African Studies on all three of UWI's campuses. By the late 1990s they ranged from courses in African literature and film to courses in African philosophy. Also, an important research project begun at UWI during the 1970s, which sought to incorporate work on African-Caribbean connections, was the Caribbean Lexicography Project established at Cave Hill under the direction of Richard Allsopp.[23] Elsewhere, in 1978 the University of Guyana, through its Extra-Mural Department, became the first in the region to offer a course in Yoruba.[24]

The creation of the Caribbean Examinations Council in the West Indies in 1974 was an important development in the continuing process to decolonise the lower levels of the education system in the Anglophone Caribbean. Its mandate was to devise and administer a system of examinations for secondary schools to replace the British system of 'O' levels; this led to the introduction of a 'Caribbeanised' history syllabus in 1978 in which pride of place was given to West Indian history. The section on 'Sugar and Slaves' included a discussion, albeit limited, of West African history and culture (Rouse-Jones 1986: 1). From this time onwards African studies has gained an increasing foothold in schools in the West Indies as the number of teachers who are UWI graduates, and who have taken courses with African content as part of their undergraduate programme, has steadily increased. Since the 1980s UWI History Departments in Jamaica and Barbados have encouraged the growth of African studies in schools by mounting a series of African History Workshops. These are intended to be a form of in-service training for teachers, and are designed to provide both materials and advice on teaching aspects of African heritage in schools. Most recently, the CXC has begun to introduce a new 'Caribbean Advanced Proficiency Examination' (CAPE) in a variety of disciplines to replace the British 'Advanced Level' examinations used for matriculation purposes. In the units on Caribbean History and Caribbean Civilisation, discussion of the role of Africa is considerably expanded.

African Studies in the Non-Anglophone Caribbean

It might have been expected that Cuba, with its history of extensive direct linkages with African states since the Revolution in 1959, would have seen extensive development of African studies over the same period. It is worth pointing out, however, that Cuban interchange with African states since the 1960s has owed much more to a search by Castro for international allies and trading partners than to any obvious Afro-centric sentiment on the part of the Castro regime, despite the fact that over half of Cuba's population is of African descent, and, as Castro himself once put it, 'the blood of Africa runs deep in our veins'.[25] In fact, initially research into Cuba's African heritage and connections was positively discouraged by the Castro regime because this was thought to conflict with efforts to build a new, post-revolutionary Cuban national identity. This harked back to an earlier period in Cuban history, exemplified by Jose Marti, in which the allegedly deracinated nature of Iberian slavery and colonialism had left a legacy throughout the Hispanic Caribbean and Latin America in the form of non-racialised national identities.[26] According to exiled Afro-Cuban scholar Carlos Moore, Afro-Cuban intellectuals who investigated aspects of Cuba's African heritage during the 1960s and 1970s (such as the extensive nature of syncretic Afro-Cuban religions in Cuba) were treated as political dissidents because their work almost inevitably lead to assertions that the Revolution had failed to tackle the issue of racism in Cuban society (Moore 1988, especially Chapter 19). Notwithstanding these difficulties a Centre for African and Middle Eastern Studies (CEAMO) was established in Havana in 1979, and began publishing its own journal, *Revista de Africa y Medio Oriente (RAMO)* in Spanish and English in 1983. The presence of hundreds of African students from Angola in Cuba during the 1980s, a by-product of Cuba's heavy military involvement in that country between 1975 and 1988, played a part in promoting these developments. They were followed by the founding of the *Casa de Africa* in old Havana in 1986 to house the research collection of Fernando Ortiz, the 'father' of anthropology in Cuba (he is credited with coining the phrase 'Afrocubano'), as well as to display the collection of gifts presented by African heads of state and other African personalities to Fidel Castro. More recently there have been attempts to institutionalise African studies at different levels in Cuba's education system, although this development still appears to be in its early stages.[27] However, one unfortunate effect of Cuba's isolation and resulting economic crisis during the 1990s was an apparent resurgence of racism and a 'polarization of ... thinking on the race question' (Sarduy and Stubbs 2000: 6), resulting in renewed resistance to the study of Cuba's African heritage as a discrete subject.

A similar sensitivity on matters of race, and resultant neglect of Africa as an appropriate subject for academic study is still evident in other parts of the Hispanic Caribbean, including Puerto Rico, the Dominican Republic, and Venezuela. In each of these societies large black populations are characterised by poverty, social marginalisation, and a relative lack of empowerment in both politics and the academy. As David Howard (2001:1-2) explains in the introduction to his recent study of race and ethnicity in the Dominican Republic:

> Dominican nationalism has been colored by a pervasive racism, centered on a rejection of African ancestry and blackness. This exclusion of an African past and the manipulation of a European colonial legacy and indigenous heritage underpin the current analysis of Dominican society. *Négitude* is associated with the Haitian population [the Dominican Republic's impoverished neighbor]. *Dominicanidad*, on the other hand, represents a celebration of whiteness, Hispanic heritage and Catholicism.

Elsewhere, in the Francophone Caribbean, the same relative underdevelopment of African Studies is evident. Currently, for example, there are no courses in African history offered at the Université des Antilles et de la Guyane in Martinique, although, as might be expected, the discourse on *créôlité* is well-established and extensive. As in the Hispanic Caribbean, it may be that the dominant discourses on French cultural identity, reinforced by the administrative status of the French Caribbean territories since 1946 as 'departments d'outre mer' of metropolitan France, have muted more direct interest in African studies there.

Conclusion: The Anti-Apartheid Struggle and After

While the battle over the form and relevance of African studies continued within the education system in the Anglophone Caribbean during the 1970s and 1980s, popular sentiment on African issues focussed primarily on the dramatic struggle against apartheid in South Africa. West Indians were drawn directly into this issue by the international controversy over sanctions, especially within the British Commonwealth, and by the question of a cricketing boycott of South Africa. Radical Pan-Africanists throughout the West Indies rallied around calls for a boycott, and waged a vocal campaign in support of sanctions. As a spin-off from this campaign, renewed efforts were made to educate the public in the Caribbean about the region's African heritage, and to promote a sense of connection with the African continent. These efforts ranged from lecture series and workshops to cultural events; at UWI, courses on South African history were also added to the curriculum. In Cuba, as already noted, direct military intervention as well as other aid to support the Marxist MPLA Government against UNITA, the South African-backed rebel group, drew that Caribbean nation into a much closer relationship with the African continent than had seemed possible a decade before.

Since the early 1990s, after the end of the apartheid era, interest in Africa has been sustained in the Caribbean through continuing campaigns by people of African descent to bolster a sense of African identity and to promote African advancement in the face of a global environment perceived to be hostile to these goals. In Barbados, for example, the government has established a Commission on Pan African Affairs, with a brief to develop practical links with the African continent and educate the Barbadian public about its African heritage. These continuing efforts at consciousness-raising have ensured that African studies options and options concerning aspects of the African heritage of Caribbean people remain popular among the region's students.

Perhaps the most enduring effect of the 'transcontinental tradition' of African studies (both organic and intellectual) on academic discourse in the Caribbean over the past forty years has been the fact that it is now widely accepted, not only at the academic but also at the popular level in Caribbean society, that an interest in, and the study of, aspects of African culture must be embedded in any credible programme of Caribbean studies. This was not generally so in the 1960s or 1970s. This means that the study of Caribbean literature or Caribbean linguistics today, for example, can scarcely proceed without reference to African influences. The result is that it is becoming increasingly difficult to identify a clear dividing line between African and Caribbean studies. This convergence is reflected in a growing interest among Caribbean scholars in emerging new disciplinary formations such as Diaspora Studies and Caribbean Cultural Studies.

When independence came to the Caribbean in the 1960s, key issues of consciousness and identity among Caribbean people remained unresolved. One of these questions concerned the significance and continuing relevance of the African heritage to Caribbean people. As this discussion has shown this question has yet to be fully confronted in many societies in the region, often due to concern that to do so might provoke a racialised political debate that would threaten the fragile 'non-racial' consensus embodied in many postcolonial national identities across the Caribbean. It is against this background that the sometimes agonised debates surrounding the educational role of African studies in the Caribbean over the past forty years should be seen. Yet a substantial population of African descent in the Caribbean region continue to feel themselves under-represented in the discourses on identity and continue to press for the valorisation of the African connection. Looking to the future, and in the current globalised context, it is apparent that new approaches, as well as renewed commitment, are required if the continuing interest among Caribbean people in the study of Africa is to be developed in the academy in meaningful and productive ways.[28]

Notes

1. Some of the material for this chapter has been drawn from an earlier paper published by the author (Cobley 2001).
2. Extensive data on the Transatlantic Slave Trade from various African ports to Caribbean destinations can be found in Eltis et al., (1999), or in an on-line data archive, 'Slave Movement During the Eighteenth and Nineteenth Centuries' at the following address: http:/dpls.dacc.wisc.edu/slavedata/index.
3. It should be noted however that in recent years the descendants of Africans have been overtaken as the majority population in Trinidad and Guyana (on the South American mainland) by the descendants of people from the Indian sub-continent. They have also

inter-mingled in some places with significant populations of Amerindian, European (especially Hispanic) and Chinese origin.

4. On various aspects of slave resistance see Beckles and Shepherd (1999).

5. Many aspects of African culture, including religious beliefs and practices and musical and dance styles are evident in popular festivals that occur in many parts of the Caribbean. See for example Berttelheim (2001). On African influences in Caribbean English see Richard Allsopp's (1996) 'Introduction' to his ground-breaking *Dictionary of Caribbean English Usage*, esp. pp. xxxi-xxxiii; for Richard Allsopp's early work on the same subject, dating back to the 1940s, see Allsopp (2002).

6. Garvey's writings were collected in two volumes edited by his wife Amy Jacques-Garvey (1986). Padmore wrote extensively on Africa in his capacity as editor of the Communist newspaper, *Negro Worker*, in the 1920s and early 1930s; he also published a book in the aftermath of the Italian defeat of Abyssinia entitled: *Africa and World Peace* (1937). 'Africanist' works by C. L. R. James include: *A History of Negro Revolt* (1969), first published 1938; and *Nkrumah and the Ghana Revolution* (1977). The contrasting views of Fanon and Césaire can be gleaned from Frantz Fanon (1965), *The Wretched of the Earth* and *Studies in a Dying Colonialism*; Aimé Césaire (1972), *Discourse on Colonialism*.

7. On the influence of Garvey's movement see Martin (1986).

8. On Afro-Caribbean intellectuals in the United States see James (1998).

9. Lewis (1939; 1950); with Michael Scott, Martin Wight and Colin Legum (1951).

10. The 'Asquith Colleges' have been described by John Hargreaves as 'Colonial universities'. They were established after the Second World War with sponsorship from the (British) Colonial Development and Welfare Fund to provide training for the rising indigenous elites in various parts of the empire. All of the others were in Africa: Khartoum University College (1947), the University College of Ibadan (1948), Makerere University College (1949), and the University College of Ghana, Legon (1948).

11. It was published as Rodney (1970).

12. W. Rodney to T. O. Ranger 30.11.65.

13. W. Rodney to T. O. Ranger 30.11.65.

14. Many of Rodney's talks from this time were published in *The Groundings with My Brothers* (1969).

15. A brief biographical note is included in Hill (1990).

16. The scheme is set out in Fierce (1991), Appendix C. Fierce also notes that some African history was taught at the College of the Virgin Islands during the late 1970s (Appendix E).

17. Aside from his teaching and research, Professor Thompson expressed his Africanist consciousness in the naming of his children. His son, Obadele Thompson (named for the ancient kings of West Africa) is a world-class sprinter who won a bronze medal for Barbados at the Sydney Olympics.

18. Williams was himself a noted historian. His most influential work remains *Capitalism and Slavery* (1964).

19. Comments by Fitzroy Baptiste in a public lecture delivered in Barbados in March 1998, Baptiste (2004).

20. The Valdez Commission on Secondary Education in Trinidad and Tobago, quoted in Baptiste (2004).

21. See, for example, Alleyne (1988); Warner-Lewis (1995, 2003); Braithwaite (1970; 1971); Nettleford (1970).
22. Copies of the *Bulletin* and of the *Journal* can be found in the Library at the University of the West Indies, Mona Campus in Jamaica.
23. The major products of this project to date are Richard Allsopp's (1996) *Dictionary of Caribbean English Usage*, and Jeannette Allsopp (2003), *The Caribbean Multilingual Dictionary of Flora, Fauna and Foods in English, French, French Creole and Spanish*.
24. Unfortunately this experiment was short-lived; for resource reasons the course was discontinued in 1982: Rouse-Jones (1986: 2-3). There have been occasional attempts to develop African language courses elsewhere in the Caribbean since that time; however none of these efforts appear to have endured for long.
25. See Díaz-Briquets (1989); Sarduy and Stubbs (2000: 1).
26. Sarduy and Stubbs (2000: 16): 'Iberians, it is claimed, instituted a more benign form of slavery than did northern Europeans because of the strong Moorish influences on, and the nature of feudalism in, the Iberian Peninsula.' Similar claims were made by the Portuguese in the colonial era, who elevated it to a justifying ideology for Portuguese colonial rule, known as 'lusotropicalism'. This idea is still invoked by Brazilian politicians to explain the alleged lack of racism in modern Brazilian society: see Bender (1978), Part One.
27. See for example the proposal made on 'Afro-CubaWeb' for the establishment of a 'Department of Afro-Cuban Studies' at the University of Matanzas: http://afrocubaweb.com/mtzsu.htm
28. One such approach is proposed in (Cobley 2001).

References

Alleyne, M., 1988, *Roots of Jamaican Culture*, London: Pluto Press.

Allsopp, J., 2003, *The Caribbean Multilingual Dictionary of Flora, Fauna and Foods in English, French, French Creole and Spanish*, Kingston, Jamaica: Arawak Publications.

Allsopp, R., 1996, 'Introduction', in *Dictionary of Caribbean English Usage*, Oxford: Oxford University Press.

Allsopp, R., 2002, *Guyana Talk: Early Essays in the Study of a Caribbean Creole*, Pamphlet, Carlex Language Consultancy, Cave Hill, Barbados.

Baptiste, F., 2004, 'Developments in African History and the African Diaspora at the University of the West Indies, 1968-1998', in R. Goodridge, ed., *Caribbean Perspectives on African History and Culture*, Barbados: Department of History and Philosophy, University of the West Indies.

Beckles, H. and V. Shepherd, eds., 2000, *Caribbean Slavery in the Atlantic World*, Kingston, Jamaica: Ian Randle Publishers and Princeton, NJ: Markus Weiner Publishers.

Bender, G. J., 1978, *Angola under the Portuguese: The Myth and the Reality*, London: Heinemann.

Berttelheim, J., ed., 2001, *Cuban Festivals: A Century of Afro-Cuban Culture*, Kingston, Jamaica: Ian Randle Publishers and Princeton, NJ: Markus Weiner Publishers.

Braithwaite, K., 1970, *Folk Culture of the Slaves in Jamaica*, Pamphlet, London: New Beacon.

Braithwaite, K., 1971, *The Development of Creole Society in Jamaica, 1770-1820*, Oxford: Clarendon Press.

Césaire, A., 1972, *Discourse on Colonialism*, New York: Monthly Review Press.

Cobley, A., 1999, 'Forgotten Connections, Unconsidered Parallels: A New Agenda for Comparative Research on Southern Africa and the Caribbean', *African Studies* 58: 2, 133-155.

Cobley, A., 2000, 'The History of Higher Education in the Anglophone Caribbean', in G. Howe, ed., *Higher Education in the Caribbean: Past, Present, Future*, Kingston, Jamaica: The University of the West Indies Press, 1-24.

Cobley, A., 2001, 'African Studies in the West Indies', *African Research and Documentation*, No. 86.

Cox, E., 1998, *Rewriting History, Number One: Rekindling the Ancestral Memory: King JaJa of Opobo in St. Vincent and Barbados, 1888-1891*, Department of History, University of the West Indies and the Barbados Museum and Historical Society Pamphlet Series, Barbados.

Díaz-Briquets, S., ed., 1989, *Cuban Internationalism in Sub-Saharan Africa*, Pittsburgh: Duquesne University Press.

Edwards, P., ed., 1989, *The Life of Olaudah Equiano, or Gustavus Vassa the African, Written by himself*, London: Longman.

Eltis, D., S. Behrendt, D. Richardson and H. Klein, 1999, *The Trans-Atlantic Slave Trade [computer file]: A Database on CD-ROM*, Cambridge: Cambridge University Press.

Fanon, F., 1965, *The Wretched of the Earth and Studies in a Dying Colonialism*, New York: Monthly Review Press.

Fanon, F., 1967, *Black Skin, White Masks*, New York: Grove Press.

Fierce, M. C., 1991, *Africana Studies Outside the United States: Africa, Brazil, The Caribbean*, Ithaca, NY: Cornell University Africana Studies Research Center Monograph Series No. 7.

Gilroy, P., 1993, *The Black Atlantic: Modernity and Double Consciousness*, Cambridge, MA: Harvard University Press.

Hill, R. A., ed., 1990, *Walter Rodney Speaks: The Making of an African Intellectual*, Trenton, NJ: Africa World Press.

Howard, D., 2001, *Coloring the Nation: Race and Ethnicity in the Dominican Republic*, Oxford: Signal Books and Boulder, CO: Lynne Reinner Publishers.

Hyam, R. and P. Henshaw, 2003, *The Lion and the Springbok: Britain and South Africa Since the Boer War*, Cambridge: Cambridge University Press.

Jacques-Garvey, A., ed., 1986, *Philosophy and Opinions of Marcus Garvey*, New York: Atheneum.

James, C. L. R., 1969, *A History of Negro Revolt*, New York: Haskell House Publishers.

James, C. L. R., 1977, *Nkrumah and the Ghana Revolution*, London: Allison and Busby.

James, W., 1998, *Holding Aloft the Banner of Ethiopia: Caribbean Radicalism in Early Twentieth Century America*, London: Verso.

Klein, H. S., 1999, *The Atlantic Slave Trade*, Cambridge: Cambridge University Press.

Lewis, C. R., 1998, *Walter Rodney's Intellectual and Political Thought*, Kingston, Jamaica: The University of the West Indies Press and Detroit: Wayne State University Press.

Lewis, W. A., 1939, *Labour in the West Indies: The Birth of a Workers' Movement*, London: Fabian Society.

Lewis, W. A., 1950, *The Industrialization of the British West Indies*, Barbados: Government Printers.

Lewis, W. A., 1965, *Politics in West Africa*, Toronto: Oxford University Press.

Lewis, W. A., M. Scott, M. Wight and C. Legum, 1951, *Attitude to Africa*, Harmondsworth, England: Penguin.

Martin, T., 1986, *Race First: The Ideological and Organizational Struggles of the Universal Negro Improvement Association*, Dover, MA: The Majority Press.

Martin, W. G. and M. O. West, 1999, 'Introduction: The Rival Africas and Paradigms of Africanists and Africans at Home and Abroad', in W. G. Martin and M. O. West, eds, *Out of One, Many Africas: Reconstructing the Study and Meaning of Africa*, Urbana and Chicago: University of Illinois Press, 1-36.

Moore, C., 1988, *Castro, the Blacks, and Africa*, Los Angeles: Center for Afro-American Studies, University of California, Los Angeles.

Nettleford, R., 1970, *Mirror, Mirror: Identity, Race, and Protest in Jamaica*, Kingston, Jamaica: W. Collins and Sangster.

Padmore, G., 1937, *Africa and World Peace*, London: Secker and Warburg.

Rodney, W., 1969, *The Groundings with my Brothers*, London: Bogle-L'Ouverture Publications.

Rodney, W., 1970, *A History of the Upper Guinea Coast 1545-1800*, Oxford: Clarendon Press.

Rodney, W., 1972, *How Europe Underdeveloped Africa*, London: Bogle-L'Ouverture Publishers.

Rouse-Jones, M., 1986, 'African Studies in the English-Speaking Caribbean', in *African Research and Documentation* No. 40.

Sarduy, P. P. and J. Stubbs, eds., 2000, *Afro-Cuban Voices on Race and Identity in Contemporary Cuba*, Gainesville: University of Florida Press.

Warner-Lewis, M., 1995, *Yoruba Songs of Trinidad*, Chicago: Karnak House.

Warner-Lewis, M., 2003, *Central Africa in the Caribbean. Transcending Time, Transforming Cultures*, Kingston: University of the West Indies Press.

Williams, E., 1964, *Capitalism and Slavery*, London: André Deutsch.

Chapter 13

Let the Drums Sound: The Teaching of African History and the History of Africans in Brazil

Mônica Lima

(translated from the Portuguese by Izelda F. Galvao)

This chapter intends to present a few thoughts on the teaching of African History and the History of the Africans in Brazil. Among the themes discussed here are: the new legislation that has made the teaching of these subjects compulsory in the schools; the reasons for the long absence of these themes from the elementary and university curricula in Brazil; the questions that arise from the wrong approach that has been historically given to these themes in Elementary Education and in the formation of educators and social scientists in Brazil; suggestions for possible strategies to introduce the themes in a satisfactory way, that is, academically up to date and adequate from the point of view of ethics and of the promotion of citizenship.

On 9 January 2003, Law # 10.639 was approved. The law made compulsory the teaching of History and Afro-Brazilian Culture, as well as of African History and History of the Africans in the public and private schools in Brazil. According to the text of this law, the teaching would include the struggle of blacks in our country, the Brazilian Black culture and the black contribution in the formation of the national society as necessary sub-themes in the study of Brazilian History.

Right away we should consider this legal measure from a certain distance and ask ourselves: Why is there the need for a law to validate the presence of such an evidently fundamental content in general History and more specifically in the History of social groups that participated directly in the formation of our country? The answer to this question seems so obvious that it almost changes the questioning into an exercise in pure rhetoric.

But what will become of us if we do not challenge ourselves to question the apparently evident, to change into a question what is given as common fact? If we do not try to show that something that has been accepted as a logical answer does not truly make sense, we will not go any further than the acceptance of a phenomenon that has been socially and historically fabricated. I believe that only by questioning, and questioning more than once, the answer to the given question, that we will get to the root of the things. Thus, we will be able to present the questions from a radical point of view, in the literal sense of the word. This constant questioning will follow the path of a reflection without visible question marks, but they will always be present, seeking to weave the background scenario in which the agents of History will be noticed and the battles fought and the upcoming battles will be revealed.

History of the Africans in Brazil and the Brazilian Identity

Since mankind began to accumulate knowledge about human societies, one knows that to elaborate and to give meaning to the history of a people means to lend to these people the tools for them to form their own identity by taking from it the raw material which is their social memory. Thus, the misleading inclusion or the deliberate exclusion of any aspect of the history might bring about an identity or self image distinct from the reality of that human group, distorted by ideological elements far from reality. The History of Brazil, or better, of Brazilian society is a clear example: for a long time historiography ignored the contribution of African cultures and societies in the formation of our society.

The root causes for this omission were prejudice and ignorance about the social life and the history of these human groups, and above all, the need to dominate them so as to enslave or colonise them. Therefore, this root cause is embedded in the relationship of those dominant groups with the African people, of those societies in which our first historians looked upon to build the official records on Brazil. The denial of this History has always been clearly associated with the forms of social control and ideological domination, besides the interest in building a Brazilian identity shed of its racial content, within the so-called desire for the whitening of our society. Typical of the second half of the nineteenth century, this desire for the whitening of the society is still present in some more backwards social sectors, although the struggle for change in the field of the teaching of History created clashes throughout the twentieth century.

The difficulty in dealing with this theme seemed such that even the more progressive sectors at times refused even to consider this question (why the absence of African History and History of the Africans in the school curricula in Brazil?). Many believed that the African struggle in Africa and in Brazil should be studied within the category 'struggle of the dominated, the oppressed', or any other title that we might want to give to the history of the excluded. Therefore, it would not deserve special attention by itself—after all, this group that has been for such a long time ignored by the school books, one would not define it in any other way except by the social place that it has occupied of exploited workers. That way, when the history of the collective masses was rescued, the Africans and the Afro-descendants in Brazil, together with all the other groups, would enter history, being gloriously placed in the condition of protagonists. Would they be in their rightful place?

In the books of Brazilian History, of Geography and Social Integration, reviewed by this so called progressive view, many slaves were portrayed as working hard in the plantations, victims of the exploitation guided by capitalist interests in expansion, or running to the 'quilombos' (hidden settlements founded by runaway slaves) in a few fleeting moments of rebellion, an almost impossible rebellion due to the masters' control of the whip. And finally in the nineteenth century, they would be worth mentioning again, upon being freed by the new agents of the dominating economic system, with an interest in turning them into consumers. In the twentieth century, they would become part of the working class, disappearing as a specific theme, and only returning to the scene in a few works of scholarship in which popular culture was briefly mentioned, in these instances, *capoeira* (an Afro-Brazilian martial art and dance) and samba (an Afro-Brazilian musical rhythm) would appear connected to these groups.

Regarding the History of Africa, as a theme in World History, it would appear linked to the period of capitalist accumulation, that is, it would appear as the place where the slaves were taken from, and later as the place for the neocolonial expansion, from the end of the nineteenth century onwards.[1] And that was all. The Africans, victims of foreign greed, became objects of pillage, subject to exploitation, domination, destruction, slavery, oppression. And when they were mentioned in History as subjects, even in tatters, they fought but always lost, they screamed but their voices were always quietened. Finally, their chance of occupying another place in history seemed to be by disappearing as a specific group and reappearing as part of the great proletarian mass that one day would take power. Would that be enough?

The reality showed that was not enough. The Africans seemed to continue objectified or almost invisible. Even when they were praised as Zumbi dos Palmares (the African slave, leader of the biggest and strongest Brazilian quilombo), even then it was a brief paragraph in History. When it came to Africa, everything was still very far, on the other side of the immense ocean.

If we reflect upon the main receivers of the teaching-learning process, the students, what continued to be done was to hinder the building of self-esteem for portraying an image of our African antecedents as always oppressed, exploited and defeated, even when they were rebellious and unbending. Who would like to identify with this image? And besides, it was a false image, if not totally, at least partially. Recent historiography supplied us with new data to correct that image. The only thing left to do now is to make sure that data gets to the classrooms.

We can observe till today there are very few subjects dealing specifically with Africa in the curricula of History courses of Brazilian universities, as well as the almost ignorance of the theme in the studies of General History in the elementary and secondary schools. Upon making its inclusion compulsory in the elementary education, we will face a tremendous difficulty: what kind of history will be taught, since the majority of the teachers in the classrooms have not had contact with it?

This does not diminish the importance of the measure. Many were we, and we are the ones who requested spaces for these themes. Now that our request has been heeded, we have to define objectives, to discuss approaches—that is, where to arrive and how to arrive? To answer these questions, we are faced with very profound issues. Well, if to rescue this memory is to create a new identity for us as a people, we have a challenge ahead of us: Who are we? Furthermore: Who do we wish to be?

Rocks in the Middle of the Road

It is not simple to figure out 'how to do', when the question involves centuries of disinformation and intellectual distancing. There is no way of recovering the Africanness of our History without recovering the History of Africa itself. And in this case, it is necessary to build references, to rescue memory, to bring up to the surface all that did not find stimulus to sediment in the individual and collective culture when it comes to the meaning of the relations with Africa in our History.

The most common images of African History were based either on ethnocentric conceptions, presenting Africa as a backwards place, uneducated, savage, land of barbarisms, or on placing the emphasis on the role as victims—victims of the slave traffic, of capitalism, of neocolonialism, and so on. As to the first instance, much has been written and much has been criticised. True, never enough, since prejudice still lingers in many different shapes, disguised in new clothing. So, it is important to unclothe it and fight it, every time it shows up. And if this prejudice exists in a less explicit manner in the academia, we cannot say the same of the media, which is a powerful means in the formation of opinions and in the creation of imagery of Africa. In this sense, we need to denounce and combat this image.

In the second instance, we need to remember that the position of victim carries in itself a very strong content of passivity, of impotence and incapacity to resist, to act and to intervene in History. It is, therefore, a question of getting used to seeing Africans always treated as objects and not as subject of History. And that affects the understanding of their trajectory.

The plain fact of whole populations having lived a long process of exploitation under the control of external agents, in cahoots with internal agents, cannot be denied. But, not to limit it in its time and in its social implications within Africa itself adds strength to the idea that Africans have always been victims of a cruel destiny, and not individuals that were involved in a historical process that generated and deepened inequalities.

To recognise these distorted facets and to clarify them is fundamental. This can only be possible with serious scholarship, whose academic quality should be evaluated, receiving from funding organisations a special stimulus. These works should be advertised, translated into many different languages, and shared. The more people who have access to them, the better. And "all our care will never be enough". But, as the song by Brazilian composer Chico César goes:

Stronger than the whips of the overseers,

Are the drums.

One, Multiple

It is very difficult to talk about Africa in the singular, or of one Africa in Brazil. The societies are many, diverse in their development, diverse in their origin, diverse in their culture. Many colours in Africa, many Africas in Brazil. One knows that the idea of 'African' did not exist among the slaves and freed Brazilians brought from the (African) continent before the nineteenth century. It is not that there were no identities among them—on the contrary, there were, and they were discovered, created and reinforced. But the idea of one Africa, as the land of them all, and of an African identity, arose attached to the forms of re-invention of identities characteristic of the 1800s, and originated at this specific moment because of their relation with the dominant society.

In the same way, we know that in the struggle for freedom from the colonial yoke in twentieth century Africa, it was fundamental to create ideological pools that emphasised common aspects, such as the idea of Blackness, of Pan-Africanism. All these ideas played a role in History, the denial of the discourse of the colonisers, and the creation of necessary integrations. But they were not absolute truths. Those who took them as black and white truths without shades of grey soon felt defeated when they saw that to belong to the (African) continent as a native did not turn them necessarily into brothers.

However, one cannot lose sight of the common aspects within the total vision, which reach into vast regions of Africa. We can refer to bigger issues, shared histories, long-lasting interactions and trade. Regionally, in greater geo-cultural and linguistic areas, there are general concepts for blackness, explicit and profound. In the same way it happened in Brazil, the contact between peoples of neighbouring regions created a shared vocabulary and shared ways of communication contributing to the creation of new resistance tactics.[2] Only historical research that focuses on aspects of this daily life, on the apparently diffuse life of these persons, will be able to bring to life the presence of these Africas in Brazil. Today we are walking in the right direction, there is productive research going on, but we need to make this research reach the university and the elementary school classrooms.

To discover these Africas, we need to awaken others' curiosity, their interest, and to stimulate their admiration. So, we need to take these Africas into our cultural and educational hubs. Besides reading, we need to listen, to see, to watch, to participate and to realise how much of these Africas we bring inside ourselves. Doing so, we will wake up in ourselves the pride of our Blackness. We will see our famous and unknown heroes again, all this for Zumbi of Palmares, and for all the Antônios Minas and Joaquins Angolas, for Manoel Congo, and for so many Marias Cabindas and Joanas Crioulas, for Luiza Mahin, for Antônio Rebouças and for João Cândido. And many, many more. Yes, we should celebrate them, not as a return to a history of names and dates, but to create points of reference.

To Recognise, To Self-recognise

There are no ready formulas to follow, the 'how to do it' does not exist, hence the need for much discussion and intellectual exchange, not only among those who are respected as 'intellectuals', but among social movements as well. We cannot, just for the sake of obeying the law, communicate misinformation in our classrooms, or address the theme in a folklorised and idealised manner. It is a great fear: to repeat models in order to make these curricular contents look like the ones that we used to work with when we taught History and cultural contributions, an easy but very dangerous road. They are different themes, therefore they should be taught differently.

Our students will certainly have a lot to say, but we should be very careful with common sense, because it can either underestimate or create myths—which, once they are debunked, will double the weight of disillusion and the wearing down of self-esteem. It is a very delicate equilibrium between the rescue of a history that will make one proud of belonging to it, and the valorisation of narrow ideas that tend to create Manichean explanations.

In the end we are left with the central question: how and what to introduce regarding these themes (African History, History of the Africans in Brazil) in our school curricula? The answer is not simple, and I could not pull it out of my magician's hat. But it is possible to present brief suggestions, acquired from some experience in teaching these themes in the elementary, secondary and university levels.[3]

We could take as one important lead the vision that approaches critical multiculturalism, that is, one that results from 'historical struggles for identity recognition in public spaces embraced by social movements, NGOs, groups and organizations that fight for social justice and recognition of the plural citizenship'.[4] This focus would try to value the discussion on the differences without failing to place them historically in their due context, as well as to locate the identities in order to foster attitudes that overcome prejudice and stimulate solidarity.

In the first place, it is fundamental to become experts, to get up-to-date on these themes instead of relying on just the little bit one knows, in order to occupy a position that has never been occupied. We have the responsibility of approaching these themes with professionalism. Thus, we should study, look for specific readings, and whenever possible, to improve ourselves by taking courses and participating in academic discussions. Our precarious work and life conditions cannot justify a lack of effort towards this goal—we are talking about the rewriting of a History that was denied to us, we are dealing with the basis of an identity that is about to be reconstructed. What is at play here is more than our competence—it is our commitment.

It is important to demand from the authorities, from the deans of teaching institutions, the support to turn this law into a reality. With the law, the legal obligation was established, but that is not enough in order to make that obligation viable and productive. There must be investment in education. University students: fight for the inclusion of these themes among the subjects of the curricula of your universities, institutes, and departments. This is possible and has already been done. Teachers: request from the school district the teaching of these courses—this is possible and it is also a reality in some places.[5] And also, create opportunities (seminars, round tables, debates, symposiums) and courses where the study of these themes and adequate teaching methodology for these themes are stimulated.[6] It might not be easy, but it will be a good start.

For the teachers in Basic Education, a few general suggestions. In the first grades of elementary school, the teacher can introduce themes of African and Afro-Brazilian cultures through legends, stories, songs, and games. There are already didactic materials (especially books)[7] to use as reference. In Social Integration courses, you should talk about the presence of the Africans in the history of Brazil going beyond slavery: guide the students to notice traces of this live presence in the music, in the feasts, in the vocabulary, in our food habits. Africans, besides being a labour source, were a people that produced culture. But it is not enough to say this. This has to be experienced in order to shake the old structures of prejudice which feed on ignorance.

On a more advanced level of the elementary school, we can work with more precise content, we can talk about Prehistory—questioning the naming of the period, since it is not writing that creates History, as during the time of human evolution that happened in Africa before other places on the planet. To explain the whys, to talk about the first African Homo Sapiens that left to populate the world. Do not leave out the splendour and pomp of the Ancient Egypt, a theme that entices students at this age, and always remind them that Egypt is located in Africa, something that seems so obvious, but ends up forgotten. Of course, Egypt was also a place of inequalities, who says that the Africans did not experience them in their own land? To try to remember the great kingdoms of Western Sudan, which during the Middle Ages raised cities, with universities, book markets, contacts with the Orient and Europe—and also enchanted so many travellers and made other peoples envious of their gold mines.[8] And, obviously, when studying the slave trade, do not limit yourself to talking about the exchange of people for riches, but also about the riches carried by these people inside themselves, in the largest process of forced migration in the history of humanity, whose consequent was a true African Diaspora throughout the New World.

In high school, when revisiting some of the themes, you should debate the great visions, situate the appearance of racism as a political and scientific project, using strategies that allow the students to construct and deconstruct ideas through research, mock trials, skits. And always point out racial inequality in Brazil. It is never too much to repeat: our poverty has a colour, our exclusion has a colour. These facts, however, should not be treated as natural. In the same way that they were fruits of a history, to create another history might change the situation.

Another fundamental point in the teaching of History of Africa and History of the Africans to Brazilian students is to think of ways to expand its dimensions, highlighting the aspects of Afro-Americanness, and introducing elements in this part of our history that are common to and different from the history of the Afro-descendants of the whole continent. We know we have a common history not only between Africa and Brazil, but also between the Africans and their descendants born in the New World. And it is not only this history that unites us, as we can see from reflection upon projects of the formation of national identities on the continent. In a recently published article dealing with discussion about the teaching of History, Hebe Mattos, author of many works on slavery in Brazil, states that 'from a more general point of view, the formation of national identities in the Americas implied a process of racialization of their populations, producing the present segregation in the United States, or transforming the reflections on the "mestiço" (mixed) nature of the populations and/or the projects of racial and cultural whitening into true obsessions of the social Latin-American thought'.[9] Then, our school curricula should try to deepen the perception of these processes in the History of America. And the training of teachers of History, Geography, Sociology, Artistic Education, and Literature should include these questions.

In this sense, I can state without fear of sounding obsolete, that militancy is fundamental for the conquest of these rights, the right to information about the history of our antecedents. It must be a militancy that demands and creates spaces not only political but also academic, and that is open to debates and not sectarian. All of us will win, the school will win, the students will win, and citizenship will be the great winner.

We know that our memory builds our perceptions of ourselves and of others, brings us back to building our identity. It is up to us to multiply initiatives like this and make sure that research, formation and production on these themes be doubled. It is about rescuing the History of Africa and, in a way, Africanising the History of Brazil. As it is beautifully said by Antônio Jacinto, Angolan militant poet:

The rhythm of the drum, I don't have it in my blood

not even in my skin

I have the rhythm of the drum, above all, in my thinking.[10]

Notes

1. We are talking about most of the works. There are honourable exceptions, such as the book *History* by Francisco Falcon, Ilmar de Mattos, Maria Alice Resende de Carvalho and Selma Rinaldi de Mattos, published by Francisco Alves in 1977, whose chapter on Africa was written under the supervision of Professor José Maria Nunes Pereira (University of Campinas).

2. In this case, and especially important, is the work of the historian Robert Slenes in his book *In the Slave Quarters, a Flower*, published by Nova Fronteira in 1999, and his article 'Malungo, N'goma Vem—Africa, covered and discovered in Brazil', in the USP (University of São Paulo) magazine, December/January/February 1991–1992.

3. Since the conclusion of my Master's Degree in African Studies from El Colégio de México (a graduate programme to train Latin Americans in research and teaching of African themes) in 1990, when I returned to Brazil and to the position of Professor of Basic Education in Colégio de Aplicação of the Federal University of Rio and began my experience teaching History of Africa to teachers.
4. Ana Canen, 'Racial Relations and Curriculum. Reflexions upon Multiculturalism', from Pedagogic Notebooks PENESB (publisher) # 3, page 68.
5. The Public School District of Rio de Janeiro, under the governorship of Benedita da Silva (black woman, politician, from a Rio shanty town who became a governor and a senator) since 2002, has been offering specialisation courses in African History for History teachers in Campos and Rio, organised by the Centre of Studies for Afro-Asians in the Candido Mendes University, a traditionally taught theme in this institution.
6. Such as the Specialisation courses offered by the Programme for the Studies of Blacks in Brazilian Society/PENESB of the College of Education of Fluminense Federal University.
7. For example, FTD Publisher, São Paulo, Brazil, published some few African legends in the series 'Mythological Adventures'.
8. To quote an important French historian, Pierre Vilar, to mention gold in Medieval Europe was to mention Africa (in his book *Gold and Money in History, 1450–1920*, Barcelona, 1974, p. 61).
9. Mattos, Hebe, 'The Teaching of History and the Struggle Against Racial Discrimination in Brazil', from Teaching History: Concepts, themes and Methodology, p. 131.
10. Poem 'The Rhythm of the Drum', published in *To Survive in Tarrafal de S. Tiago*, Luanda: Angolan Writers Union, 1989, p. 73.

References

Belucci, B., coordinator, 2003, *Introduction to the History of África and Afro-Brazilian Culture*, Rio de Janeiro: Center of Afro-Asian Studies (CEAA)-UCAM/Centro Cultural Banco do Brasil (CCBB).

Canen, A., 2001, 'Racial Relations and Curriculum. Reflexions upon the Multiculturalism', Pedagogic Notebooks No. 3, Niterói: Publisher Fluminense Federal University, 65-77.

Costa e Silva, A., 1996, *The Hoe and the Spear. Africa Before the Portuguese*, Rio de Janeiro: Nova Fronteira.

Costa e Silva, A., 2002, *Shackles and Chains*, Rio de Janeiro: Nova Fronteira.

Falcon, F. et al., 1977, *History*. Rio de Janeiro: Francisco Alves.

Gilroy, P., 2001, *The Black Atlantic. Modernity and Double Conscience*, Rio de Janeiro: UCAM/ Editor 34.

Grinberg, K., 2002, *The Backer/Guarantor of the Brazilians. Citizenship, Slavery and Civil Right in the Time of Antonio Pereira Rebouças*, Rio de Janeiro: Civilização brasileira.

Jacinto, A., 1989, *Survival in Tarrafal de São Tiago*, Luanda: União de Escritores Angolanos.

Lovejoy, P., 2002, *Slavery in Africa: A History of its Transformations*, Rio de Janeiro: Civilização Brasileira.

Mattos, H., 2003, 'The teaching of History and the fight against Racial Discrimination in Brazil', in M. Abreu and R. Sohiet, eds., *Teaching of History. Concepts, themes and Methodology*, Rio de Janeiro: Faperj/Casa da Palavra, 127-136.

Munanga, K., 2002, 'The building of Black Identity in the context of globalization', *Cadernos Penesb* 4: 61-83, Niterói: Editora da UFF.

Oliver, R., 1994, *The African Experience. From Pre-History to Today*, Rio de Janeiro: Jorge Zahar Editor.

Priore, M. del and R. Venncio, eds., 2004, *Ancestors: An Introduction to the History of Atlantic África*, Rio de Janeiro: Campus/Elsevier.

Reis, J. J., 2003, *Slave Rebelion in Brazil: The History of the Males Rebellion*, São Paulo: Cia. das Letras (reedição ampliada).

Slenes, R., 1991-2, 'Malungo, N´goma vem!: África, covered and discovered in Brazil', *São Paulo: Revista da USP* 12 (dec /jan /feb): 48-67.

Slennes, R., 1999, *In the Slave Quarters, a Flower. Hopes and Remembrances in the Formation of the Slave Family*, Rio de Janeiro: Nova Fronteira.

Vilar, P., 1974, *Gold and Money in History, 1450-1920*, Barcelona: Editorial Ariel.

Chapter 14

African Studies in India[1]

Aparajita Biswas

The programmes of Area Studies and International Studies in India were started in the mid-1950s by pioneers such as educationists Pandit Hriday Nath Kunzru and Professor A. Appadorai. The latter, considered as the doyen of Area Studies in India, gave hope and scope to the concept of Area Studies. At the request of UNESCO, Prof. Appadorai made a survey of the position of International and Area Studies in India in the early 1950s, and it was he who was responsible for drawing the attention and interest of Indian intellectuals and political scientists to the study of international relations.

The idea of introducing Area Studies as a new academic discipline in India sprouted from the success of the Indian Council of World Affairs (ICWA, of which Kunzru and Appadorai were President and Secretary-General, respectively) which was established in 1944 for the promotion of understanding of international affairs in India. ICWA was patterned after the Royal Institute of International Affairs, London. It was designed to have a well-equipped library on international affairs. One of its objectives was to provide a platform for world leaders to interact with scholars and the public whenever they visited the country. Thus the ICWA, in the first decade of its activities, inspired the launch of Area Studies as a new academic programme in India.

The initial impetus for the emergence of Area Studies in India came from the far-sighted and internationalist vision of India's first Prime Minister, Pandit Jawaharlal Nehru. After independence, Nehru stressed on the need for an enlightened awareness of the world beyond India's borders and a clear and critical understanding of situations in countries and regions, especially those of vital interest to India (Nehru 1961). It was a time when newly independent India felt the imperative need for competent Indian academic specialists regularly to watch developments in other areas of the world, interpret their significance, and give a studied second opinion or a critical evaluation of India's own external policies, apart from the work of government bureaucracy. It was also a time when India felt the need for specialists in professions like teaching, administration, journalism, business, etc. The strong motive behind the introduction of Area Studies was to train a group of competent experts in international matters through the establishment of the Indian School of International Studies (ISIS) in New Delhi, in October 1955. From its very inception, ISIS was intended to be the centre for advanced study and research in International Relations and Area Studies (Rajan 1991).

In April 1963, the University Grants Commission (UGC, a statutory body created by an Act of Indian Parliament in 1956 for co-ordination, determination, and maintenance of the standard of university education in India) appointed a committee under the chairmanship of B. Shiva Rao. The committee recognised the need for a large number of Indian scholars who would be adequately equipped with the historical, cultural, social and economic backgrounds of particular regions and also the need to give priority to the study of areas like China, Japan, South and South-East Asia, Africa, West Asia, and other countries and regions which are India's immediate neighbours. The main objectives of the programmes were (a) specialised teaching and research, and (b) the production of popular books in these areas (Government of India 1966). The committee recommended that Area Study Centres be set up in select universities where the existing faculty might participate in Area Studies Programmes.

Taking cognisance of the committee's report, a Standing Advisory Committee was appointed by the UGC to develop the programme of Area Studies in Indian Universities. It envisaged the growing need for Indian scholars with specialised knowledge of the life, institutions, culture, and languages of the regions with which India has close social, political and economic relations. It recognised that Area Studies also required intensive courses in the languages of the areas concerned and inter-disciplinary collaboration, especially in the field of social sciences. It was acknowledged that profound knowledge of the world beyond our country's borders was not only essential for the security and the prosperity of the nation but also for the improvement of the quality of the country's participation in world affairs. In pursuit of this objective, the UGC undertook the task of promoting Area Studies in some universities. The programme was expanded over the years and today, there are about 20 Area Studies Centres in the country (Reddy 1979).

The structural arrangement made by the UGC is that Area Studies Centres be established with financial support from the UGC for the first five years. Thereafter, respective state governments were expected to take over the financial responsibility of running the centres on a permanent basis. At the end of every five years, the UGC sends an expert committee to evaluate the performance of the centres and, on the basis of committee's report, the UGC sanctions additional grants as well as staff.

African Studies in India

At the outset it must be mentioned here that the foremost Indian political leaders whose views, statements and actions inspired the setting up of African Studies in India were Mohandas Karamchand (Mahatma) Gandhi and Jawaharlal Nehru. They were Africanists judged by any definition, and had a good grasp of problems and issues facing Africa. A close examination of several documents such as speeches of these two Indian leaders and a review of several resolutions of the Indian National Congress before and after India's independence established beyond doubt that India was fully aware of, and sympathetic to, African liberation movements (Biswas 1992). The issues concerning liberation of African countries and racist policies of the white regimes in Africa were among those which drew the deepest concern of the Indian national leadership.

It is also pertinent to note here that in 1893, Gandhi went to Africa and stayed there for nearly 22 years. He soon experienced the humiliating discrimination against Indians in South Africa and sensed the need for organised protest. He first experimented with the instrument of *Satyagraha* as a passive resistance movement in opposition to the unjust and discriminatory laws against South African Indians. He led the movement in South Africa for six long years.

For the first time in contemporary history, Gandhi demonstrated the effective application of a non-violent approach as a means to oppose wrong and injustice. The success of this movement in South Africa and later in India immensely inspired African and subjected peoples all over the world. In later years, Gandhi was visited by many African leaders who sought inspiration and guidance in their own struggle for self determination (Thomas 1956). Nelson Mandela of South Africa paid rich tributes to Gandhi's philosophy of non-violence as means of protest against subjugation.

Along with Gandhi, Jawaharlal Nehru was also an eminent Africanist. During the initial years of India's independence, Nehru was instrumental in shaping and defining major policy objectives and diplomatic thrusts in India's policy towards Africa. It was largely based on his personal commitment to Afro-Asian resurgence. Under his leadership, India took a definite diplomatic stand on many African issues. Firstly, it took decolonisation of African states as a continuum of the process of Afro-Asian resurgence. Secondly, it took a firm stand against racial discrimination and broke off its diplomatic and trade relations with racist regimes. Thirdly, it took a categorical stand on issues of people of Indian origin settled in Africa and made it clear that they must identify with the local majority community and should not seek any special privilege in the country of their adoption (Biswas 1992).

Moreover, Nehru expected support of the newly independent African states for the Non-Aligned Movement (NAM). It may be mentioned here that the important characteristic of India's foreign policy since the Nehru years has been the vigorous pursuit of the policy of non-alignment. In his first formal enunciation of the policy, Nehru declared that 'we propose, as far as possible to keep away from the power politics and groups, aligned against one another, which have led to the past world wars and which may again lead to disaster on an even vaster scale' (Nehru 1961).

NAM was conceptually designed around the middle of the 1950s to meet the aspirations of those newly born states who would not like to be constrained by the politics of alignment with either of the two power blocs, and who would rather prefer a path of development independent of the major power centres. After their independence, every African state, with the exception of the Republic of South Africa, had joined NAM.

From the very beginning, there was an emphasis on developmental requirements of the emerging African states. Indeed, with considerable foresight, even as early as 1949, India had established a general cultural scholarship scheme under which students from Africa and Asia were provided access to the institutions of higher studies in India, even though at that time facilities in India were not adequate to meet Indian requirements (Appadorai 1987).

Nehru always talked of Africa in emotional tones. For instance, on the occasion of Ghana's independence, while addressing the African Student Association of India, he observed:

> There is something more distinctive about independence of Ghana than perhaps of other countries. It symbolizes so much for the continent of Africa ... it moves us not only intellectually but also emotionally. There are many things happening in Africa which are rather painful to contemplate. There are many dark shadows. So it is a peculiar pleasure that out of darkness this light has come which I hope will spread (Nehru 1958).

Educational co-operation has remained the main plank of India-Africa relations ever since. Nehru was keen on promoting Indo-African understanding in the cultural field on a continuing basis. To achieve that objective, he institutionalised African studies. It was he who first thought of inducting African studies into the university framework. Way back in 1953, a proposal was made by the Ministry of External Affairs, Government of India, to set up a Department of African Studies in the University of Delhi. It was established in 1955.

Thereafter, two more African Studies Centres came up within a short period of time. These were (i) West Asian and Sub-Saharan African Studies, Jawaharlal Nehru University (JNU), New Delhi and (ii) Centre for African Studies, University of Mumbai. Among these three centres, only the Centre for African Studies, University of Mumbai, was set up by the UGC in 1971-72. The organisational pattern of all three centres differs in details. While the University of Delhi's department is a full fledged one, the Centre for African Studies in the University of Mumbai is a centre headed by a full time director. In JNU, New Delhi, the African Studies Programme is an integral part of the Centre of West Asian and Sub-Saharan African Countries. Both JNU and University of Delhi offer a Master of Philosophy (M.Phil) programme, whereas the Centre for African Studies, University of Mumbai, offers a combination degree—Master of Arts (MA in African Studies, along with other social science departments. All the centres offer PhD programmes.

Department of African Studies, Delhi

The Department of African Studies in the Faculty of Social Science at the University of Delhi was set up in December 1954, at the personal initiative of Jawaharlal Nehru, who formally inaugurated it in August 1955. While inaugurating the department, he made an extremely poignant speech. He said,

> Africa is now awake after centuries of somnolence. People of Africa are in mental ferment and physical turmoil. One has to understand not only the minds of Africans but their hearts and urges as well. It is therefore necessary for people of India to study Africa not merely as an academic subject but in all its bearings—cultural, political, economic and historical. It was most urgent for them to understand Africa, more particularly the people of Africa. Africa has history and culture growing out of its soil for thousands of years. Africa is not an ordinary subject but a subject of great significance (*Hindustan Times* 1955).

The department was the first inter-disciplinary area studies centre of its kind in India. The objective of setting up this department was primarily to conduct inter-disciplinary research, teaching and studies on the problems of the African continent. The department also provides a forum for fostering mutual understanding, friendship and co-operation between the people of India and Africa. Thus the mandate of the department extends beyond its primary function of the acquisition and dissemination of knowledge and learning on Africa.

However, being the first Area Studies department in the university system, the Department of African Studies, University of Delhi, experienced a number of problems. In the beginning, a two-year diploma course with seven papers was initiated, but soon thereafter, it was transformed into a Masters course on Africa. The main idea was to impart comprehensive inter-disciplinary instruction on Africa, to turn out a body of social scientists with specialisations on Africa. Many distinguished academics had joined the department at that time as Visiting Professors. Among them were Professor T. S. Elias, a brilliant Nigerian political scientist, Professor J. C. Graft Johnson, a well-known Ghanaian economist and Professor S. Hofstra, a leading Dutch social anthropologist.

The main problem with the diploma course was the inappropriately compiled syllabus and the perception of lesser market value when compared to regular MA degree courses in other social science disciplines. Unfortunately, even the MA course did not take off because of inadequate job opportunities available to these postgraduates. After about two years, the course was discontinued and the African course was introduced at the post-graduate level in the departments of Economics and Political Science, as an optional subject (University of Delhi 2000). Subsequently, a number of committees were formed in the 1960s to discuss the issues pertaining to the Area Studies programme. Some of these committee meetings were presided over by eminent social scientists like Professor Amartya Sen and Professor M. N. Srinivas. It was argued that the thriving execution of an African studies programme required an intermediate research degree between MA and PhD, so that a student would be able to gather information on an area on the basis of the knowledge acquired by him in the discipline.

However, the real breakthrough in the organisational pattern of area studies came from the introduction of an MPhil course in Delhi University in 1978-79.

A student with a master's degree in the traditional social science could join the MPhil course in African Studies and subsequently, proceed to a PhD degree. The department is now credited with 65 PhD dissertations and over 270 MPhil dissertations. It also offers a one-year diploma course in the Swahili language (University of Delhi 2000).

The department is now proposing to establish formal staff-student exchange arrangements with a number of universities in Africa. In March 2003, a Memorandum of Understanding was signed between the University of Delhi and the University of Khartoum, Sudan. The department has also set up a small specialised library and reading room within its premises. This is to supplement the University's Central Library which has one of the best collections of books and periodicals on Africa. Besides this, the Department of African Studies also published the bi-annual *Indian Journal of African Studies*. Contributors of articles in the journal include scholars from both in India and abroad, who have specialist knowledge of African affairs.

The African Studies Division, Jawaharlal Nehru University

In the 1950s, a small centre for African Studies was established in the School of International Studies (ISIS). With the merger of the School into JNU in 1969, this centre became part of the University. It is not a separate department like the one in the University of Delhi; rather it is a part of the Centre of West Asia and Sub-Saharan African Studies, which in turn, is a part of the School of International Studies. The main focus of this centre is on the MPhil and PhD Programmes. The centre is credited with the conferring of 25 PhD degrees and 70 MPhil degrees.

The Centre for African Studies, University of Mumbai

The Centre for African Studies is located in the Kalina Campus of the University of Mumbai (Bombay). It was set up by the UGC under the Area Studies Programme introduced in the country, as mentioned earlier. It was initially headed by the Chairman of the Area Studies Co-ordinating Committee. This committee consisted of the Heads of the Social Science Departments like History, Economics, Political Science, Sociology and Geography. The Committee was the decision-making authority of the centre between 1971 and 1983. The centre attained departmental status of the university in 1984. Initially the centre covered areas and issues pertaining to East Africa. Subsequently, on obtaining departmental status, its scope was expanded to cover all of Africa.

The Centre is committed to enhancing interest in the African region through academic and research programmes on Africa. It is one of the few academic institutions in India which has constantly upheld dialogue and co-operation among students and scholars, with a focus on policy matters. Over the years the centre has made concerted efforts at nurturing a corps of social scientists and scholars who are concerned with various aspects of Africa. The centre is inter-disciplinary in nature with a multi-disciplinary faculty. It is headed by a full time Director and functions under the guidance of an inter-departmental advisory committee, with the University's Vice-Chancellor as the chairperson. The centre offers courses and provides instruction and research guidance at the MA and PhD levels. It offers a total of eight papers in African Studies for a combined Masters Degree in Arts. Students admitted to the Centre opt for four out of the eight papers offered in combination with Political Science, Economics, History, Sociology and Geography. The advantage of this combined MA degree is that a student, while gaining basic knowledge in any of the traditional discipline, can simultaneously acquire expertise in African Studies.

The eight papers offered by the Centre are: (i) Environment and Human Geography on Africa; (ii) State Formation and Nation Building in Africa; (iii) African Economics: Problems and Prospects; (iv) Africa in World Affairs; (v) Foreign Trade Investment and Industrialisation in Africa; (vi) Governments and Politics in Independent Africa; (vii) Africa-India and Indian Ocean Region; and (viii) History of Africa. The Centre has a Documentation Unit, which is a reference library. It provides support to the curriculum and general information needs of the faculty, research staff and students. It keeps in touch with African Studies institutions, both within and outside the country. It houses a variety of information on the sub-Saharan African countries. The collection includes books, pamphlets and periodicals.

The Centre has also built a sizeable collection of primary and secondary source materials on African history, economics, geography, politics, and sociology. There is a small collection of materials on Swahili language and literature as well. Besides this, the Centre receives books and journals in exchange from various African institutions and libraries. It has signed cooperation agreements with a couple of institutions of African studies based in Africa and Russia. In addition, the faculty and students also have the advantage of substantial books and journals on African Studies at the Central Library of the University of Mumbai. The UGC contributes substantially for continuous upgrading of the Library's African collection.

The Centre publishes *African Currents*, a bi-annual in-house journal edited by the director of the Centre. The contents of the journal are a reflection of the ongoing research interests of the Centre's staff and its students. Scholars and senior academics from India and abroad have also been invited to contribute articles to the journal.

Constraints of Area Studies and African Studies in India

If one looks back at the performance of various Area Studies programmes in India against their objectives, their achievements are laudable in terms of both quality and quantity. The last four decades have produced a large number of reasonably good Indian specialists on various areas of the world. Presently, India has numerous knowledgeable area specialists. One finds these specialists occupying important positions in the fields of media, administration, journalism, business, etc. They are vocal on contemporary national and international issues of importance.

However, this does not mean that all is well with area studies in India. A number of area specialists are of the view that, by and large, the area studies programmes have not achieved their objectives. Reasons for this include bureaucratic and infrastructural impediments, insufficiency of funds, inadequate facilities for libraries and documentation, problems relating to teaching and student enrolment, and the lack of co-ordination between the area studies centres and the Ministry of External Affairs.

Moreover, although area studies in India was established as an inter-disciplinary field of study, the disciplinary profiles of the area specialists betray the marked presence of political scientists. Thus, out of twenty Africanists associated with the Area Studies Programme, fifteen are from the field of political science, two from economics, and one each from history, geography and language, and none from anthropology and sociology. It is needless to state that disciplinary specialisation has an important bearing on the selection of problems as well as the thrust and emphasis on research priorities.

A few years ago, Bimal Prasad and Urmila Phadnis, both well-known social scientists, undertook an exhaustive survey of over 700 works of Indian scholars in the field of area studies. The survey revealed the gaps and strengths of Indian contributors to area studies. It also showed that disciplines like political science and international relations have overshadowed others in area studies. Issues like African development and anthropology were ignored (Prasad and Phadnis 1988). Professor A. Appadorai, mentioned earlier as a doyen of area studies programmes in India, has realised this. In an article published in *International Studies* (New Delhi), he writes:

> In studying international affairs for some years past, I have been struck by the fact that we in this region (Africa) are too preoccupied with political problems. The important part that economic consideration elsewhere plays in the formulation and implementation of foreign policy is obvious to any one who cares to see it. Even if we do not accept Marx's economic interpretation of history in its entirety, we must admit that economic considerations do have a place in the determination of the ends and means of foreign policy (Appadorai 1987).

As mentioned earlier, the discipline of anthropology has been neglected by African studies programmes in India. Not a single anthropologist has been appointed to any of the three African Studies centres in India, although there is recognition of the brilliant contribution of anthropologists such as Clark Wissler (1870-1947), Ralph

Linton (1893-1953), Melville J. Herskovits (1895-1963) and George Peter Murdock (1897-1892) in classifying and mapping out cultures of geographical areas or regions. In addition, there are noteworthy contributions to African Studies from anthropologists like Mayor Fortes, C. G. Seligman, E. E. Evans-Pritchard, Hilda Kuper, J. A. Barnes, S. Nadel and Max Gluckman.

The other problem confronting the African studies centres as well as other area studies departments in India is a lack of funds. Area studies calls for more resources and motivation than traditional disciplines. This is partly due to the fact that independent India took to these studies rather late, for obvious reasons like the constraints of our colonial heritage. African studies and other area studies programmes in India need a regular flow of funds to meet various expenses. These include staff training, acquiring library resources, regular field trips, and visiting appointments, especially of foreign scholars.

However, what is frustrating is that unlike in Western countries, the promotion of area studies has never been a priority of the Government of India, the UGC or research agencies like the Indian Council of Social Science Research (ICSSR) and the Indian Council of Historical Research (ICHR). There is hardly any interaction between the Ministry of External Affairs, the Government of India and the area studies centres. Moreover, there is no philanthropic organisation in India like the Rockefeller or Ford Foundations. These organisations came late into India to facilitate area studies. Another problem facing area studies programmes in India is that traditional Indian academics and intellectuals have serious reservations about these programmes. They contend that area studies programmes call for more resources, especially for regular field trips to foreign countries. There is also the unfortunate absence of an African Association of India, in spite of the large presence of Africanists in India. It is indeed a disturbing reflection on the state of African studies in India that no such association has been formed even four decades after the country's first African Studies programme was established.

Now that the African Studies Programme has completed 25 years of existence at JNU and the University of Mumbai, it would be appropriate to take immediate steps to establish an African Studies Association of India. Further, there is a need to introduce Africa as a subject in the school curriculum, as in the United States. This would go a long way in laying the foundation for greater India-Africa understanding. To begin with, it should be confined to schools in Mumbai and Delhi where a short orientation programme can be arranged for the designated school teachers. A small beginning has been made: an active Africa Club exists in the prestigious Springdales School of New Delhi.

Note

1. In the course of writing this article, I have had discussions with many academics, including Africanists such as Prof. Daleep Singh, Prof. R. R. Ramchandani, Prof. Anuruddha Gupta and Prof. Shridhar Shrimali. I acknowledge their insights which have helped me complete the article.

References

Appadorai, A., 1987a, 'International and Area Studies in India', *International Studies* [New Delhi] 14 (2).

Appadorai, A., 1987b, 'African Studies in India', *International Studies* 24 (2).

Biswas, A., 1992, *Indo-Kenyan Political and Economic Relations*, New Delhi: Kanishka Publishing House.

Department of African Studies, University of Delhi, 2000, *Handbook of Information 2000-2001*, University of Delhi.

Government of India, Ministry of Education, 1966, *Education and National Development: Report of the Education Commission*, New Delhi: Ministry of Education.

Hindustan Times (New Delhi), 1955, 6 August.

Hodgkin, Thomas, 1956, *Nationalism in Colonial Africa*, London: Frederick Muller Ltd.

Nehru, J., 1958, *Jawaharlal Nehru's Speeches, vol. 11, 1953-57.*

Nehru, J., 1961, *India's Foreign Policy: Selected Speeches (September 1946-April 1961)*, New Delhi: Government of India Publication Division.

Prasad, B. and U. Phadnis, 1988, 'Area Studies in India', *ICSSR, Survey of Research in Political Science: International Relations* 15: 71-202.

Rajan, M. S., 1991, *Professor A. Appadorai and the Development of International and Area Studies in India: A Personal Memoir*, New Delhi.

Reddy, V. M., 1979, 'Area Studies in India', Presidential Address to Indian History Congress, 40th session, 28-30 December, Andhra University.

Chapter 15

The State of African Studies in Australia[1]

Tanya Lyons and Elizabeth Dimock

The purpose of this chapter is to provide up-to-date evidence on the importance of African studies in contemporary Australia. The chapter sets this discussion within a historical context and examines also the relevance of the African Studies Association of Australasia and the Pacific, Australian government policy towards Africa, and the impact that such policy has on teaching African studies in Australian universities. This chapter will show how African studies exists in Australian universities because of the dedication of a core group of enthusiastic scholars who have had the opportunity to deliver topics on Africa, and develop research in specific fields of interest in their respective university departments.

Unlike the USA where there is 'a brutally direct link between the new geo-politics and academic funding' (Bundy 2002: 67), Australia does not appear to have any government-sponsored initiative to promote the study of Africa, either in relation to the African Diaspora or indeed specific African countries or languages (West and Martin 1997; Lowe 1997). Indeed, the opposite effect was apparent in the 1990s when the Keating Labour Government initiated a closer engagement with Asia to the detriment of links with Africa. When United States President George W. Bush visited Africa in July 2003, he clearly drew links between Africa's instability and global terrorist threats.[2] Africa is logically more important to the United States than to Australia not only because of the history of the slave trade and African American demography, but also due to the desire for access to Africa's vast mineral and oil resources. Instability in Africa, whether caused by poverty, HIV/AIDS, corruption or state collapse has, as we have seen with the bombings of the US Embassies in East Africa in 1998, impacted upon US interests in Africa and in the USA. In the wake of terrorist attacks on New York and Washington and the subsequent war on terror it has become increasingly important to understand ethnic and resource conflicts, collapsed states and unstable regions. Yet, despite Australia's close ties with the

USA and support for its leading role in the war on terror (in Afghanistan and Iraq), Australia persists in its lack of interest in arguably the world's largest unstable region, where some of the roots of terror can be found (see BBC 2002).

Australia's engagement with Africa stems from the Anglo-Boer War, when Australia contributed to the British forces fighting in South Africa. However, popular folklore and reminiscences of Breaker Morant and Baden Powell have little influence on current foreign policy, and Australia's interests in Africa were, through most of the twentieth century, indirectly through London and British colonial links. Perhaps it is no great surprise that Australia has little diplomatic interest in Africa, outside of Commonwealth responsibilities. Nonetheless, the Australian academy still ought to be in a position to provide insight and analysis and offer comparative examples with other collapsing regions (for example the Solomon Islands) from an African perspective (see Reilly 2000). Yet, there are very few experts to call upon in the university sector that purport to have this detailed knowledge of African politics, economy, society and history and in particular, current affairs in Africa.[3] In 2003 there were only eleven academics teaching at least one topic directly related to Africa.[4] If Africa is in crisis, then African studies in Australia is under siege.[5]

An Overview of the History of African Studies in Australia

While the Anglo-Boer war may be seen as the beginning of Australian-African relations, the links between the two continents, as Peter Limb has pointed out, were more complex through the mid-twentieth century, extending from military involvement to immigration issues, cultural, economic and intellectual engagement (Limb 1999). Intellectual links in mid-century were enhanced by the work of Keith Hancock, whose *Survey of Commonwealth Affairs* (1937-41) and his post-war evaluation of colonial rule in Buganda have given him high acclaim as an Australian historian. Fred Alexander, whose teaching in the University of Western Australia included British Empire and European history, was another. Alexander became the foundation Professor of History at UWA in 1948 and was an eminent public figure in Perth. His interest in South Africa stemmed from a visit in 1949 as a Carnegie Fellow, which formed, thereafter, the basis of his teachings and writings on South Africa (Limb 1999).

If there was a heyday of African Studies in Australian universities it was during the anti-apartheid struggles, a time that was also characterised by liberation movements and decolonisation in Africa. As in the US and Britain, African Studies had expanded in the years following the Second World War, coinciding with the upsurge of African nationalism, the initial phase of decolonisation, and the deepening of the Cold War. Area studies, that is, African, Latin American, Asian, and Pacific studies, gained increased significance as the superpowers became involved in geo-political manoeuvres. Tertiary education was expanding in Australia and new universities were established. Courses on Africa were an integral part of humanities and social science degrees in a number of universities. The move towards African independence generated new areas of research in colonial, precolonial and eventually postcolonial studies. The effects of Cold War politics on nationalist and liberation movements in Africa and the militarisation and arms-building that paralleled these movements provided 'grist to the mill' for further research and academic courses in politics, development studies, economics and history.

During the 1970s and 1980s a further impetus drew Africanists in Australia together. Waves of migrants from Southern Africa (South Africa, Namibia, Zimbabwe), fleeing apartheid and white racist regimes, settled in the major cities. The inter-census population increase of South African-born immigrants went from 11,400 between 1976 and 1981, to 10,093 between 1981 and 1986, and to 11,951 between 1986 and 1991, after which the increase dropped significantly (Lucas 2000: 1-3). The total South Africa-born population of Australia was:

1966	9,692
1971	12,655
1976	15,567
1981	26,965
1986	37,058
1991	49,009
1996	55,821

(**Source**: Lucas (2000).

These immigrants included people from all of South Africa's racial categories, but were predominantly white, and had the economic means to re-settle in Australia. They did, however, include members of the banned African National Congress, some Indians and coloureds.[6] The multi-factored issues that crossed racial boundaries and political movements within South Africa were brought to Australia, but the anti-apartheid movement among South Africans in Australia also encompassed existing class, race and political tensions.[7] In Melbourne, for example, the one-year old Anti-Apartheid group disbanded in 1985 because of disagreements with representatives in the SWAPO (South West Africa People's Organisation) and ANC (African National Congress) offices. Intellectual debate concerning apartheid, already a feature of African studies in the universities and of increasing political significance, was thus fuelled by input from South African migrants, both permanent settlers and those who chose Australia for temporary political asylum.

Members of the African Studies Association of Australia were deeply involved, as a survey of papers presented at the annual conference between 1979 and 1985 demonstrates (AFSAAP 1985).[8] A key figure in the anti-apartheid movement in Australia, until his death in 1985, was Jim Gale, a founder member of AFSAAP and also of the Campaign Against Racial Exploitation (CARE). One of Jim Gale's achievements was his role in bringing ANC and SWAPO representatives to Australia and assisting them to establish offices here.

One might get the impression that Australian Africanists have focussed their interests on South Africa and its turbulent political history. This, however, is only part of the story. Many of the academic staff moving into university posts in the

1960s and 1970s had other interests in Africa. This new generation had completed doctoral degrees in Britain, the USA or Africa, had spent considerable periods of time conducting fieldwork in Africa, and had frequently taught in African universities. Some were involved in establishing degree courses in African History, Politics, Education and other disciplines in new universities created in Africa around the time of independence. The research interests of these new arrivals were often continued subsequent to appointment in Australian universities, and their often vibrant links with West, East, Central and Southern African countries were maintained and reflected in teaching and in conference papers.

Given this remarkable history of African Studies in Australia, one might ask why the interest in Africa has not increased, or at least maintained the earlier level of activity. It has been suggested that after Nelson Mandela walked out of prison and democratic elections were held in South Africa in 1994, the struggle was over, and we no longer needed to focus on Africa. This naïve interpretation of events was far from reality. The Rwandan genocide, to name only one tragedy, amply demonstrated the need to continue to analyse and understand Africa's politics, economics, history and society. Nonetheless, as we will see below, many Africanists either shifted to Asian Studies, now the preferred focus of the Australian government policy and many tertiary institutions, or simply, as in Gavin Kitching's case abandoned African studies.

'Giving up' African Studies

Gavin Kitching, a *former* Africanist, at the centre of a recent debate sparked by his article on why he gave up African studies (Kitching 2000), argues that the answers to the questions about Africa's failures are simply too hard. He (unfortunately) joins other scholars such as Manuel Castells who have painted rather bleak pictures of Africa's development woes and have subsequently given up asking the pertinent questions, just as they have given up hope for Africa (see Castells 2000: 112-117, cited in Bundy 2002). The questions surrounding the corruption and failure of the new leaders in postcolonial Africa were the hardest to resolve. The old theories, like dependency and underdevelopment, Kitching explains, 'could not account' for the corruption and mismanagement of many African states, or indeed state collapse. The end of the Cold War, the subsequent marginalisation of Africa combined with the forces of globalisation (see Lyons 2002) have according to Bundy (2000), 'translated into a declining public support for African Studies in the academy'. Is it then any wonder that Kitching dropped his involvement in Africa? Kitching's attempts to reconcile the external and internal constraints on Africa's development might have led him to this juncture. He argues that the new leaders in Africa were long considered by dependency theorists to be the puppets of transnational capital or victims of IMF and World Bank Structural Adjustment policies. Yet, it appears now that they were also simply inadequate as leaders. Colonisation and imperialism had for so long been the scapegoat for Africa's woes that it was difficult for Kitching to conclude that it was these leaders who were hindering development.

Kitching (2000:21) writes that he 'gave up African studies because [he] found it depressing', but emphasised it was not because he did not care what happened to Africa and Africans. His rather emotional response to an historical and political crisis on the African continent may indeed reflect a wider crisis in African Studies in Australia.

Without the exposure of Africa in university teaching curricula, there have been obvious repercussions for research output including the number of PhD students in this field of study. In fact, there would appear to be such scant interest in Africa within the Australian academy that when Kitching's article was first published in 2000, after being presented at an African Studies Conference in Adelaide, hardly an eyebrow was raised in Australia. It was not unusual for an Africanist to move into Asian studies in order to gain or maintain their academic position. Subsequently, it was not until the US-based *Chronicle of Higher Education* (by chance reprinted in an Australian newspaper almost three years later) published an account of Kitching's story and the current debate now raging in Britain and North America (see Bundy 2002, as well as the special edition of the forthcoming online journal *The African Studies Quarterly*, to be edited by Marc Epprecht), that the Australian public was made aware of a crisis in African Studies.[9] The online journal *The African Studies Quarterly* has already commissioned a special edition to explore the problems raised by Kitching, yet Australians have remained eerily silent on the issue. The fact that neither *The Chronicle*, *The African Studies Quarterly*, nor *The Australian* sought an opinion or any analysis from the African Studies Association of Australasia and the Pacific (AFSAAP), might demonstrate how insignificant this association has become, or might simply illustrate the media's inability to draw on the group of experts available in Australia who can provide up to date and relevant analysis on current affairs in Africa. Yet, it was through the pages of AFSAAP's *ARAS* that the controversy was set in motion. Kitching, in fact, argues that we could educate the media about Africa because they are grappling with the same questions but will continue to do so if African Studies is not promoted substantially. In this 'age of globalisation', Kitching points out that we in Australia should know more about Africa than we do. We couldn't agree more with him on this issue. However, it is unfortunate that Kitching felt he had to leave Africa behind (Kitching 2000; Postel 2003).

Survey of African studies in Australian universities in 2003

A recent survey of the 38 public universities in Australia has been made to determine the extent of African studies today. Our method has been to examine all topics offered in Australian universities in 2003, assessing topic titles and outlines as presented in their respective university calendars and student handbooks.

The survey has shown that only fourteen Australian universities appear to have any African Studies in their teaching programmes.[10] A total of 49 topics that mention Africa are on offer at undergraduate and postgraduate levels in these universities. Of these topics, only sixteen are specific to Africa, while another 33 include Africa within a comparative context (see Bates et al., 1993 for an example of African studies themes) (Table 1). Comparative topics include themes such as genocide, agriculture and rural poverty, sociology, philosophy, literature, history, geography, and development and world politics. The Africa-specific topics are taught in only ten universities, as indeed are twenty three of the comparative topics, a total of 39 topics.

Table 1: Universities with the Most African Studies Topics

University	Specific African Studies Topics	Comparative Topics that Mention Africa
La Trobe	4	3
Macquarie	3	0
Flinders	2	3
Western Australia	1	8
Monash	1	1
Curtin	1	0
Melbourne	1	0
Wollongong	1	0
Sydney	1	8
Uni of New South Wales	1	0
Total	16	23

Table 2: Universities Offering Comparative Topics that Mention Africa

University	Specific African Studies Topics	Comparative Topics that Mention Africa
Newcastle	0	4
New South Wales	0	2
Queensland	0	2
Tasmania	0	2
Total	0	10

The remaining ten comparative topics are taught in four other universities (see Table 2). These four universities do not offer any specific African topics, although it should be noted that there are staff with research interests in Africa in each of these universities. Furthermore, our survey has covered the year 2003 only, and topics with an African content may have been offered in other years.

Of the sixteen Africa-specific topics in nine of the ten universities nearly half (seven topics) are located in history departments. These are at Curtin University (one), Latrobe University (three), Melbourne University (one), Sydney University (one), and the University of Western Australia (one). Only four Africa-specific topics are offered in the discipline of politics, two each at Flinders and Macquarie Universities. Of the remaining topics two are in Music Studies, one each at Macquarie and Monash Universities, one is in English at Wollongong University, another one is also in English at the University of New South Wales, and one is in Archaeology at La Trobe University.

Of the 33 topics that use Africa for comparative case studies and/or brief examples, nine are in history, five in politics, three in archaeology, two in agriculture, two in Semitic studies, and one in each of the following: geography, philosophy, English, French, art history, Australian literature, Jewish studies, architecture, fine arts, anthropology, development studies and sociology.

In combining both the specific topics and comparative topics that relate to Africa we find again that the majority, sixteen, are located in the field of history. The next most popular discipline that teaches African studies themes is Political Science (nine topics); archaeology (four topics); music (two topics); agriculture (two topics); English (three topics); and Semitic Studies (two topics). The disciplines of geography, French, philosophy, art history, fine arts, anthropology, Jewish studies, architecture, Australian literature, development studies and sociology all have just one topic that mentions Africa, none of which are specifically African studies topics.

While Sydney University and the University of Western Australia both appear to offer the most topics related to Africa (nine topics each) only one topic in each case is specific to Africa. La Trobe University, however, has the highest number, four, of Africa-specific topics out of seven topics that mention Africa.[11] The other universities with African studies are Macquarie University with three Africa-specific topics, Flinders University, which offers two, and Melbourne, Monash, University of New South Wales and Wollongong which each offer one.

The survey indicates other key features. Africa-specific topics are in most cases electives and not core topics to major sequences of study. The teaching of African studies in Australian universities is dependent on a small number of academic staff; eleven Africanists deliver the Africa-specific topics across ten universities. While this is a somewhat gloomy assessment, the number of people researching African themes might be higher. However, there is no reliable database to calculate this figure.[12]

Listed in the order of the number of topics they teach, these Africanists are as follows. David Dorward taught three topics (each offered every second year) in History at La Trobe University. The topics are: (i) *Africa in the Modern World*, (ii) *Ancient Africa: Delving into the mythic past*, and (iii) *South African History*. David Dorward also teaches two additional topics, *Pox, Plagues and Pestilence*, and *Globalisation*, both of which have a significant African content. Geoffrey Hawker is located in the Politics Department at Macquarie University and teaches two topics related to Africa. These are (i) *Development, Globalisation and State-Building in Africa*, and (ii) *Africa, Politics and Globalisation*. Tanya Lyons is in the School of Political and International Studies at Flinders University and teaches two topics; (i) *Africa on a Global Stage* and (ii) *African Politics: Global Issues*. Taught for the first time in 2003 her topics attracted a total of 22 students.

Sue Kossew in the English Department at the University of New South Wales teaches one topic called *African Resistance Literature* and Anne Collett in the English Department at Wollongong University teaches one topic called *Africa and the New World*. While there are other academics located in English departments around Australia who have demonstrated an interest in Africa literature, Kossew's and Collett's topics were the only Africa-specific topics.

Reis Flora, an Ethnomusicologist in the School of Music at Monash University has taught *Music of Sub-Saharan Africa* every third year since his appointment there in 1973. The topic attracts about 45 students, which may in part reflect the wider interest in African music and drumming in Victoria. While Flora's main area of interest and research is the music of North India, he has 'always found music and dance from sub-Saharan Africa compelling',[13] and perhaps because of this, Monash University's School of Music Conservatorium owns a full ensemble of Ewe drums, including the double bells, two *atoke*, and three gourd rattles. The Matheson Library at Monash has possibly the finest collection of music from sub-Saharan Africa on LP discs and CDs in Australia.[14]

Joan Wardrop in the History department at Curtin University teaches one topic on *South Africa the Politics of Memory*. She is also involved with the African Studies Centre of Western Australia. Her colleague Jeremy Martens in the History department of The University of Western Australia teaches one topic called *An Introduction to African History*.[15]

As an archaeologist and a member of the African Research Institute at La Trobe University, Nicola Stern is well placed to teach African studies. She teaches one undergraduate topic simply called *African Archaeology*. Nicola Stern has been instrumental in the 'Blue Tuff' archaeological project in Kenya.[16]

David Phillips teaches one topic called *South Africa under Apartheid*, in the History department at the University of Melbourne. In 2003 there were 115 students enrolled, the highest number previously being 135 students. Like many African studies topics, this one has only limited support from the university and is taught by someone who was 'appointed as a British historian, who mainly teaches courses on Modern British history, Australian history, and some comparative colonial history. If [Phillips] disappear[s], so does African history from Melbourne University.'[17]

Issues relevant to the African Diaspora should be considered equally important in the general field of African studies. Thus, we have included Shane White's history topic at Sydney University entitled *The Black Experience in the Americas*. The importance of the Slave Trade and American history in understanding historical events in Africa is obvious. Recent events in Liberia can attest to this.

In sum, we have a small and eclectic list of Africanists currently teaching Africa-specific topics in Australia. How did it get to this minority proportion? And what do the results of the survey mean? In the next section, we will analyse this further.

Other Perspectives on African Studies in Australia

At the start of the twenty-first century, the generation of Africanist scholars that came in to the universities in the 1970s is a diminishing group. Natural attrition through retirement, death or promotion (to administrative positions within the university) has taken its toll (see Bundy 2002: 61).[18] But what a list this is! These scholars include: Professors Anthony Low and Deryck Schreuder, prominent imperial historians, who moved into university administration, Professors Norman Etherington, Martin Chanock, Peter Alexander, David Goldsworthy, Cherry Gertzel, Gareth Griffiths, David Dorward, Derek Wright and others. While they have each published extensively, some of their more significant contributions have been Low's early work on Buganda (Low and Pratt 1960; Low 1971, 1991, 1996); Schreuder's (1980, 1991) on imperialism and on Southern Africa; Alexander's biographies of Alan Paton (1994); William Plomer (1989); and Roy Campbell (1982); Etherington's analysis of imperialism (1984)and his ground-breaking new style, post-1995 analysis of South Africa history (2001); Chanock's examination of law, custom, gender in Zambia and Malawi in the colonial period (1985) and, more recently, the making of South African legal culture (Chanock and Simpson 1996; Chanock 2000); David Goldsworthy's contribution to the End of Empire documentary series and the histories coming out of that project (Goldsworthy et al., 1994; Goldsworthy 2002); Gareth Griffiths' work on postcolonial literatures, specifically African literature (Griffiths et al., 1989; 2000; Griffiths 2000); and Derek Wright's (1993, 1997) work on Wole Soyinka (see also Gertzel 1974, 1984, 1991). There is more to be said, however, and this section will further examine this first generation, and the institutions established by them, before looking at later changes and a younger generation of scholars.

Penelope Hetherington, whose enthusiasm and passion for Africa has not gone unnoticed, is worth noting here. Not only has she detailed her experiences in teaching African studies in her soon to be published autobiography,[19] she has demonstrated a typical process of how African studies has developed in Australia. As the author of *British Paternalism in Africa 1920-1940* (Hetherington 1976), she began teaching African history in the early 1980s. Like many Africanists in Australia, she was a university lecturer given an opportunity to develop and deliver her own topic, and she chose Africa. It was that simple. She found support for her endeavours from AFSAAP and as will be detailed below provided one of the few intellectual engagements for scholars of Africa in Australia. Her story demonstrates the vulnerability and provisional nature of African studies in Australia.

Hetherington wrote in her autobiography that she 'knew that African studies had begun to take off' (Hetherington n.d.) particularly after participating in her first AFSAAP Conference. While she was teaching African History at the University of Western Australia however, Hetherington was one of a small group of academics doing so. This situation remains today. While Hetherington was establishing herself as an Africanist at the University of Western Australia, David Dorward and Tom Spear at La Trobe University were busy establishing AFSAAP and later the African Research Institute. Around the same time Cherry Gertzel was appointed to the Flinders University School of Political and International Studies in 1975 and taught African Studies until 1993 when she retired. She was replaced by David Moore who came from Canada in 1994 before taking up a post in South Africa in 2000, whereupon the post of African studies lecturer became redundant. The position was reestablished in 2003 when Tanya Lyons began teaching two African studies topics with the support of the School of Political and International Studies and the Globalisation Programme at Flinders University.

While the disciplines of History and Politics were dominant in the 1970s and early 1980s there have been interesting disciplinary shifts in the last twenty years. The study of African literatures, important from the 1960s with the earliest publications of Chinua Achebe, Bessie Head, Ngugi wa Thiong'o and others, has expanded, and in the 1990s cultural studies, media studies (film in particular) and musicology have become more significant. In theoretical fields, postcolonial and post-structural theory, much debated and disputed, have also become important. Concerning the latter the academy is much divided. Nevertheless the boundary between representation and historic reality (inasmuch as one can even consider this a possibility), is one that must be grappled with in all disciplines. The field of postcolonial scholarship has provided teaching and research especially in English departments throughout Australia, notwithstanding cut-backs to university budgets in the 1990s. Herein lies a contradiction. Our survey shows that few such scholars are teaching Africa-specific topics, yet African literature is encompassed within general topics on postcolonial literature at undergraduate and honours degree levels. This is an indicator of how African studies has merged with other regional studies in a new academic order.

To look specifically at English departments, at the University of New South Wales Peter Alexander, Sue Kossew and Bill Ashcroft have all published in the field of Africa, African literature or postcolonial writing. Sue Thomas at La Trobe, Helen Gilbert and Joanne Tompkins at the University of Queensland, Andrew Peek at the University of Tasmania, Chandani Lokuge at Monash, Anne Maxwell at the University of Melbourne, Rosemary Colmer at Macquarie, and Paul Sharrud at Wollongong all have research interests and publications in African literature, although they do not offer teaching topics specific to Africa Studies. Derek Wright, a renowned scholar, and an authority on the work of Wole Soyinka, was unfortunately one who lost his position when the whole of the English department in the University of Darwin was closed in a massive down-sizing exercise.[20]

The demography department at the Australian National University (the ANU) is a further case in point. Through several decades this department has spearheaded research in population studies in the developing world, with Africa as a special focus since the publication of Jack Caldwell's *African Rural-Urban Migration* in 1969 and his subsequent appointment to a chair of Demography. In 1971 Jack and Pat Caldwell, together with Helen Ware, ran the Changing African Family Project from the University of Ibadan, encompassing twelve countries. From this time, African graduates were drawn into the project and during the 1990s a flow of African graduates have completed the MA in Demography at the ANU with Australian government funding, with some students going on to complete a PhD degree. While the Caldwells have now retired, David Lucas, a long-term lecturer in the department, continues, and as government funding has eased, financial support has come from the UN and more recently from the Wellcome Trust.

There has also been a shift of government interest and official funding away from Africa which has parallelled the upheaval in the tertiary education sector, associated with economic rationalism (neoliberalism) and 'user pays' ideology. Changing funding structures and the rigorous tightening of the universities' budget have been associated with the encouragement of vocational courses in the universities and in particular the expansion of technology courses, computer studies and business studies, with related negative effects on the humanities and social sciences. In the latter, departments have reduced their staff numbers by not renewing contracts and not replacing tenured staff as they retire. Promotions have in some cases been held back. Staffing levels have been halved in many humanities and social science areas, with less capacity for supervision of postgraduates with specific interests. One effect of this misery has been to encourage Africanists to apply for overseas positions, with the loss of some able scholars. Gareth Griffiths, Pal Ahluwalia, and Peter Limb have been lost to Australian African studies in the last two years, the USA and English universities benefiting from our loss.

A further shift in the early 1990s was effected by the Paul Keating Labour Government's policies which favoured a greater political and economic engagement with Asia. Asian studies received a new lease on life. Asian languages and business-oriented courses encompassing Japan, Indonesia, China and other southern and south-east Asian countries were funded in expanding departments.

Although our survey has suggested that African studies is in a perilous state, further analysis indicates that teaching programmes and the research interests of individual scholars continue to promote African studies. We would argue that the current state of African studies in Australia is not completely hopeless. Despite the small numbers of topics on offer in a small group of Australian universities, there remains a committed group of scholars who conduct research on Africa and African languages and literature and incorporate Africa into more general teaching topics.

Although the demography department at the ANU is unique in attracting students from Africa, African postgraduate students, in more random manner, have made their way to departments of history, politics and development studies programmes around the country, some sponsored by the Australian government through aid programmes. This has sadly been tightened up in recent years.

Australian universities, furthermore, have positioned themselves within Africa, particularly in South Africa, with offshore campuses and the offshore teaching of Australian degrees (such as Bond University, Monash University and the University of South Australia). None of these, sadly, engage in the study of Africa, but deliver, rather, a global education such as in business and communications to an African elite that can afford an Australian university degree.[21] We would argue that funding should be available for supporting a wider range of programmes in African universities.

A further factor concerns the increasing African-Australian population especially in state capital cities. Some university campuses have considerable numbers of African-Australian students. While there may be no particular desire by these students for courses on Africa, this may be because the courses currently on offer do not take their interests into account. More research is needed in this. The presence of a growing African-Australian community is a reminder of the complex demography and social movements of the world in 2003, and of the need for understanding diverse cultures.

Although our survey has demonstrated a small, and threatened, nucleus of Africa-specific courses in Australian universities, there is a more complex story which is perhaps less gloomy. The problem is to maintain some cohesion amongst African interests in the universities and to maintain pressure on federal and state governments for funding and other support. In this respect, links established with government, non-government organisations and other interest groups are important. In recognising the small base from which African studies operates, creating links across these other sectors seems to be important.

African Studies Association of Australasia and the Pacific[22]

Bringing together all of the eclectic disciplines, academics, researchers, organizations and interest groups is the African Studies Association of Australasia and the Pacific (AFSAAP). The Association was formed when a number of Africanists gathered together during the 1977 Australian and New Zealand Association for the Advancement of Science (ANZAAS) Conference to discuss common problems and concerns, including their physical and intellectual isolation. During the following year Dr David Dorward and Dr Tom Spear organised a conference under the title of 'African Modes of Production' at La Trobe University where they were both teaching African History. At the same meeting a decision was made to form the African Studies Association of Australia and the Pacific (AFSAAP). This coincided with a rising tide for African Studies in Australia (Gertzel 1998). Professor Anthony Low, then Vice-Chancellor of the Australian National University and an eminent Africanist, agreed to be the President of AFSAAP. An Association Newsletter was also inaugurated and the founding members agreed that the Association would endeavour to convene an annual conference.

The second conference held at the Australian National University in 1979 was a larger event and focussed on 'contemporary issues', with a decidedly political emphasis. In 1980 the conference returned to La Trobe University with the theme of promoting the teaching of Africa in schools. In 1981 the University of New South Wales hosted the conference with the theme 'Africa and the Media' and in 1982 the conference returned to the Australian National University when a new President, Dr Cherry Gertzel of the Centre for Development Studies at Flinders University, was elected. A special AFSAAP section on Southern Africa in Transition was also organised by Professor Deryck Schreuder of the University of Sydney as part of the annual conference of the Australian Historical Association. Other conferences followed at Monash, the University of Melbourne, then a bold venture in having a conference in Wellington, New Zealand where it was hosted by the African Information Centre.

These early conferences and their range of themes indicate the diversity of focus that existed in African Studies as well as the geographical spread of participants. The annual conference moved between Melbourne, Canberra and Sydney in the first decade, and later included Adelaide and then Perth. Concern about Perth's 'isolation' from the eastern states of Australia delayed the first conference there until 1991 with the theme of 'Transfers of Power in Southern Africa'. The more recent Perth conference, in 1999, had a registration of around 500 participants and was the largest AFSAAP conference held so far. Perth is the closest Australian city to Africa, a decided advantage in linking African concerns to Australian academic interests. The 1999 conference attracted a large number of South African colleagues, due largely to the efforts of Peter Limb, who, sadly, has become part of the Africanist brain-drain and has since moved to the United States. The 1999 conference also gave an artificial impression of an expansion of the Association and level of interest in Africa.[23] This however, lasted only as long as the millennium celebrations.

A cursory look at the last few AFSAAP conference programmes[24] illustrates not only that smaller conferences are being held, but that more non-Australians are interested in African studies in Australia than resident Australians. Of note is that in many cases the interest comes from our colleagues in Nigeria, Kenya, Uganda, Mozambique, and Ghana who are seldom able to obtain funding and have often had to withdraw for that reason. Australian universities are unable, or unwilling, to assist in this, although they often find funds for visiting conference delegations from Asia. There is further negative response from the government that frequently denies visas for African participants to AFSAAP conferences.

Another dilemma for AFSAAP is the declining membership numbers (approximately 85 members in 2003). The annual conference continues to bring African studies scholars from Australasia, the Pacific and around the world together, but has become increasingly dominated by non-members of the association from outside of the region (Australasia and the Pacific). While this in itself is not the problem, the challenge for the Association in maintaining its membership base is a critical factor if it is to continue.

A more positive aspect of the progress of AFSAAP during the 1990s has been the expansion of the earlier newsletter, through various name and content changes to its current state as a respected, refereed journal, the *Australasian Review of African Studies (ARAS)* which has an international editorial board, and was edited by Cherry Gertzel until 2005 when Helen Ware took over as editor. *ARAS* publishes scholarly articles across the wide inter-disciplinary field of African studies and shorter contributions on research matters/reports, professional involvement in Africa and other notes relating to Africa and Australian engagement with Africa. A more comprehensive website for AFSAAP has also been established in recent years with the support of Flinders University, Adelaide, Australia (see www.ssn.flinders.edu.au/global/afsaap).

African Research Institute, La Trobe University, Melbourne

Another institution that has helped to promote African Studies is the African Research Institute in Victoria. Founded in 1985 at La Trobe University in Melbourne, with David Dorward as Director, the African Research Institute is the first and only institute of its kind in Australia. Multi-disciplinary in approach, the aims are: to stimulate and promote research and postgraduate teaching in the field of African studies; to promote interaction and cooperation in research and teaching with members of academic or research staff of other institutions in Victoria, elsewhere in Australia and overseas; to initiate postgraduate and post-doctoral interchange between institutions; to give institutional structure to links with organisations and institutions outside La Trobe; and to provide advisory services to government and non-government bodies, such as the corporate sector, trade unions, aid agencies and the media.[25]

The African Research Institute encompassed teaching staff in legal studies (now law), agriculture, archaeology, English and history. Renowned scholars have included Professors Martin Chanock and Penny Andrews (now at the City University of New York), Dr. Nicola Stern, Associate Professor David Dorward, Professor Tom Spear (now at Wisconsin in the US) and Associate Professor Sue Thomas. Within these disciplines there has been a continuous stream of Honours, Masters and PhD candidates. The Institute is supported by an excellent African collection of monographs, serials and microform resources in the Borchardt Library (See Fisch 2003).

Visits of notable persons organized through the Institute have included Oliver Tambo and Archbishop Desmond Tutu in 1987 and 1993, each of whom addressed large crowds in the Union Hall at La Trobe University. In 1991 when the move towards multi-racial democracy in South Africa was well under way, Walter Sisulu, Deputy President of the African National Congress, and Albertina Sisulu, Deputy President of the ANC Women's League and Co-President of the United Democratic Front coalition, also visited the university. Later in 1991 Cyril Ramaphosa, then General Secretary of the National Union of Mineworkers, the largest Black trade union in South Africa, gave a luncheon address to a large audience of staff and students. Other visitors included His Holiness Pope Shenouda III, Patriarch of Alexandria and Spiritual Head of the Coptic Orthodox Church, who delivered an address to the University in 1989.[26]

Members of the African Research Institute have been involved in various co-operative teaching programmes with other institutions, particularly in distance education programmes offered through Deakin University. There has been effective liaison between the Institute and Africanists at other Victorian universities and colleges on matters relating to teaching, thesis research and library acquisitions. Professor James Polhemus, formerly Dean of Social Sciences at Deakin University, and Professor David Goldsworthy in Politics at Monash University, have both been associate members of the Institute.

The African Studies Centre, Perth

On the other side of the continent the University of Western Australia (whose now retired Vice Chancellor, Professor Deryck Schreuder, is an Africanist and member of AFSAAP) hosts the African Studies Centre of Western Australia (ASCWA). The centre was established in July 1997 after a successful African Seminar Program inaugurated in 1996.

The Centre is a multi-disciplinary and multi-campus body that organises an annual programme of seminars in all fields of African Studies; encourages the study of African studies and awareness of Africa in W.A.; maintains a web page and e-mail contact list; [and] hosts international visitors in the field of African studies. The African Studies Centre Committee has contacts on all Western Australian university campuses. It also organises social events. It works closely with the African Studies Association of Australasia and the Pacific (AFSAAP).[27]

Links with Government, NGOs, and other Interest Groups

Africanists in Australia, as individuals or by association with AFSAAP and/or the African Research Institute, have taken activist roles concerning government and non-government relations with Africa. Links have been forged with the Department of Foreign Affairs and Trade, the Australian Council for Overseas Aid and many of its constituent organisations, such as Australian Volunteers International (formerly the Overseas Service Bureau) as well as with Oxfam/Community Aid Abroad. The African Research Institute also has ties with the Africa-Australia Business Council, the South Africa Business Council and a broad spectrum of African community and special interest groups. Members of the Australian diplomatic corps have visited the Institute before departure to postings in Africa and provided briefings upon their return to Australia. Members of the African diplomatic corps in Australia are regularly invited to AFSAAP annual conferences to contribute presentations about their country or their country's perspective on broader issues concerning the continent.

The drawing together of these interest groups has been of particular importance in Australia. The small population concentrated in a handful of urban settlements dispersed around the seaboard of a large continent has made for pockets of awareness of Africa concentrated in Melbourne, Sydney, Adelaide, Perth and Canberra, which are relatively isolated from each other. In each centre there has been a history of liaison between NGOs and Africanists in the universities. AFSAAP has been a unifying factor and provided an institution from which government committees and departments have sought submissions concerning policy development. AFSAAP, along with the African Research Institute and individual Africanists, has maintained a continuing critique of government policies concerning Africa. Discussion of these matters was a formal, and informal, feature of AFSAAP conferences throughout the 1980s and 1990s, and will certainly continue if the Association survives. Papers, news and notes in the *AFSAAP Newsletter* for the years 1984 and 1985 demonstrate that this trend was already in place.[28] Items included 'Australia's diplomatic representation in Africa' (March 1984), notes on 'The Jackson Committee Report', 'The Overseas Service Bureau', 'The Australian NGO Preparatory Seminar of ICARA II' attended by an AFSAAP representative (July 1984), 'Training aid in the era of comparative advantage: African development planning at Sydney', 'ACIAR and farming systems research' (November 1984), etc.

The relationship between these sectoral interests was significant in relation to the 1984 *Jackson Report*, which marked a change in Australian policy concerning humanitarian aid and the gradual weakening of official interest in black Africa. Since that time official emphasis has been on trade rather than aid. This emphasis was entrenched by the *Simons Report on Australian Overseas Assistance* in 1997, which substantially lessened development assistance to Africa. With government focus placed largely on southern Africa and trade, the NGOs were left to take up the humanitarian aid requirements. AFSAAP, along with individual members, made submissions to the 1995 Parliamentary Enquiry into Australia's Political, Security and Trade Interests with Southern Africa, which preceded the *Simons Report*. The AFSAAP submission firmly recommended the extension of Australia's interest beyond southern Africa, but noted the importance of Australia's development of bilateral relations with South Africa at the time of the first multi-racial elections in that year.[29] AFSAAP has continued to maintain links with the NGOs.

It is perhaps ironic that as Africanists in the universities have found it increasingly difficult to obtain funding for fieldwork, particularly postgraduate funding, first-hand Australian knowledge of Africa has come increasingly through Australian NGO workers on the ground. Given the small population of Australia, an integrated emphasis on Africa, in which Africanists in the universities, that is the core of research and higher education, in close liaison with the NGOs and the government sector, would seem to be crucial to assuring a viable field of African studies in Australia and in attaining and maintaining a body of expertise on Africa.

There is trade and investment in various African countries by the Australian mining, energy, banking, service, and manufacturing sectors. The African Research Institute and individual members of AFSAAP have established links with the Australia Southern African Business Council (ASABC). Australia's trade with southern Africa has grown to roughly half that with Indonesia in recent years. There are also links between individual members of AFSAAP and the African Research Institute with AusTrade and its presence in Pretoria. These are areas where building strategic interests in Africa may be extended to the advantage of African studies in Australia.

Conclusion

Measuring the overall interest in African studies in Australia according to teaching capacity in university curricula might suggests that there is very little interest in African studies in Australia. A brief survey of Australia's mainstream media furthermore might also conclude that there is hardly any interest in Africa, and little in-depth knowledge of African issues. Shifts in government policies concerning development aid away from Africa during the last decade and the turmoil in the universities caused by cuts in university budgets have caused enormous distress to academics with interests in Africa and reduced the core community of Africanists to small numbers, with additional losses caused by a brain drain to America, Africa and Britain. Funding for African research has never been high on Australian agendas for grants, and the combined focus of vocational, business, technological courses associated with Australia's rising economic and political interests in South East Asia has made African Studies particularly vulnerable.

Perhaps the most obvious explanation for the lessening prominence of African studies has much to do with Australian foreign policy and priorities (See Ford 2002; 2003), not to mention Australia's historical past. However, with current foreign affairs concerns about collapsed states in Australia's region (The Solomons, PNG, and Fiji) there might be a need to develop closer links with Africa and Africanists who are engaged in exploring the historical and political reasons for collapsed states in Africa and its prospects for the future.

A fuller analysis indicates that the suggested malaise in African studies may not be wholly true. Community interest, such as participation in cultural events and, in the NGO sector, an interest in development issues, for example through child sponsorship programmes and so on, are significant in Australia, and these create additional links with Africa, Africans and African Australians.

Keen support for African studies in Australia has continued mainly because of dedicated academics, who continue their research and teaching on African issues. The survey of teaching on Africa in Australian universities, on which this paper has been based, while showing a very small core community of Africanists, indicates that there are considerable numbers of other academic staff whose teaching and research interests incorporate Africa. These workers, at the fringe of the community of Africanists, are the ones whom we would like to see more centrally placed. These, along with core Africanists, work in isolation in their respective universities, only coming together once a year under the umbrella of the African Studies Association of Australasia and the Pacific. It is these academics who should, as Colin Bundy (2002: 73) suggests, 'take pride' in their efforts to understand a complex world and to make it a better place. We would argue that now is not the time to give up on Africa or African Studies in Australia.

Notes

1. Since this chapter was written there have been further retirements. Professor Schreuder has retired as Vice Chancellor of the University of Western Australia, Professor David Dorward from the African Research Institute and Dr David Lucas from the Demography Department at the ANU. There has been no replacement of Dr Dorward's position and the African Research Institute is itself under threat. On the other hand, Professor Gareth Griffiths has returned to the University of Western Australia and Professor Pal Ahluwalia has resumed an Australian academic position in the University of South Australia, which will be coupled with teaching in the University of California in San Diego, USA. Promotions

include Sue Thomas to a full chair at La Trobe University and Dr. Geoffrey Hawker to Head of the School of Politics at Macquarie University.

2. US Pledge on Africa Terror, http://news.bbc.co.uk/2/hi/africa/3060379.stm

3. While the African Research Institute at La Trobe University often puts out media releases and other information, the general lack of experts has only recently become noticeable to the authors due to the increasingly large number of phone calls received from national and local radio stations wanting interviews and information on African issues.

4. Gertzel foreshadowed this contraction of African Studies as early as 1998. There were then 'at least 30 scholars in different disciplines engaged in teaching and research' (Gertzel 1998). For a comparison read Lonsdale (2000).

5. Here the Australians join a host of American and British counterparts who have been 'frustrated' in their Africanist pursuits, not only due to an 'epistemological angst' regarding 'who can speak for whom?', but due also to a gloomy sense of Africa's marginality in both the world and the academy. See Bundy (2002).

6. White settlers from Kenya and Rhodesia were also among Australian immigrants of this period. Some, including white South Africans, were supporters of apartheid policies.

7. African Research Institute archives.

8. 'Papers presented at AFSAAP conferences 1979-1985' *AFSAAP Newsletter,* 10-16. Wider problems in Southern Africa, including papers on Namibia, Zimbabwe and Mozambique were central in a symposium on Southern Africa at La Trobe in March 1985.

9. Within AFSAAP, however, there has been concern about the state of the field for ten years or more. Africanists in Australia, and AFSAAP, have attempted to influence government through submissions to the Jackson and Simons Reports, etc.

10. Many thanks to Julie Tonkin for help in collating this information. This list might include some topics that were not on offer in 2003, and might not include topics that were not available from university web-sites.

11. Two additional topics were offered as summer and winter courses by Liz Dimock on a one off basis (Gender and Imperialism in Africa and Women, Race and Gender in Africa; notably the only topics related to women or gender).

12. We can use the annual AFSAAP Conference programme to demonstrate the level of interest in African research: about 50 percent of the 55 papers listed at the 2002 conference at Macquarie University were by locals, while the remaining papers were given by members and non-members from outside Australia. Of the 62 papers listed for the 2003 Conference at Flinders University, 60 percent are being offered by participants from overseas while only 40 percent are being presented by locals. Of the total presenters only 22 percent (or 14) are actual members of AFSAAP.

13. In 2003 Flora was assisted by Chris Lesser who completed his Masters thesis (Lesser 1996) on West African drumming. Lesser is well-known in the African music performance circles in Melbourne, Australia, and he has been on a number of field trips to West Africa. I am grateful to Reis Flora for his personal correspondence detailing this information. July 2003.

14. Part of this collection includes a copy of Hugh Tracey's 'Catalogue: the Sounds of Africa Series', which includes 210 long playing records of music and songs from Central,

Eastern and Southern Africa. The library subscribes to the journal *African Music* and has been systematically purchasing monographs on music in Africa.

15. Martens has recently replaced Norman Etherington who was teaching African history at the University of Adelaide between 1972 and the mid-1980s and then began teaching history at the University of Western Australia in 1993.

16. 'Blue tuff' is the informal name given to a sedimentary horizon in the Koobi Fora Formation in northern Kenya that contains traces of activities of early African *Home erectus*.

17. Personal Correspondence from David Phillips.

18. Colin Bundy confirms that even in the United Kingdom the 'subject is dying because its practitioners are fading away' Bundy (2002: 61).

19. Penelope Hetherington, from her unpublished autobiography.

20. At the October 2003 Annual Conference of AFSAAP, Bob Turner of Bushbooks, who has attended every conference during the last twelve years, pointed out that book sales in African literatures far exceed the sale of all other categories concerned with Africa.

21. While this area of global education would provide an interesting insight into the expansion of Australian education overseas and Australia's relationship with Africa in relation to education, such a task will not be undertaken here.

22. It was during the 1979 meeting in Canberra that AFSAAP changed its name from the 'African Studies Association of Australia' to the 'African Studies Association of Australia and the Pacific' in recognition of the participation of Africanists from such diverse regional states as New Zealand, Fiji and Papua New Guinea. In 1995 the name was again changed to the more inclusive 'African Studies Association of Australasia and the Pacific'.

23. See the AFSAAP 1999 conference website http://www.arts.uwa.edu.au/ASCWA/conference99/

24. See AFSAAP 2000, 2001, 2002, 2003 Conference websites: www.ssn.flinders.edu.au/global/afsaap/conferences/

25. African Research Institute Report, 1985-1990, www.hist.latrobe.edu.au/africanresearchinstitute

26. Many of these visitors visited other universities as well as government departments in Canberra. The African Research Institute Annual Reports conveniently list visitors, but only for La Trobe.

27. The African Studies Centre of Western Australia. See their website at http://www.arts.uwa.edu.au/ASCWA/

28. The *AFSAAP Newsletter,* then published three times a year with 20-40 pages per issue, included short articles or papers, news and notes.

29. In the period following these elections a number of representatives of the new South African government made visits to Australia, addressing meetings and institutions. It is noteworthy that seven Kenyan parliamentarians spent a month in Australia in 1997 as guests of the government as part of a study tour.

References

Alexander, P., 1982, *Roy Campbell: A Critical Biography*, Oxford: Oxford Univ. Press.

Alexander, P., 1989, *William Plomer: a Biography*, Oxford & New York: Oxford Univ. Press.

Alexander, P., 1994, *Alan Paton: a Biography*, Cape Town & Oxford: Oxford Univ. Press.

Bates, R., V.Y. Mudimbe, and J. O'Barr, 1993, *Africa and the Disciplines: The Contribution of Research in Africa to the Social Sciences and Humanities*, Chicago: University of Chicago Press.

BBC, 2002, *Africa's Ground Zero (The Bin Laden Effect)*, BBC Focus on Africa.

Bundy, C., 2002, 'Continuing a conversation: prospects for African Studies in the 21st century', *African Affairs* 101: 61-73.

Castells, M., 2000, *End of Millennium, Vol. III of The Information Age, Economy, Society and Culture*, Second edition, Oxford: Blackwell.

Chanock, M., 1985, *Law, Custom, and Social Order: the Colonial Experience in Malawi and Zambia*, Cambridge: Cambridge University Press.

Chanock, M., 2000, *The Making of South African Legal Culture, 1902-1936: Fear, Favour, and Prejudice*, New York: Cambridge University Press.

Chanock, M. and C. Simpson, eds., 1996, *Law and Cultural Heritage*, Bundoora, Victoria: La Trobe University Press.

Etherington, N., 1984, *Theories of Imperialism: War Conquest and Capital*, Totowa, NJ: Barnes & Noble Books.

Etherington, N., 2001, *The Great Treks: the Transformation of Southern Africa, 1815-1854*, Harlow: Longman.

Fisch, E., 2003, 'African collections at the La Trobe University Library', *The Australasian Review of African Studies* XXV (1): 87-96.

Ford, J., 2002, 'Australia's Aid to Africa', *The Drawing Board*, 16 October 2002, http://www.econ.usyd.edu.au/drawingboard/digest/0210/ford.html

Ford, J., 2003, 'Australian-Africa relations 2002: another look', *Australian Journal of International Affairs* 57 (1): 17-33.

Gertzel, C., 1974, *Party and Locality in Northern Uganda, 1945-1962*, London: Athlone Press for the Institute of Commonwealth Studies, University of London.

Gertzel, C., ed., 1984, *The Dynamics of the One-Party State in Zambia*, Manchester & Dover, NH: Manchester University Press.

Gertzel, C., 1991, *Uganda, an Annotated Bibliography of Source Materials: with Particular Reference to the Period since 1971 and up to 1988*, London & New York: Hans Zell.

Gertzel, C., 1998, 'African Studies in Australia', *Australasian Review of African Studies* 20 (1): 4-11.

Goldsworthy, D., 2002, *Losing the blanket: Australia and the end of Britain's empire*, Carlton South, Victoria: Melbourne University Press.

Goldsworthy, D., D. A. Low, and S. R. Ashton, 1994, *British Documents in the End of Empire Series A: Volume 3. The Conservative Government and the End of Empire 1951-1957*, London: Institute of Commonwealth Studies.

Griffiths, G., 2000, *African Literatures in English: East and West*, Harlow: Longman.

Griffiths, G., B. Ashcroft, and H. Tiffin, 1989, *The Empire Writes Back: Theory and Practice in Post-Colonial Literatures*, London & New York: Routledge.

Griffiths, G., B. Ashcroft, and H. Tiffin, 2000, *Post-Colonial Studies: the Key Concepts*, London & New York: Routledge.

Hancock, W. K., 1937-41, *A Survey of Commonwealth Affairs*, Vol. 1, London: Oxford University Press.

Kitching, G., 2000, 'Why I gave up African Studies', *African Studies Review and Newsletter* 22 (1): 21-26.

Lesser, C., 1996, *Note Placement and Placement Flexibility in Asante Speech-Mode Drumming*, Unpublished MA Thesis, La Trobe University, Bundoora, Victoria.

Limb, P., 1999, 'An Australian historian at the dawn of apartheid: Fred Alexander in South Africa, 1949-1950', *The Electronic Journal of Australian and New Zealand History*, http://www.jcu.edu.au/aff/history/articles/limb.htm.

Lonsdale, J., 2000, 'African Studies in the United Kingdom', *Australasian Review of African Studies* 22 (2).

Low, D. A., 1971, *Buganda in Modern History*, London: Weidenfeld & Nicolson,

Low, D. A., 1991, *Eclipse of Empire*, Cambridge & New York: Cambridge University Press.

Low, D. A., 1996, *The Egalitarian Moment: Asia and Africa, 1950-1980*, Cambridge: Cambridge University Press.

Low, D. A and R. C. Pratt, 1960, *Buganda and British Overrule, 1900-1955: Two Studies*, London: published on behalf of East African Institute of Social Research by Oxford University Press.

Lowe, C., 1997, 'Resurrection how? a response to Michael O. West and William G. Martin's article, "A future with a past: resurrecting the study of Africa in the post-Africanist era"', *Africa Today* 44 (4): 385-423.

Lucas, D., 2000, *Community Profiles: 1996 Census*, Department of Immigration and Multicultural Affairs, Statistics Section.

Lyons, T., 2002, 'Africa at the edge of globalisation', *Australasian Review of African Studies* 24 (2): 38-48.

Postel, D., 2003, 'Out of Africa and into contention', *The Chronicle of Higher Education*, reprinted in *The Australian*, Wednesday 9 April 2003.

Schreuder, D. M., 1980, *The Scramble for Southern Africa, 1877-1895: the Politics of Partition Reappraised*, Cambridge & New York: Cambridge University Press.

Schreuder, D. M., 1991, *Imperialisms: Explorations in European Expansion and Empire*, Sydney: Sydney Studies in History, History Department, University of Sydney.

West, M. O. and W. G. Martin, 1997, 'A future with a past: resurrecting the study of Africa in the post-Africanist era', *Africa Today* 44 (3): 309-326.

Wright, D., 1993, *Wole Soyinka Revisited*, Toronto; Maxwell Macmillan Canada; New York, Maxwell Macmillan International.

Wright, D., 1997, *Contemporary African Fiction*, Bayreuth, Germany: E. Breitinger.

Chapter 16

African Studies in China in the Twentieth Century: A Historiographical Survey

Li Anshan

African studies in China has been perceived as more or less a myth to Africanists in other parts of the world. In 1981, Dr George T. Yu, an expert on China's policy towards Africa, visited China and was followed by another visit by an American delegation of Africanists in 1984. The visits started a Sino-US African Studies Exchange Programme.[1] However, owing to the language barrier and lack of involvement in the international academia by Chinese scholars, Africanists in the world are still unfamiliar with African studies in China.[2] This paper tries to give a general survey of African studies in China in the twentieth century, informative rather than critical. Divided into five parts chronologically, it will deal with history, political, and cultural studies and other related fields, with an analysis of the factors that have contributed to the African studies in China.

Contacting Africa (Before 1900)

The evidence in China and abroad indicates that China and Africa have had a long history of contact. There were frequent exchanges of products between China and Egypt in the ancient times.[3] The major ones are as follows:

(a) Austrian archaeologists found in 1993 a bit of natural silk in a female mummy of the 21st Dynasty of Egypt (1070-945 BC); only China could produce natural silk at that time.[4]

(b) The first literary encounter with Africa was by Du Huan, who was captured in the Talas Battle (751 AD) between China and the Arabs. He returned back to China by sea after about ten years. In his book he mentioned a place of blacks called 'Molin', which caused a debate about its location in Africa.[5]

(c)   Chinese archaeologists found a terra-cotta black figure in a tomb of 'Madame Pei' of the Tang Dynasty (691-907, AD).[6]

(d)   Chinese porcelains produced in dynasties of Tang, Song (960-1279, AD), Yuan (1271-1368, AD) and Ming (1368-1644, AD) dynasties have been discovered in a lot of African places. Five pieces of Tang currency were discovered in Africa as well (Ma Wenkuan and Meng Fanren 1987).

(e)   Zhu Siben, a Chinese scholar in Yuan Dynasty (1271-1368, AD), drew a map of Africa in the period of 1311-1320, which was of a triangular shape, much more true to reality than the maps drawn by Europeans and Arabs at the time (Needham 1959).

(f)   The North African scholar and historian Ibn Battuta went to China in 1346 and left notes covering various aspects on China, such as political and legal system, architecture, customs and habits, economic life and currency system, transportation and local special products, especially the political struggle within the court in Beijing (Ibn Battuta 1929).

(g)   During the years of 1405-1433, a Chinese eunuch-official Zeng Ho led a big fleet across the Southeast Asia and Indian Ocean seven times. His fleet visited the East African coast three or four times. Three persons in the mission left works that mentioned places of East Africa (Shen Fuwei 1990; Li Anshan 2000).

(h)   Later the two particular animals in Africa appeared in Chinese classics in Ming dynasty: Zebra and Giraffe.[7]

(i)   Fan Shou-yi, a Chinese official (1682–1753) who personally accompanied a missionary to Italy, passed the Cape coast and left some notes; he was most probably the first free Chinese who visited Africa (Fan Shouyi 1959).

(j)   Some Chinese in Southeast Asia were exiled to South Africa by Dutch colonists as early as the 1700s and early 1800s (Manlanie Yap and Dianne Leong Man 1996; Li Anshan 2000).

Sensing Africa (1900–1949)

Although contact, indirect or direct, began a long time ago, the study of Africa in China did not start until modern times. With the coming of the Europeans, especially the missionaries who brought knowledge of geography, the Chinese intellectuals and court officials began to hear more about the outside world. The most recent Qing Dynasty (1616–1911) witnessed the most humiliating experience in Chinese history. After China's defeat by Western countries in two Opium Wars, there was a rush by the great powers to establish their 'spheres of influence' in China, while the partition of Africa was also going on. Under the imminent partition, a new wave of alarm swept across China, especially among the intellectuals. Among them the most prominent was Lin Zexu, the official who led the burning of the opium in Canton, an incident that triggered the Opium War between China and Great Britain in 1840.

Lin ordered his subordinates to collect whatever information about the West, and the efforts produced an important book entitled *Si Zhou Zhi* (Gazetteer of the Four Continents). Illustrating geographical as well as ethnological knowledge about Africa, the book mentioned different places, states, cities, leaders and ethnic groups in Africa (Lin Zexu 1841).[8] Unfortunately he became a scapegoat of the Qing government under the pressure of the European invaders. Before his exile to the northwest region, Lin left the materials to Wei Yuan, his good friend and another famous reformer. Based on the materials, Wei compiled a big book and added new materials with his own comments.[9] Viewed as 'a landmark in China's relations with the West', this book 'represents the first systematic attempt to provide educated men with a realistic picture of the outside world' (De Bary et al., 1960: 10). Wei Yuan also introduced some knowledge about Africa in his book (Wei Yuan 1842). Another scholar Xu Jiyu wrote in some detail about Africa in his book: north, west, central, east, South Africa and the islands located in West Indian Ocean (Ai Zhouchang 1989: 167-188).

Regarding rare publications, they can be generally divided into three categories: translations or editions of world geography covering some parts of Africa, travel notes that described places in Africa, and books about Egypt (Zhang Qiwei 1904; Ren Baoluo 1907). It is easy to understand why books about Egypt were written or translated. First, it, like China, has a long history and glorious past. Secondly, it is a place where Chinese Muslims went for pilgrimage every year, and with which Chinese were more familiar. Thirdly, it is near China and people who went to Europe could pass it by land and by sea after the opening of the Suez Canal. The last and also the most important factor is that both nations had the same experience of national humiliation, since Egypt had just suffered from European invasion. Chinese intellectuals used Egypt as an example to show that a weak nation would be bullied by a strong nation (Li Changlin and Yang Junming 1995). Besides translations on Egypt, the earliest book on Africa published in China was probably *Feizhou Youqi* (Travel in Africa) by a British writer, translated by Shanghai Huibao Guang and published by Zhong-Xi Publishing Company in 1900.

Revolutionary pioneers like Chen Tianhua, Liang Qichao, Sun Yat-sen[10] and others tried every means to mobilise the Chinese at the end of the Qing dynasty. They watched carefully the activities of world powers as well as the situation in Africa. At the end of the century, the Boers were fighting against British domination, which attracted great attention from Chinese intellectuals. Both Chen Tianhua and Liang Qichao praised the Transvaal for its bravery. Chen compared the forces between the two nations, and extolled the Boers' great spirit by calling them 'heros of indomitable spirit'. He asked, 'Compared with Transvaal, Great Britain must manoeuvre an army of 300 million and fight 3000 years, then Chinese can negotiate peace with the British. Transvaal can do this, are we not as good as Transvaal?' Liang Qichao also stressed the important linkage of the Anglo-Boer War with Chinese issues (Ai Zouchang 1989, 192-195). Sun Yat-sen used the example of the partition of Morocco and wanted to show the rationale of 'reform or perish'. In other words, they wanted to wake up their nationals with negative or positive lessons from Africa.

A few newspapers in China also played a role of transmitting the information about Africa, such as *Waijiao Bao* (Newspaper of Diplomacy), *Qing Yi Bao*, and others. Newspapers and journals also published articles to remind Chinese people of what was going on in Africa. Owing to the same historical experience and fate, the Chinese media kept an eye on the scramble for Africa, especially Egypt.

After Sun Yat-sen established the Republic of China in 1911, very few books on Africa were published. *Oriental Miscellany*, an important journal started in 1904, published various articles about Africa. Some discussed the relations between Africa and big powers, some illustrated the partition, some introduced its peoples and customs, etc. Scholars also analysed the political situation there, especially topical issues of the time such as the Morocco crisis or the Italian invasion of Ethiopia, and the conflicts between European powers and African people.

However, the first book on Africa written by a Chinese scholar was published in 1936. *Ethiopia* was a survey of the history, geography, ethnic groups, politics, economy, religion and culture of Ethiopia (Wu Zuncun and Xie Defeng 1936). The first book on Ethiopia written by Soviet scholar was also translated in 1935. In early 1940s, two books on Egypt were published. One was a general history of Egypt (Huang Zengyue 1940), and the other was about the Suez Canal (Ren Mei'e and Yan Qinshang 1941).

During the Republican period, Africa was seldom touched on. There are three reasons. First, most parts of Africa were under colonial rule and had no political status in international affairs. Second, China itself was undergoing a chaotic experience, one war after another, and there was no systematic research going on. Third, very few people were interested in Africa. However, there were some reports about Chinese overseas or labourers in Africa.

Supporting Africa (1950-1965)

The founding of People's Republic of China in 1949 is generally regarded as an important part of the national liberation movement in the world after the Second World War. African studies in China began in the late-1950s, and was concentrated on nationalist independence movements. Several booklets were published about the independence movements in North Africa (Wu Xiu 1956; Luo Ke 1956; Fan Yong 1957; Yan Jin 1958; Chen Li 1959). A few academic journals had a couple of articles on the struggles against colonial rule in different countries (Na Zhong 1957; Zheng Daochuan 1957; Ma Tong 1959; Wang Junyi 1959; Wang Zhen 1959), or nationalist movements in Africa as a whole. Two universities were pioneers in African studies. Nankai University of Tian Jin, located in north China, started to probe nationalist movements in North Africa. The South China Normal University in the south began to deal with the same subject in Central Africa. The section for World History of the Department of History of both universities published several articles on African national liberation movements in *Teaching History, Teaching History in Middle School*, and other journals.[11]

Leaders of Chinese Communist Party encouraged African studies as well. On 27 April 1961, Chairman Mao Zedong met a group of African friends.[12] He admitted that he, as well as other Chinese, did not have a clear understanding of Africa:

> An institute of Africa should be established, studying African history, geography, and the socioeconomic situation. We don't have a clear understanding of African history, geography and present situation, so a concise book is badly needed. It doesn't need to be thick, about one hundred to two hundred pages are enough. We can invite African friends to help and get it published in one or two years. It should include the contents of how imperialism came, how it suppressed the people, how it met people's resistance, why the resistance failed and how it is now rising.[13]

On 4 July 1961, the Institute of Asian African Studies under the Central Party External Ministry and the Chinese Academy of Sciences was founded. Zhang Tiesheng, was appointed the first director of the Institute.

On 30 December 1963, a report on the strengthening of the study of foreign countries was issued, drafted by the Group of Foreign Affairs of the Central Committee of the Chinese Communist Party (CCP). As a direct result of this report, three institutes in three universities were set up specifically for the study of foreign countries. Peking University was chosen to set up the Institute of Afro-Asian Studies, for two reasons: Peking University had a solid foundation for humanities and social sciences, and the Department of Oriental Studies covered various languages spoken in Afro-Asian countries.[14] Ji Xianlin, a scholar who received his PhD in Germany during the 1940s, was appointed as the Director of the Institute. Professor Yang Ren-pian of the Department of History, who received his degree in France, switched from French history to African history and began to train graduate students in the field.

Besides the universities, different research institutions were involved in African studies, and the most prominent was the Institute of Asian-African Studies under a dual leadership of both the Central Party External Ministry and Chinese Academy of Sciences (later it became an institute of the Chinese Academy of Social Sciences, thereafter, CASS). For example, *African Introduction* (1962), a general survey of African geography, history, society, economy and the anti-imperialist struggle, prepared specially for the purpose of Premier Zhou Enlai's visit to Africa, was published by the Institute of Asian-African Studies and internally circulated. The institute also had two *Neibu Kanwu* (internally circulated journals): *Translations on Asia and Africa* and *Data on Asia-Africa*.

Another achievement during this early period was the introduction of international scholarship, which included two aspects: the introduction of African studies in other countries and the translation of books written by foreign scholars. Beginning from the early 1960s, there appeared introductions to African studies abroad, such as conferences, institutions, studies, etc.[15] Most of the information was published in the two journals already mentioned. *Translations on Asia and Africa* was a monthly journal that started from September 1959, while *Data on Asia-Africa* was a bi-monthly journal. Publishing a lot of introductions and articles, these two journals served as a major channel for Chinese scholars to get to know the study of the subject abroad.

The translation of books generally included four types: works by African nationalist leaders, serious works by Western or Russian scholars, reports to government, and popular readers. The first type included Egyptian President Gamal Abd El-Nasser's *The Philosophy of the Revolution* (1959), Ghanaian President Kwame Nkrumah's *The Autobiography of Kwame Nkrumah* (Nkrumah 1957) and *Neo-colonialism: The Last Stage of Imperialism* (Nkrumah 1965), *Selections of Ben Bella's Speeches, September 1962-February 1965* (1965), Senegalese political leader Majhemout Diop's *Contribution à l'étude des Problèmes Politiques en Afrique Noire* (Diop 1958), and similar works. The second type included *Afrique Noire Occidentale et Centrale* (Suret-Canale 1958), *Africa: The Roots of Revolt* (Woddis 1960), and *Africa: The Lion Awakes* (Woddis 1961), *Africa: A Social, Economic and Political Geography of its Major Regions* (Fitzgerald 1955), *The African Awakening* (Davidson 1955) and *Black Mother; The Years of the African Slave Trade* (Davidson 1961), *Les Trusts au Congo* (Joye and Lewin 1961), *Africa in World Politics* (Mckay 1963), and others. There were translations of many books by scholars in the USSR; among them the best known was *African Nations* (Moscow, 1954), a large volume on ethnic groups in Africa by two Soviet leading Africanists. Even books by American scholars were translated from Russian, such as W. E. B. Du Bois's *Africa: An Essay Towards a History of the Continent* (Du Bois 1961).[16] The third category consisted of reports prepared for the government, such as *United States Foreign Policy: Africa* (1959) prepared by the Program of African Studies at Northwestern University. Some popular readers were also translated, such as John Gunther's book, *Inside Africa* (Gunther 1955).

During this period, two important books written by Chinese scholars are worth mentioning: *History of Sino-African Relations: Primary Research* (Zhang Tiesheng 1963), and *A Concise History of Modern Egypt* (Na Zhong 1963). Zhang's work was a compilation of five articles on Sino-African relations from the Han Dynasty (206 BC to AD 220) to the Ming Dynasty (AD1644-1911). The first one was a general survey, the next two dealt with China's contact with East Africa, the fourth with China and North Africa, and the last was on Sino-African contact by sea routes. Na Zhong is a professor who graduated from the University of Al'Azhar in Egypt in 1940s. His work on Egypt started the academic study of Africa in China. A first chapter concerned the ancient history of Egypt, the rest dealt with the period from Napoleon's invasion to the Egyptian national independence movement after the Second World War.

We can see several features in African studies up to the mid-1960s. First, African studies was more pragmatic than academic, and closely linked to the political situation and topical issues at the time. China strongly supported the national liberation movements and wanted to win new friends among the independent African nations or those who were still fighting for their liberation. Secondly, besides governmental units, it was the departments of history at universities that took the lead. The main reason for this phenomenon was that the status of anthropology and political science were not recognised in China at that time. Thirdly, much research was undertaken and published collectively. Fourthly, African studies concentrated on the national independence movements or anti-colonialist struggles.[17] Tied closely to politics and strongly influenced by the official policy stance, research lacked its own orientation as well as an original viewpoint. Fifth, the introduction of African studies outside China received great attention, and almost all the important divisions of African studies in the world were introduced, and books on them were translated. There was an attempt to select works for translation on an objective basis.

Understanding Africa (1966–1976)

During the Cultural Revolution (1966–1976), China suffered a considerable setback in intellectual life. Universities were closed for several years, and later enrolled students according to their 'political performance'. There were few studies on foreign issues. Cultural and intellectual life was controlled by political criteria. These were a function of struggles concerning the various political factions. Drama, film and even ballet were rated for their political relevance, and tertiary education was considered something that had 'to consolidate the proletarian dictatorship'. Under the circumstances, few studies could be undertaken in the social sciences and humanities outside of the framework of Marxism-Leninism-Maoism. However, two things are worth mentioning.

First, the Zhong Xuan Bu, the Department of Propaganda of the Central Committee of the CCP, had its own branch to study the situation in Africa and provide support to African liberation movements. Various kinds of research conducted under the auspices of the Department contributed in various ways to decision-making at the central level. There were a few publications that were only accessible at a high official level. The institution concentrated more on information collection and data analysis than academic research.

Secondly, a great number of books were translated during the 1970s. The reason for this turn of events was that 1971 was a critical year for China. At this time, several important occurrences suggested that China was breaking away from its siege mentality and was returning to the international community. Two events are most significant: the beginning of the normalisation of Sino-American relationships marked by Henry Kissinger's secret mission to China, and the entry of the People's Republic of China to the United Nations. What did this mean for the study of Africa, or the study of the world outside China for that matter? Owing to a long-standing neglect of cultural issues, the Central Committee of Chinese Communist Party realised the serious problems in the academic field. A nation-wide meeting of publications was held in 1971, organised by the State Council, which decided to publish some important books of history, such as 24 classic histories, the history of the Republic of China, and so forth.

In order for leaders of different levels to understand foreign affairs, histories or general surveys of foreign countries were chosen for translation. This major project was carried on right into the 1980s. The books seemed to be chosen somewhat on an arbitrary basis, owing to the shortage of library collections, but some of them were of high quality. They can be roughly divided into three kinds: history, general surveys, and geography. Histories of almost all African areas were translated, such as black Africa, North Africa, Central Africa, East Africa, West Africa, Southern Africa, and Madagascar. Histories of individual countries were also selected for translation, such as Ethiopia, Somalia, Sudan, Uganda, Tanzania, the Central African Republic, Nigeria, Niger, Sierra Leone, Ghana, Gambia, Dahomey, Togo, Congo (Kinshasa), Liberia, Mauritania, Morocco, Tunisia, Mauritius, Malawi, etc., or histories of a specific people, such as the Basuto. For those countries short of works of history, general surveys were selected, such as those for South West Africa, Lesotho, Botswana, Swaziland, Zambia, Djibouti, the Horn of Africa, the Central African Republic, Luanda, Burundi, Mali, Upper Volta, Angola, Rhodesia, Libya, Congo, etc. Some geographical works were also translated.

The translations included works by famous African scholars, such as *The Independent Sudan: The History of a Nation* (Shibeika 1959), *A History of Tanzania* (Kimambo and Temu 1963), Ruth First's *South West Africa, Rhodesia: Background to Conflict* (Mtshali 1967), and similar works. Some are classics in African studies, such as *Old Africa Rediscovered* (Davidson 1960), *An Introduction to the History of West Africa* (Fage 1969). Others are rich in documents and archives, such as *A History of Sierra Leone* (Fyfe 1962), *Histoire du Togo, Histoire du Dahomey* and *Histoire du Congo* (Cornevin 1959; 1962; 1970). Many works by Soviet scholars were also translated. Two important volumes of a general history of Africa compiled by the Institute of African Studies, Soviet Union Academy of Sciences, and a four-volume *History of Black Africa* (1966) by Hungarian-born historian Andre Sik were among the most important.

Since the original purpose of the translations was not for academic study, several points should be stressed here. First, none of these translations was intended to be published openly, but only circulated internally (*neibu faxing*), although with the passage of time, all the books were sold publicly. Secondly, every translation included a preface of criticism by the translator. This step was a measure to protect the translator as well as to warn the reader. This is a typical feature of the Cultural Revolution and its resulting persecution of intellectuals. Related to this issue, most of the books were translated by a group,[18] which indicated that responsibility would be taken collectively. Thirdly, the books were chosen neither for the content, nor for the academic quality, but for the title. In every possible case, they are general histories rather than monographs of highly regarded academic works. Almost each country or area has one book chosen for translation. The uneven choice of the books (some have no academic value) resulted from two facts: a lack of knowledge regarding Africa as well as little academic research in the field, and a lack of variety of books on Africa in China.

According to the statistics, 117 books on Africa were published in 1967–1968; 111 were translations, five were for popular readers and one was a reference work. Some 95 percent of the books were translated from other languages (Zhang Yuxi 1997: 272-273).

However, the importance of these translations should not be underestimated. The choice and translation of the books were not limited to African countries, but countries all over the world. In terms of African studies in China, Chinese students began to acquire some knowledge about a continent far away from China, and came across the names of some leading scholars in the field. They gradually became familiar with the topics, interests and trends in African studies. This laid a foundation for later studies after the Cultural Revolution.

Table 1: Publications on African Studies in China

	Monograph	Translation	Popular Reader	Reference	Total
Before 1949		14	5		19
1949–1966	10	60	35	6	111
1967–1978		111	5	1	117
1979–1994	41	68	48	9	166

Studying Africa (1977–2000)

After the downfall of the Gang of Four in the 1970s,[19] university teaching and research resumed. The years 1977–2000 were the most productive period for African studies in China. There are three institutional branches of African studies in China: universities, academic institutions, and institutions attached to ministries of the government. There are two nation-wide organisations of African studies: the Chinese Association of African Studies (1979) and the Chinese Society of African Historical Studies (1980). The former is more or less concentrated on the study of current issues, the latter on African history. There is a lot of overlap between the two associations and the membership is open to everyone interested in the area. With the coordination of the two associations, African studies in China has made great progress. The 1990s witnessed an increase of centres. The Institute of West Asian and African Studies of CASS set up a Centre for South African Studies in 1995, followed by the Institute of Afro-Asian Studies at Peking University, which founded its Centre for African Studies in 1998. Xiangtan University in Hunan also set up a Centre for African Law Studies in 1998 (Hong Yonghong and Xia Xinghua 2000). The Department of Geography at Nanjing University has a research group specialising in African economic geography and Yunnan University also hosts a group specialising in African studies.

From the end of the 1970s, Chinese intellectuals restarted the study of Africa. Articles in academic journals generally covered three topics. The first is the early fight against colonial invasions or resistance during the colonial period, such as the

Mahdi movement in Sudan, the Ethiopian war against Italian invasion, the Maji Maji uprising in Tanganyka, the Mau Mau in Kenya, etc. (Pen Kunyuan et al., 1978; Jiang Xuebing 1979; Mao Tianyou 1979; Luo Hongzhang 1979; Chen Gongyuan 1980; Lu Ting'en 1981; Ding Bangying 1981). The second concerns African nationalist movements since the First World War, and especially after the Second World War, such as articles on the Pan-Africanist movement, African nationalist movements in general (Li Qingyu 1979; Hu You'e 1980; Tang Tongming 1981; Zhu Gang 1981; Tang Dadun 1981), or in particular countries, especially those of Egypt, Algeria, Ghana, Nigeria, Sudan and South Africa (Tang Tongming and Xiang Qun 1979; Zhao Jianping 1980; Wang Shaokui 1981; Tang Tongming 1981; Qin Xiaoying 1981). The third area is the study of important figures, of two main types: the first generation of nationalist leaders, such as Felix Houphouët-Boigny, Kwame Nkrumah, Gnassingbe Eyadema, Robert Mugabe, Kenneth Kaunda, Quett Masire, Leopold Sedar Senghor, Omar Mouammar Gaddafi, Ahmed Sekou Toure, Habbib Bourguiba, and so on; and influential figures who made contributions to nationalist movements in Africa such as Garvey, Du Bois, Padmore, Fanon and others. This list continued to expand in the 1980s and thereafter.

At the end of 1981, the first student in African studies was enrolled in the graduate school of the Chinese Academy of Social Sciences, followed in later years by enrolments in Peking University, Eastern China Normal University and others.[20] During the 1980s, Chinese scholars began to switch their interests to more specific topics. Lu Ting'en used various data to show David Livingstone's dual role in the exploration of Africa, as a fighter against the slave trade and as a tool of colonial expansion (Lu Ting'en 1981). Wu Bingzhen, Xu Jiming and other scholars studied the slave trade and its linkage to early capitalist development in Africa (Wu Bingzhen 1983; 1984; Wu Bingzhen 1984a; Xu Jiming 1983; 1983a; 1983b; Li Jidong 1983; Lao Jianguo 1984). Wu also criticised the viewpoints of J. D. Fage and other Western scholars regarding the slave trade (Wu Bingzhen 1983). Qin Xiaoying touched on a very sensitive subject: the role of the national bourgeoisie in African liberation movements. For a long time, the Communist tradition generally denied the positive role of the national bourgeoisie, and they had always been a target of the proletarian revolution. Using Kenya as an example, Qin argued that the national bourgeoisie could play an active role in anti-colonialist struggles. Wang Chunliang also made the same point in his study on the nationalist movement in Zaire (Qin Xiaoying 1980; Wang Chunliang 1981). Li Anshan tried to analyse the formation, characteristics, and role of modern intellectuals in West Africa (Li Anshan 1985; 1986).

In 1982, the Chinese Society of African Historical Studies published a collection of papers. He Fangchuan's paper studied the politics, economy and culture of the ancient kingdom of Axum. Zheng Jiaxing probed the early period of South African socioeconomic structure. Gu Zhangyi explored the origin and development of African nations. Nin Sao discussed in his article the issue of the 'Hamitic hypothesis' or 'Hamitic theory'. Illustrating the prosperity in ancient kingdoms and cultures such as Ghana, Mali, Sanghai, Kanem-Bornu, Kush, Nok, Benin, etc., he argued that the

African people were the creators of African civilisation and criticised the racist denotation in the hypothesis. Lu Ting'en studied the periodisation of modern African history. Ai Zhouchang's article studied several important issues in modern African history, such as the origins of the invasion of Africa by the Portuguese, the slave trade and the occupation of Africa. Using Nigeria as an example, Qin Xiaoying studied the role of reform in the independence movement in Africa (Chinese Society of African Historical Studies 1982: 26-48; 49-77; 95-109; 127-154; 155-164; 165-181; 254-280).

During the 1980s, African studies made more progress. First, several textbooks and monographs were published, such as *A Concise History of Africa* (Yang Renpian 1984), *A General History of Africa* (1984) edited by the Chinese Society of African Historical Studies, *Africa and Imperialism* (Lu Ting'en 1987), *Study on the Strategy of Economic Development in Africa South of Sahara* (Chen Zhongde and Wu Zhaoji 1987), *African Socialism: History, Theory and Practice* (Tang Dadun 1988), *Origin of the Disturbance in Southern Africa* (Ge Jie 1989), etc. *In the Mysterious Chiefdom* (Yang Rongjia 1986) is a memoir by a member of a Chinese group that undertook explorations in Cameroon. This is the first book about a black African country written by a Chinese who had personally been there. The author illustrated the chieftainship system in Cameroon and listed two important laws regarding the status of the chief. Histories of individual countries were also published, such as *The Modern History of Egypt* (Yang Haocheng 1985), a *Concise History of Niger* (Xun Xingqiang 1983), and a *Concise History of Zaire* (Zhao Shuhui 1981), amongst others.

Two important works on African geography were published. *African Natural Geography* (Su Shirong et al., 1984) was written by scholars of Department of Geography, Nanjing University. It includes two parts: a General Study and a Regional Study. In 1984, the *World Agricultural Geography* Series was published, which included 11 books on various countries (Japan, India, Australia and New Zealand, the USSR, US, Great Britain, France), an area (Southeast Asia), continents (Africa, Latin America) and a general survey on world agricultural geography. *Agricultural Geography in Africa* (Zeng Zungu et al., 1984) is comprised of two parts. The first part of seven chapters is entitled 'General Survey',and deals with natural conditions, the history of agriculture and social factors, food and cash crops, livestock husbandry, forestry and fishery. Part two, 'Area Varieties of Agriculture', consists of nine chapters and looks at agriculture in different areas. There was also a more systematic study of the African anti-colonial struggle. Articles began to touch on issues related to African nationalism (ideology, intellectuals, anti-colonial religious movements, etc.), ethnic problems, economy and development, culture and international relations.

A second major development at this time was the translation of some important works, for example, the authoritative work on African borders by the former Secretary-General of the United Nations Boutros-Ghali (Beijing, 1979). The epic *Sundiata* was also translated (1983). It is interesting that Seligman's *Races of Africa* (1930) was translated in 1966 by his Chinese student Fei Xiaotong, a prominent sociologist at Peking University, but was only published in 1982. The translator regarded this work as a 'standard reader' on the subject.[21] Among the translations, two were on the slave trade, one by a Soviet scholar named Abolamowa, (Beijing, 1983), the other, *The African Slave Trade from the Fifteenth to the Nineteenth Century: Reports and papers of the meeting of experts* (Beijing 1984). Basil Davidson's book (1978) and some biographies and autobiographies were also translated. Another big project, the translation of UNESCO's eight-volume *General History of Africa* was also started in the early 1980s. In 1984, volumes one and two were published, with the rest in the following years.

Thirdly there was the compilation and publication of reference materials. *Overview of Africa*, the first comprehensive introduction in Chinese, was openly published in 1981. This work covered geography, history, ethnic groups, political systems, economic development and Sino-African relations. Then there was the interesting study *Selection of Data of the History of Overseas Chinese in Africa* (Fang Jigen 1986), some selected reports, articles, chapters of monographs, etc. *Contemporary African Celebrities* appeared in 1987, and referred to more than 1000 important figures. Several bibliographies were compiled and printed with the help of the Chinese Society of African Historical Studies (Chinese Society of African Historical Studies and Documentation Section of Peking Library 1982; Zhang Yuxi 1990; Zhang Yuxi 1997). An *Atlas of Africa*, the largest one among all the atlases in China, was published in 1985, and included a comprehensive picture of Africa, its history, ethnic groups, economy and geography. Attention was given to African studies in other parts of the world. During the period 1982-1989, there were 105 articles or introductions about African studies globally (Zhang Yuxi 1990: 131-141). It is worth mentioning that several books on African nationalities were translated and compiled (Ge Gongshang and Chao Feng 1980; Ge Gongshang and Li Yifu 1981; Ge Gongshang and Chao Feng 1982; Ge Gongshang and Chao Feng 1984; Ge Gongshang and Song Limei 1987). Although they were not formally published, they contributed a great deal to African studies at the time.

Publications in African studies greatly increased during the 1990s. East China Normal University Press published an African Studies Series, including six monographs (Shu Yunguo 1996; Ai Zhouchang and Mu Tao 1996; Luo Jianguo 1996; Xia Jisheng 1996; Lu Ting-en and Liu Jing 1997; Liu Hongwu 1997). Several compilations of historical materials were published by the same press, including *Selection of Materials on Sino-African Relations* (Ai Zhouchang 1989), which collected travel notes, contemporary newspaper articles, letters and reminiscences, etc., *Translated Materials on Arabic Africa* (Pan Guang and Zhu Weilie, 1992), and *Documents of Pan-Africanism and the Organization of African Unity* (Tang Dadun 1995), which brought together translated documents such as resolutions, declarations and Charters of the Pan-African conferences and the OAU. All these provided data for Chinese scholars to study the related subjects. Some books on Africa were part of a series. For example, in the *Study of the British Commonwealth*, South Africa, Nigeria and Ghana (Chen Zhongdan 2000) were covered. In the History of Colonialism series, a volume on

Africa was published which dealt with the origin, the development and the decline of colonialism in Africa (Zheng Jiaxing 2000).

A general history of Africa was published in 1995, as a collective work by the Chinese Society of African Historical Studies. Divided into three volumes, it covered the ancient, modern and contemporary history of Africa (He Fangchuan and Nin Sao 1996; Ai Zhouchang and Zheng Jiaxing, 1996; Lu Ting-en and Peng Kunyuan, 1996). The publication summarised the work of Chinese scholars in the past decade (Li Anshan 1996b). A *Concise History of African National Independence* (Wu Bingzheng and Gao Jinyuan 1993) was the first systematic study of the nationalist movement in Africa. A strength of the work is that it also covered the struggle in the Portuguese colonies. Li Anshan's monograph, based on his PhD dissertation at the University of Toronto, was the first case study in African history in China. Based on his research at the Public Records Office in London and the Ghanaian National Archives in Accra, he explored four types of conflicts, arguing that colonialism was a situation of paradox where protest played an important role and in most cases caused changes in colonial policy (Li Anshan 1998a).[22]

During the 1990s, several subjects became topics of interest, covering socialism, democratisation, ethnic issues and 'tribalism', international relations, South Africa, cultural studies, economic studies, Sino-African relations, and so forth. African politics attracted great attention. With the coming of the wave of democracy, what would be the future of African socialism? As a collective project, the *New Analysis of African Socialism* began in 1989 and involved 16 authors from different units. It discussed the origin, development and typology of African socialism and compared the various socialisms on the continent. It analysed the contrast between socialism and capitalism in Africa, arguing that African socialism contributed a great deal to the consolidation of national independence, the building of national culture, and the foundations for control of the national economy, and also greatly raised the status of African countries in the world. Socialism in Africa was, however, not successful and the decline of the movement was due to several reasons: internal factors (forces of production, internal policy), the impact of the decline of socialist bloc of Soviet and Eastern Europe, and the pressure exerted by Western countries. The re-orientation of socialist countries had three options: drop out, self-adjustment, and democratic socialism. According to the authors, the rise of democratic socialism in Africa was inevitable (Tang Datung et al., 1994).

There were more studies of the process of African democratisation. *African Political Development from a Multiple Perspective* (Zhang Hongming 1999) studies different strands of political thought and their influence on the African political arena. *Political Evolution in Contemporary Africa* (Xu Jiming and Tan Shizhong 1998) is a general study of political issues in contemporary Africa. The two works also touched on the wave of democratisation on the continent. There were generally two viewpoints concerning the wave of democracy in Africa. One considered that the internal demand for a more democratic society was the major cause of the process. The two books referred to above hold this view, arguing that the disturbances that occurred during and after democratisation were either the natural outbreak of long-time oppression and mal-governance, or new conflicts generated by the process of democratisation. The other point of view argued that democratisation in Africa was the result of both the decline of the Soviet bloc and the pressure from Western countries, and that the Western system of democracy does not fit African reality (Cui Qinglian 1995; Lu Ting-en 1995).

Chinese Africanists have devoted attention to ethnic issues in Africa for a long time. There is a debate among the Chinese scholars on the use of terms 'tribe' and 'tribalism' (Wu Zengtian 1996; Li Anshan 1998b). Some think that the use of the term 'tribe' is quite appropriate (Nin Sao 1983; Ge Gongshang 1995; Zhong Hongming 1995), while others considered it a derogatory term and preferred to use concepts such as 'nation' or 'local nation' (Difang Minzhu; Gu Zhangyi 1997; Yuan Xihu 1998). Although opinions differ regarding the appropriate term to describe the phenomenon of 'ethnic conflict', all agree that this phenomenon has been an obstacle in nation-building in Africa. Li Jidong, Zhang Hongming and Xu Jiming studied the negative affect of so-called 'tribalism' and concluded that it challenged the legitimacy of the nation-state and posed a threat to political stability as well as to the unity of the nation-state (Li Jidong 1997; Zhong Hongming 1999; Xu Jiming and Tan Shizhong 1998). Li Anshan analysed the origins and development of 'local nationalism' and its relationship with nationalism and international politics. He argued that local nationalism has its origins in the pre-colonial social base, and was greatly influenced by colonial rule (especially the system of 'indirect rule'), while internal factors such as mal-governance and external interference strengthened this trend (Li Anshan 2001a, 2001b).

As for international relations, Liang Gencheng's work is impressive. *United States and Africa* tries to explore American policy towards Africa after the Second World War through the 1980s. It is divided into eight chapters: an introduction; American policy after the Second World War to the end of 1950s; the late 1950s to the mid-1960s; the mid-1960s to the mid-1970s; the mid-1970s to the beginning of the 1980s; the conflicts between America and Soviet Union after the downfall of the Portuguese colonial rule; American policy to settle the problem of southern Africa peacefully; and American policy in the 1980s (Liang Gencheng 1991). His view of American policy is generally negative. There were other articles on international relations as well, especially French policy. From 1990 to 1996, more than thirteen articles appeared on French policy towards Africa. Understandably, Sino-African relations enjoyed the most coverage, especially economic relations between the China and the continent.

In recent years, South Africa has been a major topic for Africanists in China. The fame of Nelson Mandela, both in politics and academia, has been one contributing factor for this interest. Secondly, South Africa is a large nation and its history has long interested the Chinese; Chinese scholars are familiar with Chaka, the Great Trek, the various wars involving the Boers, the Zulu struggles against the Boers, and so on. A third reason is the normalisation of diplomatic relations between China and

South Africa. Fourth, the African renaissance is now getting underway, and has also aroused interest among Chinese scholars. Even before the normalisation of China-South African relations, both sides had set up a research centre in each other's capital, which served as a kind of semi-diplomatic mission and also promoted academic exchange.[23] Biographies and autobiographies of Nelson Mandela and his ex-wife Winnie Madikizela-Mandela were written or translated (Yang Lihua 1995; Wen Xian 1995). Several books on South Africa published during the 1990s and at the beginning of the new millennium covered politics, the economy, ethnic relations and modernisation (Yang Lihua et al., 1994; Ge Jie 1994; Chen Yifei 1994; Zhu Chonggui et al., 1994; Xia Jisheng 1996; Xia Jisheng et al., 1998; Zhang Xiang 1998; Ai Zhouchang et al., 2000).

In June 1996, the Institute of West Asian and African Studies at CASS held a conference on 'Prospects of Political and Economic Development in South Africa', sponsored by the Ford Foundation. The conference was the last of a series of seminars organised by the Sino-US African Studies Exchange Program, and was a celebration and summary of 15 years of cooperation between Chinese and American African studies research institutions sponsored by the Foundation.[24] Since this conference was held after President Jiang Zemin's first visit to Africa and before the normalisation of Sino-South African diplomatic relations, it had a special significance. The papers presented were around three topics: South Africa's political transition and its prospects, South Africa's reconstruction and development plan, and the New South Africa's foreign relations (*Conference*, 1996).

As far as cultural studies are concerned, Nin Sao's work was the first on black African culture. It treated African culture in the broad sense and studied social norms and festivals, worship and religion, technology and ideology, and the pursuit of beauty through art, literature and the performing arts (Nin Sao 1993). Li Baoping tried to analyse the linkages between tradition and modernisation in Africa (Li Baoping 1997). Liu Xiuwu dealt with black African culture in historical perspective (Liu Hongwu 1997). An interesting feature of this piece is the way the writer sees how culture can play its role in creating a national consciousness. As a part of the 'Series of World Civilizations', Ai Zhouchang's *African Black Civilization* covers a wide range of topics. Part I, 'Formation of African Black Civilisation', studies different cultures, such as those of the Upper Nile (Nubia, Kush, Aksume), iron age culture in West Africa, the Bantu migration, Islam, Swahili and Hausa cultures. Part II, 'Manifestation of African Black Civilisation', illustrates different forms and expressions of African civilisation, such as arts and literature, religion and customs, ideologies and technology, etc. Part III, 'African Black Civilisation to the Future', tries to link Africa with the outside world and tradition with modernity (Ai Zhouchang 1999).

Another analysis of African society is Feng Jianwei's *Notes*. The work is unique in the sense that the author, as a news reporter, travelled to the interior of several African countries to collect materials for his research. He spent half a year and visited four countries in the Sahel as well as Ghana, and visited 150 towns, villages, units, and schools. He explored social organisation, economic patterns, class structures, political systems, and historical stages, analysed some interesting issues such as chieftainship system, and the role of the national bourgeoisie in those countries, and offered his ideas on the subject. For example, contrary to the popular view in China, he argued that the cash crop system had its positive aspects as well as negative ones (Feng Jianwei 1992). The study of modernisation has been a popular topic in China since the late 1980s. Based on his PhD dissertation, Li Jidong's book analyses the causes of delayed modernisation in Africa. Among the negative factors he identified were governance and tribalism (Li Jidong 1997). He Li'er's work on Zimbabwe was the first study in Chinese on this new independent country (1995).

Economic studies began to arouse a great deal of interest among scholars. *A Study on the Strategy of Economic and Social Development in Africa* (Zhang Tongzhu 1992) was the first comprehensive work on the subject, and a collective product of the Chinese Association of African Studies. With 16 chapters, it covers a wide range of issues, such as the relationship between development and demography, urbanisation, ecology, environment and agriculture, privatisation and nationalisation, the choice of national economic strategy, etc. The author argued that whatever overall strategy was adopted, it would be linked with the natural and social conditions of an individual country, and thus it is unwise to copy another's model without revision. African countries should develop their economy on the basis of self-reliance, while trying to win support from outside without conditions being attached (Chen Zongde 1994). There are other books about African economy. Some consider the market economy in Africa (Yang Dezeng and Su Zeyu, 1994; Chen Muo 1995), others analyse the relationship between reform and economics (Tan Shizhong 1998).

Besides the African economy in general, more specific topics have been studied. In order to meet the needs of the Forum on China-Africa Cooperation-Ministerial Conference Beijing 2000, the Ministry of Agriculture organised a group of researchers to compile a set of books on African agriculture. As 'The Series of Investment Guides for the Development of African Agriculture', it includes five volumes and four major parts: Brief History of Development of African Agriculture (Lu Ting'en 2000), Development and Utilization of African Agricultural Resources (Wen Yunchao 2000), African Afro-Product Market and Trade (He Xiurong, Wang Xiuqing and Li Ping 2000), and Generalization of Agriculture Development in African Nations (Chen Zhongde, Yao Guimei and Fan Yushu 2000). This set made good use of the achievements of the study on agriculture in Africa.

With regard to Sino-African relations, international academics are much more familiar with the names of Duyvenduk, Filesi or Philip Snow (Duyvenduk 1947; Filesi 1972; Snow 1988) than those of Chinese scholars. But the latter scholars began to study Sino-African relations much earlier. For example, Cen Zhongmian in 1935 produced an article discussing contact between China and Africa during the Tang dynasty, in which he illustrated the sea route between the Persian Gulf and East Africa (Cen Zhongmian 1935). Zhang Xinglang's remarkable collection of data indicated that there had been a long history of contact between China and Africa

(Zhang Xinglang 1940). Zhang Tiesheng dealt with the subject historically, as mentioned above (Zhang Tiesheng 1963).

Zhang Junyan studied the relations between Ancient China and West Asia-Africa by sea. His work deals with contact from the Ming (1368-1644) to the Qing (1616-1911) dynastic eras. The first three chapters deal with Sino-West Asia relations. From Chapter 4, he mentions Du Huan and other scholars who described places in Africa in their works. As far as the correct identification of the place 'Molin' in Africa is concerned, there are various opinions. Duyvenduk thought that it referred to Malindi in Kenya. The author of *Overview of Africa* argued that it was Mandi, while other scholars argue for the choice of Meroe, Morocco, Axum and other sites. Zhang supported the Morocco view for three reasons. First, Du Huan in his notes also mentioned that Molin was located in the southwest of 'Qiusaluo', the name for Castilla (Spain) in Chinese. Secondly, Du Huan indicated that Molin was reached by going through a big desert. In ancient times, east Africa was usually reached by sea. Zhang regarded the 'big desert' as the Libyan Desert and the desert on the east and west sides of Algeria. Third, other classics of the Tang dynasty also mentioned 'Molin' and its neighbour which was located to the east of Morocco. Ai Zhouchang also agreed that Molin referred to Morocco (Zhang Junyan 1986; Ai Zhouchang 1995).

Shen Fuwei published his work on Sino-African relations after a long period of research. The book deals with contact between Egypt and China in ancient times; imported African plants in China; Africa and Africans in the Chinese classics; the history of communication, etc. Many scholars believe that relations between China and Egypt have enjoyed a long history, but that China's contact with sub-Saharan Africa started much later. Shen considers that direct contact between China and sub-Saharan Africa began during the Han dynasty (206 BC–220 AD). Besides various commercial activities between the two, the first mission from black Africa to China was that from Adulis, a port city in Eritrea, which arrived at Luoyang in AD100. Since the mission was from Adulis, Ethiopia can claim to be the first African country to establish diplomatic relations with China (Sheng Fuwei 1990). Other scholars have also expressed their views on this subject (Sun Yutang 1979; Yan Renbian 1984; Zhang Xiang 1987; 1993).

Some scholars have argued that contact between China and Africa was absent for five hundred years from the mid-1400s till the 1950s (Hutchison 1975, 2). Ai Zhongchang, who has studied Sino-African relations for a long time, criticises this conclusion in his book and argues from Chinese materials that relations between China and Africa were still going on during this period (Ai Zhouchang 1989). This work by Ai Zhouchang and Mu Tao devotes six chapters to a overview of Sino-African contact from the earliest times to the present: the opening of Sino-African contact; the development of Sino-African relations (sixth to fifteenth centuries AD); century); Sino-African relations during the Ming dynasty; cultural exchange in ancient times; Sino-African relations 1500-1910; Sino-African relations in the Republican period (1911-1949); and contemporary Sino-African relations. The works claims that as early as 200 BC Silk Road was open to traders from the two regions (Ai Zhouchang and Mu Tao 1996). The Centre for African Studies at Peking University published a collection of papers entitled 'China and Africa', which includes 22 articles covering Sino-African relations from ancient times to the present, with a bibliography on the subject and a list of publications of the members of the centre (Centre for African Studies of Peking University, 2000).

As for the Chinese in Africa, three books have been published. As early as 1984, Chinese historian Chen Hansheng edited a collection of data entitled 'Chinese Labour in Africa', which is a part of *Compilation of Data of Chinese Labour Abroad*. He compiled government archives, documents, letters and various original materials concerning Chinese labour in Africa, mainly in South Africa (Chen Hangsheng 1984). Fang Jigen compiled data on the Chinese in Africa, but most of the information consisted of translations of secondary sources (Fang Jigen 1986). Th first comprehensive work on the subject, *A History of Chinese Overseas in Africa* (Li Anshan 2000), studies the origin, adaptation, and integration of the Chinese in Africa. As the first work on the subject, although published in Chinese, it has attracted international attention. The French international broadcast service reported on the publication in its Chinese programme and the book has been reviewed in *African Studies Review* (James Gao 2001) and the *Canadian Journal of African Studies* (Brose 2002).[25]

There are three major reference sources, all organised and compiled by the Institute of West Asian and African Studies, CASS. The annual *Yellow Book of the International Situation: The Report of the Development of Middle East and Africa* (Zhao Guozhong, et al., 1998-2001) usually covers the following subjects: overview of the year; political review; economic survey; international relations; and a data section. This publication began in 1998 and has appeared annually. The publication of the *Concise Encyclopaedia of Sub-Saharan Africa* (Ge Jie 2000) and the *Concise Encyclopaedia of West Asia and North Africa* (Zhao Guozhong 2000) is another important achievement in China. The content of these two works is comprehensive and the material is relatively new. They are divided into three parts respectively: a general study; individual countries studies and documents; and appendices. Part one covers five subjects: a general survey; history; political development; international relations; and economic development. Part two lists individual countries in the area. Part three includes four sections: documents; regional organisations in Africa; statistics and data; and a chronology of Sino-African relations 1949-1999. Most of the authors are experts on the subject and the material is relatively new.

During the 1990s, scholars continued to report on aspects of African studies abroad. There were articles on African historiography and the various schools such as the Ibadan school, the Dar school or the early liberal school of history in South Africa (Li Anshan 1990a, 1990b, 1993a). On specific topics, work appeared on the ancient history of sub-Saharan Africa (Li Anshan 1991), the Bantu migration (Li Jidong 1994); archives abroad and African studies in other parts of the world (Li Anshan 1990c, 1993b; Meng Qingshun 1990; Zhang Xiang 1994; Zhou Muhong

1996). Leading texts on Africa were translated, such as works by Roland Oliver and Anthony Atmore (1981), E.G. Parrinder (1974) and Audrey I. Richards (1960).

Conclusion

This discussion has attempted to show that African studies in China is making progress. We may come to the following conclusions. There have been definite achievements. The survey shows that African studies in China has transformed gradually from a politically-oriented to an academically-oriented pursuit. This is a significant change, which also indicates that Chinese scholars are likely to make more original contributions to the field in the future. Secondly, as far as the content is concerned, it ranges from narrow to broad, from liberation movements and politics to history, geography, economics, ethnography, cultural studies, and so forth. Thirdly, the quality of the scholarship is improving, from general surveys and introductions to more specific and detailed studies. Fourth, there is more contact and exchange between practical work and academic research. The government ministries need information and analysis, while academia needs funding, stimulus and feedback on research.[26] Furthermore, more and more academic exchanges are taking place between Chinese and international scholars, and this trend must surely bring African studies in China fully into the international academy.

Problems exist as well. From the list of references, we can also tell that very few original studies have been undertaken. Most of the works listed here utilised secondary materials, usually in English. What is more, very few scholars have been to Africa to visit, to teach or to conduct research. No anthropologists have visited Africa in order to conduct fieldwork there, and thus have not produced any serious ethnographic studies. Secondly, neither of the Africa-related academic association in China puts out its own journal. There was an internally circulated journal of the Chinese Society of African Historical Studies, but it was irregular and short-lived. The work is still too general, with very few country studies, except for South Africa and Egypt, let alone more local case studies. Thirdly, communication is lacking between academics and practical workers. Although both attend meetings and conferences, there is no dynamic relation between the two. Fourth, there are very few exchanges between China and the outside world. There has been some progress, but it is not enough. Moreover, Chinese scholars seldom have their research published in the English-speaking world. African studies in China is a promising field, but will need more effort and hard work in the future.

Notes

1. In 1983, the Ford Foundation funded a delegation of Chinese Africanists to visit the US. In 1985, the Ford Foundation funded the establishment of the US-China African Studies Exchange Committee, with Professor George Yu as its Chair and Professor Ge Jie as counterpart in China. Proposed by Professor George Brooks in his report on African teaching and research in Asian countries, the ASA Board in 1986 invited Professor Zhang Xiang of Nankai University in China, together with Professor Hideo Yamada from

Japan and Professor Har from South Korea to attend the ASA annual meeting and visit African studies programmes in the US.

2. So far few Chinese Africanists have published formal articles or books in English in the Western world (Gao Jinyuan 1984; He Fanchuan 1987; Ge Jie 1997; Li Anshan, 1994; 1995; 1996a; 2002). Zhang Hongming, a senior researcher in Institute of West Asian and African Studies, CASS, also published articles in French magazines. At Peking University I met two delegations from Great Britain (1996) and France (1997) respectively, and some American scholars such as Goran Hyden, Joel D. Barkan, and George Brooks. They all wanted to know about African studies in China.

3. For the ancient records, see Du Huan AD 762 [?]; Duan Chengshi (AD 850); Ma Huan (1433); Fei Xin (1436); Ibn Battuta (1929). For studies of Sino-African relations in English, see Duyvendak (1947); Filesi (1972); Snow (1988). For works by Chinese scholars, see Shen Fuwei (1990); Ma Wenkuan and Meng Fanren (1987); Ai Zhouchang and Mu Tao, (1996); Li Anshan (2000).

4. *People's Daily*, 2 April 1993, p. 7.

5. Opinions differ on the exact location of 'Molin', such as the Maghreb, Malindi or Mendi in Kenya, Meroe, Aksum. See Li Anshan (2000: 49-50).

6. Wen Wu, 1979, No.2, p. 88.

7. A zebra appeared in Yi Wu Tu Zhi (*Picture and Records of Things from Abroad*), a book from the Ming dynasty, and a giraffe in a painting by Shen Du in Ming Dynasty, which is now in the collection of the Philadelphia Art Museum.

8. It mentioned places such as the Niger River, Lake Chad, countries such as Dahomey, Tukolor, Zaria, Sokoto, cities such as Accra, Lagos, Ouidah, Cabinda, leaders such as Uthman dan Fodio, Ahmadu Bari, Mowlay Ahmad al-Mansur, etc.

9. The first edition has 50 volumes; the edition of 1852 increased to 100 volumes. Ironically, the Japanese government made great use of this book while it was neglected by the Chinese court.

10. Chen Tianhua (1875-1905), an early democratic revolutionary, went Japan to study and organise anti-Qing activities. He wrote several influential books. In 1905, he initiated the set up of Tongmen Hui (Alliance), committed suicide in order to protest Japanese policy to forbid Chinese students. Liang Qichao (1873-1929) was an early reformist, exiled to Japan after the conservative coup of 1898. He used his writing to raise support for the reformers' cause among overseas Chinese and foreign governments. Sun Yat-sen (1866-1925) was the father of the Chinese republican revolution. He led the anti-Qing activities and became the leader of Tongmen Hui and later the Guomindang (Nationalist Party).

11. In the late 1950s, the Department of History at Nankai University published several articles on the national independent movements in Tunisia, Morocco, Libya and Algeria in *Lishi Jiaxue* (*Teaching History*); the Department of History at South China Normal University published articles on Congo and Cameroon in *Zhongxue Lishi Jiaoxue* (*Teaching History in Middle School*).

12. The African friends came from the following countries: Guinea, South Africa, Senegal, North Rhodesia, Uganda and Kenya (Zhonghua Renmin Gongheguo Waijiao Bu and Zhonggong Zhongyang Wenxian Yanjiushi, 1994, 463).

13. Ibid., p. 465. On 30 December 1963, a report was issued by the Group of Foreign Affairs of the Central Committee of CCP on strengthening the study of foreign countries.

14. The People's University in Beijing was chosen for the study of 'socialist countries' which included the USSR and other East European countries, and Fudan University in Shanghai for the study of 'Western countries'.

15. Most of the introductions are published in the journal *Yafei Yicong (Translations on Asia and Africa)*, such as Conferences: 'The first International Africanist Conference', 1963, no.2; 'Selections of the special reports of the first International Africanist Conference', 1963, no.3; 'The fifth annual conference of African Studies Association in the US', 1963, no.3; 'Special reports and articles presented by delegations in the first International Africanist Conference', 1963, no.4; 'Academic conferences in East Africa', 1963, no.10. Institutions: 'About the Institute of African Studies at University of Ghana', 1962, no.5; 'Introduction of the Institute of African Studies in Spain', 1963, no.7; 'Introduction of the Institute of African Studies in Italy', 1963, no.8; 'Introduction of the Department of African Studies at Delhi University in India', 1963, no.9; 'Institute of African Studies in University of Edinburgh', 1964, no.2; 'The origin of the Institute of African Studies in Japan', 1964, no.4; 'Institute of Ethiopian Studies at Addis Ababa', 1964, no.6; 'The Institute of African studies in France', 1964, no.11; 'The Institute of African Studies in Holland', 1964, no.12; 'Centre for African studies at University of London', 1965, no.8. Studies: 'African studies in West Germany', 1963, no.4; 'Recent African research in the USSR', 1963, no.6; 'The project of African studies and coordination of Ford Foundation in the U.S.', 1965, no.3; 'African studies at Hoover Institute of Stanford University', 1965, no.5.

16. About 60 books were translated during this period, among them 29 from the USSR and East European countries. In other words, about 48 percent were translated from Russian or related languages (Zhang Yuxi, ed., 1997, 260).

17. In 1965, the Institute of Asian African Studies (later became the Institute of West Asian and African Studies, CASS) decided that studies should be concentrated on five fields: the development and characteristics of contemporary national liberation movements; the contemporary socioeconomic situation with a focus on the structure of social classes; the bourgeois ideology of nationalism; the revisionists' wrong viewpoints about national liberation movements; and the policy of imperialist countries towards the national liberation movements. *Forty Years of the Institute of West Asian and African Studies*, CASS, 1961-2001 (draft, June 2001), p. 9.

18. Such as Shandong University Translation Group, or Shanghai Foreign Language School Translation Group.

19. Jiang Qing, Wang Hongwen, Zhang Chunqiao and Yao Wenyuan formed a political clique during the Cultural Revolution. They were regarded as ultra-leftists and were very unpopular in China. Their downfall represented the end of the Cultural Revolution.

20. The first graduate student in African studies after the Cultural Revolution is the author of this article. He went to the University of Toronto in 1987 and received his PhD (History) in 1993. He returned to China at the beginning of 1994 and is now teaching at the School of International Studies, Peking University.

21. The translator Fei Xiaotong was a graduate of the London School of Economics and Politics in the 1930s and is now a famous sociologist. His attitude towards this book indicates how inadequately Chinese scholars understood international scholarship in

African studies in the early 1980s, owing to a long-term cut-off from other parts of the world.

22. A revised English version was published by Peter Lang in New York (Li Anshan 2002).

23. For example, Professor Ken Smith, the Chairman of the Department of History at UNISA visited Peking University with the arrangement of Mr Leslie Labuschagne, the Director of the South African Centre for Chinese Studies in Beijing at the time.

24. Professor George T. Yu, Chairman of the Program Committee attended the conference. The more than 30 participants from the US, South Africa and China included Professor Howard Wolpe, in charge of special mission to Burundi sent by the Clinton administration, Professor William J. Foltz, US National Intelligence Council Officer for Africa, and Mr Leslie Labuschagne, Director of the South African Centre for Chinese Studies.

25. Professor Qi Shirong, the Vice Chairman of the Chinese History Society, praised it highly in his keynote speech at the conference 'World History Studies in China in the 20th Century' held at Peking University in April 2000.

26. In October 1997, the Chinese Society of African Historical Studies held its conference in Beidaihe. At the meeting, Li Anshan and Liu Hongwu were requested by the Society to draft a letter to President Jiang Zemin, emphasising the importance of African studies. The letter was later sent to the President, who commented on the issue: 'In recent years, I have stressed many times that work on Africa should be taken very seriously. This issue should be paid great attention to, not only in politics, but also in the development of economic cooperation. The Central Committee and related units of the State Council should all support this work' (translated Li Anshan and Chen Gong Yuan 2000, 244).

References

Ai, Z., ed., 1989, *Zhong Fei Guanxi Shi Wen Xuan* (Selection of Materials on Sino-African Relations), Shanghai: East Normal University Press.

Ai, Z., 1995, 'An examination of the travel in Africa by Du Huan', *Xiya Feizhou* (West Asia and Africa), no. 3.

Ai, Z., ed., 1999, *Feizhou Heiren Wenming* (African Black Civilisations), Beijing: Chinese Social Sciences Publishing House.

Ai, Z. et al., 2000, *Nanfei Xiandaihua Yanjiu* (A Study on Modernisation in South Africa), Shanghai: East Normal University Press.

Ai, Z. and T. Mu, 1996, *Zhong Fei Guanxi Shi* (A History of Sino-African Relations), Shanghai: East Normal University Press.

Ai, Z. and J. Zheng, 1996, *Feizhou Tongshi: Jindai Juan* (A History of Africa, Volume of Modern Time), Shanghai: East Normal University Press.

Anonymous, 1991, 'Institute of African Studies of Hamburg in Germany', *Guo Wai Shehui Kexue* (Foreign Social Sciences), no. 1.

Anonymous, 1995, 'Asian-African bibliographical room in the library of Russian Academy', *Guo Wai Shehui Kexue* (Foreign Social Sciences), no. 3.

Babajee, E., 1958, *A Concise History of Mauritius*, Bombay: Hind Kitabs, (Shanghai, 1973).

Beslier, G.G., 1935, *Le Senegal*, Paris: Payot, (Shanghai, 1975).

Beuchelt, E., 1966, *Mali*, Bonn: Kurt Schroeder, (Shanghai, 1976).

Boutros-Ghali, B., 1972, *Les Conflits de Frontières en Afrique*, Paris: Edition Technique et Economique (Beijing, 1979).

Brose, M. C., 2002, 'Book review: A History of Chinese Overseas in Africa', *Canadian Journal of African Studies* 36 (1): 157-159.

Burns, Sir A., 1963, *History of Nigeria*, London: George Allen and Unwin, (Shanghai, 1974).

Cen, Z., 1935, 'Chinese sea route in Tang dynasty: from Persian Gulf to East Africa', *Dongfang Zazhi* (Oriental Miscellany), 41:18.

Centre for African Studies of Peking University, ed., 2000, *Zhongguo yu Feizhou* (China and Africa), Beijing: Peking University Press.

Chen, G., 1980, 'Mahdi uprising in Sudanese history', *Jiaoxue Tongxun* (Bulletin for Teaching), no.12.

Chen, G., 1985, *Gudai Feizhou yu Zhongguo de Youhao Jiaowang* (Friendly Contact between Africa and China in Ancient Times), Beijing: Commercial Press.

Chen, G., ed., 2000, *21 Shiji Zhongfei Guanxi Fazhan Zhanlue Baogao-Zhongguo Feizhou Wenti Yanjiuhui Chengli 20 Zhounian Teji* (Strategic Report for the Development of Sino-African Relations in the 21st Century—Special Collection of the 20th Anniversary of the Chinese Association of African Studies), Chinese Association of African Studies.

Chen, H., ed., 1984, *Huagong Chuguo Shiliao Huibian* (Compilation of Data of Chinese Labour Abroad), Vol. 9, Chinese labour in Africa, Beijing: Zhonghua Publishing House.

Chen, L., ed., 1959, *Kamailong Renmin Fandui Zhiminzhuyi de Douzheng* (Cameroon People's Anti-Colonialist Struggle)' Hebei People's Publishing House.

Chen, M., 1995, *Feizhou Shichang Zhuzhi* (African Market Organisation), Beijing: Chinese Encyclopaedia Publishing House.

Chen, Y., ed., 1994, *Kaituo Nanfei Shichang: Huanjing yu Jiyu* (Explore the Market in South Africa: Environment and Opportunity), Beijing: Chinese Social Sciences Publishing House.

Chen, Z., 2000, *Jiana: Xunzhao Xiandaihua de Genji* (Ghana: Looking for a base for Modernization), Chengdu: Sichuan People's Publishing House.

Chen, Z. and Z. Wu, 1987, *Sahala yi Nan Feizhou Jingji Fazhan Zhanlue Yanjiu* (Study on the Strategy of Economic Development in Africa South of Sahara), Beijing: Peking University Press.

Chen, Z., 1994, 'A probe into the experience and lesson of economic development of African countries: review of Study on the Strategy of Economic and Social Development in Africa', *Xiya Feizhou* (West Asia and Africa), no. 3.

Chen, Z. and G. Yao Guimei, eds., 2000, *Feizhou Geguo Nongye Gaikuang* (Generalization of Agriculture Development in African Nations), Vol. 1, Beijing: Chinese Financial Economic Press.

Chen, Z.. G. Yao and Z. Fan, eds., 2000, *Feizhou Geguo Nongye Gaikuang* (Generalization of Agriculture Development in African Nations), Vol. 2. Beijing: Chinese Financial Economic Press.

Chinese Society of African Historical Studies, 1982, *Feizhoushi Lunwen Ji* (Collection of Papers on African History), Beijing: Joint Publishing.

Chinese Society of African Historical Studies, 1984, *Feizhou Tongshi* (A General History of Africa), Beijing: Beijing Normal University Press.

Chinese Society of African Historical Studies and Documentation Section of Peking Library, ed., 1982, *Feizhou Wenti Yanjiu Zhongwen Wenxian Mulu, 1949-1981* (Bibliography of African Studies in Chinese 1949-1981), Beijing.

Chinese Society of African Historical Studies and Documentation Section of Peking Library, ed., 1996, 'Conference on Prospects of Political and Economic Development in South Africa', Organised by the Institute of West-Asian and African Studies, CASS. Sponsored by the Ford Foundation. Beijing.

Cornevin, R., 1959, *Histoire du Togo*, Paris: Edition Berger-Levrault (Shanghai,1974).

Cornevin, R., 1962, *Histoire du Dahomey*, Paris: Editions Berger-Levrault (Shanghai, 1976).

Cornevin, R., 1970, *Histoire du Congo Leopoldville-Kinshasa*, Paris: Editions Berger-Levrault (Beijing, 1974).

Cui, Q., 1995, 'Multi-party democratic model of the west does not fit the reality of black Africa', *Xiya Feizhou* (West Asia and Africa), no.1.

Dang, D., J. Xu and G. Chen, eds., 1994, *New Analysis of African Socialism*, Educational Science Publishing House.

Davidson, B., 1955, *The African Awakening*, London: Cape (Beijing: 1957).

Davidson, B., 1960, *Old Africa Rediscovered*, London: Victor Gollancz (Beijing. 1973).

Davidson, B., 1961, *Black Mother: The Years of the African Slave Trade*, London: V.Gollancz (Beijing. 1965).

Davidson, B., 1978, *Africa in Modern History. The Search for a New Society*, London: Penguin Books Ltd., (Beijing. 1989).

De Bary, W. T., W.-T. Chan and C. Tan, eds., 1960, *Sources of Chinese Tradition*, Vol.2. New York: Columbia University Press.

Desire-Vuillemin, G., 1962, *Contribution à l'Histoire de la Mauritanie de 1900 a 1934*, Dakar: Editions Clairafrique (Shanghai, 1977).

Diop, M., 1958, *Contribution à l'étude des Problèmes Politiques en Afrique Noire*, Paris: Presence Africaine (Beijing, 1961).

Ding, B., 1981, 'Maji Maji uprising', *Xiya Feizhou* (West Asia and Africa) no.3.

Du Bois, W. E. B., 1961, *Africa: An Essay Towards a History of the Continent*, Moscow (Beijing, 1964).

Du, B., 1979, 'On the black African terracotta in Xi'an', *Wen Wu* (Cultural Relic) no.6.

Du, H., AD 762 [?], *Jing Xing Ji* (Record of My Travels), preserved in Du You, *Tong Dian* (Encyclopaedia) AD 812.

Duan, C., 850, *Yuyang Za Zu* (Assorted Dishes from Yuyang) AD 850.

Duyvendak, J. J. L., 1947, *China's Discovery of Africa*, Stephen Austin and Sons. (Beijing. 1983).

Ellenberger, D. F., trans. J. C. Macgregor, 1969, *History of the Basuto*, New York: Negro Universities Press, (Shandong. 1975).

Esquer, G., 1957, *Histoire de L'Algerie (1830-1957)*, Presses Universitaires de France, (Shanghai. 1974).

Fage, J. D., 1969, *A History of West Africa: An Introductory Survey*, Cambridge University Press (Shanghai, 1977).

Fan, S., 1959, 'Shen Jian Lu' (Records of My Witness) in *Shan Xi Shiyuan Xuebao* (Journal of Shanxi Normal College), No.2, 1959, Annotated by Z. Yan.

Fan, Y., ed., 1957, *Mologe. Tunishi. A'erjiliya de Minzhu Duli Yundong* (The National Independence Movement in Morocco, Tunisia and Algeria), Shanghai: People's Publishing House.

Fang, J., 1986, *Feizhou Huaqiao Shi Ziliao Xuanji* (Selection of Data of the History of Overseas Chinese in Africa), Beijing: Xinhua Press.

Fei, X., AD 1436, *Xing Cha Sheng Lan* (Triumphant Tour of the Star Raft), Annotated by Feng Chengjun, Zhonghua Press, 1954.

Fei, Z., 1965, 'A'shandi renmin de fan ying douzheng', (Asante people's anti-British struggle), *Lishi Jiaoxue* (Teaching History), 1965. no.8.

Fei, Z., 1985, *Feizhou Ditu Ji* (Atlas of Africa), Beijing: Atlas Press.

Feng, J., 1994, *Niri'er He Kaocha Ji* (Notes on the Exploration of River Niger Area), Beijing: Beijing Language College Press.

Filesi, T., 1972, trans. D. L. Morison,*China and Africa in the Middle Ages*, London: Frank Cass.

First, R., 1963, *South West Africa*, Penguin Books (Shandong, 1978).

Fischer, W., 1962, *Ober-Volta*, Bonn: Kurt-Schroeder (Shanghai. 1977).

Fitzgerald, W., 1955, *Africa: A Social. Economic and Political Geography of its Major Regions*, London: Methuen & Co. (Beijing. 1963).

Fyfe, C., 1962,*A History of Sierra Leone*, London: Oxford University Press (Shanghai, 1973).

Gailey, H. A. Jr., 1964,*A History of the Gambia*, London: Routledge and Kegan Paul (Shanghai, 1974).

Gao, J., 2001, 'Book review: A History of Chinese Overseas in Africa', *African Studies Review* 44 (1): 164-165.

Gao, J., 1984, 'China and Africa: The development of relations over many centuries', *African Affairs* 83: 331.

Ge, G., 1994, 'Nationalism and tribalism in Africa', *Xiya Feizhou* (West Asia and Africa), no.5.

Ge, G. and F. Chao, 1980, *Feizhou Minzu Gaikuang* (Survey of African Nationalities), Institute of Ethnic Studies, CASS.

Ge, G. and Y. Li, 1981, *Feizhou Minzu Renkou yu Fenbu* (African Nationalities: Population and Distribution), Institute of Ethnic Studies, CASS.

Ge, G. and F. Chao, 1982, *Feizhou Shoulie Minzu yu Youmu Minzu* (Hunting nationalities and Nomadic Nationalities in Africa), Institute of Ethnic Studies, CASS.

Ge, G. and F. Chao, 1984, *Xifei Minzu Gaikuang* (Nationalities in West Africa), Institute of Ethnic Studies, CASS.

Ge, G. and L. Song, 1987, *Zhongfei Minzu Gaikuang* (Nationalities in Central Africa), Institute of Ethnic Studies, CASS.

Ge, J. et al., 1989, *Nanbu Feizhou Dongluan de Genyuan* (Origin of the Disturbance in Southern Africa), World Affairs Press.

Ge, J., 1994, *Nanfei: Furao er Duonan de Tudi* (South Africa: A Rich Land with Bitterness), Beijing: World Affairs Press.

Ge, J., 1997, 'China', in J. Middleton, ed., *Encyclopaedia of Africa. South of the Sahara*, Charles Scribner & Sons, Vol.4.

Ge, J., 2000, *Jianming Feizhou Baikequanshu: Sahala yi Nan* (Concise Encyclopaedia of Sub-Saharan Africa), Beijing: Chinese Social Sciences Publishing House.

Greenfield, R., 1965, *Ethiopia: A New Political History*, London: Pall Mall (Beijing. 1974).

Gu, Z., 1997, '"Buzu" or "nation"?', *Shijie Minzu* (World Ethno-national Studies) no.2.

Gunther, J., 1955, *Inside Africa*, London: Hamish Hamilton (Beijing. 1957).

Hall, R., 1969, *Zambia*, London: Pall Mall (Beijing. 1973).

He, F., 1987, 'The relationship between China and African history', *UCLA African Studies Center Newsletter*, Fall.

He, F. and S. Nin, 1996, *Feizhou Tongshi: Gudai Juan* (A History of African: Volume of Ancient Time), Shanghai: East Normal University Press.

He, L., 1995, *Nanbu Feizhou de Yi Ke Mingzhu: Jinbabuwei* (A Pearl in Southern Africa: Zimbabwe), Contemporary World Press.

He, X., X. Wang and P. Li, eds., 2000, *Feizhou Nongchanping Shichang he Maoyi* (African Afro-Product Market and Trade), Beijing: Chinese Financial Economic Press.

Holas, B., 1963, *La Côte d'Ivoire: Passe-Present-Perspectives*, Republique de Côte d'Ivoire, Ministere de l'Education nationale, Centre des Sciences Humaines, Librairie Orientaliste Paul Geuthner S.A. (Shanghai. 1974).

Hong, Y. and X. Xia, 2000, *Feizhou Fa Daolun* (An Introduction to African Law), Changsha: Hunan People's Publishing House.

Hu, Y., 1980, 'African national independence movement after World War II', *Xiya Feizhou* (West Asia and Africa) no. 3.

Huang, Z., 1940, *Aiji Gou Cheng* (A Study of Egypt), Changsha: Commercial Press.

Hutchison, A., 1975, *China's African Revolution*, London: Hutchinson.

Ibn Battuta, 1929, *Ibn Battuta Travels in Asia and Africa 1325-1354*, Trans. and selected by H. A.R. Gibb, London: George Routledge & Sons.

Ingham, K., 1958, *The Making of Modern Uganda*, London: George Allen and Unwin (Beijing. 1973).

Institute of Contemporary International Relations, 1987, *Xiandai Feizhou Mingren Lu* (Contemporary African Celebrities), Current Affairs Press.

Institute of West Asian and African Studies, CASS, 1981, *Feizhou Gaikuang* (Overview of Africa), Beijing: World Affairs Press.

Jarrett, H.R., 1964, *A Geography of Sierra Leone and Gambia*, London: Longmans (Beijing. 1973).

Jiang, X., 1979, 'The anti-British struggle of the Matabele and Mashona in modern South Africa', *Jiangshu Shifan Xueyuan Xuebao* (Journal of Jiangshu Normal College) no.4.

Joos, L. C. D., 1966, *Histoire de l'Afrique du Sud*, Paris: Editions du Centurion (Beijing 1973).

Joye, P. et P. Lewin, 1961, *Les Trusts au Congo*, Bruxelles: Societe Populaire d'Edition (Beijing. 1964).

Kalck, P., Trans. B. Thompson, 1971, *Central African Republic*, London: Pall Mall (Shandong, 1976).

Kimambo, I.N. and A. J. Temu, eds., 1969, *A History of Tanzania*, Nairobi: East African Publishing House (Beijing, 1976).

Lemarchand, R., 1970, *Rwanda and Burundi*, London: Pall Mall (Beijing. 1974).

Lewis, I. M., 1965, *The Modern History of Somaliland: From Nation to State*, New York: Frederick A. Praeger (Beijing, 1973).

Li, A., 1985, 'On the formation and development of West African intellectuals', *Xiya Feizhou* (West Asia and Africa) no.6.

Li, A., 1986, 'The characteristics of West African intellectuals and their role in national independent movement', *Shijie Lishi* (World History) no.3.

Li, A., 1990a, 'On Ibadan school: its formation. development and criticism', *Shijie Shi Yanjiu Dongtai* (Development in World History Studies) no.3.

Li, A., 1990b, 'On the formation and development of the Dar es Salaam school of history', *Shijie Shi Yanjiu Dongtai* (Development in World History Studies) no.4.

Li, A., 1990c, 'The impression of the Public Records Office in London', *Shijie Shi Yanjiu Dongtai* (Development in World History Studies) no.12.

Li, A., 1991, 'A survey of the study on ancient history of sub-Saharan Africa abroad', *Shijie Shi Yanjiu Dongtai* (Development in World History Studies) no.5.

Li, A., 1993a, 'On the early liberal historiography in South Africa', *Xiya Feizhou* (West Asia and Africa) no.1.

Li, A., 1993b, 'An introduction to the Ghanaian National Archives', *Shijie Shi Yanjiu Dongtai* (Development in World History Studies) no.3.

Li, A., 1994, 'Book review of African Eldorado: Gold Coast to Ghana', *The Journal of Modern African Studies* 32 (3): 539-541.

Li, A., 1995, 'Asafo and destoolment in colonial southern Ghana', The International Journal of African Historical Studies 28 (2): 327-357.

Li, A., 1996a, 'Abirewa: A religious movement in the Gold Coast', *Journal of Religious History* 20 (1): 32-52.

Li, A., 1996b, 'New glory. new beginning: Review of three volumes of General History of Africa', *Xiya Feizhou* (West Asia and Africa) no.1.

Li, A., 1998a, *Zhiminzhuyi Tongzhi yu Nongcun Shehui Fankang: Dui Zhimin Shiqi Jiana Dongbu Sheng de Yanjiu* (Colonial Rule and Rural Social Protest: A Study of Eastern Province in Colonial Ghana), Changsha: Hunan Educational Press.

Li, A., 1998b, 'The issue of "tribe" in African studies in China', *Xiya Feizhou* (West Asia and Africa) no.3.

Li, A., 2000, *Feizhou Huaqiao Huaren Shi* (A History of Chinese Overseas in Africa), Beijing: Overseas Chinese Publishing House.

Li, A., 2001a, 'Local nationalism in Africa: an analysis of its origin', *Beida Shi Xue* (Clio at Beida) Issue 8.

Li, A., 2001b, 'An analysis of the evolution of local nationalism in Africa', *Shi Jie Jing Ji Yu Zheng Zhi* (World Economics and Politics) no.5.

Li, A., 2002, *British Rule and Rural Protest in Southern Ghana*, New York: Peter Lang.

Li, B., 1997, *Feizhou Chuantong Wenhua yu Xiandai Hua* (Tradition and Modernization in Africa), Peking University Press.

Li, C. and J. Yang, 1995, 'Chinese narration of Egypt in the end of Qing dynasty', *Alabo Shijie* (Arab World) no. 1.

Li, J., 1983, 'On the causes of ending slave trade', *Feizhou Wenti Cankao Ziliao* (African Issues Reference Data) Issue.7.

Li, J., 1994, 'A survey of the study of "Bantu migration" abroad', *Xiya Feizhou Ziliao* (West Asia and African Data) no.2.

Li, J., 1997, *Xiandaihua de Yanwu: Dui Duli Huo de 'Feizhou Bing' de Chubu Fenxi* (An Analysis on Delayed Modernization in Africa), Chinese Economic Press.

Li, Q., 1979, 'World War I and the national liberation movement in Africa', *Nanjing Daxue Shixue Luncong* (Nanjing University History Series) no.2.

Liu, H., 1997, *Hei Feizhou Wenhua Yanjiu* (A Study on Black African Culture), Shanghai: East Normal University.

Liu, H., 2000, *Cong Buzu Shehui dao Minzu Guojia:Niriliya Guojia Fazhan Shigang* (From Tribal Society to Nation-State: The Outline of the Development of Nigerian State), Kunming: Yunnan University Press.

Liu, H., 1997, *A Study on Black African Culture*, Shanghai: East Normal University.

Lu, T., 1981, 'On David Livingston', *Beijing Daxue Xuebao* (Journal of Peking University) no. 5.

Lu, T., 1981, 'On the causes of Mau Mau uprising', *Shixue Yuekan* (History Monthly) no.2

Lu, T., 1986, *Feizhou yu Diguozhuyi* (Africa and Imperialism), Beijing: Peking University Press.

Lu, T., 1995, 'West countries' multi-party system does not fit Africa', *Guoji Shehui yu Jingji* (International Society and Economy) no.3-4.

Lu, T. and K. Peng, 1996, *Feizhou Tongshi: Xiandai Juan* (A History of African: Volume of Contemporary Time), Shanghai: East Normal University Press.

Lu, T. and J. Liu, 1997, *Feizhou Minzuzhuyi Zhengdang he Zhengdang Zhidu* (African Nationalist Parties and Party System), Shanghai: East Normal University Press.

Lu, T., ed., 2000, *Feizhou Nongye Fazhan Jianshi* (Brief History of Development of African Agriculture), Beijing: Chinese Financial Economic Press.

Luo, H., 1979, 'When did the Ethiopian anti-Italian War end?', *Xinan Shifan Xueyuan Xuebao* (Journal of Southwestern Normal College) no.4.

Luo, J., 1984, 'A comprehensive review on the impact of the Atlantic slave trade on the development of capitalism', *Jiangxi Daxue Xuebao* (Journal of Jiangxi University) no.2.

Luo, J., 1996, *Feizhou Minzu Zichanjieji Yanjiu* (A Study of African National Bourgeoisie), Shanghai: East Normal University Press.

Luo, K., ed., 1956, *Gaoju Fan Zhiminzhuyi Qizhi de Aiji* (Egypt. Holding High the Banner of Anti-Colonialism), Hunan: People's Publishing House.

Ma, H., 1433, *Triumphant Tour of the Ocean's Shores* (Ying Yai Sheng Lan), trans. and ed., U. V. G. Mills. for Hakluyt Society, Cambridge University Press, 1970.

Ma, T., 1959, 'The national liberation struggle in Algeria', *Lishi Jiaoxue* (Teaching History) no.1.

Rivieres, E. S. de, 1965, *Histoire du Niger*, Paris: Edition Berger-Levrault (Shanghai. 1977).

Ma, W. and F. Meng, 1987, *Zhongguo Guci zai Feizhou de Faxian* (The Discovery of Chinese ancient porcelains in Africa), Beijing: Forbidden City Press.

Mckay, V., 1963, *Africa in World Politics*, Harper and Row (Beijing. 1965).

Mao, T., 1979, 'The South African people's armed struggle against colonial invasion in the 17th-19th centuries', *Ya Fei Wenti Yanjiu* (Study of Asian African Issues) no.1.

Marsh, Z. and G. W. Kingsnorth, 1963, *An Introduction to the History of East Africa*, London: Cambridge University Press (Shanghai, 1963).

Meng, Q., 1990, 'Soviet's study on Egyptian modern history', *Shijie Shi Yanjiu Dongtai* (Development in World History Studies) no.2.

Mtshali, B. V., 1967, *Rhodesia: Background to Conflict*, New York: Howthorn Books (Beijing 1973).

Na, Z., 1957, 'Egyptian people's struggle against Napoleon and the national awakening', *Renwen Kexue Zazhi* (Humanities Science Journal) no.1.

Na, Z., 1963, *Aiji Jingxiandai Jianshi* (A Concise History of Modern Egypt), Beijing. Joint Publishing.

Needham, J., 1959, *Science and Civilization in China*, Vol. 3, New York: Cambridge University Press.

Nin, S., 1983, 'An analysis on the issue of "tribe" in contemporary Africa', *Shijie Lishi* (World History) no.4.

Nin, S., 1993, *Feizhou Heiren Wenhua* (Black African Culture), Hangzhou: Zhejiang People's Publishing House.

Nkrumah, K., 1957, *The Autobiography of Kwame Nkrumah*, Edinburgh: Thomas Nelson and Sons (Beijing, 1960).

Nkrumah, K., 1965, *Neo-colonialism: The Last Stage of Imperialism*, London and Edinburgh: Thomas Nelson and Sons (Beijing 1966).

Oliver, R. and A. Atmore, 1981, *Africa since 1800*, Cambridge: Cambridge University Press (Beijing, 1992).

Pan, G. and W. Zhu, 1992, *Translated Materials on Arabic Africa*, Shanghai: East Normal University Press.

Parrinder, E. G., 1974, *African Tradtional Religion*, London: Sheldon Press (Beijing. 1992).

Peng, K. et al., 1978, 'A glorious page in the Sudanese anti-colonialist struggle: the Mahdi uprising in 1881-1885', *Lishi Yanjiu* (Historical Research) no.3.

Pike, J. G., 1968, *Malawi. A Political and Economic History*, London: Pall Mall (Beijing. 1973).

Program of African Studies at Northwestern University, 1959, *United States Foreign Policy: Africa*, Washington, DC (Beijing. 1960).

Qin, X., 1980, 'Can a national bourgeoisie lead contemporary national liberation movement: an analysis of the characteristics of Kenyan proletariat and national bourgeoisie and their historical role', *Shijie Shi Yanjiu Dongtai* (Developments in World History Studies) no.2.

Ren, B., trans., 1907, *The Political History of Egypt*, Shanghai: Commercial Press.

Ren, M. and Q. Yan (1941) Suyishi Da Yunhe (Suez Canal). Shanghai: Daozhong Press.

Richards, A. I., ed., 1960, *East African Chiefs*, Faber and Faber (Beijing. 1992).

Seligman, C. G., 1930, *Races of Africa*, London: Thornton Butterworth (Beijing. 1982).

Service de l'Information du Dahomey, 1963, *Le Dahomey. Des Temps Anciens au Jourd'hui*, Service de l'Information du Dahomey (Shanghai, 1972).

Shen, F., 1990, *Zhongguo yu Feizhou: Zhong Fei Guanxi Er Qian Nian* (China and Africa: Relations of 2000 Years), Beijing: Zhonghua Press.

Shibeika, M., 1959, *The Independent Sudan: The History of a Nation*, New York: Robert Speller and Sons (Shanghai, 1973).

Shu, Y., 1996, *Feizhou Renkou Zengzhang yu Jingji Fazhan Yanjiu* (A Study on African Population Increase and Economic Development), Shanghai: East Normal University Press.

Sik, E., 1966, *The History of Black Africa*, Budapest, 1966, 4 vols., (Shanghai. 1973-1980).

Snow, P., 1988, *The Star Raft: China's Encounter with Africa*, London: Weidenfeld and Nicolson.

Stevens, R. P., 1967, *Lesotho. Botswana. and Swaziland: The Former High Commission Territories in Southern Africa*, London: Pall Mall (Shandong, 1979).

Su, S., 1984, *Feizhou Ziran Dili* (African Natural Geography), Beijing: Commercial Press.

Sun, Y., 1979, 'China and Egypt in the Han dynasty', *Zhongguo Shi Yanjiu* (Study of Chinese History) no.2.

Suret-Canale, J., 1958, *Afrique Noire Occidentale et Centrale*, Paris (Beijing, 1958).

Tan, S., ed., 1998, *Fansi yu Fazhan: Feizhou Jingji Tiaozheng yu Ke Chixuxing* (Reflection and Development: African Economic Adjustment and the Sustanability), Social Science Documentation Press./

Tang, D., 1981, 'The rise and development of Pan-Africanism and its historical role', *Xiya Feizhou* (West Asia and Africa) no. 6.

Tang, D., 1988, *Feizhou Shehuizhuyi: Lishi. Lilun. Shijian* (African Socialism: History. Theory and Practice), Beijing: World Affairs Press.

Tang, D., 1994, *Feizhou Shehuizhuyi Xingtan* (A New Analysis on African Socialism), Beijing: Educational Press.

Tang, D., 1995, *Fanfeizhuyi yu Feizhou Tonyizhuzhi Wen Xuan* (Documents of Pan-Africanism and Organization of African Unity), Shanghai: East Normal University Press.

Tang, T., 1981, 'National liberation movement in Sub-Sahara between the wars and its characteristics', *Shixue Yuekan* (History Monthly) no. 2.

Tang, T., 1981, 'On the Sudanese people's struggle for national independence', *Guiyang Shifan Xueyuan Xuebao* (Journal of Guiyang Normal College), no.2.

Tang, T. and Q. Xiang, 1979, 'On the July Revolution in Egypt', *Guiyang Shifan Xueyuan Xuebao* (Guiyang Normal College) no. 3.

Thompson, V. and R. Adloff, 1968, *Djibouti and the Horn of Africa*, Stanford: Stanford University Press (Shanghai. 1975).

Tindall, P. E. N., 1970, *A History of Central Africa*, London: Longman, (Shanghai. 1976).

Toussaint, A., 1972, *Histoire des îles mascareignes*, Paris: Editions Berger-Levrault.(Shanghai 1977).

UNESCO, 1979, *The African Slave Trade from the Fifteenth to the Nineteenth Century*, (Beijing. 1984).

UNESCO, 1981-1992, *General History of Africa*, 8 vols. (Beijing 1984-2002).

Varley, W. J. and H. P. White, 1958, *The Geography of Ghana*, London: Longmans, Green and Co. (Beijing. 1973).

Wang, C., 1981, 'The struggle for independence: with reference to the historical role of national bourgeois', *Shandong Shifan Xueyuan Xuebao* (Journal of Shangdong Normal College) no. 4.

Wang, J., 1959, 'South African people's fight against racial discrimination', *Guoji Wenti Yanjiu* (Study of International Affairs) no.4.

Wang, S., 1981, 'Wafd and the national independent movement in Egypt 1918-1922', *Lishi Yanjiu* (Historical Research) no. 1.

Wang, Z., 1959, 'Imperialist invasion into Congo and the struggle of the Congolese people', *Guoji Wentin Yanjiu* (Study of International Affairs) no.8.

Ward, W. E. F., 1957, *A History of Ghana* London: George Allen and Unwin. (Beijing. 1972).

Wei, Y., 1842, *Hai Guo Tu Zhi* (Illustrated Gazetteer of the Maritime Countries), Gu Wei Tang.

Wellington, J. H., 1967, *South West Africa and its Human Issues*, London: Oxford University Press (Henan. 1976).

Wen, X., 1995, *Heiren Jiaozi Mandela* (Mandela: Proud Son of the Black People), Contemporary World Press.

Wen, Y., 2000, *Feizhou Nongye Ziyuan Kaifa Liyong* (Development and Utilization of African Agricultural Resources), Beijing: Chinese Financial Economic Press.

West, R., 1970, *Back to Africa: A History of Sierra Leone and Liberia*. London: Jonathan Cape Ltd. (Shanghai. 1973).

Wheeler, L. D. and R. Pelissier, 1971, *Angola*, London: Pall Mall (Beijing. 1973).

Wight, J., 1969, *Libya*, Praeger, (Shanghai. 1974).

Woddis, J., 1960, *Africa: The Roots of Revolt*, London, (Beijing. 1962).

Woddis, J., 1961, *Africa: The Lion Awakes*, London, (Beijing. 1963).

Wu, B., 1983, 'A review of contemporary western scholars' viewpoints', *Shijie Lishi* (World History) no.1.

Wu, B., 1984a, 'The beginning and ending of African slave trade of 400 years', *Shijie Lishi* (World History) no. 4.

Wu, B., 1984b, 'A study on the impact of slave trade on black Africa', *Xiya Feizhou* (West Asia and Africa) no. 5.

Wu, B. and J. Gao, 1993, *Feizhou Minzu Duli Yundong Jianshi* (A Concise History of African National Independence), Beijing: World Affairs Press.

Wu, Z. and D. Xie, 1936, *Abixiniya Guo* (Ethiopia), Shanghai: Zhengzhong Press.

Wu, X., ed., 1956, Aiji Renmin Zhengqu Duli Heping de Douzheng (The Struggle of the Egyptian People to Win Independence and Peace), Beijing Popular Readers Publishing House.

Wu, Z., 1996, 'A survey of the issue of tribe in the study of black Africa in China', *Xiya Feizhou* (West Asia and Africa) no.5.

Xia, J., 1996, *Apartheid and Ethnic Relations in South Africa*, Shanghai: East Normal University Press.

Xia, J. et al., 1998, *Dangdai Geguo Zhengzhi Tizhi: Nanfei* (Contemporary World Political System: South Africa, Lanzhou: Lanzhou University Press.

Xu, J., 1983, 'Slave trade and the development of early capitalism', *Shijie Lishi* (World History) no.1.

Xu, J., 1983, 'Slave trade as an important factor to cause African backwardness', *Xiya Feizhou* (West Asia and Africa) no. 4.

Xu, J. and S. Tan, eds., 1999, *Dangdai Feizhou Zhengzhi Biange* (Political Transformation in Contemporary Africa), Beijing: Economic Science Press.

Xun, X., 1983, *Niri'er Jianshi* (Concise History of Niger), Beijing: World Affairs Press.

Yan, J., 1958, *A'erjiliya Renmin de Minzhou Jiefang Douzheng* (The National Liberation Movement of Algerian People)' Beijing: World Affairs Press.

Yang, D. and Z. Su, eds., 1994, *Feizhou Shichang Jingji Tizhi* (African Market Economy System), Lanzhou: Lanzhou University Press.

Yang, H., 1985, *The Modern History of Egypt*, Beijing: Chinese Social Sciences Publishing House.

Yang, H. and C. Jiang, 1997, *Nasai-er he Sadate Shidai de Aiji* (Egypt in Nasser and Sadat's Period), Beijing: Commercial Press.

Yang, L. et al., 1994, *Nanfei Zhengzhi Jingji de Fazhan* (Political and Economic Development in South Africa), Beijing: Chinese Social Sciences Publishing House.

Yang, L., 1995, *Mandela: Minzu Tuanjie zi Fu* (Mandela: Father of National Unity), Changchun: Changchun Press.

Yang, R., 1984, *Feizhou Tongshi Jianbian* (A Concise History of Africa), Beijing: People's Publishing House.

Yang, R., 1986, *Zai Shengmi de Qiuzhang Wangguo Li* (In the Mysterious Chiefdom), Beijing: Current Affairs Publishing House.

Yap, M. and D. L. Man, 1996, *Colour. Confusion and Concessions: The History of the Chinese in South Africa*, Hong Kong: Hong Kong University Press.

Yuan, X., 1998, 'About the term "Buzu"', *Shijie Minzu* (World Ethno-national Studies) no. 4.

Zeng, Z. et al., 1984, *Feizhou Nongye Dili* (Agricultural Geography in Africa), Beijing: Commercial Press.

Zhang, H., 1995, 'On the issue of "tribe" and tribalism in black Africa', *Xiya Feizhou* (West Asia and Africa) no. 5.

Zhang, H., 1999, *Duo Wei Shiye Zhong de Feizhou Zhengzhi Fazhan* (African Political Development form a Multiple Perspective), Beijing: Social Science Documentation Press.

Zhang, Q. trans., 1904, *Modern History of Egypt*, Shanghai: Commercial Press.

Zhang, J., 1986, *Gudai Zhongguo yu Xiya Feizhou de Hai Shang Wanglai* (The Contact between Ancient China and West-Asia-Africa), Beijing: Ocean Publishing House.

Zhang, T., 1963, *Zhong-Fei Jiaotong Shi Chu Tan* (History of Sino-African Relations: A Primary Research), Beijing: Joint Publishing.

Zhang, T., 1981, *Feizhou Jingji Shehui Fazhan Zhanlue Yanjiu* (Study on the Strategy of Economic and Social Development in Africa), Beijing: People's Publishing House.

Zhang, X., 1987, 'Four high-tides of the contacts between Africa and China in ancient times', *Nakai Shixue* (History in Nankai University) no. 2.

Zhang, X., 1993, 'Several issues in the study of Sino-African relations in ancient times', *Xiya Feizhou* (West Asia and Africa) no.5.

Zhang, X., 1994, 'African scholars pay attention to the study of environment issues', *Zhongguo Feizhou Wenti Yanjiu Tongxun* (Bulletin of Chinese Association of African Studies) no.26.

Zhang, X., ed., 1998, *Caihong zhi Bang Xing Nanfei* (A Rainbow Country. New South Africa), Beijing: Contemporary Press.

Zhang, X., 2000, *Caihong zhi Bang Xing Nanfei* (A Rainbow Country. New South Africa), Beijing: Contemporary World Press.

Zhang, X., 1940, *Zhongxi Jiaotong Shiliao Huibian* (Compilation of Data of China-West Contact), Beijing: Furen University Press.

Zhang, Y., ed., 1990, *Feizhou Wenti Yanjiu Zhongwen Wenxian Mulu. 1982-1989* (Bibliography of African Studies in Chinese. 1982-1989), Beijing: Institute of Afro-Asian Studies, Peking University. Chinese Society of African Historical Studies. Chinese Association of African Studies.

Zhang, Y., ed., 1997, *Feizhou Wenti Yanjiu Zhongwen Wenxian Mulu. 1990-1996* (Bibliography of African Studies in Chinese. 1990-1996), Beijing: Institute of West Asia and Africa, CASS, Institute of Afro-Asian Studies. Peking University. Chinese Society of African Historical Studies.

Zhao, G. et al., eds., 1998, *Guoji Xingshi Huangpi Shu: Zhongdong Feizhou Fazhan Baogao* (Yellow Book of International Situation: The Report of the Development of Middle East and Africa), Beijing: Social Science Documentation Press.

Zhao, G., ed., 2000, *Jianmine Xiya Beifei Baikequanshu: Zhongdong* (Concise Encyclopaedia of West Asia and North Africa: Middle East), Beijing: Chinese Social Sciences Publishing House.

Zhao, J., 1980, 'The national independence issue of Namibia', *Xiya Feizhou* (West Asia and Africa) no.4.

Zhao, S., 1981, *Zayi'er Jianshi* (Concise History of Zaire), Beijing: Commercial Press.

Zheng, D., 1957, 'Nasser's ideology of anti-colonialism', *Xueshu Luntan* (Academic Forum) no. 1.

Zheng, J., ed., 2000, *Zhiminzhuyi Shi: Volume of Africa* (History of Colonialism: Africa). Beijing: Peking University Press.

Zhonghua Renmin Gongheguo Waijiao Bu and Zhonggong Zhongyang Wenxian Yanjiushi, eds., 1994, *Mao Zedong Waijiao Wenxian* (Selections of Mao Tse Tung's Works on Diplomacy), Central Documentation Publishing House and World Affairs Press.

Zhou, M., 1996, 'Recent studies on Botswana abroad', *Xiya Feizhou Ziliao* (West Asian and African Data) no. 2.

Zhu, C. et al., eds., 1994, *Nanfei Jingji: Maoyi Touzhi Zhinan* (Nanfei Jingji: Guide to Trade and Investment), Beijing: Current Affairs Press.

Zhu, G., 1981, 'A probe into the process of national democratic revolution in Africa', *Xiya Feizhou* (West Asia and Africa) no. 3-4.

Chapter 17

African Studies in Recent Years in Japan

Masao Yoshida

By February 2001, the membership of the Japan Association for African Studies had surpassed 700. The Association was established in April 1964 by a group of scholars who were interested in promoting studies on Africa. This Association is unique in character as it has amongst its members many natural scientists. This came about because in the initial years of its establishment, natural scientists were the majority among those who were undertaking fieldwork in Africa. One of the earliest studies through fieldwork was conducted by the zoologists of Kyoto University in 1958, who started preliminary research on chimpanzees and gorillas in Uganda and the then Tanganyika and the Belgian Congo. Field studies on primatology have continued in Africa by generations of zoologists until today. Another group of natural scientists who started field work in Africa in the early years are geologists and the earth-scientists. Their interest centred on the formation of the Great Rift Valley and the volcanic activities in Eastern and Central Africa The other unique character of the membership of the Association has been the leading position of cultural or social anthropologists since its beginning. This point is well explained by the article written by P. M. Peek (1990) in *African Studies Review*, who introduced Japanese studies on Africa to US scholars, concentrating his writings on studies in anthropology and sociology.

However, in recent years, other fields of study have been on the increase. It is the purpose of this paper to show recent trends of study, especially in the field of the social sciences, and highlight the issues that have frequently been taken up. It is therefore not a complete survey of the studies undertaken by the members of the Japan Association for African Studies. The association holds an annual conference once a year, and at each conference about 80 academic papers are presented and discussed. The fields of such papers include: political science, law, economics, history, sociology, cultural anthropology, geography, agricultural science, literature, linguistics, arts and crafts, music, physical anthropology, zoology, primatology, botany, earth science, geology, and medical science. The annual conference is important, more as a meeting place for the different researchers than as a forum where in-depth and heated discussions take place.

The increase of the Association membership is primarily due to the liberalisation of the rule regarding the establishment of new faculties in Japanese universities, where the Ministry of Education used to impose stringent restrictions, especially regarding the qualifications for setting up post-graduate schools. This liberalisation has led to many new types of courses becoming available at universities, especially when they wanted to start something new, and this presented opportunities to intro-duce studies related to African affairs. It was under the initiative of each individual university that this expansion occurred, and not as a result of a great deal of fund-ing from the government. It may be that the universities saw the possibility of more graduates who were knowledgeable about Africa obtaining employment in the aid agencies of the Japanese government.

The Association publishes its biannual *Journal of African Studies* (*Africa Kenkyu* in Japanese). Although the contributors are restricted to the membership, and articles are normally published in Japanese only (with an English summary), the contributed papers are subject to detailed scrutiny by the scholars whom the editorial board asks to referee them, and therefore the quality of their academic standard is preserved. Membership is open to scholars, including foreigners and post-graduate level stu-dents. It is observable that young post-graduate students are starting to contribute a considerable amount to the journal articles recently.

Political Studies

Another academic association, the Japan Association of International Relations, published in its journal *International Relations* a special issue on 'Africa towards the 21st Century' in January, 2000. In its introductory chapter, Professor Masahisa Kawabata (2000: 12) stated that the most urgent themes of African Politics at present are:

(i)   The establishment of democracy;

(ii)   The formation of civil society; and

(iii) An understanding of the causes of violent conflicts and the strategies for their solution.

These three are actually the main themes for Japanese political scholars concerning Africa today.

The articles which were contributed to this special issue were written by the so-called second generation of political scientists who came into the field of African studies in the 1980s. There are three articles on the topic of civil society: M. Endo's (2000) 'Civil Society Arguments on Africa'; M. Sato's (2000) 'Civil Society in Afri-can Studies', and K. Mochizuki's (2000) 'Emergent Actors in Socio-political Sphere of the African State'. The last article does not use the term civil society, but by utilising the term 'actors', the author deals with the same phenomenon as the emergence of civil society. The 'emergent actors' to whom he refers are mainly NGOs and the local residential associations which tend to act outside the control of the state.

Next to these articles, there are two articles which deal with the issue of democracy and pressure groups in the African political sphere. K. Inoue (2000) deals with the problem of democratisation which has, in his opinion, been imposed from outside by the international regime headed by the World Bank/IMF, and the author argues that rapid democratisation in such a situation could often bring about political destabilisation. K. Makino (2000) then takes up the role of Christian churches in helping bring about the democratic transformation in many African countries. These analyses are supported by case studies, with Inoue looking at Zimbabwe, and Makino the Republic of South Africa.

The 1990s saw a number of African countries abolish their long-cherished one party system and adopt the system of plural political parties. Kenya, Tanzania, Zambia, Mozambique, Zaire, Côte d'Ivoire, and Senegal are the important examples. Also governments under military regimes, such as Ethiopia, Nigeria, Ghana, Liberia, Mali, Burkina Faso, etc., have changed to civilian and plural party-based systems. However, the transition has not been smooth and was sometimes turbulent. The existence of numerous ethnic groups, the prevalence of fissures among the nationals in accordance with disparities of wealth, and a monopoly of state power by a small group with a patron-client type of rule are all contributing factors to instability when instituting democratic political systems. Mere copying of democratic institutions which have been developed in Europe and America, namely in Western civilisation, cannot be expected to solve these problems overnight. For Japanese political scientists who come from a different political culture the problem of democratisation in Africa may be looked at as an arena in which various different views and analytical methods could be advanced. An empirical study on Kenyan political parties currently undertaken by Tsuda (2000) may provide a fresh point of view in this connection.

In the aforementioned journal issue, two articles take up the topic of violent conflicts engulfing African countries, and try to advance the theoretical understanding of conflict mechanisms, especially after the end of the Cold War period. Toda (2000) embarks on a comparative study of violent ethnic conflicts in Africa in her article entitled 'Ethnic Conflicts in Africa', and Aoki (2001) presents his analysis on the 'African Mechanism on Conflict Management and Resolution in the Post Cold-war Era', focussing on the conflict resolution attempts by the OAU and its adoption of the Declaration of MCPMR at the Cairo Heads of State Meeting in June 1993. The conclusion drawn from Toda's study is that violent conflicts erupt not because of the long standing ethnic antagonism as is commonly thought, but largely because of the monopoly of state power by a small group under conditions of the collapse of the rule of law and state legitimacy. Aoki's study advances the hope that the creation of networks by the OAU and other regional organisations for co-ordination with various actors of opposing forces would prevent the eruption of violent conflicts.

Original contributions by Japanese scholars to the understanding of recent conflict situations have been made from the fieldwork of anthropologists. The best examples of this type of analysis can be found in Fukui and Markakis (1994) and Kurimoto and Simonse (1998).

These works, especially the latter, stress the point that traditional social systems, such as age grade systems among cattle herders, have been reactivated and are made to play important roles in the new configuration of power struggles which are caused by entirely modern situations.

The emphasis on modern situations in an African context is especially strong in the works of S. Takeuchi and in the books he edited. In a chapter called 'Understanding Conflicts in Africa: Reflections on its Recent Characteristics' (2001), he calls for attention to the 'popularisation of conflicts'. Conflict does not start from ethnic antagonism but rather is promoted by 'political entrepreneurs' (Rothchild 1981) utilising patron-client networks to enhance personal gain. Ethnicity is often harnessed as a tool to strengthen this network, but is not the only means; regional differences and religion can come into play as well. The specific timing of the emergence of violent conflict coincides with the appearance of a large number of autonomous strong men who have built their strength on the democratisation process (from one party or military regime to multi-party system) and the introduction of economic liberalisation policies (from state monopoly of economic accumulation to economic competition for control of resources). The violence has been exacerbated by the easy availability of small arms from international sources.

An important research topic that has emerged as a kind of aftermath of conflict resolution is that of 'national reconciliation'. This term came into vogue in recent years, not only in Africa but also in widely scattered countries in the world where human rights violations occurred on a massive scale under dictatorial political regimes and due to internal wars in various countries. There have been attempts to grasp the characteristics and evaluations of this difficult problem of national reconciliation. The usage of this term does not reflect a consensus as to how nationals can come to reconcile with each other. It is meant to be a political corrective in place of the execution of justice, but in the practical situations there have to be inevitable compromises for implementing any action.

The monthly journal *Ajiken World Trends*, published by the Institute of Developing Economics (IDE), had a special issue in July 2002 on national reconciliation, and it tried to compare various cases worldwide. The cases taken up are the Central American states of Nicaragua, El Salvador, and Guatemala, the South American states of Peru, Chile, and Uruguay, the Asian States of Cambodia and East Timor, and the African States of South Africa, Côte d'Ivoire, and Rwanda. The South African case is presented in the article 'Truth and Reconciliation Commission' written by Y. Nagahara (2002). She points out that the philosophy of non-racialism cultivated by a long history of its freedom struggle and the traditional African philosophy of *ubuntu* made it possible to choose reconciliation through the discovery of the truth, rather than through punishment. Following this article, A. Sato (2002) wrote about the task facing Côte d'Ivoire after the massacre of 57 people in Abidjan in December 1999. Newly-elected president Gbagbo had set up the *Forum National pour la Reconciliation* and held a public hearing with more than one hundred people, including all the important political figures. Sato examines the recommendations made from the agreed points, and evaluates these undertakings as a political success. This assessment may have been given prematurely in the light of the recent events in Côte d'Ivoire.

Concerning Rwanda, S. Takeuchi (2002) examines the tasks awaiting the national reconciliation practices through the court hearings on the 1994 genocide set up by the UN and by Belgium. The Rwandan government itself had also set up a national court which judges the violation of human rights within Rwandan borders. However, this national court proceeds too slowly, and the Rwandan government has introduced a traditional type of group judgement by all the inhabitants, termed *gacaca*, in 2002. This provides for the reduction of punishment by admitting one's sin, by which the government hopes to facilitate national reconciliation.

Another topic concerning political conflict is that of 'human security'. This topic has been taken up as the study both of conflict prevention and of providing social care after human security is violated and emergency relief action becomes necessary. The study of 'human security' has been vigorously promoted by scholars such as M. Katsumata, who organised study groups gathered around the Institute of Peace Research at the Meiji Gakuin University (see Katsumata 1999). These initiatives were instrumental in the adoption of human security as one of the major objectives of the revised Japanese ODA strategies, now being formulated.

Economic Studies

The strength of economic studies amongst Japanese Africanist scholars could be said to lie in its engagement with economic history. As most of their writings are in Japanese, these works are not well-known outside Japan. Japanese economic historians are noted for their vigorous textual critiques, and much effort has been made to utilise unique sources available to the Japanese.

A good example is the doctoral thesis written by K. Kitagawa in 1999, entitled *A Historical Study of Trade Relations between Japan and South Africa*. In his thesis, Kitagawa made extensive use of the Japanese Consular Reports which started in 1881 and were sent from the offices in Cape Town, Port Said, Cairo, Bombay, London, Lyon, and other places to the central Ministry of Foreign Affairs. Kitagawa examines the reports painstakingly and uses the evidence to explain the motives underlying Japanese trade policies with South Africa. Under the strict racial segregation policy of the Union of South Africa, Japanese trading firms were not allowed to set up branches on South African soil. The Japanese Consular reports reveal that vigorous efforts were made to increase Japanese imports of South African woollens, which persuaded the South African government to finally grant permission for Japanese trading companies to acquire the right of residence in the 1930s (Kitagawa 1999: 60-71). Closer to the present age, J. Morikawa utilised unofficial documents from Japanese business organisations and NGOs and included the findings in his book *Japan and Africa: Big Business and Diplomacy*, which was published by Hurst in 1997.

There are other examples of such meticulous personal efforts to glean facts. M. Saeki (1975) obtained the amount of investment going to the various mining companies of South Africa by perusing all the issues of *The Economist* published in Britain. T. Yoshikuni went through the Town Clerk's Department files in Salisbury, searching for information on housing, when he wrote his DPhil thesis for the University of Zimbabwe, *Black Migrants in a White City: A Social History of African Harare: 1890-1925* (1989). I myself for my PhD at the University of East Africa, Kampala (1970) used the personal files of Sir Amar Maini, a one-time Legislative Councillor in Colonial Uganda, and this source enabled me to fill the information gap on the allocation of cotton to different ginners in Uganda during and immediately after the Second World War.

Coming closer to the contemporary world, many Africanist economists have started to enquire why African development has been lagging behind in comparison with Asian countries, especially those of South East Asia. Japan allocates about ten percent of the total ODA to African countries while almost 70 percent goes to the Asian countries. The search for reasons for the low development shown in many indicators of African countries has no doubt been prompted by the desire to foster an aid strategy based on a more thorough understanding of factors preventing faster economic growth, although in Japan scholars are not often directly involved in actual aid formulation.

When the IMF/World Bank regime started to impose Structural Adjustment Programmes (SAP) on African countries in the 1980s, there was a resurgence of neoclassical economic prescriptions. There was an urgent need to study the effects of these neo-classical arguments regarding Africa's economic performance. The IDE published two books in this connection, Haraguchi's *Political Economy of Africa at a Turning Point* (1993), and *Structural Adjustment and African Agriculture* (1995).

While the new free market strategies of the international financial institutions did not seem to turn the tide of economic stagnation in Africa, there were fresh attempts to find the causes of non-development while re-examining the relevant economic theories on the issue. Y. Mine's *Economics for an African Rebirth* (1999) is the best example of this trend. His approach is to take up the works of three great economists, namely A. Lewis, A. Hirschman and A. Sen, who have dealt with the political-economic problems of Africa in their own individual ways, and present their discourses for fresh examination. By referring to their theories and insights, Mine tries to illuminate the problematic of African economic stagnation within the contemporary framework of the free market economic regime.

Another economist who has energetically pursued the cause of African economic stagnation is M. Takahashi (2001), who examines the notion of the developmental state, formulated to describe the East Asian industrialisation miracle. His study discards the applicability of this type of development strategy as he examines the predatory nature of African states. He points out that the missing link of the argument is agricultural development in Africa. In comparison with the Asian peasantry, African peasants' collective action against the state has been weak and could not exert strong influence on the state for the purpose of extracting resources for investment. His attention now centres on problems of institutional barriers such as a land tenure system which erects high transaction costs around the promotion of production efficiency. His interest in rural institutions could benefit much from the sociological studies in the rural areas of Africa to which we turn later. Another economist who has been enthusiastically promoting the study of African economy, and is trying now to formulate a development theory from the African perspectives, is K. Hirano of the IDE. He has been the co-ordinator of a study group on this theme.

Agricultural and Rural Sociology

Kyoto University can be considered as the largest centre of African area studies in Japan, and its special strength lies in the field of ecological anthropology and zoology. To this, one might add agricultural and rural sociological studies. Their field researches are many and their journal articles appear in abundance. Another centre of study in this field is the Institute of Developing Economies (IDE). There are of course many scholars in various universities all over Japan who are interested in this subject, and to this, I must add the staffs of NGOs and the Japan International Cooperation Agency (JICA) research staff. They are focussing their attention on research that has an immediate policy applicability, much of which is in the field of African agricultural and rural sociology.

Recently, T. Suehara (2001) has reviewed the reasons for this expansion of agricultural and rural sociological studies. He points out that there have always been many researchers in this field, but they were not grouped together before 1984 when a review of African studies in Japan was published in that year.[1] For instance, many studies undertaken before 1984 were included in the fields of ecological anthropology, cultural anthropology, sociology, economics and economic history according to this special issue.

It is often said that the studies of this field have developed mainly through group study method with the scholars and students of different but related academic discipline undertaking field research together and deepening the knowledge of agriculture or livestock-related problems in some specific areas in Africa. Such groups were at times formed with financial backing from specific universities or institutions, but more commonly were funded by the Ministry of Education and its programme of grants-in-aid, which selects several applicants every year. An advantage of this fund is that the successful applicants can obtain preferential treatment in the next year's applications so that some groups can continue to undertake field research for three to four years in a succession.

Suehara (2001) has classified recent Japanese scholars' studies in the field of agriculture and rural sociology under the five headings, namely, (i) livelihood or subsistence activities of agriculturalists, cattle herders, and fishermen, etc., (ii) the relationship between the peasant economy and the national economy, (iii) internal relations of the rural community and traditional farming systems, (iv) development and improvement of agricultural technologies, and (v) collaborative studies by many researchers in closely linked disciplines, especially with biologists and primatologists.

Rather than following Suehara's categorisation, I would like to discuss Japanese scholars' interest in this field and the products of their research under the headings (i) concern with the character of the local community and its transformation, and (ii) concern with the environmental preservation and the search for a new path to sustainable agriculture.

The first category of studies comes out of the Japanese scholars' preoccupation with 'community' as an outmoded and disappearing entity, while at the same time serving as an important preserver of humane values, mutual help and security. Japan has witnessed a rapid change from an agrarian-based society to an ultra-modern industrial society in a matter of a hundred years. People still have memories of the home village with its rich but fast disappearing traditions while living in the hustle and bustle of the city with a cosmopolitan outlook. In its endeavour to become an industrial nation, a powerful ideological inclination has developed to do away with anything communal, and to pursue modernity and individualism.[2] But at the root of this change it has been found that the population still could not escape from the old communal obligations, and these communal attitudes and value systems persisted even in urban and industrial establishments. Many Japanese have developed ambivalent views about the existence of communal relations among themselves, and such preoccupations have given Japanese scholars strong incentives to study African rural society in its particular forms and its processes of transition.

Another issue concerning 'community' which has made the Japanese scholars, especially the economists, aware about its importance is that the introduction of free market economics in most African countries, after the failures of state-led economies, has also seemed to have failed, and the third factor, namely 'community,' should be positively utilised wherever feasible. Such a view appeared first in studies of the rural development of Southeast Asia and was re-introduced in arguments around African rural development (Hayami 1995). However, there still remains the question of 'what is the composition of community in rural Africa: is it a lineage structure, a village, a neighbourhood, a clan or what else?', and these issues have not yet clarified. Identifying community has become all the more important as aid agencies have come to stress the need for 'participatory' planning and implementation by the people of a 'community'.

Such a concern prompted a re-evaluation of rural societies of Africa in the research agenda at the Institute of Developing Economics (IDE), and the product of a group study was published in Ikeno (1999). Five chapters of this book were written by scholars of rural economy and sociology who have had at least two years of field research experience in various areas of Africa. The titles of these chapters are 'Rural communities and the actors for land tenure reforms in East Africa with special reference to Tanzania' (by M. Yoshida), 'Socioeconomic study on indigenous irrigation systems of North Pare Lowland, Tanzania' (by J. Ikeno), 'Land tenure and land issues in customary land areas in Zambia: The case of a village in Central Province' (by S. Kodamaya), 'Rural exodus in the northern Gabon: a process of de-agrarianisation' (by S. Takeuchi), and 'Searching for new frontier in the study on rural Africa: from the political-ecological point of view' (by S. Shimada). These studies, especially the first three chapters, point to a reassessment of the traditional concept of 'community' as an entity belonging to a limited geographic area with a rigidly restricted membership. African villages are often multi-ethnic, and have complex land claims and work organisations which are sometimes quite open to outsiders. As Chapter 4 of this book suggests, there is often a large outflow of young people from the villages, and therefore the situation is very fluid. As Chapter 5 points out, African peasants are vulnerable to climatic and political change, and are wanting in basic needs entitlement, but still energetically act to capture various access channels for self-improvement.

'African community', thus, should be pictured as a rather varied and amorphous entity, by no means static. A second book (Takane 2001) has already been published which is a kind of continuation of the above-mentioned research but with a focus shifted to rural societies heavily influenced by national and international transformations.

There are many other excellent products of field research on rural sociology by scholars who belong to different universities. S. Kodamaya and K. Hanzawa for Zambia, K. Ikegami and H. Tsujimura for Tanzania, T. Suehara and K. Sugimura for the former Zaire, and T. Takane for Ghana, are but a few examples of such scholars studying this subject.

Also, there has appeared a gender-focussed rural society study, of which we may see a considerable increase in the near future. The outstanding example is Sugiyama's (1987) study in the Bemba area of Zambia. She observed the mutual relations of village women and wrote: 'May I use your mortar? Micro-politics of Bemba women on the ownership and usage of daily utensils'. Including the urban areas, C. Tominaga has proposed a feminist perspective of African history, which culminated in an edited volume on the subject (Tominaga and Nakahara 2006).

As regards environmental issues and sustainable agricultural practices, there exist many articles especially by researchers associated with the Kyoto University group. Certain types of agronomical practices which show the wisdom of peasants have drawn their particular attention. M. Kakeya studied the slash-and-burn agriculture of the Tongwe people on the shores of Lake Tanganyika, and went on to examine the *chitemene* system in Northern Zambia. Kakeya, together with Y. Sugiyama, conducted detailed research on the Bemba people's rational practice of cutting wood branches for burning and spreading ashes, which has been undertaken in such a way that no ecological destruction occurred. However, in this area also, cash crop production has now become quite advanced, and Sugiyama has analysed the mechanisms of transition and the villagers' logic in explaining change (Sugiyama 2001). T. Takane (1999) has also examined villagers' logic for the various types of *abusa* labour systems in Southern Ghana in order to ascertain the rationality of indigenous agricultural practices. T. Wakatsuki and S. Hirose have concentrated on the intensive type of agriculture in the valley-bottoms and wet-lands (called *Fadama*) in Nigeria and Ghana, and has published a book on the subject, *Ecological Recovery and Rural Reconstruction in the Savanna Area of West Africa* (1997). Both the Kakeya group and the Wakatsuki group have received contracts for long-term research from the Japan International Cooperation Agency (JICA), in order to study the improvement of indigenous agronomical practices in Tanzania and Ghana respectively. The Kakeya group has been taking up the traditional cultivation practices of the Matengo people called *ngoro* (pit cultivation), and is experimenting with regard to its transfer of technology to the inhabitants of Morogoro mountain area of Tanzania.

Urban Sociology and Industrialisation Studies

While rural area research has often been chosen as a field of study by many Japanese anthropologists, scholars who study urban societies have been fewer. However, noticeably more urban studies have been produced in recent years.

S. Hino initiated an urban sociological study in the town of Ujiji in Tanzania and in Ngaundere in Cameroon in the 1960s. Younger generations have taken up Hino's initiative, and are now producing remarkably detailed and well-organised studies. M. Matsuda lived among the migrants in Nairobi city in Kenya (in a sort of urban colony called Kangemi) and eventually produced a book called *Urbanisation from Below: Creativity and Soft Resistance in the Everyday Life of Maragoli Migrants in Nairobi* (1998). The book was written in English and is a culmination of many journal articles he had written in previous years in Japanese. His viewpoint is that seemingly traditional elements of the migrant community are playing an important role in the adaptations in their everyday life. The people have been converting these elements to the means of resistance against official coercion and for struggles to live with their own creativity. Thus they create traditional-cum-modern associations that enable them to ride out the rough waves of urban life. He examines their practices, both in their home villages and their urban colony in Nairobi, and ascertains how their traditional practices have changed in the urban circumstances.

H. Wazaki and Y. Shimada have studied urban life in Cameroon, and also produced impressive studies. Wazaki and Shimada edited a book together with Matsuda entitled *A World of Urban Society in Africa* (2001). In this book Wazaki takes up the networks of associations among the Bamum people in various Cameroon cities such as Douala, and analyses the role of their dances and their rotating saving and credit associations. Shimada has previously examined the contemporary life of the people in a small Fulani kingdom called Rey-Bouba in Northern Cameroon, and in this edited book he constructs a typology of Islamic cities in the Sahel area. Wazaki has already published a detailed account of the saving associations among the Bamum in which he described the characteristics of their membership and distributive mechanisms.

Urban-rural linkages are the object of a study by M. Ogura (1988). By conducting interviews among city dwellers in Zambia, Ogura found out the frequencies of their remittances to their home villages and their annual visits, as well as their stated intentions to go back to their villages after retirement. He found that the urban-rural linkages remain quite strong.

The so-called 'informal sector' has developed rapidly in the urban centres as opportunities for formal-type employment are limited to a few, well-educated youth, and a majority of urban dwellers have to earn their living in the very small-scale 'informal' type of enterprises.

G. Ueda has studied such small-scale enterprises in Nyeri, which is a small town in a rural setting in Kenya, and examined the movement of apprentices or employees at outdoor garages. When such small enterprises are clustered in some localities, there could be a significant contribution to national economic development, and this topic deserves more study by economic geographers.

On the other side of the extremes, large enterprises sometimes form conglomerates. A good example of the study of such a large enterprise has been written by Y. Muroi (1992) who examined the United Africa Company, which formed a main component of the present-day Unilever Corporation. Later, A. Nishiura (2001) embarked on a comparative study of six large business groups in South Africa and is searching for the motive force behind the formation of such groups, comparing them with the business groups in the developing countries in general.

Concluding Remarks

There has been a remarkable expansion of African studies in Japan in recent years, both in terms of the variety and the depth of individual research and in terms of the number of centres of research activities. The liberalisation of establishing postgraduate courses in the universities has contributed to the rapid increase of graduate students who have taken up research on African subjects. The Japanese yen has greatly appreciated in value since the second half of the 1980s, and this has made the cost of field research in Africa for Japanese scholars much less expensive.

In the field of social science Japanese researchers have shown great interest in the study of certain topics, especially the causes of violent conflict, conflict resolution, and the nature of 'community' and for its role in the economic development in Africa.

Indigenous agronomical practices have been enthusiastically studied in order to ascertain if they could be utilised for the purpose of sustainable rural development. Urban societies are being studied in order to understand the working of informal types of human relations in the rapidly changing circumstances.

This chapter has concentrated on recent studies of Africa in Japan in the field of social science. I have attempted to show what the current topical emphases are, but of course there are many social scientists pursuing quite different individual themes. Also, as I stated in the beginning of this paper, there have been many field studies conducted by natural scientists in Africa, and the cooperation between the social scientists and natural scientists has been very sound. It would seem that Japanese Africanists are particularly fond of inter-disciplinary approaches, in contrast to fellow Africanists elsewhere.

Notes

1. Agriculture and rural sociology was not allocated an independent category in the *Journal of African Studies* (Africa Kenkyu) No. 25, 1984.
2. In Japan, the rural community has been depicted as an embodiment of feudalism, and both the industrialists and labour movements stressed the need for the removal of the feudal mentality.

References

Aoki, K., 2001, 'African mechanisms on conflict management and resolution in the post Cold-War era', *African Study Monographs* 22 (1): 37-52.

Endo, M., 2000, 'Civil society arguments in Africa', *International Relations* 123.

Endo, M., 2001, 'International relations in the 21st century: the challenge of African Studies', *Journal of African Studies* 57:1-4.

Fukui, K. and J. Markakis, eds., 1994, *Ethnicity and Conflict in the Horn of Africa*, London: James Currey (in English).

Hanzawa, K., 1998, 'Structural adjustment and rural changes in Zambia', *Journal of Development Studies*, (Kaihatsu Kenkyu) 9 (1).

Haraguchi, T., ed., 1993, *Political Economy of Africa at a Turning Point*, Tokyo: IDE.

Haraguchi, T., ed., 1995, *Structural Adjustment and African Agriculture*, Tokyo: IDE.

Hayami, Y., 1995, *Development Economics* (in Japanese), Tokyo: Sobunsha.

Hayashi, K., 1992, *African Historical Studies in Japan* (IDE Working Paper Series), Tokyo: IDE, (in English).

Hayashi, K., 1999, *A Study in the Political Economy of Southern Africa*, Tokyo: IDE.

Hino, S., ed., 1990, *African Urban Studies*, Vol. 1, Tokyo: ILCAA (in English).

Hirano, K., 'Extension services in economic cooperation: "green revolution" and the local-level administration', in H. Sato, ed., *Management of International Cooperation and the Local-level Administration*, Tokyo: IDE.

Hirano, K., 2001a, 'International comparative study on African agriculture: non-growing economies', in K. Hirano, ed., *Comparing Africa: The Challenges of Disciplines*, Tokyo: IDE.

Hirano, K., 2001b, ed., *Comparing Africa: The Challenges of Disciplines*, Tokyo: IDE.

Hirose, S., and T. Wakatsuki, eds., 1997, *Ecological Recovery and Rural Reconstruction in the Savanna Area of West Africa*, Tokyo: Norin Tokei Kyokai.

Ikegami, K., 1994, 'The traditional agrosilvipastoral complex system in the Kilimanjaro region, and its implication for the Japanese-assisted Lower Moshi Irrigation Project', *African Study Monographs* 13 (4).

Ikeno, J., 1999, 'Socioeconomic study on indigenous irrigation systems of North Pare Lowland, Tanzania', in J. Ikeno, ed., *Search for Reality of Changing Rural Africa*, Tokyo: IDE.

Ikeno, J., ed., 1999, *Search for Reality of Changing Rural Africa*, Tokyo: IDE.

Inoue, K., 2000, 'Globalizing democracy and political instability in African states', *International Relations* 123.

Kakeya, M., 1996, 'The present state of the slash-and-burn agricultural society: 10 years in Bemba villages', in J. Tanaka, M. Kakeya, M. Ichikawa, and I. Ohta, eds., *Ecological Anthropology in Changing Africa*, Kyoto: Academia Publishing.

Katsumata, M., 2001, 'Introduction', *Prime,* No. 10.

Katsumata, M., 2001, 'Rewriting contemporary Africa's place in the world: an Afro-Asian perspective', in E. Kurimoto, ed., *Rewriting Africa: Toward Renaissance or Collapse?* Osaka: JCAS (in English).

Kawabata, M., 2000, 'Africa: a new vision for the 21st Century?' *International Relations* 123.

Kitagawa, K., 1999, *A Historical Study of Trade Relations between Japan and South Africa*, Unpublished PhD Thesis for the Graduate School for Advanced Studies.

Kitagawa, K., 2001, *A Study in the Socioeconomic History of Southern Africa*, Osaka: Kansai University Press.

Kodamaya, S., 1999, 'Land tenure and land issues in customary land areas in Zambia: the case of a village in Central Province', in J. Ikeno, ed., *Search for Reality of Changing Rural Africa*, Tokyo: IDE.

Kurimoto, E., 2001, 'Capturing modernity among the Anywaa of Western Ethiopia', in E. Kurimoto, ed., *Rewriting Africa: Toward Renaissance or Collapse?* Osaka: JCAS (in English).

Kurimoto, E., 2001, ed., *Rewriting Africa: Toward Renaissance or Collapse?* Osaka: JCAS (in English).

Kurimoto, E. and S. Simonse, eds., 1998, *Conflict, Age, and Power in Northeast Africa*, Oxford: James Currey (in English).

Majima, I., 2001, 'Past and future of African studies: cultural and social anthropology', *Journal of African Studies* 57: 25-28.

Makino, K., 2000, 'The Christian churches and politics in South Africa', *International Relations* 123.

Matsuda, M., 1990, 'A formation process of urban colony for the Maragoli migrants in Kangemi, Nairobi', in S. Hino, ed., *African Urban Studies*, Vol. 1, Tokyo: ILCAA (in English).

Matsuda, M., 1998, *Urbanization from Below: Creativity and Soft Resistance in the Everyday Life of Maragoli Migrants in Nairobi*, Kyoto: Kyoto University Press (in English).

Matsuda, M., 2001, 'Sociology and African studies', *Journal of African Studies* 59.

Mine, Y., 1999, *The Economics for an African Rebirth*, Tokyo: Nihon Hyoronsha.

Mine, Y., 2001, 'Rewriting the political landscape of Africa: a perspective from South Africa', in E. Kurimoto, ed., *Rewriting Africa: Toward Renaissance or Collapse?* Osaka: JCAS (in English).

Miyamoto, M. and M. Matsuda, eds., 1997, *An African History, in New Series*, Tokyo: Kodansha.

Mochizuki, K., 2000, 'Emergent actors in the socio-political sphere of the African states', *International Relations* 123.

Morikawa, J., 1997, *Japan and Africa: Big Business and Diplomacy*, London: Hurst (in English).

Muroi, Y., 1992, *A History of the United Africa Company 1879-1979*, Kyoto: Dobunkan.

Nagahara, Y., 2002, 'South Africa: from "Truth and Reconciliation" to "Justice and Reconciliation"', *Ajiken World Trend* 82.

Nishiura, A., 2001, 'A comparative analysis of "Business Groups" in South Africa', in K. Hirano, ed., *Comparing Africa: The Challenges of the Discipline*, Tokyo: IDE.

Ogura, M., 1988, 'Rural-urban migration in Zambia: migrants' ties with their home villages', *Ajia Keizai* 29 (7/8).

Ogura, M., 1995, *Labour Migration and Social Change: A View from the Lives of the Zambians*, Tokyo: Yushindo-Kobunsha.

Peek, P. M., 1990, 'Japanese anthropological research on Africa', *African Studies Review* 23 (1).

Rothchild, P., 1981, *Ethnopolitics: A Conceptual Framework*, New York: Colombia University Press.

Saeki, M., 1975, 'A study in British investment towards Africa', in H. Yamada, ed., *Capital and Labour in Colonial Africa*, Tokyo: IDE.

Saito, F., ed., 2002, *Participatory Development*, Tokyo: Nihon Hyoronsha.

Sato, A., 2000, 'Lemarchand's self-fulfilling prophecy reconsidered', in D. Goyvaerts, ed., *Conflict and Ethnicity in Central Africa*, Tokyo: ILCAA.

Sato, A., 2002, 'Tasks remaining after the "Forum national pour la reconciliation"', *Ajiken World Trend* No. 82.

Sato, M., 2001, 'Small arms proliferation and peace-building in South Africa', in K. Hirano, ed., *Comparing Africa: The Challenge of the Disciplines*, Tokyo: IDE.

Shimada, S., 1996, 'The influence of rapid economic change on food production systems in Nigeria', in S. Hosomi, S. Shimada, and J. Ikeno, eds., *Food Problems in Africa: Case Studies of Ghana, Nigeria, and Tanzania*, Tokyo: IDE.

Shimada, S., 1999, 'Searching for new frontiers in the study of rural Africa: from a political ecological point of view', in J. Ikeno, ed., *Search for Reality of Changing Rural Africa*, Tokyo: IDE.

Shimada, Y., H. Wazaki, and M. Matsuda, eds., *A World of Urban Society*, Kyoto: Sekai Shisosha.

Suehara, T., 1990, *Food Production in Equatorial Africa*, Kyoto: Dohosha Shuppan.

Suehara, T., 2001, 'Agriculture, peasant & agricultural studies in Africa: a review and perspective', *Journal of African Studies*, No. 58.

Sugimura, K., 1999, 'Traders' ethnicity and rural Africa: a case study around Kisangani, Zaire', *Journal of Fukui Prefectural University* No.14.

Sugimura, K., 1999, 'Organizational principles of subsistence livelihoods and their changes in Equatorial Africa', *Journal of Fukui Prefectural University* No. 15.

Sugiyama, Y., 1987, 'May I use your mortar? micro-politics of the Bemba women on the ownership and usage of daily utensils', *Journal of African Studies* No. 30.

Sugiyama, Y., 2001, 'Agricultural policy changes and the Bemba villages of northern Zambia, 1983-2000', in T. Takane, ed., *Rural Transformation in Contemporary Africa*, Tokyo: IDE.

Takahashi, M., 2001, 'The creation of development states: arguments and reality in Africa', in E. Kurimoto, ed., *Rewriting Africa: Toward Renaissance or Collapse?* Osaka: JCAS.

Takahashi, M., 2001, 'African studies and mainstream economics: development and prospects', *Journal of African Studies* No. 57.

Takane, T., 1999, *Cocoa Producers in Ghana: the Social Aspects of Smallholder Export Crop Production*, Tokyo: IDE.

Takane, T., ed., 2001, *Rural Transformation in Contemporary Africa*, Tokyo: IDE.

Takeuchi, S., 2001, 'Understanding conflict in Africa: reflections on the recent characteristics', in E. Kurimoto, ed., *Rewriting Africa: Toward Renaissance or Collapse?* Osaka: JCAS (in English).

Takeuchi, S., 2000a, 'Hutu and Tutsi: a note on group formation in pre-colonial Rwanda', in D. Goyvaerts, ed., *Conflict and Ethnicity in Central Africa*, Tokyo: ILCAA (in English).

Takeuchi, S., ed., 2000b, *Conflicts in Contemporary Africa*, Tokyo: IDE.

Takeuchi, S., 2002, 'Introduction to the national reconciliation "phenomena"', *Ajiken World Trends* No. 82.

Toda, M., 2000, 'Ethnic conflicts in Africa', *International Relations* 123.

Toda, M., 2001, 'Political science (African studies in the 21st century)', *Journal of African Studies* No. 58.

Tominaga, C., 1989, 'Merchants of the Indian Ocean and Jetha Lila Bankers', in E. Linnebuhr, ed., *Transition and Continuity of Identity in East Africa and Beyond*, Bayreuth African Studies (in English).

Tominaga, C., and Y. Nakahara, 2006, ed., *Towards New Perspectives of African History: Wome, Gender, Feminisms*, Tokyo: Ochanomizu-shobo.

Tsuda, M., 2000, 'A re-examination of "Ethnic Crashes" and the State', in S. Takeuchi, ed., *Conflict in Africa: History and Subject*, Tokyo: IDE.

Tsujimura, H., 1999, *Rural Cooperative Societies in Southern Africa: their Role and Assistance under the Structural Adjustment Policy*, Tokyo: Nihon Keizai Hyoronsha.

Ueda, G., 1998, 'Business management logic and populism of the micro enterprise cluster: organizing Jua-Kali in Nyeri Town', in J. Ikeno and S. Takeuchi, eds., *Rethinking on the Informal Sector in Africa*, Tokyo: IDE.

Ueda, G., 1999, *Devolution and Autonomy: Dynamics of Micro Enterprise Reproduction in Nyeri Town, Kenya*, Unpublished PhD Thesis, University of London (in English).

Ueda, G., 2001, 'African studies in Japan: the case of human geography in the 1990s', *Journal of African Studies* No. 58.

Wakatsuki, T. and S. Hirose, eds., 1997, *Ecological Recovery and Rural Reconstruction in the Savanna Area of West Africa*, Tokyo: Norin Tokei Kyokai.

Wazaki, H., 2001, 'African traditional city in a nation: Bamun urbanity in the contemporary network', in Y. Shimada, H. Wazaki, and M. Matsuda, eds., *A World of Urban Society in Africa*, Kyoto: Sekai Shisosha.

Yoshida, M., 1984, *Agricultural Marketing Intervention in East Africa: A Study in the Colonial Origins of Marketing Policies, 1900-1965*, Tokyo: IDE (in English).

Yoshida, M., 1999, 'Rural communities and actors for the land tenure reforms in East Africa with special reference to Tanzania', in J. Ikeno, ed., *Search for Reality of Changing Rural Africa*, Tokyo: IDE.

Yoshikuni, T., 1989, *Black Migrants in a White City: A Social History of African Harare: 1890-1925*, unpublished PhD thesis, University of Zimbabwe (in English).

Yoshikuni, T., 2001, 'Studying African history: amidst the currents of the "End of History"', *Journal of African Studies* No. 58.

Index

Printed in the United States
200642BV00007B/124-126/A